To Tam
with blessings
W.S. Pizzuto
6/23/13

THUS WE HEARD
RECOLLECTIONS OF THE
LIFE OF THE BUDDHA

BHANTE WALPOLA PIYANANDA
&
STEPHEN LONG, D.Dh.

Thus We Heard
Recollections of the Life of the Buddha
Copyright © 2010
by Bhante Walpola Piyananda and Stephen Long

All rights reserved. No part of this book may be reproduced, transmitted, or utilized in any form or by any means, electronic or mechanical, including photocopying, recording, or by any information storage and retrieval system, without written permission from the publisher.

*The Buddha became enlightened under a Bodhi Tree;
its leaf is used throughout the book
as a symbol of his achievement.*

Published by:

METTA From Us
1847 Crenshaw Blvd.
Los Angeles, CA 90019

Distributed by:

Redwing Book Company, Taos, NM USA
www.redwingbooks.com

Library of Congress Catalog-in-Publication Data Pending
ISBN-13: 978-0-615-40950-4 (paperback)
        978-0-615-43339-4 (hardback)
Printed in the United States of America; First Printing January 2011

Cover Illustration: inspired by the ancient murals of Kelaniya Temple, Kelaniya, Sri Lanka; Cover Design: Ven. Kalabululande Dhammajothi and Nirmala Handapangoda; Illustrations: Tharaka Somaratna

"A unique being, an extraordinary man arises in this world for the benefit of the many, for the happiness of the many, out of compassion for the world, for the good, benefit, and happiness of gods and men.

Who is this unique being?

It is the *Tathagata*,
The Exalted, Fully-Enlightened One."

— Anguttara Nikaya, I, 1, 13, p. 22

This book celebrates the
2,600th anniversary
of the Buddha's enlightenment,
and is dedicated
to all members of the Sangha —
Past, Present, and Future.

TABLE OF CONTENTS

Foreword	x
In Gratitude	xii
Map of India in the Time of the Budha	xv
The Sakyas – Geneology	xvi
The Koliyas – Geneology	xvii

Chapter 1   **The First Sangha Council**   1
Sattapanniguha Caves, Venerable Ananda Achieves Arahantship, the First Sangha Council Convenes

Chapter 2   **The Birth of a Prince**   11
Recollections Begin, *Bodhisatta Deva* Saketu, Kapilavatthu, Ten Duties of a King, Parents, The Dream, Prophecies, Birth of Prince Siddhartha

Chapter 3   **The Prodigy**   25
Presentation to the King, Asitadevala, Naming Ceremony, Kondanna's Prophecy, Queen Maha Maya's Death, Ploughing Ceremony, Devadatta and the Swan

Chapter 4   **Coming of Age as Householder**   37
Simile of the Snake, *Brahmajala Sutta*, Education of a Prince, The Three Palaces, Search for a Bride, A Royal Wedding

Chapter 5   **The Four Foresigns**   51
Channa, The Old Man, The Sick Man, The Dead Man, The Holy Man

Chapter 6   **Renunciation**   63
The Greater Discourse to Saccaka, Difficult Choices, Family Conflict, Rahula's Birth, Permission to Leave, The Departure

Chapter 7   **The Ascetic**   77
The Reaction, King Bimbisara, Alara Kalama, Uddaka Ramaputta, The Five Ascetics, *Mahasihanada Sutta*, Self-Mortification, Discovery of The Middle Path

Chapter 8   **The Fully Enlightened One**   91
Dvedhavitakka Sutta, Sujata's Story, Confronting Mara, *Padhana Sutta*, Enlightenment, The Seven Stages of Purification

Chapter 9	**The First Seven Weeks** 103
	Sujata's Daily *Dana*, Veneration of the Bodhi Tree, Doctrine of Dependent Origination, *Bahudhatuka Sutta*, the Arrogant Brahmin, Mara's Return, Mara's Three Daughters, the Mucalinda Tree, the Rajayatana Tree, Two Brothers, Decision to Teach
Chapter 10	**The First Disciples** 113
	Journey to Varanasi, a Brahmin Walks on Water, Reunion with the Five Ascetics, *Dhammaccaka Pavattana Sutta*, the Sangha is Born, *Nalaka Sutta*
Chapter 11	**The Sangha Grows** 127
	Sabbasava Sutta, Yasa, Yasa's Friends, "Go forth, O Bhikkhus," *Dasadhamma Sutta*, *Bhikkhu* Ordination, the Bhadda Princes
Chapter 12	**Three Ascetics and a King** 139
	The Three Kassapas, Loving-Kindness and the Serpent, The Fire Sermon, King Bimbisara's Conversion, Veluvana Monastery
Chapter 13	**The Chief Disciples** 149
	Reverence for the Dhamma, Sanjaya's Story, Venerables Sariputta and Maha Moggallana, *Payasi Sutta*, *Nava Sutta*, *Sutta* on *Sotapanna*, *Rathavinita Sutta*, Meditative *Sutta* on *Nibbana*
Chapter 14	**Father of the Sangha** 163
	The Simile of the Ocean, Venerable Maha Kassapa's Story, Bhadda Kapilani, The Couple Renounces, Exchange of Robes, A Tale of Two Alms Bowls
Chapter 15	**Return to Kapilavatthu** 177
	Honoring One's Parents, The King's Emissaries, Minister Kaludayi, A Royal Salute, The Twin Miracles, Yasodhara's Lion of Men, The Five Precepts, Yasodhara's Devotion
Chapter 16	**Nanda and Rahula** 191
	Prince Nanda's Ordination, Reunion with Rahula, The First *Samanera*, *Maha Dhammapala Jataka*, The Clay Pot Metaphor, Rahula and Meditation, The Eight Precepts
Chapter 17	**Six Princes and a Barber** 205
	Vasettha Sutta, The Princes: Ananda, Anuruddha, Bhaddiya, Bhagu, Kimbila, Devadatta; Anuruddha's

	"have no cakes," Upali's Dilemma, Ordination, *Maha- sunnata Sutta*, Loving-Kindness Meditation	
Chapter 18	**Anathapindika**	**219**
	Kala and Sujata, from the *Kosalasamyutta* on Wealth, Anathapindika meets the Buddha, Prince Jeta's Garden, Seniority of Sangha Members, Jetavana Monastery, The Ananda Bodhi Tree, Four Kinds of Happiness	
Chapter 19	**Mission: Compassion**	**235**
	The *Dhammapada* on Affection, Venerable Nanda's Breakthrough, Sopaka's Story, Ten Questions for *Samaneras*, Sunita's Story	
Chapter 20	**Conflict and Death**	**247**
	Kalahavivada Sutta, The River Rohini Dispute, " discarding both victory and defeat," *Brahmanasamyutta Sutta*, Death of King Suddhodana, *Sala Sutta* – Meditation on Death	
Chapter 21	**The *Bhikkhuni* Order**	**263**
	The *Vandana*, the *Kosalasamyutta Sutta* on Women, *Bhikkhuni* Kalyani's Story, The Five Hundred Royal Wives and Queen Mahapajapati, Ananda's Appeal, The Buddha Establishes the Order, Khema, Uppalavanna, Kisagotami, Patacara	
Chapter 22	**Visakha**	**281**
	Four Qualities for a Woman's Victory, Visakha's Story, The Wedding, Migara, A Father's Advice, The Dress, Visakha Builds a Monastery	
Chapter 23	**Mentor to Kings**	**303**
	Cakkavatti-Sihanada Sutta, King Canda Pajjota of Avanti, King Pukkusati of Gandhara, King Bimbisara's Gift of Dhamma, King Udena of Vatsa, King Udena's Elephant Bhaddavati, King Pasenadi of Kosala, *Kosala Sutta*, King Bodhiraja of Bhagga, The Licchavis and Their Plagues, *Ratana Sutta*, Seven Conditions for a Nation's Well-Being	
Chapter 24	**Truth or Hearsay?**	**325**
	Kalama Sutta, The Blind Men and the Elephant, Good or Bad vs. Wholesome or Unwholesome, Four Great References, Angulimala, Good Teachers	

Chapter 25	**Dr. Jivaka and the Buddha's Daily Routine**	**343**

Kasibharadvaja Sutta, The Monk's Robe, Jivaka's Story, Venerable Ananda – the Buddha's Chief Attendant, *"Besajja Guru"* Medicine Buddha, The Buddha's Daily Life

Chapter 26	**The First Psychologist**	**363**

"Seeing things clearly as they are," Mindfulness, The Courtesan Sirima, Meditation – the Best Prescription, the Licchavi "Prince Wicked," Taming Sujata, The Seven Kinds of Wives, The Six Character Archetypes, *Samatha* and *Vipassana* Meditation, *Kakacupama Sutta*

Chapter 27	**Teachers, Reputations and Tolerance**	**376**

"Brahmins that should or should not be followed," Six Contemporary Teachers: Purana Kassapa, Makkahali Gosala, Ajita Kesakambali, Pakudha Kaccayana, Sanjaya Belatthiputta, Mahavira; *Brahmajala Sutta*, Cincamanavika's Lie, The Sundari Incident, Venerable Kumara Kassapa's Story

Chapte	**Sigala and Friends**	**395**

The Lay Follower, Sigala's Story, *Sigalovada Sutta*, The Six Directions, True vs. False Friends

Chapter 29	***Dhammaduta***	**415**

Swans and Peacocks, Teaching the Dhamma, Challenges of *Dhammaduta*, Venerable Tissa and the Hungry Eagle, The Buddha Always Sleeps Well, *Dighacarika Sutta*, *Patika Sutta*, Meditators vs. Scholars, Venerable Punna Goes to Sunaparanta

Chapter 30	**King Ajatasattu**	**431**

Devadatta's Influence, False Friend and Teacher, Devadatta Challenges the Buddha, Patricide of King Bimbisara, Queen Videhi's Devotion, A King's Unfortunate *Kamma*

Chapter 31	**Gain, Honor, and Praise:**	
	The Devadatta Insurgency	**445**

Labha Sakkara Sutta, *Devadatta Sutta*, Schism in the Sangha, Venerables Sariputta and Maha Moggallana to the Rescue, Devadatta's Assassins, The Buddha and the Boulder, The Elephant Nalagiri, Devadatta's Demise

Chapter 32	**The Passing of Sariputta and Moggallana**	**465**
	Saccavibhanga Sutta, Conversion of Rupasari, Venerable Sariputta's *Parinibbana,* Past-Life Unresolved *Kamma,* Murder and *Parinibbana* of Venerable Maha Moggallana	
Chapter 33	**The Final Year**	**479**
	The Courtesan Ambapali, The Magnificent Licchavi Princes, The Lifespan of a Buddha, Last Confrontation with Mara, Farewell to Vesali, Journey to Kusinara, Excellent Venerable Dhammarama, Last *Dana* at Cunda's, Miracle of the Clear Water, The Malla Prince Pukkusa	
Chapter 34	***Parinibbana***	**495**
	The *Sala* Grove, Venerable Upavana, Ananda's Questions, Subhadda, "With mindfulness, endeavor diligently to complete the task," *Parinibbana* of the Buddha, Funeral Rites, Venerable Maha Kassapa Arrives, Brahmin Drona and the Distribution of Relics	
Chapter 35	**Epilogue**	**517**
	The *Vinaya* Pitaka, The *Sutta Pitaka,* Re-collections of the Life of Buddha, "Who are you?" *Sutta,* Farewells	

Glossary of Terms	**527**
Endnotes	**533**
About the Authors	**542**

Foreword

The timeless teachings of the Buddha have been our source of inspiration, our guidelines for happy living, our motivation for practice, and our tools for higher spiritual attainment for many decades.

The question always arises: Just who was this prince who renounced the world to seek enlightenment and eventually became the Buddha?

Many books have attempted to answer this question, and many have done an admirable job. None, however, have really satisfied our desire for an eye-witness account of who he really was.

We decided that the best and only place to look for him was the *Tripitaka*, the Three Baskets of 84,000 teachings that were organized during the First Sangha Council ninety days after the Buddha passed away, and then first written down three hundred years after the Buddha's *Parinibbana*.

Our first intention for writing this book was to present a biography of the Buddha from the perspective of the *Tripitaka* itself. The ancient Pali-language Canon contains a wealth of information on this subject, and we decided to mine it for deeper clues that might enable us to discover exactly who and what the Buddha was – minus the speculations, fables, and tales from the early Buddhist commentaries.

Our second intention for writing this book was to share verbatim as many translations of the Buddha's primary messages as we could, realizing that most readers would never have the chance to read them unless they took it upon themselves to engage in countless hours of research.

Our third intention for writing this book was to share the life of the Buddha in a way that would appeal to Westerners and Easterners alike. To do that, we realized the need for a contextual story platform that would make the material both accessible and entertaining: hence the creation of the fictitious First Sangha Council sub-committee that recollected the life of the Buddha.

Thus We Heard: Recollections of the Life of Buddha became an amalgam of three kinds of books: a fully-researched biography of the Buddha, a collection of his important Dhamma messages, and a historical novel that "might have happened," but we'll never know for sure.

The nine fully-enlightened arahants on the sub-committee are real historical disciples of the Buddha that *may have* attended the First Sangha Council; we know that at least three of them actually did: Maha Kassapa, Ananda, and Upali. In regards to the other six, the records tell us they were alive at the time of the Buddha's passing away, which means that they may have attended. The characterizations of the arahants in this book are based upon information gleaned from the *Tripitaka*, as well as from insights drawn from our own understanding, plus some imagination. The conversations they have with one another are fictitious, of course, as are the events we portray as having taken place during the course of the Council. The characters that make "guest appearances" at the sub-committee meetings are real and historic, and their genuine contributions to the *Sasana* are duly recorded in the *Tripitaka*.

Since both of us have close connections to Sri Lanka, it might be expected that we would include stories about the Buddha's reputed three visits to that island in this book, but we did not. It is our intention to cover these fascinating tales in a future publication.

We hope you enjoy **Thus We Heard: Recollections of the Life of Buddha**, and gain a greater appreciation for the Fully Enlightened One and his influence on all of humanity for the past two and a half millennia.

May you be well and happy!

In Gratitude

This book would not have been possible without the guidance, assistance, and kind support of many individuals, whose names are far too many to mention here. We would, however, like to acknowledge the following for their contributions to the book and to our lives:

The venerable monks of Dharma Vijaya Buddhist Vihara in Los Angeles: Ven. Dr. Udagama Sumangala Thera, Ven. Maitipe Wimalasara Thera, Ven. Shibuya Subhuti Thera, Ven. Muruthamure Pannaloka Thera, Ven. Bambarawane Kalyanawansa Thera, Ven. Gajayakagama Kassapa Thera, Ven. Kalabululande Dhammajothi. Thanks also to the monks of Sri Maha Viharaya in Pamankada, Dehiwala, Sri Lanka, including Ven. Haupe Somananda Nayake Thera and Ven. Walpola Piyaratana. We extend our special thanks to Ven. Galaboda Gnanissara Nayake Maha Thera; to Ven. Dr. Zhi Xu; to Bhikkhunis Zu Zai Shih, Liu Kuei Ying, Sik Chi Chin, Gunasari, and Susila; and any acknowledgement wouldn't be complete without thanking the late Ven. Elle Chandawimila Thera for his many years of friendship.

We owe a tremendous debt of gratitude to Cynthia Shimazu (*Bodhicari Cintamani*) for her many hours of Dhamma research while the book was being written; and for a variety of reasons we are also grateful to W. J. B. Dedunupitiya, Ramya Gunasekera, Bhadraji Jayatilaka, Tissa Karunasiri, Mrs. Hong Tai Tai, Carol Munday Lawrence, Dr. Victor Coronado, Yoon-ja Kim, Sherry Cefali, Nampet Panichpant-Michelson, Pradeep Gunawardana, Mihiri Tillakaratne, Mihiri and Justin Hettigoda, Ayesha Bulegoda, Tiara Kaimal, and Sunil Semasinghe. Many hours of proofreading were consumed during the editing process of this book, and we offer particular thanks to Stan Levinson for his insights and deep understanding of Dhamma. We also thank Graciela Carabes, Lanka Ranasinghe, Susan Amarasekara, Heather Ortiz, and Cerissa Chaney for their dedication to the arduous task of proofreading. Thanks also to Dharma Vijaya's Board of Directors, members of the temple congregation, and the children and parents of the Sunday School for their inspiration and encouragement.

We would both like to thank the Dayaka Saba of Sri Maha Viharaya, Lakshman Senivaratne, and our friends Sunil Shanta, Kirti and Shiroshi Goonatillake, Gayan Canuka Vidanapatirana, and Vijith Gunawardena for their kind assistance during the editing phase in Sri Lanka.

We would like this book to honor two of our heroes: Col. Henry S. Olcott and the Anagarika Dharmapala. Their tireless work in restoring Buddhism in Sri Lanka and promoting it throughout the world has been a great source of inspiration.

Bhante Walpola Piyananda wishes to thank his late parents for bringing him into the world and setting him on the Right Path, and his teachers for imparting their knowledge and wisdom: the late Ven. Walpola Nanaratana Thera, the late Ven. Balangoda Anandamaitreya Nayake Thera (whose book was used as a primary reference), the late Ven. Kobala Medhananda Thera, the late Ven. Dr. Kotagama Wachissara Thera, the late Ven. Dr. Havanpola Ratanasara Nayake Thera, the late Ven. Dr. Walpola Rahula Thera, the late Ven. Dr. K. Sri Dhammananda Nayake Thera, the late Ven. Lenagala Sumedhananda Maha Nayake Thera, the late Ven. Abanwelle Pannasekara Anunayaka Thera, Ven. Dr. Kakkapalliye Anuruddha Nayake Thera, Ven. Dr. Henepola Gunaratana Nayake Thera, Ven. Weihene Pannaloka Nayake Thera, Ven. Kurunagoda Piyatissa Nayake Thera, Ven. Madawela Punnaji Thera, Ven. Dr. Welmitiyawe Kusaladhamma Nayake Thera, Ven. Dr. Kuburugamuwe Vajira Thera, Dr. Ananda Guruge, Kirthi Narampanawa, and Dr. George Bond. Bhante also thanks his venerable friends for their presence in his life over the years: Ven. Dr. Pannila Ananda Nayake Thera, Ven. Madawala Seelawimala Thera, Dr. Bellanwela Wimalaratana Anunayaka Thera, Ven. Madoluwane Sobhita Thera, Ven. Kirama Wimalajothi Thera, Ven. Dodangoda Rewatha Nayake Thera, Ven. Kirinde Dhammaratana Nayake Thera, Ven. Gantune Assaji Thera, and Ven. Hinbunne Kondanna Thera, Ven. Siyabalagoda Ananda Thera, and Ven. Halwitigala Assaji Nayake Thera.

Bhante Piyananda offers his special thanks to His Excellency Mahinda Rajapaksa, President of Sri Lanka, and First Lady Shiranthi Rajapaksa; Defense Secretary Gothabaya Rajapaksa and Ayoma Rajapaksa; Hon. Minister Dinesh Gunawardana; Hon. Minister Basil Rajapaksa and Pushpa Rajapaksa; and Hon. Deputy Minister Geetanjana Gunawardana. Other friends who deserve his gratitude are: Dr. Chandra Wickramagamage, and the Kadin family: Ana, David, and their son Daniel. Bhante also thanks his brothers Punnasekara, Ranaweera and Urdisena and his sisters Sumanawathi, Chullawati, Premalatha, and the late Gunawathi. Many thanks to Dr. Gamani Jayasinghe for his friendship, support, advice, and dedication for over thirty years. Thanks also to Dr. S. K. P. Gunawardane, Ron Bogan, Dr. Lal Fernando, Rajiv Fernando, and Dr. Jayantha Gunasekara. Last, but certainly not least, Bhante is grateful for his long friendship with his co-author, Dr. Stephen Long.

Dr. Stephen Long wishes to thank his father, John Long, and his late mother, Catherine Long, for their love and guidance. As the Buddha said, even if you carry your parents on your shoulders for an entire lifetime you can never repay them for what they have done for you; Stephen feels this way about John and Catherine. Stephen is grateful to his teachers: the late Tanouye Tenshin Rotaishi, Abbot of Daihonzan Chozen-ji in Honolulu, his first Buddhist teacher; the late Nana Veary, whose living lessons in *aloha* will be with him always; Ajarn Phra Bodhipalo of Wat Mahathat in Bangkok, Thailand, who introduced him to Theravada Buddhism; and Ven. Walpola Piyananda, who taught him the Dhamma and co-authored this book. He has no words for expressing his gratitude to Sri Bhagwan Ramana Maharshi, Sri Nisargadatta Maharaj, Lakshmana Swami, Dr. David Hawkins, Ramesh Balsekar, and David Carse for what they and others have taught him through their books, the books written about them, and the spiritual energy they generate for all mankind.

Stephen is grateful for the support of Won Joon Lee (*Vajirasena*, the "Unbreakable Warrior"), who over the years has taught him the true meaning of "noble friendship"; and he is thankful for the many blessings he has received from his son in Thailand, Thepmetawat Sirathanann (Tang). He also offers his sincere thanks to his "noble friends" Elizabeth Danysh, Claudia Woods, Dr. Barbara Wright, Karla Kral, Audrey Fu, Darlene Hutchinson, Ray and Sonya Miyashiro, Dr. Hyungsuk Choi, Sandra Hunnicut, Gregory Rand, Luc Hovan, Sean and Deborah McLean, Richard and Seritta Krafnick, Bob Felt and Martha Fielding, Stephen Madden, Mary Gamble Wyse, Sarah Danysh Rand, Tiana Silliphant, Geevani Singh, Dr. Kampol Poophawatanakij, Ven. Pyinea Nenda, Manjula Jayasekera, August Cho, Seo Joon Lee, and Nisala Premaratne for their unwavering friendship and belief in him. To his brother David Long, and his sister-in-law Judy Long, he offers his thanks for their caring and steadfast presence in his life.

Map of India in the Time of the Buddha

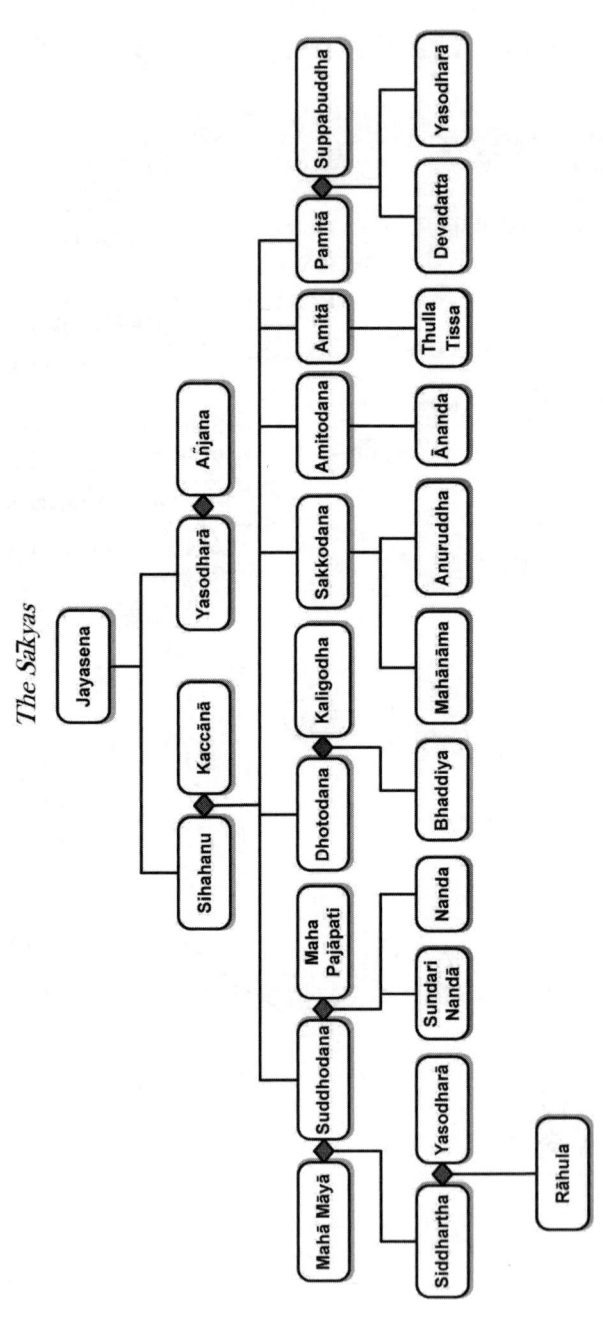

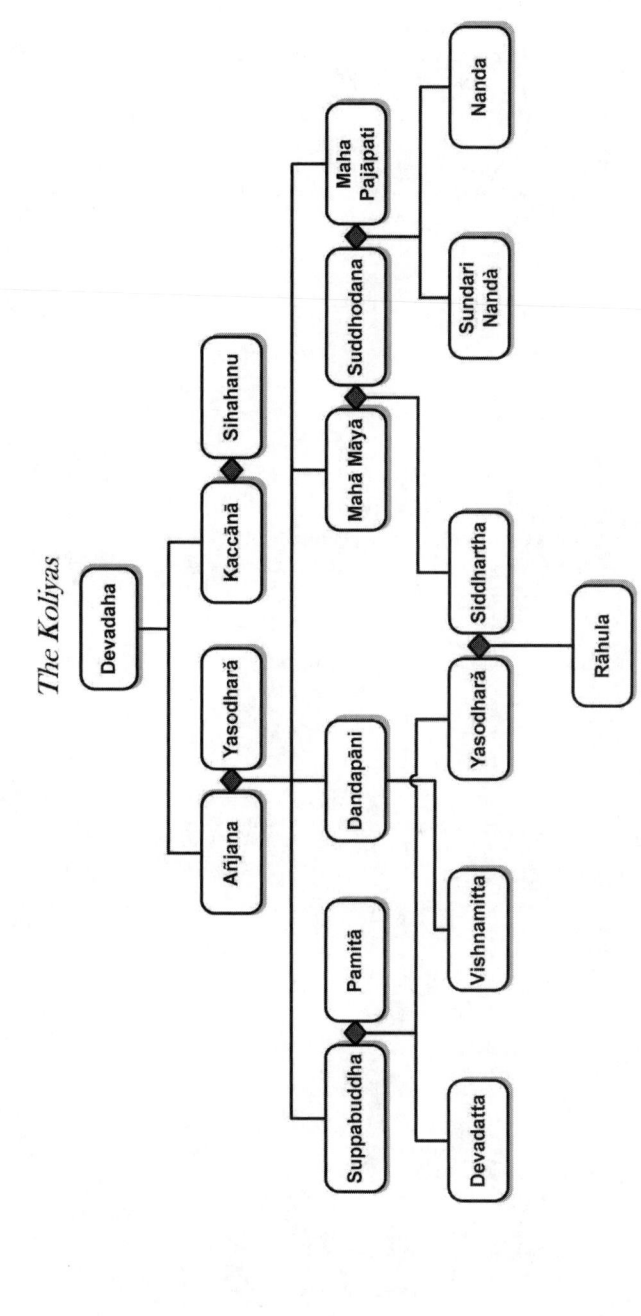

Chapter 1
The First Sangha Council

"Ninety long days have passed since my Lord left this world," reflects Venerable Ananda as he spreads out a rush mat on the earthen floor. He lowers his aged, weary frame to the hard ground of the cave chamber, and then pauses for a moment to catch his breath.

"I've had ninety days to miss his sacred presence, and to feel the sharp pain of not having asked him to stay," he whispers sadly to himself.

"Why, when I had the chance, didn't I beg him not to leave us – not to give up his body for a thousand more years? He didn't have to go. He had the power to live as long as he wished, and if I had but asked him he would have stayed. He gave me several chances to make that request, once in this very spot, and each time I somehow didn't hear the opportunity. When I finally understood, it was too late; he had already spoken his holy word, which was final and irrevocable. How can I live with this guilt? Why am I even here?"

Such are the troubled, anguished thoughts of one of the rarest of men: a near-saint, who for eighty years had lived a completely blameless and virtuous life.

Venerable Ananda and his attendant, Venerable Sopaka, have just walked from Kusinara in the north to Sattapanniguha Cave on the slopes of Mount Vebhara, which is near Rajagaha. He is exhausted from the arduous month-long journey, and the the guilt he carries weighs heavily on him.

He stretches out to rest, and almost immediately falls into a deep sleep. Ananda dreams of childhood with his beloved cousin Siddhartha, who through his own efforts, eventually became the Buddha, the Blessed One, the Fully Enlightened One.

Ananda stirs from his sleep when he hears soft footsteps approaching. He opens his eyes and sees the kind, radiant face of Venerable Maha

Kassapa, the revered monk the Buddha had relied upon to maintain the *Sasana*.

Ananda smiles at his old friend and raises himself up on one elbow, feeling a sharp pang in the well-worn joint.

"Welcome, my dear Venerable Ananda; we have all been waiting for you. How was your journey?" asks Maha Kassapa, his voice glowing with kindness and compassion.

"The trip was long, but not unpleasant. The hardest thing wasn't the walking or the usual hardships of travel, but the thoughts that tormented me the whole way. After all, once in these very caverns the Master gave me a chance to ask him to live for a human *kappa*. Several times the opportunity arose in the last year of his life, but I misunderstood. Since he was saying that a *Tathagata could* live out the maximum life span for a human, I just assumed that he *would*, and not leave us. Due to my lack of mindfulness I didn't hear him and now he's gone," laments the travel-weary monk. "How much longer must I endure this life without our Master?" he asks, doing his best to hold back a tear.

"You'll be with us another forty years, my old friend. I know that very soon the doubts and troubles in your mind will cease – very soon. By the way, in the *Mahapadana Sutta*[1] it's told that when Prince Siddhartha was born, the celestial *devas* commented that in the current human era the maximum span of life is only a hundred years. They said that the Buddha's life would be short. The idea of living for eons came from the lives of previous Buddhas. I'm sure you remember this, my friend."

"*Forty more years?* I know you can see the future, Maha Kassapa, but are you sure I will live to one hundred-twenty? The Master himself only made it to his eightieth birthday," responds Venerable Ananda.

"Forty years seem to go by fast when you attain the state of arahant, my brother. Being so completely absorbed in the present moment you virtually lose consciousness of the passage of time; in fact, the knowing is that *there is no time*. I know you are tired and frustrated, but you must not give up faith in your eventual success," replies Maha Kassapa, who at age eighty-three has been an arahant for decades.

"That's just it – *eventual*. You invited five hundred arahants to attend this important First Council, and the only one still struggling with attachments is me. The assembly starts tomorrow morning and I'm concerned about my qualifications. Until I'm an arahant, I don't even belong here."

"Your qualifications are beyond question, Ananda. Your memory alone qualifies you to be here; in fact, this council wouldn't even be possible without you. Who else keeps the Buddha's eighty-four thousand Dhamma teachings alive in his memory? Keep striving, friend, you just may have a big surprise in store for you."

Arahant Anuruddha walks into the small chamber and greets his first cousin; then he bows respectfully to Maha Kassapa. "Welcome, Venerable Ananda; I heard that you had finally arrived. How are you keeping?"

"For an eighty-year-old monk who has recently lost his Master, I'm doing as well as can be expected, thank you. I'm just concerned that I'm the only one here who isn't enlightened, and I'm still weighed down by the fact that I'm responsible for the Buddha prematurely leaving his body."

"How can you possibly say that you are responsible when you know better than anyone the Master's teaching on 'dependent origination'?" asks Anuruddha. "Conditions are responsible for other conditions, and in the Master's case, the conditions that brought about both his birth and his death are complex beyond our reckoning. You certainly can't take the blame for his passing when he did. Mara, the evil one, probably blinded you whenever the Master hinted about his passing away. If Mara had clouded your mind, how could you possibly have thought to ask the Lord to prolong his life?"

"There is still the case of my not being an arahant. Who is responsible for that?" is Venerable Ananda's frustrated response.

"The same law applies, cousin. All of the conditions required for that event to occur simply haven't yet arisen. If you give it your supreme effort now, however, you may bring about that last, most important, condition for your success. I urge you not to give up hope, but to strive with all your might. I also urge you to let go of your sense of guilt; I can see that's one of the main obstacles holding you back. Go into the forest where you will find peace and solitude. I assure you, it's not too late."

"I agree with your cousin, Ananda. I think that tonight you should give it your best attempt," says Maha Kassapa.

Ananda shakes his head, discouraged that after forty-three years as a monk he hasn't been able to claim the grand prize of his arduous training. "I'll try again, my dear friends, and then I'll try yet another time. I won't give up; it's not in my nature. Your encouragement gives me confidence, and I know that being negative will only keep me from my goal."

"Don't you remember the story of Vakkali?" asks Anuruddha. "Yes, of course you remember! You're the one who remembers every syllable the Master ever spoke." Venerable Anuruddha chuckles and shakes his head, thinking of Ananda's legendary memory.

He continues, "The monk, Vakkali[2], was so attached to the Buddha's form that he refused to take his eyes off of him – even for a moment. You recall that he never left the monastery; he was obsessed about being in the Master's presence all the time, and he followed him around like a baby duck. The Buddha was aware of Vakkali's attachment, and he knew that it was keeping him from attaining enlightenment. He told Vakkali, 'If you see the Dhamma, you see me. Now go out and meditate.' Vakkali understood, and he went off to the forest to practice, even though he was very reluctant about leaving his Master. He practiced hard, eventually saw the Dhamma, and finally achieved his goal of arahantship. So, Venerable Ananda, I suggest you go off by yourself and meditate. I have a good feeling about tonight."

With great effort Ananda stands. He picks up his spare robe, folds it, and walks slowly and with great resolve toward the cave entrance. Maha Kassapa and Anuruddha smile at him, and they affectionately pat him on the back as he leaves the chamber.

As Ananda walks through the vast cave complex he is greeted with supreme respect by many of the arahants who have assembled for the great event. Each of them gives him a knowing smile. One of them winks at him and says cheerfully, "This is your lucky day, Venerable Ananda. We're all pulling for you."

Ananda bows to the kind arahants and silently thanks them for their encouragement. He continues walking and eventually arrives at the edge of the dense forest.

Walking under the dark green canopy, he makes his way through the thick underbrush. He is cheered by the sound of many birds. A pair of monkeys in a tree is having a conversation above his head, and

Ananda gets the feeling they are talking about him. He looks up and sees one of them pointing at him with her slender, furry finger. Her mate looks down at him, claps his hands joyfully, and calls out a greeting. Ananda smiles at the friendly creatures, and his curiosity is aroused by their seemingly intuitive nature. "Perhaps they know something I don't," he muses to himself.

Coming to a small stream he looks down into the water as he carefully steps on the smooth flat stones to reach the other side. Small red and yellow fish are swimming in the flowing current as he bends down for a refreshing splash, cupping his hands. He accidentally catches one of the tiny fish in his joined palms as he is about to raise them to his face. The fish seems startled as he gently places it back into the stream. He dips his hands in again and sluices the cool, fresh water on his forehead and temples.

On the other side of the stream he finds himself in a small glade filled with sunshine. At the edge of the clearing is a graceful *sala* tree in full bloom that looks inviting. Going to the tree, he refolds his robe and places it between two of the massive roots that splay out over the ground. He slowly sits down and adjusts his body to fit the cozy space; the closeness of the roots makes him think of a mother's womb. He reflects that this must be the way a baby feels just before it is born. He folds his legs into the lotus posture, straightens his back, and closes his eyes. It doesn't take him long before he is deep in meditation.

Patches of light dance with the shadows as Ananda strives in concentration with all his might. He watches his breath carefully at the end of his nose, and soon he is in the first *jhana*. He goes deeply into that joyful, timeless, inner space, and relaxes into the rhythm of his breathing.

The sun sinks lower, descending below the horizon, and the glade slowly fills with darkness. New sounds of night are all around, replacing the chatter of monkeys and the songs of birds. A jackal cries out somewhere in the distance, and a leopard suddenly growls in response. Ananda, though, is unaware of these nocturnal voices, and he descends further in his meditation to the second *jhana*. After a while his senses cease sensing, thoughts stop thinking, and perceptions stop perceiving. His absorption is finally complete.

At some point he enters the third *jhana*, and he eventually reaches the fourth, the highest and last. He has now reached the realm of being and non-being. Afterwards he passes through the phase of consciousness and no-consciousness, and leaves behind the void. He is not even aware that he has never been to this sacred place before, because he is aware of nothing. He is in new spiritual territory as he ventures out to the farthest reaches of space.

All the forest sounds suddenly cease, as if nature is holding its breath. A sense of anticipation is in the atmosphere, but Ananda is unaware of it. He has reached the place of oneness, where he has become all that is – and nothing at the same time.

Just as dawn is breaking he returns to consciousness of his body, and he decides to lie down and have a short nap. Mid-way to the lying down posture, with one of his legs still in the air attempting to stretch and his head not yet all the way to the ground, he suddenly feels an explosion in his head and a ripping feeling in his chest. The light that shines at the back of his cranium is almost too intense, and even with his eyes closed, he is blinded by the luminosity of a thousand suns. An opening occurs in the center of his being, and all defilements disappear forever.

In an instant "Ananda," the "person," is gone.

An arahant has taken "his" place.

The old monk sits up straight and remains in the sea of bliss that engulfs him for a seeming eternity. In his mind he travels the universe and sees that it has no end – and no beginning as well. He arrives at the awareness where he realizes that there is no "he" to see; no "Ananda," no "I," and no "other" as well.

Extremely surprised, he joyously exclaims out loud, "I made it! And just in time!"

Ananda slowly stands up, stretches his tired, stiffened limbs, and folds his patchwork robe. He pats it affectionately, as if thanking it for supporting his struggle through the night. Then he smiles at the *sala* tree and its cradle of roots, bows before it with great respect, and turns away.

He walks back through the glade, which is filled with the pale new sun of morning, and ambles down to the silver brook. He bends down and splashes his face with water from the crystal pure stream, and tears form in his eyes when he sees the small red and yellow fish. "You look different today, my friends, even more beautiful than yesterday. But then, everything looks different now. I see you, my swimming brothers, and I see nothing but myself. That's all I can see in every direction – myself!" He smiles broadly with the realization that "he" is all there is, and all of a sudden he notices that the tiredness and weariness of the day before is completely gone.

With renewed energy he walks back to the cave complex, and he senses that all eyes are upon him. Everyone stops and stands still when they see him approaching. Ananda realizes that the old saying that "it takes an arahant to know an arahant" is true. He now understands what an arahant truly is because he has become one, and everyone who lovingly watches him can see it. All of a sudden there is silent applause, as if all five hundred arahants offer their ovation, even though no one has even lifted their hands. Ananda hears their joyful praise, though it isn't expressed in sounds. The arahants are cheering him at the top of their silent voices, and words of congratulations are showered upon him from the purified minds of the saints who gather around him.

Ananda smiles at each one in appreciation, and thanks them all with his radiant eyes. Words are completely irrelevant now, which comes as a surprise to the one who maintains each and every utterance of the Buddha in his mind. He knows that he will be reciting those blessed words soon, and he feels happy that after countless rebirths his spiritual destiny has at last been fulfilled.

He walks back to his silent chamber deep in the cave complex, sits down on the floor, and sinks deeply into meditation. He notices that the silence is different now, more potent and alive. "He" is neither here nor there, and yet "he" is everywhere. He enjoys the peace, and savors the great sense of accomplishment that his mind is settled once and for all.

He doesn't know how long he remains in that blissful state when he hears, "Venerable Ananda, it's time for the council to begin. Your presence is required at once," his attendant Sopaka announces gently.

Ananda smiles warmly at his old friend as he stands. He straightens his back, and then walks regally from the chamber. There is a tranquil look of contentment on his face that wasn't there the day before. His realizes that all feelings of guilt are gone, just as "he" is now gone.

The council is already assembled when Ananda enters the hall. All eyes turn toward him, and he stands still. With great enthusiasm the arahants express their happiness at his arrival. His cousin Anuruddha approaches him and says, "If the Buddha was still alive he would congratulate you himself for your great achievement. Please allow me to express those congratulations on his behalf."

In unison, all of the Sangha members say, "*Sadhu! Sadhu! Sadhu!*"

Venerable Maha Kassapa, chairman of the council, stands at the podium and calls out, "Venerable Ananda, now that you have achieved your goal, you can rightfully participate in this auspicious event, which is only for arahants. Your presence at this council is critical, for you are the one who knew our Lord the best, and the one who witnessed the unfolding of his blessed life for most of its eighty years. Your unparalleled ability to memorize all of his *suttas* and teachings will help us systematically organize them for the benefit of all future generations. Please take your seat."

Ananda smiles, and with his customary humility he seats himself at the back of the hall. He knows that even though he is a senior monk, he is the most junior arahant in the council. After all, his enlightenment took place only a few hours before.

Maha Kassapa says, "Come, Venerable Ananda, your place is here by me at the front of the council. You need to be heard by all." To the assembled arahants he says, "Please recall that the Lord himself said that Venerable Ananda has the greatest memory, is the most learned in regards to the Dhamma, and in fact is the actual guardian of the Dhamma."[3]

Ananda stands up and walks humbly toward the platform. He approaches Maha Kassapa, who points to the place at his right hand. Ananda seats himself, and his countenance shines radiantly with the light of ultimate spiritual fulfillment.

Maha Kassapa goes to the front of the platform and addresses the council, "One of the reasons I have called this meeting is because I realize the supreme importance of maintaining law and order in the Sangha. If the Buddha's teachings are to remain alive and relevant, then Sangha members need to be governed in such a way that their behavior reflects the sanctity of the Dhamma.

"Three months ago I was on my way to see the Lord Buddha for the last time. I encountered an ascetic who was holding in his hand a coral-colored *mandarava* flower, which grows in the heavens and blooms only on rare occasions. I knew at that moment that I was too late to pay my last respects to the Master while he was still alive. I walked on, and before too long I came upon a monk named Subhadra.

"He saw my solemn expression, and told me not to be upset because of the Buddha's passing. He even said that I should be glad – that all the monks should be glad – because we were now free to do as we wished.[4] Astonished to hear such a disrespectful statement coming from a monk, I realized that the Sangha was in great danger of corruption and decay. I couldn't, of course, allow that to happen."

Maha Kassapa pauses while his remarks have a chance to settle into the minds of the arahants. "We will, therefore, review the *Vinaya* Rules of Discipline and Conduct for the Sangha, and reinstate them for all future generations of monks." This statement is met with nods and gestures of approval from the five hundred enlightened monks in the assembly hall.

"Another reason for calling this council is to organize the Buddha's vast and precious teachings. Presently, all of the Lord's *suttas* and other teachings are in no particular order; they are scattered about much in the same way different varieties of flowers are strewn across an altar before worship. With the help of Venerable Ananda and his prodigious memory, we will review each and every one of the Buddha's teachings and group them together – like to like – so they will be easier to preserve, and more convenient to study.

"We will first address the disciplinary rules of the Sangha, as recorded in the *Vinaya*. Venerable Upali, please come to the podium. We wish to question you about these rules and make sure that the Master's teaching is intact and complete."

Upali walks up to the platform and readies himself for questioning. For a long time he has been the expert on the *Vinaya*, and he was proclaimed "Foremost" in this regard by the Lord Buddha himself.[5]

"I will ask you five things about each rule, Venerable Upali. Your answers will establish the rule's validity, and determine whether or not it will contribute to the longevity of the Buddha's *Sasana*. If there are no rules there is no order, and the life of the *Sasana* will be short. The five questions are: What is the reason to apply this rule? Who is the person it applies to? Where did the offence take place? What is the applicable rule? What are the sub-rules that may also apply?"

"Very well, Venerable Maha Kassapa, I am prepared to answer your questions," replies Upali.

The first council has officially begun.

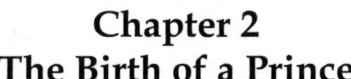

Chapter 2
The Birth of a Prince

The First Sangha Council, called and organized by Maha Kassapa, is being held near the city of Rajagaha, which means "house of the king." It was the capital of the Magadhan king, Bimbisara, the present king's father. An impressive forty kilometer enclosure called the Cyclopean Wall surrounds the actual city. It stands tall with watchtowers, bastions, thirty-two large gates, and sixty four posterns.

Rajagaha was well-known to the Buddha who had lived on and off for a total of twelve years in one of his main monasteries, Veluvana, which was nearby. Gijjhakuta, the "Hill of Vultures," is in the area, the site where the Buddha delivered many of his most memorable discourses.

Pippali Cave, one of the Buddha's favorite places for meditation, is just on the outskirts of Rajagaha, and the Karnada Tank where the Buddha used to bathe is close by. Each of the arahants in attendance had fond memories of Rajagaha, and Venerable Maha Kassapa knew that they would enjoy gathering there for the auspicious First Sangha Council.

For over two decades Maha Kassapa, being somewhat of a recluse, was known for living alone in the forests. It was highly unusual for him to engage in organized activities of any kind. Since the Buddha's passing, however, he had felt so strongly about maintaining order in the Sangha that he decided to call this first council and was acting as chairman.

The Buddha had called Maha Kassapa[1] the monk who was "Foremost in Austere Practices" because of his insistence to live humbly outdoors, exposed to the elements. He could have chosen to live in the comfort of a monastery, but he preferred the freedom and solitude of the wide open spaces. His selection of the Sattapanniguha Cave for the council site was a compromise solution since it offered the benefits of seclusion, natural beauty, and close proximity to the city of Rajagaha.

Sattapanniguha Cave is actually a cluster of seven connecting caves, which surrounds a wide clearing where King Ajatasattu had erected a large pavilion. This temporary structure will serve as the assembly venue for the council. The five hundred arahants will use the labyrinth of caves as their residences, except for those who prefer to live alone in the nearby forest.

There is ample water for the council because of Saptadhara, an underground network of seven streams. There are also hot springs, which will enable the monks to have hot baths throughout the council proceedings.

Ananda walks slowly back to his chamber in the cave complex after the sumptuous luncheon King Ajatasattu has just offered for the five hundred arahants. Ananda's personal attendant, Sopaka, gently guides the revered elder along the stony path. Sopaka is also an arahant, and has been one for thirty-eight of his forty-five years.

Ananda appears radiant and full of life. He is smiling broadly, expressing the unfathomable inner joy of realization. He bows humbly and offers benedictions to his fellow arahants as he passes them along the way.

Maha Kassapa walks toward him from a convergent pathway, calling out to him. "Ananda, please come to my chamber for your rest. Anuruddha, Upali, and a few others will be joining us, and Bakkula is bringing some special herbs from the Himalayas; he guarantees that they will keep your voice from failing you when it's your turn to speak. You're going to need those vocal cords working at full strength in order to recite all those *suttas*."

"Thank you for your concern and support; I accept your kind invitation," replies Ananda. "Upali, as usual, did an excellent job explaining the *Vinaya* rules today. I'm sure that by the time we conclude this council we will have them all in order."

"Yes, it will be good to review the complete *Vinaya* and Dhamma so we can group them into baskets," responds Maha Kassapa.

"I was thinking that even though the council will give priority to the Dhamma and the *Vinaya*, we may want to create a record of the Buddha's life as well," suggests Ananda.

"You know how the Master felt about his former personal life. He usually discouraged stories about it, wanting to keep the focus on the message and not the messenger," responds Maha Kassapa in a serious tone.

"I am well aware that the Master didn't want a personality cult to develop when he was gone, but I don't see anything wrong with creating a historical account of his life. This will probably be our only opportunity since those of us who were eye-witnesses probably won't be around for another council. I think the story of his life might serve as an inspiration for those who will study the Dhamma and enter the Sangha later on," says Ananda.

"The Buddha wasn't just an ordinary person, you know; he made this very clear to us many times. He taught us about *anatta*, the fact that there is no permanent individual 'I.' You are talking now about creating a story about an 'I,'" exclaims Maha Kassapa.

"I know that if I were born a thousand years from now I would very much want to know where the Dhamma came from, and to be able to learn about the person who was first to expound it," replies Ananda.

"When you put it that way, I see that it is actually a good idea, in spite of my initial response to the contrary. It just might be an excellent complement to our council work. Even though I'm not so sure he would have wanted it, I will form a sub-committee for this purpose. Our completed biography can be shared with the general assembly at the end of the council," responds Maha Kassapa. "I will summon ten monks with the memory gift to attend our recollections."

"Thank you, Maha Kassapa. You have just taken complete responsibility for recording the Master's teaching, his Sangha rules, *and* his life story."

As they approach a steep point near the edge of a cliff, Sopaka takes one of Ananda's elbows, Maha Kassapa the other, and together the three of them descend some steps to another pathway leading down into the caverns.

They all duck their heads as they enter the vast antechamber. Maha Kassapa leads the way through a narrow corridor to his personal cave. Upali, Punna, Anuruddha, Bhaddiya, Maha Kaccayana, and Bakkula are already there.

"We have just been discussing the formation of a sub-committee to record the life of the Master. We feel that it will be a noble complement to the organization of the *Vinaya* and the Dhamma," explains Maha Kassapa as he settles on the floor.

"That is an excellent idea," declares Bakkula. "Those of us who were close to the *Tathagata* must do this now before we're all gone!"

"My sentiments exactly," adds Ananda.

"It's no coincidence that those of us gathered here now are the perfect members for that sub-committee. Sopaka, please call a group of memory monks to the chamber so we can begin tonight," requests the chairman. Sopaka gets up and leaves the cave.

"While we're waiting for them I'll finish brewing the Himalayan tea for Ananda. I heard from a source in the higher realms that these herbs will give him much strength, and preserve the timbre of his famous voice," says Bakkula.

Ananda can't help but laugh at this remark considering the fact that Bakkula was now one hundred-five years old; he didn't ordain in the Sangha until he was eighty. If Himalayan herbs were one of the elder's secrets for health and longevity, Ananda is more than willing to give them a try.

Bakkula opens his shoulder bag and takes out a cloth pouch containing the herbs. He puts some of them into a pot of water boiling over an open fire, and a few minutes later he pours some of the fragrant brew into an earthen cup and hands it to Ananda, who accepts it with a smile.

"Thank you, Bakkula. Being the one who is 'Foremost in Good Health,'[2] you always know what is best for us."

"Since I hear you'll be with us another forty years, we have to make sure you are healthy and full of energy," replies the kindly arahant as he pours tea for the others.

"I see the word has already spread about my predicted lifespan," says Ananda with a chuckle.

Before too long, Sopaka returns to the chamber with ten memory monks following behind him. They bow deeply to the senior monks and silently take their seats against the cave wall.

"Let's begin. The Buddha's father, King Suddhodana, had four brothers and two sisters. Bhaddiya, you are the son of Dhotodana, King Suddhodana's next oldest brother and Princess Kaligodha, the chief Sakyan lady of her time. Anuruddha, you are the son of Sukkodana, the King's third-oldest brother; and Ananda, you are the son of Amitodana, the King's fourth-oldest brother. This makes the three of you the Buddha's first cousins, and you were there from the very beginning. Which one of you will kindly start off our recollections?" asks Maha Kassapa.

Ananda answers, "I will begin the story of the Master's life by saying that I was born on the very same day he was. I learned about the prophecies that were made about him before he was born, and the circumstances of his birth from my parents, aunts and uncles. Much later on, the Master told me himself about his decision to become a Buddha."

"I'm very interested in hearing about that decision," requests Upali, sitting up to pay closer attention.

Ananda continues, "The Buddha's last prior existence before being born here as Prince Siddhartha was as a *Bodhisatta* named *Deva Setaketu*. One day there was a gathering of all the *deva* kings from the ten thousand world-systems, and they approached *Deva Setaketu*. They told him that since he had fulfilled the three levels of the Ten Perfections it was a propitious time for his last birth, when he was destined to become a fully enlightened Buddha.[3]

"The Ten Perfections, you remember, are: *dana*, generosity; *sila*, virtue; *nekkhamma*, renunciation; *panna*, wisdom; *viriya*, committed energy; *khanti*, patience; *sacca*, truthfulness; *adhitthana*, determination; *metta*, loving-kindness; and *upekkha*, equanimity. These ten perfections required mastery on three successive levels of development with each one increasing in intensity and difficulty. The Buddha told us that he had mastered these ten perfections by cultivating and practicing them with compassion, skillful reason, selfless motivation and purity of mind on the three successive levels. He had mastered each of the perfections three times, for a total of thirty completions.[4]

"The *deva* kings said that after the *bodhisatta* attained supreme enlightenment he would liberate *devas*, humans and *Brahmas* from *samsara*. They made their request for him to take on human form.

"The *bodhisatta* did not hastily give his consent to this request. Instead, he followed the tradition of previous *bodhisattas* and made the five great investigations. The first investigation was, 'Is this the appropriate time for the appearance of a Buddha?' The second, 'Is this the appropriate island or continent for the appearance of a Buddha?' The third, 'Is this the appropriate country for the birth of a Buddha?' The fourth, 'Is this the family into which the *bodhisatta*, in his last existence, is to be reborn?' And the fifth investigation is, 'What is the life span of the *bodhisatta*'s future mother?'"[5]

"What were the results of those five investigations?" asks Sopaka.

"After carefully examining the current conditions, the *bodhisatta* determined that it was indeed a propitious time for him to be born and for becoming a Buddha," responds Ananda. "He said that he would take human form in the city of Kapilavatthu as the son of King Suddhodana and Queen Maha Maya. He immediately took his leave of the *devas* and *Brahmas*, and then he entered the *Nandana Vana* Celestial Garden to rest and prepare for his rebirth."

"Why was Kapilavatthu selected as the birthplace of the future Buddha? And why were the king and queen chosen to be his parents?" asks Bakkula.

Anuruddha answers, "When the *bodhisatta* investigated these questions he saw that the continent called *Jambudipa* was the only one on which previous Buddhas had appeared. This was one of the requirements for establishing his place of birth. The *Bodhisatta* then searched for an ideal spot where former Buddhas had been born, which was another requirement. When he saw the Middle Country of *Jambudipa* he realized that it was indeed the place where ancient Buddhas had appeared in the past. He next examined this area closely and determined that Kapilavatthu, the royal city of the Sakyas, was the best-suited place.

"He saw that its king, Suddhodana, was a direct descendent of Mahasammata, the first elected primeval king, and that his lineage was pure Sakyan. He saw that the queen was a perfect vessel to be the mother of a future Buddha because she had accumulated merit and fulfilled the perfections throughout one hundred thousand eons. The *bodhisatta* saw that all of the required conditions had come into confluence, and that it was the perfect time to be reborn as the next Universal Buddha.

"In addition to what I have just explained, I personally think that the *bodhisatta* saw *Jambudipa*, India, as the ideal place for teaching the Four Noble Truths and the other important doctrines of the Dhamma. There is now, as there will be again in the distant future, a great deal of suffering in this ancient, blessed, but also troubled country."

The arahants nod their heads in agreement to Anuruddha's profound prediction.

"What do you remember of Kapilavatthu in those days? What was it like when Siddhartha was born?" asks Bakkula eagerly.

"I'd be happy to answer those questions since I was fifteen years old at the time of Prince Siddhartha's birth," replies Bhaddiya, who was now ninety-five years old. He had served as the king's Regent for a few years since his father, Prince Dhotodana, had already passed away; this put him next in line for the throne when King Suddhodana retired. The Buddha had called Bhaddiya "chief among monks of aristocratic birth." "I remember those times very well; after all, it's only been eighty years," he continues. "At that time, everyone in the kingdom was talking about Siddhartha's birth, the physical signs on his body, the predictions about his future, and of course, the king's hopes and aspirations for his long-awaited son.

"Kapilavatthu was the capital of the beautiful kingdom of the Sakyas which stretched from the foothills of the Himalayas all the way to the Ganges River. The Anoma River flowed down from the Himalayas and ran right through the middle of the kingdom, providing fresh pure water for the rice fields and pastures. The Sakyas were farmers as well as cow-herders, and Suddhodana himself, even though he was king, occasionally worked in the paddy fields. The Sakyan people were well known for being good looking; they produced strong, handsome men and stately, beautiful women.

"My uncle, Suddhodana, governed his people with honor by adhering to the 'ten duties of the king,' which are just as valid now as they were eighty years ago," concludes Bhaddiya.

"For the record, what are those ten duties?" requests Punna. "I'm sure you performed them well when you ruled as the king's Regent."

"I was young then, and it was before I became a *bhikkhu*; but looking back at that time I think I performed them passably," says Bhaddiya with modest candor. "The first of the ten duties[6] is *dana*, or liberality, generosity, and charity. The ruler shouldn't have craving and attachments to wealth and property; he should use them for the welfare of the people.

"The second is that he must have a high moral character, demonstrating his *sila*, or virtue. He should never destroy life, cheat, steal, or exploit others. Nor should he commit adultery, tell lies, or take intoxicants. These are similar to the Five Precepts as later taught by the Master.

"The third duty is that he must sacrifice everything for the good of the people. This is called *pariccaga*. He must be prepared to give up his own personal comfort, name, fame, and even his life in the interest of his subjects.

"The fourth duty is *ajjava*, or honesty and integrity. The king must be free from fear or favor in the discharge of his duties. He must be sincere in his intentions, and must not deceive the public.

"Number five is *maddava*, or kindness and gentleness. He must possess a genial temperament and treat his subjects with loving-kindness.

"The sixth duty is *tapa*, or austerity in habits. The king must lead a simple life, practice self control, and not indulge in excessive luxury.

"Number seven is *akkodha*, or freedom from hatred, ill-will, and enmity. The king should never hold a grudge against anyone.

"The eighth duty of the king is to practice *avihimsa*, or non-violence, which means that he should promote peace by preventing war.

"The ninth duty is the practice of *khanti*, or patience, forbearance, tolerance, and understanding. He must be able to bear hardships, difficulties and insults without losing his temper.

"Finally, the tenth duty of the king is to live by the rule of *avirodha*, or non-opposition and non-obstruction. This means that the king should not oppose the will of the people, and he should never obstruct any measures that are conducive to the welfare of the people," says Bhaddiya.

"I sincerely hope that rulers in the future will take these ten duties to heart and put them into practice. If they do, the world will surely have peace," says Punna. "Bhaddiya, please continue with your description of Kapilavatthu."

"Around the city of Kapilavatthu there was a wall used for defense," begins Bhaddiya. "The palace and the ministers' houses were inside the wall, and they were all made of baked brick with terra cotta roof-tiles. There were several wells around the city that supplied fresh water, and they too were surrounded by brick walls for security. There were four massive iron gates in the walls, and each one was nineteen feet wide. The streets were paved with stones and were always kept clean by the king's maintenance crews.

"East of us was Koliya, another small kingdom, which was also populated by Sakyas; its king at the time was Anjana. The capital, Devadaha, was named for the beautiful lake that was once used by the Sakyan princes for recreation. King Devadaha was King Anjana's father, and he too was named after the lake, which was so beautiful that the city actually grew up around it. Long ago many of the Sakyans who went there for enjoyment were reluctant to go back home to Kapilavatthu, so they stayed by the lake and eventually established Koliya."

"I bet you used to swim in Lake Devadaha when you were a young man," says Bakkula.

"Yes. Ananda, Anuruddha, Devadatta, Nanda, Siddhartha and I, being first cousins, spent many happy days swimming and paddling around in that lake," replies Bhaddiya.

"What about the family?" inquires Sopaka. "The Master didn't talk about his family very much, and his son Rahula didn't either. Why was that?"

"The Buddha considered everyone to be part of his family, and he didn't distinguish others from those of his own flesh and blood. Of course he loved his family, but he saw no reason to grant them extra favor because they were his relations," responds Anuruddha.

"Can you tell us anything about the Buddha's mother, or should I say his *two* mothers?" asks Punna.

"King Anjana's elder daughter was Maha Maya, and his younger was Mahapajapati," answers Bhaddiya. "Both women were extremely beautiful. Even though it was common for a king to have more than one consort in other parts of India, the Sakyas were monogamous. However, as a reward for putting down a rebellion on the border, Suddhodana received a special boon from his father, King Sihahanu, and he was allowed to marry both sisters with all rites and rituals.

"Queen Maha Maya did not conceive for twenty years. She was thirty-six years old when she gave birth to Siddhartha. Queen Mahapajapati, the younger sister, had two children by Suddhodana: Sundarinanda, a daughter born before Siddhartha, and later a son, Nanda."

"I have always enjoyed hearing the story of Queen Maha Maya's dream," comments Bakkula. "Will you give us your version, please?"

Anuruddha speaks up, "Allow me to explain the dream, since it has always been of great interest to me, too. I have pondered about it for eighty years, since the telling of the dream has become such an integral part of the history and lore of Kapilavatthu. Every villager tells a different story, and I'm happy to give you mine, which was actually told to me by my aunt, Queen Maha Maya herself. I was only a young boy of seven, but I will never forget the sweetness in her voice and the love she expressed for her unborn child." The esteemed monks nod their approval, thinking that they are finally going to hear the truth.

"In August, on the ninth waxing day of the moon, the entire kingdom of Kapilavatthu was celebrating the annual festival of the constellation Uttarasalha. This festival was unique because the participants abstained from alcoholic beverages. The entire city was decorated with elaborate floral displays, and every home had bouquets of fragrant, colorful flowers on their doorsteps. Other types of ornaments made of painted wood adorned the city walls, the exteriors of the palaces, and even the trees that lined the roads.

"Dancing, prayers, and religious rituals went on for several days. Queen Maha Maya didn't participate in the festivities that year; instead she did charity work and gave food to the poor. On the final day of the festival she went to see the sage Asitadevala at his tranquil park near the river. She took part in the traditional religious observances that he conducted. Afterwards, she came home and had dinner with her sister, Mahapajapati. Maha Maya had practiced loving-kindness all day and she was in particularly good spirits. After dinner she paid her respects to the king in his bedroom, and then retired to her own royal chamber."

Anuruddha has the complete attention of everyone in the room. The memory monks, whose eyes are closed, are absorbing the event through their inner sight.

"Maha Maya told me she fell asleep easily that evening, and the light of the full moon shined in on her through the open window," continues Anuruddha. "She said that when her dream began her bed was suddenly lifted up and carried out through the window into the sky. She watched as the *devas* transported her to the very top of the Himalayas. The view was spectacular as she drifted over the highest peaks with moonlight glistening on the snow and glaciers. The celestial *devas* finally set the bed down gently next to Lake Anotatta. They bathed her in the lake and dressed her in shimmering clothes that glittered with multicolored jewels.

"Then she saw a milky white baby elephant carrying a full-blooming lotus blossom in its raised trunk. She instinctively felt a deep love for the animal. The elephant circled her bed three times as if paying homage to her, then it trumpeted and melted into the right side of her body. She said this was the moment the future Buddha was conceived, and a thunderous earthquake shook the ten thousand worlds.

"When she awakened the next morning she told the king about her dream. Curious about what it meant, he called a group of Brahmin astrologers to the palace and asked them to interpret it for him. One of them said that Lake Anotatta, where the queen had been taken, was the source of many of Asia's rivers: the Brahmaputra, the Ganges, the Mekong, and others. He said that as water flowed from its source to nourish the world, so would their son nourish people spiritually, purifying their minds with the supreme truth and making them receptive to higher realms of spirit.

"Another of the Brahmin astrologers confirmed that their son would either become a Universal Monarch; or, if he renounced the householder's life, he would become a Universal Buddha.

"It was said that from the moment of conception forty thousand *devas* came to the queen's chamber to protect her and her unborn child from any kind of harm. Being chaste and pure, Maha Maya became totally free from any form of sensuous desire, and her womb became like a sacred *stupa*. She never suffered any pain or discomfort during her time of confinement.

"She said that with her inner gaze she often looked at the fetus of her unborn son. She saw him seated cross-legged, leaning against her backbone for support; he looked like a true speaker of the Dhamma, seated upon a Dhamma throne."

All of the arahants are silent, giving Anuruddha their complete attention; they are greatly moved by the story of the Lord's coming into a physical body for the last time.

"I remember my mother telling me about the Master's birth in the Lumbini Gardens," continues Anuruddha. "She was in the queen's traveling party on its way to Devadaha City. According to custom, an expectant mother would go to be with her parents for the delivery of her child. You were there too, Bhaddiya, am I correct?"

"Yes. I was fifteen years old and just as excited as everyone else about the imminent royal birth. Along with your mother, my mother, and the Buddha's half-sister Sundarinanda, a host of guards and hundreds of attendants and servants accompanied the queen, who was carried in a golden palanquin. Young Princess Sundarinanda was very excited that she was about to have a brother, and she kept asking the queen when he would arrive. The queen lovingly smiled at her niece, saying, 'Soon, my dear child, soon.'"

Bhaddiya pauses for a moment as he remembers the blessed occasion as if it was just yesterday, then continues, "As you all know, the queen never made it all the way to Devadaha. When she saw the stunning beauty of Lumbini Gardens, she requested that the procession stop so she could enjoy it. She really loved nature, and she wanted to rest for a while among the *sala* trees. Lumbini, mid-way between the two cities, was a popular place for relaxation and recreation that people from both kingdoms enjoyed.

"Every *sala* tree in the grove was in full bloom. Birdsong filled the air along with the fragrance of untold numbers of flowers. As the queen's palanquin approached the center-most tree of the grove, *devas* and *Brahmas* proclaimed that the future Buddha would be born that day. Thousands of heavenly creatures congregated in the grove to witness the blessed event, while the entire universe resounded with celestial music, singing, and the sonorous tones of conch shells.

"I was told that when she descended from her palanquin, almost immediately she felt a sudden urge to grasp a branch of the blooming *sala* tree. We all marveled when we saw the branch bending down to her like a cane stalk. In her dress of gold-threaded brocade she looked serene, majestic, and full of joy. She then felt the unmistakable signs of impending childbirth, and her ladies in waiting cordoned off the area with curtains. The rest of us withdrew.

"Instantaneously, flowers began falling from the sky and musical instruments started playing. The *bodhisatta*, adorned with both major and minor physical marks, was then delivered clean and pure from the *stupa*-like lotus-womb of Queen Maha Maya. It was the full moon of Vesakha when it was in conjunction with the constellation Visakha. Immediately, two fountains of pure spring water materialized in the sky to clean the already spotless bodies of the *bodhisatta* and his mother. The natural world and the entire universe paid homage to the future Fully Enlightened One."

The arahants, who are in deep meditation, view the events internally as they are being described. Bhaddiya continues, "There was a pond in the park and there were seven lotuses lined up that stretched from one side to the other. I know many of you have heard that the Buddha was born while his mother was standing and holding on to the branch of the *sala* tree. This is true. You have also heard that the four great guardian deities received the child in a golden net and presented him to his mother. This is true as well. You have heard that the young prince stood up and faced the ten directions, and then walked seven steps producing a fully-blooming white lotus with each footprint. I will say to you my brethren that the babe Siddhartha, even though he was undoubtedly very special, was like any other babe; the lotus blossoms they said that appeared under his feet were nothing more than symbols of his purity.

"The Buddha later explained the symbology of the lotus[7] saying that it grows beneath the surface of the water in deep mud, much like human beings who are often born into unfavorable circumstances. He also told us that the water in the pond is a metaphor for the society in which the individual grows. Regardless of one's birth and upbringing, the individual, like the lotus, is able to emerge from his or her circumstances without surrendering to harmful or unwholesome influences. A life can blossom for everyone to appreciate and enjoy," concludes Bhaddiya.

"I'm glad you cleared up the detail about the lotus footprints, and put it in the proper realm of symbolism, Bhaddiya," says Ananda. "The Buddha was a human being, and his message of purification is for all people, for all time. He actually came into the world as a purification element, and to inspire us all to strive for perfection and the realization of *Nibbana*."

"Yes, Ananda, this is so," says Maha Kassapa. "The seven lotuses at the birth of the Master also symbolize the seven stages of purification, which he later completed before attaining full enlightenment. Punna, will you please explain these to us?"

"Very well, Venerable Sir," answers Punna, the second-youngest arahant member of the group; he is seventy years old. "I will quote from the *Rathavinita Sutta*:[8]

> "'Purification of virtue is for the sake of reaching purification of mind;

> 'Purification of mind is for the sake of reaching purification of view;
>
> 'Purification of view is for the sake of reaching purification by overcoming doubt;
>
> 'Purification by overcoming doubt is for the sake of reaching purification by knowledge and vision of what is the path – and what is not the path;
>
> 'Purification by knowledge and vision of what is the path and what is not the path – is for the sake of reaching purification by knowledge and vision of the way;
>
> 'Purification by knowledge and vision of the way is for the sake of reaching purification by knowledge and vision;
>
> 'Purification by knowledge and vision is for the sake of reaching final *Nibbana* without clinging.
>
> 'And it is for the sake of final *Nibbana* without clinging that the holy life is lived under the Blessed One.'"

"Thank you for that explanation, Punna. Without purification there truly is no hope of attaining Truth, and the Dhamma makes this very clear. I think this has been enough for our first day, my brothers," says Maha Kassapa. "I suggest that we go to our separate quarters and reflect on what has been said, and meditate on the Master's holy life. Tomorrow we will continue."

The arahants all stand and respectfully bow to their seniors. One by one they silently leave the chamber. In the darkness of the passageway it seems that there is a faint blue glow around each of their forms. There is no need for torchlight since they illuminate their way with the pure radiance of their own realization.

Chapter 3
The Prodigy

Every day for the past two weeks the council has been questioning Upali about the *Vinaya*. They are nearing the end of the rules section of the agenda, and the committee in charge of organizing these materials is now busy grouping them by subject.

"Upali, you look as fresh as you did on your first day of the council," remarks Ananda as they step down from the platform. Upali takes Ananda's elbow and guides him through the crowd to the exit of the assembly hall. The sun is low on the horizon, and torches are being lit around the perimeter of the cave area.

"Thank you, Ananda, for your kind words. Where would any of us be right now without your consistent support throughout the years? My energy level is probably the result of a fresh appreciation of the Master's unfailing wisdom and uncanny insight. If he hadn't established the *Vinaya* rules when he did, I doubt if the Sangha would last much beyond our lifetimes. I'm glad Maha Kassapa arranged to have these disciplinary issues sorted out once and for all. Some of his questions were extremely difficult; I'm grateful that you were there to fill in some of the blanks in terms of who, what, when, why, and where."

"I'm happy I was able to help. We can all rest easier now that we know for sure that the Sangha will outlive us," replies Ananda, as he and Upali walk toward the eastern caverns. They duck as they enter the first chamber and continue down the dark corridor until they reach their destination.

Maha Kassapa greets Upali and Ananda at the entrance to his cave and asks, "Do you feel up to continuing our story of the Buddha's life?"

"That would be agreeable to me, Maha Kassapa, if it is convenient for you and the others," replies Ananda.

"They are already assembled, and the memory monks are waiting."

Ananda smiles and gives the chairman a nod of appreciation for his remarkable prescience.

Upali, Maha Kassapa and Ananda are greeted warmly by their fellow committee members and the memory monks. When they are all seated on their mats Ananda says, "Cousin, I believe you had just finished talking about the Master's birth. Why don't you continue with a description of the king's welcome at the palace?"

"Very well, Ananda," replies Bhaddiya. "As you can imagine, all of Kapilavatthu was jubilant when the queen returned to the capital. The queen's parents, King Anjana and his wife, and other relatives had joined the procession at Lumbini Gardens, and they followed the golden palanquin into the city. Preparations were busily underway for the grand festival to celebrate the royal birth; the king had been wishing and praying for an heir for twenty years, and his happiness was now complete.

"I was there when the queen presented the newborn boy to his father at the city's garlanded western gate. The king wept with joy as he took him in his arms, and a great cheer went up from the assembled multitude. Queen Maha Maya was radiant beyond description, and she showed no signs of the fatigue that usually accompanies childbirth. She was elated by the warm reception and didn't hesitate to join the festivities with great enthusiasm. It was due to her purity and devotion that she was chosen to be the mother of the future Buddha, and she knew that her aspirations from previous births had finally been fulfilled."

"We should note that on the same day the Master was born there were six other inter-related births," comments Maha Kaccayana. "You, Ananda, were born on that day as the son of Prince Amitodana, who was a younger brother of King Suddhodana. The other births were of Princess Yasodhara, Prince Siddhartha's future wife; Channa, his charioteer; Minister Kaludayi, the Master's childhood playmate who later became an arahant; the Maha Bodhi Tree at Gaya; the Master's royal stallion Kanthaka; and four huge jars of gold, which were never depleted no matter how much was removed from them."[1]

"I would say that those seven simultaneous entrances made it quite an auspicious birthday, Venerable Sirs," remarks Sopaka, chuckling, "undoubtedly the greatest in history." All of the arahants smile and nod in agreement.

"When the prince was born it was as if the entire manifest universe celebrated the event with unprecedented, spontaneous natural phenomena," adds Anuruddha. "There were all sorts of miraculous healings, flowers blooming, musical instruments playing, water flowing and turning sweet, elephants trumpeting, and believe it or not, people everywhere speaking kindly to one another."

"Wouldn't it be great if a Buddha was born every day!" exclaims Maha Kaccayana, beaming.

Punna says, "The ascetic Asitadevala was the king's spiritual guru and advisor; he had also guided the king's father, King Sihahanu, for many years. I remember the Lord saying on one occasion that the ascetic was so well-respected by the king that he regularly had his mid-day meal at the palace. Was he already there when the queen arrived with the newborn prince?"[2]

"No," answers Bhaddiya. "In his deep meditation Asitadevala had gone up to *Tavatimsa*, the celestial realm, where he was enjoying the bliss of *jhana*. When he emerged from this state *devas* were rejoicing in such an outlandish manner that he was taken aback; he asked them what had happened. With great excitement they announced that a son had been born to King Suddhodana, and that he would one day become the Fully Enlightened Buddha. Upon hearing that news the ascetic immediately came back into his body and went directly to the palace.

"He went directly before the king and said, 'I wish to see your newborn son; bring him to me.' The king gave the order at once and had the young prince brought before the revered teacher. The king held the baby in front of Asitadevala with the intention of making the child pay his respects to the ascetic. However, without warning the baby placed his sacred feet directly on the aged hermit's head. I saw it with my own eyes."

"That must have caused quite a reaction," says Sopaka, who, since he was a child, was always very proper when it came to matters of showing respect.

"Indeed it did," replies Bhaddiya. "With the child's feet on his head the ascetic started to laugh; and then very quickly his laughter turned to tears. Asitadevala immediately put his palms together and bowed before the infant son of the king. When the king saw how moved his teacher was by his son's bold act he turned the baby around and placed the infant's feet on *his own* head.

"Then he spoke to his son and said, 'This is the first time I pay homage to you.' The king asked Asitadevala, 'Why were you so happy one minute, and then so sad the next?'

"The sage answered, 'I'm completely overjoyed that a future Buddha has been born into the world, but at the same time I'm grief-stricken that I won't live long enough to hear his Dhamma message.'"

"How did the king take this news?" asks Punna.

"The king, of course, desperately wanted a direct heir for his throne, and his astrologers had already told him that his son would either become a Universal Monarch – or a Universal Buddha. After hearing Asitadevala's pronouncement, I'm sure my uncle was very much distressed," replies Bhaddiya. "The king was a good man and a good ruler, but he wanted what all householders want: a son to carry on his name, and to inherit and expand his kingdom."

"I heard that Asitadevala convinced his nephew to renounce the world after meeting the infant prince," remarks Sopaka.

"Yes, this is true," responds Bhaddiya. "After leaving the palace that day he went straight to his sister's house where he convinced his nephew, Nalaka, that he should immediately become a wandering ascetic and prepare himself for the arrival of the future Buddha. Asita also told Nalaka that one day he would hear the news that Prince Siddhartha had renounced his throne and family. At that time he should find him and ordain in his order."

Punna says, "My mother told me that without a moment's hesitation Nalaka, who was an heir to a fabulous fortune, did as his uncle advised. He retired to the Himalayas where he practiced austerities for twenty nine years. When he finally heard the news about Siddhartha's renunciation, he did in fact, seek him out. By the time he found him, Siddhartha was already enlightened and had become the Buddha. Nalaka asked to be ordained in the Sangha, and soon afterwards he became an arahant. Asitadevala had, by this time, already passed away, just as he predicted he would."

"Tell us about the baby's head washing and naming ceremony," requests Ananda.

"As is custom," begins Bhaddiya, "the king organized a large ritual that included one hundred-eight Brahmins who would perform the ceremony of washing the infant's head, and giving the prince an auspicious name. The king began the rite by offering each of the Brahmins specially-prepared milk-rice. Afterwards, eight Brahmins were selected from the one hundred-eight who would actually make the predictions. These eight examined the infant's body and saw the thirty-two primary physical marks, and the eighty minor physical marks that distinguished him for greatness. Seven of the Brahmins repeated what had been said earlier, that the child would either be a Universal Monarch or a Universal Buddha.

"Only one Brahmin, the youngest one named Kondanna, who happened to be Punna's uncle, said that he had no doubt the young prince would become a Fully Enlightened Buddha," says Bhaddiya.[3]

Punna says, "I wasn't born until ten years after that event, and I didn't meet my famous uncle until I was nearly forty and we were both Sangha members. My mother had often spoken of my uncle's tremendous faith in the prince, and how he looked forward to eventually hearing the Dhamma from the lips of one who had been a baby when they first met."

The arahants on the sub-committee reflect for a moment on the faith of their old friend Kondanna, who had passed away several years before.

"When Uncle Kondanna made his pronouncement there was an irrefutable air of absoluteness about it that was very convincing. So after further discussion amongst themselves, the eight Brahmins all proclaimed that the infant prince would undoubtedly renounce the worldly life and become a Buddha. Since King Suddhodana had so earnestly prayed for a son, an heir to the throne, they selected the name 'Siddhartha,' which means 'he who has completed his task.' The king's need for an heir had now been satisfied," concludes Punna.

"The king must have been very distraught by the untimely death of his beloved wife, Queen Maha Maya, seven days after Prince Siddhartha's birth," comments Bakkula.

"That is true," answers Bhaddiya. "The king was extremely worried when his queen, who had seemed the picture of health before and after the prince's birth, started getting weaker by the day. Even so, she remained serenely joyful. All of a sudden she called all of her family members to her royal bedchamber and announced that in a few moments she would pass away. Her parents wept, as did her sister, Mahapajapati, and everyone else in the room – especially the king. Queen Maha Maya asked her sister to take care of her son, and Mahapajapati accepted the new responsibility with loving grace. The queen then asked to hold Siddhartha, and the nurse placed him in her arms. She held the infant tightly, kissed him many times, and then handed him to her sister.

"Then she said, 'If I have offended any of you in any way – especially you, my husband and king – please forgive me.' A few seconds later she closed her eyes and peacefully passed from this life." Bhaddiya pauses for a moment and then continues, "I was in the chamber that day, and I will never forget the grief, the wailing of many voices, and the sound of the king's tortured sobs."

Maha Kaccayana states, "It had been told that the mothers of all twenty-seven former Buddhas had left their bodies seven days after giving birth. The boddhisatta *Deva* Setaketu, as we know, saw his future mother's death as one of his five investigations before agreeing to be born as a human for the last time. Her former lifetime desire to one day become the mother of a Buddha had been fulfilled, and there was no longer any reason for the queen to remain alive. Similar to other mothers of Buddhas, Queen Maha Maya was instantly re-born in the *Tusita* heaven where she watched over her son throughout his entire life."[4]

The arahants in the cavern are very still at this point. They see with their inner eye the passing away of beloved Queen Maha Maya.

Ananda breaks the silence, "The prince was, of course, much loved, and very well cared-for by his step-mother, Queen Mahapajapati. She assigned many servants to protect him and attend to his needs. My first memories of Siddhartha are the two of us playing in the queen's apartments when we were about four or five years old. I can't remember exactly what we were doing, but I recall distinctly the queen's presence in the room. I noticed how she watched his every move. The servants absolutely loved the child, and they indulged him in every way."

"How could they not? I remember him very clearly as the most amazing child I had ever seen. He seemed like a fully-aware and mature adult, and sometimes he even acted like a wise sage from the Himalayas," says Bhaddiya.

"Do you remember the king's plowing festival, when Siddhartha and I were about seven or eight years old? I was there that day with my mother, not with the prince, and I later heard two different stories about what happened. Bhaddiya, could you please give us your eye-witness account?" asks Ananda.

"Of course," answers Bhaddiya. "The plowing festival was one of the great events of the year, and it seemed that the entire population had turned out that day. The ritual included the Brahmin priests who blessed the land and the seeds, praying for a good harvest. The king had a solid gold ceremonial plow, his ministers had ceremonial plows of silver, and about a thousand farmers and land-owners used their own work plows. They all engaged in various contests such as who could plow the most furrows and who was fastest.

"The king wanted Siddhartha to witness the event – I think to inspire him in regards to his birthright, and to impress him with the glory of Kapilavatthu. The prince's nurses set up a couch for the young prince under a rose-apple tree. From there he could watch the elaborate ceremony and the contests. The nurses stayed with him and watched him very carefully, as usual. At some point, however, they got caught up in the excitement, and drifted closer to the plowing contests for a better view of the men. They completely forgot about the young prince, and left him unattended.

"While the nurses were carried away in their enthusiasm, the prince slipped off his couch. His attention was drawn to a lizard at the edge of the field. The reptile was busily eating ants from a large anthill as fast as his little red tongue could dart in and out of his mouth. The prince was fascinated, and shocked at the same time, to see the ants running wildly trying to escape. Then he noticed a big snake slithering toward the unsuspecting lizard. The snake caught the lizard and began to swallow it whole.

"Siddhartha was stunned. He couldn't believe the act of savagery he had just witnessed. He watched the bulge made by the lizard slowly working its way down the satisfied body of the stretched-out snake. In the next instant, a huge brown hawk with a white head and sharp beak swooped down and grabbed the snake. The writhing reptile was swiftly carried off to the bird's lair," says Bhaddiya.

"I'm sure this traumatic event made a big impression on the young prince," says Sopaka.

"Indeed it did, as it was the beginning of what I call 'the big change' that came over Siddhartha. This was the first time he had actually seen with his own eyes the ugliness and suffering that can lurk behind beauty and peace. He viewed this scene with an even mind, and went back to his couch to think about it; he immediately went into deep meditation. An enormous wave of compassion for living beings swept over him, and transported him to the first *jhana*," concludes Bhaddiya.

"I hope the king didn't discover that the crown prince had been abandoned. I'm sure the nurses' punishment would have been quite severe," says Sopaka.

"He did, in fact, discover their transgression, but what happened next caused him to forget to punish them," replies Bhaddiya with a smile.

"Out of the corner of his eye the king saw the nurses playing and having a good time with the farmers at the edge of the field," continues Bhaddiya. "They were completely swept away in the moment. When the king didn't see the young prince with them he panicked and sent his attendant to find out where he was.

"The servant and a group of guards set off in search for Siddhartha. A minister spotted him under the rose-apple tree, and saw that he was completely absorbed in contemplation. The minister also saw that even though the sun had long passed over its zenith, the young prince still sat in the shade of the tree. Siddhartha should have been sitting in full sunlight, but the tree's shadow remained on him while he meditated. Needless to say, the minister was amazed.

"The minister immediately ran to the king with the good news, saying that he had found his young son and wanted to show him. The king was curious and anxious at the same time. A group of us followed the minister and the king, who found his son in the first stage of *jhana*. We were all completely stunned to see that the prince's body had actually levitated about a foot above the couch. The king slowly approached his son, bowed before him, and said, 'I pay homage to you a second time.'[5] Afterwards King Suddhodana stayed on his knees and watched his son meditate." concludes Bhaddiya.

"No wonder the king forgot to punish the nurses," says Anuruddha. "He was undoubtedly surprised by the prince's extraordinary abilities, and at the same time concerned that the prophecy might come true."

"While we were watching, Prince Nanda ran up to his brother and poked him in the ribs to get his attention. Siddhartha immediately came out of his reverie, and ran off to play with his beloved little brother. The king dearly loved both of his sons, and he was happy to see the two of them enjoying each other's company. He was probably in too good a mood to mete out punishment for the nurses that day," adds Bhaddiya.

"Prince Siddhartha truly loved his brother and his big sister, Princess Sundarinanda," says Ananda. "He doted on both of them and gave them many gifts. He didn't know until he was older that he actually had a different birth mother; he thought all three of them were the children of Queen Mahapajapati. I believe that the king wanted Queen Maha Maya's death to be kept secret from the crown prince for as long as possible; I don't think the king's mind was ever far away from the predictions about his son. I'm told that after the incident at the plowing festival he really started to be on the lookout for any tell-tale signs that Siddhartha might one day become an ascetic."

"This is true. The king started to obsess about how to prevent his son from learning anything about suffering," says Bhaddiya.

"What about your cousin Devadatta. Did you see him much when you were a child?" asks Punna.

"No, only occasionally," replies Ananda, "but I do remember him as being very proud as a young boy. I recall one particular day when Siddhartha and I were playing with some lower-caste children. Devadatta shouted at the prince and said 'Don't pay any attention to that young boy – he's way below our class!'

"Prince Siddhartha looked directly at Devadatta and said, 'Doesn't he have arms, legs, a mouth, nose, ears, and a body just like yours?'

"Devadatta thought about it and said, 'Yes, but so what? He's still a low-caste nobody. I will have nothing to do with him, and neither should you!'

"Siddhartha looked at him and said, 'How can you speak that way about someone who is a boy just like you? What's the difference between you and any other human being?'

"Devadatta sneered at Siddhartha and answered, 'Haven't you been listening to the Brahmins and the teachers? For thousands of years we have been rulers, and all the others have been who they are. That's just the way it is, Siddhartha; everyone has their place and they must stay in it. Furthermore, the castes should never mix – it pollutes us.'

"Siddhartha pondered Devadatta's statement for a moment and then said, 'Your blood and my blood and his blood are the same color; there is no difference in our blood. Maybe castes should be based on something else – like a person's actions. If someone performs wholesome acts they would be high-caste. If someone performs unwholesome acts they would be low-caste. One should be judged differently according to their actions, Devadatta. Otherwise there really is no difference between people,'" concludes Ananda.

"It's amazing that the Master already had these ideas at such a young age. He was born with exceptional reasoning skills which eventually led him to knowledge of the Dhamma," says Bakkula.

"Due to his countless past lives he came into this world prepared to become the Fully Enlightened One and to teach the Dhamma. When we discuss his education I'm sure we'll find many more examples of this kind," comments Maha Kaccayana. "Please continue about Devadatta, Ananda."

"He was very competitive, and always had to be the best, no matter what. He started to become jealous of Siddhartha because everyone always praised him. There was so much anger inside Devadatta, and it started to make him cruel. He began demonstrating a total lack of compassion for anyone or anything."

"Your last comment brings us to the famous story of the swan. Are all of you familiar with this one?" asks Anuruddha.

Some arahants nod in agreement; others shake their head, unaware of the story. "Why don't you relate this story since you were there, Anuruddha," says Ananda.

"Very well," responds Anuruddha. "One day Siddhartha, Devadatta, and some of the other royal children were playing games in the palace park. Since I was in my late teens, I sometimes watched them, and it turned out I was there that day. Devadatta was carrying around his bow and arrow, boasting of his hunting prowess. Prince Siddhartha was watching him carefully, knowing that he liked to kill innocent animals.

"Earlier in the day Siddhartha had said to him, 'Devadatta, you know it's not right to take life just for amusement.'

"Devadatta replied, 'Men are supposed to kill; that's our job. We are of the warrior caste, but you're just a weakling with no courage.'

"Prince Siddhartha looked at him with a stern expression, and said, 'Everyone, including animals, wants to live. Don't you understand that? Please don't kill innocent creatures. You don't want to be harmed, so you shouldn't harm others. You should treat others as you would want them to treat you.'

"Devadatta just shook his head and laughed at Siddhartha, 'What are you talking about? They can't do anything to me. I'm a prince!' Then he went off to another part of the park.

"Later, a great white swan suddenly crashed to the ground. Its cry was pitiful. Siddhartha quickly ran to where the bird had fallen, carefully picked it up, and began stroking its feathers to calm it. The beautiful bird's wing had been pierced right through by Devadatta's arrow. The prince gently removed the arrow from the injured wing and caressed the poor creature. Devadatta came running toward the prince and tried to grab the bird. Siddhartha turned so he shielded the swan, keeping it away from its intended murderer.

"Devadatta began yelling at the prince, 'Give that bird to me – it's mine! How dare you interfere with my hunting?'

"The prince answered calmly, 'No. I will never give it to you. If the swan had died by your arrow then it would be yours. But now, since it is alive, it belongs to me. I saved it.'

"Devadatta argued and tried his best to get the bird from him, but the prince was adamant and refused to budge. Finally Devadatta said, 'I'm going to tell your father.'

"Siddhartha replied, 'Go ahead and tell him. It's your right.'

"Devadatta went before the king to make his complaint. He was sure he was right and that the king would side with him. We followed the two boys to the king's chamber and they each told their version of the story.

"The king considered the matter carefully and said, 'I think it would be a good experience for you boys if you would take this matter to court. You can argue your case before the learned judges and then let them decide.'

"So Siddhartha and Devadatta went before the court and Devadatta went first saying, 'I shot this swan myself with my own bow and arrow. It clearly belongs to me. I brought it down, so it's rightfully my property.'

"When it was Siddhartha's turn, he said to the court, 'Birds are free; they only belong to the sky. If a bird is killed by a hunter then he belongs to the hunter. But if a bird is injured he belongs to the one who finds him and tries to save his life. I have no intention of keeping this swan after he is healed; I will release him back to the sky. For now, however, he's mine.'

"The judges deliberated for a while and finally their spokesman said, 'We rule in favor of Prince Siddhartha. The bird belongs to him.'

"Siddhartha smiled, bowed politely to the judges, and took the bird back to the palace with him. Devadatta was furious. The court's decision so enraged him that he carried this anger to the end of his days. Within a short time the bird was cured and released back to nature," concludes Anuruddha.

"Over the years more anger built up each time he lost to Siddhartha. From that day on, he seemed determined to make each meeting with the prince into a contest," adds Ananda. "He was consumed by jealousy, and he harbored such strong feelings of animosity that his mind began to turn to unwholesome thoughts of revenge."

"We all know where those unwholesome thoughts eventually led him, Ananda," says Punna, shaking his head.

"Yes, his actions led to his ultimate downfall, according to the law of *kamma*. The Buddha, however, remained compassionate to the end, and he never retaliated against Devadatta for his misguided plots and schemes. We'll talk about all of this later, I'm sure," replies Ananda.

"I think this is a good place to pause, Venerable Sirs. Upali, you have one more day of questioning tomorrow, and then the following day we can start on the Dhamma discourses. How does that sound, Ananda?" asks Maha Kassapa.

"It sounds fine to me, Venerable Sir. And on that note I will bid you all a good night. May the bliss of your meditations this evening reach sublime heights," says Ananda with a warm smile.

The arahants then proceed to leave Maha Kassapa's chamber. Once again, the faint blue light of their inner radiance lights their way through the dark caverns.

Chapter 4
Coming of Age as a Householder

The council has completed its questioning of Venerable Upali on the *Vinaya*; Maha Kassapa and the Rules and Discipline committee are satisfied that it has been reorganized in such a way that will withstand the test of time. It has been an arduous three weeks for Upali, the rules specialist, but he knows that the contributions he and the other arahants have made will be great and long-lasting.

Upali concludes his presentation to the council by saying, "I'm sure you all remember the Buddha's simile of the snake.[1] The Lord compared the grasping of the Dhamma with the grasping of a large snake. If you grab a snake by the middle of its body, its head can easily turn to strike you, causing you suffering or death. On the other hand, if you grasp the head of the snake, even though its body may wrap around your limbs, it cannot strike or cause you harm.

"The same goes with the Dhamma. If you grasp it *incorrectly*, it can cause a great deal of damage to yourself or to others. If you grasp it *correctly* it will reward you, as well as those you teach. The same can be said for the disciplinary rules of the *Vinaya*. Grasp their intentions, contexts, and meanings incorrectly, and the misunderstanding could cause irreparable harm to the Buddha *Sasana*. Grasp the truth upon which they were based correctly, and the Buddha *Sasana* will last forever."

The arahants at the council are familiar with the metaphor, and they nod in full agreement. Arahant Upali steps down from the platform and takes his seat with the others in the assembly hall.

Maha Kassapa then addresses the five hundred Sangha members, "At our next session Venerable Ananda will begin reciting the Dhamma discourses. Please make sure you grasp their meaning correctly, use your discrimination to see if they are spoken correctly, and then memorize them word for word. The meaning of the Dhamma cannot be recorded and passed down with errors; its purity must be preserved with precision."

With the completion of the *Vinaya* review, it is time to begin the main task of the First Sangha Council, the reorganization of all of the Dhamma materials. Up until this time the discourses of the Buddha were classified for memorization based on the "teacher's nine-fold instruction." In this system they are loosely grouped as prose, song, textual analysis, verse, inspired utterances, sayings, birth-stories, wonderful events, and questions and answers.[2] Ananda has been going over the body of *suttas* and other teachings in his mind, and he seeks a more practical way of grouping them. This task has been made much easier since he became an arahant, and a new system is beginning to take shape. He feels a canon might eventually be formalized, and he is looking forward to discussing his ideas with his fellow arahants.

Early the next morning Sopaka approaches Ananda in the quiet of his cave chamber. Ananda is sitting cross-legged in deep meditation, and the loyal attendant is reluctant to disturb him. He clears his throat and waits.

Ananda stirs and says softly, "I know, it's time for the council meeting. More and more I am drawn inward. I imagine there will come a time when I don't wish to return."

"Undoubtedly that time will come, Venerable Sir, but not before you have completed this important work. Everyone is depending on your remembrance of the Dhamma discourses so the memory monks can preserve them for the future. Have you decided where you will begin today?"

"I thought we would go over the longest discourses first, Sopaka. They will be the most taxing for the memory monks, so we might as well get most of them out of the way at the beginning," he replies.

"I think that would be a wise choice, sir. How many would you classify as 'long discourses'?"

"I've been going over them in my mind, and I counted thirty-four extremely long ones that would fit this category."

Sopaka shakes his head in disbelief. "How you can isolate thirty-four *suttas* out of eighty-four thousand teaching elements is beyond my comprehension, sir."

"Don't ask me how I do it, Sopaka. It's just something I was born with, a peculiar mental ability, if you will."

"Undoubtedly your memory is one of the reasons you were born on the same day as your cousin, Prince Siddhartha. You yourself are an integral component of the Buddha's work in his last birth," replies Sopaka.

As Ananda prepares to leave for the assembly, he says, "Is our subcommittee gathering again this evening to continue our story of the Lord Buddha's life? It's been one week since we last met."

"Yes, I received a message saying that we'll meet in Maha Kassapa's chamber after sunset. All of the members will be present, and I know everyone is looking forward to hearing more."

Ananda stands up, stretches his limbs, and looks inspired. He says smiling, "I know exactly how I'm going to start my part of the program today."

Sopaka accompanies the elder, who has been like a father to him since he was seven. When they reach the outdoors they both squint in the first rays of sunlight as Sopaka leads the way across the stony clearing to the assembly hall entrance.

King Ajatasattu is standing with members of his retinue, and he is conversing with a group of arahants. When he sees Ananda approaching he hurries toward him and bows to touch the revered monk's feet with great respect.

"Venerable Ananda, I understand you will be beginning the Dhamma discourses today. Venerable Maha Kassapa has given me permission to listen from the edge of the pavilion. It will be a great honor to hear you speak again," says the king.

"Your Majesty, it is good to see you, as always. Thank you for your many kindnesses in regards to sponsoring the council. We're all grateful for your hospitality."

"It is indeed a great opportunity for me to be able to offer *dana* to the five hundred esteemed arahants who have gathered here for the most important work of our lifetime," responds Ajatasattu. "This is indeed an auspicious historical event."

"And your name will be remembered forever because of your part in it, Your Majesty," says Ananda.

The king bows deeply and puts his palms together in reverence. Ananda places his right hand on Ajatasattu's forehead, giving him his blessing. He can't help but remember that the king had murdered his own father, King Bimbisara, who was the Buddha's great friend and patron. After killing his father he seized the throne of Magadha for himself. Ananda feels no judgment for the man; he only feels compassion, knowing that Ajatasattu's future rebirths will be extremely unpleasant as a result of his *kammic* actions.

When they are assembling in the hall, Maha Kassapa's attendant approaches Ananda and calls him to the platform. In unison, the arahants utter the words, "*Sadhu! Sadhu! Sadhu!*" Ananda bows gracefully to his Sangha brothers in return.

"Venerable Ananda, please take your place at the podium," says Maha Kassapa as he rises from his seat. He leans over and whispers to his old friend, "I hope you have taken plenty of Bakkula's herbs from the Himalayas; your voice is going to need its full strength today." Ananda winks and nods at him, smiling.

"You may begin where you like, Venerable Ananda," announces the chairman in front of the assembly.

"The purpose of this council is to organize the Lord's discourses into a categorized system that will make them easier to learn, memorize, and transmit to future generations," begins Ananda. "I will start today with what I call his 'long discourses,' because of their great length. I will begin with the one that I think provides the best overview of the Buddha's entire life's work and teachings. It is called the '*Brahmajala Sutta*:[3] The Supreme Net.'

"'Thus I heard: Once the Lord was travelling along the main road between Rajagaha and Nalanda with a large company of some five hundred monks. And the wanderer Suppiya was also travelling on that road with his pupil, the youth Brahmadatta...'"

Ananda then begins to recite the whole of the great *Brahmajala Sutta*, which sets forth a comprehensive summary of the Master's work. The subject matter is "What the Teaching is Not," and it deals with the roots and causes of wrong views. The Buddha reminds his listeners, among other things, that it is possible to become sidetracked on one's way to attaining *Nibbana*; therefore, he cautions them not to become attached to any view that does not lead all the way to the supreme goal. The Buddha talks about sixty-two views that were in existence during his time, and how each one claimed to be the only truth, and refuted the validity of all others. Without finding fault in any of the views, the Buddha tells his listeners that he clearly understands each of them, and he knows where they will ultimately lead. He points out that none of them will help one succeed in becoming enlightened, and that only by remaining unattached to all views will one be free, and therefore able to successfully find a way through the dense jungles of the mind, all the way to liberation.

"In regards to the sixty-two views the Buddha said:

>"'These viewpoints thus grasped and adhered to will lead to such-and-such destinations in another world. This, the *Tathagata* knows, and more, but he is not attached to that knowledge. And being thus unattached he has experienced for himself perfect peace; and having truly understood the arising and passing away of feelings, their attraction and peril, and the deliverance from them, the *Tathagata* is liberated without remainder.'"4

It takes Ananda several hours to complete the entire discourse. When he is finished, he steps down from the platform. Sopaka approaches him, "Are you tired, Venerable Sir? Would you like to rest?"

Ananda answers, "There is no more tiredness for me, Sopaka. I am free!"

Sopaka smiles at his beloved teacher while Ananda gladly accepts a cup of Himalayan potion from his friend Bakkula.

"Whenever you are ready, we still have time for another discourse," says Ananda to Maha Kassapa.

"Save some of your strength; you will need it later on when you tell us more of the Master's life," replies Maha Kassapa. "King Ajatasattu has catered our lunch in the forest today, so let's proceed."

The arahants wind their way down the hill in a long queue, and enter the shady forest where a great repast is waiting. Hundreds of servants have been busy preparing the food, and they are now ready to serve the king's guests. The arahants partake of their meals in silence while enjoying the soft breeze that cools them. The king himself supervises the luncheon, and with his own hand serves the senior monks.

After the lunch break, and for the next few hours, Ananda recites another of the long discourses.

Later, when the sun has gone down, Ananda and the other subcommittee members gather in Maha Kassapa's chamber to continue their recollections of the life of the Buddha.

"Tell us about Siddhartha's education, Ananda. I think this is where we left off last time," requests Maha Kaccayana.

"I was his classmate while we were growing up, and I received the same education he did. Siddhartha excelled in everything, of course, and even though I was a good student, I was no match for him."

"Why wasn't Prince Siddhartha sent away to study as was custom in those days?" asks Punna.

"He actually had his heart set on going to Taxila, a great center of eclectic learning in the northwest, far away from Kapilavatthu. It boasted of teachers from all of the great systems in the known world, including Greece. King Suddhodana, however, felt that such a liberal and sophisticated place might provide his son with too many opportunities to become attracted to an ascetic way of life. Other close friends of Siddhartha's and mine were sent to Rajagaha or Varanasi, but the king's teacher, Asitadevala, warned him of their intellectual and spiritual temptations, and advised him to keep the prince in Kapilavatthu where he could keep a closer eye on him," explains Ananda.

"What did your parents want for you?" asks Maha Kaccayana.

"They wanted me to be with Prince Siddhartha, so I wound up studying with him in the palace – along with dozens of other youths from aristocratic families. I loved my cousin dearly, and I would have refused to be separated from him anyway. The king hired the best possible tutors for us, including Visvamitra. His ministers recommended him as the best available, and the most acquainted with all fields of learning. Queen Mahapajapati was the one who broke the news to the prince that he was not to be allowed to study abroad, and Siddhartha was definitely disappointed. Still, he made the most of his home schooling, and he mastered everything he was taught."

"Visvamitra was a scholar of the Vedas and the Vedanta, wasn't he?" asks Punna.

"Yes, and even though he wasn't a Brahmin the king wanted his son to have a solid foundation in the teachings of his cultural forebears. Visvamitra, however, soon learned that the young prince already knew the four Vedas, all of the Sastras and Sutras, and was even able to teach them to others. He was amazed at the young man's accomplishments, and the fact that no one had ever taught him before," says Ananda. "For the martial skills and politics the king hired Ksantadeva, the son of Suppabuddha, who was an expert in both fields. The king often relied on both instructors to guide him in the administration of his Sakyan kingdom."

"What were some of the other subjects the Master studied – besides the Vedas and polity?" asks Maha Kaccayana.

"He excelled at mathematics, and he was particularly good with languages and writing. One day the prince picked up a sandalwood tablet, ink, and a golden pen encrusted with jewels. With no prior instruction he asked his teacher, 'which form of writing, sir, do you wish to teach me? Is it Kharosthi or Pushkarasan?' He held the golden pen aloft and mentioned sixty four other languages, and then he demonstrated writing all of them for the tutor. While he was just a teenager Siddhartha even invented a new alphabet called *'Brahmi'* script.[5] Visvamitra was at a complete loss, because he knew he had nothing to teach the prince," says Ananda. "I was there that day, and I can assure you that this is true."

"What about the martial skills – particularly archery?" asks Punna.

"When Ksantadeva met the prince for the first time he also realized there was nothing he could teach him. After watching him a few minutes he said, 'Prince, if you wish, you may practice on your own.' The teacher wound up teaching the rest of us, while Siddhartha trained alone. His archery skills had no equal. I know you've heard those fantastic stories about him shooting arrows through plates of iron, and I must tell you that they are myths. I will say, however, that he could win any normal contest hands down; he virtually had no peer," replies Anuruddha.

"Was Devadatta jealous growing up with someone so gifted and skillful?" asks Sopaka.

"Yes, you could literally see his frustration growing by the day. He was already a terrible bully by the time he was ten, and his arrogance and cruelty grew rapidly from that time onward," says Anuruddha.

"Remember the famous swan story? You can just imagine how competitive Devadatta was when Siddhartha started besting him in every contest. He rarely spoke a civil word to any of us; he became completely consumed and motivated by his negative inclinations," says Ananda.

"One day Devadatta became so enraged that he killed a baby elephant that had been a gift to Siddhartha from the Licchavi princes of Vesali. The prince, as you know, dearly loved every living creature, and he was greatly disturbed by the animal's murder. He kept his composure, however, and never even quarreled with Devadatta over this incident," remarks Anuruddha.

"When did the king build the three palaces for Prince Siddhartha?" asks Bakkula.

"He was sixteen years old when his father built him the three palaces, and there have never been any equals in terms of luxury and refinement. The king hired the most celebrated architects, masons, sculptors, carpenters, and painters in the land to construct the Ramya palace for winter, the Suramya palace for summer, and the Subha palace for spring. The palaces were about the same size, but each one had a different number of tiers in the towering spire," answers Anuruddha. "The spire of Ramya palace had nine tiers, Suramya had five, and Subha had seven. The height of the roofs and ceilings of each palace was also different, and they were perfectly matched for the season, keeping the interior spaces cool, warm, or dry."[6]

"Did you spend a lot of time in those palaces, Anuruddha?" queries Punna.

"Oh yes, you could always find me wherever the prince was. Imagine the two of us at sixteen and twenty-three years old – enjoying the most luxurious life possible. Female musicians provided music continuously, and the finest food and wines were served at all hours of the day and night. The palaces themselves were superb works of art, and each one had magnificent paintings suitable for each season. The winter palace, for example, had paintings of blazing flames on its walls, central planks, and roofs. When you gazed at them they dispelled the feeling of coldness. Seasonally appropriate textiles decorated the three palaces: wools, velvet and silks for the winter, cool sheer cotton for the summer, and a combination of both for the rainy season. Each palace was also furnished with garments that matched the different climates.

"The rooms of each palace were festooned with ornaments made of pearls, flowers, and precious gems. The ceilings of Ramya palace were canopied with sheer fabric, and were adorned with stars of gold, silver, and rubies. These stars created bright and flaming colors in the torchlight.

The summer palace was a virtual water park, with lakes, pools, and earthen-ware pots filled with lotuses of all shades. Perfumed water was also kept in gold and silver containers that adorned every room. I remember the prince liked to wear blue garments in the summer to match the color of the water, of which he was very fond. Aquatic birds like swans, ducks, and herons were kept in the ponds so there would always be birdsong.

"The palace for the rainy season was designed using medium proportions so that either heat or cooling could be created depending on the weather. I particularly liked this palace because of the way we could change our garments and re-configure the doors and walls to match the alternating stormy and pleasant climatic conditions. Sometimes Siddhartha and I would climb the golden stairs to the seventh tier and stand there in the wind, howling with our loudest voices at the thunder, challenging the lightning with our youthful bravado."

"Did the prince entertain often during those days?" asks Upali.

"Let me answer that question, sir. I, too, was Prince Siddhartha's cousin, and although I was fifteen years older than he was, I was often a guest at his endless parties," responds Bhaddiya.

Ananda laughs and says, "*Often a guest*, he says! I'm not sure if you ever went home, dear cousin. I don't remember a single party that you didn't attend, and you were always the one who played the comic, amusing all of us with your clever jokes and anecdotes. You also liked your wine, if I remember correctly."

Bhaddiya smiles, reflects, and says, "Yes, those were definitely the days of wine, music girls, and excessive amusement. The prince encouraged all of us to enjoy ourselves. I particularly liked the summer palace and its water park with the small boats. I was the one who promoted our sailing competitions that usually ended in capsizing one another."

"But you know, even during those hilarious times the prince would often disappear and go off by himself. I would go looking for him and find him in unexpected places, sometimes deep in meditation," says Ananda.

"Even then he was concerned about life outside, knowing that the palace environment was totally artificial. I think he sensed that suffering was never far from his cloistered enclave," remarks Anuruddha.

"Anyway, that lifestyle began to come to an end when Channa, his charioteer, took him on those excursions beyond the palace walls. I know there are a lot of stories about the Master's first exposure to sickness, old age, death, and ascetics – and how he had absolutely no idea of their existence until those four occasions with Channa. Prince Siddhartha was far from uninformed, and he was the most intelligent individual that any of us have ever known. I'm certain he knew full well the hard facts of life well before that time. It's just that on those outings with Channa he seemed to have been particularly sensitive – and definitely ready, if you will – to fully examine them for the first time," says Ananda.

"I think you're getting a bit ahead of your story, cousin," remarks Anuruddha. "Before the prince began examining the truths inherent in the four signs, he married and lived quite happily for a number of years."

"You are correct, venerable cousin," replies Ananda. "I only wished to point out that even though the prince was surrounded by luxury from a very early age, there was always something different about him. He oftentimes seemed to retreat to an interior world all his own, into which none of us could penetrate. To portray him as completely unaware of life outside the palace is absurd. Prince Siddhartha was very well aware of everything going on around him, and in the rest of the known world as well. The prince experienced a deep connectivity to all things, all people, and all places, and to believe stories about him being oblivious to reality is just another myth."

"So tell us, Ananda, how was a wife chosen for the young prince," requests Maha Kaccayana.

"Shortly after the completion of the three palaces, the king's elder advisors came up with the suggestion that it was time for the prince to get married. Their reason was the fact that the Sakyan kingdom would soon need an heir for the next generation.

"The king asked the elders, 'so which maiden do you think would be worthy of the prince?'

"Each elder in turn said, 'my daughter is beautiful and worthy of the prince.'

"The king now had many applicants, so in order to be diplomatic he said, 'I must first ask the prince what sort of maiden he wishes.'

"When the king put the question to Siddhartha, the young prince said that he would think about it, and give him an answer in seven days.

"A week later the prince went to see his father and described his ideal bride in detail. The prince said that a maiden who would be worthy would not be an ordinary one. She must be free of envy, ever truthful, ever vigilant, and thoroughly pure in birth and lineage. She must also be accomplished in writing and in composing poetry.

"The prince went on to say that she must be beautiful, but not be proud. She must also be benevolent, and disposed to giving alms. She must have no ill-repute, fault, wickedness, or affectation."

"Our young Prince Siddhartha definitely knew the kind of maiden he was looking for, didn't he?" comments Upali.

"He certainly did. I'm convinced that he knew from the beginning that there could only be one possible candidate in the world. That's why he made his list the way he did – to make sure he got the woman he knew was destined for him. Anyway, the prince continued by saying that she must be religious, and be pure in body, speech and mind. She must be attentive to her religious obligations and dutifully respectful towards her in-laws. She must be pleasant to her maids and dependants, and be devoted to her friends. When the prince finished his long list of qualities I'm sure his father was quite taken aback," says Ananda.

"So how did the king go about finding a maiden who could possibly fit those requirements?" asks Bakkula.

"The king sent his emissaries throughout Kapilavatthu, as well as to the neighboring kingdoms, to find someone who could fit the prince's description. The search lasted several weeks, and finally they came to report that they had found only one suitable candidate: the daughter of Suppabuddha, who by then had become the king of Koliya when his father King Anjana passed away. The young princess also happened to be Devadatta's sister.

"In order to be diplomatic, King Suddhodhana arranged a formal ceremony for Prince Siddhartha to choose a bride from a number of candidates – including the one chosen by the emissaries and the daughters of the elders and other aristocrats. During the ceremony the prince noticed only Princess Yasodhara, and he made his choice known to his father. Shortly afterwards the king dispatched a messenger to her father to formally ask for her hand in marriage to his son," continues Ananda.

"Don't forget to mention the conditions, cousin," says Anuruddha.

"Suppabuddha's response message said, 'The prince is thriving at home. We have a family custom not to give a daughter to anyone who is not an expert in the martial arts. The prince has not proved his proficiency in the use of bows, elephant riding, and wrestling. I shall only give my daughter to one who is expert in these esteemed skills,'" explains Ananda.

Anuruddha continues, "The king dispensed with elephant riding and wrestling. He suggested that there should be an archery exhibition where Prince Siddhartha could demonstrate his prowess with an exceptionally heavy bow. The exhibition was arranged, and the prince exceeded everyone's expectations. Siddhartha may not have shot an arrow through a hundred plates of iron, as the legends say, but he did complete the demonstration with one hundred percent accuracy. I was there on that occasion, and I saw with my own eyes the prince's extreme concentration and its resultant success.

"After the archery performance Yasodhara's parents were convinced that Prince Siddhartha could marry their daughter. Yasodhara later told me that Devadatta thought otherwise, and he stridently expressed his views that same evening to his parents and sister.

"During the family meeting Devadatta said, 'I think Siddhartha is completely wrong for my sister. He's often moody and goes off by himself all the time. Don't forget the predictions at his birth. I think that one day he'll abandon his wife and go off and live like a hermit. He'll hurt you, Yasodhara. Don't marry him.'

"Yasodhara told me she answered her brother calmly, 'I know that you have always been jealous of Siddhartha, and that you're saying these things just to keep him from being happy. I want to marry Siddhartha, and if I can't have him then I'll have no other. I know I can make him happy, and then he'll never want to leave me.'

"Suppabuddha carefully considered the statements of both his children, and eventually gave his daughter permission to marry the prince. Preparations for the wedding began almost immediately," concludes Ananda.

"The wedding must have been an amazing spectacle, from what I've heard," says Punna.

"Nothing like it had ever been seen before in Kapilavatthu – or perhaps in any kingdom of India, for that matter," begins Anuruddha.

"Preparations for the event took nearly three months, and extra provisions had to be brought in from as far away as Rajagaha. The bride's family came with a party of several thousand, and the gifts they brought were carried on the backs of four hundred caparisoned elephants. Scores of graceful, well-trained female attendants were brought to serve the royal couple in their three palaces, many of them accomplished in the musical arts.

"The wedding ceremony took place in the grand reception hall of the king's palace, and it was presided over by a host of Brahmin priests. The princess wore a gown made of sheer white silk spun with gold. She looked breathtaking that day; never before had I seen a young woman of such beauty and radiance. The prince was outfitted in the costliest velvet robes of indigo blue and magnificent jewels. Upon his head he wore a crown of rubies and diamonds, one of which was of oval shape and the size of a peacock egg.

"After the feast, which lasted nearly two full days, the couple retired to their summer palace where they were left in seclusion for a fortnight. It was reported that the prince and princess were exceedingly happy," concludes Anuruddha.

"So the marriage turned out to be a love match," says Bhaddiya. "After the honeymoon, Ananda, Anuruddha, and I and some of the prince's other friends were invited to the summer palace for a celebration that lasted nearly a week. I can attest to the fact that the royal couple was inseparable; they never parted for a single moment. Even in the midst of the revelry they acted as if they were completely alone."

"I remember that joyous week as if it were yesterday," continues Ananda. "The prince and the princess were so devoted to one another, so much in love. Meanwhile we entertained ourselves inside the palace, on the wide verandas, in the parks, and even in the ponds. We swam and floated on rafts that were decorated like miniature mansions, complete with pillows of silk and sunshades of golden gauze."

"Our lives continued in that carefree, peaceful way for many years," says Anuruddha. "I forgot to mention that the prince and princess were both eighteen years old when they married, and together they enjoyed the full splendor of their youth. We were all very happy in that life of wealth and luxury, and then the prince began to show signs of dissatisfaction – not with the princess, but with life in general. He began to brood and sink into deep thought. We started to worry about him, but his father truly became concerned. His reaction was to give even more gifts to the couple, lavish them with more and more luxury, as if that were possible. He also increased the number of guards on the palace gates."

"We went with the prince and princess from palace to palace as the seasons changed, and the music played on for eleven years. There was barely a moment between the ending of one party and the beginning of the next," concludes Bhaddiya.

"In all fairness to the crown prince, I think we shouldn't fail to mention that throughout his late teens and twenties he served as an advisor to his father on political and economic matters. He also assisted him in several areas of his kingdom's administration," says Ananda. "When he was officially made *yuva raj*, or crown prince, he took on even more state duties."

"Don't forget the social projects Prince Siddhartha created for Kapilavatthu's underprivileged. One of his primary interests was the public hospital he and Princess Yasodhara founded, which took care of those who couldn't afford medical care. There were also the agricultural programs he dreamed up that helped the farmers with new techniques that would increase their crop yields. There was also what I call the prince's 'science projects,' where he experimented with new municipal technologies, particularly management of water resources. In many ways the prince was a great help to his father, and the kingdom prospered from his tremendous foresight, sound ideas, and practical economic reforms. To paint the picture of the crown prince as a spoiled party boy wouldn't do him justice at all," comments Bhaddiya.

These last statements cause the arahants to pause and consider a different dimension of the prince's privileged early life that perhaps foreshadowed the future Buddha's teaching. It also helps them better understand the sound advice and positive guidance he later gave countless individuals who made their livelihood in a wide array of disciplines.

The chairman stands up and says, "I think this is a fitting place to end for now. The sun will be up soon, and Ananda will be reciting another long discourse. We'll say good-night now, my friends, and may your meditations be full of joy and peace."

Chapter 5
The Four Foresigns

Five days pass, and another ten of the long discourses have been recited. Ananda's voice is still good, and his memory, of course, is as lucid and powerful as ever. The sub-committee is gathered in Maha Kassapa's cave chamber, and the arahants are discussing Prince Siddhartha's life from the time of his wedding to the occurrence of the famous Four Foresigns.

"As we've already said, Prince Siddhartha was far from ignorant about life outside the palace walls. To believe that his charioteer, Channa, had to explain the harsh facts of old age, sickness, death, and the existence of asceticism to the young man is absurd. The prince already knew full well of these realities, and it makes no sense to portray him as so caught up in his life of luxury that it had never occurred to him to think about them," says Anuruddha.

"On many occasions we discussed these things. Oftentimes a friend would get sick, an elder relation would visit the palace, a friend's grandparent would pass away, or a band of wandering ascetics would pass through Kapilavatthu. Also, by this time the prince had found out that his birth mother had passed away seven days after he was born, so death was no stranger to him. Don't forget that he and Yasodhara had founded a hospital that cared for the poor, and he had also engaged in a great deal of social work to improve the life of the lower castes.

"The fact is, we all had ample opportunity to learn about the down side of life, and we discussed the subject of suffering many times. The prince's knowledge of these four aspects of life is not the issue: how he *reacted* to them when he and Channa made those four forays outside the palace walls *is*," comments Punna.

"Ananda, I know your memory is far superior to mine, but I remember one of the Buddha's discourses when he visited the Brahmin Rammaka's hermitage. He actually said, '...*Bhikkhus*, before my enlightenment, while I was still only an unenlightened *Bodhisatta*, I too, being myself subject to birth, sought what was also subject to birth; being myself subject to ageing, sickness, death, sorrow, and defilement, I sought what was also subject to ageing, sickness, death, sorrow, and defilement.'[1] The Lord could not have uttered those words if he hadn't had some deep understanding way before his renunciation," comments Maha Kaccayana.

"Venerable Sir, I also believe this is so. But up until this time the prince lived a very happy life, enjoying his wealth, his family, his beautiful wife who was expecting their first child, perfect health, and all that could be desired as a householder. As we have already stated, Siddhartha had always been a contemplative, and daily meditation practice had long been his routine. Those of us who were close watched as he grew in spiritual awareness over the years, and we knew of his deep interest in teachers, ascetics, and the Vedic scriptures. We also recognized the fact that even though he didn't talk about them frequently, he had deep spiritual aspirations that he one day hoped to fulfill," says Ananda.

The arahants are silent for a moment and then Bhaddiya says, "Before the excursions with Channa, the prince had been in a reflective mood for weeks; as if there was some problem he was trying to solve. We tried talking with him, and we did our best to distract him, but he just wanted to be alone most of the time. He told us that he was trying to understand something, trying to think it through."

"Later, of course," continues Ananda, "we realized that he had been thinking about the nature of suffering and impermanence, but he said nothing about it at the time."

"Let me tell you the story the way Channa once told it to me," says Anuruddha.

The arahants give the revered monk their undivided attention, waiting to hear the truth from one of the prince's relatives and contemporaries.

"Channa told me that one day the prince asked him to prepare his chariot for a visit to one of his favorite parks near Kapilavatthu. This request was nothing particularly unusual considering the season and good weather, so Channa happily complied.

"Channa steered the chariot and its four magnificent thoroughbreds through the palace gates and onwards toward Prince Siddhartha's destination. The prince's usual company of sixteen guards and attendants followed at a discreet distance on horseback. As they passed, the townspeople, happy to see the prince, bowed to him with great respect, and waved him on with smiling faces.[2]

"About half way to the park they passed a decrepit old man, sickly and shivering. He was bent down like an old rafter, supporting himself on a walking stick.

"'Stop!' the prince cried out. 'What's the matter with that man?'

"Channa was surprised at the question, since the answer seemed so obvious, and he looked at the prince quizzically. He answered as normally as possible and replied, 'That's just an old man, my lord.'

"'I understand that people get old, Channa; I've noticed the white hairs in my father's beard. But I've never seen a man in such bad shape as this one,' said Siddhartha, who seemed to have a strange new tone in his voice.

"Channa told me that the prince dismounted from the chariot and approached the old man. Seeing the beloved prince, the old man immediately struggled to his knees to touch the prince's feet; his shoulders were stooped from a life of hard work.

"Siddhartha kneeled down beside the poor old man and put his arm around his bending frame. There were tears in the prince's eyes and his blessed face was filled with concern. The old man seeing this said, 'Please Your Highness, do not weep for me; I am not worthy of your tears. I am old and will soon be gone from this world. I am alone, my wife and children are dead, and I will be happy to leave.'

"The prince looked the old, wizened man directly in the eye and asked him, 'Have you suffered much in this life?'

"The old man replied, 'No more than anyone else, Your Highness. I've had happy moments, too. I had my youth as you now have yours, and my pleasures as well.'

"'Where are you going?' asked the prince.

"The old man stopped to think a moment then said, 'Nowhere, Your Highness. I have no home since my son passed away, and I am on my way to beg for my daily food.'

"Channa said that the prince shouted to him, 'Have my servants take this old father back to the palace and give him food. Make sure they find some kind people who will care for him. I will pay for any expenses.'

"The old man looked up at the prince in total disbelief. His mouth was agape, completely speechless. Channa issued the prince's command, and Siddhartha watched as the servants carefully lifted the old man on to one of the horses behind a guard.

"'Don't worry, father; you have a home now, and you will have your daily food.'

"The guard rode slowly back to the palace with the old man riding behind him, holding tightly to his waist. When the man turned around and waved to the prince there were tears of joy in his eyes.

"Channa said that the prince then commanded him, 'Take me back to the palace now.' He had regained his normal composure, but he seemed distant; his mind was elsewhere.

"Channa said, 'We didn't even get to the park, my lord; are you sure you want to go back so early?'

"The prince replied, 'Just take me home. I've had enough for today.'

"Channa said that he was deeply concerned about his master. On the way back to the palace the prince's mood seemed withdrawn; he was turned so deeply inward that Channa knew it would be useless to attempt conversation.

"Channa took Siddhartha back to the palace and when the prince was walking toward the entrance he heard him say, 'Damn this thing called birth! Everyone who is born is eventually faced with old age; no one can escape!'

"Channa just stood there in the chariot, completely dumbfounded. He told me the prince had completely changed; he was no longer the same happy, carefree young man he had known all his life. Remember, Venerable Sirs, that Channa was born the same day as the prince, and he knew his master well," says Anuruddha.

"What happened then?" asks Punna.

"Word about the incident soon reached the king and he sent for Channa, asking, 'How was your outing in the park? Did the prince practice archery? Was he happy?'

"Channa, being completely guileless, said, 'We never made it to the park, Your Majesty. Half way there the prince wanted to return to the palace. He did not seem happy, sir.'

"The king then asked Channa to explain, and Channa gave a complete account of the encounter with the old man.

"King Suddhodana, troubled by Channa's report, walked away without saying a word. I later learned from the queen that the king had seven disturbing dreams that night. The following morning he called the Brahmins to interpret them for him. One of the seers said the dreams were foretelling the prince's departure from the palace. It also signaled the eventual renunciation of his family and position, and the attainment of supreme enlightenment; he would then set the wheel of Dhamma in motion for the sake of gods and humans.

"The king was beside himself when he heard this news, and he went immediately to see Minister Kaludayi, seeking his advice. Kaludayi, too, was born on the same day as the prince and they had grown up together. The king also talked to the queen and asked her what could be done. In both cases the king was advised to increase the prince's amusements. He told the queen to urge everyone attending the prince to use every possible device to keep him engrossed in pleasure. The king also assigned special guards to closely observe his son," concludes Anuruddha.

"Unfortunately for the king, after a few weeks the prince grew tired of being amused and once again asked Channa to prepare the chariot for an excursion to the park," says Ananda.

"This time Channa chose a more remote route – one he thought would be deserted at that hour. He wanted to avoid another similar incident that he would have to report to the king," remarks Anuruddha.

"This time they encountered a sick man, one who was in the advanced stages of leprosy. When the prince spotted him on the side of the road he immediately ordered Channa to halt the chariot. Siddhartha got down and walked over to the man, and without hesitation he reached for his diseased hand.

"'Prince Siddhartha, please don't touch him! He is infected with leprosy!' screamed Channa.

"The prince ignored his charioteer's plea and took the man's hand in both of his. The sick man tried to pull back, but Siddhartha held on to him.

"'Please, Your Highness, it's not good for you to touch me. Not only am I of the lowest caste, I am a pariah. No one is to touch me,' implored the sick man.

"The prince looked at the man's hand and saw that where his fingers and thumb had been there were now stumps. Sores were festering, red and yellow liquid oozed from them. The man's face was pockmarked and scarred, and his nose was no longer a nose. Siddhartha simply held the infected hand and looked into the man's eyes, not caring that pus was touching his own fair skin.

"'Have you had this condition long, my friend?' asked the prince.

"The man replied, 'For nearly ten years, Your Highness.'

"Prince Siddhartha asked if he had had any medical attention, and the man told him that there was nothing that could be done for the disease. With deep sadness in his voice the man said, 'The doctors are helpless to cure it.'

"'Where do you live? Do you have a family?' asked the prince.

"'I live with the others who also have this condition – in a desolate place with no water. My wife, who mercifully is not infected, stays with me, but my two daughters are with relatives in the town; they are forbidden to come anywhere near me,' replied the man.

"'Channa, have my servants bring food and medicine to this man, and find out where these people dwell so we can provide our patronage,' ordered the prince.

"The poor man sunk to his knees and kissed the prince's sandal. With great emotion he said, 'Bless you, Your Highness. You are saving us by relieving our suffering.'

"The prince was also full of emotion. He walked back to his chariot with a deeply furrowed brow. 'Take me back to the palace, Channa," he commanded.

"'We never even got to the park, Prince; are you sure you wouldn't like to go for just a little while? Practicing archery would be good for you,' responded Channa.

"'Just take me home. I am in no mood for sport today,' was his terse reply.

"Channa said that when he took the prince back to the palace Siddhartha got off the chariot and said, 'Damn this thing called sickness! Everyone eventually gets sick. There is no escape!'

"Channa, as ordered by the king, reported the incident as soon as he and the prince returned to the palace. This time the king was more disturbed than ever. He cried out, 'What can be done for my son? What can I do to save him?' His response to Channa's report was to order even more pleasures for Siddhartha, and to increase the number of guards at the palace gates," concludes Anuruddha.

"Moved by these incidents, the prince's compassion was growing," comments Punna. "It would continue to grow, wouldn't it? We are all arahants because of his great compassion. I don't imagine the leper was as lucky." The sub-committee members are silent for a moment as they ponder the unfortunate fate of the leper.

"Tell us, Anuruddha, about the third excursion," requests Bakkula.

Anuruddha takes a sip of herbal tea and continues, "We noticed a change in the Prince. He pursued his pleasures with such intensity that we were astonished. He also dived into his administrative duties and social projects with extreme vigor. It was as if he was trying to drown himself in activity, and stamp out the knowledge that was growing in his mind.

"Unfortunately, the relentless pursuit of amusement and hard work didn't last. After about two weeks he seemed to run out of steam, and once again Siddhartha called for his chariot. The king got the news and sent out his guards to make sure the road to the park was cleared of anyone who was sick or old. The king had no way of knowing, however, that the prince would choose another road, and he ordered Channa to drive the chariot toward the river. When they arrived at the Anoma there was a poor family gathered on the banks, preparing a funeral pyre for their father. He had passed away the day before, and the shrouded corpse was lying with its feet in the river, as is the custom.

"The man's wife and three young children were wailing. Other relatives were beside themselves with grief. The prince ordered Channa to stop the chariot. When he stepped down and approached the bereaved family they immediately silenced their voices and dropped to their knees.

"Siddhartha walked over to the corpse and pulled the muslin fabric back to expose the man's head. He looked down at the grey, ashen face, its expression frozen in the last painful agonies of death. The prince gasped, suddenly overcome with emotion. Channa and the prince's attendants just stood there, not believing their eyes.

"'Please, Your Highness, let us leave here at once. It is not good for you to see these things,' said Channa, who had moved beside his lord.

"The prince just stared at his charioteer, momentarily unable to speak. Finally he told Channa, 'Have servants bring sandalwood paste for the fire, and food for this poor family.'

"Siddhartha turned to the widow and said, 'Was your husband sick a long time? Did he suffer?'

"The widow answered, 'He was fine yesterday morning. Then he complained of stomach pain after eating lunch, and he was dead by mid-afternoon,' she replied. 'We all ate the same food, so I have no idea what happened. During the last two or three hours his pain was unbearable, and nothing I did seemed to help.' After saying these words she broke down in sobs.

"The Prince answered, 'It seems that death chooses at whim when not to be a stranger. Life seems to be only a temporary condition, my dear friends, and we must face death when it comes.'

"Siddhartha walked back to the chariot told Channa to take him back to the palace."

"Channa begged him, 'Please, Your Highness, let's go to the park. It's been many weeks since you've had any amusement.'

"'That's not true, Channa,' was his reply. 'All I've been doing is amusing myself, and nothing satisfies me! I want to go home now.'

"Channa did as he was ordered. He turned the chariot around and headed back to the palace. When they arrived, Channa told me that the prince looked him in the eye and said, 'Damn this thing called death! Eventually all humans die. There is no escape!'

"The charioteer immediately reported this third aborted excursion to the king. Suddhodana simply closed his eyes and wept. Later he hired more music girls, and told his ministers to devise even more pleasures for his son. He went to the queen for consolation, but her comfort was fleeting, and the worry always returned," says Anuruddha.

"How was it possible to provide the prince with even more amusements than before? The prince's palace must have been filled to the brim with entertainers and all sorts of pleasures by then," says Bakkula, raising his eyebrows.

"The palace was literally teeming with female dancers and musicians, and the servants organized the most lavish banquet imaginable," begins Bhaddiya. "The chefs prepared the prince's favorite foods, and the rarest delicacies were brought in from Varanasi. Even though it was summer, we had ice for our wine, carried down from the Himalayas on the backs of peasants. Princess Yasodhara was in charge of the preparations, and she herself choreographed the timing of each successive performance, each new course of food and drink.

"All of the prince's closest friends were called – we had no choice but to be there. Siddhartha's cousins were also commanded to attend; they even summoned the princess's brother, Devadatta. By this time we were all so steeped in amusements and pleasures that we had little appetite for more. However, since it was the king's command we did our best to entertain the prince, and that night my comic abilities were taxed to their limits," continues Bhaddiya.

"I remember the party lasting until sunrise, and the prince danced and carried on to the last. Finally, seeing that the entertainers and guests were drunk from exhaustion and wine, the prince retired to his private chambers where the princess had gone hours before," says Ananda.

"I will never forget that evening," says Anuruddha. "I eventually took a pillow out to the veranda and lay down to sleep. Early in the afternoon I heard footsteps, and opening my eyes I saw the prince picking his way through the party's debris. Dancing girls and musicians seemed to have dropped wherever they were when the prince left the party.

"The girls were disheveled in various stages of undress with their costumes out of place. The prince later told me that he thought they looked like dead bodies strewn about randomly in the charnel ground. Their makeup was smeared, and I saw several who had drooled spittle on themselves. Two or three had been sick and vomited on their saris. Even though the most fragrant perfumes in the world were in vessels throughout the palace, there was such an overwhelming stench of humanity mixed with wine that I nearly gagged. I could see by the look on the prince's face that he was completely disgusted," says Anuruddha.

"I think the aftermath of that party was the real turning point for Prince Siddhartha. After that night he no longer wanted entertainment of any kind. He sent the music girls and dancers home, and told them he no longer needed them. This put a large number of young women out of work – not to mention the caterers, provisioners, and entertainers whose livelihoods abruptly ended. The prince became increasingly more reclusive, and he doubled or tripled the time he spent in meditation. He would go off by himself to the far corners of the palace gardens, giving orders that he was not to be disturbed," relates Bhaddiya.

"When questioned by the king, we were all at a loss, unable to explain the prince's behavior," says Ananda. "The queen visited her son on a number of occasions trying to counsel him. She told me about a conversation she had with him one day.

"'Why, son, has this sudden change come upon you?' she asked. 'Is there anything your father or I can provide that will make you happy?'

"He answered, 'I understand now that the purpose of my life is not just to make myself happy, mother. How can I be happy when there is so much suffering in the world? Am I to forever pass my days in search of fleeting moments of pleasure, knowing that they will soon fade?'

"The queen asked Siddhartha what he wanted from this life, if not happiness.

"He responded, 'I want to be free from *desiring* happiness. I get what I want, get bored with it, and then I want something else. Every pleasure ends in dissatisfaction, mother. I want to be free from this fruitless cycle.'

"The queen had no answer for her troubled son. She loved him with all her heart, but this time she knew it was not in her power to give him what he wanted," says Ananda.

"What about the fourth fore-sign? When did that take place?" asks Punna.

"About three months after the last banquet Siddhartha summoned Channa," begins Anuruddha. "The loyal charioteer dreaded that something else might happen, but he went ahead and prepared for another excursion to the park. The king made sure there were no sick people, no old people, and no cremations on any route the prince may choose to take. He sent his guards in advance to clear the way of anything that looked unpleasant. The roads had all been cleared when the royal chariot left the palace."

"As they approached the park's entrance they passed through a wooded area. To one side there was a path to the Himalayan foothills. As fate would have it, just when the prince's party passed that path an ascetic, wearing only a loincloth, was entering the main road. He had matted hair and his dirty fingernails were long and unkempt. He carried a water-pot in one hand and a trident staff in the other. The prince spotted the old ascetic and told Channa to stop the chariot.

"He immediately jumped down and walked up to the hermit, bowing low to show his respect. The old ascetic looked kindly at him and touched the prince's forehead in blessing.

"'You are very troubled, my son. The temporary nature of your pleasures has disturbed your peace of mind. You seek a way out of your misery, but you are conflicted by your duties and obligations,' said the wandering recluse.

"'Everything you say is true, holy one. My mental condition must be very transparent,' said the prince.

"'Only fear and attachment keep you trapped, householder. Once you conquer those you will be free,' responded the hermit, whose strange, light blue eyes were shining brightly.

"'You seem full of peace, reverend sir. How long have you been following your path, and what is your goal?'

"'I started on this path when I was forty nine, and now this body is seventy. I know that I will pass away in a year, but until that time I won't give up striving for liberation, which is freedom from all desires, attachments, and fears.'

"The prince listened very carefully to the old man, who then said, 'When someone dies he takes nothing with him. He leaves all material things behind, and his friends and relatives can only go as far as the charnel grounds. The man who dies only takes with him the results of his good or bad actions. Old age, sickness, and death cannot be avoided by anyone who is born. Even the serpent sheds his skin and gets a new one.'

"'I have to find a way to stop this cycle of *samsara*,' responded the prince with a tone of desperation in his voice.

"The old recluse looked directly into Prince Siddhartha's eyes. Without saying a word he smiled warmly at him and walked away. The prince stood there and watched the ascetic amble down the lonely road. Then he said to Channa, 'Take me back to the palace. I have met a truly peaceful and holy man today. I have no further need for sport.'

"Channa gazed at the prince, but no words came out of his mouth. He felt a faint pre-sentiment that this might be one of their last excursions, and a wave of sadness momentarily overcame him. He readied the chariot and the prince climbed up.

"The prince said, 'Do not worry about me, Channa. Everything is moving forward exactly as it should be.' Channa was dumbfounded.

"They returned to the palace, and as Siddhartha dismounted from the chariot he said to himself, 'It is good! I have met a holy man who lives in the world but is not of it; he desires only liberation. Yes, it is good that I have seen him!'

"As Channa reported the day's events, the king wept, stricken by deep grief. The charioteer didn't know at the time that these Four Foresigns would dramatically change the world – as well as his own life," concludes Ananda.

"Yes, my dear friends. The prince's Great Renunciation was just around the corner, and celestial beings throughout the Universe were joyous with anticipation," says Maha Kassapa. "Let us retire now to our chambers."

One by one the arahants follow the now-familiar trail to their silent space deep in the womb of the earth. Each one reflects on what that renunciation has meant to him.

Chapter 6
Renunciation

All five hundred arahants are gathered in the assembly hall. It is the end of the day and Ananda stands calmly at the podium. He shows no sign of fatigue, even though he has just spoken for several hours. His face is as full of radiant joy as it was at the beginning of his recitation.

He addresses the council and says, "We have now finished most of the thirty-four long discourses of the Buddha. The *Maha Parinibbana Sutta* will be saved for the end of the council meeting, as will a few of the others for later sections of our assembly. We will now begin the recitation of what I call the 'middle length discourses,' and after having gone over all the *suttas* in my mind I have determined that there are one hundred fifty-two of these.

"As you know, we have a sub-committee that is documenting the life of the Buddha as we remember him. The last time we met we completed a discussion of the Four Foresigns, and when we meet this evening we will tell the story of the Lord's renunciation from the world. To give a fore-taste of tonight's meeting I will recount 'The Greater Discourse to Saccaka,'[1] says Ananda.

He begins with, "Thus I heard. On one occasion the Blessed one was living at Vesali in the Great Wood in the Hall with the Peaked Roof…"

The five-hundred arahants listen with rapture to Ananda's recitation of this popular *sutta*.

> "'…Has there never arisen in Master Gotama a feeling so pleasant that it could invade his mind and remain? Has there never arisen in Master Gotama a feeling so painful that it could invade his mind and remain?'
>
> "'Why not, Aggivessana? Here, Aggivessana, before my enlightenment, while I was still only an unenlightened *Bodhisatta*, I thought: 'Household life is crowded and dusty; life gone forth is wide open. It is not easy, while living in a home, to lead the holy life utterly perfect and

pure as a polished shell. Suppose I shave off my hair and beard, put on the yellow robe, and go forth from the home life into homelessness.'"

At the end of the discourse Ananda steps down from the podium and Sopaka accompanies him to Maha Kassapa's chamber. The other members of the sub-committee follow.

When they are all together Maha Kassapa says, "Please tell us about the events leading up to the Master's renunciation. That was, perhaps, one of the most important events in the Lord's life up until the attainment of *Nibbana*. It was the moment that closed the door on his life as a householder, and opened the door for Prince Siddhartha's quest for enlightenment. Surely, without that moment, all arahants here and elsewhere would never have attained supreme bliss. Each of us would still be fated to endless rebirths as seekers of sense pleasures.

"Ananda, would you like to begin? Or would you like to start, Anuruddha? Bhaddiya? All three of you are the prince's cousins, and you were with him during that time. Your eye-witness accounts are critical." The three cousins look back and forth at one another, each one willing to defer to the other.

Finally Anuruddha speaks up, "If I may, Venerable Sirs, I would like to begin telling the sacred story of Siddhartha's journey of renunciation. Much of this journey is inward, and the familiar accounts primarily deal with outer circumstances. I think the world would like to know about the prince's state of mind and his emotions during that time. The tremendous conflicts he faced when he tried to balance the pull of his strong inner urgings with his equally compelling outer attachments and obligations should also be recorded."

"Then please begin, Venerable Sir," replies Maha Kassapa.

"Try to imagine, if you will, the inner life of the Master during that period," begins Anuruddha. "Ever since his birth he had been the subject of a series of prophesies about his destiny. He was aware of these prophesies, of course; they were not a secret. He knew that they foretold that he would either become a Universal Monarch or a Universal Buddha. As a young man born into his position he would naturally prefer the former. It would not only bring honor to his father, his clan, and himself; it would also give him the opportunity to put into effect the compassionate social programs he envisioned for the world. He could institute numerous reforms that would eliminate the harmful effects of the caste system, improve the position of women in society, protect the rights of all religions, and ultimately lead humankind on the path to universal brotherhood. Prince Siddhartha believed in each of these causes, and if he were to become the Universal Monarch he could bring about many of these changes for his society.

"A Universal Monarch could also regulate the economy, which would provide for the fair accumulation and distribution of wealth. He could virtually eliminate poverty and armed conflicts; sponsor learning and advancements for farmers, tradesmen, and businessmen; and alleviate physical suffering by providing medical services for all. In essence, if he chose the route of Universal Monarch he could, by decree, unify the known world under the ideals of compassion, virtue, generosity, non-violence and contemplation – ideals he championed later as the Buddha.

"On the other hand, he knew that if he followed his inner voice, he had within him the intellectual and spiritual seeds that could eventually germinate a universal Dhamma – one that could benefit all beings from that time forward. This Dhamma would provide a path, which if followed, would lead to the end of suffering. Siddhartha knew that to make this a reality he would have to give up everything, including his wife, his unborn child, his family, his wealth, and his royal position. He knew that seeking his enlightenment would be a rough road, and that there would be many obstacles.

"There is no doubt in my mind that Prince Siddhartha knew with certainty that he would meet with success either way. After much soul-searching, however, he saw that if he were to become a Universal Monarch the worldly transformation he could effect would not be permanent. He also understood that this reversal might take ten generations, a hundred generations, or only one generation; and in the end, all of the benefits he had brought about for humankind would eventually disappear.

"If he were to choose the route of Universal Buddha, however, the Dhamma that would arise from his direct experience of reality would be everlasting. Siddhartha realized that everything manifest in the physical universe is temporary and impermanent; the truth of the Dhamma is not. He ultimately chose the path that would lead to permanent liberation from suffering, but it would be at the expense of his personal worldly happiness and gratification. We are today the beneficiaries of this wisdom," concludes Anuruddha.

"Thank you, Venerable Sir, for that succinct summary of the prince's two choices. It truly illuminates the background for the decision that he ultimately made, and it makes it clear that at the end of his deliberations he chose to take the long-term path of the greater good for the greater number of beings. His choice represents the deliberate selection of the permanence of ultimate truth over the impermanence of personal glory," says Maha Kassapa.

"Don't forget that Princess Yasodhara was with child during this time, which put even more pressure on the prince," says Bhaddiya. "Siddhartha discussed the possibility of his renunciation with the princess on a number of occasions. Much later, she herself said to me, 'One day the prince came to me with a heavy heart; it must have been six months before the first of the four Foresigns.'

"He said to her, 'Beloved wife and partner through countless lives, I am torn between two life choices. On one hand I have you, the responsibilities of my family, and my father's kingdom. On the other, I have these unrelenting dreams and powerful urges to undertake the quest for enlightenment. If I choose the first I will remain caught in the world of *samsara* with all its attachments for perhaps many more rebirths. If I choose the second I will give up everything I have, but by doing so I could end future suffering, which is caused by rebirth. What am I to do?'

"She answered, 'Why does it have to be one or the other? Why can't you enjoy the pleasures and responsibilities of a householder's life while pursuing your spiritual goals at the same time? You are the most gifted man of your generation, Siddhartha, why can't you do both?'

"His honest reply to her was, 'What do you think I've been trying to do these past few years, Yasodhara? You know these yearnings are not new; I've discussed them with you many times. I simply don't know how I can properly fulfill my traditional obligations and still seek enlightenment. I know it will require every ounce of energy and effort if I am to be successful.'

"She pleaded with him, 'Please, please try, dear husband, because I don't know if I could live without you. I know if you renounced your birthright your father would be devastated; he might not recover. And who would succeed him on the throne? Besides, when we married you promised to love me forever, and not to leave and follow your dream when it suited you.'

"The prince responded, 'You're making this very hard for me, Yasodhara. You have no idea how painful this conflict is; it's tearing my heart in two. I wish I didn't feel this way. I also wish the Brahmin seers hadn't said that I would eventually have to make this choice. One day I will have to decide.'

"'Then let's hope that 'one day' is many, many years from now. When the time is right, I will give you my permission and you will be free to go. In the meantime I know you'll do what is right for us and your father's kingdom,' said the princess. She was completely honest about her feelings, and so was the prince," concludes Bhaddiya.

"I didn't realize they had such frank discussions with one another about the possibility that he would renounce," comments Upali.

"They did. In fact, they talked about it for a number of years. My mother used to tell me how this worried the king and queen, and how devastated they would be if Siddhartha abandoned them," says Anuruddha.

"She told me about one occasion when she was with the king and queen in their private chambers. Prince Siddhartha entered the room and bowed before his parents.

"They could all see the torment on the prince's face. The queen, obviously distraught, asked, 'What troubles you, my son? You look like you haven't slept in days.'

"He answered, 'You always read me very well, mother. It's true that I've not been sleeping well. I keep having these vivid dreams – as if beings from other worlds are trying to tell me what I should do. They keep me awake.'

"'What do they tell you to do, Siddhartha?' inquired the king.

"'They tell me that the time to leave is drawing near,' replied the prince.

"'Don't pay any attention to those silly voices, Siddhartha. They're only phantoms in your imagination,' said the worried queen.

"'But, mother, they're so real. I also hear them in my meditations. They're not frightening; they just compelling. They insist that it's time to leave,' confessed the prince.

"'Leave? What do you mean, leave? I'm about to retire and turn the kingdom over to you, son. Next year you'll be thirty; you know this is our plan. You will be king, Siddhartha; you will hardly have the freedom to leave,' said Suddhodana, nearly trembling with fear.

"'I know I'll have to leave sometime, father. It's not only the voices I hear in my dreams and meditations, but I have a strong sense of why I was born. I feel like I have to leave one day to accomplish a mission,' said Siddhartha.

"'You need to put those thoughts out of your mind, my son. Your father needs you to carry on the Sakyan line and rule his kingdom after him. You are still so young. If you must leave, then let it be much later when you have produced your own heir and he is fully grown,' pleaded the queen.

"'I cannot promise anything, mother, but I know for certain that I will be leaving one day. I don't know exactly when, but I don't think it will be too long from now,' said the prince.

"'How could you do this to us? We're all depending on you Siddhartha! You have your duty to do, and I cannot allow you to simply leave. Where are you going?' asked the king.

"'I will go to seek enlightenment, father. I'm just letting you know now so you will be prepared. It's inevitable,' said the prince.

"My mother, the king's sister, just stared at the three of them. She was in shock," says Anuruddha.

"Then the queen, crying, said, 'I can't believe that you would be so selfish as to leave us to seek your own enlightenment. What about us?'

"'It's not just for my own enlightenment, mother, but for yours, too, and to find a way to end suffering for everyone,' responded the prince with tears in his eyes.

"'Do you know how arrogant that sounds?' was the queen's harsh reply.

"Prince Siddhartha did not respond. He simply bowed to his parents and left the room. The king, queen and my mother frantically looked back and forth at one another, not wanting to accept what they had just heard."

"Thank you, Anuruddha," says Maha Kassapa. "I've always been very curious about Devadatta during this time. Did the prince ever discuss renunciation with him?"

"When the cousins were together Devadatta was sometimes with us, and the prince talked about it from time to time – especially after that last big party," replies Bhaddiya.

Ananda says, "One day at the water park we beached our sailboats on the island in the middle of the lake. While we were relaxing in the sun Siddhartha said, 'You know, before too long I won't be here with you.'

"Shocked, I asked him what he meant by that," interjects Anuruddha. "He answered, 'Anuruddha, you know what I mean; I've talked about this before. I may renounce the world and go off on my own.'

"Then Devadatta said, 'I think you should do it, and the sooner the better. Why waste time just hanging around here being crown prince when you could be meditating in some jungle?'"

Bhaddiya says, "I asked Devadatta how he could encourage Siddhartha like that, knowing what it would do to Yasodhara. Devadatta had a smirk on his face, stifling a laugh."

"'Devadatta is right,' said Siddhartha. 'If I'm going to do it eventually, then why not just go ahead and leave? It's bound to happen sooner or later. I might as well just make up my mind and take off.'

"'Don't worry about my sister, Siddhartha. She can handle it; and besides, I'll be there to help her raise your child. I think you should go and do what you have to do – for the good of all, right? Isn't that what you've been saying?' asks Devadatta.

"'Yes, that is what I've been saying,' responded the prince with a sigh. He stood up, walked over to the water's edge and pushed off in his small sailing skiff. The cool breeze filled his sail, and before too long he was nearly all the way across the lake.

"Devadatta said coldly, 'Let him go. We'll all be better off without him. Ever since he was born everyone put too much hope and energy into that spoiled boy. If he leaves, the sun will still rise and set; life will go on.'"

"Anuruddha and I looked at one another knowingly. We had learned long ago that it was useless to try to argue with Devadatta. Together we jogged over to our sailboats, jumped in, and pushed off, catching a brisk wind from the west. We left Devadatta alone on the small island pondering life in Kapilavatthu without his arch rival, Siddhartha," says Ananda.

"Later that evening Devadatta went to his sister, Princess Yasodhara, and told her about that conversation," continues Ananda. "He said, 'I told you not to marry Siddhartha. We all knew he would leave you one day.'

"She told me that she stayed calm and said, 'You have always been jealous of my husband, Devadatta. I know you very well; you'll be happy if he leaves. You think this would give you an opportunity to take his place, but you are wrong. You have no interest in my happiness, or in the happiness of our family. You are selfish and misguided, and your hatred for Siddhartha has twisted your mind. When Siddhartha leaves, it will be with my blessing. If that day should come, and I suspect it will, we will all play our roles in the outcome, including you.'

"She said that Devadatta looked at her as if she was crazy. She knew that deep down her brother had a sense that his future was intertwined with that of the prince's. She felt that he had a golden opportunity to change his ways, but at the same time she knew the jealous demon within him aroused his emotions against Siddhartha. He told her, 'I don't believe a word you're saying, Yasodhara, but if it turns out to be true, it will be an outcome of my choosing.'

"Yasodhara said that she looked her brother directly in the eye and said, 'So be it.'

"The princess had an amazing sense of prescience; I witnessed it on numerous occasions," says Ananda. "So did the prince's half-brother, Nanda."

"Speaking of Nanda, I remember a conversation I had with him long ago at Jetavana during a rains retreat. I was always curious about the Lord's renunciation, so I asked him about it. After all, it was the very beginning of the *Sasana*," says Maha Kaccayana. "I'll share that conversation with you if you like." The arahants on the sub-committee nod their approval.

Maha Kaccayana begins, "I asked Nanda if Prince Siddhartha had ever confided in him before he decided to renounce.

"He answered, 'Yes, he came to me on three or four occasions wanting to talk about it. He reassured me that it wasn't just some whim, but he was considering a lifetime commitment to the ascetic way of life. I loved my brother dearly, and couldn't imagine life without him. Also, I knew I wasn't cut out to be king, nor did I even want the crown. However, if Siddhartha left, there would be tremendous pressure on me to take on that responsibility.

"Nanda asked Siddhartha, 'Do you know what will happen to me if you renounce and leave?'

"'Yes, brother Nanda, and I know that you'll be fine. You'll make a fine king, and after I achieve my goal, I promise I'll come back to advise you from time to time,' was Siddhartha's reply.

"Siddhartha knew that Nanda was nervous – frightened, really – at the prospect of having to be king. All his life Siddhartha had been trained for that role, and since he was a child he had repeatedly demonstrated that he would make an ideal king. Remember, it was prophesied he would be the Universal Monarch. Whoever took Siddhartha's place on the throne would naturally be nervous, and Nanda simply wasn't prepared.

"Nanda asked, 'Why in the world would you want to give up your unbelievably rich life? You have everything – including about a thousand beautiful girls who stumble over each other just to serve you!'

"Siddhartha answered, 'I know you think I'm insane for even considering it, and you're not alone in that view. What I want you to understand is that I really have no choice. Leaving won't be just for my own selfish good – it will be for all of you.'

"'Siddhartha, you have everything in the world; you have all the gifts the gods can give. Why would you want to throw it all away?'

"'You will understand later, Nanda, but now you can't see it. At the beginning you will be sad along with the rest of the family, but I foresee that in the future we'll be together again. Just let me go. That's all I ask of you, brother,' said the prince.

"'For what it's worth, you have my blessing for your quest, Siddhartha. You're making me be king in your place, and I will do my best for the sake of our people. But you still need to get father's and Yasodhara's blessings; they'll be much harder to obtain.'

"Prince Siddhartha told him that he was trying to find a way to leave on good terms, and to make sure there was an understanding that he wasn't abandoning anyone. The prince spent several months speaking to everyone in the family about his leaving. He spoke with the king's senior ministers, too. He wanted all of us to understand that he really had no choice about this quest of his. He tried to convince us that it was for the good of all, but I have to admit, most of us didn't understand him. We could only see what he wanted to throw away, and we couldn't understand the reasons why. It seemed like such a waste."

Maha Kaccayana concludes his story about Nanda, and Anuruddha says thoughtfully, "My cousin Nanda was such a good man, and a wonderful monk."

Ananda says, "Yes, he was one of the best, but how could he not have been? After all, he was the Buddha's half-brother, nearly as tall and handsome as the Lord. Remember that he won the distinction of being called 'the best in self control' by the Master himself; that was, of course, after conquering his personal battle with his strong attraction to women."

"Remember all those parties at Siddhartha's palaces? Nanda had a hard time leaving the music girls alone. I have to give him credit, though; he did, in fact, overcome his obstacles and succeeded in becoming an arahant," replies Bhaddiya.

"What about the birth of Prince Rahula?' asks Punna. "I think we've now arrived at that point in our recollections."

"I was the closest person to Rahula since the day he was born, so I'll tell you what I remember. Prince Siddhartha was beside himself with worry throughout the princess's pregnancy," says Ananda.

"Why? She was a perfectly healthy young woman in the prime of her life," says Upali.

"The prince couldn't forget the fact that his own mother, Queen Maha Maya, had died seven days after giving birth to him. He feared the same thing would happen to Princess Yasodhara," answers Ananda.

"When she went into labor the prince carried her into her chamber and she asked him, 'Does it matter to you if we should have a daughter instead of a son?'

"'Sons and daughters are both good, Yasodhara, and either one will be equally loved,' he responded. The princess smiled and squeezed his hand as he gently placed her on the bed.

"'When we see each other again you will be a father and I will be a mother. This is the one and only time in our lives when this will happen,' said the princess.

"Siddhartha nodded, kissed his wife on the forehead, looked deeply into her eyes, and left the room, as was the custom.

"For many hours he paced back and forth outside her chamber. He heard Yasodhara cry out in pain, and he winced each time. His thoughts were about birth, sickness, old age, and death. He felt enormous compassion for all living beings that were trapped in the never-ending cycle of existence. Siddhartha was acutely aware that even his newborn child awaited the same fate, and he felt helpless that he could do nothing to prevent its future suffering.

"Finally, he heard the first cry of the newborn babe. A few minutes later the mid-wife came to the door and told him he could enter. Siddhartha rushed to his wife's side. She smiled at him, and held up their son for his approval. The prince took the baby in his arms and tears of both joy and anguish streamed down his face. He said, 'How can I possibly leave now? This is the strongest tie to bind me to this worldly life.'" Ananda pauses for a moment before continuing his story.

"Apparently Mahapajapati told the king about Siddhartha's statement, so he named his grandson, 'Rahula,' which means 'fetter.' He hoped that Rahula would keep the crown prince tied to his home," says Bhaddiya. "This unusual name caused trouble for many over the years, because it was interpreted somehow as 'unloved.' This couldn't have been farther from the truth. I assure you that the prince loved his son as much as any father has ever loved a child. We must remember that the name also carried the connotation of 'eclipse,' because of the planet Rahu. According to legend, Rahu sometimes hid the moon or the sun from view. At that moment Siddhartha's emotions were in a state of confusion. Although he knew exactly what he could achieve, his plans were temporarily eclipsed by the love he experienced for his son.

"Siddhartha joined the palace festivities celebrating the joyous event. King Suddhodana was jubilant; he had both an heir and an heir for the succeeding generation.

"The prince, however, continued to be tormented until the seventh day after Rahula's birth; only then was he assured that his wife's life was in no danger, and he could release his fear," remarks Anuruddha.

"The prince doted on his son from the very beginning, and he enjoyed every minute with him," begins Ananda. "For the time being Siddhartha was joined with his wife, parents, and the rest of the kingdom in the unifying happiness of having Rahula in the family. A month or so later, however, his old longings began to surface. He started talking of leaving again.

"One day he had a formal meeting with his father to announce his departure. His stepmother, Queen Mahapajapati was also present. He said to the king, 'I shall be leaving soon.'

"'I cannot give you permission, my son. I forbid you to go. You have a lifetime commitment to the throne – or at least until Rahula is old enough to succeed you,' responded Suddhodana sternly with great emotion.

"'Father,' said the prince thoughtfully, 'I have three things to ask of you. If you can give me but one of them I will remain here as the servant of your people for the rest of my life.'

"King Suddhodana was momentarily overjoyed. He realized that if he could grant one wish out of three, Siddhartha would give up his plans. He was confident that he could provide anything on earth the prince might desire. 'I agree. What are the three things?'

"'The first is: give me a solution to avoid sickness for the rest of my life.' The king heard this first request and his face turned pale.

"'Second is: give me a solution to avoid old age. I wish to remain young and strong and never change.' The king closed his eyes as the impossibility of these two requests dawned on him.

"'The third is: give me a solution to avoid death. I do not wish to die; I want to stay alive forever.' The king began to weep, realizing that he could not fulfill any of his son's requests.

"'You know I can't give you those things, Siddhartha. Please be realistic. Ask for something I can grant you; I'll give you anything you ask.' By this time the king was in a state of shock, realizing for the first time that he was actually going to lose his son. He looked to Queen Mahapajapati for support, but she looked as helpless as he was.

"'You have already given me everything the material, mental, and emotional worlds can provide, father. There is nothing more to ask other than the three things I seek. If you cannot grant at least one of my requests, then I must ask again for your permission to renounce. I must find a solution to these three conditions of life.'

"The king, his heart breaking, said, 'My permission is granted, son. I ask you one favor in return.'

"'What is it, father?' asked the prince.

"'When you have found solutions for these conditions, and when you have attained the enlightenment you seek, please come back to me,' said the king, sobbing.

"'I give you my word.' Siddhartha went down on his knees and touched his father's feet. When he did so, he could feel tears dropping onto the back of his neck.

"Then he stood up and looked pleadingly into the eyes of his stepmother, Queen Mahapajapati. She said, 'Although it grieves me greatly, I, too, give you my permission, son.' After saying this, the prince's shoulders relaxed, and he smiled with relief as he bowed down before the queen."[2]

Ananda is beaming with joy when he finishes relating this last.

"Why are you smiling, Venerable Sir?" asks Bakkula.

"I am smiling because if the Master, my cousin, hadn't had the strength to give it all away, I wouldn't have attained this unalterable, irrevocable state of bliss! He paved the way for all of us, and we owe it to that very moment in his life."

Each of the arahants acknowledges their same appreciation.

"What about Princess Yasodhara? Did she give the prince her blessing?" asks Punna.

"I can answer that question, sir, since I lived in the midst of the turmoil created by the prince's announcement," answers Anuruddha. "That very night the prince approached his wife and told her of his decision.

"'Our son Rahula is four months old, and I can wait no longer. We have been talking about this moment for several years, beloved; this comes as no surprise. Will you give me your blessing now and let me go?' asked the prince.

"With tears in her eyes the princess said, 'You have been my partner for many lifetimes, my beloved husband. Yes, I give you my blessing. You will never be happy until you have found the solution you seek, and I will never be happy until you are. Please bless our son and leave whenever you are ready. I have prepared your robes.' She reached out and handed Siddhartha a neatly tied bundle.

"'You have been my helpmate over the eons, my dearest wife, and I thank you. I will return when I have found the answers, and all of our lives will greatly benefit. You'll see,' said the prince.

"So the stories that had been circulating that Siddhartha left the palace like a thief in the night are completely untrue," interjects Ananda. "Like a dutiful husband and son he received the appropriate blessings and permissions before his departure."

"Did the prince leave that night?" asks Bakkula.

"Immediately after receiving Yasodhara's blessing, he held and kissed his son for the last time. Then he went to the stables and told Channa to get his horse ready. Late that full moon night, while Kapilavatthu was sleeping, Siddhartha mounted his stallion, Kanthaka, and left the city with Channa seated behind him. The guards opened the gates for them and saluted, not suspecting that this nighttime ride was anything out of the usual.

"Kanthaka carried the two men to the River Anoma, and without hesitation waded across. Siddhartha then removed his royal clothes and put on the robe Yasodhara had made for him. The story you have heard about the prince cutting off his own hair with his sword is quite accurate; and Kanthaka did, in fact, pass away from grief a few days after returning with Channa to Kapilavatthu.

"Channa asked his Master, 'Lord, will you return to us?'

"'Yes, Channa, I will return, and you will join me again. We were born on the same day, as was Kanthaka, Yasodhara, Kaludayi, and Ananda. When I have obtained a solution to the problem of suffering and the endless cycle of rebirth I will come for you. Go back to the palace and present my clothes to my father. Tell him that all is well.' Channa remarked later that he had never seen his Master look so radiant. He described him as happy – even beyond happy; he was also resolved, determined, clear, and confident.'

"Siddhartha, now wearing the yellow robe of a monk, smiled at his boyhood friend, and then turned from Channa and walked silently into the forest. His gait was regal, full of strength and commitment. The faithful charioteer, with tears in his eyes, waved a silent farewell.

"That renunciation, my dear friends, was the birth of the *Sasana*," concludes Ananda.

"I think we'll pause here, Venerable Sirs. The council will meet again tomorrow morning at dawn." With these words from Maha Kassapa the arahants stand up in unison and file silently from the chamber, each one deep in reverie.

Chapter 7
The Ascetic

"How did the prince spend those first days after his renunciation?" asks Sopaka when the sub-committee reconvenes the following evening. "I can only imagine what was going through his mind. After all, he had just left his wife and infant son, his parents, his kingdom, and his luxurious lifestyle. It must have been hard for him to adapt to living out in the open."

"First let us discuss the reaction in Kapilavatthu when everyone found out their beloved prince had left them," interjects Bakkula.

"In all my life I have never seen such a strong reaction to a single event – other than the prince's birth, that is. The people were devastated. It was as if the entire kingdom had suddenly gone into mourning; everyone was shocked into silence. No one could believe their prince was no longer with them; Siddhartha was so well loved, and now his light was gone. I, for one, went into a severe depression, and if I'm not mistaken, I think you did too, Anuruddha," says Ananda.

The prince's cousin shakes himself out of his thoughtful mood before answering, and then says, "We were all sort of numb. Nanda and I tried to console ourselves with large quantities of wine and music girls, but it really didn't help. After a few days of drunken stupor I realized that I wasn't doing the prince any honor by behaving that way; after all, he was living in a jungle somewhere on roots and berries. I finally realized he was probably happy, and that made me less depressed."

"The king and queen barricaded themselves in their private quarters in the palace. My mother said they didn't eat for about four days, and the king completely ignored the affairs of state," says Bhaddiya.

"Princess Yasodhara surprised everyone by being so accepting and serene. She played with Rahula as if nothing had happened, and all of a sudden she started wearing only yellow clothes and eating one meal a day. My mother told me that she had even taken to sleeping on a mat on her bedroom floor, thinking that if her husband slept on the bare ground in the forest she would do the same in the palace. She let it be known that since her husband was living the life of an ascetic, then she would live like one, too; and just in case any man might want to court her, she declared that she would be celibate for the rest of her life," says Ananda.

Bhaddiya says, "There were rumors going around that Devadatta was trying to take advantage of the situation, and had planned a palace coup. People saw him in Kapilavatthu gloating over the fact that his brother-in-law had abandoned the throne. He was heard saying, 'Who is going to lead this kingdom now? The pride of Kapilavatthu has forsaken us, and no one has been trained to take his place. He made my own sister a single mother at the age of twenty nine. I guess he showed us who he really is just in time. What if he had thrown away his country after becoming king?'"

"Eventually the king issued an official statement saying that Prince Siddhartha had left Kapilavatthu and renounced his position with his and his mother's blessings. The king didn't want the common people to feel worse than they already did by imagining strife and dissent within the royal family. He also made it very clear that rumors about Devadatta were untrue; the king said that he was still a loyal supporter of the present monarchy," says Anuruddha. "This was a very wise decision, which helped console the people and avoid any more confusion. In his statement the king also mentioned that his son had become an ascetic out of compassion for all beings, and that one day he would return to show the way to enlightenment to his former friends and subjects."

"The Brahmin Kondanna, the youngest astrologer of the group who had prophesied the prince's future, came out with a statement of his own praising Siddhartha for his brave decision. Kondanna reminded everyone that he was the one who had unequivocally said the prince would one day become a Universal Buddha. 'He's made his commitment, which is irreversible and destined for success,' said Kondanna, and very shortly afterwards he himself renounced the world. Along with four of his associates he left Kapilavatthu to live as an ascetic in the forest," says Bhaddiya.

"My uncle, Kondanna, wanted to be prepared for the prince when he started teaching," says Punna. "It's amazing how much confidence he had in the Master even then."

"There were a lot of people in those days that would have followed the prince anywhere. In Kapilavatthu a number of young men wanted to run off and join Siddhartha. The only thing that stopped them was their parents," says Anuruddha.

"Yes, and after the Master's enlightenment the movement really gained momentum, and young men started joining him in droves; but I'm getting ahead of the story," says Ananda.

"After the king's announcement, life in Kapilavatthu gradually returned to normal, and the prince's renunciation was finally accepted," says Anuruddha.

"One thing I could never quite understand was how the king just let him go off like that with no guards or attendants to watch over him," says Punna.

"It's not generally known, but almost immediately after the king learned of his departure he sent spies to follow the prince. He ordered them to keep at a discreet distance and not to disturb him, but they were there nonetheless, and they reported to His Majesty on a weekly basis. It has never been made clear, however, if the prince knew he was being watched; if he was aware of the spies, he never said anything," says Ananda.

"There was very little to report for the first seven days. Prince Siddhartha was alone, and he seemed to be enjoying the peace of his new life. He stayed in a beautiful mango grove for a week and practiced meditation. He ate only fruit he picked himself. On the seventh day he began walking to Rajagaha," continues Anuruddha.

"He caused a stir when he arrived in the Magadhan capital. Even though Siddhartha was dressed in the robes of an ascetic there was no mistaking the fact that he was of royal lineage. Word had already reached Rajagaha about the prince's renunciation, so people were speculating that this unfamiliar ascetic might actually be him. People compared him to a full moon, Brahma, the god of love, and even the king of gods. They were captivated by the handsome figure of the future Buddha as he walked about their city. News about him soon reached the Magadhan king.

"King Bimbisara sent three of his administrators to investigate at once. After observing him for a while, two of them stayed to watch the prince while the third went back to report to the king. He told the king that the recluse had been given alms food, and that he was sitting at the entrance to the cave at the top of Mount Pandava. He was peacefully eating his meal, absolutely without fear, like a lion.

"The king, overcome by curiosity, summoned his chariot and went at once to see the ascetic. When the chariot could go no further up the mountain the king dismounted and continued on foot. He approached the serene figure of the recluse and obtained his permission to sit with him; after a few moments he engaged him in friendly conversation.

"Impressed with the man, the king asked, 'What is your lineage, Venerable Sir? I can see that you are no ordinary hermit.'

"Siddhartha looked at the king and said, 'I was born crown prince of the Sakyan kingdom near the foothills of the Himalayas. I recently renounced my birthright and have become an ascetic. I no longer have any desire for worldly enjoyment.'[1]

"The king considered for a moment before saying, 'Being of noble virtue, allow me to offer you wealth, prestige, and an opportunity to rule my kingdom with me.'

"Siddhartha smiled warmly at the king and said, 'I thank you for your generosity, but what you are offering is exactly what I just renounced. I intend to strive until I find the enlightenment I seek.'"

"The king bowed before the ascetic and said, 'Having seen with my own eyes your great aspiration for *Nibbana*, I firmly believe that you will accomplish your goal. If I may; please allow me to make one request, Venerable Sir.'

"The prince nodded his agreement, and the king continued. 'Once you have attained Buddhahood please visit my country first, so that we may benefit from your Dhamma.'

"Siddhartha said, 'I will see you again, Your Majesty. Your faith in me is well-noted, and I believe, justified.'

"The king bowed and went back down the mountain the way he had come," concludes Anuruddha.

"Did the prince remain long in Rajagaha?" asks Punna.

"Almost immediately after the king left him, Siddhartha started walking again," answers Ananda. "He continued traveling for several days, occasionally stopping to speak with ascetics he met along the way. He paused briefly at the hermitage of the female Brahmin ascetic Sakya,[2] who offered him food and garments. He also visited the hermitages of Revata[3] and Datruma Dandika Putta,[4] each of whom treated him with kindness and respect.

"Eventually he found his way to the ashram of Alara Kalama,[5] a popular teacher who had at that time three hundred devoted students. Alara's brother saw the prince approaching and he was filled with awe at the *Bodhisatta's* demeanor. He immediately reported that he had seen the Sakyan prince and said, 'The son of Suddhodana, desiring to escape from sorrow and attain supreme wisdom, is coming here. Let us welcome him.'

"Alara Kalama indeed welcomed him, and offered him a seat on a clean grass mat. After observing the young ascetic, Alara said, 'Venerable Gotama, long ago I heard of your intention to renounce your life as a prince and become a recluse. I see now that you have done it. Other kings in the past gave up their kingdoms when they were old, but you have renounced at a very young age.'

"'All earthly rulers and their endeavors appear to me as unstable and ultimately destined for destruction. I now look for the true road to happiness,' replied the prince.

"Alara Kalama said, 'You may live here, brother. My teaching is such that an intelligent man can master it himself before too long, putting it into practice, just as I have done.' The prince considered Alara's words, and he perceived that this learned teacher had mastered his teachings through his own direct experience, and not by faith alone.

"'I've had everything the material world can possibly offer, but it is of no use to me in my search for what is permanent,' replied Siddhartha. 'Will you accept me as your pupil?'

"The seer said, 'I will accept you, and I will instruct you in what I have realized myself. It will be up to you to exert yourself to arrive at your own understanding.'

"The prince was happy that he had found a teaching that was not based on mere speculation. He could examine it himself, using his own energy to discover its truth, and apply it to his personal quest. He bowed before Alara Kalama, officially recognizing the bond between student and teacher," concludes Ananda.

"What did Alara Kalama teach our Lord?" asks Punna.

Ananda begins again by answering, "He told the prince that the first thing he had to do was to eliminate the five hindrances; this would calm the mind, preventing it from being disturbed by outside events. He said the hindrances were lustful desires; ill-will, hatred and anger; torpor and languor; restlessness and worry; and skeptical doubts. Alara asked him if he thought he could get rid of these five hindrances.

"Without hesitation Siddhartha replied that he believed he could eliminate them without too much difficulty, and that getting rid of them was the very reason for adopting the reclusive lifestyle in the first place.

"Alara then told him to go into seclusion and concentrate on getting rid of these unwholesome tendencies. He wanted Siddhartha to experience for himself the joy and happiness that arises when they are gone. This was the first stage of his meditation practice, and Alara said that more will be explained when this task was mastered.

"Siddhartha went off by himself to practice the technique, and in very little time he mastered it. He went back and reported this to his teacher, who then taught him the second step; then the third step when he had mastered the second; and then finally the fourth step when he had mastered the third. He mastered the first three *jhanas* in a matter of just a few weeks.

"After mastering the fourth meditative step Alara Kalama said to the prince, 'You have worked your way up the *jhanas*. With the first *jhana* you reached the stage of joy and happiness, and with your newly acquired discrimination, you determined that it was far more pleasurable than any sensation you had ever experienced before.

"'With the attainment of the second *jhana* you went beyond thinking and exploring the new sensations; and then you surpassed them with a feeling of joy and happiness from concentration alone.'

"'With mastery of the third *jhana* you eliminated joy completely, and with mindfulness and purification you were able to stay in an ecstatic state that pervaded your entire body.'

"'After you mastered the fourth *jhana* your mind was totally composed with equanimity, and you experienced neither pain nor pleasure, gaining you complete control of your mind. You are now ready to move on to the advanced stages of meditation.'

"Alara Kalama was impressed by Siddhartha's ability to master his techniques in such a short time. 'What you have learned so far is the way to get past the world of sense pleasures, but your mind is still in the world of form. The next task is to further develop your mind so it can reach the world of the formless. This is the highest attainment you can reach, and in it the highest state of happiness.'

"With great enthusiasm he asked Alara, 'How can I reach this formless world?'

"'Since all forms are finite, the formless is infinite like space. You now need to direct your complete concentration to space, exploring it fully to see if you can reach its end. For this technique first move up the four *jhanas* as before, and then go beyond – to space,' replied the great teacher." Ananda pauses for a moment while the arahants on the subcommittee reflect on this phase of Siddhartha's quest.

"Since we have all been there on our own inward journeys, we can empathize with the difficulties faced by the prince at this critical juncture," says Maha Kaccayana.

"Yes, we can," agrees Ananda. "Siddhartha went back and practiced as he instructed, but not finding the end of space puzzled him. He reported this to Alara Kalama who explained, 'You assumed that space had to be finite, as is form. This is incorrect. I advise you to try again and reach for the place where space becomes consciousness, and then go beyond that.'

"Siddhartha did as he was told, and in his inner explorations he discovered that consciousness has no form, therefore beyond it was 'nothingness.'

"Siddhartha went to his teacher and told him what he had experienced and Alara said, 'It has only been a few months and you have now reached the same level as I, Siddhartha. I have nothing more to teach you. Please join me and help me teach others so they, too, can experience nothingness,' said the revered teacher.'"

Bhaddiya says, "Siddhartha went back to his place of solitude and pondered this request. After a while he reached the conclusion that all of the states he had attained were temporary. He also saw that no matter how blissful the states were, he eventually had to come back to the material world and become entangled with the senses once again. It did not take him to the place where suffering was permanently eliminated.

"When Siddhartha reported this realization to Alara Kalama, expressing his gratitude for what he had been taught, he told him that he had to move on to find the final solution to his problem. The teacher said, 'When you find the solution, then please return and teach it to me.'"

"The great seer was completely open and honest with Siddhartha, who graciously took his leave from the *ashram*," says Punna. "He refused to settle for a half-way solution to the problem he had dedicated his life to solving."

"Exactly," exclaims Anuruddha. "Once Siddhartha set his mind upon something nothing could deter him. Any 'normal' person would have been happy to have reached the exalted states taught by Alara Kalama. Siddhartha, however, was committed to the total annihilation of suffering on the level of the permanent and absolute. Nothing short of this would satisfy him.

"So Siddhartha went back on his quest and eventually wound up at the hermitage of Uddaka Ramaputta,[6] who had seven hundred dedicated students.

"He approached Uddaka and said, 'Friend, I wish to live a holy life in this system of yours.'

"Uddaka welcomed him warmly, as had Alara Kalama, and Siddhartha was surprised to find out that their meditation techniques were almost identical. Both moved the student up through the four levels of *jhana*, and both went beyond. The only difference between the two teachers was where they stopped: Alara's went to 'nothingness,' and Uddaka's went one step further to a place he called 'neither perception nor non-perception.'

"Uddaka taught him the technique for reaching this state, and the *Bodhisatta* further explored his mind during meditation. Before too long, with great absorption, Siddhartha was able to penetrate this new level. He dived deep into the realm of 'nothingness,' and then to 'neither perception nor non-perception.' He declared, 'I have understood! I have seen the course!' However, after mastering this stage Siddhartha found that it, too, was non-substantial and inconclusive in terms of reaching his goal of *Nibbana*," concludes Anuruddha.

"I understand that Uddaka also offered to share the leadership of his sect with him, which had been passed down to him from his father, Rama," adds Bakkula.

"This is so," agrees Ananda, "and Siddhartha graciously responded by saying, 'I thank you for the honor you wish to bestow upon me, and for your advanced teaching, sir. However, I must leave you to continue my search, because after attaining 'neither perception nor non-perception' I still returned to the world of the senses. I did not find what I was looking for: *Nibbana*, emancipation. I must find a way to cease returning.' The kind, compassionate teacher gave his blessing, and so, after having spent a few months with Uddaka, Siddhartha moved on."

"Siddhartha must have been frustrated and somewhat discouraged at this point. He had had high hopes for both of these esteemed teachers, but they could not help him realize the final solution to suffering," comments Maha Kaccayana.

"I think this is very true in regards to his state of mind; the Master told me so on a number of occasions. He also said that he was forever grateful to his first two teachers; they had assisted him greatly in the accomplishment of those first stages of meditation. He said that without their instruction in the *jhanas,* he would have had to seek them through the method of trial and error which would have taken a lot more time," says Ananda.

"Where did Siddhartha go after he left Uddaka?" asks Punna.

"He proceeded through the kingdom of Magadha, eventually reaching the village of Senani in Uruvela. He fell in love with the natural beauty of the surrounding area, deciding that it was an ideal place to strive for *Nibbana,*" replies Ananda.

"Magadha at that time was a center for numerous hermits and ascetics who practiced extreme forms of self-mortification. They lived in caves that dotted the slopes of Mount Vebhara. These yogis believed that the body and its sensations were their enemies. They hoped to attain liberation through achieving mental control over the body by contorting it into extreme postures and denying it nourishment. Siddhartha walked into a campsite where a group of these ascetics was living, and he joined their community," says Anuruddha.

"Were Kondanna and the other four ascetics part of this group?" asks Sopaka.

"No, they weren't, but they happened to be passing through the same part of Uruvela in search of their daily alms," answers Upali. "They heard about the young ascetic who had recently taken up residence in the forest, and thinking that it might be Siddhartha, they sought him out.

"When they found him Kondanna approached Siddhartha bowing low, touching his feet and saying, 'I have been waiting for this moment for nearly thirty years, Your Highness. I was one of the Brahmin astrologers who prophesied your future. I am here with my colleagues Bhaddiya, Vappa, Mahanama, and Assaji. When I heard of your renunciation I became a recluse and convinced these others to do the same; we have been waiting for you ever since.'

"'I thank you for your patience, Kondanna. I will do my best to make sure your wait was a profitable one,' replied Siddhartha. 'I only ask that you do not call me 'Your Highness,' for that person is no more.'

"'With your permission, Venerable Sir, we will wait upon you, seeing to your needs. We feel very strongly that your enlightenment is imminent and we wish to be there when that event occurs. We want to partake of your Dhamma from the beginning,' replied Kondanna.

"The *Bodhisatta* silently nodded his consent, and together they began their morning round of alms collection," concludes Upali.

"Returning to their camp they shared their meager meal, and then the prince went off by himself to a shady spot in the forest," begins Punna. "He cleared away some underbrush and placed his mat on the ground. When he sat down that day to meditate he began what turned out to be five-years of constant self-torture of the body. The prince was nothing if not thorough in everything he did. We might say that he began this practice with as much enthusiasm as he had begun his training with Alara Kalama and Uddaka. He followed the way of the ascetics who believed that if they could completely control their physical bodies, they could control their minds. Since Siddhartha was determined to control his mind, he experimented with a number of physical techniques that involved the breath, pressing his tongue to his palate, fasting to the point of starvation, and others."

Ananda speaks, "Tomorrow at the council I will be reciting a discourse called the '*Mahasihanada Sutta*:[7] The Great Discourse on the Lion's Roar.' This *sutta* goes into great detail about Siddhartha's self-mortification in his own words."

"Then perhaps we could continue this discussion afterwards," suggests Maha Kassapa.

The arahants nod their agreement to Maha Kassapa's suggestion, and prepare to leave his cave chamber.

The following morning at dawn five-hundred arahants gather in the assembly hall to begin the day's session. Maha Kassapa calls the meeting to order, and then motions Ananda to stand at the podium.

He begins.

> "Thus I heard. On one occasion the Blessed One was living at Vesali in the grove outside the city to the west...now on that occasion ...the Blessed One said...the

Tathagata has these...powers, possessing which he claims the herd-leader's place, roars the lion's roar in the assemblies, and sets rolling the Wheel of Brahma...

'...I recall having lived a holy life possessing four factors: I have practiced the extreme of asceticism; I have practiced the extreme of coarseness; I have practiced the extreme of scrupulousness; I have practiced the extreme of seclusion.

'Such was my asceticism that I went naked, rejecting conventions, licking my hands, not coming when asked, not stopping when asked; I did not accept food brought or food specially made or an invitation to a meal; I received nothing from a pot, from a bowl, across a threshold, across a stock, across a pestle, from two eating together...; I accepted no fish or meat, I drank no liquor, wine, or fermented brew. I kept to one house, to one morsel; I lived on one saucerful a day; I took food once a day, once every two days...once every seven days, and so on up to once every fortnight;...I was an eater of greens or millet or wild rice or hide-parings or moss or rice-bran or rice-scum or sesamum flour or grass. I lived on forest roots and fruits; ...I clothed myself in hemp; ...in shrouds, in refuse rags, in tree bark, in antelope hide; ...in bark fabric, in wood-shaving fabric, in head-hair wool, in owls' wings. I was one who pulled out hair and beard...I was one who stood continuously, rejecting seats. I was one who squatted continuously...I was one who used a mattress of spikes for my bed; ...I dwelt pursuing the practice of bathing in water three times daily including evening. Thus in such a variety of ways I dwelt pursuing the practice of tormenting and mortifying the body. Such was my asceticism.

'Such was my coarseness...that just as the bark of a...tree, accumulating over the years, cakes and flakes off, so too, dust and dirt, accumulating over the years, caked off my body and flaked off...

'Such was my scrupulousness...that I was always mindful in stepping forwards and stepping backwards. I was full of pity even for the beings in a drop of water....

'Such was my seclusion...that I would plunge into some forest and dwell there. And when I saw a cowherd or a shepherd or someone gathering grass or sticks, or a woodsman, I would flee from grove to grove, from thicket to thicket, from hollow to hollow, from hillock to hillock...so that they should not see me or I see them...

'I would go on all fours to the cow-pens when the cattle had gone out and the cowherd had left them, and I would feed on the dung of the young suckling calves... Such was my great distortion in feeding.

'I would plunge into some awe-inspiring grove and dwell there...when those cold wintry nights came...I would dwell by night in the open and by day in the grove. In the last month of the hot season...I would dwell by day in the open and by night in the grove. And there came to me spontaneously this stanza never heard before:

> *'Chilled by night and scorched by day,*
> *Alone in awe-inspiring groves,*
> *Naked, no fire to sit beside,*
> *The sage yet pursues his quest.'*

'I would make my bed in the charnel grounds with the bones of the dead for a pillow. And cowherd boys came up and spat upon me, urinated upon me, threw dirt at me, and poked sticks into my ears. Yet I do not recall that I ever aroused an evil mind of hate against them. Such was my abiding in equanimity...

'By such conduct, by such practice, by such performance of austerities, I did not attain any superhuman states, any distinction in knowledge and vision worthy of the Noble Ones. Why was that? Because I did not attain that noble wisdom which when attained is noble and emancipating and leads the one who practices in accordance with it to the complete destruction of suffering.'"

Ananda continues reciting the discourse until the end, and there is not one arahant present who is not greatly moved by these words of the Lord, which express so vividly his extreme personal experiences of austerity.

When he concludes the *sutta* Ananda steps down from the podium and returns to his seat in the assembly. Maha Kassapa stands and says,

"We will resume the next discourse after our noon meal. King Ajatasattu is waiting to present *dana* to the venerable arahants."

With this announcement the five-hundred arahants begin filing out of the assembly hall toward the *dana* ceremony. Bakkula catches up with Ananda and Anuruddha and says, "Might we continue our discussion about the Lord's asceticism as we walk? I have questions about the end of this six year period."

Anuruddha answers saying, "Yes, of course, Venerable Sir. What are your points of inquiry?"

"If the Master lived for all those years the way he described it in the discourse you just recited, how did he manage to survive?" asks Bakkula.

"I learned later that Kondanna and the other four ascetics in the group would sometimes boil mung beans or garbanzo beans and force the Master to drink the water. Other times they would boil rice and pour the leftover water into the Lord's mouth. Since the *Bodhisatta* wouldn't take anything solid, this was the only way they could keep him alive," answers Anuruddha.

"The Master was nearly unconscious most of the time, and he would often collapse from hunger. He was so thin that if you touched his belly you could feel his backbone. His skin became yellow and sallow, and his hair fell out in clumps from malnutrition. If Kondanna and his friends hadn't forced the Lord to take some sustenance he would have died, for sure, and none of us would be here today," adds Ananda.

"When the future Buddha was very, very close to death as a result of his *tapas,* a thought occurred to him. He said to himself, 'I cannot, surely, by this severe form of austerities and mortifications realize that higher noble state which leads to the perception of the highest noble truth. For the realization of that enlightenment there must be another path.'

"Then he reflected on that early childhood meditation under the rose-apple tree during his father's plowing ceremony. He recalled the extreme feelings of bliss, and he asked himself, 'Why should I fear that bliss, for it does not arise out of sensual pleasures and evil deeds. It is not easy to realize that bliss with this exceedingly emaciated body.[8] What if I were to take solid food and rice gruel?'" explains Anuruddha.

Ananda begins, "Just at that moment a boy who was tending his cows saw the *Bodhisatta* lying prostrate on the ground. He assumed that the poor emaciated man was dead. He ran home to his parents, who had often provided alms to the ascetics. They returned with their son to where Siddhartha was lying unconscious, and they felt for the breath under his nostrils.

"He isn't yet dead, but he will be soon if he doesn't take some nourishment. Son, go home and get some warm milk and we'll make him drink it,' said the boy's mother.

"The young boy ran home and quickly returned with the warm milk. His mother placed the Lord's head upon her lap and poured a few drops between his lips. In this way she and her family tended to the Master. They eventually got him to eat solid food, which brought him back to health," says Ananda.

"Why didn't Kondanna and the other members of the group accompany the Master when he went to Gaya to make his final attempt at enlightenment?" asks Bakkula. "If they were so devoted to him why didn't they continue to serve him and support him in his supreme efforts?"

"If I might answer your first question, Bakkula," begins Anuruddha, "when Kondanna and the other ascetics saw the Master begin to take nourishment they became disappointed with him. They felt that he had given in to the needs of his body, abandoning his quest for enlightenment.

"Kondanna said to the others, 'Let us leave Siddhartha to the pleasures of the senses. He has failed himself, and he has failed us.' With that the five ascetics abandoned him and moved on to Isipatana in Varanasi."

"The Lord knew that in terms of mortifying the flesh, he had gone beyond the point where any ascetic had ever gone before," says Ananda. "The Boddhisatta said, 'I did not attain any superhuman knowledge and insight that would give me a glimpse of the ultimate goal: freedom from suffering...I have lost the trail and must go back and retrace it.' From that time forward the Master began to practice the Middle Path, avoiding the extremes of pleasure and self-torture. He had lived the life of both extremes, and now he knew that neither one would lead to enlightenment, but only to death and rebirth."

At that moment Maha Kassapa approaches the three arahants saying, "King Ajatasattu is waiting to offer you food, brothers. We will have plenty of time for further discussion about the Middle Path later on. There is no need to be hungry; the Master learned that lesson the hard way."

Maha Kassapa leads the way to the *dana* hall where the king and his retinue are preparing to offer the midday meal.

Chapter 8
The Fully Enlightened One

After lunch, which was presented again by King Ajatasattu, the arahants file back into the assembly hall where Ananda prepares to recite another of the Buddha's middle length discourses.

Ananda approaches the podium and begins by saying, "Our sub-committee recording the life of the Buddha has just concluded the chapter about the Lord's period of self-mortification, and his return to health after nearly starving to death. Shortly after his recovery, just before he made his final effort, he perceived two kinds of thought, each one leading to entirely different outcomes. Speaking of that, the Lord delivered the '*Dvedhavitakka Sutta*:[1] Two Kinds of Thought,' to recount that understanding. I will begin…"

The arahants give their full attention to Ananda, many of them closing their eyes to listen. The memory monks are alert and completely absorbed in the moment.

"Thus I heard. '*Bhikhus*, before my enlightenment, while I was still only an unenlightened *Bodhisatta*, it occurred to me: Suppose that I divide my thoughts into two classes. Then I set on one side thoughts of sensual desire, ill-will, and cruelty; and I set on the other side thoughts of renunciation, non-ill will, and non-cruelty.

'As I abided thus, diligent, ardent, and resolute, thoughts of sensual desire, ill-will, and cruelty arose in me. I understood thus: These thoughts have arisen in me. They lead to my own affliction, to others' affliction, and to the affliction of both; they obstruct wisdom, cause difficulties, and lead away from *Nibbana*. When I considered these thoughts, they subsided in me. Whenever any of these thoughts arose in me, I abandoned them, removed them, and did away with them.

"'*Bhikkhus*, whatever a *bhikkhu* frequently thinks and ponders upon, that will become the inclination of his mind. If he frequently thinks and ponders thoughts of sensual desire, ill will, or cruelty, he has abandoned the thought of renunciation...If he frequently thinks and ponders upon thoughts of renunciation, non-ill will, and non-cruelty; he has abandoned thoughts of sensual desire, ill-will and cruelty.'"

Ananda continues to the end of the discourse. Afterwards, the arahants take a short recess for rest and refreshment.

Later, when the day's proceedings have concluded, the subcommittee re-convenes in Maha Kassapa's chamber.

"This morning's discourse on the two kinds of thoughts is a good example of the Buddha's infinite wisdom," comments Punna. "Hopefully men and women will take care in choosing their thoughts, for by doing so they choose their reality – whether they are aware of it or not."

"If one follows the Dhamma's practical applications one cannot help but have a happy successful life – at the very least. If one follows the Dhamma's spiritual applications, then one has a good chance of ultimately attaining emancipation, *Nibbana*," adds Maha Kaccayana.

"Very true, Venerable Sir. Now we are ready to hear what happened in the Buddha's life after his six-year period of self-mortification. Where should we begin, Ananda?" asks Maha Kassapa.

"I think the story of Sujata would be a good place to start," replies Ananda after a pause. Maha Kassapa and the other arahants smile, knowing that this evening they will hear about their Lord's successful effort to attain enlightenment.

Ananda begins, "When Siddhartha left the community of ascetics in Senani, he walked along the banks of the Neranjara River until he came to a hillock situated under the wide shade of an ancient banyan tree. The place was appealing to him, so he seated himself in a grassy spot between two roots that had grown out horizontally from the tree's massive trunk.

"The ascetic Siddhartha reflected on the fact that he was virtually no closer to his goal of *Nibbana* than he had been six years before when he renounced his worldly life. He had followed the two best teachers in the land, but their training hadn't been able to take him all the way to his goal. Then he followed the path of self-torture, but it nearly killed him. He wracked his brain trying to think of a solution to the problem of existence, and to find a practical course that would lead to his release from the endless cycle of rebirth and suffering.

"Out of nowhere a thought suddenly occurred to him, 'In the future I do not need to follow the path of any teacher. I have within me all that is necessary to find a solution on my own. If I apply my energy, using my willpower and determination, I will surely be successful.'

"He spent most of that night in deep meditation under the banyan tree. Feeling relaxed and happy, he lay down and slept the last hour or two before dawn. While sleeping he had five dreams. Analyzing their combined meaning he realized that he would attain enlightenment that very day. He smiled, thinking about his imminent release.

"Nearby lived Sujata, the daughter of a wealthy merchant.[2] She was a beautiful young woman, virtuous, kind, and compassionate," continues Ananda. "When she was just sixteen years old she made a vow that if she were to marry a husband of equal status and have a son, she would make an annual offering to the deity of the very tree under which Siddhartha was resting.

"Her wishes had been fulfilled. She was now happily married, and the mother of an infant son. That night she was preparing special milk-rice, which she would offer the following morning.

"She said to her servant girl, Punna, 'Go to the ancient banyan tree, clear a place beneath it, and spread the mats in preparation for the offering.'

"Punna went to do as she was ordered, and when she came near the tree she saw the seated figure of an ascetic deep in meditation. It appeared to her as if light was shining from his golden body. The light illuminated the tree and its surroundings with a gleaming radiance. She was afraid to approach the serene and noble presence. Punna's first thought was that the tree god had come down to wait for her mistress's offering. She quickly cleared the leaves and spread out the mat, and then ran back home to report the news to Sujata, who was overjoyed.

"Sujata dressed herself in her finest sari and ornaments. The two young ladies carefully arranged their offering of milk-rice in an elaborately-crafted golden bowl, and then covered it with a pale ivory silk cloth.

"When they reached the banyan tree Sujata slowly approached the ascetic, and with her head bowed low, she placed the golden bowl of milk- rice in his hands saying, 'Please, Venerable Sir, accept these gifts. Just as my desire was fulfilled, may your ambition also be realized.' She also presented a vase filled with perfumed water, which the *Bodhisatta* accepted graciously with a nod.

"The two young ladies paid their respects by touching their heads to the ground in front of him. They rose to their feet, backed up slowly, and turned to walk away. Then a thought occurred to Sujata and she went back and knelt before the Lord and asked, 'Are you really the god of this tree?'

"'No, child,' was his reply with a faint smile.

"'Well then, who are you?' asked Sujata.

"'I am called Siddhartha, of the Sakyan clan,' responded the Prince.

"Her face showed surprise when she heard his reply, and she said, 'I've heard of you, my lord. I know you left your kingdom to search for enlightenment. I am certain you will achieve your goal and become the Buddha.'

"The young girl bowed once again and stood up to go. The Master looked at her with great compassion and nodded his thanks for her good wishes.

"When she was a few steps away Siddhartha called out to her and said, 'Please take this golden bowl with you. I have no need of such an object.'

"'It is my custom to make an offering of food along with the vessel it is served in,' she replied. 'You may do with it whatever you wish.'

"The two young ladies took their leave. Siddhartha carried the bowl of milk-rice to the river and then bathed. Afterwards he robed himself and ate his meal," continues Ananda.

"Then the Lord put his resolve to the test," adds Sopaka.

"He certainly did," says Ananda. "He picked up the empty golden bowl and threw it into the Neranjara River. He said, 'If this bowl floats upstream, then I will surely be successful in my attempt to attain enlightenment today.'

"When he tossed the bowl it was as if the sun itself grabbed it in its rays, so intense was the golden reflection as it hit the water. Siddhartha watched carefully as the swiftly-flowing river actually carried the bowl upstream instead of dragging it along with the current. After a while the bowl sunk beneath the surface of the water and disappeared.

"The Lord smiled, thinking that on that very day he himself was to move against the current of life, and with his own direct experience penetrate the cycle of birth and death. He also thought about the impermanent nature of all material things as he considered the fate of the golden bowl. He felt happy, thinking that earlier it had belonged to Sujata, then to him, and perhaps later it would belong to some lucky person who happened to find it. Then the Lord spent the rest of the day in a grove of *sala* trees meditating and gathering his strength."

"I can only imagine his thoughts as the sun began to go down and he approached his moment of truth," says Maha Kassapa.

"He later said that his mind became as tranquil as a mountain lake, remaining as pure and reflective as a polished mirror," says Ananda. "Towards dusk he had an inclination to walk towards a magnificent pipal tree on the other side of the river. He waded across the shallow river, and when he approached the tree he encountered a farm worker named Sotthiya. The humble man was carrying a bundle of freshly-scythed river grass on his shoulders. Sotthiya took one look at Siddhartha and was dazzled by his powerful yet peaceful countenance. The *Bodhisatta* smiled compassionately at him, and silently the peasant took the bundle of grass and spread it out for the Master under the tree.

"It was upon that very bundle of grass that the Lord took his seat with great determination saying, 'I will not arise from this place until I have attained my goal, which is full, irrevocable enlightenment,'" says Ananda

"The Master then closed his eyes and began his long night of concentration," says Maha Kassapa. "We know very well where that concentration led, and about the demons he had to first overcome."

"The king of those demons, Mara, approached the Lord during the early evening with words of kindness and feigned compassion," begins Ananda. "He asked, 'Why are you striving so hard, Prince Siddhartha, and for what? The path you have chosen is obscured by many difficulties; very few have conquered it. Why don't you just enjoy your birthright and the incomparable, happy life that was provided for you by the gods themselves?' Siddhartha ignored the demon and continued breathing softly, deep in his tranquil bliss.

"Mara then said, 'Devadatta has conquered Kapilavatthu and is now ensconced in your royal bed. He has murdered your entire family while you sit here doing nothing. Don't you have any will to avenge him?' Mara then caused apparitions of Yasodhara and Rahula to appear before the prince; they were being tortured and subjected to great pain. Siddhartha also saw the bloody bodies of the king and queen who had been beheaded and dismembered.

"Siddhartha continued to ignore the powerful demon, knowing that what Mara had spoken, and the visions he had caused to appear, were nothing more than illusions. The Lord remained unmoved. At this point Mara became frustrated and he started to argue with the Master. He tried his best to distract him with his armies and temptations," continues Ananda.

"Why don't you tell us in the Buddha's own words from the *Padhana Sutta*,[3] how he responded," requests Maha Kassapa. "I know you will recite this discourse later, but I think telling it here would provide clarification for our recollections."

"Very well, Venerable Sir," says Ananda as he searches the files in his legendary memory for the requested *sutta*.

> "The Buddha began by saying, 'The foremost of your armies is that of Sense Pleasure, the second is called Dissatisfaction. The third is Hunger and Thirst, and the fourth is Craving. The fifth is the army of Sloth and Torpor, and the sixth is Fear. The seventh is Doubt and the eighth is Conceit and Ingratitude. Then there is also Gain, Praise, Honor and Undeserved Fame obtained by wrongful means, (which is nine). And Self-Exaltation and Disparaging (is ten). These, O Mara, are your forces, the attackers of the evil one. One less than a hero will not be victorious over them and attain happiness.'"

Ananda pauses briefly as the arahants reflect on the Ten Armies of Mara; then he continues.

> "The Lord, relaxed and composed, continued to address the demon by saying:

"'There are monks and hermits who have drowned in defilements and never see that path which the well-conducted ones tread. I can see the troops all around me, with Mara mounted on an elephant, and I go forward into the struggle. Even though the whole world, inclusive of its gods, cannot beat that army of yours, I am going to destroy it with the power of wisdom like an unfired clay pot with a stone. With disciplined thought and firmly grounded mindfulness I shall travel from country to country training numerous disciples. Alert and energetic in the practice of my teaching, contrary to your wish, they will attain that which having attained they will not come to grief.'

"Then Mara, who by now was in a complete rage, shouted at his armies, 'Come and seize this low-born human! Bind him and cast him off. He is nothing more than a worm.' With these words Mara caused a blazing shower of flames, blinding the Lord with smoke. He threw countless thunderbolts and assailed the Master with a host of deadly weapons. The Master sat there unmoved, showing no emotion.

"Seeing that nothing he did had any affect on Siddhartha, he shouted at him, 'How dare you sit in my rightful seat! Get up or I will tear your heart in two!'

"The Lord looked at Mara with limitless compassion, much as a father would look at a young son playing at his feet. He said, 'I have come here to teach the world the lessons of death and decay, and to help many beings cross over from this painful existence of suffering. I shall vanquish your armies by means of wisdom. There is no need of a witness. The earth itself is my witness.'

"The Lord stretched out his right hand and touched the ground. At that moment a great earthquake arose, and a terrifying noise roared through the sky. Thunderbolts cracked and crashed and struck terror into the heart of the king of demons. Mara covered his eyes and wailed piteously before dematerializing from view; his armies scattered like dust in a strong wind. Siddhartha was once again left alone, untroubled, and determined." Ananda says these last words with great emotion. It seems like fire shines from his eyes as he sees in his mind the forces of evil evaporate before the goodness of his Master.

"That was the end of Mara and his armies – at least for the time being," says Bakkula.

"I wish I could have been there to witness the Lord's moment of Supreme Enlightenment," says Maha Kaccayana. "I know that untold numbers of *devas* and *Brahmas* had gathered from the four corners of the universe, but there were no human observers."

"We have the Master's account which will have to suffice," says Upali.

"Ananda, please tell us in your own words, as well as in the Master's, the story of that auspicious night," asks Maha Kassapa.

"No words can properly do justice to the telling of this event, but I will do my best. It's like comparing the most beautiful painting of a sunset to the true splendor of the actual, impermanent, and artful expression of nature itself."

"Don't underestimate the potency and beauty of your words, Ananda. I would rather hear this account from you than from anyone else; after all, you were the one who had the opportunity to hear it directly from the Master's lips," says Punna.

"Then I will begin Venerable Arahants. After the departure of Mara and his armies, the Lord remained serenely seated in the lotus posture under the broad green branches of the pipal tree. He concentrated his mind on the task at hand, and focused his combined energies on the attainment of full enlightenment. The *Bodhisatta* knew without doubt that this was the time he had prepared for all his life, and for countless lifetimes in the past.

"The sun went down, and the full moon of Vesakha began to rise. The sky was amazingly bright and clear that night and only the most brilliant stars appeared. The moonlight was reflected in the radiance of the Master's golden skin. The forest went completely silent, as if every living creature was doing its small part to support the unfolding event. The entire cosmos was watching with great anticipation; countless celestial beings were focusing their meditative attention on the man who was about to transcend life, death and rebirth.

"I will use the Master's words as well as my own. He said that he 'entered upon and abided in the first *jhana*, which is accompanied by applied and sustained thought with rapture and pleasure; but such pleasant feeling that arose in him did not invade his mind and remain. At this stage he was completely detached from lust and evil in all its forms, and his mind was full of reasoning and investigation.

"'After a while reasoning and investigation ceased, and with the stilling of applied and sustained thought, he entered upon and abided in the second *jhana*...With the fading away as well of rapture...he entered upon and abided in the third *jhana*. At this level, being detached from joy, he became impartial and mindful.

"Finally, he entered into and dwelt in the fourth *jhana*, 'with the abandoning of pleasure and pain...But such pleasant feeling that arose in (him) did not invade his mind and remain.' At this point the Lord was completely detached from both happiness and sorrow, and his mind was firmly established in faith, energy, mindfulness, concentration, and the light of wisdom.

"After attaining the four *jhanas* the Master said that when his 'concentrated mind was thus purified, bright, unblemished, rid of imperfection, malleable, wieldy, steady, and attained to imperturbability, (he) directed it to knowledge of the recollection of past lives.' The Lord once compared his mind at this time to gold that had been refined to its purest state; it becomes supple and pliant, and with it the jeweler can craft anything he desires. A *Bodhisatta's* mind can similarly be directed at will to anything it wants to know, see, or create. With his newly-acquired supernormal knowledge, in an instant he destroyed ignorance forever. This enabled him to see the activities, events, and experiences from all of his past existences – from the first, to the last as Setaketu *Deva*.

"The Master said that 'this was the first true knowledge attained by me in the first watch of the night. Ignorance was banished and true knowledge arose, darkness was banished and light arose, as happens in one who abides diligent, ardent, and resolute. But such pleasant feelings that arose in me did not invade the mind and remain.'

"Siddhartha didn't stop there. He next began to 'concentrate on the death and rebirth of beings, which (he) could see with (his) clear supernormal vision. Thus with the divine eye, which is purified and surpasses the human, (he) saw beings passing away and reappearing, inferior and superior, fair and ugly, fortunate and unfortunate, and (he) understood how beings pass on according to their actions.' The Lord saw that beings whose thoughts, words, deeds, and beliefs were misguided, false, and self-centered were reborn, according to their degree, in low states of existence. By the same token, he saw that beings whose thoughts, words, deeds, and beliefs were noble, generous, and upright were reborn, according to their degree, in high states.

"The Lord said that this was the second true knowledge attained by him in the second watch of the night.'

"When Siddhartha's mind reached this exalted state he concentrated on the knowledge of the destruction of the defilements, and he realized the discomfort of suffering in its entirety. He said, 'I directly knew it as it actually is: 'This is the origin of suffering';...'This is the cessation of suffering';...'This is the way leading to the cessation of suffering';...When I knew and saw thus, my mind was liberated from the taint of sensual desire, from the taint of being, and from the taint of ignorance. When it was liberated there was the knowledge: 'It is liberated.' I directly knew: 'Birth is destroyed, the holy life has been lived, what had to be done has been done, there is no more coming to any state of being.' The Master was completely released from the defilements of lust, hatred, and ignorance forever.

"Thus, in the last watch of the night the *Bodhisatta* realized the way leading to the cessation of suffering with the Noble Eightfold Path, namely: right view, right thought, right speech, right action, right livelihood, right effort, right mindfulness, and right concentration. This knowledge completed his aspirations for attaining full enlightenment to the utter joy of humans and gods.

"The man who had become the Buddha that evening said:

> "'For many a birth in this existence, I was traveling through fruitlessly to find the builder of this structure, for repeated birth is suffering. I have seen the builder, and never again will this structure be built. All the rafters are broken and the top of the structure is shattered. My mind is fixed on dissolution, and I have mastered the cessation of lust, hatred, and ignorance.'"[4]

When Ananda completes these last words he pauses and looks around the cave chamber. Each one of the arahants is in deep *samadhi*. Concentrated in unparalleled understanding, they are focused on the ultimate liberation of the Buddha. Their own enlightenment enables them to truly comprehend the universal significance of emancipation.

Bhaddiya breaks the silence, "Earlier when we discussed the Master's birth at Lumbini I mentioned the legend of the seven lotuses. Baby Prince Siddhartha supposedly stepped on them just a few moments after he was born. These lotuses symbolized the seven successive stages of purification, which Siddhartha needed to complete before attaining Buddhahood. Enlightenment is the final event in this series of seven.

"The Master attained the first, 'purification of virtue,' at the time he renounced the world and put on the robes of the *bhikkhu*.

"After he partook of Sujata's offering of milk-rice he spent much of the day purifying the eight attainments of *jhana* and the five mundane psychic powers. They had become unclean and dim during his six years of asceticism. The re-establishment of these attainments and powers constituted the *Bodhisatta's* second purification, which is 'purification of the mind towards mastering one's moods.'

"After the *Bodhisatta* moved to the Bodhi tree and vanquished Mara, in the first watch of the night he developed the knowledge of his past existences. He perceived and penetrated the phenomenon of mind and matter, and he destroyed all beliefs in personality. This is when he achieved the third purification, which is 'purification of view towards the elimination of all belief systems.'

"During the middle watch of the night when he discerned the birth and death of beings according to their thoughts, words, and deeds he realized distinctly the law of *kamma*. This realization enabled him to become free of doubts, and it is when he achieved the fourth purification, which is 'purification of doubt towards the attainment of faith in the Dhamma.'

"In the last watch of the night when the *Bodhisatta* dwelt on the twelve factors of the Doctrine of Dependent Origination, there arose in him the complete understanding of the defilements of *Vipassana*, or insight. Some meditators mistook the defilements for the true Path, but the *Bodhisatta* saw through them to the truth. This is when he achieved the fifth purification, which is 'purification of discernment towards an understanding of the true path versus the false path.'

"During the last watch of the night he completed the final stages in the Path of Purification. The sixth is 'purification of knowledge and vision towards a commitment to the Way.' The seventh is 'purification of wisdom towards attaining enlightenment and the Truth.' Upon completion of the seventh, the *Bodhisatta* achieved enlightenment. In this manner, the series of the seven purifications constitutes the right and proper way to *Nibbana*," concludes Bhaddiya.

"Since the dawn will be breaking soon, I suggest we stop our discussions here," says Maha Kassapa.

Ananda says, "Before we break for the night, please allow me to quote from one of the Buddha's discourses about his state of enlightenment."

Maha Kassapa nods his consent, and Ananda speaks:

> "Having directly known all the world,
> All in the world, exactly as it is,
> He is detached from all the world,
> Unengaged with all the world.
>
> "'He indeed is the all-vanquishing sage,
> The One released from all the knots,
> Who has reached the supreme state of peace,
> *Nibbana*, without fear from any side.
>
> "'He is the Buddha,
> With taints destroyed, untroubled,
> With all doubts cut off,
> Who has attained the destruction of all *kamma*,
> Liberated in the extinction of acquisitions.'[5]"

After a few moments of profound silence Maha Kassapa says, "I know we all deeply feel the significance of tonight's recollections, and that we will wish to reflect privately on their impact not only on our own lives, but on the lives of all who will one day come into birth."

Ananda and the other arahants rise silently and make their way toward their own chambers. There is no need for torchlight; once again the pale violet auras of the venerable monks provide their illumination.

Chapter 9
The First Seven Weeks

The Sangha members file out of the assembly hall for their morning tea break. On this day King Ajatasattu provides the refreshments under the shade of a banyan tree half way down the slope of Mount Vebhara. The weather is scorching hot, but wherever the arahants gather a cool breeze seems to find them.

It has gradually become the custom of the members of the sub-committee to get together for an informal meeting during this recess period. It gives them an opportunity to go over their previous discussion if there are points that need clarifying, or to continue where they left off. Maha Kassapa has requested that the memory monks also attend these gatherings.

"I so enjoyed our recollection of the Master's enlightenment last evening, Ananda," says Bakkula. "I never tire of hearing his joyous proclamation after attaining full liberation. The image he uses of a builder and his structure is brilliant; it makes the false mental construct of the persona so visual for the listener, and much easier to comprehend."

"With that one statement he forever destroys the myth of the permanent individual self, and he makes it clear that what one takes for one's 'I' is nothing more than a fabricated invention of the conditioned mind," adds Anuruddha.

"Indeed, Venerable Sir," says Punna. "Since we have a little time before the council resumes perhaps we could talk about the Master's first seven weeks after enlightenment."

"An excellent suggestion, Punna," says Maha Kassapa. "The Buddha was completely alone after his great liberation, and I often wonder how he obtained food to sustain his body."

"The Lord once told me that the young woman, Sujata, brought fruits, beans, and milk-rice to him every day" says Ananda.

"How did that come about?" asks Sopaka.

"The day following the Lord's awakening Sujata's maid, Punna, met the farm worker, Sotthiya, in the marketplace," begins Ananda. "She had been acquainted with him since she was a child. Sotthiya said to her, 'Have you heard the news that Gotama Siddhartha, the former prince of the Sakyan clan, is sitting under the big pipal tree across the river? Yesterday afternoon I saw him there and made a seat for him out of river grass. I thought he was a god since light was shining all around him. Did you feel the earthquake last night? And those strange noises? Did you see those flashes of lightning in the sky? The heavens were definitely in an uproar over something. Do you think it had anything to do with the prince?'

"Punna replied, 'Yesterday my mistress and I went to give an offering of milk-rice to the god who lives in that tree. We spoke to the man who was sitting there and he told us he was the Sakyan prince you just mentioned. Last night all those noises and lights in the sky kept me awake. I have no idea what they were. What do the people in the village think?'

"'I spoke to some folks who had seen the ascetic in the grove, but they didn't dare go near him. They were frightened by the earthquake and all the lightning flashes. They're convinced the prince must have caused it all.'

"Punna hurried home to tell Sujata. When she heard Punna's news she told her to gather the best mangoes from the orchard. Sujata thought that if the prince had meditated all night maybe he had become enlightened; in any event, he must be hungry.

"The two young women hurried toward the pipal tree. When they saw Siddhartha Sujata said with excitement, 'Look, Punna, do you see that glowing aura around him? There seems to be six colors: blue, yellow, red, white, orange, and a combination of all of them!'

"Punna answered, 'Yes, I can see it!'

"The two young women approached the seated Buddha, and Punna unfolded a mat. He said not a word, nor did his gaze waver as Sujata put the plate of perfect ripe mangoes in front of him. Sujata and Punna bowed with the greatest respect and went home.

"In the same manner, for the next forty-nine days the two women brought the Buddha his daily food. He said to me later that he silently blessed them, and that Sujata would one day become a *sotapanna*, a stream-enterer. In fact, before the Buddha passed away he commented that the meal Sujata offered him before his enlightenment was the greatest act of generosity the world had ever seen.[1] It wasn't until the fifth week after his enlightenment that the Buddha began speaking again. At that time he thanked Sujata and Punna for their offerings, and eventually they became life-long devotees," concludes Ananda.

"That's indeed a beautiful story, Ananda; one of many that over time will be told about the life of our Lord. We should record as many of them as possible in this recollection," says Maha Kaccayana.

"This is where all of our memories will come in handy, not just mine," replies Ananda, smiling. "Coming back to the first week after the Buddha's enlightenment, in order to stabilize his mind and body after the tremendous impact of realization, the Lord stayed seated under the pipal tree and enjoyed the bliss of emancipation. Now, of course, we call it the 'Bodhi Tree,' the word 'bodhi' meaning 'enlightenment.' Even though several of the villagers went near the tree to see him, no one ever approached the Buddha except Sujata and Punna."

"Ananda, I think this is the appropriate place to introduce the Buddha's doctrine of dependent origination," says Bhaddiya.

"Yes, Venerable Sir, a very appropriate place," agrees Ananda. "At the end of the first week the Lord rose from his blissful state of contemplation, and in the first watch of the night he started to analyze the nature of the law of cause and effect from beginning to end.

"He saw clearly that everything that exists is conditioned upon the arising of every other thing that exists. This applies to individuals, thoughts, feelings, ideas, material objects, and even the universe itself with its endless worlds and dimensions. In a few moments I am going to recite one of the Buddha's discourses. It explains the process in the Lord's own words."

The gong rings out calling the arahants to the council. They put away their tea bowls and prepare to return to the hall.

"I'm looking forward to hearing the discourse, Ananda. Which one will you recite?" asks Bhaddiya.

"It's the '*Bahudhatuka Sutta*:[2] The Many Kinds of Elements,'" responds Ananda.

When they enter the hall Ananda goes to the podium, closes his eyes, and begins, "Thus I heard: On one occasion the Blessed One was living at Savatthi in Jeta's Grove, Anathapindika's Park. There he addressed the *bhikkhus* thus: *'Bhikkhus.'* – 'Venerable Sir,' they replied. The Blessed One said this:

"'…in what way can a *bhikkhu* be called skilled in dependent origination?'

"'…a *bhikkhu* knows thus: When this exists, that comes to be; with the arising of this, that arises. When this does not exist, that does not come to be; with the cessation of this, that ceases. That is, with ignorance as condition, formations come to be; with formations as condition, consciousness; with consciousness as condition, mentality-materiality; with mentality-materiality as condition, the six-fold senses; with the six-fold senses as condition, contact; with contact as condition, feeling; with feeling as condition, craving; with craving as condition, clinging; with clinging as condition, being; with being as condition, birth; with birth as condition, ageing and death, sorrow, lamentation, pain, grief, and despair come to be. Such is the origin of this whole mass of suffering.

"'But with the remainderless fading away and the cessation of ignorance comes cessation of formations; with the cessation of formations, cessation of consciousness; with the cessation of consciousness, cessation of mentality-materiality; with the cessation of mentality-materiality, cessation of the six-fold senses; with the cessation of the six-fold senses, cessation of contact; with the cessation of contact, cessation of feeling; with the cessation of feeling, cessation of craving; with the cessation of craving, cessation of clinging; with the cessation of clinging, cessation of being; with the cessation of being, cessation of birth; with the cessation of birth, ageing and death, sorrow, lamentation, pain, grief, and despair cease. Such is the cessation of this whole mass of suffering.' In this way, a *bhikkhu* can be called skillful in dependent origination.'"

Ananda continues reciting until the discourse is completed. Afterwards he says, "I would like to quote briefly from another *sutta* that demonstrates how this system works in regards to happiness:

> "'Overcoming suffering leads to confidence; confidence to rapture; rapture to joy; joy to tranquility; tranquility to happiness; happiness to concentration; concentration to knowledge and vision of things as they truly are; the knowledge and vision of things as they truly are to repulsion; repulsion to non-attachment; non-attachment to deliverance; deliverance to the extinction of passions, or arahantship.'"[3]

After the lunch break Ananda begins another discourse. The recitations, ensuing questions and discussions continue until dusk. Maha Kassapa finally sounds the gong to officially end the day's session.

The arahants on the sub-committee walk swiftly towards Maha Kassapa's cave chamber. They are eager to continue their earlier discussion, and to hear more about how the Buddha spent his first seven weeks after enlightenment. They know that from the Buddha's enlightenment forward they, as well as many of their brothers in the Sangha, will start appearing as characters in their recollections.

When they are seated, Maha Kassapa says, "It always amazes me when I think of the Lord going forwards and backwards on the wheel of *samsara* during his first night after emancipation. He managed to map the arising of suffering, and then reverse it to reach suffering's ultimate cessation. By putting it into a systematic order it could be followed by both the *bhikkhu* as well as the layman. This had never been done before, and it was a tremendous accomplishment of *vipassana*."

"Indeed it was, Venerable Sir," says Bhaddiya, "and if one follows it, comparing it to events in one's own life, it can ultimately lead to the end of one's *samsaric* journey."

"It also applies, as was said during the council, to all things, both mental and spiritual. The Buddha's teaching of impermanence, *anicca*, goes hand-in-hand with this principle, and it helps to explain the arising and passing away of all phenomena. I'm sure that scholars of the future will study this principle, and finding it useful, will elaborate on its applications," adds Punna.

Ananda begins, "Let's get back to the period immediately following the Buddha's liberation. It is well known that during week number two he stood and gazed at the Bodhi Tree for seven days without looking away. He did this to show his gratitude to the tree for sheltering him and sharing its energy while he struggled to attain his enlightenment.

The Buddha realized the importance gratitude plays in the creation of reality, and he never missed an opportunity to teach this principle to those who approached him for instruction.

"During the third and fourth weeks he contemplated various aspects and applications of the higher doctrine. As we said, the Buddha spoke for the first time during the fifth week. His first conversation was with a somewhat arrogant Brahmin who approached him while he was seated under a banyan tree.

"The man greeted the Lord and then asked, 'What are the qualities that make a person a Brahmin?'

"The Buddha, immediately perceiving the underlying assumptions behind the man's question, said, 'A true Brahmin is a person who is free from all forms of evil; completely lacking in arrogance and defilements. He is committed, well-versed in Vedic knowledge, and lives his life based on high moral standards. He understands and shares the sacred theories correctly; he is impartial and fair.'[4]

"The Brahmin immediately caught the subtle reproach and went away from the meeting deep in thought."

"Didn't Mara make a reappearance at this time?" asks Punna.

Ananda nods and begins, "Mara, who was completely defeated and humiliated after his last confrontation with the Master, approached him while he was seated under the Goatherds' banyan tree.[5] He tried to insult him by saying, 'Why are you sitting alone and depressed in the forest? Don't you want company? Have you committed some sort of a crime? Are you grieving over your lost wealth?'

"Very calmly the Buddha answered, 'I am meditating. I have forever cut off the root cause of suffering, and I am free from any kind of grief. There are no longer any attachments or desires.'

"Mara said, 'If you are holding on to the thought that this is 'mine,' even if you call it 'my freedom,' then you cannot possibly escape from me.'

"The Buddha responded, 'There is no "I," and there is nothing called "mine." If you don't see it this way, you who cannot see the truth, then you are not following my thought.'

"Then Mara asked, 'If you have realized immortality, then why don't you go off somewhere by yourself? Why do you want to correct the imperfections of others?'

"To this the Buddha said, 'If any approach me who wish to cross the bridge of existence from death to the deathless, then I will teach them the truth with no attachment whatsoever.'

"Mara, frustrated and angry, left the Buddha's presence without taking his leave. He realized that the Master had destroyed forever all of the avenues of illusion and evil, and he had no hope of successfully defeating him," concludes Ananda.

"What about Mara's three daughters? Didn't they make an appearance during this time?" asks Bakkula.

"Yes, the three temptresses named Tanha, Arati, and Raga, don't know what to make of their father's wrathful and despondent mood when he described his confrontation with the Buddha to them," responds Ananda. "They tried to console him by saying, 'Don't worry, father; we will tie that man up with a rope of lust and passion like a mad elephant; no one can resist our charms. We'll bring him to you so you can demonstrate your supreme dominance over all.'

"Mara responded by saying, 'The Well Gone One is no longer susceptible to lust; he is completely free of defilements, and has moved beyond my influence. You have no idea how impotent this makes me feel. I curse him!'

"Mara's three daughters made themselves up and adorned their bodies until they were satisfied that no man could withstand their appeal.[6] They approached the Buddha and said, 'We will sit here at your feet and serve you, monk.' The Master, of course, paid them no attention.

"Having been thoroughly ignored, they went away to discuss how they could win over the Buddha, still having confidence in their seductive allure. Tanha said to her sisters, 'Men love variety. We should transform ourselves into thirty different young girls. I can't wait to see him fall off his high horse and spring for that irresistible bait.' The three evil daughters laughed out loud agreeing to this devious strategy.

"In a flash, thirty beautiful young girls wearing garments of transparent silk and ornaments of gold and gleaming jewels appeared before the Buddha. They started to dance for him in a seductive manner. One by one they paraded themselves before him and plied every female charm they knew. The Buddha took absolutely no notice of them. He sat silently in deep meditation as before.

"The three sisters then disguised themselves as all sorts of females, but to no avail. Close to admitting defeat they said to one another, 'Surely the Well Gone One is immune to lust; he has passed beyond the reach of our father, Mara. Any other man, be he monk or Brahmin, would have lost his senses and gone mad with desire. Let's go back and try one more time.'

"One by one Tanha, Arati, and Raga approached the Buddha who sat impervious, like granite. He didn't even blink an eye. He finally said, 'Go away, you phantoms of grief. To what benefit did you try to tempt me? Those temptations only work on one who is not yet free from passion, hate and delusion. As for me, I am free of all of these.'

"This statement enraged them to such an extent that their disguises vanished in a flash of flame. They were left standing there looking like the demonic old hags they really were," concludes Ananda.

Upali says, "I can just imagine the intense anger and frustration they felt. They had no idea what they were up against when they challenged one who had completely eliminated all defilements and vestiges of human lust. Never had they encountered a supremely enlightened one such as our Lord."

"At the end of that week," begins Ananda, "the Buddha sat at the foot of the Mucalinda tree where he enjoyed the bliss of his exalted, emancipated state. A violent, cold storm hit the area that lingered for several days. The giant cobra that lived in that tree coiled its body in such a way that he created a canopy over the Buddha, protecting him from the rain and wind. When the storm passed the cobra uncoiled himself and slithered back up into the tree.[7]

"After spending a week at the Mucalinda tree the Master moved on to the Rajayatana tree. He seated himself at its base for a week while enjoying his emancipation. We'll never know exactly what went through his mind during these weeks, but I imagine he was trying to decide how to teach the Dhamma."

"Ananda, was this when the two traveling merchants arrived from Kalinga?" asks Bakkula.

"Yes, two brothers[8], Tapassu and Bhallika, were passing through the region when their five hundred carts suddenly stopped, as if stuck in mud. Since the ground was even and dry, they couldn't figure out what caused them to halt. Standing there perplexed, they were visited by a mysterious stranger who said, 'Young men, the Buddha has recently attained full enlightenment, and he is staying at the base of the Rajayatana tree, which is nearby. I advise you to honor him with an offering of alms food. This will bring you success and happiness for a long time to come.'

"The two men were delighted to hear about this extraordinary opportunity to make merit, so they examined their stores and found that they had rice cakes and dough made with honey that they could offer. Obtaining directions, they proceeded immediately to the designated tree.

"After they prostrated themselves before him, the Buddha accepted the alms food. He ate the rice cakes and honey-dough silently, and then he delivered a suitable sermon to the two generous brothers. Together they said, 'Reverend Sir, we take refuge in the Blessed one and his teachings. May the Blessed One receive us as his lifelong disciples.'

"The Lord nodded his acceptance, and Tapassu and Bhallika became the first disciples in the world to take the Two Refuges: the Buddha and the Dhamma. Since the Sangha had not yet come into being, they could not take refuge in the Triple Gem.

"Then one of them said, 'Master, from your boundless compassion, please give us something that we may worship.'

"The Buddha smiled and plucked a hair from his head with his right hand. He handed it to the two men, who were delighted with the gift. They paid their obeisance to the Lord and continued on their journey. Later they constructed a *stupa* in which to enshrine the hair, which they encased in a golden casket," concludes Ananda.

The arahants pause to reflect on their Master's compassion, and then Anuruddha says, "We have all visited that *stupa* in the village of Pukkharavati."

"I believe that it was after meeting the two brothers that the Master made his decision in regards to teaching the Dhamma, and to whom," says Punna.

Ananda answers, "That is so. For several days the Buddha contemplated whether or not to teach the fruits of his realization. He knew that his teaching was difficult, and that most people wouldn't be able to comprehend it. He saw that understanding it was nearly impossible if the listeners' minds were clouded with defilements, impurities and attachments."

"At one point he almost decided that he would not teach the Dhamma. He saw that if others couldn't comprehend it, his efforts would be wasted and the exertion would only cause him fatigue," interjects Punna.

"That is correct," agrees Ananda. "He began to survey the wide array of human intelligence, and he saw that there were in fact some individuals whose faculties were more highly developed than others. He decided that they might be able to grasp his teaching.

"He used the example of lotuses. The Buddha said that all lotuses grew out of the mud on the bottom of the pond, but each one would grow upwards at its own pace, and in accordance with its own nature. He said that some lotuses would never make it to the water's surface. Others would make it to the surface, but would wilt before blooming. There were perhaps even fewer that would not only break through the surface, but rise above the water and come into full bloom. The full-blooming lotuses were like the people to whom the Dhamma would appeal, so he decided to teach it."[9]

"The Lord actually said, 'Open is the door to *Nibbana* and immortality. May those who have ears hear the Dhamma and be freed,'" quotes Upali.

"The Buddha became resolved, and he said to himself, 'Go into the world and preach the doctrine. There will be people who can understand'"quotes Ananda.

Maha Kassapa says, "I think this takes us to a very pleasant place to begin our discussion tomorrow. We will encounter many of our old friends as the Lord proceeds from Buddha Gaya with his message of compassion and wisdom."

The arahants know that they themselves will soon show up in their sub-committee recollections. Some of them had been there since the very beginning of the *Sasana*, and all nine, in their own way, were pillars of its development and essential links to its future.

Chapter 10
The First Disciples

The five-hundred arahants are listening to Ananda recite some of the shorter discourses of the Buddha. The sun is about to set, and he is just completing the *sutta* on the difference between the Buddha and an arahant. There is no decline in his energy level even though he has been standing at the podium for nearly ten hours.

> "'The *Tathagata*, *bhikkhus*, the arahant, the Perfectly Enlightened One, is the originator of the path unarisen before, the producer of the path unproduced before, the declarer of the path undeclared before. He is the knower of the path, the discoverer of the path, the one skilled in the path. And his disciples now dwell following that path and become possessed of it afterwards…'"[1]

The gong rings ending the council for the day. Bhaddiya says to Bakkula as he stands to depart, "I simply don't know how he does it. I know those Himalayan herbs do some of the work, but after all, he's eighty-one years old."

"I assure you, Venerable Sir, that the herbs are only for the throat – they have nothing to do with stamina. His energy undoubtedly comes from the unlimited source of power within; that with which he became endowed when he became enlightened," replies the one hundred-five-year-old arahant who had become almost a legend because of his perennial good health.

"I actually don't think I could stand up there that long," says Bhaddiya. "It's funny, but when we were growing up Ananda was always the one who wanted to rest and take it easy. Now he's become a superhuman."

"As the Lord said on several occasions, when required, we're automatically given necessary abilities that arise from unforeseen conditions," responds Upali. "This applies to arahants as well, even after their enlightenment. Your cousin proves that the ability to tap into unlimited energy was latent within him all along. When he became an arahant it was simply activated."

Bhaddiya shakes his head in amazement as they continue walking toward the cave where they will continue their discussion of the life of the Buddha. Upali suddenly stops, saying, "If you don't mind, Venerable Sir, I would like to pause and enjoy the beauty of the setting summer sun. We'll be down below the surface of the earth soon enough."

Bhaddiya smiles at his friend as they pause to watch the colorful spectacle of nature unfolding in the northeastern hills of India. "By the way, your *double entendre* just now didn't escape me – the 'below the surface of the earth' remark; another reference to our impermanence and mortality, no doubt."

Upali laughs and says, "Was that a delayed reaction, Venerable Sir?"

Before Bhaddiya can answer the two arahants are startled to hear the sound of the gong coming from the assembly hall. They look at one another puzzled, knowing that the gong means they should return to their seats at once. Without hesitation they retrace their steps to the hall, joining their fellow Sangha members who are equally perplexed by the call.

When they arrive, Maha Kassapa is standing at the podium. Several attendant monks are spreading mats in the center of the platform. He says to the re-assembled arahants, "Forgive me if I have caused you any inconvenience, but I have had many requests for making at least a few of the life of Buddha sub-committee discussions open to the whole council. It just occurred to me that this evening's segment would be an appropriate one. I have asked that the hall be re-configured so members of the sub-committee can sit on the platform and conduct their meeting. This will give all of you an opportunity to ask questions, offer suggestions, or make corrections if you feel so inclined."

The arahants seem to be pleased with the opportunity to hear this evening's recollections. The sub-committee members take their places on mats in the center of the platform. Ananda begins, "Our previous discussion ended with the Lord meeting the two brothers, Tapussa and Bhallika. After this event the Buddha decided to preach the doctrine, knowing for certain that there were those who could understand.

"The first person he thought of was his teacher Alara Kalama, for whom he felt such tremendous gratitude. He wanted to demonstrate it by sharing the Dhamma and his enlightenment experience with him. The Buddha used his supernormal powers to determine Alara's whereabouts, and he intuited that the teacher had passed away seven days before.

"He next thought of his second teacher, Uddaka Ramaputta; he also felt inclined to show him his deep gratitude for the knowledge he had gained through him six years prior. Once again he scanned with his mind to find Uddaka's present location, and he discovered that the revered ascetic had just passed away the very night before.

"His mind then turned to the five ascetics with whom he had practiced austerities. Even though they had abandoned and ridiculed him when he gave up the practice of self-mortification, he was inclined to find them and teach the Dhamma to them. He knew their minds were ripe, and that they had the ability to realize *Nibbana*. He also wanted to show his gratitude to them for their care when he was undertaking his severe *tapas*. He looked into his mind and saw that they were currently at the Deer Park of Isipatana in Varanasi, still practicing their austerities," says Ananda.

One of the arahants in the audience stands up and asks, "Did the Lord travel to Varanasi alone, or did someone accompany him?"

"The Buddha had no attendants during this time, and he later told me that he actually preferred to make the one hundred seventy-mile journey alone. On the way he passed through the towns of Rohitavastu, Uruwalvakalpa, Arunalaya, and Sarathi carrying with him the bowl that had been offered to him by the two merchant brothers. He received alms from kind householders along his route. He met the ascetic Upaka on the road between the Bodhi Tree and Gaya," says Ananda.

Upali says, "Ananda, please allow me to quote their conversation from the *Mahavagga* in the *Vinaya*." Ananda consents by nodding his head.

Upali begins:

> "The approaching naked ascetic said, 'Your reverence, your sense-organs are quite pure, your complexion very bright, very clear. On account of who have you, your reverence, gone forth, who is your teacher, or whose dhamma do you profess?'

"The Buddha replied in verse:

> "'Victorious over all, omniscient am I,
> Among all things, undefiled,
> Leaving all, through death of craving freed,
> By knowing for myself, whom should I follow?
>
> "'For me there is no teacher,
> One like me does not exist,
> In the world with its *devas*
> No one equals me.
>
> "'For I am perfected in the world,
> The teacher supreme am I,
> I alone am all-awakened,
> Become cool am I, *Nibbana* attained.
>
> "'To turn the Dhamma-wheel
> I go to Kasi's city,
> Beating the drum of deathlessness
> In a world that's blind become.'

"Upaka replied to the Buddha, 'According to what you claim, Your Reverence, you ought to be the victor of the unending.'

"The Buddha answered the ascetic, again in verse:

> "'Like me, they are victors indeed,
> Who have destroyed the obstructions;
> Vanquished by me are evil things,
> Therefore am I, Upaka, a victor.' [2]

"As the naked ascetic shook his head, he said, 'It may be so, your reverence,' and he went off, taking a different road," concludes Upali.

"I don't think the ascetic understood the Buddha at all," comments Punna. "After hearing his words he went off on a different road to avoid him. This is quite unlike some of the others the Lord met during this time."

"Quite true, Punna," agrees Bakkula. "Remember the story of the lotuses; each one grows and develops according to its own nature and conditioning. This ascetic's lotus blossom seems to have withered just as it reached the surface."

Ananda begins, "The Buddha continued traveling and finally reaching the Ganga River. During the cool part of the day he paused on the bank to reflect and meditate. While enjoying the bliss of solitude, he gazed out over the river and saw a Brahmin ascetic approaching him, walking on the water.

"When the ascetic reached the Blessed One he said with great pride, 'Did you observe what I did just now?'

"The Lord answered, 'Indeed I did. I saw you walking on the water, all the way across the river. How did you come to learn how to do that?'

"Proudly, the ascetic replied that he had acquired this powerful ability by practicing austerities for twelve years with a great teacher at a hermitage high in the Himalayas. He said that he had fasted six days each week and had stood on one leg. Pleased with himself, he said, 'It takes great effort to be able to walk on water.'

"The Buddha smiled compassionately at the Brahmin and said, 'It sounds like you went to a lot of trouble to learn your magic feat; but you could have saved yourself twelve years if you had just asked the ferryman over there to take you across the river for one-half *pice*.'

"The Brahmin, totally deflated, walked away from the Lord and unhappily reflected on his twelve wasted years."

Bakkula begins, "I was told that after that incident the Buddha crossed the river with the help of the ferryman. Then he stayed for a while with a community of ascetics. After a time, a particularly bold ascetic walked right up to the Lord and asked, 'Who are you, monk? Are you still working on your *tapas*?'

"He replied, 'I am Gotama Buddha, the Fully Enlightened One. I have no need to practice austerities.'

"Then the matted-haired ascetic, who wore nothing but a small piece of cloth, told the Buddha that he should bathe in the Mother Ganga because it would purify him of all of his past, present, and future misdeeds and sins.

"The Buddha responded, 'If what you say is true then the crocodiles, fish, frogs, and turtles who were born in the river and live there all their lives must be saints.'

"The ascetic looked at the Buddha with a shocked expression and replied, 'What you just said is nonsense. It is impossible for river creatures to become saints.'

"The Buddha said, 'Very true, honorable recluse. It is only by washing away the defilements from one's thoughts, words and actions that one can acquire the status of sainthood. Washing in the Ganga will clean your body of dust, but cleaning your mind of impurities requires great effort and discipline.'

"The ascetic walked away in a state of confusion, and the Buddha went back into *samadhi*," concludes Bakkula.

The arahants smile hearing this favorite tale. Maha Kassapa speaks, "Then the Buddha continued on to Varanasi to meet his old friends, the five ascetics. I would have liked to have been there to witness that encounter, which, of course, became the birth of the Sangha."

"If I may, I'll provide an account which was related to me by the Lord himself."

"Very well, Anuruddha."

"On the way to Deer Park he stopped for alms in a small village," begins Anuruddha. "The group of five ascetics recognized the Buddha as he approached and said, 'The recluse Gotama is coming. He has reverted to a life of abundance, giving up the practices of true asceticism. Let's not greet him or even stand up when he arrives. We won't take his robe or bowl. We can put out a seat for him and he can sit down or not.'

"As the Buddha got closer the ascetics became curious, impressed by his luminous form and imposing demeanor. One of them ran up to the Lord and humbly took his bowl and robe. Another quickly brought water so he could wash his feet, and a third brought a foot-stool and a foot-stand. The Buddha calmly sat down and began to wash his feet. Because of his radiant appearance the ascetics couldn't refrain from addressing him as 'Your Reverence.' The Buddha said nothing as he finished washing his feet. The five hermits didn't know what to make of the dramatic change in Siddhartha, and they couldn't help but notice the aura of light that surrounded him.

"Finally the Buddha said, 'Do not address a Truthfinder by name, or with the epithet, 'Your Reverence.' A Truthfinder, monks, is a perfected one, a fully awakened one. Give ear, monks, the deathless has been found; I will instruct and teach the Dhamma.'[3]

"Kondanna, their leader, asked, 'But you, reverend Gotama, did not come to a state of enlightenment, to the eminence of truly noble vision of knowledge, by this practice of austerities. So how can you come to this state when you live in abundance, and are wavering in striving?'

"The Buddha said, 'A Truthfinder, monks, does not live in abundance, and he does not waver in striving. A Truthfinder is a perfected one, a fully awakened one. Do you admit that I have never spoken to you like this before?'

"The ascetics replied with honesty, 'You have not, Lord...'

"The Buddha continued, 'Give ear...you will abide in it.' The group of five monks listened intently to the words of the Buddha, and their minds were aroused with what he told them," concludes Anuruddha.

Maha Kassapa speaks up, "Ananda, would you recite briefly from the *Dhammaccaka Pavattana Sutta*?[4] This was the Buddha's first sermon, and it set the wheel of Dhamma in motion."

"Yes, of course, Venerable Sir," responds Ananda. "When the Buddha expounded this *sutta* it was just dusk on the full moon day of Asalha. Many deer had come very near the ascetics' camp, and they stood there in silence as if they, too, were preparing to listen to the Lord's words.

> "'...*Bhikkhus*, these two extremes ought not to be practiced by one who has gone forth from the household life. What are the two? There is devotion to the indulgence of sense-pleasures, which is low, common, the way of ordinary people, unworthy and unprofitable; and there is also devotion to self-mortification, which is painful, unworthy, and unprofitable.
>
> "'Avoiding these two extremes, the *Tathagata* has realized the Middle Path: it gives vision, it gives knowledge; it leads to calm, to insight, to enlightenment, to *Nibbana*. And what is that Middle Path...? It is simply the Noble Eightfold Path.
>
> "'The Noble Truth of suffering is this: Birth is suffering; aging is suffering; sickness is suffering; death is suffering; sorrow, lamentation, pain, grief and despair are suffering; association with the unpleasant is suffering; dissociation from the pleasant is suffering; not to get what

one wants is suffering – in brief, the five aggregates of attachment are suffering.

"'The Noble Truth of the origin of suffering is this: It is this thirst or craving which produces re-existence and re-becoming bound up with passionate greed. It finds fresh delight now here and now there, namely: thirst for sense pleasures; thirst for existence and becoming; and thirst for non-existence or self-annihilation.

"'The Noble Truth of the cessation of suffering is this: It is the complete cessation of that very thirst, giving it up, renouncing it, emancipating oneself from it, and detaching oneself from it completely.

"'The Noble Truth of the Path leading to the cessation of suffering is this: It is simply the Noble Eightfold Path, namely: right view, right thought, right speech, right action, right livelihood, right effort, right mindfulness, and right concentration.

"'…This suffering, as a noble truth, should be fully understood, and has been understood.'

"'…This origin of suffering, as a noble truth, should be abandoned, and has been abandoned.

"'…This cessation of suffering should be realized, and has been realized.

"'…This Path leading to the cessation of suffering, as a noble truth, should be cultivated, and has been cultivated.

"'…when my vision of true knowledge was fully clear, then I claimed to have realized the perfect enlightenment that is supreme in the world with its gods, its Maras and *Brahmas*, in this world with its recluses and *brahmanas*, with its *devas* and humans. And a vision of true knowledge arose in me thus: My heart's deliverance is unassailable. This is the last birth. Now there is no more becoming or rebirth.'

"'This the Blessed One said. The group of five ascetics was glad, and they rejoiced at his words.'"

"Thank you, Ananda," says Maha Kassapa.

Ananda bows to the chairman with respect.

Punna adds, "My uncle Venerable Kondanna said that when he heard the Buddha's words there arose in him a crystal clear perception of the fact that all that arises is subject to cessation. He immediately became a *sotapanna*, or stream-enterer."

"He will go down in history not only as the first *sotapanna*, but as the very first Sangha member as well," says Upali.

"Venerable Kondanna told me once that all he could do was just sit there, stunned, enjoying the bliss of the first stage of realization. He requested entrance into the Lord's Sangha, and he received the higher ordination when the Buddha said, 'Come, O monk. Well uttered is the truth. Lead the noble higher life for the right elimination of suffering,'" says Maha Kaccayana.

"Mahanama and Assaji volunteered to go out and collect alms for the group, so they went to a nearby village," begins Ananda. "In the meantime, the Lord taught his Dhamma to Vappa and Bhaddiya, and very soon the crystalline perception of the truth dawned on them, and they became *sotapannas*. They asked for ordination, and the Master complied in the same manner.

"When Mahanama and Assaji returned with the meal the six of them ate together. Then the Buddha spoke with Mahanama and Assaji and they soon attained the status of stream-enterer. They asked for ordination, and the Lord granted their request."

"All of a sudden there were five venerable monks in the Sangha," comments Maha Kaccayana.

Ananda continues, "The Buddha gave his second discourse to the newly ordained monks. He chose to discuss how the self is not real. He began by saying, 'Monks, the body is not the self; nor are feelings, perceptions, activities, or consciousness the self. All five of these are prone to distress, which causes one to want them to be other than what they actually are.

"The Buddha asked, 'What do you think, Kondanna; is the body permanent or impermanent?'

"'It is impermanent, Venerable Sir,' he replied.

"'Is that which is impermanent satisfactory or unsatisfactory?'

"'It is unsatisfactory, Venerable Sir.'

"'How about feelings, perceptions, activities, or consciousness; are they permanent or impermanent?' was the Buddha's next question.

"The five monks answered, 'Impermanent, Venerable Sir.'

"'Do you think it is correct to consider those things that are impermanent, unsatisfactory, temporary, and of a changeful nature as 'this is mine, this am I, or this is my self?'

"'No, Venerable Sir,' was their reply.

"'Therefore, monks, whatever body, feelings, perceptions, activities, or consciousness, whether it be past, future, or present, internal or external, gross or subtle, low or high, far or near, none of them are "mine. I am not them, nor are they my self." Thus you should see these things correctly, and with wisdom, as they are.'[5]

"The five new monks listened carefully to the Buddha, intent on understanding. Their eyes were closed, and they completely absorbed this new knowledge into the very pores of their being.

"The Buddha continued,

"'Perceiving these things to be true, monks, the learned and noble disciple becomes disenchanted with the body, feelings, perceptions, activities, and consciousness. And through this disenchantment, he becomes dispassionate; in the absence of passion, he becomes free; when he is free, he becomes aware of that freedom, aware that rebirth is exhausted, that the holy life has been lived, and that there is nothing more to do.'

"The five former ascetics rejoiced in this Dhamma taught by their Master. During the course of hearing this discourse each one of the monks became free of their defilements forever, and without attachment to anything they achieved arahantship," concludes Ananda.

"And then there were six arahants in the world," comments Maha Kassapa.

Kumara Kassapa stands up and says, "And *now* there are five hundred arahants in this room alone, and many more scattered throughout the entire country. How many there were before today and how many more will come after us is a matter of conjecture. Each one is a living testament to the efficacy of the Buddha's teaching."

"Thank you, Venerable Sir, for that observation," says Maha Kassapa. "I think Nalaka, the nephew of the sage Asitadevala, makes his appearance in our story now."

"You are correct, Venerable Sir," replies Ananda. "After Asitadevala predicted infant Prince Siddhartha's future he advised Nalaka to become an ascetic. His uncle told him that one day when he heard someone talking about a Buddha, he should go to join him. He said, 'Follow this Master, this Lord, and adhere to the practices of a pure life.'

"Nalaka believed his wise uncle. He lived a good and wholesome life, and he looked forward to the appearance of the hero who would conquer suffering. In time the news did reach him that the Buddha had appeared. Nalaka immediately went off to find the Lord, his meditative intuition guiding him to the Deer Park in Varanasi. The Buddha, knowing that Nalaka was on his way, was expecting him.

"When he arrived at the Buddha's camp he approached the Lord with great respect. He bowed before him, touched his feet, and said, 'Exalted Buddha of Gotama lineage. Now that I have seen you with my own eyes I realize that the words spoken to me by my uncle thirty five years ago are perfectly true. I can see that you have reached the perfection of all things. I wish to ask you a question, if I may.'

"The Buddha nodded and Nalaka began, 'I have lived for all of these years as a wanderer, and now I would like to live as a monk. Please, what is the highest state of wisdom?'

> "The Master replied, 'I will explain this state to you, but I'll say from the start that it is hard to reach, and difficult to put into effect. You must be alert and full of effort.
>
> "'Develop equilibrium of the mind. Going through life you will always get both praise and blame, but do not let either one affect your mental poise. Always remain calm, and free from pride.
>
> "'Keep your sensual desires in check and be without aversion or attachment to any beings, however weak or

strong they may be. Refrain from comparing yourself to others, and abstain from killing or causing others to kill.

"'Free yourself from the impulses of 'I want' or 'I'll have.' Eat moderately, do not be greedy, and have few needs.

"'A person of wisdom follows the pattern of collecting alms food, eating alone in the forest, and strenuously applying himself to meditation practice.

"'He spends the night in this practice, living under a tree, and then repeats the pattern the following day. He never gets excited or distracted by the gifts and invitations people offer him.

"'He gratefully accepts whatever food is given to him, not showing any preferences.

"'Wandering with his begging bowl in his hand he does not talk; he appears to be almost simple-minded, but he is not. He accepts even the smallest gift without scorn or pride.

"'When a person is desireless, when a monk has extinguished the river of becomings, when he has given up all the activities of duty and obligation – the "ought to's" and the "ought *not* to's" – then the proverbial fever is past.

"'Be razor sharp. Keep your tongue relaxed; your stomach quiet and restrained.

"'Let go of attachments completely by freeing your mind. Don't spend too much time thinking about things that are irrelevant. Allow no defilements, no ties, and no dependencies; keep strictly to the practices of a pure life.

"'Living alone in the silence of solitude is wise; a source of pleasure.

"'When you, a follower, hear the sound of the meditation of wisdom, you will grow in confidence, modesty, and strength of practice.

"'Listen to the sound of water running through chasms and rocks. The minor streams are the ones that make a lot of noise, but the great rivers flow silently.

"'That which is hollow resounds, and that which is full is still. Foolishness is like a half-filled pot; the wise person is an entire lake full of water.

"'The hermit can talk of many things with good sense and precision. He can describe reality, the way things are, from a position of direct knowledge.

"'Remember that a true person of knowledge retains self control and speaks only a little; then you have found a person of wisdom. For such a one, silence is appropriate and deserved because such a person has found the silence of wisdom.'"

When Ananda finishes reciting the *Nalaka Sutta*,[6] complete silence fills the room. The arahants had long respected Nalaka as the monk who had epitomized the practice of moral perfection, and they voicelessly thanked him for his devotion.

"Does anyone know what happened to Nalaka after the Buddha delivered this discourse?" asks Bakkula.

"He returned to the Himalayas and leaned against a golden rock for seven months while practicing meditation. He attained arahantship at the end of this period of *sadhana*," answers Upali.

"After Nalaka's death, the Buddha and a group of his monks cremated his remains, and had a *stupa* built over the site. The Lord had great respect for Nalaka's tremendous faith. He gave up great wealth, renounced the world to become a hermit, and waited for the Buddha to appear for thirty five years," adds Anuruddha. "I went with the Lord at that time, and participated in Nalaka's final rites."

Maha Kassapa stands up and says, "I believe it is time to retire to our chambers, Venerable Sirs. This evening's open sub-committee meeting has been a marvelous shared experience. Let us go to our places of meditation and reflect on the Master's timeless Wheel of Dhamma. In your inner space envision the momentum it picked up with each rotation during our lifetimes, and with your mind's eyes see it rolling forward into the vast and distant future where it will benefit untold numbers of beings."

The arahants rise to their feet, salute one another, and depart from the Assembly Hall. It is now well past midnight and the stars are clear and bright. There is no moon. Suddenly, a great meteor flashes across the heavens. All eyes watch as it vanishes over the peaks, and each and every arahant pauses to receive the cosmic sign as a blessing from the Lord.

Chapter 11
The Sangha Grows

Two hours before sunrise the arahants gather for the early morning session. They will have their devotions, chants, Buddha *puja*, and then a brief group meditation. The main session follows with recitation of the discourses, questions, and other council business.

Maha Kassapa rings the gong. The sound reverberates throughout the assembly hall and its deep tones echo beyond to the surrounding valley. He begins by leading all those present in the Three Refuges and the *Vandana* to the Buddha, the Dhamma, and the Sangha. Then they chant a portion of the *Sabbasava Sutta*,[1] which has become the morning standard for Sangha members in monasteries throughout all of India. It is a daily reminder for monks regarding the use of their very small number of personal requisites. As they chant together their eyes are closed; the strong vibration of the sacred words of the Buddha can be felt for miles around the area:

> "'...Here a *bhikkhu*, reflecting wisely, uses the robe only for protection from cold, for protection from heat, for protection from contact with gadflies, mosquitoes, wind, the sun, and creeping things, and only for the purpose of concealing the private parts.'
>
> "'Reflecting wisely, he uses alms food neither for amusement nor for intoxication nor for the sake of physical beauty and attractiveness, but only for the endurance and continuance of this body, for ending discomfort, and for assisting the holy life, considering: 'Thus I shall terminate old feelings without arousing new feelings and I shall be healthy, blameless and shall live in comfort.'
>
> "'Reflecting wisely, he uses the resting place only for protection from cold, for protection from heat, for protection from contact with gadflies, mosquitoes, wind, the

sun, and creeping things, and only for the purpose of warding off the perils of climate and for enjoying retreat.'

"'Reflecting wisely, he uses the medicinal requisites only for protection from arisen afflicting feelings and for the benefit of good health.'

"'While taints, vexation, and fever might arise in one who does not use the requisites thus, there are no taints, vexation, or fever in one who uses them thus. These are called the taints that should be abandoned by using (the requisites of a *bhikkhu*).'"

Maha Kassapa concludes the chanting with the Reflection after Using the Requisites:

"'Just as the robe, alms food, resting place, and medicine are dependent upon and made up of mere elements, the individual that uses them also is not a permanent being, not a permanent life, void of self and made up of mere elements.'"

The monks begin meditating after the recitation. Later, Maha Kassapa rings the gong again, and the arahants rise and begin walking toward the clearing at the edge of the forest. They have breakfast under the canopy of a sprawling tamarind tree.

Ananda and Sopaka are walking together when Bakkula and Punna catch up with them. "Let's meet immediately after breakfast to continue our discussion. Since there will be an organizational meeting to start sorting the *suttas* that Ananda has already recited, we'll have a good two hours before the general council session begins," says Bakkula.

"Excellent, Venerable Sir," replies Ananda. "Sopaka, why don't you inform my two cousins and Upali and Maha Kaccayana. Let them know about our new plans – and don't forget the chairman and the memory monks." Sopaka goes off to inform the other sub-committee members about the unscheduled meeting.

King Ajatasattu has sent his chief minister to officiate today, and he busies himself giving orders to the cooking and serving staff. The milk rice and savories are finally ready and are offered to the esteemed arahants.

The sub-committee decides to meet under the tamarind tree after the breakfast things have been cleared away. When the meal is finished and the members are assembled Maha Kassapa says, "Ananda, I think we are ready to hear about Yasa from Varanasi."

"Indeed we are," responds Ananda. "Yasa, as you know, was an authentic sybarite. He was extremely wealthy and had three huge palaces for the three seasons, very much like Prince Siddhartha's, and he only employed female servants and musicians. He so indulged himself in sense pleasures that during the four-month rainy season he and his musicians would stay in his entertainment hall on the top floor of the palace and never once go downstairs. Regardless of his excesses, he was gentle in word, deed, and thought. He had vast wealth and a large number of friends and followers.

"One day when his senses were completely sated Yasa fell asleep in the middle of a party. Seeing that the host was asleep, his companions decided to also take a nap. Later on Yasa woke up and saw everyone fast asleep around him. The beautiful female musicians no longer looked appealing; many were lying with their hair disheveled, saliva dripping from their mouths, muttering to themselves. To Yasa the place looked like the charnel grounds with bodies strewn about haphazzardly. Then he had an insight and saw the uselessness of his life; he became thoroughly disgusted with himself."

Punna adds, "He actually became frightened because of the way he had been using his time. He said to himself, 'I am in danger; I am truly afflicted.' He told me later that he put on a pair of golden slippers and quietly left his palace. He walked through the city gates and went directly to the Deer Park where the Buddha was staying. He said that it was as if supernatural powers had suddenly made him invisible. He didn't see anyone while he was walking, and no one tried to stop him."

"Quite so," says Ananda. "As he approached, the Lord called out to him and said, 'O Yasa, there is no danger here; there is no affliction. Come here and I will preach the doctrine to you.'"

"It was obvious that the Lord had been expecting him, since he called him by name," comments Sopaka.

Ananda continues the story, "The Buddha often knew when someone was approaching, and he would ask us to prepare in advance for some unannounced arrival. It used to surprise me to no end, and then I began to expect the unexpected visitor.

"Yasa was elated by the Buddha's kind reception. He removed his golden slippers and saluted the Master with great respect. The Buddha first taught Yasa about charity and morality; then about the hollowness, impurity, and unhappy by-products of sensual desires; and then the advantages of renunciation.

"When the Buddha saw that Yasa's mind was pliable, open, joyful, calm, and able to hear and understand the Four Noble Truths, he taught the Dhamma to him. Yasa perceived it clearly and experienced a pure vision of truth. He realized that everything that arises is subject to passing away. At that moment Yasa became a *sotapanna*, and he enjoyed the bliss of that state. He realized then that the sensual pleasures he had been chasing all his life were nothing compared to his newly-attained spiritual realm."

"I'll continue for a while, if I may," requests Anuruddha. Ananda nods his acquiescence, and his cousin begins. "Yasa's mother, Sujata, had risen early that morning and gone to Yasa's mansion."

"Excuse me, Anuruddha, is this Sujata the one who offered milk-rice to the Buddha on the morning of his enlightenment?" asks Sopaka.

"I'm glad you asked that question, which will avoid confusing the two women in the future," responds Anuruddha. "*This* Sujata, Yasa's mother, looked around for her son, and when she didn't find him she became worried and informed her husband. Yasa's father immediately sent out his guards to look for him while he himself went towards Isipatana in search of his son. He came upon footprints in the road and could tell that they were made by Yasa's golden slippers. He followed their trail to Deer Park and the Buddha saw him approaching

"The Buddha said to Yasa, who was sitting by his side, 'Your father is coming.'

"Yasa replied, 'I will remove myself for a moment while you speak with him; I don't want his attention diverted from your teaching. I know he will benefit by hearing you, Lord.' Yasa then went and hid behind a tree. In a few moments his father, Senanigama, reached the Buddha.

"'Sit down householder,' said the Buddha. Senanigama bowed and paid his respects to the Lord before seating himself.

"'Have you seen my son, Yasa?' asked the worried father.

"'He is nearby,' replied the Buddha.

"The father was delighted to learn that his son was safe, so he relaxed and his mind became receptive. The Buddha used the opportunity to teach the Dhamma to the millionaire, and when he was finished Senanigama achieved *sotapanna*. He said, 'Very grand, Sir, very grand! It is like turning up something that has been upside down; like opening up something that has been hidden; like showing the path to a person who had lost his way; like holding up an oil lamp in the dark for those with eyes to see. The Blessed One gave me such an illuminating exposition of his teaching that I implore him to accept me from today as his lifelong disciple. I take refuge in the Buddha, the Dhamma, and the Sangha.'" Anuruddha smiles as he finishes this part of the story.

"And so Senanigama, Yasa's father, became the first lay person to take refuge in the Triple Gem: the Buddha, the Dhamma, *and* the Sangha," says Maha Kaccayana, smiling, "the first of probably millions over the course of time."

Anuruddha begins again, "At this point the Buddha called to Yasa, who came out from behind the tree and respectfully greeted his father. Senanigama was overjoyed to see him and said, 'Dear son, your mother is in tears worrying about you, and I'm afraid she'll die!'

"The Buddha explained to Senanigama that his son was now free from three of the ten fetters, and he asked him if he thought Yasa should renounce the life of householder. The happy father said that he should, and he invited the Buddha for *dana* at his residence the following day.

"Yasa then asked for ordination, which the Buddha granted while his father watched with great joy. Immediately afterwards he achieved the exalted state of arahantship. Now there were seven arahants in the Sangha. The next day they went to Senanigama's palace for the mid-day meal, and Yasa's mother and his former wife were relieved to see that he was safe and sound," concludes Anuruddha.

"After the meal the Buddha taught the two women about charity, morality, and other virtues, and in due course he taught them the Four

Noble Truths. Yasa's mother and former wife immediately understood. They became *sotapannas* and took refuge in the Buddha, the Dhamma, and the Sangha. These women were the first female lay disciples of the Buddha," says Punna.

"The news spread quickly about Yasa's renunciation," begins Ananda, "and before long his close friends Vimala, Subahu, Punnaji, and Gavampati, also sons of millionaire merchants, learned that Yasa had shaved his head, donned the robes of a monk, and joined the Sangha. They talked among themselves and decided that he wouldn't have done it if the teaching hadn't been worthy and extraordinary, so they found Venerable Yasa, who took them to the Buddha and requested that he teach the Dhamma to them.

"After the preliminary teaching, the Buddha expounded the Four Noble Truths. Almost at once the four wealthy young men understood the doctrine with crystalline clarity, becoming *sotapannas*. They requested ordination, which the Buddha granted. Soon they became arahants, and now there were eleven in the growing Sangha of the Blessed One," concludes Ananda.

"A short while later, another fifty former associates of Venerable Yasa, all of them sons of rich noble families, came to see their old friend requesting an introduction to the Buddha," says Bakkula. "The teaching of the Buddha had the same effect on all of them, and they, too, quickly attained the state of *sotapanna*. Afterwards they asked for ordination, and were graciously received by the Buddha. When they became arahants there were then sixty-one enlightened monks in the Order."

"It's amazing how quickly the first arahants perceived the diamond-like quality of the Dhamma and attained enlightenment. It was as if a match were put to a bale of cotton, so swiftly did the Buddha's spiritual flame ignite their ripe minds," comments Maha Kaccayana.

"It was often like that with the Lord, so great was his power to transmit not only the truth, but the tremendous energy required to attain its full realization. Having a Fully Enlightened Buddha in the world is a blessing for all living creatures – an unprecedented opportunity for attaining the zenith of spirituality. Hopefully the flame of transmission will stay alight so countless generations in the future can achieve the same liberation," says Maha Kassapa.

"If human beings immerse themselves in materialism and sense pleasures they have no hope of ending the cycle of death, rebirth, and more suffering. The Buddha's Dhamma is the antidote for the cycle of rebirth, and an elixir for a happy, healthy, and successful life," adds Punna.

"This brings us to the point in our story when the Buddha realized the potentially wide appeal of his teaching," says Ananda. "He was convinced that there were people who could grasp the Dhamma when it transformed the lives of these sixty intelligent men. With knowledge of the Dhamma their attachment to experiencing any 'me,' 'mine,' or personal 'I' had ended. Using what the Buddha taught had freed them forever from the trap of personal identity. As a result, they were able to live in a state of complete bliss and happiness, putting an end to the creation of new *kamma*. This wisdom enabled them to be of service to others, and this is when the Buddha conceived the idea of sending them out to share the Dhamma with those who wished to hear it. They were, in fact, our first missionaries."

"Ananda, will you recite what the Buddha said to the sixty arahants when he sent them out to the four corners of India?" requests Maha Kassapa.

"Very well, Venerable Sir. Just after the first rainy season retreat in Isipatana, The Lord addressed the monks, saying:

> "'Go forth, O *Bhikkhus*, and wander forth for the gain of the many, for the welfare of the many, in compassion for the world, for the good, for the gains, for the welfare of gods and humans. Proclaim, O *Bhikkhus*, the Dhamma glorious, preach a life of holiness, perfect and pure.
>
> "'Let not two of you go by the same road. Monks, teach Dhamma which is lovely at the beginning, lovely in the middle, and lovely at the end, which is complete both in letter and spirit. There are beings with little dust in their eyes, who by not hearing the Dhamma, are deteriorating; there are also those who will understand the Dhamma, and they will flourish. I, too, monks, will go alone to the village of Senani in Uruvela to teach the Dhamma.'"[2]

"In this manner the sixty monks were sent out to teach the Buddha's blessed Dhamma," says Maha Kassapa. "Before they departed, the Buddha spoke to them very seriously about ten important things to always keep in their minds. Venerable Ananda, please recite the *Dasadhamma Sutta*[3] for us."

"With pleasure, Venerable Sir," and he begins:

"'There are ten things that a monk should reflect upon always. What are these ten?

"'I am now changed into a different mode of life; I am no longer a layman.

"'I must stay motivated to serve others.

"'I must now behave in a different manner.

"'Does my mind keep reminding me about the state of my virtue?

"'Do my discerning fellow-monks, having tested me, reproach me regarding the state of my virtue?

"'There will be a parting and separation from all those who are dear and loving to me.

"'Of *kamma* I am constituted. *Kamma* is my inheritance; *kamma* is my origin; *kamma* is my kinsman; *kamma* is my refuge. Whatever *kamma* I perform, be it good or bad, to that I shall be heir.

"'How do I spend my nights and days?

"'Do I take delight in solitude?

"'Have I gained super-human knowledge which can be specially known to noble ones so that later when I am questioned by my fellow monks I will not be embarrassed?'

"'These are the ten things that a monk should reflect upon always.' Thus spoke the Exalted One. The monks were pleased with and appreciated the Exalted One's words.'"

"Thank you Ananda," says Maha Kassapa. "I would like to quote some of my favorite verses in the Daily Advice to Sangha members from the *Dhammapada*. I have said them to myself every day for decades:

"'Abstaining from all evil,
Doing what is good,
Purifying one's mind,
This is the teaching of all the Buddhas.

"'Patience is the highest practice,
Nibbana is supreme,' say the Buddhas,
A true monk does not harm others,
A true renunciate oppresses no one.

"'Not despising, not harming,
Restrained according to the monastic discipline,
Moderation in food, dwelling in solitude,
Devoted to meditation,
This is the teaching of the Buddhas.'" 4

The soft breeze blowing through the leaves of the tamarind tree suddenly stops when Maha Kassapa finishes his recitation; the atmosphere becomes silent and still. The arahants notice a sudden shift in energy, and they look at one another with a sense of joy. Finally, Anuruddha says, "I feel the Master's presence so strongly right now. I know that since he has already attained *parinibanna*, it is impossible for him to be with us. If it were possible, however, I'm sure he would remind us of the importance of these words…"

The other arahants smile, thinking of their Lord's wisdom, compassion, and great love.

After a while Maha Kassapa takes a deep breath and continues, "So the sixty arahants proceeded out from Isipatana. Before too long they began to bring suitable candidates to the Buddha for both lower and higher ordination. They sometimes had to travel great distances, and both the monks and the men who sought ordination became fatigued.

"The Buddha considered this and decided that he would delegate the power of ordination to the monks so they could avoid excessive travel. He formulated instructions for doing so. Upali, would you kindly explain the protocol the Master established in this regard?"

"The Buddha addressed the monks, 'From this day forward, O monks, you may confer lower and higher ordination in the regions and provinces where you teach. This will be the procedure: First, hair and beard are to be shaven off; saffron robes are to be donned; one robe is to be worn over the left shoulder. Then the candidate salutes the feet of the monks, and kneels with folded hands reciting these lines:

> "'I take refuge in the Buddha. I take refuge in the Dhamma. I take refuge in the Sangha.'
>
> "'For the second time, I take refuge in the Buddha. For the second time, I take refuge in the Dhamma. For the second time, I take refuge in the Sangha.'
>
> "'For the third time, I take refuge in the Buddha. For the third time, I take refuge in the Dhamma. For the third time, I take refuge in the Sangha.'"[5]

"Was it during this time that Mara appeared again and attempted to harrass the Lord?"[6] asks Punna.

"Yes he did, Venerable Sir; twice, in fact. On both occasions, however, Mara fled from the Master in utter defeat," answers Bakkula.

"Venerable Ananda, when did the Buddha travel onwards to Uruvela?" asks Sopaka.

"I'm not sure exactly how long the Master stayed in Varanasi, but I know it was at least until the end of the rainy season," answers Ananda. "He eventually proceeded on to Uruvela alone, carrying only his alms bowl. While en route he stopped to rest in a wooded area. While the Buddha was meditating there was a disturbance in the woods, which was being caused by thirty princes of the Bhadda clan. These princes had been good friends since childhood, and it was their custom to get together whenever they could and enjoy themselves. Twenty nine of the princes had brought their wives on this particular outing, and the unmarried one brought a prostitute. While everyone was drinking and carrying on, the prostitute stole their valuables and ran off through the woods. The princes chased her, scouring the area looking for her.

"Out of breath, they approached the Buddha and said, 'Venerable Recluse, have you seen a woman?'

"The Buddha answered, 'Princes! Of what use is a woman to you, young men?'

"They told him about their careless partying and the prostitute's theft. The Buddha said, 'Princes! What, in your opinion is better for you: searching for a missing woman, or searching for your own self?'

"Together they replied, 'Venerable Ascetic! It is better for us that we seek ourselves.'

"Then the Lord said, 'Princes! Sit down and I, the Buddha, will teach you the Dhamma.'

"The princes replied, 'Yes, Glorious Buddha.' And after making proper obeisance to him the thirty Bhadda princes sat and listened to the Lord. The Buddha taught them, as he had others, in regards to charity, morality, the hollowness, impurity, and unhappy by-products of sensual desires, and the advantages of renunciation.

"He also told them, 'One should not pry into the faults of others, into things done and left undone by others. One should rather consider what by oneself is done and left undone.'[7]

"During the discourse, the minds of the princes became adaptable, calm, freed from hindrances, eager, gladdened, purified, and pellucid. Then the Buddha taught them the Doctrine of the Four Noble Truths. Many of the princes attained the state of *sotapanna*, some of them attained *sakadagami*, and a few attained *anagami*.

"The princes, overjoyed in their newly-attained spiritual states, exclaimed, 'Glorious Buddha! May we receive admission as members of your Order?'

"The Buddha at once complied. He stretched out his hand and said, 'Come, monks! Receive the ordination you have asked for, my dear sons. The Dhamma has been well taught by me, so strive to engage in the practice of the higher life in order to bring about the end of suffering.' With this statement the thirty princes were granted high ordination, and they became virtuous *bhikkhus*," concludes Ananda.

"Excuse me, Venerable Sir, but I can't resist asking a question about the twenty-nine wives that were left in the woods. What happened to them?" asks Bakkula.

Punna answers, "The Buddha once told me that the wives were at first very distraught, disappointed, and angry. They were brought to him later, though, and after speaking with them, each one became a lay disciple and took the Three Refuges. Afterwards, they returned to their homes and were generally supportive of their husbands' decisions to renounce the life of a householder. Later on these devoted women worked hard for the benefit of the Sangha whenever an opportunity arose."

Maha Kassapa smiles and says, "The regular council session will begin shortly, and our presence is required. We can continue this profitable discussion later in my chamber. I feel like it's just about time for my appearance in our story. I'm sure it will be amusing."

As the arahants proceed to the assembly hall each of them carries with him a greater knowledge about the origins of the Sangha. During the time they spent in the shade of the tamarind tree that morning they had each gained an expanded appreciation of the banner they carry, and the banner that would be carried on long after they leave this world.

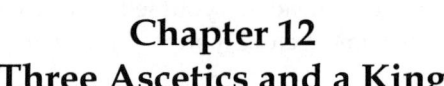

Chapter 12
Three Ascetics and a King

It is now six o'clock in the evening and Maha Kassapa sounds the gong signaling the end of the day's council session. Ananda has recited several more of the Buddha's *suttas*, some of medium length, and others of varying lengths and topics.

The arahants disburse for the evening, most of them returning to their chambers to meditate. A small group makes its way to Maha Kassapa's quarters to continue its work recollecting the life of Buddha.

This evening a different group of memory monks will be in attendance. The usual group will be gathering to recite the material they have already heard to another group of monks. It is in this way that they hope to ensure the accuracy of the oral transmission. Maha Kassapa, in his wisdom and with great foresight, has established strict policies for the memory monks, who are called *bhanakas*.

Inside the cave chamber the arahants take their seats. Silently they wait for the last two members to arrive. The Buddha had often said that if one was not talking about the Dhamma, then silence was best. He stressed the importance of avoiding irrelevant speech, emphasizing his preference for silence over idle conversation.[1]

Ananda enters the chamber with Sopaka. He seats himself on the rush mat and breathes a sigh of relief. "This pair of eighty year-old legs just isn't what they used to be, I'm afraid. Before, I could easily walk with the Master and cover thirty miles in one day; I would think nothing of it. These days, standing eight or nine hours at the podium takes more effort than walking those thirty miles."

"That's the impermanent nature of the body, Venerable Sir," says Punna. "Even the Lord's was eventually used up."

"Don't I know that all too well," replies Ananda. "And one day this one will be used up, too."

Maha Kassapa calls the meeting to order. "We are making excellent progress in our recollection of the life of the Lord, my brothers. I believe we are now up to the point where my character makes its entrance."

"You're getting way ahead of yourself, old friend. A number of other characters will come before yours – like King Bimbisara," says Upali, chuckling.

"Oh yes, of course, His Majesty – and the three ascetics. I almost forgot," laughs the chairman. "I don't want to give the impression that my non-existent ego wants to jump the queue."

"We might have considered that as a possibility, Venerable Sir, if your ego hadn't been annihilated and cast to the wind several decades ago," says Bakkula, smiling broadly.

Maha Kassapa good-naturedly continues, "Ananda, why don't you begin where we left off yesterday. I'll leave it to you to decide which characters appear this evening."

Ananda bows politely to the chairman saying, "The three ascetic Kassapas,[2] no relation to you Venerable Sir, lived in hermitages near the town of Uruvela. These ascetics were also known as '*jatilas*' because of the turbans they wore. The Buddha, who was traveling alone, went to visit the ashram of Uruvela Kassapa, the leader of five-hundred matted-haired ascetics who worshiped fire. He approached Uruvela Kassapa and said, 'If it is not inconvenient for you, sir, will you let me spend one night in your fire room?'

"'Great monk, there is no inconvenience to me, but there is a ferocious and venomous cobra living in the fire room. I wouldn't want him to harm you,' says Uruvela Kassapa solicitously.

"The Buddha made the same request a second, and then a third time, and to Uruvela's objections the Lord merely responded, 'The cobra will not harm me, Kassapa.'

"Finally, Uruvela gave his permission, and the Buddha entered the fire room and spread out his mat. He immediately sat down and began to meditate. The cobra, annoyed that a stranger had invaded his space, reared up, spread his hood, and hissed, threatening the Buddha with death. The Master calmly sent forth loving-kindness toward the cobra, and its anger was instantly neutralized. We all know that loving-kindness emanates a powerful force-field that can not only be felt, but can even be seen by certain gifted individuals."

After reflecting a moment Anuruddha speaks up, "Maha Kassapa, if it wouldn't be out of place here, I would like to recite one of the Master's meditations on loving-kindness. As we know, this is the most powerful energy on earth, and it can subdue anyone or any thing – even a hostile, death-threatening cobra."

"Proceed, Venerable Sir."

Anuruddha nods and begins.

> "'Having seen that all beings,
> Like oneself, have a desire for happiness,
> One should methodically develop
> Loving-kindness towards all beings.
>
> "'May I be happy and free from suffering!
> And, always, like myself,
> May my friends, neutral persons,
> And those hostile be happy, too.
>
> "'May all beings in this village,
> In this state,
> In other countries,
> And in all the world systems be ever happy.
>
> "'May all persons,
> Individuals, beings,
> Creatures in all world systems
> Be ever happy.
>
> "'So, too, may all women, men,
> Noble ones, non-noble ones, gods, humans,
> And beings in the lower worlds be happy.
> May all beings in the ten directions be happy.'"[3]

The arahants smile in appreciation of the Master's meditation. "Thank you, Anuruddha. Please resume your story, Ananda," says Maha Kassapa.

"In the other room Uruvela Kassapa and some of his disciples were speculating on whether or not the cobra would destroy the Buddha's life. 'Too bad,' said one of them, 'he was so handsome.'

"The next morning the Buddha opened the door and to everyone's utter amazement, he walked out unharmed. The vicious cobra, now docile and tame, was coiled up in his alms bowl. He walked up to Uruvela saying, 'Here is your friend, Kassapa.'

"'How did you survive, great monk? How did you subdue that cobra?' asked Uruvela Kassapa in disbelief.

"'The power of loving-kindness can overcome anything; even you can learn how to manifest it,' replied the Buddha.

"The matted-hair ascetic, Uruvela Kassapa, not accepting the Buddha's challenge, thought to himself, 'This great monk has amazing psychic powers. He was able to use them to tame that ferocious cobra. Nevertheless, he cannot possibly be a sanctified one like I am.'

"Uruvela, impressed by the Buddha's supernatural powers, said, 'Great monk, please feel free to stay here in my hermitage with us. I will personally provide you with regular meals.'

"The Buddha said nothing in response. He simply put the pet snake back in the fire room and walked toward a grove where he decided to stay for a while. During the last watch of the following night a group of four powerful guardian gods came to visit the Buddha, illuminating the entire grove with their spiritual splendor.

"The next morning Uruvela Kassapa approached the Buddha to invite him for the daily meal. He asked the Lord who his resplendent visitors were the night before, and the Buddha said, 'They were the Divine Kings of the Four Regions, O Kassapa. They came to me to hear the Dhamma.'

"Kassapa once again thought to himself, 'Even though, great monk, you have tremendously developed psychic powers, you are not a sanctified one like I am.'

"On another night, the ruler of the *Tavatimsa devas*, Sakka himself, came with the utmost respect to personally offer his obeisance to the Buddha. Afterwards he stood off to one side while the Lord expounded the Dhamma to him. Sakka's magnificent halo was even brighter than those of the combined Divine Kings, and though it was midnight, the grove was bright as noonday.

"When Uruvela learned who the Buddha's nighttime visitor was he once again remarked, 'The ascetic is definitely a great monk, and has highly developed psychic powers, but he is not a sanctified one like I am.

"Several more incidents of a similar nature occurred with ever-increasing celestial splendor, and each time the Buddha's connection with supernormal powers was clearly demonstrated. Uruvela Kassapa continued to remark that even though his psychic powers were great, the Buddha wasn't fully-enlightened like he was.

"Finally, the Buddha spoke directly to Kassapa. He said, 'Kassapa, first of all, if you think you are enlightened, you are mistaken. Secondly, if emancipation is your goal, then you are not on the right path.'

"'What do you mean?' asked Uruvela, his voice betraying irritation.

"'You may be well-accomplished in your spiritual practices, Uruvela, but your ego stands in the way of any further progress,' answered the Lord.

"'My ego? How can you say that, great monk, when I renounced everything and became an ascetic decades ago?' exclaimed Uruvela.

"'Conceit, Uruvela; pride. This is one of the ten fetters that bind you to existence. It completely vanishes upon the attainment of arahantship. Even though you claim such exalted status for yourself, you haven't yet reached that level,' said the Master.

"Uruvela looked downcast and ashamed, having been reproached by the Buddha in this fashion.

"'Further, Uruvela, when one has no more "I"-making, "my"-making, and the underlying tendency to conceit either in regard to this conscious body or in regard to external objects; when he thus enters and dwells in the liberation of mind, which is liberation by wisdom, then he is called one who has cut off craving and removed the fetters; one who, by fully breaking through conceit, has made an end of suffering.' The Buddha finished this statement and looked at Uruvela Kassapa with great compassion.

"Kassapa, filled with emotion, said, 'Then please ordain me and make me your disciple. Surely you will show me the correct path.'

"The Buddha replied, 'Kassapa, in case you have forgotten, you have five hundred followers. What will become of them? You are responsible for their welfare.'

"Kassapa, acknowledging his responsibility, went to speak to his followers. Telling them that he had decided to follow the Buddha, he urged them to do the same thing. It didn't take too much to convince them because they had all heard about the Buddha subduing the cobra. They also had seen the groves surrounding the *ashram* all lit up at night by the radiance of the Buddha's many celestial visitors.

"Without hesitation, every one of the five hundred disciples threw his fire-worshipping garment and his ritual implements into the Neranjara River. Afterwards they followed Uruvela Kassapa to receive ordination from the Buddha," says Ananda.

"What about the other two Kassapas?" asks Punna.

"Nadi Kassapa lived a ways downstream with three hundred followers. When he saw the garments and other paraphernalia floating down the river he became alarmed. He was hoping that no harm had befallen his eldest brother, so he sent two of his followers ahead to find out what had happened to Uruvela and his group. Then he himself departed for his brother's hermitage. When Nadi arrived, Uruvela Kassapa explained that he and his followers had just ordained in the Buddha's Sangha.

"Nadi Kassapa and his three hundred disciples immediately went to the Buddha and requested ordination. They, too, threw their fire-worshipping garments and sacrificial objects into the Neranjara River, and then the Buddha admitted them into the Sangha," says Ananda.

"Imagine what the third brother, Gaya Kassapa, must have thought when he saw the first mass of ascetic debris floating down the river – and then seeing a second mass drifting downstream," says Punna, smiling.

"He must have been terrified. I'm sure his first thought was that some religious sect war was being waged against the ascetics – that someone was attempting to wipe them all out," says Bakkula.

Ananda continues the story, "He sent scouts upstream to check out the situation, and then with his two hundred followers he set out for Uruvela Kassapa's ashram. When he reached the hermitage his elder brother reassured him that he, Nadi, and their followers were quite well. Then he explained their new relationship with the Buddha and their admittance to the Sangha.

"Gaya and his ascetic followers immediately sought out the Buddha and asked for ordination. The Buddha gave his consent and they were duly admitted. The Buddha now had over one thousand disciples. They all proceeded to Gaya Head where he expounded the Fire Sermon. After listening to this discourse all of them became arahants."

Maha Kassapa says, "Upali, why don't you recount this important discourse for us since it is in the *Vinaya*. '*The Fire Sermon*'[4] is traditionally told to newly-ordained Sangha members to admonish them about disavowing the senses. As you have just heard, the effect it had on these newly-ordained ascetics was instantaneous."

Upali nods and begins.

> "...The Blissful One dwelt, together with the thousand monks, and he addressed them thus: 'All things, monks, are on fire. And what, monks, are all these things which are on fire?'

"'The eye, monks, is on fire; forms are on fire; eye-consciousness is on fire; impressions received by the eye are on fire; and whatever sensation: pleasant, unpleasant, or neutral, which originates in dependence on impressions received by the eye that also is on fire. And with what are these on fire? With the fire of passion, say I, with the fire of hatred, with the fire of delusion; with birth, old age, death, sorrow, lamentation, pain, grief, and despair are they on fire.'

"'The ear, monks, is on fire; sounds are on fire...

"'The nose, monks, is on fire; smells are on fire...

"'The tongue, monks, is on fire; tastes are on fire...

"'The body, monks, is on fire; body-consciousness is on fire...

"'The mind, monks, is on fire; mental objects are on fire...

"'Perceiving this, monks, the learned and noble disciple becomes disenchanted with the eye, with forms...with the ear, with sounds...with the nose, with smells...with the tongue, with tastes...with the body, with touch...with the mind, with mental objects...

"'And through this disenchantment, the noble disciple becomes dispassionate; and by the absence of passion, free; and when free, aware of that freedom; aware that rebirth is exhausted, that the holy life has been lived, that what was to be done has been done, and that there is nothing more to do in this body-mind existence.

"'While this exposition was being delivered, the minds of the one thousand monks, relinquishing attachment, became free from defilements.'"

Upon finishing the discourse, Upali bows respectfully to his fellow arahants and takes his seat.

"Thank you, Upali. Ananda, when does the Buddha make his way to Rajagaha?" asks Maha Kassapa.

Ananda begins, "With his retinue of monks, which now included the Kassapa brothers and their followers, he came to Rajagaha and settled under the banyan trees at Suppatittha shrine in the Palmyra Sapling Grove," answers Ananda. "Seven years before he had made a promise to

King Bimbisara that he would return to his kingdom as soon as he achieved his goal of full enlightenment. It didn't take long before the king heard that the Venerable Gotama was nearby, and it pleased him to know that he had honored his earlier request. He learned that the Buddha was expounding a powerful new doctrine, proclaiming a pure higher life. The king thought it would be good to pay him a visit.

"King Bimbisara, along with a large group of Brahmin householders, went to the Palmyra Sapling Grove where he respectfully saluted the Buddha. Some of the Brahmin householders paid homage to the Blessed One, some exchanged greetings with him, some extended their hands in reverential salutation, some pronounced their name and clan, and some kept silent and sat down to one side.

"There was some confusion in the minds of the Brahmin householders in regards to who was the leader: the Buddha, or Uruvela Kassapa. Knowing their minds, the Buddha addressed Uruvela Kassapa and said, 'O monk from Uruvela, what made you abandon fire worship and sacrifice?'

"Uruvela Kassapa answered, 'Sacrifices are said to procure sights, sounds, tastes, and other enjoyments. Through you I learned to know these as defilements and fetters, so I gave up all faith in offerings and sacrifices.'

"The Buddha said, 'If your heart finds no delight in the five sense pleasures of sight, sound, smell, taste, and touch, what sense object in this world of *devas* and humans still delights you? Answer me that, Kassapa.'"

"'Glorious Buddha, because I have distinctly perceived *Nibbana*, which has the characteristics of peace and freedom from attachments, I no longer enjoy offering sacrifices, nor do I take delight in the daily practice of fire worship,' replied Uruvela Kassapa.

"After giving his answer, Uruvela Kassapa got up from his seat and prostrated himself at the feet of the Blessed One. Then he said twice, 'Reverend Sir, the Blessed One, you are my teacher and I am your pupil.'

"The Brahmin householders now knew, beyond a shadow of a doubt, that Uruvela Kassapa was following the Buddha's spiritual guidance. Knowing their minds, the Buddha expounded to them the doctrine of the Four Noble Truths, and several of those gathered realized the Doctrine. A large percentage of them made it known that from that moment forward they wished to be lay disciples of the Buddha," says Ananda.

"King Bimbisara, I believe, was one of those who realized the Doctrine and became a *sotapanna*, wasn't he?" asks Punna.

"Yes, Venerable Sir," replies Ananda. "After the Buddha's discourse the king spoke to him and said, 'Ever since I was a young prince I have had five aspirations.'

"'What were those aspirations, Your Majesty?' asked the Buddha.

"'The first was that I would be a consecrated king. The second was that a Fully Enlightened One would visit my country. My third aspiration was that I would associate with the Buddha. My fourth was that the Buddha would preach his Doctrine to me. And my fifth aspiration was that I would understand his Doctrine. All five of these are now fulfilled,' answered the king.

"The king expressed his supreme happiness, and said, 'I now take refuge in the Buddha, the Dhamma, and the Sangha. May the Blessed One accept me henceforth as a lifelong lay disciple, and may he, with his community of monks, accept an invitation for alms at my palace tomorrow.'

"The Buddha accepted his invitation in silence, and the following day he and his one thousand monks went to the palace for their midday meal. They took the seats prepared for them, and the king himself served the Buddha and his Sangha members."

"Ananda, did the king present the Bamboo Grove to the Lord on this occasion?" asks Bakkula.

"Yes. The king wanted the Buddha to be as near to him as possible, so he considered several sites for a hermitage. He finally decided on Veluvana, the Bamboo Grove, which he deemed was most suitable for a variety of reasons.

"The king took a golden jug and poured scented water over the Buddha's hands to mark the dedication of the park. Then he said, 'I cannot keep myself away from the Triple Gem, and I wish to come into the presence of the Buddha on all occasions, appropriate or not. The Palmyra Sapling Grove where you are currently residing is too far from the city. Reverend Sir, I hereby dedicate the Bamboo Grove, our Veluvana Park, to the fraternity of monks led by the Buddha. May the Blessed One please accept this gift.'

"The Buddha accepted the gift and gave another discourse. In this talk, he told the monks that from that day forward they, too, could accept the gift of monasteries. After the king and the Brahmins paid their respects, the Buddha and the monks left the palace," concludes Ananda.

"It is good that we are recollecting this story in the privacy of your chamber, Maha Kassapa, rather than in the assembly hall where King Ajatasattu might hear it," says Punna.

"Perhaps, but this won't be the last time we talk of King Bimbisara, Venerable Sir. He was, after all, one of the Lord's closest associates and disciples. It may be good for his son, King Ajatasattu, to be present the next time we discuss his father. It might help him come to terms with his dreadful plight more fully, and inspire him to strive even harder to make amends. He now lives a virtuous life, trying hard to redeem himself for the sins he committed against his parents. He can never be fully expiated, however, until his unfortunate *kamma* has been totally exhausted. I'm afraid he will have to live with the consequences of his misguided deeds until the end of his life – and for countless others in the lower unpleasant worlds," says Maha Kassapa.

"The laws of *kamma* work that way – especially when the misdeed involves the ill-treatment of a parent," says Upali.

The arahants solemnly reflect on their own fond memories of King Bimbisara and his gracious hospitality. Then Maha Kaccayana suggests that it would be an appropriate time to discuss the different types of *kamma*, and their subsequent effects.

"I think you would be the best one to explain these, Maha Kassapa," says Punna.

"Actually, I think this is enough discussion for this evening, my brothers. The hour is very late, and we still need our time alone for meditation. Let us re-convene in the assembly hall at dawn tomorrow," says Maha Kassapa.

The arahants stand and make their way to their own solitary chambers where they will enjoy the balance of the night in the spiritual bliss of their enlightenment.

Chapter 13
The Chief Disciples

The First Sangha Council, held in the cavern complex near Rajagaha, enters its sixth week; Maha Kassapa is pleased with its progress so far. Several thousand of the Buddha's eighty-four thousand *suttas* and other teachings have already been recited and vetted. The memory monks are in the process of sorting them by length, topic, and other criteria under the auspices of a sub-committee devoted to Dhamma organization.

The council begins at dawn, as usual, with Maha Kassapa sounding the gong, its deep, sonorous tones reverberating throughout space. After completing their devotional chants the chairman says, "May these verses become part of the daily Sangha services for generations of monks to come." The arahants chant with him this affirmation of the Buddha in unison:

> "'This Dhamma is for one who wants little,
> not for one who wants too much.
> 'This Dhamma is for one who is contented,
> not for one who is discontented.
> 'This Dhamma is for one who loves seclusion,
> not for one who loves society.
> 'This Dhamma is for one who is energetic,
> not for one who is lazy.
> 'This Dhamma is for one who is mindful,
> not for one who is unmindful.
> 'This Dhamma is for one who is composed,
> not for one who is restless.
> 'This Dhamma is for one who is wise,
> not for one who is unwise.
> 'This Dhamma is for one who delights in freedom
> from impediments, not for one who
> delights in impediments.'"[1]

The session continues with more recitations from the discourses that were grouped by topic, and from some that were grouped by number. Ananda is as focused as ever. He has just completed "Reverence for the Dhamma," and Maha Kassapa stands saying, "The sub-committee recollecting the life of the Buddha will be discussing the Master's two Chief Disciples today: Venerable Sariputta and Venerable Maha Moggallana. To show our great respect for these two revered leaders of the *Sasana*, the sub-committee's dialogue will be held in the center of the pavilion during this afternoon's assembly session. All of you are invited to participate."

This announcement is met with smiles of approval from all of the five hundred arahants. Each one of them has their own personal memories of these two pioneering giants, and it is apparent from their reactions that several of them will wish to participate by sharing their own experiences.

Lunch is offered by Queen Vajira in the king's absence. The queen is the daughter of King Pasenadi of Kosala, and the mother of Prince Udayibhadda, King Ajatasattu's only son. She is a devoted follower of the Buddha, and often comes to offer *dana* to the council members.

When the luncheon is finished and the arahants have chanted *Buktanumodana* in gratitude for the *dana*, the Queen and her companions pay their respects and retire. Maha Kassapa instructs attendants to clear the space in the center of the assembly hall, and to spread mats for the sub-committee members. When this is done Ananda and the others take their places and prepare to begin.

"Venerables Sariputta and Maha Moggallana entered the Sangha shortly before I did," begins Maha Kassapa. "The Buddha knew exactly when they would make their appearance, as he had known them well from numerous previous lives. He knew the important roles they would play in the infancy of the *Sasana*, and was well-aware of the tremendous long-term influence they would have in regards to the future dissemination of the Dhamma. Venerable Sariputta, in particular, was highly adept in regards to detailed analyses of the Lord's teaching. His interpretations have made their way into many of the very discourses we are reviewing here now. His early systemization of the discourses also provided us with the framework for our current task of organizing the Dhamma. Venerable Ananda, if you will, please tell us how these two arahants found the Buddha."

"There was an ascetic named Sanjaya who was living in the city of Rajagaha," begins Ananda. "As a prominent religious leader in the region he had a following of two hundred-fifty ascetics who were following his instruction. Two of these were Venerables Sariputta and Moggallana. Both young men were from wealthy Brahmin families that had been close for seven generations. Venerable Sariputta was born in the village of Upatissa, which is near Rajagaha. His father was Vanganta, and his mother was Rupasari, after whom Sariputta was named. Venerable Moggallana was from the village of Kolita, and he was named after his mother Moggali.

"The two ascetics were childhood friends; in fact, they were born on the same day. One day, when they were in their early thirties, they went together to see a mime play, and during the performance they realized the impermanence of all things. It was then that they decided to renounce the world and train as disciples of Sanjaya. Their intention was to find a practice or doctrine that would help them realize *Nibbana*, the Deathless State. After quickly mastering the teaching of Sanjaya, they understood clearly that his doctrine would *not* help them attain *Nibbana*.

"They made a vow with one another that they would search diligently for the teaching that led to *Nibbana* and that the one who found it first would immediately inform the other."

Bhaddiya comments, "These two were what the Buddha would refer to as *kalyana mitta*, or 'spiritual friends'; they were partners who supported one another in their search for truth. Please continue the story, Ananda."

"One day shortly after making their mutual vow," begins Ananda, "Sariputta happened to observe Venerable Assaji as he entered Rajagaha for his daily collection of alms. This is the same Venerable Assaji who was one of the first five *bhikkus* ordained at Isipatana. The young Sariputta was impressed by the venerable's demeanor, regal posture, and composure as he walked through the city. Sariputta watched the monk carefully, and was in awe of the man's dignity, grace, and humble manner.

"He wanted so much to approach Venerable Assaji to question him about his teacher and about *Nibbana*, but his good manners and upbringing restrained him. He decided to follow the monk and wait until he was finished collecting alms. When he sensed the monk was ready to take a seat and have his meal he offered a stool that he had been carrying. He also offered the monk water from his pot, treating him with great respect as a student would treat his teacher.

"When he thought it was appropriate, Sariputta said, 'Friend, your faculties are clear and serene; your complexion, clear and bright. Under whom have you become a monk? Who is your teacher? Whose teaching have you accepted?'

"The Venerable Assaji answered, 'Friend, I have gone forth under the Perfectly Self-Enlightened Buddha, the scion of the Sakyan clan who renounced his throne to become a recluse. He is my teacher.'

"'What does your teacher, the Buddha, profess? What does he teach?' asked the ascetic Sariputta.

"Venerable Assaji paused a few moments in order to mentally compose a response that would adequately convey the essence of the *Sasana*. He replied modestly, 'Friend, I am but a junior member of the order, having come into the *Sasana* quite recently. I will not be able to explain the Dhamma extensively; I can only tell you its essential meaning in brief.'

"The young ascetic said, 'You may speak in brief *or* in detail. Tell me only the meaning, if you wish. It is the essential meaning alone that I seek,'" concludes Ananda.

"Venerable Sariputta was the most earnest seeker of truth I ever met," comments Punna. "He never wavered from his course – from beginning to end."

"This is why the Buddha gave him the title 'Foremost in Wisdom.'[2] He was able to discern the deeper meaning beneath every aspect of the Dhamma from the first moment he heard it," adds Bhaddiya. "Please continue, Ananda."

"Venerable Assaji outlined the basis of the doctrine by saying,

> 'Whatever is rooted in cause,
> the Blessed One has explained such cause,
> and also the cessation of such cause.
> Such are the teachings of the great monk.'[3]

"No sooner had the ascetic Sariputta heard the first two lines of this stanza that he attained *sotapanna*. A clear and pure vision dawned on him of the doctrine that whatever arises is subject to cessation," says Ananda.

"The fact is," adds Maha Kaccayana, "Venerable Sariputta heard the last two lines of the stanza in a completely different state of consciousness than he had heard the first two lines. He was transformed by hearing just a few syllables of the Master's sublime teaching."

"He couldn't wait to tell his friend Moggallana about his discovery," resumes Ananda. "He even said to Venerable Assaji, 'This is the very teaching that my friend and I have been searching for. Because we have not heard this teaching, *Nibbana* has been unattainable; we have suffered a great loss, and have wasted much time. Please tell me where the Buddha is now so I can take my friend to him. I have a bound duty to inform him when I have found someone who has reached the Deathless State of *Nibbana*.' Venerable Assaji told Sariputta that the Buddha was residing at Veluvana Park. After respectfully showing his gratitude, Sariputta said he would find his friend and take him to the Buddha at once."

Maha Kassapa begins, "Venerable Maha Moggallana once told me that when Sariputta came running towards him he couldn't help but notice that his friend's face had completely transformed. He knew for certain that Sariputta had found a source for the true knowledge of *Nibbana*. He told how Sariputta shared his encounter with Venerable Assaji, and then repeated the stanza about the Dhamma that the monk had shared with him. By the end of hearing the verses he also had realized *sotapanna*, exclaiming with great joy, 'Let us go and find the Buddha immediately. He is our Master, our Benefactor!'

"Sariputta told him that they must first go and inform their teacher Sanjaya. He said they owed him that much because of the kindness he had shown them, and the teaching he had given them.

"Moggallana told Sariputta, 'You are correct, my friend.' Together they went to see Sanjaya, but on the way they happened to meet his two hundred fifty students who were gathered nearby. The two friends were eager to share the good news with them. Their energy, excitement, and changed demeanor convinced each and every one of them that they had made an important discovery.

"All of the students expressed their wish to see the Buddha right away. One of them said, 'While living in the hermitage we have come to depend on the two of you. We have been watching your behavior and disposition, knowing that you would settle for nothing less than the teaching that would lead to the ultimate truth. We will go to the Buddha with you.'

"Moggallana and Sariputta continued on their way to see Sanjaya so they could tell him about the Buddha and his doctrine.

"After sharing their big discovery with their teacher, Sanjaya's first response was, 'Why do you want to go and see this new teacher? You don't know anything about him.'

"Sariputta said, 'Just a few words of his teaching elevated us to a new level of consciousness, and we are certain that his Dhamma will lead us to *Nibbana*, the state we seek. I ask you, teacher, to come with us.'

"Sanjaya's reply was, 'If you must follow this new path, then go ahead and leave. I cannot go with you.'

"Sariputta pleaded with his teacher, 'Why wouldn't you want to rise above what you already know? The Buddha can lead you. You have been kind to us, so I ask you to come and see for yourself.'

"'You and your friend are free to go, Sariputta. I just hope you won't exert your influence over the rest of my students,' was his response.

"The group of ascetics gathered around Sanjaya, Sariputta and Moggallana, and one of them said, 'We will all go with these two friends, teacher. After hearing about the Buddha and his Dhamma we can no longer be happy here. We wish to go where there is hope for achieving full enlightenment. Please come with us dear teacher.'

"Once again Sanjaya refused. He finally said, 'You are free to go and follow your own path. I cannot go with you; I have my own beliefs and system of practices.'

"The two-hundred-fifty ascetics paid their deepest respects to their teacher and then walked away, leaving the hermitage deserted and Sanjaya desolate. Under the weight of raging grief he sat alone by his sacred fire. He felt betrayed and victimized by the two young ascetics who had suddenly caused his entire world to collapse." When Maha Kassapa finishes, he pauses to reflect on the great loss poor Sanjaya must have felt.

Anuruddha speaks, "The story of Sanjaya reminds me of a parable Venerable Kumara Kassapa likes to tell about people who are not willing to let go of their views. It is in the '*Payasi Sutta*: Debate with a Skeptic.'[4] Would you share this parable with us?"

"Gladly, Venerable Sir. I told Prince Payasi this parable long ago, and he told me he would never forget it," replies Kumara Kassapa as he stands to tell the tale.

"Two friends, seeking their fortune abroad, hear about a town that had recently been deserted. One of them said to the other, 'Let's go to that deserted town; surely we can find something of value there.'

"They went to the town and found a pile of flax that had been left in the street. 'Let's make a bundle of this flax and take it with us; we can make linen out of it,' suggested the first friend. And so they did.

"They continued on their way and eventually they discovered a pile of linen cloth in another street. 'This linen cloth is what we wanted to use the flax for; let's throw away the flax and take this linen with us,' suggested the first friend.

"The second friend replied, 'I've carried this flax all this way, and besides, it's already bundled up. I'll keep this flax; you do as you like.' So the first friend bundled up the linen and took it with him while the second carried his bundle of flax.

"The same situation came up again and again when each time they discovered something of value in another street. After the linen, they came upon cotton, then cotton cloth, then iron, tin, lead, and silver. Each time the first friend said, 'This is what we wanted, what we've been carrying this for. Let's throw this away, and take what we've just found with us.' The second friend replied each time, 'I've carried this flax all this way, and besides, it's already bundled up. I'll keep this flax; you do as you like.'

"Each time the first friend let go of what he was carrying to pick up the more valuable object that was available. His friend just kept carrying around the bundle of flax. Finally they got to a place where there was gold in the street. The first friend said, 'I'll throw away my silver and you throw away your flax. This gold is what we wanted all those other things for!'

"The second friend said once again, 'I've carried this flax all this way, and besides, it's already bundled up. I'll keep this flax; you do as you like.'

"The first friend picked up the gold and returned to his home content and full of joy. The second friend returned with his bundle of flax. The man who brought home the gold made his family happy, but the second friend with the flax got looks of scorn and words of ridicule from his disappointed wife – which he well deserved!" The arahants in the assembly hall chuckle at the folly of being so attached to views that it prevents one from finding the treasure of happiness.

"Thank you, Venerable Kumara Kassapa, for sharing that story with us. It certainly applies in the case of Sanjaya. He chose to keep his old views rather than take the gold offered by the Buddha," says Maha Kassapa.

Ananda then continues, "When Sariputta and Moggallana were on their way to see the Buddha he saw them approaching from a distance. He said, 'Here are the two friends who will be my two chief disciples.'

"The two friends prostrated themselves at the Buddha's feet and eagerly asked for ordination. The Buddha said, 'Come, O monks, well preached is the doctrine. Practice the higher religious life for the ending of suffering.' The other former students of Sanjaya were also admitted to the Order.

"The Buddha immediately proclaimed that the two new monks would become his chief disciples. The other monks were surprised that the newcomers should be shown such a great honor. The Buddha explained that for countless lifetimes Sariputta and Moggallana had strenuously exerted themselves to win this eminence.

"Seven days after his ordination Venerable Maha Moggallana became an arahant. He had been meditating for several hours when drowsiness suddenly began to overtake him. The Buddha knew this, and he appeared before him, exhorting him to be zealous. Later that day Maha Moggallana attained enlightenment.

"Seven days after that Venerable Sariputta also attained that lofty goal. At that time, he was fanning the Buddha while the Lord expounded a discourse on the nature of the body to Dighanakha, Sariputta's nephew," says Ananda. "He had asked Dighanakha to contemplate the body so that desire and concern for the body could be abandoned. He then went on to explain impermanence and the doctrine of dependent origination. Sariputta described his experience this way:

> "'The Blessed One, The Buddha, The One with Vision,
>   Was teaching the Dhamma to another.
>   Whilst the Dhamma was being taught,
>   I lent an ear keen on the goal.
>   That listening of mine was not in vain,
> For I am released from all sources of corruption.'[5]

"From that time forward for the next forty-four years the two venerable monks were indispensable to the Buddha and his work," concludes Ananda.

"May I share a personal story about Venerable Sariputta?" asks Anuruddha.

"Certainly, Venerable Sir," answers Maha Kassapa.

"Many, many years ago I was having a discussion with Venerable Sariputta, telling him with a great sense of pride about my ability to see one thousand world systems with my divine eye; I also boasted about my unshakable energy, and my clear, untroubled mindfulness. Venerable Sariputta looked me directly in the eye and said, 'Your so-called *deva* eye is conceit, your claims to energy are nothing but conceit, and your mindfulness is simply worrying, and nothing more.'

"Shocked to hear the Buddha's chief disciple scold me like that, I asked him, 'What should I do?' He simply said, 'Abandon all those thoughts – they will get you nowhere,' concludes Anuruddha.

"Venerable Sir, did you follow his advice?" asks Maha Kaccayana.

"Yes, I did, and it wasn't too long before I was able to achieve arahantship. I feel like I owe it to his very sobering words," answers Anuruddha.

"I know that you were particularly close to Venerable Sariputta, Venerable Ananda. He held you in particular regard because you were the Buddha's attendant, and he himself would have happily undertaken that responsibility. I think in one of the discourses the Buddha asked you if you approved of Venerable Sariputta. Would you mind telling us how you answered that question?" requests Punna.

"It is very true that Venerable Sariputta and I were devoted friends, and I certainly approved of him wholeheartedly. When the Lord asked me that question I said, 'Who, sir, that is not childish or corrupt or stupid or of perverted mind, would not approve of him? Wise is he; his wisdom comprehensive, joyous, swift, sharp, and fastidious. Small is he in his desires, contented, loving seclusion, detached, and of rampant energy. A preacher is he, accepting advice, a critic, and a scourge of evil.'" Ananda smiles as he relates this passage and the other arahants beam.

"I think we all share your view of our beloved Venerable Sariputta," says Upali.

"Indeed we do," says Bakkula. "I remember the time when a number of Sangha members complained to the Buddha that Venerable Sariputta was engaging in certain rites and rituals that were not appropriate; in particular, his practice of bowing to two directions and then prostrating his body and worshiping before sleeping.

"The Buddha then said to the monks, 'Each night Venerable Sariputta looks with his divine eye to see in which direction his first teacher, Venerable Assaji, and I, the *Tathagata*, are residing. Then, after paying obeisance to Assaji and to the *Tathagata*, he is careful to make sure that his feet are not pointing toward either one of us. Then he goes to sleep placing his head in one of the other two directions.' The monks who complained were silenced at once by this explanation."

"Venerable Sariputta always quoted the *Nava Sutta*,[6] which says that one should honor those from whom they learned the Dhamma. I'll recite one verse for our recollection," says Upali.

> "'As the *Devas* pay devout homage to Indra,
> So should one revere the person
> Through whom one has learned the Dhamma.'"

"Venerable Sariputta's patience was almost as legendary as his goodness and humility," says Bhaddiya. "I'll never forget the time a group of men were praising his noble qualities, and a young Brahmin challenged them. He said that Venerable Sariputta had never before shown anger because he had never been provoked. So the brash young man walked up behind the revered monk and bashed him on top of the head with a stick. All Venerable Sariputta said was, 'What was that?' and he didn't even turn around to see who or what had struck him. He just kept on walking as if nothing had happened.

"After a while the young Brahmin was so overcome by guilt that he got down on his knees and begged Venerable Sariputta's forgiveness. The monk forgave him without thinking about it twice. The Brahmin wished to make further amends so he invited Venerable Sariputta to his home for the noonday meal. The elder accepted the invitation.

"When the meal was over and Venerable Sariputta was preparing to leave, he saw that there was an angry mob in front of the Brahmin's house. They were holding sticks and stones, and they were threatening to punish the Brahmin for his ill treatment of the highly-respected monk. Venerable Sariputta walked over to them and asked, 'Who did this man hit? You – or me? I have already pardoned him, so why should you feel anger when I feel none?' The mob dispersed at once, having witnessed his magnanimous act of forgiveness and compassion,"[7] concludes Bhaddiya.

"It was the custom of my dear friend Venerable Sariputta to be last when we traveled so he could look after any aged or sick monks who were slow," begins Ananda. "Many of the younger and more able-bodied monks would hurry ahead and claim the best spots in the shelters for themselves and their preceptors. One night Sariputta arrived late, only to find that there was nowhere for him to sleep. So he wound up spending the night at the foot of a tree.

"At three o'clock in the morning the Buddha got up to meditate. As was his custom he stepped outside to breathe in the morning air, and he spotted Venerable Sariputta under the tree. He walked up to him and said, 'Chief Disciple, what are you doing out here?'

"Venerable Sariputta answered, 'I'm just resting, Master. Do you need anything? Can I get something for you?'

"The Buddha asked, 'Was there no where else for you to rest this night?'

"Venerable Sariputta replied, 'No, Master, but this tree is a good place for me.'

"'Sariputta, please get up and come to my room and sleep. I'm already awake, and I won't need it any more tonight.'

"He said, 'I couldn't do that, Master. The other *bhikkhus* might think you are showing me favoritism, and that would cause them unhappiness. I'm just fine here.'

"'Very well, my friend,' said the Buddha, and then he went to his place of meditation.[8]

Upali interjects, "That morning the Buddha gathered all of the *bhikkhus* together and asked them who should have priority in terms of accommodation. He received all sorts of answers based on noble birth, caste, attainment of certain levels of *jhana*, and so forth. This caused the Lord to declare that since birth, caste, and social status were of no importance in the Sangha, then seniority would be the *Vinaya* rule from that point forward; it would be determined by age and how long the *bhikkhu* had been ordained."

"Our dear, modest Venerable Sariputta didn't want to be singled out for any special treatment, of course, but I'm sure he appreciated knowing that from that point onward he would have a comfortable place to rest after a long day's journey," says Bhaddiya.

Maha Kassapa comments, "He would never complain, and as we all know, would never say a word on his own behalf. He worked so hard keeping everyone and everything in order, and I know that rule made his life a bit easier."

"The first time I met Venerable Sariputta we had a marvelous conversation about living the divine life," says Punna. "The odd thing was, we had never met before – I had never even seen him – and I didn't know I was speaking to the Buddha's Chief Disciple. After our conversation I asked him his name, and when he told me I was overjoyed to have had the opportunity to share the Dhamma with such a wise, experienced *bhikkhu*. Our dialog has since become known as the *Rathavinita Sutta*:[9] The Relay Chariots."

"Thank you, Venerable Punna. Venerable Sariputta told me himself that he had previously heard of your reputation as a gifted teacher. He actually walked all the way to Blind Men's Grove in Jetavana and waited the entire day to meet you and have that conversation," adds Ananda. Punna modestly lowers his head, saying nothing.

Upali says, "I think we should mention that Venerable Sariputta had three brothers: Cunda, Upasena, and Revata. He also had three sisters: Cala, Upacala, and Sisupacala. All six of his siblings received ordination from the Buddha, and all eventually attained arahantship. The only member of Venerable Sariputta's family who did not follow the Buddha was Rupasari, his mother. She was bitter about being left alone without any of her children, and she often insulted Venerable Sariputta by telling him that he had ruined her family. His patience with his mother, however, knew no limits; he remained compassionate toward her and, of course, didn't judge her for her feelings."

"We will tell the story of Rupasari's eventual acceptance of the Buddha's teaching later in this recollection," says Maha Kassapa, and the other arahants nod their approval. "There are countless anecdotes that could be recollected about Venerable Sariputta, and I know there will be other occasions to share some of them. Let's talk for a while about Venerable Maha Moggallana."

"Tell us something of Venerable Maha Moggallana's famous supernormal powers," requests Bakkula.

"There were many monks who were highly skilled in various supernormal powers, but they usually mastered only one or two of them. You yourself, Venerable Anuruddha, are a master of the divine eye. Venerable Maha Moggallana had that power as well as mastery of recollecting past births, astral travel, and communicating with divine beings," says Punna.

Anuruddha says, "He also had *iddhi*, or the power of penetrating others' minds to read their thoughts. On one occasion the Buddha made a comment that a monk in the group was corrupt. Venerable Maha Moggallana used his power to investigate the minds of the group of monks. He surveyed the gathering and, sure enough, he spotted the one the Buddha spoke of.[10]

"He often used his gift of the divine eye to observe beings in other realms, and his gifts of the divine ear and eye enabled him to have conversations with the Lord from great distances. Venerable Maha Moggallana's gift of astral travel became invaluable to the Buddha when he was transmitting the *Abhidhamma*, or higher teachings, to *devas* in the *Tavatimsa* heavens. For three months the beloved monk traveled back and forth to inform the Buddha of the progress of his Sangha.

"There are several legendary instances of Venerable Maha Moggallana's power over the laws of physical matter. And last, but not least, was his spectacular ability to transform his appearance when the need arose," concludes Anuruddha.

"His supernormal powers served him all the way to the end of his life," says Ananda, "but we will save that story for later."

"I believe it's time to adjourn for the evening, brothers. Venerable Ananda, please share the short *sutta* that reflects the esteem the chief disciples held for each other. I think that would be a fitting finale for this evening's stirring recollection," says Maha Kassapa.

Ananda begins, "Once when the Buddha was dwelling in Savatthi, the chief disciples were dwelling in Rajagaha. One day Venerable Sariputta noticed the serene, pure and bright countenance of Venerable Maha Moggallana. He asked him how he had spent his day. Maha Moggallana replied that he had enjoyed some Dhamma talk with the Blessed One. The Blessed One and Venerable Maha Moggallana had cleared their divine ear and eye elements and were able to communicate even though they were in two different places.

"Venerable Sariputta remarked, 'Friend, compared to you I am like a few grains of gravel compared to the Himalayas. You are of such great spiritual power and might that if you so wished you could live on for an eon.'

"Venerable Maha Moggallana replied, 'Friend, compared to you I am like a few grains of salt compared to a barrel of salt. For you have been extolled, lauded, and praised in many ways by the Blessed One...,'[11]" concludes Ananda.

Maha Kassapa rises from his seat and says, "Tonight we have briefly recollected the lives of the Buddha's two chief disciples. Their contributions to the *Sasana* can be matched by no others. May their legacies live forever in the minds of future Sangha members and lay people alike."

Without another word, each member of the general assembly rises from his seat and silently departs from the hall. There are tears of joy in their eyes as they recollect their own personal memories of the revered chief disciples of the Buddha.

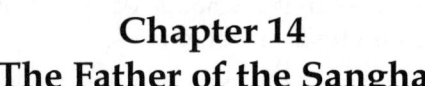

Chapter 14
The Father of the Sangha

"Before we recess to receive *dana* from the king, I would like to recite one of my favorite discourses of the Buddha: 'The Simile of the Ocean.'[1] This *sutta* was addressed to Paharada, a seafaring tribal chief."

Ananda begins, "Thus have I heard….

"'I suppose, Paharada, the members of your tribe find delight in the great ocean.'

"'They do, Lord.'

"'Now, Paharada, how many wonderful and marvelous qualities do your people…perceive in the great ocean so that they can take delight in it?'

"'There are, Lord, eight wonderful and marvelous qualities…in the great ocean in which we delight. These are the eight:

"'The great ocean slopes away gradually, falls gradually, and inclines gradually, not in an abrupt way like a precipice.

"'The great ocean is stable and does not overflow its boundaries.

"'The great ocean does not tolerate a dead body; if there is a dead body in it the great ocean will quickly carry it to the shore and cast it on the land.

"'When the mighty rivers reach the ocean they lose their former names and designations. They are reckoned from then on as the great ocean.

"'Though all the streams of the world flow into the great ocean, and rain falls into it from the sky, it neither appears to increase nor decease in its volume.

"'The great ocean has but one taste, the taste of salt.

"'In the great ocean there are many and variegated precious substances: pearls, gems, lapis lazuli, shells, quartz, corals, silver, gold, rubies and cat's eyes.

"'The great ocean is the abode of vast creatures, some of which are hundreds of feet long.

"'These, Lord, are the eight wonderful and marvelous qualities which we perceive in the ocean, and in which we take delight. I suppose, Lord, the monks take delight in this Dhamma and Discipline?'

"'They do, Paharada.'

"'But, Lord, how many wonderful and marvelous qualities do the monks perceive in this Dhamma and Discipline, in which they take delight?'

"'There are, Paharada, eight qualities, and these are:

"'Just as the great ocean slopes away gradually, falls gradually, and inclines gradually, not in an abrupt way like a precipice, even so is this Dhamma and Discipline. There is a gradual training, gradual practice, and gradual progress; there is no penetration to final knowledge in an abrupt way."

"'Just as the great ocean is stable and does not overflow its boundaries, even so when I have made known a rule of training to my disciples they will not transgress it even for life's sake.'

"'Just as the great ocean will not tolerate a dead body, but quickly carries it to the shore and casts it on to the land, even so the Sangha will not tolerate within its ranks a person who is immoral, of bad character, of impure and suspicious conduct, secretive in his actions, not a true ascetic, not chaste, rotten to the core, lustful and of vile behavior. In such a case the Sangha quickly assembles and expels such a person.

"'Just as the mighty rivers on reaching the great ocean lose their former names and designations, even so, when members of the four castes – nobles, Brahmins, commoners, and servants – go forth from home into the homeless life in this Dhamma and Discipline, they lose their former names and lineage and are reckoned only as ascetics following the son of the Sakyas.

"'Just as in the great ocean neither a decrease nor an increase will appear though all the streams of the world flow into it, and rain falls into it from the sky, even so, if many monks attain final *Nibbana*, there is no decrease or increase in it since *Nibbana* is neither a state nor a place nor a substance.

"'Just as the great ocean has but one taste, the taste of salt, even so this Dhamma and Discipline has but one taste: the taste of liberation.

"'Just as in the great ocean there are many and variegated precious substances, even so in this Dhamma and Discipline there is much that is precious: the four foundations of mindfulness, the four right efforts, the four bases of success, the five spiritual faculties, the five spiritual powers, the seven factors of enlightenment, and the Noble Eightfold Path.

"'Just as the great ocean is the abode of creatures of vast size, even so is this Dhamma and Discipline the domain of great and noble beings: the stream-enterer (*sotapanna*) and one practicing for the realization of the fruit of stream-entry; the once-returner (*sakadagami*) and one practicing for the realization of the fruit of once-returning; the non-returner (*anagami*) and one practicing for the realization of the fruit of non-returning; and the arahant and one practicing for arahantship.

"'These, Paharada, are the eight wonderful and marvelous qualities in the Dhamma and Discipline, which are perceived by the monks again and again, and in which they take delight.'"

Ananda steps down from the podium and returns to his seat. Maha Kassapa sounds the gong and the arahants begin to file toward the *dana* pavilion where King Ajatasattu is waiting with his ministers and staff.

Ananda taps Maha Kassapa's arm on the way out of the assembly hall and says, "You finally get to make your entrance into the story today, my friend. We all know how humble and austere you are, but be prepared for some of the accolades you will be forced to endure."

Maha Kassapa looks warmly at his friend and smiles. "You know, Ananda, you and I haven't always seen things eye to eye – at least on the surface. Did you ever figure out which one of us is the needle-peddler and which one is the needle-maker?"

"I can't believe you actually remember the exchange with that misguided nun, Thullananda![2] It's been years!"

"You're not the only one with a good memory," Maha Kassapa responds with good humor.

"If I recall correctly, and I always do, you went on and on about your meditative and spiritual attainments, which you felt compelled to tell me were corroborated by the Buddha himself. If I hadn't known you better I would have said that your ego was bruised by the remark you overheard," replies Ananda.

"Just for the record, dear friend, it was *your* ego I was concerned about that day. I wanted to make sure you didn't get carried away by that nun's praise," responds Maha Kassapa, chuckling.

"By the way, the night before this council began I became a needle-maker like you, so the needle-peddler is gone; we are both fully-awake arahants now, and there are no more egos and their annoying personalities to be concerned about. Anyway, I was just warning you that your humility and modesty will probably be put to the test today; it's a good thing your ego has been extinguished because I might be worried about you," jokes Ananda.

"It's a good thing you finally achieved enlightenment, or I still might be calling you a 'youngster.'" Maha Kassapa laughs when he says this and his eyes twinkle as he remembers an incident from the past.

"I reminded you then, and I'm reminding you now that white hairs are growing from this old head, my friend, so I think you can dispense with any 'youngster' comment," says Ananda, smiling.

"I still think of you as that youthful *bhikkhu* who wasted his time with monks who were unworthy of you," replies Maha Kassapa. "If you still engaged in such practices I would call you a 'youngster' again!"

"Those days are long gone, Venerable Sir, as is the nun Thullananda who inspired this conversation," says Ananda. "No need for any more lectures about your lofty status in the Sangha and in the eyes of the Buddha; we'll confirm all of that tonight in our sub-committee meeting."

Maha Kassapa can't help but grin at his old colleague's good-humored remark.

They walk on in silence where the king is waiting to serve them. They take their seats according to seniority, and the rest of the arahants follow suit. They soon begin to chant the blessing for the provider of the meal.

Later that evening in the privacy of Maha Kassapa's cave chamber, the sub-committee members are arriving to continue their work. The memory monks are already seated, eyes closed, preparing to receive the precious words that they will record indelibly in their minds.

"As I said earlier, tonight it's your turn to appear on the scene, my dear brother," says Ananda to Maha Kassapa. The "Father of the Sangha" smiles modestly and says, "So be it."

Ananda says, "Maha Kassapa, I will talk about your family background and early life, but I think you should give us a first-hand account from the point when you meet our Lord."

Maha Kassapa is about to protest, but instead he quietly acquiesces Ananda's suggestion.

"Pipphali, as he was called by his Brahmin father, Kapila, and his mother, Sumanadevi, was born in the village of Mahatittha in Magadha," begins Ananda. "He was the only son of a wealthy family that owned sixteen villages and reigned over them like kings. The young man was indulged in every luxury imaginable – including an inexhaustible supply of gold dust to rub on his body after bathing.[3]

"When he was twenty years old his parents expressed their wish that he should marry. This was a natural request, being the custom for countless generations. The parents wanted to ensure that their line had an heir to carry on the management of their estates. The young man's mind, however, was set on leaving the worldly life and becoming an ascetic. The parents wouldn't give up, however, and they were determined to see their son married. After repeated and relentless attempts to try to change his mind, Pipphali devised a clever plan to outwit his parents.

"With his own hands he fashioned a solid gold statue of a perfect young woman. He took it to his parents and said that he would marry if a girl could be found who was as beautiful as his creation. He said, 'If you can find a woman like this, then I will remain in the home life.' He thought he was pretty safe with his ingenious plan."

"I guess you underestimated the power of your parents' intention, didn't you, Venerable Sir?" quips Bakkula.

"Apparently I did," answers Maha Kassapa, smiling.

"They hired eight Brahmins," continues Ananda, "and paid them handsomely with promises of more if they could find a human likeness of the golden statue. They told them to take the statue to the far ends of the earth if necessary. Lo and behold when they took the figure to the Madda country, which is known for its beautiful women, they found your future wife, Bhadda Kapilani."

The senior monk shrugs his shoulders. "Who knew?" says Maha Kassapa.

"Bhadda was only sixteen at the time – four years younger than you were," says Ananda. "Her parents agreed to the marriage proposal, and the Brahmins couldn't wait to come back and inform your parents. They were thrilled when they heard the news."

"I understand, though, that your future wife also didn't want to get married," says Upali.

"It's true, she didn't. She wanted to live an ascetic life the same as I did – perhaps this is why our *kammic* ties from the past brought us together again in this lifetime," says Maha Kassapa.

"I heard one story of a past life the two of you shared – during the time of the former Buddha Vipassi.[4] You had been a poor Brahmin couple – so poor that you only had one upper garment to share between the two of you," says Ananda. "It seems that even though you were extremely poor, you didn't indulge yourselves in subjective, personal suffering. Both of you, one after the other, had listened to Buddha Vipassi preach a moving sermon, and you, Venerable Sir, wanted to offer his order of monks your upper garment, which was all you had. You hesitated at first because it was also your wife's only upper garment, but ultimately you gladly offered it to the monks."

"It was recorded that after you performed that tremendous act of generosity you shouted ecstatically, 'I have vanquished! I have vanquished!'" says Sopaka.

"The king, who had been listening to the Buddha Vipassi's sermon from behind a curtain, heard your shout of victory and inquired about you. After learning your story, he sent fine sets of garments to you and

The Father of the Sangha

your wife and he appointed you court chaplain, handsomely rewarding your spontaneous act of generosity," adds Bhaddiya.

"There are many accounts of lives that you and Bhadda shared, Maha Kassapa, and it seems that you were destined to share this last lifetime together as ascetics," comments Bakkula.

"It certainly worked out that way," replies Maha Kassapa, his eyes shining brightly.

"In another life, Venerable Sir, you were my father," says Anuruddha. "My three brothers were Gotama Buddha, Venerable Sariputta, and Venerable Maha Moggallana. All four of us wanted to become ascetics, and even though you and my mother resisted at first, you gave us your permission when you came to understand our true intentions. Later, my mother and you also renounced the world and became ascetics."

"It may be interesting to note for the record that the instance you just mentioned, Anuruddha, was only one of six times when Maha Kassapa was the Buddha's father in past lives. He was also his brother in two other lifetimes," adds Upali.

Ananda begins, "To continue with our story, while your parents were busy planning your wedding you wrote a letter to Bhadda explaining that your true desire was to become an ascetic and seek enlightenment. She also wrote you saying that she wanted the same thing for herself. The only thing is, your parents intercepted both of your letters and you never learned the truth until after the ceremony.

"Not wanting to dishonor your parents' pledges, you went ahead and married Bhadda Kapilani, not knowing that you both had the same ultimate intentions."

"Yes, but we never consummated our marriage," adds Maha Kassapa.

"You once told me that after the wedding you and Bhadda slept in the same bed, but each night you placed a garland of fragrant flowers between you to make sure you didn't yield to sensual desire. You loved one another deeply, and lived happily this way for years. As long as your parents were alive you didn't have to work and look after the family's estates. When they died, though, you and your wife took charge of managing the large property."

"I understand your situation rapidly began to change when you were inspecting the farms one day," says Maha Kaccayana knowingly.

Maha Kassapa nods, reflecting on the memory of that day forty-five years before.

"You saw, as if for the first time, birds feasting on worms and other small creatures after furrows had been plowed in the fields. You were horrified," says Ananda.

"All of a sudden it struck me that the source of my wealth was the destruction of innocent creatures," says Maha Kassapa. "I asked one of the farmers, 'Who will have to bear the consequences of all of those small deaths?' The farmer answered, 'I suppose you will, sir.' I went home and reflected on the *kammic* burden I was creating. I decided it was best if I gave all my wealth to my wife and renounced the world once and for all."

"Coincidentally, your wife had just had a similar experience watching the birds eating insects from your beds of drying sesame seeds," says Ananda. "She also came into contact with her *kammic* responsibility for those small violent deaths, and realized that she would have to endure countless more rebirths. When you told her of your intention to give her your wealth and become an ascetic she announced to you that her intention was exactly the same.

"So you had pale-yellow cloth and clay bowls brought to you from the marketplace, and you shaved each others' heads. You made a joint proclamation when you left your home: 'We dedicate our going forth to those who are arahants in the world!'" concludes Ananda.

"Apparently you slipped by your first village unnoticed," says Anuruddha. "But by the time you got to the second one you were recognized. Your laborers and their families started weeping, and they fell down prostrate before you and said, 'Oh, dear and noble ones! Why do you want to make us helpless orphans?'

"You answered by saying, 'It is because we have seen the world as a house on fire; therefore, we go forth into the life of renunciation.' You gave your serfs their freedom and continued on your way, leaving your former villagers in tears."

"I understand that your beautiful wife was walking a few steps behind you, as was the custom," says Bakkula. "But then you considered that this might be unseemly to others, and not setting a good example, so you told Bhadda that you needed to split up and go your separate ways."

"I'll never forget that moment as long as I live," says Maha Kassapa. "Bhadda looked at me with those beautiful eyes of hers and smiled with infinite understanding. She bowed gracefully and then circled around me three times. She said, 'Our close companionship and friendship that has lasted for an unfathomable amount of time comes to an end today. Please take the path to the right and I shall take the other road.'" Maha Kassapa is silent for a while as he recalls that pivotal moment in his life.

Ananda says, "Bhadda eventually found her way to the Buddha and heard his discourses at Jetavana monastery. As there was not yet an order for nuns, she took up residence with a group of female ascetics not far from Jetavana. When the Order of *Bhikkhunis* was established five years later she became ordained, and not long afterwards she attained arahantship."

Anuruddha adds, "I know it may be legend, but maybe not; however, it is said that when you and Bhadda went your separate ways the earth shook, and the Buddha perceived it. He said it meant that an outstanding disciple was on his way to him. The Lord then set out on the road himself and walked five miles toward Mahatittha, which is between Nalanda and Rajagaha. He went to meet the one who would become 'Foremost in Austerities.'[5] I think you should tell the story from this point yourself, Venerable Sir," says Anuruddha as he nods to the chairman with respect.

"Very well," agrees Maha Kassapa with a sigh. "On the road between Nalanda and Rajagaha the Buddha sat under a fig tree to wait for my arrival. When I approached the Lord and perceived his aura from a distance, I knew at once that I had found my master. Without wasting a moment I rushed toward him, fell at his feet and said, 'The Blessed One is my teacher; I am his disciple. Please give me permission to enter your order, Lord.'

"He looked down at me with the greatest compassion and granted my request by saying, 'O *Bhikkhu*.' Then he said three very important things to me, which pertained to my future involvement with the Sangha, and my training as a monk:

"He first said that I needed to take into consideration the different ages, backgrounds, abilities, strengths, and weaknesses of the variegated members of the Sangha before I drew my conclusions and advised them.

"Secondly, he said that whenever I listened to the Dhamma, that I should listen to it with eager ears, attend to it as a matter of vital concern, and apply my whole mind to comprehend it.

"Thirdly, he told me that I should always be mindful of my body and its senses, as well as my thoughts and my actions.

"After the Buddha gave me these admonishments we walked together toward the Bamboo Grove in Rajagaha. On the way the Buddha wanted to rest, so we stopped by the root of a tree. I folded my double robe in four and requested the Master to sit on it, saying that it would bring me much benefit for a very long time.

"The Master sat on my robe and said, 'Your robe of patched cloth is soft, Kassapa.'[6]

"Hearing this I replied, 'May the Blessed One accept this robe of patched cloth out of compassion for me.'

"The Master said, 'But Kassapa, can you wear these hempen, worn-out rag robes of mine?'

"Full of great joy I said, 'Certainly, Lord, I can wear the Blessed One's rough and worn-out rag robe. I will prize it above the whole world.'"

"You know, Maha Kassapa, that you are the only monk who ever exchanged robes with the Master. No ordinary human being would have been fit to have worn the Buddha's cast-off robe. I think it is safe to assume that there was some sort of special significance in this act," says Bhaddiya.

"The Buddha never said anything to me about any 'special significance.' At the time it just seemed like a natural and compassionate thing for him to do. After all, I was a newly-minted disciple that very day, and perhaps he acted spontaneously just to be kind to me. I don't give it any meaning at all, even though I am grateful that it happened," says Maha Kassapa.

"I think it showed two very important things, Venerable Sir: one to you, and one to the rest of us. For you, from that day forward you never deviated from your path of austerity, which made your life an example for all Sangha members," begins Anuruddha. "And for the rest of us, it was an act that indicated that the Buddha, after his passing, would transfer the mantle of Sangha leadership to you."

"You know very well that the Buddha named no successor upon his *parinibbana*. He said that the Dhamma and *Vinaya* would be our leaders, and I believed him. I *still* believe him," responds Maha Kassapa emphatically.

"The very fact that you organized and offered to chair this first council is a significant act of leadership, Venerable Sir," says Bhaddiya. "I understand very well the reasons why you called this council, and I don't think for a moment that you did it to show that you were the new king of the Sangha. I must say, though, that I am supremely happy that you are called 'Father of the Sangha' by many. I am also happy you have taken on the responsibility for making sure that both our Order and the Dhamma are preserved, and that all future generations will have the benefit of guidance from the Lord's life and wise teachings.

"One more thing should be noted here: you have seven of the thirty-two marks of a great being on your body, Maha Kassapa. The Buddha, of course, had all thirty-two. None of us here, or any of the other arahants, either alive or deceased, has or has had more than one or two. I think this is another indication that you are not only the chosen, but the fittest leader," concludes Bhaddiya.

Maha Kassapa sits with his head down and says nothing. He wonders why anyone should refer to such personal details regarding his physical body, and his modesty doesn't allow him to attach any significance to the marks whatsoever. His entire life he had never given them a single thought, even though much had been made of them by others ever since he was born.

Seeing his friend's acute embarrassment Ananda says, "If we may return to the story, brothers, I would like to say that it was only seven days after Maha Kassapa's ordination that he attained the goal he was striving for: arahantship. This is what you later told me yourself. 'For seven days, friend, I ate the alms food of the country as one unliberated; then on the eighth day the final knowledge of arahantship arose in me.'"

The members of the sub-committee pause to reflect on Maha Kassapa's day of ultimate day transformation, and remember their own as well.

"The Lord depended on you to preach the Dhamma to the Sangha members, Maha Kassapa. He even said, 'Exhort the monks, Kassapa. Give them a discourse on the Dhamma, Kassapa. Either I, Kassapa, or you, should exhort the monks or give them a discourse on the Dhamma.'[7] As you know, not every arahant has the ability to expound the Dhamma with skill and effectiveness the way you do," says Punna.

"You did tell me earlier, Ananda, that I should be prepared for accolades today. Accolades I could possibly accept, but comments like these enter into the area of the unseemly," says Maha Kassapa, shaking his head.

"Just take it all in stride, my dear friend; we only have this one opportunity for recollecting the events of the Lord's life. Who knows when – or if – we'll all be together again after this council is adjourned. Anyway, our meeting this evening is nearly over, and I'm sure you can handle the remaining compliments, if there are any," responds Ananda compassionately.

"Our venerable brother's reticence and modesty are as legendary as his inability to take criticism, and his penchant for an austere natural life in the woods," says Maha Kaccayana with a smile. "Even the Buddha couldn't convince him to be easier on himself and live in a comfortable monastery. However, I think we can spare him any further compliments this evening. After all, he is the chairman of the First Council, and we should grant him a bit of dignity."

"I'll choose to ignore that remark about 'inability to take criticism' and chalk it up to the inexperience and sensitive egos of the monks who started those rumors. I would also be grateful to all of you if we could close this session for the evening and retire to our meditations. It's been a long day, and I know, for me, a bit of a challenge," says Maha Kassapa, obviously wanting to end the discussion that had challenged his modesty to the limits.

"Before we close I would like to relate just one more story about Maha Kassapa, which I think should be included in our record," interjects Bakkula.

"If you must, Venerable Sir, then proceed," agrees the chairman reluctantly.

"Several years ago the Buddha and Maha Kassapa were making their alms round in a village not far from here. The physical likeness of the Lord's form and Maha Kassapa's has been commented on time and again. In fact, Maha Kassapa is only slightly shorter than the Master, and people often confused the two. On a couple of occasions even the celestial *devas* and *Brahmas* got them mixed up," begins Bakkula.

Maha Kassapa raises his eyebrows as he thinks back to the incident about to be described.

"Maha Kassapa led the Buddha down a street he had frequented many times. An elderly woman came out of her house, walked up to the Buddha, and put food into his bowl – ignoring Maha Kassapa.[8]

"Then, all of a sudden she looked up and stared at the Buddha – then stared at Maha Kassapa – and realized that she had put her food in the wrong bowl! Her intention was to offer alms to Maha Kassapa, not to anyone else. The old woman went up to the Buddha, put her hand in his sacred bowl, and withdrew the food she had offered him!" says Bakkula.

"What did the Buddha do – or say?" asks an incredulous Sopaka.

"The Lord just stood there, silent and composed as ever. His eyes were cast down in front of him, as usual. He didn't react at all," answers Bakkula, smiling.

"What did the woman do with the food she took out of the Master's bowl?" asks Maha Kaccayana.

"She walked over to Maha Kassapa and without a moment's hesitation put it in his bowl!" exclaims Bakkula. "Can you imagine how our modest, circumspect chairman must have felt?"

"That must have been a very uncomfortable moment for you, Venerable Sir," says Upali to the chairman.

"You have no idea!" exclaims Maha Kassapa, almost groaning.

The arahants in the cave chamber ponder what they themselves might have felt had it happened to them.

"Actually," says Maha Kassapa, "I was mostly concerned that that poor woman had created bad *kamma* for herself with her action. The Buddha simply looked at me and smiled. Then he led the way down the street to the next house, and allowed the householder who was waiting there to place food in his bowl. It was as if nothing untoward had ever happened, and he never spoke of it afterwards."

"What about the old woman? What did she do?" asks Anuruddha.

"After she put the food in my bowl she bowed to me with great respect and walked back into her house. She never knew she had performed such a great offence," responds Maha Kassapa, chuckling.

"I'm sure the Master would have said the woman was innocent since her intention was not to offend the Buddha; she didn't even know he *was* the Buddha. She only wanted to give food to our chairman," says Bakkula, laughing.

"I guess we could say that intentions and etiquette are separate issues, and it has never been the practice of the Sangha to criticize the bad manners of anyone – except for misbehaving monks," says Upali with a smile, "and I know you have criticized your share of those, honorable chairman."

Maha Kassapa smiles back at Upali with twinkling eyes.

"Anyway, it's a good story, and I thought it would make a nice finish to our talk this evening. I hope you don't mind too much, Venerable Sir," says Bakkula to the chairman.

"Not at all, my friend" responds Maha Kassapa good-naturedly.

After a moment's pause Maha Kassapa says, "I thank you all, not only for your participation in this important process, but also for your understanding of my stern, old-fashioned ways. I know you believe me when I say that ever since I met the Buddha forty-three years ago I have done my best to protect the Sangha, maintain the purity of the Dhamma, and live a life that would be a good example for others. If I have failed in any of these, I humbly ask your forgiveness," concludes Maha Kassapa with great humility.

"Forgiveness is not necessary, Venerable Sir. Your vast contribution will go down in history as incomparable beyond all measure," says Ananda. "Modesty, or no modesty, that is a fact."

"During the course of these proceedings I'm sure that a few of you will have your own chance to be exposed the way I was today. I wish you good luck in keeping *your* composure," says Maha Kassapa. "I also wish you all a good night, and a pleasant meditation."

The arahants pay their respects to their seniors and depart as silently as they had arrived.

Chapter 15
Return to Kapilavatthu

While enjoying an early morning walk, Maha Kassapa and Ananda pause for a few moments to watch the sunrise at the edge of the precipice just outside the western cave chambers. The clear morning sky is filled with the brilliant hues of the new day, and Maha Kassapa takes a deep breath.

"I'll be glad when I can sleep outside again, brother. I'm still not used to the confines of my cavern, with its damp stale air," says the chairman of the council. "The last watch of the night is the hardest for me. I find myself awaiting the pale announcement of the dawn, but it never comes in to dispel the darkness."

"We'll be on our way in a few months, dear friend, after the work of the council is completed. You'll never have to sleep in a cave again, I assure you," responds Ananda cheerfully.

Maha Kassapa takes a moment to reflect before continuing. "I'm looking forward to our sub-committee discussion today. I've decided to break the assembly at dusk so we can begin our Lord's journey to Kapilavatthu at twilight. I thought we might meet outdoors this evening – and enjoy the fresh air and full moon. What do you think?"

"I think that's an excellent idea, Venerable Sir. In fact, it's been my thought for quite some time that in the future all full moons should be occasions for remembering the Buddha, and for showing our gratitude for his liberating Dhamma. So many events in the Master's life took place on full moon days – including his arrival in Kapilavatthu; it's very fitting that we should have this part of the recollection under the watchful eye of the night," responds Ananda.

"I think there's still enough time for me to have a quick bath in the hot springs before council starts. If you'll excuse me, brother, I'll indulge this old body and meet you in the assembly hall in half an hour," says the chairman.

"Enjoy yourself, old friend. This will give me a few moments to organize my mind for today's discourses," replies Ananda.

Maha Kassapa quickly moves down the trail towards the hot springs. Ananda smiles as he watches the still-youthful figure of the eighty-three year-old chairman skillfully picking his way over the rocks to the oasis down below.

After the morning devotions Ananda stands at the podium and says, "Today in our sub-committee meeting we will revisit the momentous occasion when the Master journeyed for the first time to his home town of Kapilavatthu as the Fully Enlightened Buddha. Our Lord reminded us a number of times of the debt we all owe our parents. I will start this morning by reciting one of the discourses in which he makes this very clear. He begins:

> "'...Monks, one can never repay two persons, I declare. What two? Mother and father.
>
> "'Even if one should carry about his mother on one shoulder and his father on the other, and so doing should live a hundred years; and if he should support them, anointing them with unguents, kneading, bathing and rubbing their limbs, and they meanwhile should even void their excrement upon him, even so could he not repay his parents. Moreover, monks, if he should establish his parents in supreme authority, in the absolute rule over this mighty earth abounding in the seven treasures, not even thus could he repay his parents. What is the cause of that? Monks, parents do much for their children: they bring them up, they nourish them, and they introduce them to the world.'[1]"

Ananda continues reciting to the end of the *sutta*, and each and every arahant in the assembly offers a silent paean of gratitude to the mother and father who brought him into the world. Many of them share the same thought: of the countless parents they have had throughout the limitless span of their past lives, the mother and father of this lifetime was their last.

Later, Maha Kassapa sounds the gong at the very moment the sun sinks below the horizon. The arahants make their way from the assembly hall, some of them going directly to their cave chambers to meditate.

A few of them take a stroll through the neighboring forest; and still others fold their robes and sit to watch the symphony of sunset colors change from orange to red to purple, and finally to violet as the sky prepares itself to receive the full moon.

The arahants on the sub-committee walk to the place Maha Kassapa has selected; it has a view of the valley below, and an unobstructed vista of the open darkening sky. Mats have already been prepared for them, and the memory monks are seated, waiting patiently in meditation. One by one the fully-awakened ones gather and take their places: the cousins Ananda, Anuruddha and Bhaddiya; and also Bakkula, Punna, Maha Kaccayana, Upali and Sopaka.

Maha Kassapa is the last one to arrive. He apologizes for keeping everyone waiting, and explains that he had been attending to some last minute arrangements for the following day's *dana* ceremony. He seats himself in the lotus posture and begins, "This evening we will recount one of the most important chapters in the life of our Lord: his triumphal return to Kapilavatthu. The three cousins will play key eye-witness roles in relating the story, I'm sure. If any of you have accolades for the three of them, then this might be the appropriate place to give them." The sub-committee members laugh at this remark, remembering the previous day's discussion that was laced with colorful accolades for the chairman.

"Ananda, why don't you begin by telling us about the king and his emissaries," suggests Maha Kassapa.

"First of all, dear friend, on behalf of my fellow committee members I would like to thank you for selecting this perfect meeting place for our discussion tonight. We will all enjoy the rising of the full moon while reflecting on the early days of the rising *Sasana*. The teachings of the Buddha and its radiant rays of compassion have penetrated the farthest reaches of space, and have softened even the hardest of hearts in the darkest of places," says Ananda in a voice that communicates both his joy and his immense gratitude for the present moment.

Maha Kassapa smiles warmly at his old companion saying, "If the world could attain to even one tenth of the pure compassion in your heart, Venerable Sir, then there would never be another conflict of any kind."

The other arahants close their eyes and send Ananda their silent blessings as he begins to speak.

"The Buddha had been residing at the Veluvana Monastery here in Rajagaha, administering the elixir of Dhamma to the many humans, *devas*, and *Brahmas* that came daily into his presence. Many of the humans had taken refuge in the Triple Gem, and many had become *sotapannas, sakadagamis, anagamis,* and arahants. Many fine sons from the good families of Magadha and Anga had been granted ordination in the Sangha; it was as if a great festival of emancipation was being held every day.

"King Suddhodana heard the news that his son had become the Fully Enlightened Buddha, and that he was living and teaching at Veluvana, liberating multitudes by the clarity of his Dhamma," says Ananda.

Anuruddha speaks, "I was with the king and queen when the ambassador from King Bimbisara of Magadha came to call on them, telling them about Prince Siddhartha's transformation. The ambassador had personally been to see the Lord at Veluvana on his last visit to Rajagaha, and had heard him teach the Dhamma. It was amazing for us to hear his account of the Buddha, his teaching, and the spiritual realizations that were spontaneously taking place in his presence.

"I asked the ambassador directly, 'Are you sure this is *our* Prince Siddhartha? My cousin?'

"He said, 'Absolutely. If you recall, I met him here at court about ten years ago. How could I forget a prince of his stature? He was an imposing figure then, but now, words cannot express the aura emanating from his divine presence.'

"King Suddhodana just sat there speechless for a few moments before he said very slowly and seriously, 'I must see my son again before I die.' He turned to one of his most trusted ministers and said, 'Go to Rajagaha and invite the prince to come home. Tell him his father's greatest wish is to see him, and to pay homage to him.' Queen Mahapajapati also conveyed her wishes to see her stepson, and they urged the minister to proceed to Veluvana without delay," concludes Anuruddha.

Ananda continues, "The minister departed that very night on horseback with a large number of retainers and attendants. We all waited for news, and after several weeks had passed with still no report, the king sent another minister, who also traveled with a large entourage. One after another he kept sending them, a total of nine ministers, but none of them ever sent back word or returned home."

"What was happening, as we all know, was that the ministers and their attendants would arrive and very quickly realize the benefits of the Buddha's teachings. Afterwards they would seek ordination and attain arahantship," says Anuruddha. "At that point the ministers would forget about their householder duty to the king and remain with the Lord in the bliss of enlightenment. Eventually, the king heard the news about all of his emissaries renouncing the world and joining his son, and he decided to send Minister Kaludayi, his last hope. After all, nine emissaries and all of their attendants had been sent to invite the Buddha home, but none ever came back. The king was desperate."

Ananda says, "Kaludayi was born on the same day as the Buddha, and they had been intimate friends since they were infants. He was an administrative official of the court, and one of the closest associates of the royal family. Like everyone else he had heard the fantastic stories of the previous emissaries and their entire retinues attaining arahantship, and he had become very excited about seeing his old friend who was now the Buddha. He wanted to see the Lord for himself because he, too, hoped he might also have a chance for becoming enlightened.

"Kaludayi said to the king, 'Your majesty, I will go and deliver your message to the prince, but first I must ask your permission to enter monkhood.'

"The king was horrified to hear such a request from the one he regarded as his last hope. He said, 'My dear son Kaludayi, whether you enter monkhood or not, I implore you to first do your utmost to convey my message to my son. You must convince him to come and see me before I die; my only desire is to pay homage to him.'

"Kaludayi agreed, and within a day he left Kapilavatthu for Rajagaha with many retainers and attendants," continues Ananda.

"When he arrived at Veluvana Monastery the Buddha was teaching a large number of people," says Anuruddha. "Kaludayi and his group stayed way in the back of the crowd, listening intently. At the end of the Lord's discourse, Kaludayi and each and every one of his retainers requested ordination from the Buddha."

Ananda says, "A week before the full moon day of March, arahant Kaludayi approached the Buddha and addressed him with sixty verses he had composed.[2] He pleaded with him to make a visit to the royal city of Kapilavatthu to grant his father's wish. The sixty verses extolled everything Kaludayi could think of to try to entice the Buddha to make the journey: the pleasant time for travel, the plants, fruits, peacocks, elephants, scenic vistas, and all sorts of other attractions along the road that he thought might interest the Lord.

"'Will you come to Kapilavatthu, Lord?' asked Kaludayi.

"The Buddha responded by saying, 'Of course, friend Kaludayi, I will go to visit my parents. You and I were raised with the tradition that the one thing most worthy of worship on this entire earth is our parents. I may be the Fully Enlightened Buddha, but I am still my father's son. He and the queen were my first teachers, my *pubbacariya*, and I will go to honor them as a good son should.'"

Anuruddha says, "Kaludayi was grateful for the Master's positive response, and a few days later the Buddha started out for Kapilavatthu with a large company of arahants. Walking three miles each day, the journey took about eight and a half weeks. Kaludayi thought he should proceed ahead to let the king know the Buddha was on his way, so with a few dozen retainers, now all arahants, he traveled quickly to Kapilavatthu."

"Sariputta and Maha Moggallana had been on a teaching excursion in another city with a group of arahants," interjects Bhaddiya. "Maha Moggallana saw with his divine eye that the Buddha had departed for Kapilavatthu. Wanting to be there in person to witness the Lord's arrival, they immediately set out for the Buddha's home town by another road."

"The king was overjoyed to see Venerable Kaludayi when he arrived, and had him sit on his royal throne while he personally served him his noon meal," begins Ananda.

"The king asked, 'Beloved Kaludayi, where is the Buddha?'

"Kaludayi replied that he was on his way in the company of many arahants and would arrive in a few weeks.

"The now very happy king said, 'Please go to my son and tell him that I anxiously await his arrival. I will make all the necessary arrangements.'

"Kaludayi started out to rejoin the Buddha on the following day. When he reached the Lord he informed him of his father's joy, and the Lord smiled. After a long, two-month journey the Buddha and his arahants finally arrived in Kapilavatthu on the full moon day of Vesakha."

"Members of the Sakyan clan had decided that Nigrodha Park would be the ideal place to accommodate the returning prince and his followers," adds Bhaddiya. "They organized a welcoming parade for the Buddha, which began with a procession of royal children. The princes and princesses came next in their full ceremonial dress; the rest of the Sakyan clan followed, each person holding offerings of flowers and aromatic powder. They proceeded with great dignity and fanfare to Nigrodha Park."

Ananda continues by saying, "Prince Nanda and Princess Sundarinanda, the Buddha's half brother and sister, were excited and overjoyed. Anuruddha, Bhaddiya, and I were in the procession with them, and we could hardly wait to see our beloved kinsman."

"I haven't heard any mention yet of Princess Yasodhara. Where was she during this event?" asks Sopaka.

"For seven years she had been a recluse," replies Anuruddha. "On the day the Buddha arrived she felt that she was too emotionally volatile, and she didn't want to take the chance of breaking down in front of everyone. She decided that she would wait until she could greet the Buddha in a more private setting."

The arahants consider this statement for a moment, pausing to reflect on the princesses' state of mind during that time.

Ananda continues, "I regret to say that our senior Sakyan family members, including my own, being proud and somewhat haughty, thought it was beneath them to bestow great honors on a junior member of the clan. When it was time for salutations, they told the younger members to go forward and pay homage to the prince while they stayed in the back of the crowd. Devadatta was in agreement with them so he also stayed back with the elders. When the Buddha saw this arrangement he thought to himself, 'My relatives have grown old in years for nothing; they do not pay reverence to the *Tathagata*. They are conceited and totally ignorant of the real nature of a Fully-Enlightened Buddha.'

"It was very rare for the Master to ever display of his supernormal powers, but in this instance he deemed it not only fitting, but necessary to demonstrate the might and power of the Buddha for his clansmen.

"To dramatically reveal his new and exalted status, in seconds he created a bridge-like walkway in the sky, which was studded with precious gems of all colors. He walked back and forth over this bridge preaching the doctrine to the crowd below. Then he raised his voice and declared that the ten thousand world systems be illuminated. Instantly, to the delight of both *devas* and *Brahmas*, the universe was filled with blazing light," concludes Ananda.

"Suddenly water and fire began to simultaneously pour out of twelve parts of his body; and a shower of particles from the Buddha's feet rained down on the heads of Sakyan royalty," relates Anuruddha. "It was a strange and wonderful spectacle that I will never forget as long as I live. King Suddhodana was the first to go forward and worship the Buddha. He bowed and addressed him, 'Glorious, exalted son, on the day you were born I paid homage to you when you placed your feet on the head of my guru, Asitadevala. Several years later at the plowing ceremony I paid homage to you when I witnessed your meditation under the rose apple tree. This will be the third occasion on which I pay homage to you – this time as the Fully-Enlightened Buddha.'"

Ananda says, "The king knelt before his son and placed his head on the ground in front of him. Each and every member of the Sakyan clan had no choice but to follow suit – including me, Anuruddha, Bhaddiya, and of course Devadatta, who, begrudgingly was the very last to do so. Channa was at the back of the crowd that day, too, and he was overjoyed to see his master again. He fell to his knees and cried tears of joy."

"The crowd eventually disbursed, and none of the Sakyan family members had extended an invitation to the Buddha and his arahants for the next day's meal," says Bhaddiya. "The king simply took it for granted that his son would come to the royal palace; after all, it was his home, and Suddhonana, too, didn't think to formally invite him. I know that I, for one, simply assumed that the Lord would visit the palace and take his meal, so I don't blame the king."

"The next day the Buddha and his arahants went into the city of Kapilavatthu for their alms collection," begins Ananda. "It was shocking that no one went forward to receive him. The Buddha wondered whether the Buddhas of the past, when they visited their home towns, had started with the rich families and then proceeded on to the poor – or if they had simply gone from door to door in the order in which they passed. He realized that it was the latter, so he continued in this tradition. The townspeople were horrified to see their former Crown Prince begging from house to house. They watched him from the balconies of their multi-storied mansions in a state of total disbelief.

"King Suddhodana heard the news that the Buddha had entered the city and was collecting alms; he was overcome by despair. He rushed to the palace gate where his chariot was waiting, and he sped to the place where the Buddha was passing. When he got there he dismounted, walked over to his son and said, 'Why do you want to slight me, your father? Why are you begging for food? Can't I give food to you and all these monks?'

"The Buddha told his father, 'This is the practice of our lineage, O Great King.'

"Embarrassed and hurt, the king retorted, 'Isn't our lineage the royal clan of Sakyas of the warrior caste? Not one member of that lineage has ever begged for food.'

"The Buddha explained, 'Your lineage is the royal lineage, O Great King. But when I renounced the world seven years ago I also renounced that lineage and the caste to which it belongs. Ours is the lineage of the Buddhas, and we have no caste. All of the Buddhas before me begged for their food, and thus do I.'

"Then the Buddha uttered the following stanza:

"'Arise! Be not negligent! Lead a righteous life.
The righteous live happily both in this world and in the next.'[3]

"At the conclusion of this stanza the king attained *sotapanna*," concludes Ananda. "I was standing behind the king and witnessed his transformation with my own eyes. Anuruddha and Bhaddiya were next to me."

"After his attainment of *sotapanna*, King Suddhodana took the alms bowl from the hands of the Buddha and said, 'Please come with your monks to the palace and allow me to serve you your meal; we have been expecting you,'" adds Bhaddiya. "The Buddha's silence indicated his consent, and he led the way to the palace followed by his saffron-robed Sangha members."

Ananda speaks, "Princess Yasodhara was watching from the balcony of her private chamber as the Lord entered the palace courtyard. Prince Rahula was with her and she pointed to the Buddha, uttering the following verses:

> "'His red sacred feet are marked with excellent wheels;
> His long heels are decked with marks;
> His feet are adorned with cowries and parasol.
> Thus is your father, lion of men.
>
> "'Delicate and noble Sakyan prince,
> His body is full of marks,
> A hero among men, intent on the welfare of the world.
> Thus is your father, lion of men.
>
> "'Like the full moon is his face;
> Dear to gods and men, he is like an elephant among men,
> His gait graceful as an elephant of noble breed.
> Thus is your father, lion of men.
>
> "'Of noble lineage, sprung from the warrior caste,
> His feet honored by gods and men;
> His mind is well established in morality and concentration.
> Thus is your father, lion of men.
>
> "'Long and prominent is his well-formed nose;
> Like a heifer, his eyes are extremely blue,
> Like a rainbow are his deep blue-black eyebrows.
> Thus is your father, lion of men.
>
> "'Round and smooth is his well-formed neck;
> His jaw like that of a lion, his body, like the king of beasts,
> His beautiful skin of bright golden color.
> Thus is your father, lion of men.
>
> "'Soft and deep is his sweet voice,
> His tongue red as vermillion;
> His white teeth are twenty in each row.
> Thus is your father, lion of men.

"'Like the color of kohl is his deep blue-black hair,
Like a polished golden plate his forehead;
White as the morning star his beautiful tuft.
Thus is your father, lion of men.

"'Just as the moon crosses the sky,
Surrounded by a multitude of stars,
The Lord of Monks is accompanied by his disciples.
Thus is your father, lion of men.'[4]

"Prince Rahula recounted these verses to me later, and I committed them to memory," says Ananda.

"I'm sure that one of these days, people will often be reciting this beautiful poem to their children," comments Maha Kassapa.

Bhaddiya continues, "We all entered the great hall, and King Suddhodana escorted the Buddha to the seat of honor. The monks were then seated in pre-arranged places. When everyone was settled the Buddha again uttered the following stanza:

"'Lead a righteous life; lead not a corrupt life.
The righteous live happily both in this world and in the next.'[5]

"Upon hearing this verse King Suddhodana attained *sakadagami*, while Queen Mahapajapati attained *sotapanna*."

Anuruddha adds, "Then, with his own hand, the king began to serve his son the Buddha. Queen Mahapajapati also participated in serving the meal. She could barely disguise her intense feelings of joy and pride at having her beloved Siddhartha, her Fully-Enlightened stepson, in their presence again. All of the family members, including myself, were overcome with emotion. When the food offering was over everyone in the palace, except for Princess Yasodhara, went to the feet of the Buddha and paid their respects."

"The princess didn't take part in the king's first *dana* ceremony for the Lord?" asks Sopaka with a look of surprise.

"No, she didn't," answers Bhaddiya. "Her female attendants implored her to leave her chamber and come down for the food offering, but she refused. She said to them, 'If I have any virtue, let the Noble One himself come here. I will make my obeisance to him then, not before.'"

"Please don't judge the princess harshly, my brothers," begins Ananda. "You must understand her fragile state of mind on that day. She hadn't seen her former husband since Prince Rahula was four months old, and even though she resided in a royal palace she had been living a very austere life. She chose to live the same life her beloved prince was living after he renounced the world. There was never any question in regards to her virtue. She simply needed some time to get used to the fact that her beloved Siddhartha was now a Universal Buddha.

"I spent a lot of time with her prior to the Buddha's arrival, and we talked about how she might react during their first meeting. She honestly didn't know how she was supposed to behave, and she couldn't decide whether to deck herself out in jewels and royal finery – or keep to her austere way of life and stay in the background. She knew that all eyes would be upon her if she made a public appearance, and she just couldn't bear the scrutiny."

"After everyone paid their respects," begins Bhaddiya, "the Buddha said, 'Since this is the first reunion with my family in seven years I would like to commemorate it by offering Five Precepts to follow so you can lead wholesome, virtuous lives. In the future, whenever you gather to perform devotions to the Buddha, the Dhamma, and the Sangha, repeat these precepts in remembrance of this day:

"'The first is: I undertake the precept to refrain from killing; I will live my life for the benefit of all living beings.

"'The second is: I undertake the precept to refrain from stealing; I will be generous with all, and always happy to share.

"'The third is: I undertake the precept to refrain from sexual misconduct; I will protect the body, caring for it in all ways.

"'The fourth is: I undertake the precept to refrain from lying; I will speak the truth, gently, and behave in an honorable way at all times.

"'The fifth is: I undertake the precept to refrain from using intoxicants; I will always keep the mind clear and clean.'

"All of us in the grand hall repeated these precepts, one after the other, when they were spoken by the Lord," says Bhaddiya. "Ever since that day we begin each and every one of our devotional services in this manner."

"The Buddha rose from his seat and handed his alms bowl to his father, the king," continues Ananda. "With Sariputta and Maha Moggallana following, he led the way up the grand staircase to Princess Yasodhara's private apartments. He turned to King Suddhodana and the rest of us and said, 'Let no one utter any word to hinder or restrain Princess Yasodhara while she is paying homage to me. Let her continue as long as she wants.'

"He entered her room and seated himself on a silk-covered dais that had been prepared for him. A moment later, Princess Yasodhara rushed into the room. She immediately fell to the ground and grabbed both of the Lord's feet with her hands. With all of her strength she held them tightly in her arms, and pressed her forehead to them again and again. She continued worshiping the Master's feet to her heart's content, and it seemed like nearly half an hour passed before she was done. The princess and I were very close friends, and I was touched to the core by her devotion and great love.

"The king commended the princess to the Buddha by saying that her love for him had been continuous, and her virtue and loyalty were extraordinary. 'Out of respect for you she gave up what you gave up, my son, and she refused any overtures toward her, remaining unblemished and free from lust of any kind.'

"The Buddha told his father that he was not the least bit surprised that Yasodhara, mother of Rahula, had maintained her loyalty and dignity. He said that she had also been loyal and devoted to him during many previous rebirths, and as an example he told the *Candakinnara Jataka*[6] parable. He commented that Yasodhara had ripened and matured in wisdom, and that she was perfectly capable of protecting herself.'

"The Lord looked upon his former wife with great compassion; then he smiled at her and left her chamber without another word. He was followed by his Chief Disciples and the other Sangha members who had accompanied him, and they returned on foot to Nigrodha monastery," concludes Ananda.

Maha Kassapa stands and says, "I know that we all are enjoying the full moon and the silver vista of the valley. I propose that during the next full moon we gather at this same spot and have our discussion just as we have done tonight."

"That is an excellent suggestion," responds Maha Kaccayana, "because I know that as we proceed with our story we will encounter the full moon motif again and again. As you said earlier, Ananda, it is an excellent way to remember the radiant light of the Dhamma."

"The full moon is now approaching the eastern horizon, which means that dawn is not far away. Let us adjourn now for quiet time in solitude before the council convenes again," says Maha Kassapa. "I see that you three cousins have escaped a barrage of accolades this evening. Perhaps those will come later," he adds good-naturedly.

The three cousins smile at one another. One by one the arahants walk silently toward the cave entrances. Each one is reflecting on the story they have just recollected of the Buddha's triumphal return to Kapilavatthu; the impact this event would have on the hearts and minds of his family was yet to be told.

Chapter 16
Nanda and Rahula

The following morning after Ananda recites several more discourses and other teachings, Maha Kassapa approaches the podium and makes an announcement:

"Many of our arahant brothers from Varanasi arrived here last night and are encamped in the forest below; they have made a pilgrimage to the council to pay their respects to the senior Sangha members. Recognizing the important work being done here they wish to demonstrate their support for our endeavors. King Ajatasattu and Queen Vajira are officiating today over a special *dana* ceremony in the glade of banyan trees by the stream. I suggest that we break now so we have ample time to get down the hill and greet our esteemed guests before the meal."

When the arahants begin leaving the assembly hall, Maha Kassapa walks up to Ananda and says, "This is why I was late for our subcommittee meeting last night. I had to meet with the king's ministers to go over arrangements for this luncheon."

As they walk down the hill they see hundreds of royal attendants and servants scurrying about preparing for the *dana* ceremony. Tents of various colors have been erected in the center of the glade, and rush mats are spread beneath them in dozens of neat rows. There is a fresh banana leaf in front of each mat, which will serve as the plate for the food offerings. A clay water cup is placed upside down in the center of each leaf. Three fragrant jasmine blossoms, signifying the Triple Gem, are carefully arranged on the right side of each cup. Flowers of varying hues are in scores of baskets hanging from the tent poles, and dozens of others are interspersed around and between the rows of mats and banana leaves.

While descending the hill the senior *bhikkhus* trail behind Maha Kassapa and Ananda. The many arahants who arrived the night before are waiting to receive them in two long queues. As Maha Kassapa, Ananda, and the most senior *bhikkhus* make their way between the queues of arahants, the pilgrims bow before them and touch their feet.

The king and queen have made sure that that the dining area is lovely to the eye and pleasing to the spirit. The queen is particular about small details, and she herself is hurrying about with her female attendants. She is adjusting a flower here, a banana leaf there, checking the appearance of the serving staff, and seeing to the numerous other components of the *dana* ceremony that she wishes to be perfect.

She signals the king when she is satisfied that all is ready. He approaches Maha Kassapa, Punna, and Ananda and says, "May I escort you to your seats, Venerable Sirs."

The three senior monks nod and follow their host to their seats in front. Behind them the rest of the arahants file in and take their seats according to seniority. The fragrance of the profusion of flowers is almost overwhelming. Maha Kassapa places his hands together in front of him and begins to chant. The other arahants follow suit, and the king and queen stand with their eyes closed, basking in the energy generated by the rhythmic, lyrical, cadences.

Later, when the meal is over and the last blessing has been chanted, Maha Kassapa stands to indicate that it is time to leave. The senior monks follow his lead, as do the rest of the monks behind them. Single file they pass by the king and queen to express their thanks. Ananda says to the queen, "You created a truly beautiful experience for us today, Your Majesty. The ceremony was a work of art in every respect."

The queen bows low to show her appreciation for the revered monk's praise, and says, "It has been a great honor to serve you and your esteemed Sangha members, Venerable Sir. The brethren of the Buddha are always so dignified and refined in their eating habits; and it always amazes me how so many people can eat their meal at the same time and yet it is so quiet. A few weeks ago the king and I served a ceremonial meal to a group of Brahmin priests, and they were so uncircumspect in their habits – so much talking, smacking of lips, licking of hands. The Buddha's Sangha members are quite different."

Upali says, "The Buddha gave us very specific instructions for eating that are all recorded in the *Vinaya*. There are actually thirty disciplinary rules for taking food, including being silent while doing so. They include things like not licking the hands, smacking the lips, taking too much in one mouthful, and so forth. The Master wanted the dignity and decorum of the Sangha members to always be beyond reproach."[1]

The queen puts her hands together and bows low in appreciation for Upali's explanation.

The queue of arahants proceeds back to the assembly hall where there will be another session that will last until evening. The arahants who made a pilgrimage to the council bid their farewells and begin their journey back to Varanasi.

Later, in Maha Kassapa's cave chamber, the arahants assemble to continue recollecting the life of the Master.

Ananda says, "I believe this evening it is time to recount the story of Prince Nanda, the Buddha's half-brother. He was present during the ceremonial procession upon the Buddha's arrival in Kapilavatthu. He was also present at the alms-giving when the Lord came to the palace – as was his sister, Princess Sundarinanda. He was anxious to have some private time with his brother, but because he was busy with a host of rather momentous personal events, he didn't have an opportunity to visit Nigrodha Park."

"Three days after the Buddha's arrival," begins Anuruddha, "King Suddhodana performed the ceremonial rites and rituals for Prince Nanda that involved five auspicious, interrelated ceremonial occasions in his honor: the ceremony of uncoiling his youthful hair and styling it to befit the heir to the throne; the ceremony of investiture and coronation as Crown Prince; the ceremony of bestowing a residential palace upon him; the marriage ceremony to Princess Janapada Kalyani; and the ceremony of erecting the royal white umbrella of the Crown Prince."

"We were all involved in these ceremonies, but the Buddha did not attend," continues Ananda. "Afterwards Prince Nanda hosted a *dana* ceremony for the Master and all of his arahants at his new palace. When the meal was completed the Buddha preached a sermon and rose to leave. He handed Nanda his bowl, and led the way out of the palace.

"Prince Nanda had great respect for his elder brother, but he didn't know what to do with the alms bowl. He told me later that he wanted to ask the Buddha to take it back, but somehow he wasn't able to. So he just kept following him, carrying it. At any moment he expected the Lord to turn around and ask for his bowl, but he just continued walking, saying nothing."

Bhaddiya begins, "Nanda's bride was informed by her maids that the Buddha was taking her new husband away, so she called out to Prince Nanda from her balcony and said, 'Your Highness, please come back quickly!' This appeal weighed heavily upon the prince's heart because he cared deeply for his new bride," Bhaddiya pauses for a moment and then adds, "The prince, as we all know, was very attached to the company of females."

The arahants smile when they hear this last statement made by the prince's cousin. They all knew that previously Bhaddiya had also enjoyed the company of many women.

Ananda smiles and says, "When they reached Nigrodha Park the Buddha turned to Nanda, who was still holding the bowl, and said, 'Would you like to receive ordination and become a monk?'

"Prince Nanda was completely caught by surprise. Out of respect, and not able to express his unwillingness to become a *bhikkhu*, Nanda said, 'Very well, Exalted brother, I will receive ordination.'

"The Buddha wasted no time and ordained Prince Nanda on the spot," concludes Ananda.

"That ordination must have created quite a stir in the palace," comments Maha Kaccayana.

"That is an understatement, Venerable Sir," says Bhaddiya. "The king was absolutely devastated – as was Queen Mahapajapati, Nanda's mother. It had taken the king years to get over his eldest son's renunciation, and now the same fate had befallen his second son! He was beside himself with grief, and couldn't help but be somewhat angry with the Buddha, even though he had attained the spiritual state of *sakadagami*."

"We all remember, my brothers, that at the *sakadagami* stage anger is not yet completely extinguished," comments Upali. The other arahants nod their agreement.

"Prince Nanda's new bride was the one who was really upset. She was abandoned on her wedding day!" exclaims Anuruddha. "She didn't have the spiritual understanding of a *sotapanna*, so she took the news very badly. I heard that she was inconsolable for months and went into a severe depression."

"The furor over Nanda's ordination was nothing compared to what came next, I'm sure," says Bakkula, who had been silent until now.

"You are definitely right about that," answers Anuruddha. "Four days later the Buddha went with all of his arahants for the mid-day meal at his father's palace. Princess Yasodhara was present on that occasion, as was her son, Prince Rahula. He hadn't yet been officially reintroduced to his father, so the princess had said to him, 'My darling son, look at that gracious *bhikkhu* who is attended by so many arahants. He is your father. Before he renounced the world there were four pots of gold that were always replenished, no matter how much was removed. They disappeared at the very moment of his renunciation. Go, approach your father, Rahula, and ask him for your inheritance.'

"The shy young boy of seven approached the Buddha, and feeling the warmth of his father's love, he said, 'O Venerable One, it feels good to be near you. Even your shadow is pleasing to me.' Without any prompting Rahula sat down next to his father who looked at him with great affection while he finished his meal. Afterwards, the Buddha preached a discourse on the merits of providing alms food, and then he rose from his seat and began to walk from the great hall."

Ananda says, "Young Rahula stood up and started following his father, who had so far not said a word to him. Then the boy said, 'O Venerable One, please give me my inheritance.' The Buddha just looked at him, smiling. I was there that day, as usual, and watched along with everyone else as the young prince followed the Buddha from the palace. We all got up from our seats and continued watching that amazing procession. The Lord led the way with the small boy at his side who continued to say, 'O Venerable One, please give me my inheritance.' He said this not in the annoying, whining manner of a child, but in the manner of a young prince with confidence, asking his father for his due."

"No one stopped the boy from following the Buddha, and the Lord never asked him to return home," begins Bhaddiya. "So they just continued walking all the way back to Nigrodha Park. I might also mention that no one from the palace came after the boy to try to dissuade him from following the Lord. I don't think anyone would have dared. They were probably in a state of shock as they watched the surrealistic father-son reunion unfolding right in front of them."

Ananda says, "Years later the Lord told me that when Rahula asked him for his inheritance he knew that the thought of worldly wealth had been planted in the child's mind. Instead, he decided to give his son the spiritual inheritance of the noble ones, which were the seven treasures: faith, moral conduct, self-respect, self-preservation, education, selfless generosity, and wisdom.[2]

"When they were back at Nigrodha Park the Buddha turned to Sariputta and said, 'Chief Disciple, Prince Rahula has come to ask for his inheritance. You may ordain him.'

"'How am I to ordain him, Reverend Sir?' asked Sariputta, taken completely by surprise by the Lord's request.

"'You will be his preceptor, and Maha Moggallana will be his instructor. Give him the Three Refuges and train him as a *samanera*, or novice in the Order,' was the Buddha's reply.

"So it came to pass that Prince Rahula became *Samanera* Rahula; actually, he was the *first samanera*. He would not be granted higher ordination until he was twenty years of age. In the meantime, the young prince was given to the two Chief Disciples to train and instruct, and the boy took to it instantly," concludes Ananda.

"He enjoyed being taught so much that he earned himself tremendous respect as the one called 'greatest in obedience and discipline,'" says Upali.

"It didn't take long before news of Rahula's extraordinary ordination reached the palace," adds Anuruddha. "When Yasodhara heard of it she shut herself up in her room for several days. She had been so attached to the young boy that she couldn't bear to be away from him even for a few hours. You can imagine how the poor woman felt."

"The princess's reaction, however, was nothing compared to King Suddhodana's. I'm sure it would have been much worse if he hadn't been a *sakadagami*, but all the same it nearly broke his heart. He suffered physical agony along with severe emotional stress," says Bhaddiya.

"His last remaining hope was his grandson if his dream for an heir who would become a Universal Monarch was to be realized," begins Ananda. "Now that this was impossible, the continuity of his Sakyan line was highly doubtful. He could endure the pain no longer, so he went to see the Buddha. After paying him homage he addressed his son by saying, 'Most Glorious Buddha, my royal son, I would request a favor from you.'

"The Buddha answered, 'O Royal Father, the Fully Enlightened Buddhas of the past granted favors to their parents. What is your wish?'

"The king replied, 'Most revered son, when you renounced the world I suffered immense sorrow, as I did again just four days ago when my other son Nanda became a monk. Please understand that this love a father has for a son pierces through the skin. Then it cuts through the flesh, veins, bones, and marrow. The favor I request, therefore, is that Noble Ones would refuse to ordain a son who doesn't have the permission of his parents.'" Ananda lowers his head as he finishes reciting the king's statement. For a moment he relives the agony suffered by his beloved uncle.

"The Buddha didn't answer his father at that time," says Upali. "He remained silent as the king bowed before him and took his leave. Later, in consideration of King Suddhodana's request, he made a proclamation for the *Vinaya*: '*Bhikkhus*, a child who doesn't have the consent of both parents should not be given admission or ordination into the Order. Whoever should let such a person receive admission or ordination has committed an offense of wrong-doing.'"[3]

"Not long after this incident the Buddha and his arahants went again to the king's palace for their daily alms meal," begins Ananda. "The king shared a story with the Buddha, saying, 'Most Glorious son, when you were arduously engaged in practicing austerities, messengers I had sent to keep an eye on you came back and told me that you had died of starvation.'

"The Buddha said, 'Royal father, did you believe what your messengers told you?'

"The king replied, 'I did not. I rejected their words and told them that it is impossible for my son to die until he first attains *Nibbana*.'

"The Buddha then explained how the king, in a previous life, had been chieftain of the Maha Dhammapala village. He had rejected the words of a famous teacher named Disapamokkha when this man told him that his son, young Dhammapala, was dead.

"The Buddha said to the king, 'Disapamokkha even showed you bones that were supposedly evidence of his death. You refuted the teacher by telling him that in your clan no one died while still young. So at this late stage of your worldly existences, my royal father, you certainly would not believe the words of mere messengers.' After this explanation the king requested that the Buddha tell him more of this story, so the Lord recounted the *Maha Dhammapala Jataka*.[4]

"When the Buddha finished his *Jataka* story the king attained the lofty spiritual state of *anagami*, and was firmly established as one who would not return to this world," concludes Ananda. "Having reached this stage he was finally free from all anger, and could accept the realities of life that he had so resisted and had caused him so much pain."

"This Dhamma contains within it the power to heal and transform," reflects Punna. "The Dhamma can be applied by anyone to every conditioned situation no matter how negative or painful. Growth in the Dhamma comes as a result of the acceptance of impermanence, and seeing things clearly as they are." The arahants nod their agreement to this wise comment by their senior member.

Ananda says, "I might mention that during this first visit to Kapilavatthu, Nigrodha Park was gifted by the king to the Buddha and his Sangha for a monastery. Bhaddiya, I think that it was also during this visit that the Buddha visited your elegant mother, Princess Kaligodha, and spoke a discourse to her."

"And immediately afterwards she attained the state of *sotapanna*," responds Bhaddiya, smiling.

Ananda nods and begins, "In regards to Rahula, from the very beginning the Lord took a great interest in the training and education of his son, and he sometimes instructed him himself. Rahula responded by becoming an excellent student who quickly mastered all he was taught. He developed a habit, even at this tender age, of waking in the morning and throwing a handful of sand in the air. Then he would say, 'May I have today as many words of counsel as the number of these grains of sand.'"

Maha Kassapa speaks, "A kinder, more cheerful, obedient, and respectful child was never born. Rahula was always a great blessing to our Sangha brethren, and for years he trailed behind either the Buddha or Sariputta, eager to learn whatever he could.

"As an example of the training given to Rahula by the Buddha, shortly after his ordination the Lord sat down with him and taught him this lesson about the precept of truthfulness:

"The Buddha had picked up a small clay pot and showed it to his son. 'Rahula, do you see the small amount of water at the bottom of this pot?'

"'Yes, Lord.'

"'That small amount of water is the same as the small amount of training had by those who can lie intentionally without shame.' Rahula looked intently at the bottom of the pot as he tried to comprehend the Master's words.

"Then the Buddha threw the water out of the pot and said, 'Did you see that small amount of water I threw away?'

"'Yes, Lord.'

"'It is the same as the training thrown away by those who can lie intentionally without shame, Rahula.'

"Then the Buddha turned the pot over and said, 'Do you see this pot that I turned upside down?'

"'Yes, Lord.'

"'This overturned pot is just the same as the training of those who can lie intentionally without shame.'

"Then the Buddha turned the pot upright and said, 'Do you see this empty pot?"

"'Yes, Lord.'

"'This empty pot is the same as the training of those who can lie intentionally without shame.'

"'Rahula, anyone who can lie intentionally, without shame, could stoop to doing just about anything. Therefore, train yourself by saying, 'I will not tell a lie, not even as a joke.'

"Then he asked his son, 'What is the purpose of a mirror?'

"'The purpose of a mirror is to be able to look at yourself.'

> "'Exactly. It is just the same as the way you should look at yourself before acting, either with your body, your speech, or your mind. Think, "If I do, say, or think this thing, will it harm myself or others?" If your answer is, "Yes, if I do, say, or think this thing, it will bring harm to myself or others," then don't do, say, or think it. But if you can answer truthfully, "No, if I do, say, or think this thing, it will *not* harm myself or others," then go ahead and do, say, or think it. Therefore, Rahula, train yourself by thinking, "We will act only after looking again and again at ourselves, and only after reflecting on the possible outcome."'[5]

Maha Kassapa concludes his recitation and Maha Kaccayana says, "I think this is a good time to mention how the Buddha introduced Rahula to the practice of meditation."

"Excellent idea, Venerable Sir; why don't you tell the story," suggests Maha Kassapa. Maha Kaccayana begins:

"In a nutshell, here's how the Buddha advised his son:[6]

> "'Rahula, you should develop your mind so it is like the four elements: earth, water, fire, and air. If you do this, then any pleasant or unpleasant sensory impressions that may arise and try to grab your attention will not persist; they will simply fade away. It is just the same as when people throw filthy things on the earth, or in the water, air, or fire; none of these elements ever become troubled, worried, or disturbed. This is the way you should train your mind.'

> "'Also, Rahula, develop meditation on loving kindness; for when you develop meditation on loving kindness, any ill-will will be abandoned.'

> "'Develop meditation on compassion; for when you develop meditation on compassion, any cruelty will be abandoned.'

> "'Develop meditation on appreciative joy; for when you develop meditation on appreciative joy, any discontent will be abandoned.'

"'Develop meditation on equanimity; for when you develop meditation on equanimity, any aversion will be abandoned.'

"'Develop meditation on foulness; for when you develop meditation on foulness, any lust will be abandoned.'

"'Develop meditation on the perception of impermanence; for when you develop meditation on the perception of impermanence, the conceit "I am" will be abandoned.'

"'Develop meditation on mindfulness of breathing, for when mindfulness of breathing is developed and cultivated, it is of great fruit and great benefit,'" concludes Maha Kaccayana.

"These basic instructions have been of great assistance to beginning meditators," comments Bakkula.

"How did things go with the Buddha's family from this point?" questions Sopaka. "I can understand why they were upset, but I can't imagine they stayed that way very long."

Anuruddha answers, "After the king attained the state of *anagami*, he was much more composed and in control of his emotions. The anger was gone, of course, and his attachment to wanting things his way gradually became less and less so he could more clearly see things as they actually were. He loved Princess Yasodhara dearly, and he tried to comfort her the best way he could. She hadn't yet begun her own process toward enlightenment, so she had a tendency to languish in deep sadness for quite some time."

"Our uncle, King Suddhodana, made it his personal project to get Yasodhara to lift her spirits – knowing that ultimately she was the only one who could do this," says Bhaddiya. "He visited her nearly every day and talked to her about the nature of impermanence. He stressed the fact that Prince Rahula wasn't 'hers,' and that she couldn't expect to control his life forever. She complained that he was too young to be out on his own, and she was worried about the many dangers on the road – too many things could go wrong and he could be harmed. The king reassured her that the Buddha and his Chief Disciples were looking after Rahula very well, and that his safety wasn't an issue.

"The Buddha also sent Sariputta to see the princess and his stepmother, the queen. The revered Chief Disciple taught them Dhamma, suggesting ways they might practice on a daily basis for their unfolding spiritual awareness.

"On one occasion when he was teaching, he said, 'I know that both of you royal ladies are virtuous and have always led exemplary lives. I would like to offer you a way of living moment-by-moment that will help you stay in a happy frame of mind.' The two ladies smiled, hoping that Venerable Sariputta might have a solution for their existential doldrums.

"He said, 'I am going to instruct you in Eight Lifetime Precepts, which are training rules you can follow daily, hourly, or even minute-by-minute as you watch your mind, emotions, speech, and actions, and then make conscious choices about how to proceed. The first Five Precepts you already know and practice; they are a part of this set:

"I undertake the training rule to abstain from taking life.

"I undertake the training rule to abstain from taking what is not given.

"I undertake the training rule to abstain from sexual misconduct.

"I undertake the training rule to abstain from false speech.

"I undertake the training rule to abstain from intoxicating substances, which cause loss of mindfulness and control.

"I undertake the training rule to abstain from malicious speech.

"I undertake the training rule to abstain from harsh speech.

"I undertake the training rule to abstain from useless speech.

"When Sariputta finished giving them the Eight Lifetime Precepts, Princess Yasodhara said, 'Venerable Sir, as you said, we already practice the first Five Precepts. Why did you add the last three?'

"Sariputta answered, 'To demonstrate the fact that most of what we might want to say has little value. The Buddha always tells us that noble silence is best. One constantly hears thoughts and voices in the mind, but these thoughts can be counter-productive and even destructive – and can negatively influence your life, or the lives of others.

"If you constantly watch your speech and thoughts you will eventually be able to weed out those that don't serve you or others – and be much happier. Becoming the guardian of your minds and your tongues will soon become second nature to you. Those unnecessary conversations in the mind will subside, and you will abide more and more in a place of peace,' continued the Chief Disciple.

"The princess and the queen took Sariputta's advice to heart, and combined the Eight Lifetime Precepts with their practice of meditation. Before too long they were able to accept the dramatic changes that had taken place in their families – and move forward with their lives. They committed themselves even more fully to social service activities and higher spiritual pursuits," concludes Bhaddiya.

"One day the Buddha suggested that Sariputta take Rahula with him the next time he visited the palace," says Ananda. "Sariputta thought this was an excellent idea, and I was lucky to be with the two royal ladies when they arrived.

"Sariputta wanted Rahula's visit to be a surprise, and it definitely was. When the young monk walked into the room the queen and the princess practically sprung from their seats and rushed toward him. I could see that they really wanted to hug him and smother him with kisses, but they did their best to restrain themselves. They knew full well that Rahula no longer belonged to them, but was now a part of the Sangha. It was heartbreaking, in a way, to see their tears and feel their strong urges to touch him and caress him.

"When they regained their composure they approached the prince with great joy and went down on their knees in obeisance to him. Rahula beamed with love and affection for both of them, and I could tell that he wanted to jump into their arms and return their affectionate feelings. After all, he was just seven. But he, too, restrained himself, remaining poised and very much the dignified young monk that he was.

"Queen Mahapajapati was the first to speak. She said, 'My goodness, Venerable Rahula, how you have changed! I think you've not only grown in stature and beauty, but in awareness and spiritual depth as well. There is light all around you!'

"The young monk did his best not to blush, and answered, 'Every day I am instructed in the Dhamma, and in the proper behavior of one who follows the Buddha. I'm learning so much, grandmother, and I'm truly happy with my new life.'

"Princess Yasodhara frowned for a moment, thinking that her son had already forgotten her. Rahula picked this up immediately, and very quickly turned to his mother and said, 'I could never have adapted so quickly to life with my father if you hadn't trained me and loved me as you have, dear mother. I will always honor you and love you for the personal sacrifices you have made on behalf of our family. I know you appreciate the great opportunity I have for developing myself under my father's and Venerable Sariputta's guidance.'

"The princess's expression changed instantly upon hearing these kind words and she said, 'I can't help but miss you, my dear son. We have never been apart until now. I know you have been given the inheritance I asked you to claim. You will find it to be greater than any material wealth you could have inherited. You are in good hands, and I won't worry any longer.' Then she said that one day she might join him in the Order, and they could work together to purify their minds and uplift the suffering people of their land. I was impressed by the way the two royal ladies behaved that day, and I was nearly overwhelmed by young Rahula's precocious emotional maturity," concludes Ananda.

Maha Kassapa stands. "I think this is a good place to break for the evening, my brothers. I wish that Nanda and Rahula had lived to be here at the council; their contributions would have been enormous in terms of recounting the Master's life. But that wasn't to be."

Each of the arahants pauses for a moment to think about their beloved, departed friends; in three of their cases, their departed relatives. There is no sadness in their reminiscences, because sadness, along with all other ego-related conditions, have ceased for them. They feel gratitude for having known the princes, and the other dear ones that were mentioned in the evening's recollections.

Chapter 17
Six Princes and a Barber

Ananda is in the midst of reciting the *Vasettha Sutta*[1] to the five hundred arahants.

"'...There were two young Brahmins, one called Vasettha and the other Bharadvaja...they started a conversation regarding the factors that make one a Brahmin.

"Bharadvaja said, 'It has to do with one's family. If one's bloodline is pure, and there has been no intermarriage with other castes for seven generations, then one is a Brahmin.'

"But Vasettha said, 'I disagree. If one's actions are good, and one's duties are observed, then one is a Brahmin.'

"They both stuck to their theories, and neither could convince the other that he was right. Vasettha suggested that they ask someone else's advice and said, 'There is a hermit called Gotama, a prince of the Sakyas, of whom it is said, he teaches a perfect, pure life. Good, indeed, is the sight of such saints! Let's go to this man Gotama and ask him to clear up this question, and we will take his answer to settle our dispute.'

"So the two young men went off to look for this Master they had heard of. When they found him they greeted him politely, and then Vasettha spoke to him and said, 'Sir, we are both students of the orthodox teachings, and we are both recognized and accepted as experts in the study of the Vedas...But even so, Gotama, there is one question about which we are in disagreement, namely, the importance of heredity in regards to who is a Brahmin...So please explain it to us and tell us what a Brahmin is.'

"The Buddha answered, 'I shall explain to you in accordance with the fact that amongst the different kinds of living things there are diverse species. If you look at the trees or grass, insects, four-footed animals, reptiles and snakes, fish and water life, birds and the breeds that fly, you can see that all of them are of different species. However, among human beings there are not different kinds and species – they are all the same type. From the neck to the groin, from the shoulder to the hip, from the back to the chest – human beings are all of one kind....In the case of humans, differences are only by convention.'

"'When a man is a farmer, or he lives by a particular craft, or makes his living by trading merchandise, or gets paid for serving other people, we call him by what he does, and we do not call him a Brahmin. He could be a thief, a soldier, a priest, or a king, and we also call him by what he does, and we do not call him a Brahmin.'

"'I do not call a man a Brahmin because of his mother or because of his breeding. Just because a man is entitled to be called "Sir" does not mean that he is free from habit and attachment. He who is free from attachment, he who is free from grasping, is the person I call a Brahmin.'

"'I also call the following persons a Brahmin: one who has freed himself and thrown off his shackles and there is no more agitation; one who has cut off the strap of ignorance and harness of false views, and who has removed obstacles and is enlightened; one who doesn't get annoyed, endures insults and violence, and whose strength and army is endurance; one in whom there is no anger and no ignorance – only strength of restraint and the power of pure action, no habitual repetition, no rebirth. These persons I call Brahmin.'

"'These persons I call Brahmin as well: one whose sense-desires roll off and leave no trace in him; one who is deep in wisdom, proficient in determining the right path from the wrong path, who has reached the ultimate goal; one who has no need of mixing with other people, whether property owners or wandering monks; one who commits no act of violence; one whose wanting, hating, pride, and envy have dropped away; one who speaks words which are meaningful and true; one who never steals; one who has no expectations from this world or any other; one who has no doubts and has plunged into the absence of death; one who has gone beyond the impurity of both merit and demerit, who is free from grief and defilement and is pure; one who has crossed over and gone beyond, being contemplative, passionless and doubt-free; one who has abandoned sense-pleasures, including that of constant becoming; one who has let go of cravings; one who avoids delight and aversion; one who has fully comprehended how beings come to be and how they cease to be, is unattached, and enlightened.'

"'All titles, names, and races are merely worldly conventions. They have come into being by common consent. This false belief has been deeply ingrained in the minds of the ignorant for a long time, and still these ignorant ones say, "One becomes a Brahmin by birth."'

"'On the contrary, no one is *born* a Brahmin; no one is *born* a non-Brahmin. A Brahmin is a Brahmin because of what he *does*, and a man who is not a Brahmin is not a Brahmin because of what he *does*. The wise men see action as it really has come to be. They are proficient in the fruits of action and they are seers of dependent origination. The world exists because of causal actions, all things are produced by causal actions, and all beings are governed and bound by causal actions.'

"'A Brahmin is a result of self-restraint, wholesome living, and self-control. This is the essence of Brahmin.'

"Vasettha and Bharadvaja said to the Buddha, 'The Truth has been explained by Venerable Gotama in various ways. Therefore, we take refuge in him, his Dhamma, and his Sangha. May the Venerable Gotama accept us as lay followers who henceforth have taken refuge in him for the rest of our lives.'"

Ananda finishes reciting the *sutta*, and then Maha Kassapa strikes the gong, its powerful sound echoing in the valley below. "This is the end of our assembly meeting tonight, my brothers; we shall meet again at dawn. I wish all of you a peaceful rest and a luminous meditation."

The five hundred arahants leave the hall, and the sub-committee members retire to Maha Kassapa's cave chamber for further discussions.

When everyone is comfortably seated Maha Kassapa says, "Ananda, I believe this might be where you and your relatives enter the story. You too, Upali; maybe this is where you have to endure your share of accolades."

Ananda, Anuruddha, Bhaddiya, and Upali chuckle good-naturedly and prepare themselves for their entrance in the story.

"Who would like to begin their account of joining the Sangha?" asks Maha Kassapa of the four relevant arahants in the chamber. The four esteemed senior members look back and forth at one another, and then Bhaddiya answers saying, "I think we should give Ananda a rest this evening. I'll begin telling the story."

Ananda smiles in appreciation, and then relaxes against the rock wall of the cave.

Bhaddiya begins, "The Buddha left the Kapilavatthu area with his large following of monks and journeyed toward Rajagaha. On the way he stopped to rest at the Anupiya mango grove in the Malla country. Right about this time King Suddhodana summoned an assembly of the royal Sakyan clans and said, 'Now that my noble son has become Buddha, I urge each and every royal household to present me with a prince, and I will arrange for their ordination in the Buddha's presence.'

"The leaders of the Sakyan clan signified their assent, and soon afterward several hundred princes of the royal families went with the king to the Anupiya Mango Grove and received ordination. Some of the Sakyan families that had given sons to the Buddha discovered that the families of the Princes Ananda, Anuruddha, Bhagu, Kimbila, Devadatta, as well as my own, had not yet complied with the king's wishes. They had not sent any of their own princes for admission to the Sangha, even though three of us were sons of the king's brothers. Our families were censured, and outrage was expressed at their non-compliance," says Bhaddiya.

Upali speaks, "You can't really blame those young princes for not wanting to be ordained. Eighty-year-old King Suddhodana had gone into retirement with no male successor; and since his next eldest brother Prince Dhotodana had already passed away, Prince Bhaddiya was next in line. At the time he was quite busy acting as the king's Regent. The other princes were, to put it bluntly, oblivious to what was going on outside their private worlds of pleasure-seeking. They had no consciousness whatsoever of real life in the kingdom, and if anyone is to blame it is their families who spoiled them."

Anuruddha says, "I know you are not passing judgment on us, dear friend, and I am the first to admit that you are completely accurate. I, for one, didn't have a clue about anything outside my palace walls and the lives of my royal friends. We were all self-centered and completely self-indulgent. It's been so long ago that it hardly seems possible, but it's true nonetheless."

"That, my dear cousin is an understatement," says Bhaddiya, laughing quietly. "Since childhood I was Anuruddha's most intimate friend, and I think it's fitting that I relate a particular story about him at this point."

Anuruddha grins, knowing which story his cousin is about to tell about him and says, "Is that story particularly relevant to our discussion about the life of our Lord?"

"I think it will help the world to understand the 'before' and the 'after' much better, Venerable Sir. I hope you don't have any serious objections," answers Bhaddiya, smiling broadly.

"No, go ahead and tell it. If you think it was embarrassing when we talked about your life, Maha Kassapa, it was nothing compared to what you are about to hear about mine," says Anuruddha, laughing.

"Anyway," begins Bhaddiya, "the six princes you just mentioned, including Anuruddha and I, were playing a game of marbles one day. You were quite young then, maybe nine or ten years old; I was older, of course. Our stakes were 'loser provides cakes.' On this particular occasion, much to his vexation, Anuruddha kept losing. Each time he lost he sent one of his attendants to his mother and asked her to provide cakes. After losing his fourth game, his mother ran out of cakes and had no choice but to send word, 'We have no cakes.'

"Believe it or not, my dearest and closest friend, cousin Anuruddha, did not understand the words 'have no cakes.'[2] He thought it was some new kind of cake, the 'have no' cake. So he sent his attendant back with the instruction to bring the 'have no' cakes. Anuruddha's mother knew full well that her son had no comprehension whatsoever of 'have no,' since he had always gotten everything he had ever asked for. See what I mean by indulged?"

The arahants in the room laugh heartily upon hearing this tale, and Anuruddha just sits there smiling.

Bhaddiya continues, "Anuruddha's mother decided to teach the boy the meaning of 'have no,' so she sent golden containers that were empty – there were no cakes inside them. Lo and behold, when they were opened the golden containers were filled with the finest cakes imaginable! The guardian *devas* of the city remembered the meritorious deeds performed by dear Anuruddha in a previous existence, so they miraculously caused cakes to appear."

"Lucky young man," comments Upali, smiling.

"Very lucky indeed," says Bhaddiya. "Anuruddha lost the next game, opened the golden containers, and served them to us. They were, by far, the best cakes we had ever eaten! So Anuruddha, confused, went home and asked his mother, 'Do you love me?'

"She looked at him sweetly and answered, 'More than my heart.'

"So the spoiled boy said, 'If you love me, then why haven't you ever given me 'have no' cakes before? From now on I want nothing else!'

"Anuruddha's mother summoned the young attendant and asked him, 'Young man was there anything in the containers? They were empty when I handed them to you.'

"The servant replied, 'When the prince opened the golden boxes they were filled to the brim with the most beautiful cakes I have ever seen.'

"Anuruddha's mother then realized that her son must be a special man of power and glory, and had accumulated a great deal of merit from past good deeds. Ever since that day his mother sent him empty golden containers when he requested cakes; and each time Anuruddha opened them they were filled with celestial 'have no' cakes." Bhaddiya concludes this story with a hearty laugh.

"How could a spoiled prince like that have any comprehension of monkhood or ordination?" asks Maha Kaccayana.

"I didn't," replies Anuruddha. "When my brother, Prince Mahanama, told me that our family had to send a son to the Buddha for ordination, I didn't even know what he was talking about. Of course, I was quite a bit older by this time, but I still hadn't learned the meaning of 'have no.'"

"I can attest to his ignorance – or rather I should say his 'innocence,' Venerable Sirs," says Upali, smiling broadly. "I was his barber, and as we are all aware, barbers know everything about their patrons. Everything. We shouldn't be too hard on Anuruddha, though; each of the other five princes was just as spoiled."

The arahants couldn't help but laugh upon hearing this statement, including Anuruddha.

"I thought we would be hearing accolades tonight, Venerable Sir. I didn't know we would be hearing tales that would be quite so revealing," says Maha Kassapa, chuckling. "Please Anuruddha, continue with your story."

"So I asked my brother, Prince Mahanama, 'What is ordination? What is it all about?'

"My brother answered by saying, 'One who receives ordination is required to have his head and beard shaved, wear dyed clothes, sleep on a bed of bamboo, and go around receiving alms food.'

"I was completely horrified and said, 'O brother, if that is the case, I couldn't possibly receive ordination!'

"Mahanama considered the matter and said, 'Then you had better learn the business of human affairs, and stay home to manage our household. Between the two of us, one has to be ordained. It's the king's command!'

"I'm sure I had a big question mark on my face, so my brother explained what he meant by 'the business of human affairs.' This involved, of course, the whole process of preparing, planting, and harvesting rice – among many other things.

"I said to him, 'If it is as you describe, then the business of human affairs is never-ending! When would one ever be able to enjoy the sensual pleasures, and not have to encounter all those anxieties of life?'

"Mahanama answered, 'It's quite true that worldly affairs never end. Our fathers and grandfathers all died before they ended theirs, and it's probably our fate, too. The fate for at least for one of us; the one who ordains might have a chance at enlightenment.'

"It suddenly dawned on me that ordination might be just the answer to escaping having to deal with those harsh realities, so I said, 'If this is so, my brother, since you already understand the ways of human affairs, you had better remain at home and take care of the management of our family property. I shall renounce the household life and be the one to lead the ascetic life with the Buddha.'"

"You were so naïve, Anuruddha, I'm sure you didn't even know what you were saying at that time," says Bakkula.

"Maybe I did know. Something inside me said that this was the direction I had to take, and all of a sudden I felt absolutely compelled to do it," exclaims Anuruddha.

"I approached my mother and told her of my decision. She was adamantly against it and refused to give me permission to be ordained – in spite of the king's orders. She loved me so much, and couldn't bear to have me – or my brother – leave her. I asked her a second time and she still refused. I asked her a third time, and she very shrewdly said that she would grant her permission only if the king's Regent and my closest friend, Bhaddiya, would also be ordained," says Anuruddha

"Anuruddha's mother was quite certain that I couldn't be persuaded to accept ordination because of my royal duties, and the fact that I was very happily next in line to be king. She was pretty clever to condition her permission this way," says Bhaddiya.

Anuruddha says, "I immediately went to Bhaddiya and told him that my receiving ordination depended on him. His answer was quite blunt, 'You can do as you please, but leave me out of it.'[3]

Bhaddiya speaks up, "In my heart I really wanted to tell Anuruddha that we could receive ordination together, but at the time I was so attached to my life of power and luxury that I couldn't bear to give it up. He was persistent, however, and he kept pleading with me while I kept saying 'No.' I finally told him to wait for seven years. I said that at that time I would give up my kingship and we could both be ordained. I thought that would keep him quiet. He surprised me, though, and said he couldn't wait that long. So I said, 'Wait for six years, how about that?'

"I've got to hand it to Anuruddha for his perseverance. He simply wouldn't let up on me. I continued to negotiate downwards the time he requested, from six years to five years to four, and finally down to only one year," continues Bhaddiya.

"I kept telling Bhaddiya I couldn't wait. He was now down to where he agreed to seven months, and I still continued my pleading. He went down to six months, five, four, three, two, only one month, but I wouldn't budge. I guess I was wearing him down."

"My final offer, so to speak, was seven days, and Anuruddha finally accepted. I needed at least a week to hand over the reigns of the kingdom to my cousin, Mahanama, who was Anuruddha's older brother and the next in line to the throne after me. Besides, I wanted to have one last fling roiling in the realm of the senses," concludes Bhaddiya with a big grin.

"We six princes – along with Upali – indulged in unrestricted sense pleasures for seven marvelous days," says Ananda, smiling.

"Oh yes, Ananda, you were one of them, too. I almost forgot," laughs Maha Kaccayana. "I can hardly imagine you indulging yourself like that! The images it brings to mind are absolutely startling!"

"When we left Kapilavatthu we were escorted to the border by regiments of elephanteers, charioteers, cavalry and infantry. When they turned back to the capital the seven of us continued on through Malla on our own. That was our first step toward renunciation," says Anuruddha.

"Our second was the magnificent clothes and jewels we wore, which we exchanged for simple yellow robes and bare feet. We bundled all of our belongings together and handed the sack to Upali. I said, 'Dear friend Upali, you may return home now. We no longer have a use for these things, but they should set you up for life," adds Bhaddiya.

"But I didn't want them to leave without me," says Upali. "I wept, rolling around on the ground in protest, but to no avail. When the princes wouldn't budge, I eventually got up, paid my tearful respects, and headed for home. I had only gone a short distance, however, when I realized that my Sakyan employers back in the capital might think I had murdered the princes, stolen their property, and come back a rich man. After all, I was only a barber; and I was the one who wielded a razor! So after thinking about it long and hard I hung the garments and jewelry in a tree, saying to myself, 'Good, now I have given these things to charity. I can rejoin my princes.'"

"When we saw Upali approaching us I immediately noticed that he was empty-handed. My first thought was that he must have gotten robbed," says Ananda.

"I explained my reasoning for abandoning their fine property, and they pretty much understood that I might have actually been accused of robbing and killing them. So we all went together to the Anupiya Mango Grove to see the Buddha," comments Upali, smiling.

"When we got to where the Buddha and his arahants were encamped we approached him slowly, perhaps still thinking we might be able to back out at the last minute and go home," says Ananda. "When the Lord saw us coming he called out and told us to come forward.

"'Greetings to you, my friends and cousins! Why have you come?' asked the Buddha.

"I spoke up and answered for the group, saying that we had come to fulfill the obligations of our families and be ordained in his Sangha," says Ananda. Then the Master asked, 'And why, friend Upali, have you come?'

"Before I could answer Devadatta spoke up and said, 'Upali is our servant. We will need him to shave us and clean our robes.'

"The Buddha replied, 'In my Sangha we have no servants, Devadatta. We are all equal as monks, and we take care of ourselves. So Upali, now that you are out of a job, what will you do?'

"I told him I didn't know. I couldn't go home since their relatives might arrest me thinking I had robbed and killed them. Then the Buddha asked me if I wished to be ordained. I said that I was only a servant, but he said, 'In my Sangha we have no caste system, Upali. I ask you again, do you wish to be ordained?'

"I was astonished and replied, 'Yes, Lord, if you will accept me.' Then he said, 'In that case I will ordain you first.'

"Devadatta protested saying, 'If you ordain him first then he will be our senior, and we'll have to defer to him in matters of rank.' The Buddha looked at Devadatta with great compassion and said, 'So be it.' Then he ordained me, and afterwards he ordained the rest."

"If I know my Sangha history rightly, I seem to remember that it took all of you quite some time to attain enlightenment. Is this correct?" asks Bakkula.

"In my case it took two rainy season retreats – nearly two years," answers Anuruddha. "Sariputta was very helpful in guiding me through the *jhanas*, and the Lord himself helped me to attain the eighth stage. I was at the bamboo grove in Ceti when he instructed me, and he said to come back later that year for the rains. He sensed that it was the right place for me, and he was right. At the end of that season I attained arahantship."

"Bhagu, Kimbila, and I took about the same amount of time, and we were also instructed by the Master. We had the kind and generous guidance of several of the senior monks as well," says Bhaddiya.

"After I listened to my dear Venerable Punna I attained *sotapanna*, and I have been grateful to him ever since. You put me on the first rung of the ladder, my beloved teacher, and then from there I inched my way up," says Ananda to Punna with great affection. "And, of course, I didn't achieve full enlightenment until just a few weeks ago – the night before this council convened. I was beginning to think it might never happen."

"We know you wondered if you would ever make it, but we always knew you would," says Bhaddiya. "As the Lord always said, time is an illusion, and when the fruit is ripe it drops of its own accord."

"I know the Lord kept you by his side all those years, my dear Ananda, to make sure you would attain the fruits of your labors. And as his Chief Attendant, you also had many responsibilities that the rest of us didn't have to shoulder. Remember when he recited the *Mahasunnata Sutta*[4] to you?" asks Punna.

"Yes, I do," replies Ananda, nearly glowing.

"Why don't you tell us in the Master's own words what he said," requests the one who put Ananda on the right course.

Ananda takes a sip of Bakkula's Himalayan tea and says, "The Buddha told me:

> "'Ananda, a disciple should not seek the Teacher's company for the sake of discourses, stanzas, and expositions. Why is that? For a long time, Ananda, you have learned the teachings, remembered them, recited them verbally, examined them with the mind, and penetrated them well by view…
>
> "'But talk…on wanting little, on contentment, seclusion, aloofness from society, arousing energy, virtue, concentration, wisdom, deliverance, knowledge and vision of deliverance: for the sake of such talk a disciple should seek the Teacher's company even if he is told to go away.'"

"The Master never told you to go away, my dear friend," says Maha Kassapa. "He continually drew you close and closer to him, always valuing your mind, your loyalty, your caring, and your willing attitude. He never stopped counting on you to make sure his personal needs were met, and for faithfully remembering his words. The Buddha knew that one day you would achieve the prize you sought because you refused to give up, and you never acted as if you were disappointed. You just did your duty to the best of your ability, never complaining, never thinking about yourself. You are truly a remarkable man, my friend."

The other arahants in the chamber warmly express their agreement. Ananda lowers his head and reflects on the words of the chairman. Finally he sits up straight, smiles, and says, "You were determined to give me an accolade this evening, weren't you?"

The brother monks in the chamber smile at one another with great affection. Maha Kassapa keeps silent, but the twinkling in his eyes shows not only the love he feels for his friend, but his acknowledgement of the truth to Ananda's statement about the accolade as well.

"You haven't yet mentioned Devadatta," queries Sopaka.

"The Lord's brother-in-law meditated diligently for quite some time. He eventually mastered the four *jhanas* and gained some degree of supernormal power. Unfortunately, he never went beyond that stage," says Bhaddiya.

"Our old friend Devadatta could never quite get over not being number one, and always in the shadow of our great Master. It was Devadatta's pride and conceit that kept him from realizing his true potential. We all know what eventually became of him, but we'll save that part of his story for later," says Maha Kassapa.

"Devadatta obviously never quite understood the meaning of the *sutta* you recited late this afternoon, Ananda," says Upali. "He simply couldn't let go of his ingrained definition of a Brahmin, which until the end he staunchly believed was hereditary. Even though he deferred to me when he knew he had to, I could always sense the underlying resentment he felt."

"Bhagu and Kimbila, what ever happened to them?" asks Sopaka.

"After they attained arahantship they went off to the Himalayas and were never heard from again. I presume they spent the rest of their lives meditating and enjoying the bliss of emancipation while generating the protective energy of loving-kindness for all beings. This act is a great, immeasurable contribution, and should never be looked down upon as something unimportant or 'less than.' As the Lord said on a number of occasions, great skill at preaching the Dhamma isn't the only way to serve mankind," says Anuruddha.

Ananda says, "That is absolutely correct. Generating loving-kindness energy for the benefit of all is, perhaps, the greatest service. Please allow me to quote one of my favorite poems of the Buddha on this subject:

"'Skilled in good, wishing to attain a state of calm,
so should one behave:
Able, upright, perfectly upright, open-minded,
gentle, free from pride.

'Contented, easily supportable; with few duties,
of light livelihood; controlled in senses,
discreet, reserved, not greedily attached to family.

"'Whatever beings there are: timid, strong, and all other,
long, or huge, average, short, or large;
Seen or unseen, living near or far, born or coming to birth:
May all beings be well and happy.

"'Let one not deceive another, nor despise anyone anywhere.
Neither in anger nor ill-will, should one wish another harm.

"'As a mother would risk her own life
to protect her only child,
So should one, to all living beings,
cultivate a boundless heart.

"'Let one's love pervade the whole world,
without any obstructions,
Above, below and across, free of obstruction,
enmity, hostility.

"'Standing, walking, sitting, or lying down;
whenever awake,
One should develop mindfulness,
as this is the highest abode.

'Not falling into error, virtuous, and endowed with insight;
Giving up attachment to sense-desires,
one is not again subject to birth.'"[5]

The arahants in the cave chamber sit with their eyes closed listening to Ananda's powerful, profound words. Each of them can feel the vibration he is sending out to the universe, the sharing of the essence of his compassionate being.

"Good night, my brothers," says Maha Kassapa. "More words should not follow these tonight."

Chapter 18
Anathapindika

The members of the sub-committee meet during the morning break. Each has with him his small cloth bag of eight requisites, which includes two extra robes, a twig from the *neem* tree for cleaning teeth, a razor for shaving, a needle and thread, a water filter, and a cup for drinking water. They also have their alms bowls. These are all the worldly possessions they own, which is nothing compared to what some of them left behind.

"I'm told we'll be leaving right after the *dana* ceremony. Kala and his wife Sujata will personally escort us down the hill to their villa," says Punna to Maha Kaccayana.

"I think this two-day retreat will be good for all of us. Living in a cave can be a boon for one's meditation, but I'm ready for a change. It was very kind of Kala and Sujata to offer us their home."

"It is a fitting time and a fitting place for going over this part of the Master's life. Having known Anathapindika well, I'm sure he would have been very happy," says Punna.

Maha Kassapa has decided to halt the proceedings for two days so the five hundred arahants, the large staff, and numerous volunteers could have a much-deserved rest. It has been several weeks since the council had begun, and not a single day so far had been reserved for retreat. Most of the arahants were going to the Bamboo Grove Monastery where they could spend some sorely-missed time in seclusion.

Kala, the son of Anathapindika, had learned from his friend King Ajatasattu that during the retreat the sub-committee would continue recollecting the story of his father's friendship with the Buddha. Kala expressed his wish to be present, and the king obtained permission for him from Maha Kassapa. The chairman not only invited Kala and his wife to be present, but to participate in the discussions as well.

Even though Kala and his wife, Sujata, lived in Savatthi where they were both born and raised, about half of Kala's business was in Rajagaha so he maintained a lavish mansion there. He also had many relatives in Rajagaha, his father having married the sister of the wife of his trading partner, a leading financier of Rajagaha. Kala's cousins in the area were numerous, his business in Rajagaha was prosperous, and he enjoyed spending time there whenever he could.

Several years before, Sujata had fallen in love with the hot springs near the Sattapanniguha caves on the slopes of Mount Vebhara. She had persuaded her husband to build a spacious villa near the springs so she could bathe at her leisure and enjoy the cool breezes and views of the valley below. Even though they didn't use the villa but three or four times a year they maintained it in a state of constant readiness for whenever the mood struck them to visit. They had kindly offered it to the arahants of the sub-committee for their use during the council retreat; they themselves would stay in their mansion in the city and commute for the discussions.

Kala and Sujata are sponsoring the *dana* ceremony that day, and true to their usual opulent style, it will be a feast for the palate as well as for the eyes and ears. They have erected white cotton tents next to the assembly hall, and furnished them with the usual mats, banana leaf plates, flowers, and jars of fragrantly scented water. The mats this time are made of cloth in the six colors of the Buddha's aura, and they alternate throughout the enclosure in a rainbow pattern. The colors of the flowers match the mats, as do the costumes of the serving attendants.

Kala and Sujata wish to present fine new robes to their esteemed guests after the meal, so camphor-lined chests have been placed off to the side. They are filled with newly-sewn saffron-colored robes made of linen mixed with silk.

At the conclusion of the ceremony they will escort the members of the sub-committee to their villa, and begin the discussion of the Buddha's special relationship with generous Anathapindika.

The arahants file into the assembly hall after their morning break and Ananda walks with Maha Kassapa to the podium.

"After the *dana* ceremony today we will take a recess from our council proceedings for two days and two nights. My wish is that all of you will return with renewed enthusiasm for the work we have yet to complete. Venerable Ananda, I believe you are going to begin this segment with one of the Buddha's *suttas* on wealth," says Maha Kassapa to his friend.

Ananda steps closer to the podium, places a hand on either side for support, and begins reciting from the *Kosalasamyutta*.[1] "The Buddha spoke the following words to King Pasenadi of Kosala:

"'Where are you coming from, great king, in the middle of the day?'

"'A financier in Savatthi has died intestate, and I have come to convey his heirless fortune to the palace. There were eighty *lakhs* of gold, not to mention silver, and yet that householder's meals consisted of red rice with gruel; he wore a three-piece hempen garment, and went about in a dilapidated little cart with a leaf awning,' responded the king.

"'So it is, great king, that when an inferior man gains abundant wealth he does not make himself happy and pleased, nor does he make his mother and father, wife and children, workers, servants, nor his friends and colleagues happy and pleased. Nor does he establish an offering for ascetics and Brahmins, one leading upwards, of heavenly fruit, resulting in happiness, conducive to heaven. Because his wealth is not being used properly kings or thieves take it away, or fire burns it, or water carries it away, or unloved heirs take it. Such being the case, great king, that wealth, not being used properly, goes to waste, not to utilization.

"'But, great king, when a superior man gains abundant wealth he makes himself happy and pleased, and he also makes his mother and father, wife and children, workers, servants, and his friends and colleagues happy and pleased. He establishes an offering for ascetics and Brahmins, one leading upwards, of heavenly fruit, resulting in happiness, conducive to heaven. Because his wealth is being used properly kings and thieves do not take it away, fire does not burn it, water does not carry it away, and unloved heirs do not take it. Such being the case, great king, that wealth, being used properly, goes to utilization, not to waste.

> "'As cool water in a desolate place
> evaporates without being drunk,
> so when a fool acquires wealth,
> he neither enjoys himself nor gives.
>
> "'But when the wise man obtains wealth
> he enjoys himself and does his duty.
> Having supported his kin,
> free from blame that man goes to a heavenly state.'"

When Ananda finishes reciting the eloquent *sutta*, Sopaka steps up to assist him from the platform, and with the other senior members they proceed to the sumptuous *dana* ceremony in the tents next door.

The arahants enjoy the meal and the elegant, colorful atmosphere of the canopied enclosures, and afterwards make their way to their retreat destinations.

Kala, Sujata, and their servants personally escort the sub-committee members and the ten memory monks down the trail to the spacious villa overlooking the verdant valley. They enter the mansion and are greeted by the sound of flowing water. When he constructed the building Kala had his engineers divert the course of a small rivulet flowing down from the spring to a pool and fountain in the courtyard. The melodious, gurgling sound was pleasing to the ear, and relaxing for the mind.

Sujata said, "This is your home whenever you have time to visit, Venerable Sirs; if you need anything, all you have to do is ask Kala or me, or our overseer, Bala." The tall, burly, uniformed major domo goes down on his knees and touches his forehead to the earth in front of his esteemed guests. He stands and then leads the way to the great room on the first floor, which has been prepared for the afternoon's discussion.

The sub-committee members and the memory monks take their places on the amply upholstered silk mats that have been placed in a circle in the center of the massive room.

"Thank you Kala and Sujata for loaning us your home; we truly appreciate your kind hospitality. You are acquiring great merit for providing us with this lovely space to recount the Master's life," says Maha Kassapa.

The couple bow together and acknowledge the chairman's words of thanks. Kala says, "We are grateful for the rare opportunity of being in your presence at this auspicious event."

"Who will begin this discussion?" asks the chairman when everyone is settled.

Without a moment's hesitation Ananda speaks, "Anathapindika was a great friend for many years; in fact, Venerable Sariputta and I were with him when he died.[2] Allow me to tell you how he came to meet the Buddha."

The arahants, Kala, and Sujata give Ananda their undivided attention.

"Anathapindika used to come often to Rajagaha where he and his trading partner, your uncle, had established a solid working relationship for selling merchandise both here and in Savatthi. As a result, they both became exceedingly wealthy. On one occasion Anathapindika came here to Rajagaha with five hundred cartloads of goods for sale. As was their custom, when he got eight miles from the city he would send word to your uncle that he was on his way. Usually there would be a grand reception upon his entrance to the city, and much would be made of the new merchandise, which would immediately be put on sale.

"This time, however, when he and his caravan reached Rajagaha your uncle was nowhere to be seen, and there was no grand reception. Anathapindika was puzzled. When he arrived at your uncle's mansion that evening he found his friend busily arranging a banquet. Your uncle barely noticed him, and all he said was, 'How are your children? Are they in good health?' Anathapindika didn't know what to think, and your uncle continued moving about and issuing instructions for a big feast to be held the following day.

"Your father thought that a big wedding reception was about to take place for one of his partner's sons or daughters; perhaps King Bimbisara himself was going to be the guest of honor. Your father said, 'Wealthy man, you usually put aside everything to welcome me and get our business going. What is happening?'

"Your uncle answered, 'I'm making arrangements for a grand almsgiving ceremony. I have invited the Buddha and his Sangha for their meal tomorrow.'"

Kala politely interrupts Ananda and says, "If I may, Venerable Sir, I would like to tell this part. My father told me this story countless times."

Ananda nods and Kala continues, "When my father heard the word 'Buddha,' something sort of went off in his mind – in his whole body, actually. He told me he experienced a rapturous feeling of joy that infused his whole being. He was ecstatic!

"My father asked, 'Wealthy man, did you say the 'Buddha?' My uncle said 'Yes.' Three more times my father, as if swept away by some powerful force, said, 'Wealthy man, did you say the 'Buddha?' And three more times my uncle answered in the affirmative. Under normal conditions Uncle would have been concerned about my father's almost incoherent state, but not on that day. He was too pre-occupied with the organization of the *dana* ceremony to give it much notice.

"My father said, 'In this world it is rare indeed even to hear the word 'Buddha,' much less to have one in one's midst. Is it possible for me to go now and pay homage to him?'

"'Not right now, Anathapindika. The Buddha's monastery is close to the charnel grounds and it would be dangerous for you to go there this late. You will be able to go and pay homage to him in the morning,' was Uncle's reply.

"My father could think of nothing else but the Buddha from that moment forward. He couldn't even eat his dinner. Thinking about the Buddha he went to sleep early, wanting to get up early to go see him. Three times during the night he woke up and contemplated the Buddha, and his devotion to him seemed to grow by the hour. Every time he woke up he thought it was dawn and time to go see the Lord, but each time he realized it was still night.

"At the close of the last watch, immediately before dawn, he got up and walked along the balcony until he reached the mansion's main entrance. He noticed that the doors were already open, which was out of the ordinary. Then he went downstairs to the ground floor and went out into the main street of the city.

"When he got to the city gate he found that it was already open as well, which was also unusual. He kept walking in the direction of the Buddha's monastery, and as it was still dark, he strayed off the path and wound up in the charnel grounds. He accidentally stepped on a corpse, which caused the foul smell to rush up into my father's nose. Then the stray dogs and jackals started howling. He was startled and became frightened. His devotional faith in the Buddha, however, enabled him to quickly return to his full senses and find the path to the monastery. He said that he felt a guiding presence walking next to him and he thought, 'Why should I be afraid? I'm on my way to see the Buddha,'" says Kala, smiling.

Sujata speaks, "Knowing my father-in-law, it's hard for me to imagine him venturing out like that in the dark. He was so pampered and sensitive; I can visualize his horror upon finding himself lost in the charnel grounds, and stepping on a dead body must have sent him over the edge."

Kala begins, "My father considered, 'How shall I know if the Buddha is truly the Fully-Enlightened One?' His first thought was that no one knew his real name, Sudatta, and if the Buddha called him by that name he would know for sure.

"When he saw my father approaching the Buddha made his way through the monastery to wait for him. As he came closer the Buddha called out, 'Come, dear Sudatta!' My father was overjoyed when he heard his given name, and he rushed forward and prostrated himself before the Buddha's feet.

"He was still flustered from the dead corpse experience, so he could only manage to say, 'Most Exalted Buddha, have you enjoyed a sound sleep?'" Kala pauses after saying this.

Ananda interjects, "I was just steps behind the Master at that moment and I heard him say, 'Having expelled all evil, with all defilements having been eradicated, all sorrow has ended and the arahant, at all times, night and day, truly sleeps and lives in ease of mind and body.'[3]

"Then the Buddha taught Anathapindika about charity and morality. When he knew Anathapindika's mind had become adaptable, calm, and free from hindrances he taught him the Four Noble Truths. Upon hearing the Buddha's teaching Anathapindika attained the stage of *sotapanna*.

"I will never forget your father's words or the look on his face when he exclaimed, 'Glorious Buddha! I recognize and approach the Buddha, the Dhamma, and the Sangha for refuge and shelter. May the Glorious

Buddha take me as a devotee from today until the end of my life. So I can gain merit and experience delight, please accept my offering of a meal tomorrow.' The Buddha remained silent, signifying his acceptance.

"Anathapindika, joyous and exultant, paid his deepest respects to the Lord, and returned to his brother-in-law's mansion," concludes Ananda.

Kala begins, "At noon that same day the Buddha came to my uncle's house for the lavish banquet that my uncle had prepared. My father was overjoyed to see the Buddha again, and he told him that he looked forward to offering him *dana* the following day. This would also be served at my uncle's residence, and my father intended to provide the Buddha the grandest luncheon imaginable."

Ananda says, "It didn't take long for the news of your father's invitation to the Buddha to spread all over the city. Everyone came forward with offers to assist your father with the luncheon ceremony, including your uncle, and even King Bimbisara. Your father, naturally, wouldn't accept help or financial assistance of any kind. He insisted on sponsoring the *dana* himself, even though it would be held in your uncle's mansion."

Kala speaks up saying, "On the following day the Buddha and his arahants came for the *dana* ceremony and my father was beside himself with joy and excitement. He served the Buddha with his own hand, and said to him, 'Please spend the rainy season retreat in Savatthi, Lord, together with all your *bhikkhus*. I wish to serve you every day.'"

"The Lord answered enigmatically, 'Devotee Anathapindika, Fully-Enlightened Buddhas are pleased to reside in secluded places,'" says Ananda, smiling.

"My father explained to me later that he had immediately grasped the meaning of the Lord's phrase, and responded, 'Glorious Buddha, your devotee understands full well indeed!' From that moment forward my father could think of nothing else but providing the Buddha and his Sangha with a suitable monastery in Savatthi. He hastily disposed of his merchandise in Rajagaha and headed towards home. Along the way he said to everyone, 'Plant gardens, build shelters for rest and lodging. Build monasteries and keep reserve provisions for alms-giving. A Buddha has blossomed forth in the world! That Buddha will be coming along this way at my request!' He was so happy he couldn't contain himself," exclaims Kala.

"Because of your father's good name, his wealthy associates and childhood friends created intermediate facilities all along the Buddha's intended route to Savatthi. At their own expense, accepting no monetary help from Anathapindika, they did indeed build shelters and monasteries and put aside stores of provisions. Anathapindika insisted on donating in-kind construction and other materials, and he spent one *lakh* of gold, or one hundred thousand gold coins, for each of the intermediate stations, which were erected every six miles. After getting construction started on these stations, he returned home to concentrate on building the Buddha the magnificent monastery he had promised," says Anuruddha.

"Those shelters were put to very good use by me and thousands of other Sangha members over the years. I've stayed in every one of them," says Upali.

"So have I," says Ananda, "and we all have good memories of the beautiful monastery Anathapindika built in Savatthi. I've often reflected on the perfection of his chosen site, and have felt gratitude to him for being so diligent in securing it for the Sangha."

"Once my father set his mind on something it was very difficult to shake him off his course," says Kala, laughing. "Prince Jeta, the owner of the site he selected, was King Pasenadi's son, and a very powerful man in our country. When my father determined that the prince's garden was the most appropriate place for the monastery, he immediately went to see him and made an offer for it. Unfortunately, the prince told my father that it wasn't for sale. It is true that the prince loved nature, but he didn't really spend that much time in the park, and he had never constructed any buildings or monuments there. He knew my father was very wealthy, so maybe he was just trying to get as much out of him as he could."[4]

"I believe he told your father, 'Wealthy man, I could hardly give you my garden even if you were to lay gold coins edge to edge over it,'" says Bakkula.

"Yes, that's what he said. My father took advantage of the prince's somewhat ambiguous statement and said, 'Your Highness, you have quoted your terms for the sale of your garden.' The prince denied it, saying, 'I have not said a word about the sale of my garden.' They got into quite a heated argument, and my father took the matter to court.

"The judges pondered hard over the case, and somehow they finally ruled in my father's favor. He didn't waste any time, and within the hour my father ordered cartloads of gold coins to be taken from his treasury to the garden. Then he had them laid edge to edge, perimeter to perimeter. I went out there that day to see this sight for myself, and I can assure you that it was unbelievable. You all know how large the site is, so just try to imagine acres and acres of gold coins completely covering the entire property. You could hardly look at it when the sun was shining – it was almost blinding," continues Kala.

"As it turns out, not the *entire* property," says Upali.

"That's true," answers Kala. "One very small area near the garden gate was still left to be covered, so my father ordered more gold to be brought out. Just at that moment the prince and his guards showed up on horseback and surveyed the glittering scene. I'm sure he was just as blinded as the rest of us; he just sat up there on his horse with his mouth open. Suddenly he started to laugh, and his face grew brighter by the minute. No one had ever seen a completely golden park before, nor had anyone ever spent so much money at one time. I think the sight caused the prince a twinge of guilt, and he later told me that he realized my father's devotion must have been to a truly noble cause. He called out to my father, 'Anathapindika, enough...enough...please don't lay any more gold coin. Please be so good as to leave this part for me to donate a towered archway for the monastery.'"

Ananda speaks, "Anathapindika really didn't have to comply with the prince's wishes. He had more than enough gold to cover the small amount of ground that was still left uncovered, and then he could have said that the monastery – including its gate – was all from him. So great was his devotion to the Buddha that he realized having Prince Jeta associated with the monastery would help spread the Buddha's fame – and his teachings. He agreed to the prince's proposal, and allowed him to build a multi-tiered, arched gate for the monastery. He also named the park Jetavana in honor of the prince."

"The monastery turned out to be one of the most beautiful ever developed," says Bhaddiya. "Even our palaces in Kapilavatthu were no match in terms of design and practicality. Anathapindika had only the necessary trees cut down, wanting to make sure there was as much cool shade as possible. The perfumed chamber for the Buddha is the centerpiece of the entire plan, and it is surrounded by dwellings for thousands of *bhikkhus*. There are assembly halls with terraced roofs for Sangha meetings, small buildings for storage, lavatories, covered breezeways, separate bathrooms for cold and sweat baths, water tanks, and several pavilions scattered throughout the property. Anathapindika spared no expense. Nothing was left out that he thought might make the Buddha and his Sangha members as comfortable as possible."

"Your father spent eighteen *crores* on the land, and another eighteen *crores* to build the monastery, which is the equivalent of three hundred sixty million gold coins. No one has ever donated this much to the Sangha," said Punna. "That doesn't include the intermediate stations, on which he spent another four million eight hundred thousand gold coins."

"When the monastery was completed, Anathapindika sent word to the Buddha that it was ready. Soon afterward the Lord departed from Veluvana monastery and began his journey to Savatthi. He and his *bhikkhus* stopped one night at each of the shelters along the way," concludes Ananda.

"Kala, please tell us about the grand reception at Jetavana," requests Maha Kassapa.

"My father meticulously planned the grand occasion for weeks. He went to King Pasenadi and asked him if his beloved, seven-year-old daughter, Princess Sumana, could participate. The king gave his permission and the princess and her entourage were the first to greet the Buddha when he arrived; they presented him with bowls of scented water and flowers. The Lord preached the Dhamma to them, and almost immediately they attained the state of *sotapanna*.

"I had the honor of escorting the Buddha and his Sangha members to the monastery. I had with me a group of my friends, the young sons of the leading businessmen of Savatthi. We accompanied the Buddha right up to the gates. Excited townspeople holding flowers lined the way to the monastery, anxious to catch a glimpse of the Buddha. Waiting at the gates was my father, who was dressed in all his finery. He was accompanied by all of his family and friends, the wealthiest men of Savatthi. There stood my sisters, Cula and Maha Subhadda, and my mother, Punna Lakkhana, wearing full ceremonial dress emblazoned with jewels. Mother was accompanied by her friends, the wives of the wealthy men of Savatthi; each one carried a gold or silver cup filled with sweet scents and other offerings.

"Leading a long procession of *bhikkhus* and townspeople the Buddha passed through the magnificent gates into the monastery precincts. The forest literally glowed with a golden hue; perhaps it was a residue from all the gold my father had spread on the ground. It was as if liquid gold pigment had been washed over everything. A luminescent aura surrounded the Buddha that followed him as he moved past the trees and buildings. I'll never forget that day as long as I live," says Kala.

"I was in the ladies party with my mother-in-law and her friends," begins Sujata. "There has never been a more beautiful gathering in Savatthi before or since. It wasn't beautiful only because it was opulent and everyone was richly dressed; it was also beautiful because of the way we *felt*. The joy that welled up within us made everything radiantly golden with the purity of love."

Kala smiles affectionately at his wife and says, "At the conclusion of the reception my father approached the Lord and invited him for *dana* on the following day. The Buddha accepted with his customary silence. When the Buddha and his Sangha members arrived for *dana*, my father served his guests the finest imaginable food and drink. At the end of the meal he approached the Master and said, 'Most Glorious Buddha, please tell me how this monastery in Jetavana Grove should be dedicated.'

"The Buddha replied, 'It would be proper for you to dedicate the monastery to all *bhikkhus* who have arrived, are still arriving, and may arrive from the four directions for all time.'

"My father so dedicated the monastery, and symbolized the act by ceremoniously pouring water over the Buddha's hands," concludes Kala.

Ananda says, "The Buddha spoke the following poem after Anathapindika's gracious dedication:

"'They ward off cold, heat, beasts of prey,
creeping things, gnats and rains in the wet season.
When the dreaded hot wind arises, that is warded off.
To meditate and obtain insight in a shelter and at ease —

> A dwelling-place is praised by the Awakened One
> as chief gift to the Order.
> Therefore a wise person looking to his own weal,
> Should have dwelling-places built,
> so that learned ones can stay therein.
> To these, food, drink, raiment and lodgings
> he should give to the upright with mind purified.
> Then these will teach him Dhamma dispelling every ill;
> He, knowing that Dhamma,
> here attains *Nibbana* without obstructions.'"[5]

"Just one last thing about the monastery," interjects Punna. "Whenever the Buddha was not in residence, Anathapindika missed his presence terribly. He once asked the Lord for some tangible thing to enshrine there. He said that people wanted something they could venerate, to which they could make their offerings of flower garlands and other objects of devotion. The Buddha spoke to him about relics, but since he wasn't yet deceased, he said that the best thing to do would be to venerate the Bodhi Tree.

"The Buddha said, 'Venerating the Bodhi Tree will show your gratitude for the shelter it provided me during my struggle for enlightenment. It will become a symbol of gratitude for all of the blessings one has received, and represent taking refuge in the Triple Gem.'

"To accommodate Anathapindika, Venerable Maha Moggallana caught a fruit from the Bodhi Tree at Gaya as it was falling to the ground. He planted a seed from it in a golden jar and it soon grew into a healthy sapling. Then he brought this sapling from Uruvela and gave it to Venerable Ananda, who made arrangements for it to be planted near the gate tower of the monastery.

"Venerable Ananda asked King Pasenadi to consecrate the tree, but the king said, 'If I consecrate this tree, future enemies who might disagree with my policies, wanting to dishonor my reign, may wish to destroy my legacy. Therefore, they might also want to destroy this Bodhi tree if they knew I had a hand in planting it. Therefore, I will defer the honor of consecrating the tree to Anathapindika since it was he who is responsible for the monastery's existence.'"

Punna continues, saying, "King Pasenadi, under the Buddha's influence, had become a very wise ruler and politician. His ego had been sufficiently tamed by practicing the Dhamma, so he no longer required gratification based on conceit. Anathapindika in turn asked Venerable Ananda to plant the Bodhi tree."

"Several years later when the tree was fully grown, I asked if the Lord would spend a night under the sacred tree to more-fully consecrate it with his presence," says Ananda. "Anathapindika was fond of meditating under that tree until the day he died, and it was there that he enjoyed re-living the memories of his association with the Lord."

"That tree made my father happier than all the gold he ever had," says Kala with tears in his eyes. "To this day it is known as 'The Ananda Bodhi.'"

Ananda smiles when he hears the name of "his" tree, but not wanting the attention of the discussion to shift to him, he promptly says, "When your father knew he was dying he asked Venerable Sariputta to visit him, because he didn't want to trouble the Buddha. I went with Venerable Sariputta who expounded the Dhamma to your dear father. His physical pains left him as he concentrated his mind on the virtuous life he had led. Later on, he actually got up and offered us *dana* for the last time. He died that same night." Everyone in the room reflects for a moment on the great Anathapindika. Kala and Sujata, full of emotion, wipe away tears.

For the next two days the sub-committee continues recollecting the almost numberless occasions when Anathapindika played a role in the Buddha's life.

On the final evening Maha Kassapa says to Kala, "Your father might be called 'too generous' because he gave so much away that he eventually spent his entire wealth."

"That may very well be true, but his attitude remained positive in the face of all adversity, and he never neglected to serve the Buddha and his Sangha whenever he had an opportunity," replies Kala.

"Of course, being the industrious man he was, his fortune was soon re-built. He continued his life-long practice of daily *dana* for large numbers of monks, and he always looked for ways to provide for the welfare of the Buddha," says Bakkula.

Ananda speaks, "The Buddha once preached the following discourse to our dear friend, Anathapindika, which I think should be recorded here in our recollection:

"'There are four kinds of happiness which may be achieved by a lay person who enjoys sensual pleasure, depending on time and occasion: the happiness of possession, the happiness of enjoyment, the happiness of debtlessness, and the happiness of blamelessness.

"'The happiness of possession is when a man acquires wealth through his energetic striving, amasses it by the strength of his arms, and earns it by the sweat of his brow; this is righteous wealth, which was righteously gained. In this way he experiences happiness and joy.

"'The happiness of the enjoyment of wealth, which has been righteously gained, is when a family man enjoys his wealth and performs meritorious deeds.

"'The happiness of debtlessness is when a family man is not indebted to anyone, to any degree, whether small or great.

"'The happiness of blamelessness is when a person is endowed with blameless conduct in deed, word, and thought.

"'These, householder, are the four kinds of happiness that a lay person may achieve.'"[6]

Maha Kassapa rises from his seat saying, "On behalf of our subcommittee members I thank you, Kala and Sujata, for your gracious hospitality these past two days and nights. We have enjoyed your villa, and are grateful for your invaluable contribution to these recollections of the Lord's life.

"It can be said that the two of you have truly taken to heart the Buddha's teaching about happiness and wealth. I know that you will continue to be blessed by your unfailing practice of generosity, and by the wise ways in which you use your great gifts. Kala, your father will be an example of the correct use of wealth for all time. He knew quite well the advantages and the talents he had been given, and he never failed to do whatever he could to alleviate the suffering of those who were less fortunate.

"He also knew the tremendous responsibility that great wealth carries with it, and he dedicated his life to sharing it and spending it where it counted most: on meritorious deeds, and on those who spend their lives seeking spiritual perfection for the ultimate benefit of all."

"Venerables, we thank you for blessing us with your presence these past two days," says Kala. "We shall never forget the time we were permitted to spend with you." Kala and Sujata prostrate themselves before the esteemed arahants and return to their mansion in the city.

Silently the arahants retire to their private spaces in the villa to contemplate all they have discussed, and to meditate on loving-kindness, generating a strong force-field of happy and positive energy for all. Each of them knows that they have acquired the greatest wealth there is: the irrevocable, eternal peace of *Nibbana*.

Chapter 19
Mission: Compassion

Maha Kassapa sounds the gong and the assembly comes to order. He says, "I hope all of you had an enjoyable, restful retreat these past two days, and that you are now refreshed and ready to resume our important work. Venerable Ananda, please begin your recitation."

Ananda begins, "Today I will start with a recitation of verses from the Dhammapada on the subject of affection:

> "'Whoso gives himself to things which ought to be shunned and exerts not where he ought to exert, he, a seeker after pleasures, giving up his own welfare, envies those who are intent upon their own welfare.'
>
> "'Seek no intimacy with the beloved and never also with the unloved; for not to see the beloved and to see the unloved, both are painful.
>
> "'Therefore hold nothing as dear; for separation from the dear is painful. There are no bonds for them who have nothing beloved or unloved.
>
> "'From endearment springs grief, from endearment springs fear; for him who is wholly free from endearment there is no grief, whence fear?
>
> "'From affection springs grief, from affection springs fear; for him who is wholly free from affection there is no grief, whence fear?
>
> "'From attachment springs grief, from attachment springs fear; for him who is wholly free from attachment there is no grief, whence fear?
>
> "'From craving springs grief, from craving springs fear; for him who is wholly free from craving there is no grief, whence fear?'"[1]

Ananda pauses to allow the beautiful, timeless words of the Buddha to reverberate in the hearts of his listeners. The arahants, free from all fetters of endearment and attachment, are therefore free from grief and fear, and know fully the deep truth of these sayings.

Time passes quickly with further recitations from the Buddha's vast collection of teaching elements. Before any of the council members realize it the sun has gone down, and Maha Kassapa adjourns the assembly.

The sub-committee convenes shortly afterwards in Maha Kassapa's cave chamber. "I don't know about you, Venerable Sirs, but if I weren't already completely past all attachments, I might be tempted by the comforts of silken mats and pillows. To be honest, I got rather used to the sound of our courtyard fountain in Kala and Sujata's villa," says Anuruddha, smiling.

"I understand what you mean. I am happy that none of us are still attached to any of those pleasantries. Having no preferences or aversions is a great freedom," says Punna.

Maha Kassapa speaks, "I believe the Buddha's half-brother, Nanda, is about to make a re-appearance in our recollections, am I right?"

"That is correct, Venerable Sir," answers Ananda. "I may be mistaken about the time, but I believe that it was shortly after the Buddha accepted the monastery from Anathapindika that Nanda began complaining to his fellow *bhikkhus* of being extremely unhappy. He was depressed, and his mood was causing his health to fail. He said, 'Friends, I am not happy living the life of a *bhikkhu*; I am practicing the precepts reluctantly, without true dedication. I don't think I can continue living this way, so I intend to give up and return to a layman's life.'

"The Buddha soon heard this news and sent for Nanda, asking him, 'Have you told your *bhikkhu* friends that you are unhappy, and that you intend to give up your robes and become a layman again?'

"Nanda hung his head and said, 'It is true, my Lord.'

"'Why, Nanda, do you feel you can't continue to keep your precepts and observe the training rules?' asked the Buddha.

"'I can't get over thinking about my beautiful wife, Princess Janapada Kalyani. As you know, I left her on our wedding day when she was calling to me from her balcony. Thoughts of her tears torment me, and I can't concentrate,' admitted Nanda honestly. 'I shall give up and return to live with her as husband and wife.'

"'Come with me,' said the Buddha, and using his supernormal powers he immediately lifted up Nanda by the shoulders and transported the two of them to the *Tavatimsa* Heaven. On the way they stopped in the Himalayas. They walked over to a spot by the side of the path, and the Buddha pointed to the charred remains of a female monkey sitting on the burned-out stump of a tree. Her ears, nose, tail, and other parts of her body were burnt and ragged.

"The Buddha said, 'Nanda, who looks prettier and lovelier – your bride, Janapada Kalyani, or this burned female monkey?'

"Nanda looked at the Buddha with surprise and said, 'Well, my bride, of course!'

"They continued on their way to *Tavatimsa* Heaven where Sakka, the king of gods, greeted them with great respect. Sakka led them into a chamber where five-hundred celestial nymphs attended on them. These nymphs were ravishing, and the Buddha knew that Nanda would instantly be enamored. He said, 'Nanda, who looks prettier and lovelier – your bride, Janapada Kalyani, or these five-hundred celestial nymphs?'

"Nanda couldn't take his eyes off of the nymphs, and he answered with a big smile, 'Why, these nymphs are far more beautiful,'" says Ananda.

"Why do you think the Buddha showed Nanda the celestial nymphs when lust and passion was his problem to begin with?" asks Upali.

Bakkula, the one Foremost in Good Health, speaks, "The Buddha was acting as a doctor in this instance. In order to cure a disease the physician sometimes gives the patient a big dose of what originally caused it. This brings the disease to its peak, and then the physician can affect a cure by purging it from the system."

Ananda continues, "That is correct, Venerable Sir; the Lord was an excellent physician – and psychologist. The Buddha told Nanda, 'You can have these five hundred celestial nymphs if you obey your training rules and take delight in practicing your precepts.'

"Nanda said, 'Most exalted elder brother, if you give me your assurance that I can actually possess these nymphs then I shall undertake to observe the training rules and practice meditation with great vigor!'

"The Buddha took Nanda back to the monastery and Nanda went off to his dwelling place. It didn't take long before the news of Nanda's renewed sense of purpose spread, and monks in the community began to doubt and scorn him, saying, ' Nanda is a great servant of the senses; he is a great buyer of lustful sense pleasures.'

"When Nanda heard these taunting words from his fellow monks he became disgusted and filled with shame. He retired to a secluded place in the monastery and strove with earnestness and diligence to meditate with his mind pointed toward *Nibbana*. His hard work paid off and it didn't take him very long to attain arahantship," says Ananda.

"I understand that the Lord knew immediately of his brother's attainment," says Sopaka.

"That is correct. Shortly afterwards Arahant Nanda went before the Buddha to release him from his promise of letting him have the five hundred celestial nymphs. He said, 'Exalted brother, I had you make a promise so that I could satisfy my unsavory desires, and have thereby committed a misdeed. I now release you from that promise.'

"The Buddha replied, 'I knew of the very instant you achieved arahantship, Nanda, and at that moment I was released from your promise,'" continues Ananda.

"Apparently some of the other *bhikkhus* didn't believe Nanda had achieved the goal of arahantship," says Upali.

"No, they didn't," agrees Ananda. "They went to Nanda and rebuked him for telling lies. They also reminded him that just a short while before he had informed them of his intention to disrobe and become a layman again. Nanda was not disappointed with their reaction and disbelief; in fact, he didn't really blame them. The doubting monks went to the Buddha and brought the matter to his attention. He told them that Nanda had, in fact, achieved the highest attainment of arahantship, and then he recited the following two verses:

> "'*Bhikkhus*, just as rainwater can penetrate and flood a badly roofed house, so the mind, which has *not* been trained by tranquility and insight meditation, is liable to be inundated with defilements, and can be flooded with the rainwater of lust, malice, delusion, and conceit.
>
> "'On the other hand, *Bhikkhus*, just as rainwater *cannot* penetrate and flood a properly roofed house, so the mind, which *has* been trained by tranquility and insight meditation, *cannot* be inundated with defilements, and *cannot* be flooded with the rainwater of lust, malice, delusion, and conceit.'[2]

"By the end of these verses a number of those *bhikkhus* attained *sotapanna*, so the whole episode was of great value to many people – not just to Nanda," concludes Ananda.

"I think several of them eventually attained the final stage of arahantship, and are participating in this very conference," adds Maha Kassapa. "Sopaka,[3] I think your first encounter with the Lord came around this time. Would you mind telling us about it?"

"I would be happy to, Venerable Chairman," replies Sopaka. "For a number of reasons my childhood was not a happy one. My father died when I was only four years old, and because we were destitute my mother re-married a man who turned out to be truly wicked. For some reason he despised me from the very beginning, and he would make up excuses to beat me. My mother was powerless to stop him because of our financial condition and we depended on him. He repeatedly abused me whenever she was out. I know she loved me, but she was helpless to protect me from him.

"After two years together she became pregnant, and had a baby girl. I had hoped that my little sister would soften my step-father's heart, but even though he loved her dearly, his attitude toward me didn't change. In fact he seemed to hate me even more; he scolded me relentlessly when I ate, sat, or spoke. He would suddenly get the notion to hit me for no reason whatsoever. I couldn't even sleep because he would come at me in the night and try to strangle me. I got into the habit of sleeping with my hands grasped around my neck so he couldn't grab my throat and kill me.

"One day my little sister began to cry in her cradle as all babies do. My stepfather heard her and immediately assumed that I had done something to harm her, so he rushed toward me. He grabbed my ear, nearly twisting it off, and gave me a violent blow to the head with his clenched fist. When I started to cry my sister cried even louder, and this enraged my step-father all the more," says Sopaka.

The other arahants in the cave chamber listen intently and with great compassion to Sopaka's sad story of abuse.

"I tried my best to stop crying, and then I just lay on the floor quietly weeping, nursing my ear," continues Sopaka with great feeling. "My mother wasn't at home at the time, so I was completely defenseless. My stepfather kept yelling at me, accusing me of harming my little sister. Then he grabbed a rope from the corner of the room, roughly picked me up, and dragged me from the house, screaming for my life. I struggled desperately and somehow managed to get away from him, running as fast as my small legs would carry me. I didn't know where I was going; I just knew I had to get away from that evil man or he would surely kill me.

"He finally caught up with me at the charnel grounds, grabbing me by the neck. I remember that there was an overpowering stench, coming from a decomposing body nearby. The sounds of jackals were everywhere, howling as they fed greedily off the decaying corpses. My stepfather dragged me to where a naked body lay; I couldn't tell if it was male or female. In spite of my screaming, weeping, and begging he threw me down and tied me to that corpse with the rope. Then he just stood there laughing at me until he became tired of the amusement. Eventually he turned and walked off, leaving me to certain death," says Sopaka. The arahant pauses a moment to reflect on the once terrifying memory.

"I laid there sobbing until I no longer had the strength to cry any more," begins Sopaka. "I could hear the sounds of the jackals devouring that stinking nude corpse. When I screamed out they would stop for a while, but when I got quiet again they started tugging at it, eating it ravenously. I was soaked with the putrid excrescence of the decaying body, and nearly lost consciousness many times.

"Whenever I could gather my strength I would scream out for my mother, the person I loved most in the world; the only person that cared about me. At one point a vicious jackal bit off a piece of flesh from the corpse, and one of its sharp teeth cut into my back. I screamed as loudly as I could from both the pain and the horror. I knew for certain that any moment I would die, as the jackals continued to feast. I closed my eyes preparing myself for death, and at that very moment everything became completely quiet and still. I slowly ventured to open my eyes and I saw him standing there, the Buddha."

"How did he know you were there? How did he find you?" asks Upali.

"He told me later that he actually heard me screaming, even though I was a great distance from his monastery. He came as quickly as he could, and with great compassion said, 'Child Sopaka! Do not be afraid, I will save you. The *Tathagata*, the venerable father, will be your refuge.'

"While he started to untie me from the revolting mess that had once been a human body, he said, 'I came in search of you, child. Do not be frightened; I will soon make you free.'

"I was in a complete state of shock; my body was frozen stiff from fear. I couldn't even stand up. The Buddha said with his voice full of love and compassion, 'Sopaka, get up! Regain your senses.' Then he stroked my head and took my hand. I somehow got hold of my mind, and then began to cry like the seven-year-old child I was.

"He helped me up, and then led me by the hand to the stream between the monastery and the charnel grounds. He took me into the cool, flowing water and bathed me with his own hands. He asked, 'What happened to you, child?' So I told him my fearsome story.

"He said, 'Child, you are safe now with me. Let's go and get you some clothes and food.' When he held my hand I felt completely safe and I went willingly with him to the monastery."

Ananda speaks, "That night when I finished meditating it must have been just after midnight. As usual, I went to the Buddha's inner quarters to pay obeisance to him before going to sleep, but he wasn't there. I stood in the doorway looking around and wondered where he had gone. Then I saw him approaching in the distance leading a little naked boy by the hand. I watched as the Buddha entered his room; the tired child simply crumpled and lay down at his feet. I thought it was very strange that he had his hands clenched around his neck.

"The Buddha asked the child, 'Are you going to sleep?'

"'Yes, lord, I know I can sleep next to your feet without any fear,' Sopaka replied.

"Then the Buddha told him, 'You can take your hands from around your neck; no one will harm you here.'

Sopaka adds, "Then the Buddha told Ananda, 'I saved this poor boy's life tonight. I bathed him and brought him here to protect him. Let him stay in the monastery until I can find his parents and obtain permission for his ordination. Please take him to your room and find some clothes for him. Let him eat, and then find him a suitable place to sleep.' Without saying a word I embraced the Buddha's feet and then Ananda picked me up and carried me."

Ananda continues, "The poor, innocent child weighed next to nothing. I took him to my room, dressed and fed him, and then he curled up on a mat at the foot of my bed and went to sleep.

"The following day Sopaka's frantic mother came to the monastery looking for her missing child. Her husband, of course, hadn't told her what had happened the night before; he just said that the stupid boy had run off and he didn't know where he was. She went before the Buddha and the Lord summoned me to bring the child. She tearfully embraced her son, and the child clung to her in desperation. The Lord spoke to her saying that there was no point in looking for children and other kinsmen without looking for herself first. When he finished his talk she realized the state of *sotapanna*.

"After this conversation with your mother the Buddha smiled at you and asked, 'Would you like to live a life of peace and contentment, free from fear, and filled with happiness?'

"'Yes, Lord, and I would like to follow you for the rest of my life,' answered the prodigious young boy.

"The Buddha then turned to the child's mother and said, 'Do you give permission for your son to be ordained?'

"She replied, 'Yes, Lord. I know that I cannot protect him from my husband. I would be grateful if you would let him do as he wishes and join your Sangha.'

"The Buddha ordained Sopaka as a *samanera* on the spot," concluded Ananda.

"Don't forget the ten questions,"[4] says Upali.

"Yes, the ten questions that are now part of the training for all new *samaneras*," responded Ananda. "Sopaka, you were the first to be asked. After two years in the monastery the Buddha sent for you and proceeded to ask you ten questions. Your answers proved beyond any doubt that you were truly a prodigy. For the record, I'll relate the Buddha's ten questions and your remarkable responses:

>"'What is one?' asked the Buddha of Sopaka.
>"'One is all beings subsist on food.'
>
>"'What is two?'
>"'Two is mind and matter.'
>
>"'What is three?'
>"'Three is three kinds of feelings.'
>
>"'What is four?'
>"'Four is the Four Noble Truths.'
>
>"'What is five?'
>"'Five is the five groups of grasping.'
>
>"'What is six?'
>"'Six is the internal six-fold base.'
>
>"'What is seven?'
>"'Seven is the seven factors of enlightenment.'

"'What is eight?'
"'Eight is the Noble Eightfold Path.'
"'What is nine?'
"'Nine is the nine abodes of being.'
"'What is ten?'
"'He that is endowed with the ten attributes is called an arahant,' concluded the small boy.

"As a reward for answering these ten questions correctly, the Buddha gave Sopaka the higher ordination of *bhikkhu*. To our extreme surprise, Sopaka very quickly attained the state of arahantship," concludes Ananda.

The other arahants in the cave chamber look at Sopaka, now a man in his mid forties. By this time he had been a fully-enlightened arahant for most of his life, and he still had many years to grace the world with his radiant presence.

"You were given the greatest imaginable gift that night, Sopaka," says Maha Kassapa.

The arahant nods and smiles at the chairman with great warmth and affection and says, "The Buddha was like a father to me, and Rahula, like my brother. All of you are my brothers, and all living beings in the universe are my family. I could never fully express my gratitude to the Master or to all of you – especially to you, Venerable Ananda. You cared for me as if I was your own child that first night – and you've been watching over me ever since."

"And now you watch over me," says Ananda softly with great joy. The two arahants stare into each others hearts, communicating what could never be adequately said in words.

The committee members turn toward the cave entrance when they see torchlight approaching in the passageway. One of the chairman's lay volunteers ushers in a special guest, Sunita, who bows low to the Sangha members, who in turn bow to him.

"Come in, Venerable Sunita. You have made your entrance at exactly the right time, which doesn't surprise me one bit," says Maha Kassapa, smiling.

To the committee members he says, "I have asked Sunita to join us this evening so he could tell us his story of meeting the Buddha. I think that no recollection of the Buddha will be complete without Sunita's first encounter with the Blessed One. It demonstrates the Lord's infinitely compassionate attitude towards conventional social mores better than any other tale I can think of. Sunita, please have a seat and share your story with us; we are grateful to be able to hear it directly from you."

Sunita seats himself comfortably on a mat. "All of you know my background; I was born a *candala*, a member of the untouchable class. I had no education; in fact, by law I wasn't allowed to learn. It would have been a high offence if I had been caught writing or speaking even one word from the Vedas. I wasn't allowed to enter a place of worship, and if I had ever been overheard reciting one of the Vedic prayers my tongue would have been cut out. This was the law.

"I was born near here in the Rajagaha area, and people like me who belonged to the untouchable caste survived by cleaning the streets, drains, and toilets. We were the ones who disposed of dead animals, and who did other unmentionable work that no one else would do. We wore scraps of cloth, which barely covered our nakedness, and we weren't allowed access to the public wells. To touch the water reserved for the higher-caste people was to pollute not only the water, but the casted people who used it as well. Any contact would result in their having to perform extensive rituals to cleanse themselves, and there would be severe punishment for us as well.

"I collected night soil, human waste, from the public drains, and carried it to the fields in two large buckets suspended on a pole I carried on my shoulders. You can imagine how filthy I was, and the foul ugly smell that exuded from every pore. Flies and other insects covered not only my buckets, but my entire body as well. My hair was matted and unkempt, my skin as black as the night from dirt and excrement. I was never but an inch away from starvation; you could see every bone in my body as it protruded against my leathery, sundried skin. I had no home; I simply slept on the side of the road wherever I happened to wind up at the end of the day."

Sunita pauses for a moment and takes a sip of herbal tea. The other arahants in the room, three of whom had been born royal princes, listen intently to the kind, venerated monk, reflecting on the prejudices that permeated the established caste system of their time.

"I was a bit late on my rounds collecting night soil one morning, and when I looked up the street I saw a group of monks approaching me.

There was a beautiful golden aura surrounding them, and I could tell by their bearing that they were of the higher castes. Please keep in mind that I was not allowed to make eye contact with anyone outside my caste, nor was I to let my shadow fall across theirs. I was immediately afraid, and started looking for a place to hide. Feeling ashamed of myself I didn't want the monks to see me, and I didn't want to be accused of unlawfully looking at them.

"There was no alleyway or shelter nearby, so I walked over to the nearest wall, put down my pole, and stood there with my arms folded in front of me, bowing as low as I could. I hoped with all my heart that they would simply pass me by, and not ridicule me or complain that I was fouling the air they breathed or the earth they walked on.

"I could sense the group of monks as they approached, and I couldn't believe it when I heard a voice call out, 'Dear friend; would you like to join us?' My fear was now combined with a tentative feeling of joy, but I couldn't bring myself to raise my head and speak to the man.

"The Buddha had stopped right in front of me, waiting for an answer. I said, 'I am a *candala*, my Lord. I am not even allowed to speak with you, much less join you. Nonetheless, no one has ever spoken kindly to me before, and I am grateful for your words; they bring joy and light to my heart.'

"The Buddha stood there patiently waiting for me, and I found myself feeling stronger and happier by the second. I finally ventured to say, 'If you would have this miserable, wretched untouchable, I would gladly go with you and become a monk.'

"The Lord said, 'Come, O monk!' which was my ordination, right then and there.

"I followed the Buddha and the other monks to their monastery, and I was shown where to bathe. After shaving my head Ananda brought me fresh clean robes and showed me how to dress. You were so kind that day, my dear friend, and not a day goes by that I don't bless you for your limitless compassion."

Ananda, a former prince, looks up at Sunita and says, "You were so grateful for every smile, every sweet word, every encouragement, and every bit of respect that you so deserved. You blossomed very quickly, didn't you?"

Sunita smiles lovingly at the Lord's chief attendant, and replies, "When I was taken to his presence the Buddha gave me an object for meditation, and told me to find a secluded corner of the monastery and contemplate upon it. I was so grateful for his kindness; I felt like I owed it to him – and to all of the Sangha members – to try my very best, and strive hard for the highest goal. Believe it or not, by the end of that very night I became enlightened, an arahant. It was far beyond my wildest dreams; in fact, before meeting the Buddha I had no dreams at all."

Ananda says, "You came and found me after your supreme moment, and I'll never forget your first words:

> "'People found me disgusting, despised me, disparaged me. Lowering my heart, I showed reverence to many.
>
> "'The compassionate Teacher, sympathetic to all the world, said: "'Come, monk.' That was my formal Acceptance.
>
> "'Then, as night was ending and the sun returning, Indra and Brahma came to pay homage to me, hands palm-to-palm at their hearts:
>
>> 'Homage to you, O thoroughbred of men;
>> Homage to you, O man supreme,
>> whose fomentations are ended,
>> You, dear sir, are worthy of offerings.'"[5]

After a moment's pause, Maha Kassapa says, "From that moment forward people of all ranks and backgrounds respected and paid homage to you. Your attainment set an example for all time about hope and the fulfillment of spiritual dreams. You have showed the world the true meaning of what it means to be a Brahmin, dear friend. You also demonstrated the fact that social conventions have no meaning when held in the light of the unlimited compassion and vision of the Buddha."

The other arahants reflect on the chairman's kind words as they look at their brother, Sunita, with purest of love shining in their eyes. Sopaka and Sunita, two of the lowliest of men by birth, had reached the very pinnacle of human evolutionary potential thanks to the love of the Buddha.

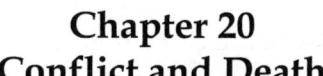

Chapter 20
Conflict and Death

Ananda stands with both hands on the podium while reciting the *Kalahavivada Sutta*:[1]

"'Sir,' said a questioner, 'whenever there are arguments and quarrels there are tears and anguish, arrogance and pride, and grudges and insults to go with them. Can you explain how these things come about? Where do they all come from?'

"'The tears and anguish that follow arguments and quarrels,' said the Buddha, 'the arrogance and pride, and grudges and insults that go with them, are all the result of one thing. They come from having preferences, from holding things precious and dear. Insults are born out of arguments, and grudges are inseparable from quarrels.'

"'But why, Sir, do we have these preferences, these special things? Why do we have so much greed? And all the aspirations and achievements that we base our lives on; where do we get them from?'

"'The preferences, the precious things,' said the Buddha, 'come from the impulse of desire. So too, does greed, and so too do the aspirations and achievements that make up people's lives.'

"'From where, sir, comes this impulse of desire? From where do we derive our theories and opinions? And what about all the other things that you, the Wanderer, have named – such as anger, dishonesty and confusion?'

"'Anger, confusion and dishonesty arise when things are set in pairs of opposites. The person who vacillates between opposites must train himself in the path of knowledge. The habit of grasping is based on wanting things. If there were no wanting, there would be no possessiveness,' said the Buddha. 'It is perception, which is rooted in consciousness, which is the source of all the basic obstacles.'

"'...The wise man has realized which things are dependencies and he knows that these are only crutches and props. And when he has realized this, he has become free. He does not enter into arguments, and so does not enter the round of endless becomings.'"

After the recitation is finished Maha Kassapa sounds the gong, indicating it is time for morning recess. Stepping down from the platform he says to Ananda, "I sense from the *sutta* you just recited that tonight we will be hearing about the war between the Sakyas and the Koliyas. It fits right in with the timeline of our current discussions."

"As usual, dear friend, you are quite correct," replies Ananda, smiling as the two esteemed arahants proceed to the enclosure where midmorning tea is being served.

Later that evening in Maha Kassapa's cave chamber the nine subcommittee members meet to continue where they had left off. The chairman suggests that Anuruddha tell the background story about the conflict between the two states, Sakya and Koliya, and give Ananda's voice a rest.

"I'd be more than happy to, Venerable Sir." responds Anuruddha. The memory monks close their eyes and enter their practiced meditative state for recording.

"The Rohini River lies between the two states, as it flows down from the Chure Range in the Himalayas. It eventually joins the Rapti River at Gorakhpur. It isn't a major artery for transportation, but it does provide water for irrigating the farmlands. There is a small reservoir where water is stored during the rainy season for use during the growing season. All the royal agricultural lands, including the estates of my family and Ananda's and Bhaddiya's as well, depend on water from the Rohini.

"During the time in question the water level in the Rohini was very, very low, and the crops were withering. The farmers were concerned, fearing there wouldn't be enough water for everyone. One of the Koliyan farmers said, 'Friends, if the small amount of water in the reservoir were to be divided there won't be enough for all our fields. At this critical stage in the growing season we need you to let us have all of the water in the reservoir.'

"One of the Sakyan farmers replied by saying, 'Do you expect us to go begging door to door from your houses when your granaries are full and ours are empty? Our crops are dying, too, and we need the water just as badly as you do!'

"The argument quickly heated up between the two groups of farmers, neither side willing to yield to the other. The hostilities spread like wildfire, quickly escalating to insults between the clans. Both sides were equally acrimonious towards the other, and eventually the farmers started exchanging blows as fighting broke out.

"The farmers returned to their respective cities and reported the matter to their Ministers of Agriculture, angrily demanding that action be taken against those who had insulted and threatened them. By the time the situation came to the attention of their chiefs, both sides were heatedly demanding war. As a result, the Sakyas of Kapilavatthu, led by my brother Prince Mahanama, prepared to wage war on the Koliyas and they came out shouting war cries. The Koliyas did the same, with Prince Vishnamitta at their head. Prince Vishnamitta was the son of Prince Dandapani, the younger brother of King Suppabuddha. Both sides quickly prepared for the inevitable battle," concludes Anuruddha.

"It always amazes me how quickly small disputes can become wars when self-centered motives, fueled by strong emotions, take over the mind," observes Punna.

"The Buddha was astute, as always, when he proclaimed in the *sutta* we heard this morning that opinions and conflicting points of view all arise out of desire and greed," comments Upali. "The sad thing, especially where politics is concerned, is that conflict usually ends in bloodshed. The emotionally-stirred-up mind of the group is so dangerous."

"Well put, Upali," says Anuruddha.

"I thank you for your consideration of my voice, but I'm fine Venerable Sirs, and I would like to continue the tale," says Ananda. His cousin nods his assent.

"At the time the Buddha was residing at the Jetavana Monastery in Savatthi," begins Ananda. "The morning of the day the two armies prepared to go to war, he surveyed the world and saw that a great amount of blood was about to be spilled. He realized that if he were to go to the Rohini River he would be able to bring the two opposing armies to their senses, and prevent the war that was about to begin.

"He spent the day in the Fragrant Chamber, and around sunset he departed for the battlefield. Using his supernormal powers he transported himself instantly to a spot just upriver from where the two opposing armies were unsheathing their swords. The fading sunlight gleamed on the bare blades that would soon be bathed in blood.

"The Buddha walked serenely down the bank of the narrow river toward the site where the two armies were making their last minute battle preparations. The Sakyan generals were the first to recognize him, and one of them called out, 'It is our kinsman, the Buddha. It is not proper for us to let our weapons fall on the bodies of others in his presence.' They immediately dismounted from their horses and put away their swords and spears. The Koliyan generals also recognized the Lord, and they, too, got off their horses and sheathed their weapons.

"The Buddha waded into the river and standing mid-stream he asked, 'Why have you all come to this place?'

"General Mahanama answered, 'We have come to wage war on this sandy plain.'[2]

"Then the Buddha asked, 'Royal Highnesses, what is the actual cause of your strife?'

"The two opposing generals answered simultaneously, 'The water of this Rohini River is the cause of it.'

"'What is more valuable - the water in this river or the earth?' questioned the Buddha.

"'Compared to the water in this river, the earth is much more valuable,' answered Mahanama.

"'What is more valuable - the earth or human life?' asked the Buddha.

"'Of course, human life is more valuable,' answered Vishnamitta.

"'Just for the sake of some water from this Rohini River, that you yourselves agree is of small value, you would wish to destroy human lives by fighting one another? Not the slightest amount of pleasure could be found in worthless conflicts and wasteful strife,' said the Buddha.

"The Lord then told them a parable about conflict, and how no good can ever come of it. As they listened intently to the words of the Buddha the emotions of the generals and their two armies began to cool, and they gradually came to their senses. The tale was the well-known one about the quail sage and the hunter. I will tell this story now so it can be included in our recollection," says Ananda.

"Long ago there lived a very wise quail.[3] He taught many important practical lessons to his great family of birds, and because of his renowned wisdom they called him the 'Sage.' The quail family lived together in a beautiful green forest. They had everything they needed, and they lived happy, contented lives.

"One day a hunter came into the forest and began tricking the quail with his clever bird calls. Thinking he was one of them, they came near him, and in the blink of an eye the hunter tossed his net over them. He scooped them up, put them in his basket, and took them to market.

"Every day the quail hunter came, capturing many of the members of the quail family. They became very fearful and disturbed, and decided to go to the sage and ask him what to do.

"The quail sage thought about it and then said, 'As soon as the net gets thrown over you, stick your necks in between the ropes, flap your wings, and fly up into the sky. You'll have the combined strength to do this if you work together. Then fly into the nearest bramble bush and let the net drop in a tangled heap. Then you can scurry out from under it to safety.'

"The next day the hunter came to the forest, and using his bird calls as usual, he threw the net over a covey of quail. Much to his surprise, the birds poked their heads through the holes and flew away with the net. Frustrated, he watched his payday disappear. He followed the flying birds and found his net on a bramble bush, tangled and in dire need of repair.

"For many days he kept trying to capture quail, but the birds worked together as a unit and thwarted his efforts every time. Soon the hunter's wife became angry. She called him bad names, saying he was useless and couldn't provide for his family. He responded with confidence, 'Don't worry, dear wife; one of these days those birds will stop cooperating with one another. Losing their mutual trust, they'll be right back in my basket.'

"It wasn't long before a quarrel developed between two of the birds. A silly incident caused it, but neither one was willing to stop and make peace. Instead, they kept on bickering and allowed the petty disagreement to escalate. They couldn't resist trading hurtful insults with one another.

"The sage leader of the quail overheard the birds arguing. He knew that in such a state of mind they were in grave danger because they were no longer in the mood to work together. He spoke to the whole flock saying, 'Those of you who want to live together in peace and in a spirit of mutual cooperation – follow me, and we will go elsewhere. Those who don't – you're on your own, but beware.'

"The next day the hunter came upon the group of quail that had been bickering. He threw his net over them and immediately some of them started arguing with one another. One of them said, 'You never do your share of the work!' The other one shot back, 'I do more than you!' While they were busy arguing the hunter quickly bundled them all up in his net and stuffed them into his wicker basket. He smiled to himself knowing that his wife would be pleased.

"After telling the story the Buddha said to the generals, 'Even in ancient times, those who survived were the ones who learned to work together, settling their arguments peacefully. Those that didn't learn this lesson perished.'

"The minds of the generals were now significantly calmed as the impact of the Buddha's story began to hit home. The Buddha, seeing that they still weren't quite ready to disarm, preached a more serious *sutta* to them, known as the *Attadanda Sutta*.[4] I will recite it for you now:

> "'Fear results from resorting to violence – just look at how people quarrel and fight!...
>
> "'Seeing people struggling, like fish writhing in shallow water with enmity against one another, I became afraid.
>
> "'At one time, I had wanted to find some place where I could take shelter, but I never saw any such place. There is nothing in this world that is solid at base, and not a part of it that is changeless.

"'I had seen them all trapped in mutual conflict and that is why I had felt so repelled...

"'When a man does not identify himself with mind and matter at all, when he does not grieve for what does not exist, then he cannot sustain a loss in this world.

"'When he does not think, 'This is mine' or 'That belongs to them,' then, since he has no egoism, he cannot grieve with the thought of 'I do not have.'

"'If you ask me to describe a man who is unshakeable, I say that where there is no harshness, where there is no greed, no trace of desire, and when a man is the same in all circumstances, then you have what I would call the praiseworthy condition of an unshakeable man.

"'A man of discernment, without a flutter of desire, does not accumulate – he has no conditioning – he has stopped all effort of every kind; so everywhere he sees peace and happiness.

"'The wise man does not rate himself with the distinguished, the lowest, nor with ordinary people; calm and unselfish, he is free from possessiveness: he holds on to nothing and he rejects nothing.'"

When Ananda finishes reciting this powerful *sutta* the arahants in the cave chamber reflect gratefully on the fact that each of them is completely free from the destructive shackles of possessiveness.

Bhaddiya speaks, "In addition to helping the two warring factions come to their senses and put down their arms, two hundred fifty royal princes were given to the Sangha that day by each side. The Buddha ordained them and took them with him to the Bamboo Grove near the city of Kapilavatthu. From that day onward they accompanied the Buddha when he went for alms food, alternating days between the Sakyan and the Koliyan capitals."

"At first those five hundred *bhikkhus* weren't happy with their families' decision to force them to join the Sangha," says Maha Kassapa. "Soon they were complaining that their wives, families and business affairs were being neglected, and that they were bored. The Buddha, knowing the state of their minds, looked after them personally as a mother would look after her children. He preached to them on a regular basis, and before too long all of them attained *sotapanna*. Eventually, all of these royal sons attained arahantship, and several of them are attending this very council."

"I think we'll soon be hearing about their royal wives," comments Bhaddiya knowingly.

"The Buddha's view on conflict can be summed up by four lines from the Dhammapada," interjects Bakkula. The arahants pause to listen carefully as the aged, but perennially-healthy arahant recites their Master's well-known verses.

> "'Victory begets enmity;
> The vanquished dwell in pain.
> Happily the Peaceful live,
> Discarding both victory and defeat.'"[5]

"Excellent summary, Venerable Sir. Before we move on I'd like to offer one last note on the Buddha's views on conflict," says Ananda. "I am reminded of one of the discourses from the *Brahmanasamyutta Sutta*[6] on the subject of abuse. A Brahmin named Akkosaka Bharadvaja approached the Buddha to complain about the large number of his clansmen that were leaving home to join the Lord's Sangha. He felt they were being stolen from their families who needed them. This man was well-known for being particularly abusive, and this encounter with the Lord was no exception. I will quote from the *sutta*:

> "'Angry and displeased he approached the Blessed One and abused and reviled him with rude, harsh words.
>
> "'When he had finished speaking the Blessed One said to him: 'What do you think, Brahmin? Do your friends and colleagues, kinsmen and relatives, as well as other guests come to visit you from time to time?'
>
> "'Sometimes they come.'
>
> "'But if they do not accept the food you offer them, then who does it belong to?'
>
> "'If they do not accept it from me, then the food still belongs to me.'

"'So, too, Brahmin, I – who do not abuse anyone, who do not scold anyone, who do not rail against anyone – refuse to accept from you the abuse, scolding, and tirade you let loose at me. It still belongs to you, Brahmin! It still belongs to you, Brahmin!

"'Brahmin, one who abuses his own abuser, who scolds the one who scolds him, who rails against the one who rails at him – he is said to partake of the meal, to enter upon an exchange. But I do not partake of your meal; I do not enter upon an exchange. It still belongs to you, Brahmin! It still belongs to you, Brahmin!'

"'The king and his retinue understand the ascetic Gotama to be an arahant, yet Master Gotama still gets angry,' said Akkosaka Bharadvaja to the Buddha, who then recited these verses:

> "'How can anger arise in one who is angerless,
> in the tamed one of righteous living,
> In one liberated by perfect knowledge,
> in the Stable One who abides in peace?

> "'One who repays an angry man with anger,
> thereby makes things worse for himself.
> Not repaying an angry man with anger,
> one wins a battle hard to win.

> "'He practices for the welfare of both –
> his own and the other's –
> When, knowing that his foe is angry,
> he mindfully maintains his peace.'

"'When this was said, the Brahmin Akkosaka Bharadvaja took refuge in the Buddha, the Dhamma, and the Sangha. 'May I receive the going forth under Master Gotama; may I receive the higher ordination?'"[7]

Ananda finishes reciting the *sutta* and the other arahants chuckle over the irony of the situation. "Venerable Bharadvaja often laughed about the fact that he went to the Buddha to complain about the excessive number of his clansmen who had been ordained – and at the end of the Buddha's discourse he himself asked for it," says Punna, smiling.

"Yes and the venerable practiced well, becoming an arahant!" adds Sopaka.

"Thank you for that recollection, Ananda, and for your comments, dear brothers. Moving on with our story, I believe that from the Rohini River the Buddha went to stay for a time at the Bamboo Grove Monastery near Kapilavatthu," says Maha Kassapa.

"That is correct, Venerable Sir. I think he knew that he would soon be needed at his father's palace," adds Sopaka.

"Very true," says Ananda. "Just a few days after the disagreement over the water in the Rohini River, the Buddha received word that King Suddhodana was on his deathbed. I went with him, as did Rahula who was by that time twelve years old. Nanda, the Buddha's brother, Sariputta, and several other monks also accompanied the Lord when he made that last visit to see his father."

"Bhaddiya and I went with you, too, Ananda. All three of us were the king's nephews, and it was an important time for the family to gather," says Anuruddha. "While I was growing up King Suddhodana treated me like his own son, and I loved him dearly."

"When we arrived at the palace the sun had just set, and the mood was very dark and somber," begins Ananda. "Queen Mahapajapati, Princess Sundarinanda, and Princess Yasodhara greeted us in the courtyard, paid their respects to the Buddha, and led us up the grand stairway to the king's private chamber."

"The three royal ladies were very composed, considering the circumstances, and their demeanor was lovely, as usual," adds Anuruddha. "Even with her shaved head and yellow robes Yasodhara still looked young and beautiful; she exhibited none of the fragile emotions that had surfaced in the past. All three ladies had obviously been meditating, and their spiritual understanding had advanced to a higher level."

"Many members of the royal household accompanied us to the king's chamber, but the Buddha signaled all of them to wait in the anteroom. Just the Buddha, the six of us *bhikkhus*, and the three women entered the royal bedchamber. The king was sleeping when we walked in, but he woke up almost immediately. His eyes sought out the Buddha first, and then they drifted to Rahula and Nanda," says Ananda.

"Even though it was obvious that the king was in great pain, he smiled at us and tears formed in the corners of his eyes. His face was lined and weather-beaten, and his flesh hung loosely on his tired frame. He had lived a wonderful, long life of eighty-five years, and I'm sure he didn't begrudge the fact that death was about to take him," says Anuruddha. "After all, he had already achieved the third stage of attainment, *anagami*."

Ananda speaks, "I'll never forget the king's first words when we gathered around him. He said, 'Tonight I'm the happiest man in the entire world. One of my sons is a Universal Buddha, another is an arahant in his Sangha, and my grandson is well-established on the path to enlightenment. I'm so proud of all three of you; and you as well my dear nephews: Ananda, Anuruddha, and Bhaddiya. My Blessed Son, you prevented a disastrous war with the Koliyas that could have destroyed my kingdom and our race. I am grateful for this generous act.'

"The king looked directly at the Buddha and said, 'Forgive me for long ago wanting you to become an emperor, son. It was my ego that required gratification, and my unenlightened mind used the excuse that it was for our royal line. What you became is much, much more, and your Dhamma will benefit countless people for all time.'

"The Buddha looked down at his father and said, 'There is no need to ask for forgiveness, Your Majesty. We have all played the roles our destinies called for, each of them determined by our previous births and conditioned by billions of factors that coalesced into the fabric of our joined earthly experience. You are a good man, father, and you have been a good king for your people. Now I want you to think of your past good deeds, and focus only on loving-kindness.'

"The king smiled faintly at his Blessed Son, and closed his eyes as a grimace of pain suddenly passed across his face," says Ananda. "The next few moments were some of the most powerful of my life."

"I will share this part of the story if you don't mind, Ananda. I know you would prefer to just listen," says Bhaddiya, who had once served as the king's Regent.

Ananda closes his eyes and nods, accepting his cousin's kind gesture.

"The Buddha placed his right hand on the top of the king's head. Without any instructions from him each of us touched the dying man's body. Nanda held his father's right hand. Rahula held his left hand. Anuruddha and I walked down towards the king's feet and each one of us held an ankle. Sariputta put both of his hands under the small of his back. Finally, our dear Ananda placed both of his palms on the king's heart.

"The three royal ladies lowered their heads as the six of us *bhikkhus* transmitted healing energy and eternal light to the king's failing earthly vessel. The king's body almost immediately relaxed, and the twisted expression left his face. The pain was suddenly gone. A golden aura began to fill the room as the intensity of the spiritual power flowing through us grew and expanded. The king's body literally glowed from within, and his face betold of sublime inner visions and indescribable ecstasy. His breathing, which had been faint, suddenly grew strong and youthful again. Our hands began to radiate heat as if on fire."

Before he continues his story, Bhaddiya pauses for a few seconds to reflect on the sacred moment of forty long years before. "The king slowly opened his weary eyes, and he focused them on the Buddha with a look of unspeakable love and gratitude. We all knew that he had just attained arahantship. We simultaneously removed our hands from his body, and the king silently said goodbye to each of us. He looked again at his son, the Buddha, and then closed his eyes for the last time.

"The Buddha reached over and placed his hands over his father's eyes as if offering a final blessing. The king's widow, Queen Mahapajapati, his daughter, Princess Sundarinanda, and Princess Yasodhara were weeping softly. There were tears in the eyes of Ananda and Rahula, but for the most part we *bhikkhus* remained quite composed. We smiled at one another, knowing that the king had passed the greatest challenge of human existence, attaining *Nibbana*," concludes Bhaddiya.

Ananda says, "For two days and two nights the king's body lay in state under a golden canopy in the palace courtyard. A continuous procession of people, both noble and commoner, slowly passed his royal bier to pay their last respects. Thousands of loving friends, subjects, relatives, and members of the Sangha said goodbye to the great king whose destiny it was to have been the father of the Buddha."

Anuruddha continues, "On the third day we held his funeral service outside the city walls in the royal park. The grand event was sponsored by the new king, Mahanama, my brother. The kings and queens and princes of all of the neighboring states attended, as did the Buddha and every member of the Sangha from all of the monasteries within a two-day's walking journey."

"In fact, every *bhikkhu* and lay person in the region, once they learned of the king's death, wanted to go and pay their respects – not only to King Suddhodana, but to the Buddha himself," says Maha Kaccayana. "I was not with the Buddha in Kapilavatthu at the time, but in Koliya. I traveled to the funeral along with my Sangha brothers in the company of Prince Vishnamitta, the general of the Koliyan military forces. Devadatta also accompanied us on this journey.

"When we arrived at the ceremony King Mahanama and Prince Vishnamitta greeted one another as brothers, their earlier conflict just a memory of the past, thanks to the compassionate intervention of the Buddha. The king's bier of sandalwood was draped in silken fabrics in the royal colors. The Sangha members filed past, and they were followed by the aristocrats. The soldiers, merchants, traders, craftsmen, farmers, and even all the servants in the land came to bid the king farewell. I am quite sure that every able-bodied person in the kingdom attended the solemn event.

"When the last person paid their final respects, King Mahanama lit the funeral pyre and we all watched as the great king's body was consumed by flames. Each of us had our remembrances of beloved King Suddhodana, the man who, because of the Buddha, would now become one of the most celebrated monarchs in history," concludes Maha Kaccayana. "Later, King Mahanama erected a *stupa* on that spot in memory of the Buddha's father, who was also his uncle."

"Ananda, I think this would be a good place to recite the *Salla Sutta*,[8] a Recollection on Death," suggests Maha Kassapa. "Would you mind?"

"Not at all, Venerable Sir.

> "'Life is unpredictable and uncertain in the world.
> Life here is difficult, short and bound up with suffering.

> "'A being, once born, is going to die, and there is no way out of this. When old age arrives, or some other cause, then there is death. This is the way it is with living beings.

"'When fruits become ripe they may fall in the early morning. In just the same way a being, once born, may die at any moment.

"'Just as the clay pots made by the potter tend to end up being shattered, so it is with the life of mortals.

"'Both the young and the old, whether they are foolish or wise, are going to be trapped by death. All beings move towards death.

"'They are overcome by death. They go to the other world. And then not even a father can save his son, or a family their relatives.

"'Look: while relatives are watching, tearful and groaning, men are carried off one by one, like cattle being led to the slaughter.

"'So death and ageing are endemic to the world. Therefore the wise do not grieve seeing the nature of the world.

"'You cannot know his path as to where he has come from, or where he is going to. So it makes no sense to grieve for him.

"'The man who grieves gains nothing. He is doing no more than a foolish man who is trying to hurt himself. If a wise man does it, it is the same for him.

"'Peace of mind cannot come from weeping and wailing. On the contrary, it will lead to more suffering and greater pain.

"'The mourner will become pale and thin. He is doing violence to himself, and still he cannot keep the dead alive; his mourning is pointless.

"'The man who cannot leave his sorrow behind him only travels further into pain. His mourning makes him a slave to sorrow.

"'Look at beings who are facing death, who are living out the results of their previous deeds; people are terrified when they see that they are trapped by death.

"'What people expect to happen is always different from what actually happens. From this comes great disappointment; this is the way the world works.

"'A man may live for a hundred years, or even more, but in the end he is separated from his relatives, and he too leaves life in this world.

"'So we can listen and learn from the noble man as he gives up his grief. When he sees that someone has passed away and lived out his life, he says 'he will not be seen by me again.'

"'When a house is burning, the fire is put out by water. In the same way the wise man, skilful, learned and self-reliant, extinguishes sorrow as soon as it arises in him. It is like the wind blowing away a tuft of cotton.

"'The person who is searching for his own happiness should pull out the cart that he has stuck himself in, the arrow-head of grieving, of desiring, of despair.

"'The man who has taken out the dart, who has no clinging, who has obtained peace of mind, passed beyond all grief, this man, free from grief, is still.'"

"Thank you, dear friend," says Maha Kassapa. "I imagine that Sangha members of the future will continue reciting this *sutta* at funerals and memorial services. Its message of the fragile impermanence of the body is, perhaps, the most compelling wake-up call there is for all human kind."

"Perhaps people will one day see death not as an enemy, but as a dear friend waiting for them at the very end of a party they call life," adds wise Punna. "Men and women have always had a tendency to be in denial about death, and to devise all sorts of ways to make it appear that it couldn't possibly come to them. Great empires, monuments, fortunes, careers, and noble works are often created out of an attempt to gain immortality. The prevalent, but acutely false notion of the immortality of the self, came about because the ego simply does not want to die. It refuses to accept the fact that the body that carries it, the conditional human vehicle, is destined to return to the elements from whence it came. The truth of the matter is: death is the very last fact of life that each and every ego has to come to terms with, alone. The Buddha's words are a great help in this respect."

Maha Kassapa rises from his seat and says, "It's now very late, my brothers, and we are ending on a serious note tonight. I'm grateful that each of us here has been able to shed all vestiges of attachment to these old and brittle mortal forms. We are able to live each moment in the true light of Dhamma, and devote our energies to the service of all humanity."

The chairman pauses for a moment while the arahants collect their thoughts. Then he says, "Council starts at dawn tomorrow morning, my friends; until then..."

Ananda and the other subcommittee pay their respects to the chairman and make their way through the dark, cavernous labyrinth to their own, not yet final, places of rest.

Chapter 21
The *Bhikkhuni* Order

Maha Kassapa rings the gong to commence the dawn devotions. The five hundred arahants begin chanting the Three Refuges and the Vandana in unison.

> "'I pay homage to the Blessed One, the Perfected One, the Fully Awakened One.
>
> "'Such indeed is the Blessed One: perfected, fully awakened, endowed with knowledge and virtue; having walked the right path, the knower of worlds; incomparable guide of willing persons; teacher of gods and humans; awakened and blessed.
>
> "'Well taught is the Dhamma of the Blessed One; of immediate advantage; timeless; inviting us to experience it, leading us onward; to be known individually by the wise.
>
> "'Wholesome in conduct is the Sangha of disciples of the Blessed One. Honest in conduct is the Sangha of the Blessed One. Wise in conduct is the Sangha of the Blessed One. Proper in conduct is the Sangha of the Blessed One. These four pairs of persons, eight individuals, this is the Sangha of the Blessed One. Worthy of offerings and hospitality, gifts and homage, it is an incomparable field of merit for the world.'"[1]

Maha Kassapa says, "Today our *dana* will be hosted by Sujata, the wife of Kala, son of Anathapindika. She wishes to offer this *dana* to the Council members as well as to her dear friend and Dhamma sister, *Bhikkhuni* Kalyani, who will be joining us along with one hundred *bhikkhunis* from her nunnery in Rajagaha.

"I have asked *Bhikkhuni* Kalyani to participate in our discussion of the life of the Buddha today, which will be held in the general assembly. She is the former wife of Nanda, and was one of the first to be ordained in the *Bhikkhuni* Order. She will give an eye-witness account of the founding of this Order, so we will hear about our dear friend Venerable Mahapajapati and the other ladies who so bravely paved the way for women to serve in the Sangha as ordained nuns. I feel it is important that we include her story so it can be preserved for all time."

The five hundred arahants smile and silently express their gratitude for this opportunity to hear about the origins of the *Bhikkhuni* Order first-hand.

Maha Kassapa continues, "Venerable Ananda will now recite a *sutta* from the *Kosalasamyutta*,[2] as a preface to our discussions after lunch. It will demonstrate the Lord's true appreciation of women, and his total lack of gender discrimination. The Buddha was truly an egalitarian; to him caste, gender, social and family background had no meaning. In this and many other respects, given the prevailing social prejudices, he was far ahead of his time."

Ananda begins to speak:

"'At Savatthi, King Pasenadi of Kosala approached the Blessed One, paid homage to him, and sat down to one side. Shortly afterwards a man approached King Pasenadi and informed him in a whisper: 'Sire, Queen Mallika has given birth to a daughter.' When this was said, King Pasenadi was displeased and the Blessed One, having understood that King Pasenadi was displeased, recited these verses:

"'A woman, O lord of the people,
may turn out better than a man:
She may be wise and virtuous, a devoted wife,
offering respect to her husband's family.

"'The son to whom she gives birth may become a hero,
O lord of the land.
The son of such a blessed woman
may even rule the realm.'"

Ananda completes this *sutta* and continues his recitations until the morning recess. During the break, Ananda engages in a conversation with his two cousins, Anuruddha and Bhaddiya.

"I haven't seen *Bhikkhuni* Janapada Kalyani in over twenty years," begins Anuruddha.

"I saw her two years ago at Venerable Nanda's funeral. Time has been kind to her, and you would never guess that she was sixty years old," says Bhaddiya.

"I, too, haven't seen her for ages," adds Ananda. "I'm looking forward to hearing her story for our recollection."

The gong sounds, signaling the end of the tea break, and the three cousins join the other council members who are returning to the assembly hall. Ananda continues reciting *suttas* and other elements of the Dhamma until it is time for lunch.

The *dana* ceremony hosted by Sujata is up to her usual standards of perfection, and she extends to all of the Sangha members the warm felicitations of her husband Kala, who is away in Savatthi attending to business. She is dressed very simply that day, with no jewelry or other ornaments, a noticeable change from the opulent way she had dressed on past occasions.

When Maha Kassapa thanks Sujata for the *dana* she says, "Please don't forget, Venerable Sir, that our villa near the hot springs belongs to you and your Sangha members whenever you feel like using it."

The chairman nods his thanks and says, "We had a very successful retreat at your villa, Sujata, and we may indeed ask to use it again before the council ends. Come, we have special seating arranged for you and your attendant ladies so you can listen to our proceedings. I also want to thank you for bringing *Bhikkhuni* Kalayani to the council today. Her participation will be of great value."

Smiling, Sujata says, "*Bhikkhuni* Kalyani has been like a sister to me, and a teacher, ever since her ordination. Over the years, whenever I am in Rajagaha I spend as much time with her as I can; her presence in my life has been a great blessing." Sujata bows low to Maha Kassapa, and then she and her ladies are escorted to their seats.

The platform in the assembly hall has been reconfigured to accommodate the sub-committee and its special guest. *Bhikkhuni* Kalyani enters the hall with her group of one hundred *bhikkhunis*. She goes directly before the Sangha and says, in the age-old tradition of Sangha members greeting each other:

> "'If by body, speech or mind
> I have carelessly done wrong,
> May I be forgiven,
> O, Venerable Monks of great wisdom.'"

When she approaches the platform, the three cousins stand up to greet her. She bows respectfully to each of them, and Ananda is the first to speak, "Your attainment sits well on you, Venerable Kalyani."

"It's wonderful to see you, Venerable Ananda, and you too Venerable Bhaddiya and Venerable Anuruddha," begins *Bhikkhuni* Kalyani. "I'm glad that some of the Lord's relatives are still here to tell the story of his life, and I thank you for your invitation to participate."

After paying her respects to the other Sangha members Venerable Kalyani seats herself in the place indicated for her, and the meeting comes to order. Maha Kassapa signals for her to begin.

Arahant *Bhikkhuni* Kalyani begins to tell them about Queen Mahapajapati's request. The arahants in the assembly hall lean forward on their mats so they won't miss a single word.

"After the death of King Suddhodana, the queen increasingly yearned to be ordained in the Buddha's Sangha," says *Bhikkhuni* Kalyani. "She no longer had any interest in the affairs of state, and since the administration of the palace was under the new king, she no longer had any meaningful duties.

"To keep busy the queen engaged herself with even more zeal in the many social projects she and Princess Yasodhara had initiated. The Sakyan people were greatly benefitted by her dedicated efforts at improving their lives.

"Queen Mahapajapati had asked the Buddha on three occasions for ordination into his Sangha, but each time he refused. Every time she asked him she returned to the palace saddened and confused. She simply couldn't understand why the man she had raised as a son would refuse her request, and to be quite frank, the Buddha never really gave her a reason."

Ananda speaks, "The Lord told me on several occasions that he had made the decision to one day admit women into the Sangha. However, he wanted to make sure they comprehended the sacrifices they would be making, and fully understand that living the life of a nun would not be easy. Renunciation was a difficult thing, and such a serious commitment should never be undertaken lightly.

"His step-mother was in the vanguard; she was the first to struggle against the many obstacles that prevented female ordination. I know that it must have deeply pained the Master to turn down a request from the woman who had raised him from birth. His natural tendency would have been to grant her whatever request she might make," concludes Ananda.

Bhikkhuni Kalyani says, "I could empathize with how the queen felt in those days. After my husband Prince Nanda left to join the Sangha, I felt completely alone, and I drifted in and out of depression for a number of years. I hoped that he would come back to me one day, but when he attained arahantship I finally accepted the fact that our relationship was over. At that point I had to cope not only with the loss of my husband, but with the knowledge that I would never have any children as well. There was no direction or purpose in my life. I had foolishly prided myself on my physical beauty, but what good did that do me then?"

Kalyani glances over at her group of *bhikkhunis*, and the look of love that passes between them is seen by everyone in the assembly hall. The arahants sit spellbound as she continues her tale.

"The former wives of the five hundred royal princes who had been given to the Buddha by the Sakyas and the Koliyas went to see the queen," says *Bhikkhuni* Kalyani. "They, too, felt empty and alone, bereft of a purpose in life; so they begged her to ask the Buddha one more time for ordination. They hoped that if she were allowed to be ordained, then they might also be accepted into the Sangha. Out of desperation they pleaded with her to be their spokesperson.

"Our beloved queen was in a deeply despondent emotional state. She wanted ordination more than anything in this world, so she listened to our appeals with great compassion and understanding. She had misgivings, considering her previous three failed appeals, but in the end she decided that if we made a joint plea the Buddha might show his mercy.

"After pondering a few minutes she finally said, 'The Buddha is ninety miles from here at his monastery in Vesali. If we shave our heads, put on yellow robes, and go all that way as a group, then he can't possibly refuse our request.'

"We all agreed with her immediately, and became excited at the prospect of success. The queen sent for her hair dresser, and in one day all five hundred of our pampered, well-groomed heads were shaved – including hers. Princess Yasodhara was in our group that day and considered going with us, but she decided to wait until a *bhikkhuni* order was already established before she herself sought ordination. She still had her on-going social projects to look after, and she wanted to make sure they would continue after her inevitable departure and renunciation. Even though she wasn't going to join us, she gave us encouragement and prayed for a positive outcome.

"We immediately started making preparations for our journey. We attired ourselves in yellow robes, obtained alms bowls, and were just about to set off – barefoot, penniless, and unaccompanied. Our relatives were horrified, as were the kings of our two states. They couldn't believe that five hundred well-bred, royal ladies could survive the harsh trip. They were worried because they felt our lives would be in danger.

"King Mahanama, knowing that the queen and the rest of us were not to be dissuaded, arranged for five hundred palanquins to carry us – with a guard of two hundred men and a large staff of servants to take care of us. The queen considered this, however, and said, 'Suppose it is not fitting for us to approach the Buddha in such an opulent fashion? It might be inappropriate or disrespectful to him, and give him grounds for denying our request. I think we should go very simply, and on foot.'

"We discussed the matter among ourselves, and many of us were opposed to her idea. After all, we had never traveled in that manner before, and the prospect was a bit terrifying. However, in the end it was decided that we would indeed walk those ninety miles without footwear and make our appeal as mendicant nuns. At this point we knew for certain that our lives would be a complete waste if we didn't have our wish fulfilled, so we felt we had to demonstrate our determination and sincerity of purpose.

"We set off early in the morning barefooted, a group of women who had never known an hour of hardship or inconvenience. Our families couldn't bear the thought of us starving, so they made arrangements to provide food for us along the way. They had supply lines follow us, and later we found out that they had dispatched a few discreet guards who kept their distance, respecting our desire to travel alone.

"The news of our departure from the royal households spread like wildfire throughout the land. I must say that we looked a pitiful sight – more so with each passing day. When night fell we slept in our robes on the side of the road, and before too long we were covered in filth. Fortunately, we were able to bathe in a river from time to time, but not every day."

Maha Kassapa asks, "Venerable Kalyani, how long did it take you to get to Vesali traveling this way?"

"We covered the ninety miles in a little over two weeks," answers Kalyani. "Luckily, none of us became ill during the journey, but to be very honest, many had second thoughts about our objective when they had to sleep on the ground every night. Fortunately, our families provided our daily meal – otherwise I'm sure we would have starved to death. The people in the countryside were accustomed to seeing male ascetics or the Buddha's disciples traveling from place to place, and they generously provided food for them; but we weren't yet the Buddha's disciples, and there was no established cultural tradition that provided for women like us."

The arahants in the assembly hall stir in their seats as they imagine the vast procession of royal ladies on the dusty country roads.

"What happened when you arrived at the monastery in Vesali?" asks Bakkula.

"We stopped at the gates of the Kutagara Monastery, but we didn't dare enter. Our delicate feet that had never been without slippers were swollen and blistered with sores; many of us had infections which oozed pus, attracting flies. We were filthy and haggard beyond description. It's a miracle none of us went completely insane during the hard journey, but we tried our best to compose ourselves befitting our former royal status. You have no idea how we suffered for the sake of obtaining *bhikkhuni* ordination," says Kalyani. The expression on her saintly face told of the memory of that fateful journey.

"Venerable Ananda, if you don't mind would you be so kind as to tell this part of the story since you played such an important role in the outcome?" asks Kalyani.

Ananda nods and replies smiling, "It would be my honor. I was traveling with the Buddha at the time, even though I wasn't yet his chief attendant. Fortunately, I was the first one in the monastery to see you and your tired group when you arrived. I was shocked to see Queen Mahapajapati and the rest of you standing at the gate. You were in a very pathetic condition."

"Venerable Sir, we were indeed so happy to see you," says Kalyani. "The look of surprise on your face was indescribable; I'll never forget it."

"I was way beyond surprised, I'll tell you that!" replies Ananda. "When I recovered enough to speak I said, 'O my dear aunt, why are you in such a miserable state? Have both the Sakyas and Koliyas gone bankrupt?' Overjoyed at seeing her nephew, and relived they had all arrived safely, the queen started to weep and tears streamed down her dust-streaked face. She said, 'I know the Buddha didn't give us permission to shave our heads and put on yellow robes, but we walked all the way from Kapilavatthu to plead with him for ordination. I am prepared for his rebuke should he be displeased. This is our fervent desire, Venerable Ananda, and I beg you to intercede with him on our behalf.'

"I was so moved by her desperate plea and her deplorable physical condition that I answered, 'Please stay here at the gate until I come back. I will do the best I can.' I must say that I didn't know what answer to expect from the Master, given his past refusals to admit *bhikkhunis* into the Sangha. Full of hope I approached him in the Fragrant Chamber.

"I said, 'Most Exalted Buddha, your step-mother Mahapajapati is standing at the gate along with five hundred royal wives from Sakya and Koliya. Their feet are swollen and wounded; they are weeping from exhaustion, and filthy from walking all the way from Kapilavatthu. They want nothing more than higher ordination. I pray, Lord, that you will have mercy on them and grant their request.'

"The Buddha said in response, 'Ananda, please arrange for the lodging and comfort of the queen and the five hundred royal ladies. From the way you described them, it sounds like they need to be fed, have a bath, and get some rest. I'm sure the lay devotees in the area can find places to accommodate them. Later we will talk about her request.'

"I went directly to Mahapajapati and said as calmly as I could, 'The Buddha has not refused your request for ordination. At the moment, however, he is most concerned about your well-being, and he has asked me to make arrangements for you and your ladies. The queen smiled at me with her tear-filled eyes, and I immediately went to do what I could to accommodate them," says Ananda.

"That night we were well-cared for by the lay people. Baths were drawn, delicious food was brought in, and doctors were called to look after our swollen, damaged feet. We were all very hopeful, so it was difficult to sleep even though we were completely exhausted," says Kalyani.

Ananda continues, "When I returned to speak with the Buddha he said, 'This is not the right time to admit women into the Sangha, Ananda. We need to be prepared for such a major undertaking, and properly organized in terms of security, education, housing, health-care, and devotional practices. I advise you to place your interest elsewhere.' I was refused, but I didn't have the heart to tell the queen and the other women that the Buddha had said 'no.' I felt I had no choice but to keep pleading with him, but he refused me again a second, and then a third time."

"Your courage in that situation was admirable, Ananda," says Punna. "Most of us would have taken the Lord's answer as final and given up — but not you!"

The arahants in the assembly hall smile when they hear this remark. They know very well Ananda's legendary tenacity when it comes to an issue of compassion.

"No, not me," exclaims Ananda. "I simply couldn't. I didn't accept the fact that the Buddha was refusing his own step-mother, who was also my favorite aunt! I just knew I had to find a way, so I kept trying."

"So how did you wind up convincing him?" asks Sopaka.

"I thought about the matter long and hard, and I finally came up with a new approach. I went to the Master again and said, 'Most Exalted Buddha, is it possible for women to attain arahantship by going through the stages of *sotapanna*, *sakadagami*, and *anagami* while leading the holy life within the structure of the Buddha *Sasana*?'

"The Buddha answered, 'Yes, Ananda, it is possible for women to attain arahantship in the manner you describe.'

"So then I asked, 'Are men and women equal, in terms of their capability of becoming enlightened?'

"The Buddha answered quite simply, 'Yes.'

"I was actually surprised by his quick reply, so I said, 'If this is so, Master, then I highly urge you grant your stepmother's request for ordination. After all, she cared for you as her own after your mother died, cleaned up after you, and bathed you with her own hands.'

"The Buddha answered, 'Ananda, I will consider your request.'

"There was nothing more to be said, so I left him alone, not wishing to disturb him while he was in the process of consideration. The next morning I went back to the Fragrant Chamber, as usual, and paid homage to the Buddha. Feeling a bit apprehensive, I waited a while before asking him for his answer. Finally I had to say, 'Have you made your decision yet regarding the ordination of nuns?'

"The Buddha said, 'Ananda, if Mahapajapati accepts Eight Special Rules[3], then let such acceptance mean her admission to the Sangha. I wish to make it clear, however, that these rules must be adhered to for life.'

"I was absolutely stunned," says Ananda. "When I recovered, I said, 'What are those Eight Special Rules, Master?'

"The Buddha explained the rules to me, and I noted that they mostly had to do with guaranteeing the protection of the *bhikkhunis*, their training procedures and discipline, and establishing traditions of respect between Sangha members. I also noted that they were in accord with certain social conventions of the day out of respect for the general society. I was so grateful to the Buddha for his favorable response, and I bowed before him with great emotion saying, 'Thank you, Lord.'

"After the Buddha gave me these Eight Special Rules I went immediately to Mahapajapati and told her of the Buddha's favorable decision. Then I recited the rules to her. She said, 'Venerable Ananda, just as a young man or woman would accept a garland of fragrant flowers from a loved one, so also am I prepared to adhere to these rules for life.'"

"At that moment Queen Mahapajapati became the very first member of our *Bhikkhuni* Order," begins Arahant Kalyani. "Her first thought, however, was not about herself; she was concerned about the five hundred royal ladies she had just led on a painful ninety-mile journey. She immediately went to the Buddha, prostrated herself before him and said, 'what shall I do, Lord, with these women who also wish to be ordained?'

"The Buddha looked at his stepmother with great compassion, and he smiled at her with his radiant eyes. He said, 'Now you have what you came for, Mahapajapati. You overcame many hardships to get it, and your determination is admirable. I'm sure you will do well.

> "'Make an island for yourself!
> Strive hard and become wise!
> Rid of impurities and cleansed of stain,
> You shall enter the celestial abode of the Noble Ones.'"[4]

"Thank you, Lord," was her simple reply as she cried tears of gratitude.

"Then the Buddha gave her certain instructions and she hurried off to give us the good news," continues Kalyani. "At the same time the Lord called his *bhikkhus* together and told them that he had just approved the admission of *bhikkhunis* into the Sangha. He also told them three things about co-existing with *bhikkhunis*, and I'll paraphrase them for our recollection:

"First of all he told them to accept and respect the *bhikkhunis* as if they were their own mothers or sisters.

"Secondly, he told them to protect the *bhikkhunis* and see to their security, as well as to refrain from engaging in any sort of dialog that would breed dissention.

"The third thing he told them was to encourage the *bhikkhunis* to attain *Nibbana*.

"Then he told them to arrange an ordination ceremony for us, and the five hundred royal women were hastily gathered before the Buddha and his *bhikkhu* Sangha. The monks proceeded to ordain us, with Venerable Mahapajapati named as our preceptor. The Buddha gave a discourse on meditation at the conclusion of the ceremony, and Venerable Mahapajapati immediately realized the state of arahantship. Each and every one of my five hundred sisters attained various stages of realization too – from *sotapanna* to arahant."

Upali, smiling broadly, comments, "That was quite an historic day, wasn't it?"

"Indeed it was, Venerable Sir. Five hundred and one lives were completely transformed, and the ripple effect was almost instantaneous," says Kalyani.

"Where did you go from there?" asks Bakkula.

"All of us newly-ordained *bhikkhunis* returned to Sakya and Koliya, and with royal patronage we established nunneries in both states. King Mahanama generously donated land, labor, and construction materials for a *bhikkhuni* monastery in Kapilavatthu, and Prince Vishnamitta did the same in Koliya. When the nunneries were completed many women from both kingdoms – and from all of the other kingdoms in the region – joined us, and received ordination as well. The word spread very fast.

"After we were well-established, we sent *bhikkhuni* emissaries out to Licchavi, Magadha, Anga, Kasi, Vatsa, and Kosala who sought and received royal patronage and built nunneries in each of those kingdoms. The *bhikkhuni* population grew rapidly, and new nunneries were continually being built to keep up with the demand. Throughout the entire process we established clear channels of communication with the *bhikkhus* in neighboring monasteries. We cooperated with them in countless ways, and on many programs that benefitted the surrounding lay communities. There was very little friction between the two groups, and we all got along surprisingly well."

The monks and nuns in the assembly hall listen with great interest and smile at one another, remembering those early days of establishing mutual trust, devotion, and growth.

"When did Princess Yasodhara join the Sangha?" asks Upali.

"About two years after Queen Mahapajapati and I were ordained she joined us and resided in the monastery in Kapilavatthu. She continued her social service projects as a *bhikkhuni*, and we all participated whenever she needed extra volunteers. She was even more valuable to the kingdom as a *bhikkhuni* than she ever had been as a member of the royal household. And I must say, Venerable Yasodhara literally burst into full bloom spiritually, quickly attaining the state of arahantship," answers *Bhikkhuni* Kalyani.

"Was she able to see her son, Venerable Rahula?" asks Sopaka.

"Yes. They kept in contact and saw each other from time to time," responds Kalyani. "I remember one occasion when I had gone with her to Savatthi and she wanted to visit Venerable Rahula. I very much wanted to see him, too. The three of us were enjoying our time together until Venerable Yasodhara suddenly came down with a horrible stomach illness.

"Venerable Rahula went immediately to his preceptor, Venerable Sariputta, and asked him what could be done for his mother. Venerable Sariputta immediately consulted with Dr. Jivaka who recommended a concoction of roasted mango with sugar. Venerable Rahula procured the doctor's prescription and gave it to his mother, who was cured very quickly by the savory remedy. Kind Venerable Rahula was always very solicitous of his mother as long as she lived."

"I believe your former wife, Bhadda Kapilani, also ordained about this time, Venerable Chairman," comments Anuruddha.

"Yes, she did. For five years she had been living as a wandering ascetic – ever since the day she and I walked away from our estates and went our separate ways. She was biding her time until the Buddha established the *bhikkhuni* order, and as soon as the nunnery was established in Kapilavatthu she ordained there joining its first members," answers Maha Kassapa. "I'm happy to say that she soon attained the state of arahantship. The Buddha once called her the disciple who was 'Foremost in Recalling Past Rebirths.' I was able to see her from time to time, and we remained close friends until she passed away – not too many years ago."

Ananda speaks, "It wasn't long before a number of great, and foremost *bhikkhunis* came upon the scene. Kalyani, why don't you briefly tell us about some of those illustrious members of the Sangha. I believe we have some time before we adjourn the meeting."

Bhikkhuni Kalyani pauses for a moment and then begins the story of Venerable Khema, who was once King Bimbisara's queen. "Queen Khema was renowned for her great beauty, and at first she hesitated about visiting the Buddha because she had heard that he looked down on comely physical attributes. The king finally convinced her to visit the Bamboo Grove Monastery, and during their meeting the Buddha conjured up a vision of a beautiful goddess who quickly aged into an ugly old crone. Queen Khema immediately understood the meaning of impermanence, and was forever relieved of her conceit. Then the Buddha taught her from the doctrine, and she became an arahant. She went immediately to the palace and received permission from the king to receive ordination as a *bhikkhuni*."[5]

Kalyani then tells the story of Venerable Uppalavanna,[6] the beautiful daughter of a millionaire. "Since she had too many suitors her father thought she should become a *bhikkhuni*. Uppalavanna liked the idea, and was very willing to enter the order of nuns. One day while she was contemplating the wick of an oil lamp she became an arahant. She was gifted with enormous psychic powers, and often performed great services for the Buddha and other members of the Sangha.

"One of my favorite stories is about my dear friend, Venerable Kisagotami," continues Kalyani. "She was from Savatthi and had married a young rich man. A son was born to them, but he died when he was still a toddler. The dear mother was overcome by grief, and couldn't accept the fact that her child was dead. Carrying her dead son in her arms she went about the city asking for medicine to cure her son of death. She seemed to be completely out of her mind when she encountered a wise man who told her to go and see the Buddha, who happened to be nearby.

"She went before the Buddha begging him to restore her child to life. He said, 'If you bring me some mustard seeds from a house where there has never been a death, then I will do as you ask.'

"Kisagotami was full of hope as she went from house to house in search of the mustard seeds. The people were more than willing to give her the seeds, but at each house when she asked if there had been a death, she was told that indeed there had been. Eventually she realized that there was not one family who hadn't encountered death. Her attitude changed completely and she became less and less attached to her son. She realized that the Buddha had taught her a very important lesson: everything that is born must eventually pass away. She eventually parted with her child's lifeless body, and allowed it to be cremated.

"She returned to the Buddha in a totally different state of mind. She said, 'Kind sir, mustard seeds I could find, but a house where there had been no death did not exist.'

"The Buddha said, 'It is good that you now know that you are not the only mother who has ever lost a son. Death comes to everyone; it is the very nature of life.'

"Kisagotami, perceiving the impermanent nature of human existence, asked the Buddha for ordination as a *bhikkhuni*. He granted her request, and she worked hard developing her meditation skills and performing her religious duties. One day when she was meditating on the flame of a lamp she said to herself, 'Even as it is with these flames, so also it is with living beings in this world: some shine brightly for a long time, while others go out almost immediately. It is only those who have attained *Nibbana* that are never seen again.'

"The Buddha saw with his supernormal powers that Venerable Kisagotami was close to achieving *Nibbana* so he focused his energy on her. She continued meditating on the impermanent nature of things and achieved arahantship," concludes Kalyani. "She and I became very close friends, and whenever I was in Savatthi on one of my missions I would stay with her. She just passed away recently, and I will always remember her kindness and great understanding."

Maha Kassapa speaks, "If you don't mind, can you please tell us about *Bhikkhuni* Patacara?"[8]

"Ah, yes, dear Venerable Patacara," sighs Kalyani. "Her life before becoming a *bhikkhuni* is perhaps the most tragic story that I have ever heard. She was the daughter of a wealthy banker in Savatthi, but she had the misfortune of falling in love with one of her family's servants. He was a good man, but because of caste differences she knew that her family would never accept him. Her father had tried to force her to marry someone of her own rank, but she couldn't bear the thought of being with another man. Ultimately she ran away with the servant and they married.

"After a while Patacara discovered that she was with child. As is the custom here, she wished to give birth in the home of her parents. She discussed the matter with her husband, but he was afraid her parents wouldn't let her come back to him, and he refused to let her go. She decided to go anyway, so she left word with her neighbors and set out alone. When her husband found out he ran after her, catching up with her before she reached Savatthi. That night she gave birth to a son, and no longer having any need to visit her parents they returned to their home together.

"The following year she found herself with child again. Once more she pleaded with her husband to let her go home to deliver the child. He refused her request for the same reason as before, so once again she started out alone. Her husband went after her, but before he reached her she gave birth to a second son. By the time her husband caught up with her a great storm came upon them. Her husband went to gather sticks and kindling to build a fire. When he reached into a thicket he was bitten by a poisonous snake and died on the spot.

"Poor Patacara spent the night alone, cold and afraid, caring for her infant and small toddler. She did her best to keep them warm without a fire. When the storm ended it was morning, and she went looking for her husband. She found his dead body and was grief stricken. The only thing she could do was to continue on to her parents' house with her two babies. Reaching the river she found the ford was swollen and flooded. She had no choice but to cross it, so she left her newborn son on the riverbank on a pile of leaves.

"She waded out into the swiftly-flowing river holding her other son over her head. When she reached the other side she set him down in a safe place. When she was half way back to get her newborn, she heard the cry of a hawk and saw it swoop down, grab her infant son, and fly away. The baby cried at the top of its lungs, but she was helpless to save him. As she screamed and shouted at the hawk her toddler son thought his mother was calling him to come to her. She was still in the middle of the swollen river when the toddler entered the fast-moving current. Helplessly she watched as he was immediately swept away.

"In a state of shock she swam to the other side of the river; there was nothing she could do but slowly walk towards her parents' house. When she got near Savatthi she heard people talking about a disastrous fire that had happened the night before; the three people who were trapped in their house had died. When she arrived at her parents' home she discovered that it was their house that had burned down.

"Patacara completely lost her mind. She wandered around for days weeping and lamenting, completely delirious with grief. She didn't even know enough to cover her nakedness, and people drove her from their doorsteps.

"One day she stumbled upon Jetavana Monastery where the Buddha was preaching. People tried to stop her from entering, but the Buddha called out to her and said, 'Patacara, come forward.' A man threw a robe over her shoulders to cover her naked body, and she walked toward the Master. She flung herself down and worshiped at his feet. He said, 'Here there is no fear for you. Here there is refuge for you.'

"Patacara instantly responded to the sweet voice of the Buddha; she stopped weeping and calmed down. Once again the Buddha spoke to her, 'Sister, awaken to your senses; look at me with your proper senses. I shall help you. I shall dispel your grief.'

"The woman, mad with sorrow, looked intently at the face of the Buddha. Softly she said, 'Lord, I am the most unfortunate woman on earth. I have no one. I have lost my husband, my two children, my parents, and my brother. I am a mad woman.'

"The Buddha said, 'Sister, you are not mad. You are awakening from a terrifying dream. Sister, it is your mind that sees both good and bad dreams. Sister, tell me the dreams you saw.' Patacara then described the unfortunate incidents that had resulted in the deaths of all of the members of her family.

"The Buddha then asked, 'Sister, were those children truly yours?'

"'Lord, of course they were mine; they were born of my flesh and my blood. Those children were mine,' she responded between sobs.

"'Good Patacara, you are grieving because of the feeling that they were yours and because you loved them dearly. There are thousands of young children dying. You are not sorrowing for them because they are not yours. Sister, when there are thousands of young children who die, why should you grieve for only two of them? According to their *kamma* they have left you and are gone.

"'Sister, it's because of the loss one feels by separation from another that one cannot bear such separation. Why do you create madness and fall into a state of confusion? Your liberation is in your hands. I shall help you. Go to the nunnery in Jetavana and look at the nuns there. Like you, they too have gone through trouble, persecution, and disaster. Coming to me they received ordination. Now they are tranquil, leading contented simple lives.'"

"Listening to the Buddha, Patacara got over her madness and returned to normal. She walked peacefully to the nunnery, was ordained, and soon became a *sotapanna*. She was an inspiration to all of us in the Order because her story was so tragic. She eventually attained arahantship, and led a peaceful meditative life. She spoke very little, and always emanated healing energy for poor women, men, and children who have had to survive unspeakable hardship and tragedy, just as she had," concludes *Bhikkhuni* Kalyani.

Maha Kassapa speaks, "I am sure that all of us tonight feel grateful for your presence, and for sharing your personal account of the establishment of the noble *Bhikkhuni* Order." The chairman then rises to his feet and the arahant *bhikkhuni* bows before him. Then she turns and bows to the other arahants in the assembly, all of whom feel privileged to have heard her story.

Silently, Arahant Kalyani, with supreme grace, walks from the assembly hall with her one hundred *bhikkhunis* following her.

Chapter 22
Visakha

The First Sangha Council is proceeding on schedule during the days following *Bhikkhuni* Kalyani's visit. There have been no more special guests, and Ananda continues his recitations.

One day at sunrise the arahants notice a great deal of activity in the large clearing at the base of Mount Vebhara. They watch as campgrounds for workers are set up, and as cartload after cartload of supplies and building materials start to arrive. It appears that construction is about to begin on a large new structure and a smaller one south of it. Hundreds of workers are being gathered for the building project, which arouses the curiosity of everyone up on the mountain.

There are guesses, but no one really knows what's being built, and the chairman, if he does know, won't say. When asked, with his eyes twinkling, all he will say is, "I'm not telling anyone anything."

Finally, one evening just as the council is about adjourn, Maha Kassapa makes an announcement. "I know that all of you have been wondering about the construction project in the clearing down below. Forgive me for not being forthright when you have asked me, but I was pledged to secrecy. The elegant pavilions you see were built elsewhere and are being miraculously assembled at the base of the mountain by our foremost patroness, Visakha. She will come from Savatthi to host a *dana* ceremony for us tomorrow.

"For many years this kind woman has devoted her life to performing acts of generosity for the Sangha. And now, she can't resist the opportunity to serve the senior-most members during this auspicious First Council. The morning schedule will proceed as usual. In lieu of recitations tomorrow afternoon, the sub-committee recollecting the life of the Buddha will meet with her in the smaller of the two pavilions where we will record an eye-witness account of her association with the Master."

The chairman sounds the gong concluding the council proceedings for the evening. Each and every one of the arahants knows Visakha personally, some better than others. At one time or another all of them have been the recipients of her *dana* in the form of meals, medicine, robes, monastery accommodation, and in countless other ways, thanks to her huge financial contributions over the years.

Ananda, Visakha's close friend, is looking forward to seeing her again. He walks up to the chairman and asks, "Why did you keep her visit a secret?"

"She asked me to, Ananda. She wanted it to be a surprise – for you most of all! I gave her my word, friend. Anyway, she will arrive in the morning, and in her usual grand style, I'm sure," answers Maha Kassapa laughing.

Ananda and the other arahants proceed to their individual chambers in the cave complex. The members of the sub-committee have decided to cancel their meeting that evening, preferring to wait to hear Visakha's recollections of the Buddha the following day.

The next morning at dawn Ananda approaches the podium and begins reciting a *sutta*. As usual, it is one that would presage the sub-committee's subject matter that day:

> "'On one occasion the Blessed One was dwelling at Savatthi in the Eastern Park and he visited the mansion of Visakha. The Blessed One asked her:
>
> "'Visakha, when a woman possesses four qualities she is heading for victory in the present world and is successful in this world. What four?
>
> "'Visakha, when a woman is capable at her work she manages her domestic help, she behaves in a way that is agreeable to her husband, and she safeguards his earnings.
>
> "'But when she possesses four other qualities she is heading for victory in the other world and is successful in regard to the other world. What four?
>
> "'Visakha, when a woman is accomplished in faith, virtue, generosity, and wisdom.

"'And how is a woman accomplished in faith? When she places faith in the enlightenment of the *Tathagata*.

"'And how is a woman accomplished in virtue? When she follows the Five Precepts.

"'And how is a woman accomplished in generosity? When a woman dwells at home with a mind devoid of the stain of stinginess, freely generous, open-handed, delighting in relinquishment, one devoted to charity, delighting in giving and sharing.

"'And how is a woman accomplished in wisdom? When a woman possesses the wisdom which sees into the arising and passing away of phenomena; which is noble and penetrative, and leads to the complete destruction of suffering.'"[1]

Ananda continues his recitations until mid-morning. During the break the arahants begin their trek down the mountain to arrive in time for Visakha's *dana* ceremony. When Ananda leaves the podium it is obvious that he is very happy about visiting with his old friend again.

The arahants, curious about the palatial new pavilions, give them a close examination when they arrive at the clearing. The structures appear to have been constructed for the express purposes of serving *dana* to the monks that day, and as a venue to hold the sub-committee recollections that will follow. Visakha is waiting at the entrance of the larger pavilion where lunch will be served. She is with her retinue of perhaps three hundred ladies – all of them female relatives: her daughters, grand-daughters, nieces, grand-nieces, and others. She is about fifty years old, but she has ten sons and ten daughters, who will each eventually have ten sons and ten daughters of their own. In time her grand children would also have big families, so her direct descendants will number in the thousands.

She greets the senior members of the Sangha council with great reverence, bowing low and touching her forehead to their feet. The ladies in her entourage follow her lead, demonstrating the perfect respect she has taught them to have for *bhikkhus*. Her face is radiant, reflecting a happy life which has come from practicing virtue and generosity. She is truly in her element whenever she has an opportunity to feed Sangha members, and she has fed thousands of them during the past forty years.

"What an amazing surprise to see you here. You've come a long way just to give us *dana*, my friend." As he gazes up at the high-beamed ceilings festooned with silk banners and tinkling golden bells Ananda asks, "And what are you going to do with these magnificent pavilions after today?"

She beams with joy as she answers, "I bought the land from King Ajatasattu, and believe it or not. I have the great privilege of constructing another monastery here. This larger pavilion will be its centerpiece, and hopefully it will be used as the main hall for other great Sangha councils in the future."

Ananda can only shake his head as he looks around at the elaborately decorated space. There is no comparison between the *dana* preparations Visakha has made to those of either King Ajatasattu or Kala and his wife Sujata. As usual, she has outdone herself thinking of every possible amenity for the monks, sparing no expense to make sure they will be comfortable and well fed.

Visakha has already given so much to the Sangha during the course of her life, and this new monastery will be yet another monument to her generosity. The Buddha called her his "Foremost Female Lay Disciple," and with good reason, reflects Ananda.

The monks are seated and begin the traditional chanting. Visakha and her female attendants sit with their hands pressed together in front of their foreheads in the devotional act of worship. They are completely absorbed in the powerful vibrations generated by the sacred *suttas*. When the meal is consecrated Visakha herself serves the senior-most monks and then supervises the serving of the balance of the *bhikkhus*.

At the conclusion of the *dana* the sub-committee members and the memory monks, along with Visakha and her female offspring, retire to the elaborate second pavilion. The nine arahants seat themselves on a teakwood platform, which is covered in Kashmiri carpets and silk cushions. Visakha and her ladies, each and every one of them dressed in white cotton with simple gold ornaments, settle themselves near the platform. Visaka's second and third-generation decendants are eager to hear their beloved matriarch's story, even though it won't be their first time or their last to do so.

Maha Kassapa says, "Friend Visakha, on behalf of the Sangha members I thank you for traveling all this way to offer *dana*, and for attending our meeting to share your recollections of the Buddha."

Visakha, composed and exuding her legendary confidence, says, "It is one of the greatest honors of my life to serve you and to be here at this first Sangha council. I was fortunate to have personally known the Buddha for decades, and I enjoyed a close association and friendship with him until his *parinibbana* a few months ago. I still deeply miss his presence in my life, so telling my part of the story today will be a great comfort for me."

Ananda speaks, "I would like to say, as a preface to Friend Visakha's tale, that in her previous births – and in those of her grandparents and parents as well – a vast amount of favorable merit had been accumulated. This merit endowed her not only with the potential for great spiritual advancement in this lifetime, but also with the opportunity to perform countless services for the Buddha and his Sangha. This gift for service was enabled by the fortunate material circumstances into which she was born, and by the fact that she has always used her wealth wisely, chiefly for the benefit of the *Sasana*. All of us owe a great debt to her."

Visakha places her hands together, closes her eyes, and bows low to her dear friend in appreciation for his kind words.

The chairman says, "Visakha, please be so kind as to start your story, beginning with your first meeting with our Lord."

The matriarch nods in acquiescence, pausing for a moment before beginning. "When I was just a young girl of seven the Buddha visited our hometown, Bhaddiya, which is in Anga. As he so often did, he went there to teach the Dhamma to someone he had seen with his universal vision as being ripe for the attainment of *Nibbana*. This time it was the Brahmin named Sela.

"My grandfather, Mendaka, was one of King Bimbisara's five wealthiest subjects. When he heard about the Buddha's arrival in Bhaddiya he said to me, 'Granddaughter, go and welcome the Buddha. By doing so, you will accrue great merit for both yourself and your family.

Take your attendants and maid-servants and go to him.' Even at age seven, something resonated deep within me when I heard the word 'Buddha.' I immediately agreed to his request.

"My attendants and maidservants numbered in the hundreds, and together we set out in coaches drawn by thoroughbred horses. When we were nearing the place where the Buddha was staying some inner voice told me that it would be disrespectful to arrive by coach; this might be considered egoistic and tasteless. So we dismounted some distance away and approached the Buddha on foot. My grandfather accompanied us and he held my hand as we walked forward.

"When we reached the Buddha I paid my respects, as did my ladies and my grandfather. Then we sat and listened to him teach the Dhamma. The Lord's discourse was spoken in words appropriate for a seven-year old, and upon hearing it I attained *sotapanna*. So did my happy grandfather, Mendaka, and all of my attendants and maidservants.

"With great enthusiasm my grandfather invited the Buddha to his mansion for the next day's alms-meal, and the Lord accepted with his customary silence. Grandfather Mendaka was never anyone to do anything in a half-way manner, so he ordered a lavish banquet for the Lord for each of the next fifteen days. As long as the Buddha stayed in Bhaddiya we wanted to provide for him and see to his needs."

"Please tell us, if you would, your personal impressions of the Buddha at that first meeting," requests Maha Kassapa.

Tears fill the kindly woman's eyes as she recalls that first encounter with the Lord. "Words cannot possibly describe his physical presence. I was only seven years old at the time, but I remember knowing that I was with a being that was like no other in the world. To say that his eyes were kind and loving would be the same as saying that the sun is a small flicker of light. I was completely overwhelmed by his beauty, and enveloped in his radiance. It felt as if a soft woolen blanket had been wrapped around me on a cold night. I experienced such indescribable comfort and peace that I never wanted to leave him. His voice was silken in texture, and just hearing the golden tones in which he spoke meant as much to me as the content of his message."

Visakha pauses for a moment to further reflect on the Master and says, "On that day he became my father, my mother, and my closest friend. He looked into my eyes for a moment and a powerful energy was transmitted that changed the course of my life. No more blessed person has ever lived, and no mortal has been as fortunate as I. Knowing him filled me with inspiration and confidence. Many words have been said about his physical beauty, so there's no need to go into that aspect now. Suffice it to say that he was indeed a lion among men, as Yasodhara had said so poetically to young Rahula. The Buddha was in every respect the very pinnacle of human evolution and potential."

The arahants and Visakha's female progeny are momentarily taken aback by the grand matron's eloquence. Each of them recalls their own impressions of the Buddha's magnificence, and the tremendous effect his presence had had on their own lives.

"Didn't your father have to move to Kosala?" asks Upali.

"Yes, the move came about because King Pasenadi wrote to his brother-in-law, King Bimbisara of Magadha. He asked him to relocate one of his five wealthiest men to Kosala because he didn't have any subjects of great wealth in his own kingdom. Of course, King Bimbisara really didn't want to lose any of his wealthy men, but he knew it would offend King Pasenadi if he said 'no' to his request.

"King Bimbisara consulted with his senior ministers in the hopes of finding a diplomatic solution to his dilemma. Eventually they suggested a compromise, which was to send a son of one of the five wealthiest men. Both kings agreed to this solution, and the lot fell to Mendaka's son, my father Dhananjayan. My father didn't really want to move so far away from home, but grandfather insisted. He told him he had no choice since he couldn't refuse the king. To help make his parting easier grandfather told father that he would give him all the wealth he could ever possibly want, so my father reluctantly agreed."

"Politics!" exclaims Bakkula. "They're always rife with greed, obligation, attachment and compromise. Thank goodness we don't have politics in the Sangha!"

The arahants around him nod in complete agreement.

"When I was seven, father moved his entire household to Kosala where we actually founded our own town," began Visakha. "He didn't think Savatthi was big enough for our family and all our retainers. He asked King Pasenadi for some land about eight miles away from the city where we could spread out. This became the town of Saketa, where I lived until I got married at sixteen. My father built a huge mansion for us, and since we had several thousand farm employees, administrators, servants, and attendants he also built homes for them, along with granaries, barns, stables, pleasure pavilions, a school, and other structures. Saketa literally grew up around our family estate."

"Speaking of getting married, how did you meet your husband?" asks Bhaddiya.

"Punnavadhana was the son of wealthy Savatthi householder Migara. When he came of age his parents decided he should marry. Migara hired search experts and sent them out to find a bride. The scouts looked first in Savatthi, but they didn't find anyone suitable. Then they started looking outside the city and wound up in Saketa.

"They stopped to rest in a pavilion near a lake where my friends and I happened to be playing. Suddenly there was a huge downpour and my girlfriends and maids ran for cover. I, however, remained perfectly poised and walked slowly to the pavilion. I wound up getting soaking wet. Migara's scouts saw me calmly walking in the rain, and they approached me to ask why I didn't run for shelter.

"I said to them, 'A dress can be bought with no difficulty. If I were to run I might slip and fall, which could damage my body. This would make make me worth less as a potential wife.'[2] Can you imagine my saying such a thing?" As Visakha laughs at herself, the others join in, shaking their heads in amazement.

"You were nothing if not precocious," says Ananda. "And you still are!"

The arahants smile as they enjoy listening to Visakha share her memories. She continues her story, "Apparently I made quite an impression on the scouts because after a few minutes they threw a bridal garland into the air. I knew exactly what their gesture meant, so I indicated that I was open to their proposal by sitting down. They put the ceremonial screen around me, and after I went back home the scouts went directly to see my father."

"What did he have to say about their proposal?" asks Upali.

"Even though he felt that Migara's family wasn't our equal in wealth, they were our equal in birth and social status. He told the scouts to go back and tell Migara that his petition was accepted," answers Visakha. "Overjoyed to have found such a good catch for his son, Migara sent an urgent message to my father telling him when he would come to fetch me. My father responded that he would make suitable arrangements for the wedding and dowry, and asked Migara to prepare for my arrival in his home."

"I hear your wedding was quite an event," comments Anuruddha, smiling.

"That would be an understatement," replies Visakha, laughing.

"My future father-in-law, Migara, went to inform King Pasenadi about the marriage, and the king said that he would personally attend to honor both families. As a result, my dear father spent the next three months – the entire rainy season – housing, feeding, and entertaining the king, his guards, our friends and relatives from Rajagaha, and Migara's large group from Savatthi. The number of people to care for was enormous. The king didn't want to be an imposition, but my father insisted that it was an honor to be his host for as long as he chose to stay with us.

"When my golden wedding dress was finally completed, which was a major project in itself, I went with great ceremony to my bridegroom. Just before our time for departure my father took me aside and gave me ten items of advice in regards to serving my husband and his family. We didn't know it at the time, but Migara was in the next room and overheard our conversation."

"Your father was very wise to give you that advice, Visakha. It was also wise of him to send eight trusted retainers who would watch out for you in your in-laws' home," says Ananda. "Tell us about your big send-off."

"I put on my bridal dress which was made of gold, lace and jewels. Father paid a fortune for it – several million gold coins. I don't think there had ever been one to equal it before – and certainly my daughters never got one like it, although each of theirs was unique and quite magnificent," says Visakha smiling at her ten beautiful daughters.

"In front of King Pasenadi and the entire wedding assembly my father gave me one hundred and fifty-four cartloads of gold, five hundred maidservants, five hundred coaches drawn by thoroughbred horses, and countless other items that he thought would be useful in my new life as a married woman," says Visakha. "Before we started out for my new home my father instructed his herdsmen to harness the finest oxen to my carts. Then they herded hundreds, if not thousands, of the finest milk cows, bulls, and other livestock into our procession. My new husband and I were at the head of the parade; the coaches, carts and maidservants followed next, and then came the animals. Our entourage stretched out about four miles – literally half the distance to the city."

"You must have made quite an entrance in Savatthi," comments Punna.

"Indeed I did," laughs Visakha. "When we arrived at the city I didn't know if I should stand up in my coach or remain seated. Then I remembered my gorgeous wedding dress and decided that everyone should have a chance to see it. So I stood. The townspeople waved and cheered and threw flower blossoms. They loved the dress, and they thought I was the most beautiful young girl they had ever seen.

"My husband was very proud of me that day, as was my father-in-law. We no sooner got to my new mansion than gifts started to arrive. Everyone in Savatthi, rich or poor, wanted to send me something on my wedding day. I was deeply touched by their warmth and generosity, but I didn't really need anything, as you can well imagine. So I immediately had all of the gifts re-distributed among the people of Savatthi, and they truly appreciated my first act of generosity in their community."

"I understand you performed another act of charity on your wedding night," laughs Ananda.

"Not charity, exactly; I suppose you could call it more an act of compassion motivated by duty," smiles Visakha. "I was just getting ready for bed when my maidservant told me one of my father-in-law's thoroughbred horses was about to give foal. I dressed appropriately, walked to the stable, and went to comfort the laboring new mother. I told my maidservants to hold the lamps so I could see better, and I delivered the foal myself. Then I had the servants bathe the mother in hot water and apply oil to her exhausted body. The foal was a healthy male, and he immediately began suckling. After I was satisfied that both mother and son were comfortable I went back to my chamber to join my new husband."

"This little act of compassion came back to haunt you, didn't it?" says Bhaddiya, smiling knowingly.

"In a way it did, but it all worked out for the best as you'll hear when I get to that part," responds Visakha.

"My wedding reception, which included religious ceremonies, started the next morning and went on for seven days," continues Visakha. "Even though the Buddha was staying in nearby Jetavana Monastery, my father-in-law didn't invite him because he was a supporter of the local group of naked ascetics. I didn't complain, but I felt it was disrespectful not to include the Buddha, since he was my teacher and spiritual benefactor. At one point during the first day Migara called me and said, 'Go and make obeisance to the arahants.'

"Hearing the word 'arahants,' I eagerly went to see who he was talking about. When I saw that gaggle of naked men I was horrified! I said to Migara, 'How could these shameless men be arahants? I'll have nothing to do with them!' I turned on my heels and left my father-in-law with his mouth open, mortally embarrassed in front of his assemblage of naked gurus."

"I imagine those naked gurus, as you called them, complained bitterly to Migara about your behavior and wanted you thrown out of the house!" exclaims Upali. "They were probably unhappy with the fact that you were a disciple of the Buddha, and they feared losing Migara's patronage."

"They even went so far as to call me a demon woman," laughs Visakha. "My father-in-law tried to placate his naked gurus by telling them that I was young and didn't know any better. He apologized profusely on my behalf and asked them to have patience with me. He also knew that there was no way he could simply throw me out of his house on my wedding day. Besides, I'm sure he couldn't bear to see all the wealth my father had bestowed on me leave his home so quickly."

All of Visakha's daughters and other female relatives laugh heartily upon hearing these remarks. Her eldest daughter says, "My mother has always had a strong personality, and has never been afraid to speak her mind. That day she certainly set the tone for her future life in my grandfather's house!"

"Especially when she perceived a slight to the Buddha – taking into account the fact that she was already a *sotapanna*," adds Ananda, smiling.

Visakha continues, "The next day I tried to make amends with my father-in-law, knowing that I had embarrassed him to the core. I cooked a special milk-rice for him and served it myself on a gold plate with a gold spoon. He was pleased by the attention, and he enjoyed the meal. A servant approached me after going to the front door, and I turned to see a *bhikkhu* standing there with his alms bowl. I was standing in Migara's line of vision so I moved aside so he could see the saffron-robed monk. I hoped his heart would be moved, and that he would offer the *bhikkhu* some food. Unfortunately he just sat there looking down at his plate and pretended not to see the noble Sangha member. It really made me irritated!"

"What did you do then?" asks one of Visakha's young granddaughters, enjoying her grandmother's colorful tale.

"I went over to the *bhikkhu* and said, 'Empty-handed I pay homage to you, Venerable Sir. My father-in-law lives only on old food.' When Migara heard this remark he jumped up out of his seat and stormed at me saying, 'How dare you say I eat excreta?' Then he screamed at his servants and said, 'Expel this woman from my house! I won't tolerate her any longer.' Fortunately, all of the servants in the house were in my employ so they didn't dare lift a finger or say a word," says Visakha, smiling mischievously.

"I guess you thoroughly upset your new father-in-law," says Sopaka, grinning.

"No doubt I did! I walked over to him and said, 'You have not brought me to this house like some common water carrier. I am a good daughter whose parents are still living, and I will not obey your unlawful command. To make sure I am treated justly, my father sent with me eight trusted patrons to hear any cases that might rise against me. With your permission I will call them now.' Then I had my servant bring these eight men to our presence; they were all honest householders beyond reproach.

"Migara said, 'Gentlemen, Visakha hasn't yet been in my house a week and she's already insulted me. She just said that I eat excreta.'

"One of these trusted elders turned to me and asked, 'Is this true?'

"'No, elder, it's not true. Since Migara refused to offer alms to a *bhikkhu* who was standing at the door I said to the monk, 'My father-in-law lives only on old food.' What I meant by that statement was that he performs no deeds of merit in his present existence, but is living only on the fruit of his past merit.'

"The elder turned to Migara and said, 'Our daughter is not at fault in this case. Why should you be angry with her?'

"Migara stammered, 'From the first night in this household Visakha ignored her husband and left the house.'

"The elder said to Visakha, 'Is this true?'

"'I attended to the birth of a thoroughbred foal that night in the stables. I thought it was my duty to do so.'

"The elder said, 'Sir, your daughter-in-law was dutiful in performing a service for you. Why should you take it as an offence?'

"Migara, by this time, was huffing and puffing, his face turning red as a pomegranate. He said, 'I wish to complain about her father. I overheard him tell her ten things on her wedding day that I strongly object to. I said nothing until now, but I think I have no choice but to bring these up. The first thing he said was not to take the fire from the inside of the house. How would it be possible not to give fire when needed by our next door neighbor?'

"So I said, 'He did not mean 'fire' in the ordinary sense. When my father said 'don't take fire from inside the house,' he meant that the affairs of my parents-in-law and their family should not be divulged to outsiders. If I were to do that I cause unnecessary trouble at home.'

"Migara retorted, 'Her father also said that she should not take fire from outside the house into the house. How would it be possible for us not to bring fire into the house from outside if our fire went out?'

"The elder asked, 'Daughter, is this true?'

"I stayed calm," says Visakha, "and answered, 'My father once again did not mean 'fire' in the usual sense. His meaning was: what others say in criticizing the family should not be told to the family. This would cause unnecessary trouble at home.'

"Migara started to speak again, but I interrupted him and said, 'Since you are obviously going to go through the whole list of ten things my father said to me, I will save us some time and explain them all at once.'

Her daughters and female relatives are laughing again, as the arahants smile in amusement at the young bride's spunky character.

"The third thing he said to me was, 'You should lend only to those who return what they borrow.' This is to not let defaulters get the better of me.

"The fourth thing he said was, 'You should not lend to those who do not return what they borrow.' This is to not let any defaulters exploit my goodness.

"The fifth was, 'You should give to those whether they repay you or not.' He said this to make me liberal in regards to poor relatives or friends who may come to me in need. I should make gifts to them rather than loans.

"Number six was, 'You should sit peacefully.' This means that I should show deference to my father-in-law and my mother-in-law by standing up when they approach me.

"Seven was, 'You should eat peacefully.' This means I shouldn't eat until my parents-in-law and my husband have finished eating their fill.

"The eighth was, 'You should sleep peacefully,' which means that I should only go to bed after I have attended to the needs of my parents-in-law.

"Number nine was, 'You should tend to the fire.' My father meant that I should consider my parents-in-law and my husband as the household fire, and they should always be held in reverence.

"The last item of advice was, 'You should worship the deities of the house.' By these words my father wanted me to always offer alms to *bhikkhus* who would stand at my door – and to eat only after I have fed them.'[3]

"One of the elders frowned and said reproachfully, 'Sir, how can you ignore *bhikkhus* who stand at your door seeking alms food?'

"Migara could find no words for the elder, so he simply remained silent and fumed. The leader of the elders then said to him, 'Sir, do you have any other complaints against our daughter? In spite of her innocence, why did you try to expel her from your household?'

"Before my father-in-law could answer I said, 'Elders, I didn't think it was wise to obey my father-in-law's rash command. Now that you have cleared me of any wrongdoing, I am more than happy to go.'

"Migara was speechless. I went to my private chamber and told my servants to pack my things at once," says Visakha.

"Were you really going to go?" asks Maha Kaccayana.

"Of course I was going to go. I wouldn't stay five more minutes in a house that didn't respect noble *bhikkhus*," is Visakha's quick reply.

"In the meantime, Migara called my eight household elders, and sent word for me to come downstairs. When I walked into the room he said, 'Dear daughter, forgive me for being so reckless in my emotions.'

"With that statement I saw a perfect opportunity to set things straight forever. I said, 'Dear Father-in-law, I do forgive you, but I have one condition if I am going to stay here under your roof.'

"He said expectantly, 'Anything, daughter, what do you want?'

"I said, 'I am an unshakable devotee of the Lord Buddha, and I wish to make offerings to his Sangha members as often as I like. If you don't give me permission to do so I will leave this house immediately.'

"Migara said, 'Dear daughter, you are at complete liberty to do as you wish.'

"Without saying another word I summoned my maids and my coach. We immediately went to the Buddha and I paid my respects. I invited him to our house the next day for the noon meal. I was so happy to see the Master again that I forgot all about the unpleasant altercation with my father-in-law.

"The Buddha arrived at our mansion the next day in the company of a large number of his *bhikkhus*. Migara's naked ascetics heard about the *dana* ceremony, so they showed up with some of their followers. They obviously wanted to keep a close eye on their primary benefactor. They did manage to prevent Migara from serving food to the Buddha, but they couldn't prevent him from hearing the Buddha's message – even though they put a curtain between him and the Buddha when he was just about to start preaching," says Visakha.

"Did those naked ascetics really think that a mere curtain could separate a man from the Buddha Dhamma?" asks Maha Kassapa rhetorically.

"At the end of the discourse my father-in-law attained *sotapanna*. He drew that silly curtain aside, went directly to where I was seated at the feet of the Buddha, and took refuge in the Triple Gem. He said to me with great emotion, 'From now onwards you are my Mother.' I must say that I was pleased by his quick change in attitude, but a glance from the Buddha told me to keep my ego in check."

Visakha concludes these remarks and looks around at her brood of white-clad females. She sighs and says to them, "I know you've heard these stories a million times, and I want to thank you for indulging me yet again."

One of her daughters looks at her with great love and says, "You have always been an inspiration to us, mother, and even if you told your stories a billion times we would never get tired of them. Besides, each time you tell them they get better – and today's version is particularly brilliant given your esteemed audience."

The arahants smile at the warm expression of love between Visakha and her daughter. They see that she is as kind and compassionate towards her family as she is towards the Buddha Sangha.

"After recognizing me as his mother, Migara went and prostrated before the Buddha. He held his feet and kissed them adoringly. Then he said to the Lord, 'Today I have learned the true meaning of offering gifts to the noble ones. My daughter-in-law has brought great benefit to my house.'

"I invited the Buddha and his monks to another *dana* ceremony on the following day. When my mother-in-law listened to the Buddha, she became a *sotapanna*. From that day onwards my house has always been open to the Buddha, the Dhamma, and the Sangha."

Visakha smiles, feeling grateful for the many opportunities she has had to be of service to the Triple Gem. Her being radiates happiness, which is the result of accumulated merit during the course of her past rebirths, as well as from this life as a close associate of the Buddha.

Ananda says, "Don't forget to tell us about the way Migara showed you his gratitude for bringing the Buddha into his life."

"I couldn't possibly leave that part of the story out, could I Venerable Sir? After all, you played a part in it at the end," laughs Visakha.

The arahants and Visakha's offspring know exactly what she is referring to. Visakha begins, "Migara, overjoyed in the bliss of *sotapanna*, thought my bridal dress was way too cumbersome and ornate for most occasions – not to mention uncomfortable to wear, especially when sitting. He got the idea to have another dress made for me embellished with gold and jewels – one that I could wear night or day.

"He paid a king's ransom for that amazing dress. When it was finished he had me bathe in sixteen pots of scented water, and then wear it for the first time in the presence of the Buddha. I showed my appreciation to my father-in-law, of course, but to be perfectly honest I didn't really need or want his expensive gift. I already had the wedding dress, which was way over the top by anyone's standards, but it was nothing compared to this new one Migara had made for me. I wore it from time to time on ceremonial occasions just to make him happy," says Visakha.

"Grandmother," says one of the small girls, "tell us the funny story about what happened to that famous dress."

Visakha laughingly says, "Yes, the dress story wouldn't be complete without telling what happened to it." She smiles at Ananda when she says this, and continues, "The people of Savatthi considered me to be a lucky woman, and of course I was, and I still am! I never get sick, I have the strength of ten elephants, I have no grey hairs, my children have never caused me a problem, and abundance simply happens around me. Everywhere I go there is abundance and plenty. I view abundance as my natural state, and I suppose people think it rubs off on them. The people of Savatthi always want me to be the guest of honor whenever there is an important event, and back in those days they always requested that I wear Migara's dress."

"I wish you had commissioned some artist to draw a picture of your dress, or make a statue of you wearing it so we could know what it looked like," says one of her lovely daughters.

"I never even gave it a thought, dear one; I was always so busy that such a trifle never crossed my mind. Anyway, one day I wore it to a large function at the Buddha's monastery. I thought it would show a lack of modesty to wear it in the Lord's presence, so I took it off and handed it to my trusted maidservant. Underneath I wore a simple white silk gown. I went before the Buddha and made my prostrations, then listened to one of his great discourses," says Visakha.

"I'll continue from here, if you don't mind," says Ananda, and Visakha smiles warmly at her old friend.

"Visakha's maidservant went off and forgot the legendary dress. The function ended and Visakha busied herself by making her daily rounds in the monastery. She was always providing medicine for sick monks, visiting junior *bhikkhus* and *samaneras*, and attending to all sorts of service details. Just before leaving the monastery she turned to her maidservant and said, 'Bring me my dress.' The girl gasped saying, 'My lady, I have forgotten it!' Visakha simply said, 'Then go fetch it.'

"Before the maid ran off, though, Visakha said to the girl, 'If, for any reason, Venerable Ananda has moved the dress, tell him that the dress belongs to him.' She knew that I usually put any articles that were forgotten in a safe place – sort of like a lost-and-found room. When the maidservant approached me asking for the dress, I told her that I had hung it up at the end of the stairway. The girl then said that if I had moved it, her lady considered it donated to me. The girl immediately left to tell Visakha what had happened," says Ananda.

Visakha speaks up, "When my maid told me the news, I said that having the expensive dress would probably cause trouble for Venerable Ananda. After all, what could he do with such an outlandish dress embellished with gold and jewels? I decided then and there that I would sell it and buy something useful for the Sangha with the money. So I retrieved it from Venerable Ananda and took it to the goldsmith for an appraisal. I won't even tell you the ridiculous value he put on that silly dress, but I decided to put it up for sale at the price he quoted anyway.

"I told my maid to drape it on the back of an elephant and then had it paraded through the streets of Savatthi. The price was posted on a sign on top of the elephant's head. I wasn't surprised it didn't sell; I knew no one could afford to buy it. That was when I decided to buy it myself at my asking price, and give the proceeds to the Sangha. I had my treasurer load up a large cart with gold, and took it to the monastery to offer it to the Buddha."

"A cartful of gold being rolled through the streets of Savatthi must have drawn quite a bit of attention," comments Upali with a laugh.

"Not nearly as much attention as the dress had drawn on the back of that elephant!" shoots back Visakha, greatly amused. "Looking back on that day, people must have thought I had gone bankrupt and had been forced to sell it."

"So what happened when you took the gold to the monastery?" asks Sopaka.

"I told the Buddha what had happened with the dress, and that I didn't think it was proper to wear it again. I said that I had sold it, and asked him how I could use the gold for the benefit of the Sangha. Without a second thought the Lord said, 'It would be fitting if you built a monastery near the eastern gate of this city.' I clapped my hands for joy hearing this idea from the Master's lips. I immediately went out and bought a suitable piece of land near the eastern gate, and then immersed myself with architectural designs and making preparations for construction.

"One day I heard the Buddha was walking toward the northern gate. This usually meant that he was leaving Savatthi, and there was no way of knowing when he would return. I rushed to him at once saying, 'Please wait until the monastery is completed before you go out of town, Lord. I want you to oversee its building to make sure it is to your liking.'

"When he looked at me I knew at once that he couldn't wait. I said, 'If you can't be here, then please leave some *bhikkhu* behind who can supervise in your absence.'

"The Lord then said, 'Visakha, take the alms bowl of the *bhikkhu* of your choice.' Venerable Ananda knows that he's always been my favorite, but I thought about the construction project and realized that Venerable Moggallana, with his vast psychic powers, might be the best one for the job. I know you didn't mind, Venerable Sir," says Visakha, looking fondly at her old friend.

"Of course I didn't mind, Visakha," says Ananda. "I was planning to go with the Buddha on his journey anyway, and besides, Venerable Moggallana was the best choice. Am I not right?"

"Indeed you are," answers Visakha. "Venerable Moggallana made sure things were expedited very quickly, very carefully, and very safely. Not a single worker had an accident, and there were no mishaps with late-arriving materials, laborers, the weather, or any other unforeseeable crisis that inevitably arises while working on such a project."

"The Buddha and I were gone nine months and when we returned the monastery was completed," says Ananda. "I couldn't believe my eyes when I saw what you had built, Visakha. It was splendid; a real achievement in design and construction. There were five hundred rooms for monks' residences on the first floor and five hundred more on the second. You also had five hundred meditation cubicles, several meeting spaces, an auditorium, and numerous other useful amenities."

"I asked the Buddha if he would kindly stay in the new monastery during the coming rainy season retreat, and he agreed. I offered *dana* to the Buddha and his Sangha in thanks," adds Visakha.

"From that point onwards for the next four months you provided *dana* on a daily basis, and saw to our every conceivable need," adds Ananda. "I remember the robes you gave to each and every *bhikkhu* one day, the quality of which was unmatched by any we had ever received. I must say, though, that you went a bit overboard with your generosity that full moon day in November. You offered the monastery to the Buddha in a grand ceremony none of us will ever forget."

"Yes, I suppose I did get a bit carried away, but it was because I was so happy! I had actually built and donated a monastery to the Buddha! I danced around the courtyards all through that full moon night; I know it probably wasn't very proper, but I couldn't help myself. Everyone probably thought I had gone completely mad. The truth is, my cherished ambitions from previous births had finally been realized, and I couldn't contain my excitement. I have no doubt that I made a total spectacle of myself," exclaims Visakha using a voice that fully communicates her happiness. "I'm surprised the Buddha didn't give me a scolding for my unseemly behavior! But he would never have done that, knowing how utterly happy I was."

"I wouldn't exactly call your performance a 'spectacle,'" says Ananda, "at least in the classical sense of the word. But you definitely conveyed your immense pleasure to everyone. You were free as a bird, and you sang and danced around as if you were completely by yourself. I'll never forget the way you were that night, Visakha, and I say that with the greatest possible respect."

The arahants and Visakha's offspring are beaming with happiness as Ananda recalls her memorable moonlight performance. They all know the high spirits of the Buddha's foremost matron, and they know she is capable of doing just about anything.

Visakha grins and says, "You know, I'm so happy that I could get up and dance right now! Would you like me to sing you a song? Just imagine: we are sitting in one of the first buildings of a brand new monastery. I get to do the whole thing all over again!"

Maha Kassapa says, "I regret having to put an end to this delightful occasion, but it is very late, and council starts again at dawn. As always, Visakha, we are grateful to you for everything, especially for coming here to be with us today.

"I hope I haven't kept you venerables up too late! I've been having such a good time – especially with all my girls here with me. When I think of the new monastery without the Buddha, though, it does sadden me a bit," says Visakha as her eyes begin to tear.

Visakha manages to compose herself quickly. She and her female relatives rise together and prepare to take their leave. Very solemnly, she leads the way as they pay obeisance to the arahants as they depart.

It is a happy ending to a memorable day, and the arahants return to their chambers even more blissful than usual. The steep climb up the mountain doesn't take as long as it might have, and this is undoubtedly due to the jubilant spirit of *metta* that permeates the atmosphere.

Ananda stops on the path to reflect for a moment and says to himself, "The Lord would have been very pleased."

Chapter 23
Mentor to Kings

The arahants on the sub-committee are already gathered in Maha Kassapa's cave chamber after another long day of recitations in the assembly hall.

"Maha Kassapa, it was such a delight to have Visakha with us yesterday," says Ananda. "The high energy she brought to the council was so welcome, as are the gifts she has been bringing to the Sangha for so many years."

"I'm glad you enjoyed your surprise," responds Maha Kassapa, smiling.

"I'm always amazed when I think about the wealthy and influential people that have been attracted to the Buddha and his teaching since the very beginning," says Maha Kaccayana. "The *Sasana* has been very fortunate to enjoy the patronage of some of the most powerful people of our day, while at the same time the Buddha epitomized the egalitarian ideal. Many times over the years he stressed the fact that what makes one a true noble is what one *does* – rather than what one *has* or *is* – or the status of the family of one's origin."

"Being born into a royal clan, it was natural for aristocrats to gravitate towards the Buddha – not to mention the fact that his presence was so magnetic that all who met him were attracted to his goodness, no matter who they were, or where they came from," says Bhaddiya.

"He was able to mentor most of the great leaders of our era," begins Anuruddha, "guiding them in the proper use of their worldly power. In many ways the Buddha started from the top down in terms of preaching to the kings and princes of the world; and then the Dhamma filtered from the heads of state to their subjects who followed their virtuous examples. There were never any threats or coercion, as there have been in the past with other teachings."

Upali says, "The Buddha's teaching is universally applicable; it applies equally to kings, queens, tradesmen, householders, servants, and street sweepers. Simply by observing the basic Five Precepts, which can be understood by everyone, a better life can be had by all."

"You are quite right, my friend," says Bakkula. "All social problems result from the fact that the Five Precepts are not kept by everyone. They're so basic: refrain from killing, stealing, lying, sexual misconduct, and intoxicants. All criminal activity, legal actions, wars, broken homes, and wrecked lives can be traced to the transgression of one or more of these five simple training rules for wholesome living."

"The Buddha never said 'you *must* follow these precepts *or else*,' which would generate fear in the hearts of his disciples," adds Punna. "He only said 'If you want to end suffering in your life I *suggest* you follow these precepts.' He even instructed followers to use the words 'I will refrain…' rather than 'I swear to never…' Knowing human nature the way he did, he understood that people might break the precepts from time to time. He made it clear, though, that if they were broken, the individual could always make fresh new commitments to keeping the precepts and to improving their lives."

Ananda says, "The *Cakkavattisihanada Sutta*,[1] sums it up brilliantly, even though it includes some additional precepts. First it speaks of the consequence of not keeping the precepts. Although I have already recited this earlier in the council, I'd like to share a few lines now:

> "'…Thus, from not giving of property to the needy,
>   poverty became rife,
> From the growth of poverty, the taking of
>   what was not given increased,
> From the increase of theft, the use of weapons increased,
> From the increased use of weapons, the taking of life
>   increased,
> From the taking of life increasing, lying increased.
> From the increase in lying, the speaking evil
>   of others increased,
> Sexual misconduct increased, harsh speech
>   and idle chatter increased,
> From the increase of harsh speech and idle chatter,
>   covetousness and hatred increased,

> From the increase in covetousness and hatred,
>   false opinions increased,
> From the increase in false opinions, incest, excessive
>   greed and deviant practices increased, and
> From the increase of excessive greed and deviant
>   practices,
> Lack of respect for mother and father, for ascetics and
>   Brahmins, and for the head of the clan increased,
> And in consequence, people's life-span decreased,
>   and their beauty decreased...'

"So we see, my friends," continues Ananda, "how breaking one precept can lead to breaking another, which leads to another, and so on. The breaking of precepts can be like a slippery slope for the individual as well as for the state, and it's difficult to reverse the downward motion. Later on in that same *sutta*, however, the Buddha tells of a change that can stop the destruction of a wholesome life. It goes like this:

> "'And then the thought will occur to those beings:
> It is only because we became addicted to evil ways
> That we suffered...so let us now do good!
> What good things can we do?
> Let us abstain from the taking of life, and...
> Let us refrain from taking what is not given,
> From sexual misconduct,
> From lying speech,
> From harsh speech,
> From idle chatter,
> From covetousness,
> From ill-will,
> From wrong views:
> Let us abstain from three things: incest, excessive greed,
>   and deviant practices;
> Let us respect our mothers and fathers, ascetics and
>   Brahmins, and the head of the clan;
> Let us persevere in these wholesome actions.'
> And so they will avoid these things, and thusly
> They will increase in life-span and in beauty.'"

Ananda continues, "After taking the refuges the Buddha gave the precepts to Brahmin, king, and commoner alike. If their minds were ready, and they had the capacity to understand, he then expounded the Four Noble Truths, the Noble Eightfold Path, and the doctrines of dependent origination, impermanence, and elimination of the 'I' concept; each one being building blocks, one on the other, for the development of the mind; in concert they establish a way of life that brings nothing short of true happiness. It's all so simple really, and yet as deep as the deepest ocean."

"Very true, Ven. Ananda, and very well put," says Ven. Upali. "Once a new disciple took refuge in the Triple Gem and subscribed to the Five Precepts, the Buddha could explain his higher doctrines, which was usually the case in the kings he mentored."

"The Buddha taught the Dhamma to a number of kings," begins Punna, "and some like King Bimbisara of Magadha and King Pasenadi of Kosala became lifelong supporters and devotees. King Ajatasattu is now a sincere devotee, though at one time he was under the influence of Devadatta, who led him to commit grave offenses that have done great harm to his *kamma*. I'm sure we will discuss this later when we go more into detail about the Devadatta insurgency."

"At this point in our recollection, perhaps we should discuss the kings and queens with whom we have had an association," suggests Maha Kassapa. "No account of the Buddha's life would be complete without stories of their interactions with the Lord. These royal relationships were catalysts for spreading the Buddha's message of compassion and wisdom to the masses. Who would like to begin?"

After a pause Maha Kaccayana says, "I don't mind starting this discussion by telling the story of King Canda Pajjota of Avanti. Before joining the Sangha I actually served on his staff, and I knew him well. He was a very powerful king and all of his neighbors were afraid of him – for good reason. He waged war on Gandhara, and he once imprisoned the king of Vatsa. King Ajatasattu also felt threatened by him, which caused him to build additional fortifications in Rajagaha against a possible invasion.

"King Pajjota never met the Buddha personally, but we heard about him from the first traveling arahants who spread his message. After my father died I became the king's chaplain, and King Pajjota sent me and seven others to invite the Buddha to Avanti. When we listened to him preach the Dhamma we immediately asked for ordination; before too long we attained arahantship."

"Did you stay with the Buddha from that time on?" asks Sopaka.

"No, the Buddha asked us to return to Avanti so we could teach the Dhamma to the people in that area. The king soon became a devoted follower of the Buddha, and with his royal patronage I was able to help found a number of monasteries in his kingdom. He contributed to the Sangha in a host of valuable ways," concludes Maha Kaccayana.

"You just mentioned Gandhara, Venerable Sir," says Bakkula, "so we should tell the story of that king too. This also happens to have been a powerful monarch who never personally met the Buddha before becoming a devoted follower."

"That's right," says Anuruddha. "Please tell us his story."

Bakkula begins, "King Pukkusati[2] of Gandhara became a close friend of King Bimbisara through the exchange of gifts and letters. The two kings established trade relations between the two countries, which allowed duty-free transactions. Taxila, the Gandharan capital, was and is one of the foremost places of learning. King Bimbisara's son, Prince Abhaya, sent his adopted son, Jivaka, to Taxila for medical school and he became the personal physician of King Bimbisara and the Buddha.

"One day King Pukkusati decided to send his friend King Bimbisara a fine gift of priceless Kashmir cloth in five colors. Please keep in mind the fact that the two kings had never met in person, but they grew close over the years through correspondence, developing a strong mutual respect for one another. The cloth was specially wrapped and sent with the express instruction that King Bimbisara was to open it in front of his ministers.

"The king did as he was asked, and when he opened the box he and his ministers were duly impressed by the fine gift, which was of inestimable value. King Bimbisara then decided to send a gift in return, but custom dictated that his gift had to be finer than the one he had received. The practice of gift exchange had evolved into a game of one-upmanship, if you will. The king pondered long and hard to decide on just the right gift, and nothing he could think of seemed fitting or adequate."

"Bakkula, what did he finally wind up sending the king?" asks Sopaka.

"He decided that the gift of the Buddha Dhamma was the most priceless thing he could send. He had a large sheet of paper-thin pure gold fabricated. He performed rituals in preparation for presenting the Triple Gem in written form, as he wanted it to be by his own hand. He shut himself up in his private chamber, giving orders that he was not to be disturbed. He knew that he was about to engage in a sacred task, one that would require every ounce of his concentrated power of meditation.

"In his inspired letter to King Pukkusati, he said that a Buddha had arisen in the world. He explained the Buddha's Dhamma, and praised the noble ones of the Sangha. He also described in detail the sixteen kinds of mindfulness on breathing, which is *anapanasati* meditation. At the end of his long letter he stated, 'The teaching of the Exalted One with its threefold training of virtue, meditation and wisdom, is beautiful in the beginning, beautiful in the middle, and beautiful in the end. It is the teaching that will certainly lead to liberation from *samsara*. Friend Pukkusati, I myself would choose to ordain as a monk in the Buddha's Sangha, but for a variety of reasons I cannot do so at this time. However, if ordination is possible for you, I would urge you to renounce the world and become a monk.'"

Ananda says, "King Bimbisara performed an incredible act of merit when he conceived of this plan."

Bakkula continues, "The king had the letter encased in several consecutive caskets of gold, silver, and other precious materials, and he sent it to King Pukkusati on the back of a royal elephant in a grand procession, which he himself led all the way to his border. He told his minister to say to the king, 'Please receive this gift, not in the presence of your queens, but privately.'

"When the Gandharan king received the sacred gift he did as he was requested, and took it to the upper terrace of his palace where he opened it alone. He told his guards not to let anyone enter his chamber. As he began to open the box he realized the importance his friend had placed on the gift, given the elaborate way it had been wrapped – not to mention the way it was delivered. He began to read the letter, marveling at the beautiful script of King Bimbisara's hand.

"When he read the first line, 'There has arisen an Exalted One in this world,' the hairs on his entire body stood on end. He realized the tremendous opportunity he had to read this message, and he studied every word very carefully. With each line he became more ecstatic and joyfully contemplative. By the end of the document he decided that he would, in fact, renounce the world and become a monk," says Bakkula.

"Imagine a king, with all his worldly power and glory, deciding to renounce his throne and become a monk just because he read the Dhamma message in a letter," says Bhaddiya, smiling broadly.

"He practiced *anapatasati* meditation the way it was described in the letter, and stayed in his private chamber for fifteen days enjoying the bliss of *jhana*," continues Bakkula. "His subjects began to worry about him, but he had given explicit instructions that he was not to be disturbed. Finally, he cut off his hair with his sword and threw it down to his subjects below, along with his ruby crown. The people in the palace had no idea what was taking place upstairs. The king dressed himself in the clothing of common people and walked away from his palace undetected. The guards later found the king's private apartment empty.

"They searched the city and eventually found the king. Prostrating themselves at his feet they begged him not to leave. They were weeping and rolling on the ground with grief. The king finally drew a line in the sand and told them not to cross it. He made it very clear that he was walking away from his former life alone, and that he was not to be followed.

"Then he walked barefoot for hundreds of miles to Savatthi. His tender feet became cracked and blistered, and he was greatly fatigued. He had no way of knowing that at the time, the Buddha was staying nearby at Jetavana Monastery. From the letter he received from King Bimbisara, he assumed that the Buddha was residing in Rajagaha, so he continued walking all those extra miles," continues Bakkula.

"It's rare to find a man whose confidence in the Buddha is so strong that he would undertake such an inspired journey; it was completely unprecedented," says Upali.

"It was late when King Pukkusati reached Rajagaha," resumes Bakkula, "so he inquired of the townspeople where wandering ascetics were permitted to stay. They told him of a potter's shed, gave him directions, and with the potter's permission he entered and spent the night.

"During the third watch of that night the Buddha surveyed the world of living beings and he saw King Pukkusati. He realized that the king had gone to Rajagaha to become a monk because of reverence for him. He also saw that the king had the capacity for spiritual attainment, and that he would soon pass away. The Buddha decided that he would go to Rajagaha to see the faith-filled king and personally give him further instructions.

"The Lord took his alms bowl and robe and used his supernormal powers to travel to the potter's hut," continues Bakkula. "He covered his spiritual glory so he could approach the king who needed rest before he could fully comprehend his Dhamma message. The Lord's appearance was very modest when he stood at the doorway of the dilapidated hut and asked the ascetic's permission to enter.

"King Pukkusati said, 'My friend, this hut is small, but quiet. Please come in and make yourself comfortable.' The Buddha entered the humble dwelling, which was filthy and filled with broken pots, ashes, and animal droppings. The Buddha made himself a bed of straw and spread out his robe, and then he calmly sat down as if he was in the Fragrant Chamber of one of his monasteries.

"The Buddha and King Pukkusati went into meditation. It was the Buddha's intention to help the king attain liberation, so he silently supported him with his energy, and together the two of them entered the fourth *jhana*.

"Later, the Buddha asked the king to whom had he dedicated his monastic life, and who was his teacher. The king answered that he had dedicated himself to the Buddha. Then the Buddha asked him where the Buddha was residing, and the king answered, 'The Blessed One resides here in Rajagaha.'

"Then the Buddha said, 'If you were to see the Buddha would you recognize him?'

"The king answered honestly, 'No, I would not recognize him.'

"The Buddha realized that the king was now sufficiently rested, and his mind was ready to hear the Dhamma. So the Buddha began a discourse. While the Master preached, the king attained the status of *anagami*. When this occurred the king knew immediately that he was in the presence of the Buddha, and that he had heard the Dhamma delivered by the Blessed One himself. He was overjoyed, to say the least," says Bakkula.

"What did the king do then?" asks Sopaka.

"He immediately prostrated himself before the Lord and asked him for ordination," replies Bakkula. "The Buddha then asked him, 'Do you have your own robe and alms bowl?'

"The king said, 'No, Lord, I do not, but I will leave now and obtain them.'

"King Pukkusati went at dawn to find the two requisites. Just after the king left the hut the Buddha decided to make his presence known to the people of Rajagaha. He emitted from his body his six-hued rays of light, which soon filled the entire city. News that the Buddha was in town spread quickly, and it eventually reached King Bimbisara who rushed immediately to the poor potter's hut to pay his respects.

"When he reached the humble dwelling, King Bimbisara asked the Buddha about the purpose of his visit. The Buddha told him of his friend King Pukkusati, and the fact that he had walked all of those extra miles just to meet the Buddha face to face. He explained that out of compassion for him, and for his spiritual welfare, he had journeyed to help him.

"King Bimbisara, greatly excited, said, 'Lord, where is the king right now?'

"The Buddha replied, 'He has gone out to find a robe and an alms bowl so he can be ordained.'

"Without another word the Buddha then vanished into thin air, and went back to the Fragrant Chamber at Jetavana Monastery in Savatthi. Meanwhile, King Pukkusati was looking through piles of discarded pieces of cloth for the robe he intended to make. While he was doing so he was suddenly attacked by a mentally deranged bull and gored to death. He fell to the ground and landed in a rubbish heap. He was immediately reborn in the Brahma realm and there attained arahantship," says Bakkula.

"King Bimbisara must have been horrified when he discovered the sad fate of his friend," says Upali.

"Yes, he mourned for his friend and lamented the fact that they had never met," continues Bakkula. "He had King Pukkusati's body bathed and dressed in clean white garments, and then he honored him with a state funeral. After he was cremated King Bimbisara built a *stupa* interring his ashes."

"The fate of King Pukkusati demonstrates the fact that *kamma* cannot be reversed once it has been set in motion. The king was gored by a bull because of past actions; even the Buddha couldn't have stopped it," says Bhaddiya.

Maha Kassapa says, "King Pukkusati of Gandhara will be remembered forever as one who heard the good news that the Buddha was in the world, and due to his *saddha*, gave up everything to pursue a life in the Dhamma."

"This is just one more example of the tremendous spiritual power of the Triple Gem, and how it can transform lives," says Ananda. "More good news is that personal transformation can take place even without the Buddha's personal presence. One can simply follow the Five Precepts and move on up the spiritual ladder as the Dhamma is revealed in the heart."

"Who else would like to tell a story of one of the Buddha's kingly disciples?" asks the chairman, ready to focus again on the topic at hand.

"I will tell you briefly about King Udena of Vatsa, whose capital is Kosambi," says Punna.

The arahants listen intently as Punna begins, "Udena's origins were quite interesting. His father was King Parantapa of Vatsa, but before Udena was born his mother, the queen, was kidnapped. She was left in the forest near the hermitage of the former king of Allakappa, who had renounced his throne and was now an ascetic. When the queen gave birth, the ascetic kindly took Udena under his protection and raised him. When Udena was grown, one day the ascetic divined that King Parantapa was dead. This is when Udena's mother finally divulged her son's true identity.

"The ascetic was a master of elephants and he taught Udena how to tame them. Together they assembled a large herd so Udena could return to Vatsa to claim his throne. Udena was successful in this undertaking and secured his kingdom.

"King Udena married Samavati, the adopted daughter of his treasurer, the millionaire Ghosaka. Samavati was a devotee of the Buddha, having learned his doctrine from her attendant, Khujjuttara. Samavati had realized the state of *sotapanna* along with hundreds of her attendants, and she did much to spread the Dhamma in Vatsa. For political reasons King Udena took Princess Vasuladatta, daughter of King Canda Pajjota of Avanti, as his second wife. He also married a third queen, Magandiya, who in the past had felt insulted by the Buddha when he refused to marry her after her father had begged him to. She used her position as queen to try to get revenge." says Punna.

Bhaddiya speaks, "Queen Samavati was actually very instrumental in introducing the king to the teachings of the Buddha, correct?"

"Yes, this is true. Even though the king wasn't interested in religion, Samavati gradually brought him under the influence of the Buddha and his teaching. He wound up supporting the spread of the *Sasana* in his kingdom in many ways – including the building of monasteries," replies Punna.

"Queen Magandiya didn't approve of this, did she?" asks Sopaka, knowingly.

"Not at all. In fact, through various schemes she tried her best to poison the mind of the king against Samavati," answers Punna. "At one point the king actually took up his bow and arrow and was about to kill Queen Samavati and all of her attendants because of Queen Magandiya's lies. The women projected the potent energy of loving-kindness towards him and he calmed down. The king later realized Samavati's innocence, and he begged her for forgiveness.

"This didn't stop Magandiya, however. One day she set Samavati's palace on fire, burning her and all her ladies to death. King Udena was overwhelmed with grief because he truly loved Samavati. When he learned that Magandiya was responsible for the murders he had her executed,"[3] concludes Punna.

Ananda says, "One of my favorite stories is about King Udena and his elephant, Bhaddavati."

"Oh, yes, the king's prized elephant," begins Punna. "The king rode on Bhaddavati when he eloped with Queen Vasuladatta, and afterwards he always said that he owed his life, queen, and kingdom to this great beast that could travel tirelessly fifteen leagues a day. He treated the elephant with great respect, having her stall perfumed with costly fragrances and decorated with colorful fabrics. The king personally fed her royal food, honoring her as a favored member of his court.

"When the elephant grew old, however, the king forgot about her and she was neglected. He stopped seeing her and she nearly starved to death, pining away for the king. One day while visiting Vatsa, the Buddha entered Kosambi to collect his alms food. The elephant saw the Buddha from a distance and walked slowly toward him. She fell at his feet and he could tell by her sorry state that she had been abandoned by the king.

"In his great compassion for all beings the Buddha sent word to the king that he shouldn't mistreat Bhaddavati this way, reminding him that he had at one time loved the elephant as a member of his own family. The king felt remorse for his neglect and restored Bhaddavati to her previous high status,"[4] concludes Punna.

The arahants smile, reflecting on their memory of the great beast that had long since passed away.

"King Pasenadi of Kosala was a great devotee of the Buddha," says Anuruddha. "He visited the Lord frequently, and their talks were many and varied, as well as quite intimate and frank. I'll never forget the time the Buddha suggested that he shouldn't eat so much."

"If you'll allow me, I'll relate one of the stories from the *Kosalasamyutta*,[5] which records several dialogues and references to this king." The arahants nod their approval and Ananda begins:

> "'On one occasion in Savatthi King Pasenadi had eaten a bucket measure of rice and curries. Then, while huffing and puffing the king approached the Blessed One, paid homage to him, and sat down to one side.
>
> "'Then the Blessed One, having understood that King Pasenadi was full and was huffing and puffing, recited this verse:

"'When a man is always mindful,
Knowing moderation in the food he eats,
His ailments then diminish;
He ages slowly, guarding his life.'

"'The Brahmin youth Sudassana was standing behind the king who then addressed him, saying, 'Come now, dear Sudassana, learn this verse from the Blessed One and recite it to me whenever I am taking my meal and every day I will give you a hundred gold coins as a perpetual grant.'

"'Yes, sire,' the Brahmin replied eagerly, both startled and pleased by this windfall. Having learned this verse from the Blessed One he recited it whenever King Pasenadi was taking his meal.

"'The king gradually reduced his intake of food to at most a pint-pot measure of boiled rice and curries. At a later time, when his body had become quite slim, the king stroked his limbs with his hand and said, 'The Blessed One showed compassion towards me in regard to both kinds of good – the good pertaining to the present life, and that pertaining to the future life.'"

The arahants beam in appreciation of the Buddha's wise words for good health as well as for spiritual growth.

Ananda continues, "While we're speaking of King Pasenadi, I would like to mention the time he and King Ajatasattu engaged in battle, and King Pasenadi was defeated:

"The *bhikkhus* approached the Lord and informed him of what had happened. The Buddha said:

"'*Bhikkhus*, King Ajatasattu of Magadha has evil friends, evil companions, and evil comrades. King Pasenadi of Kosala has good friends, good companions, and good comrades. Yet for this day, *bhikkhus*, King Pasenadi, having been defeated, will sleep badly tonight.

"'Victory breeds enmity,
The defeated one sleeps badly.

> The peaceful one sleeps at ease,
> Having abandoned victory and defeat.'⁶

"In a second battle," continues Ananda, "King Pasenadi defeated King Ajatasattu and captured him alive. Then it occurred to King Pasenadi:

> "'Although this King Ajatasattu of Magadha has transgressed against me while I have not transgressed against him, still, he is my nephew. Let me now confiscate all his elephant troops, all his cavalry, all his chariot troops, and all his infantry, and let him go with nothing but his life.'

"The following morning a number of *bhikkhus* returned from their alms round and reported all of this to the Blessed One.

"Then the Blessed One recited these verses:

> "'A man will go on plundering
> So long as it serves his ends,
> But when others plunder him,
> The plunderer is plundered.
>
> "'The fool thinks fortune is on his side
> So long as his evil does not ripen,
> But when the evil ripens
> The fool incurs suffering.
>
> "'The killer begets a killer,
> One who conquers, a conqueror.
> The abuser begets abuse,
> The reviler, one who reviles.
> Thus by the unfolding of *kamma*
> The plunderer is plundered.'"⁷

"It always amazed me," begins Maha Kaccayana, "how the Buddha's wisdom applied to literally every facet of life – including political strife and war."

"How true that is, Venerable Sir," says Ananda. "And while I still have my mind on King Pasenadi, I will tell one more story, if you don't mind." The arahants on the sub-committee voice no objection, so he begins:

> "Once in Savatthi a great sacrifice had been set up for King Pasenadi of Kosala. Five hundred bulls, five hundred bullocks, five hundred heifers, five hundred goats, and five hundred rams had been led to the pillar for the sacrifice. And his slaves, servants, and workers, spurred on by punishment and fear, were busy making the preparations, wailing with tearful faces."

"Excuse me for interrupting, Venerable Sir," says Bakkula. "How could such a strong follower of the Buddha engage in such cruel animal sacrifices?"

"King Pasenadi, being a product of his time, had one foot on each side of the fence, so to speak, and still viewed those Brahmin beliefs he grew up with as valid," answers Maha Kassapa. "He thoroughly believed in the Triple Gem, but being a ruler, he also had to think of the prevailing culture. He understood that his beliefs could not be imposed on all his people."

Bakkula seems satisfied with this explanation so Maha Kassapa says, "Ananda, please continue."

> "In the morning a number of *bhikkhus* just returning from their alms round approached the Buddha and reported what they had seen in regards to the preparation for the king's great sacrifice. The Buddha recited the following verses:
>
>> "'The horse sacrifice, human sacrifice,
>> These great sacrifices, fraught with violence,
>> Do not bring great fruit.
>
>> "'The great seers of right conduct
>> Do not attend the sacrifice
>> Where goats, sheep, and cattle
>> Of various kinds are slain.
>
>> "'But when sacrifices free from violence
>> Are always offered by family custom,
>> Where no goats, sheep, or cattle
>> Of various kinds are slain:
>> The great seers of right conduct
>> Attend a sacrifice like this.

> "'The wise person should offer this,
> A sacrifice bringing great fruit.
> For one who makes such sacrifice
> It is indeed better, never worse.
> Such a sacrifice is truly vast
> And the *devatas* too are pleased.'"[8]

"Thank you, Ananda," says Maha Kassapa. "We should say, for the record, that after hearing the last discourse, the Buddha's timely advice prevented King Pasenadi from going forward with his wasteful animal sacrifice."

Ananda speaks, "There's just one more story that I would love to recite before we close on King Pasenadi."

"That's the second or third time you've said 'just one more,' Venerable Sir," says the chairman smiling. "Are you sure this is the last one?"

"I'm certain," answers Ananda, grinning.

> "Once in Savatthi King Pasenadi had gone with Queen Mallika to the upper terrace of the palace. The king said to the queen: 'Is there, Mallika, anyone more dear to you than yourself?'
>
> "'There is no one, great king, more dear to me than myself. But is there anyone, great king, more dear to you than yourself?'
>
> "'For me too, Mallika, there is no one more dear than myself.'
>
> "Then the king descended from the palace and approached the Blessed One. Having approached, he paid homage to the Blessed One, sat down to one side, and related his conversation with Queen Mallika. Then the Blessed One, having understood the meaning of this, recited this verse:
>
> > "'Having traversed all quarters with the mind,
> > One finds none anywhere dearer than oneself.
> > Likewise, each person holds himself most dear;
> > Hence one who loves himself should not harm others.'"[9]

"Thank you, Ananda, for demonstrating the Lord's ability to give advice to his kingly devotees on many diverse subjects," says Maha Kassapa. "Are there any more stories of kings that any of you would like to recollect?"

Anuruddha speaks up, "The stories are countless, but I don't think we should forget the Mallas and the Bhaggas. I know we'll hear more about the Mallas later, so I'll just mention that the Buddha and his Chief Disciple Maha Moggallana visited the Bhagga kingdom on numerous occasions. King Bodhiraja Kumara became a devout follower of the Lord, and many of his kinsmen also took refuge in the Triple Gem."

"I don't think we could possibly conclude this topic without mentioning the Licchavis," says Maha Kaccayana.

"You are right, Venerable Sir," says the chairman. "Please tell us about them."

"Vesali, the large capital of the powerful Vajjian confederacy, was a prosperous city, and its inhabitants were strong followers of both Brahmanism and Mahavira, the founder of Jainism," begins Maha Kaccayana. "There was a time not too many years ago when a severe famine beset the city and people began to die in droves. Corpses littered the city, and evil demons roamed freely throughout the land. Dead bodies piled up and a vicious plague broke out; not a single family was left unscathed by the horror of these three simultaneous disasters."

"I remember those days," says Punna. "I knew many people in Vesali that died from that triple calamity, which left their families in ruin."

Maha Kaccayana continues, "The people were desperate, and they gathered at the assembly to beg the king to find a solution. Nothing like the present catastrophe had visited the city for seven generations. King Mahali humbly asked them if they thought the fault was his, but they told him they didn't hold him responsible.

"The assembly was desperately seeking a remedy, and someone said, 'A Buddha has been born in the world, and he is preaching his doctrine. He is endowed with supernormal powers, and I'm sure that if he visited us our calamities would vanish.'

"This suggestion was met with unanimous approval, but there was uncertainty as to whether or not the Buddha would actually come to Vesali. Someone said, 'Buddhas are full of compassion and sympathy; he couldn't possibly refuse. We must send our request for help.'

"It was said that the Buddha was staying in Rajagaha, so King Mahali, who was already a devotee of the Buddha, approached King Bimbisara with appropriate gifts and requested that he use his influence to get the Buddha to come to Vesali.

"King Bimbisara told him that he had no control over the Buddha, and that they could invite him to Vesali themselves. So King Mahali went directly to the Buddha and explained the calamities that had befallen his kingdom. He begged him to come and set matters straight," concludes Maha Kaccayana.

Ananda speaks, "The Buddha perceived that if he were to go to Vesali and preach the *Ratana Sutta*,[10] thousands upon thousands of people would be saved from suffering. He agreed to go. As a result, King Bimbisara took it upon himself to see to the Buddha's accommodations on the journey. He had the road decorated with flowers, banners, and plantain trees. The Buddha set out with five hundred *bhikkhus*, and in five days they reached the bank of the river.

"King Bimbisara had a ship waiting to take the Buddha across, and a message was sent to the Licchavi princes on the other side that they should arrange to accompany the Master to Vesali. The Licchavis, therefore, made similar preparations for his reception on their side of the river and were waiting for him.

"King Bimbisara waded into the water up to his neck as the Buddha boarded the ship. He said to the Lord that he would wait on the riverbank until his return. The Licchavi princes waded into the water on the other side, and paid homage to the Lord when he set foot on their lands. At that moment a great rainstorm suddenly started, and the ensuing deluge washed the city of Vesali clean of all its filth and decomposing corpses. King Mahali, his adviser, and a great host of retainers escorted the Buddha into the city.

"The Buddha then said, 'Ananda, as a preventative measure, learn this *Ratana Sutta* from me, and recite it as you go throughout the city accompanied by the Licchavi princes, who will carry offertories in their hands.'"

Maha Kassapa adds, "*The Ratana Sutta* is one of the most powerful *paritta* recitations there is. Nothing can overcome its invincible protection from evil, or its ability to restore well-being. Would you please quote a few of the important stanzas for us, Venerable Sir?"

Ananda nods and begins his recitation:

> ""Whatever beings are here assembled,
> Whether terrestrial or celestial,
> May all these beings be happy
> And listen closely to my words.
>
> "'Pay attention all you beings:
> Show kindness to the humans
> Who day and night bring you offerings.
> Therefore guard them diligently.
>
> "'Whatever treasure is here or beyond
> Or the precious jewel in the heavens,
> None is equal to the Perfect One.
> In the Buddha is this precious jewel.
> By this truth may there be well-being.
>
> "'As a post firmly grounded in the earth
> Cannot be shaken by the four winds,
> So is the superior person, I say,
> Who definitely sees the Noble Truths.
> In the Sangha is this precious jewel.
> By this truth may there be well-being.
>
> "'Like woodland groves in bloom,
> in the first heat of summertime,
> Is the sublime Dhamma he taught,
> Leading to *Nibbana*, the highest good.
> In the Buddha is this precious jewel:
> By this truth may there be well-being.
>
> "'Noble, knower of *Nibbana*, boon-giver,
> Boon-bringer, he taught the great sublime Dhamma.
> In the Buddha is this precious jewel:
> By this truth may there be well-being.
>
> "'The past extinct with no new becoming.

Their minds detached from future existence,
Old seeds destroyed, craving uprooted;
The wise are extinguished like a lamp.
In the Sangha is this precious jewel:
By this truth may there be well-being…'"

Ananda finishes reciting the lines and then says, "I recited this *sutta* the way the Buddha instructed me. While I chanted I sprinkled blessed water, and when I uttered the first line the demons started to flee. I continued until they were completely gone. The Buddha then recited this *sutta* in the assembly hall of the Licchavis, and all of the families in the entire city were rid of plague, pestilence, and famine. Thousands of sentient beings on numerous planes were immediately emancipated, and peace was restored. Happiness and prosperity returned to the kingdom."

"Didn't the Buddha continue to expound this *sutta* for seven days?" asks Upali.

"Yes, and each day more and more sentient beings were emancipated until the Buddha was satisfied that there was no more danger, and that health and happiness were firmly re-established," answers Ananda.

"The Buddha saved the kingdom through the power of the truth of his words," adds Sopaka.

"I'm sure this *sutta* will be used by countless generations for protection and restoration of peace and harmony; it is effective if both reciter and listener are compassionate and full of faith," says Ananda.

"As a result, the King of Licchavi was well-established in the Dhamma, and many monasteries and shrines were built," says Maha Kaccayana. "Some Licchavis joined the Noble Order and attained arahantship, while generals, noblemen and commoners alike took refuge in the Triple Gem."

"Let's not forget that the Buddha once taught the Licchavis the seven conditions that would lead to the well-being of a nation," says Bhaddiya. "Before his *parinibbana* the Lord said that these same seven conditions applied to all types of communities, including the Sangha. If these seven conditions are followed then the community or nation would not decline, but would endure and prosper."

"When King Ajatasattu was just about to wage war on the Licchavis, the Buddha asked me if they were still following those seven conditions, and I replied that they were. The Buddha then said that they would not be defeated – that in fact, defeat was impossible for them," says Ananda. "I will recite those seven conditions now for this record:

> "'The first is to gather together for discussions frequently; keeping the lines of communication open and clear.
>
> "'The second is to meet in harmony and unity, depart in harmony and unity, and work in harmony and unity.
>
> "'The third is to respect and follow all laws, or if a law is found to be incorrect, work to change it in a lawful manner.
>
> "'The fourth is to respect and listen to worthy leaders, both religious and secular.
>
> "'The fifth is to refrain from committing or advocating violent crimes, such as rape, destroying another's property, or killing.
>
> "'The sixth is to respect, protect, and maintain the shrines and religious sites.
>
> "'The seventh, and final, is for the leader to preserve his or her personal mindfulness, so that in the future the good among the people will come to him, and the good who have already gathered will feel at ease with him.'"[11]

Ananda finishes reciting, and then pauses while the arahants reflect on these seven conditions and their supreme value for all varieties of communities and their leaders.

"The Buddha's influence in the world through its kings and princes is unprecedented," says Maha Kassapa. "My most sincere hope is that political, business, and community leaders of the future will heed the Buddha's words and put them into practice. The words are timeless, and applicable for all world systems throughout the universe."

The members of the sub-committee instinctively know that their discussion for the evening is concluded. The stories that could be related are uncountable, but nothing more is needed to further enhance what has already been said in regards to the Buddha's advice to kings.

They rise from their seats and file silently out of the chamber, each one deep in thought, anticipating the bliss of their nightly meditation.

Chapter 24
Truth or Hearsay?

Ananda stands calmly at the podium in the assembly hall. A huge thunderstorm is passing overhead and heavy rain pounds on the roof, making it impossible for him to be heard. He closes his eyes in quiet meditation as he patiently waits for the downpour to pass. The five hundred arahants follow Ananda's example and join him in contemplation. A deep sense of peace permeates the atmosphere while the squall outside rumbles, and lightening streaks across the sky in a violent display of energy.

After the storm passes and the noise fades to a faint rhythm of light raindrops, Ananda begins to speak:

"The Buddha once visited a small town called Kesaputta in the kingdom of Kosala. The inhabitants of this town were known by the common name Kalama. When they heard that the Buddha was in their town, the Kalamas paid him a visit and told him:

"'Sir, there are some recluses and brahmanas who visit Kesaputta. They explain and illumine only their own doctrines, and despise, condemn, and spurn others' doctrines. Then come other recluses and brahmanas, and they, too, in their turn, explain and illumine only their own doctrines, and despise, condemn and spurn others' doctrines. But for us, Sir, we have always doubt and perplexity as to who among these venerable recluses and brahmanas spoke the truth, and who spoke falsehood.'

"The Buddha replied, 'Of course you are uncertain, Kalamas. Of course you are in doubt. When there are reasons for doubt, uncertainty is born. So in this case, Kalamas, don't go by reports, by legends, by traditions, by scripture, by logical conjecture, by inference, by analogies, by agreement through pondering views, by probability, or by the thought, "This ascetic is our teacher." When you know for yourselves that, 'These qualities are unskillful; these qualities are blameworthy; these qualities are criticized by the wise; these qualities, when adopted and carried out, lead to harm and to suffering' – then you should abandon them...By the same token, when you know for yourselves that, 'These qualities are skillful; these qualities are blameless; these qualities are praised by the wise; these qualities, when adopted and carried out, lead to welfare and to happiness' – then you should enter and remain in them."

"'Kalamas, one who is the disciple of the Noble One, free from lust, free from hate, free from confusion, intelligent and aware, abides with a heart full of selfless love, compassion, joy and equanimity. He abides in the entire boundless cosmos, covering with a heart full of selfless love, compassion, joy and equanimity, broadened and expanded, free from limitations, without enmity, without hatred.'"

Ananda goes on to recite the rest of the powerful *sutta*, putting emphasis on the following stanzas:

"'Now, Kalamas, one who is a disciple of the Noble Ones – his mind thus free from hostility, free from ill will, undefiled, and pure – acquires four assurances in the here-and-now:

"'*If there is a world after death*, if there is the fruit of actions rightly and wrongly done, then this is the basis by which, with the break-up of the body, after death, I will reappear in a good destination, the heavenly world.' This is the first assurance he acquires.

"'*But if there is no world after death*, if there is no fruit of actions rightly and wrongly done, then here in the present life I look after myself with ease – free from hostility, free from ill-will, free from trouble.' This is the second assurance he acquires.

"'If evil is done through acting, still I have willed no evil for anyone. Having done no evil action, from whence will suffering touch me?' This is the third assurance he acquires.

"'But if no evil is done through acting, then I can assume myself pure in both respects.' This is the fourth assurance he acquires.'"[1]

At the end of Ananda's recitation Maha Kassapa stands and says to the council, "We generally don't discuss the content of any of the *suttas* after hearing them, but I sense that there are things that some of you would like to say about the *sutta* to the Kalamas. In my opinion, it is a very important discourse."

The arahants in the assembly hall nod their heads in approval of the chairman's suggestion.

Punna stands and says, "I agree with you, Venerable Chairman. Hearing Venerable Ananda recite the *Kalama Sutta* today reminds me how revolutionary the Buddha was in his thinking. No one ever before had dared to say that one's direct experience of the truth was valid; most claimed that their views, derived from scriptures, hearsay, or teachers were more valid than the individual's direct experience."

"If I may add," says Kumara Kassapa, standing, "the statements in this *sutta* prove that the Buddha had such confidence in his Dhamma that he knew it would stand up to scrutiny of any kind – *including* that of the individual's direct experience. The Dhamma needs no validation from scriptures or teachers; it validates itself in the lives of those who live it!"

Revata stands, "The freedom of thought encouraged by the Buddha is unprecedented, and simply unheard of prior to his appearance. The freedom he teaches is absolutely essential because emancipation or enlightenment depends upon the individual's own realization of Truth – and not upon his belief systems. There are countless things in which to believe, including a creator being, the efficacy of doing good works, or the concept of grace; but none of them leads to *Nibbana*. In other words, whatever one believes in, or no matter how many times one supplicates a man-made anthropomorphic god, it won't make any difference in terms of achieving the ultimate goal of arahantship, or enlightenment."

Sunita raises his voice to say, "Thank you, Venerable Ananda, for putting your emphasis on the 'life after death' issue covered in the *sutta*. By the Buddha's repeated refusal to answer this question and either confirm or deny its existence, he made it very clear that the most important thing is how we live our lives now. An afterlife may or may not exist, and the Buddha didn't totally rule out this possibility; however, the 'here and now' is what really matters, as are the choices we make and the commitments to do that which is wholesome. Things will still be 'as they are,' and one needs to cultivate the ability to see things clearly in order to be free from suffering. This was a completely revolutionary idea, and it will have repercussions for millennia, I am sure."

Culapantaka, a gifted arahant who at one time couldn't even memorize a four-line stanza after four months of trying, rises from his seat saying, "The *Kalama Sutta* clearly says a number of things on the subject of truth and scriptures. First of all, the Buddha says in essence, 'Do not take anything as true without thorough investigation.' He also says, 'Use your own judgment; scripture is only an aid, not a substitute for thinking.'

Upavana, who was blessed with having fanned the Buddha before his *parinibbana*, adds, "This *Kalama Sutta* also says that one should stay focused on one's inner experiences and their consequences, rather than on conceptual ideas of truth and falsehood."

"Very well said, Venerable Sir," says Subhuti, who had been a monk since the day his uncle Anathapindika dedicated the Jetavana Monastery to the Buddha. "That goes along with another paraphrased statement, 'Belief in dogmas or dependence on supernatural powers is not necessary in order to be good.' The Buddha made it very clear that beliefs are merely ingrained, reinforced opinions, either of the individual or of the collective group, and that they didn't have anything to do with absolute truth. Beliefs can be the products of one's society, culture, religion, family, or peer groups, but they are still only real in the minds of the believers; they have no intrinsic reality of their own!"

Vangisa, a born poet who had the gift of quick wit and who could extemporaneously compose lyrical verses in praise of the Buddha, says, "It is very interesting to note that we only need to believe a statement if we *don't* know if it is true. If we *know* it is true, belief is unnecessary. We believe only the unknown; we don't have to believe the known."

"Let's not forget the Buddha's parable about the blind men and the elephant," says Kumara Kassapa.

"Why don't you briefly tell us this tale for the record," says Maha Kassapa. "You are the one who is best-known for your parables, and rightly so, I might add."

"Thank you for your kind words, Venerable Chairman. This example, however, is directly from the Buddha, and is not my own," replies Kumara Kassapa.

> "Long ago there was a king in Savatthi who called his chief attendant and said, 'Gather all of the men you can find who were born blind and bring them together in one place. When you have done so I want you to show them an elephant.'
>
> "The attendant did as he was ordered, and he presented one blind man with the elephant's head, another with its ear, another, its tusk, another, its trunk, another, its body, another, its foot, another, its hindquarters, another with the tail, and the last one with the tuft at the end of the tail, saying to each, 'Here is an elephant.'
>
> "When the attendant had shown the blind men the elephant he went to the king and said, 'I have presented the elephant to the blind men, Your Majesty.'
>
> "The king went over to the blind men and the elephant and said, 'So you have all seen the elephant?'
>
> "The blind men answered, 'Yes, Your Majesty, we have seen the elephant.'

"The king said, 'So tell me what an elephant is like.'

"The first man who had been presented the head said, 'An elephant is like a large water jar.'

"The man who had been shown the ear said, 'An elephant is just like a wide, shallow wicker basket.'

"The one who had been presented the tusk said, 'An elephant is exactly like a plowshare.'

"The blind man who was shown the trunk replied, 'An elephant is just like a plow pole.'

"The one who had been shown the body said, 'An elephant is like a big store room.'

"The man who had been shown the foot said, 'An elephant, Your Majesty, is just like a post.'

"The blind man who was shown the hindquarters replied, 'An elephant is just like a mortar.'

"The blind man who had been shown the tail replied, 'An elephant, Your Majesty, is just like a pestle.'

"The man who had been shown the tuft at the end of the tail replied, 'An elephant is just like a broom.'

"When the nine men were finished telling the king about the elephant they started arguing, then shouting and screaming at one another – each one had his own opinion about what an elephant was like. The bickering turned to fighting and before too long they started to brawl. The king looked on in amusement, laughing.[2]

"The Buddha said, 'So you see, *bhikkhus*, those wanderers of various sects are like the blind, unseeing when they say, 'Dhamma is like this!' or 'Dhamma is like that!' Then he said:

"'Some recluses and Brahmins, so called,
Are deeply attached to their own views:

> People who only see one side of things
> Engage in quarrels and disputes.'"³

"I think the Buddha illustrated the subject of opinions and beliefs very beautifully in this parable," concludes Maha Kassapa. The arahants in the assembly hall shake their heads at the foolishness of the blind men in the story; many of them remember hearing it from the Buddha's mouth when he first told it.

Revata laughs and says, "Don't forget that if we want to maintain a *belief*, we have to call it a truth. On the other hand, if we want to maintain a *truth*, we don't have to call it a belief."

"The Buddha said that rather than have a belief about something, one should test it based on its goodness – or lack thereof," says Kumara Kassapa. "In deciding what is good, the Buddha advises one to think of the consequences, whether it is in regards to a thing, an action, a word, a thought, an idea, or even a person. If it is harmful to oneself or to others, it is *not* good. If it is beneficial to oneself or to others, it *is* good. With this test it is possible to be, do, think, or have good – without beliefs or dogmas."

Culapantaka says, "The Buddha said that dogmatic beliefs actually have the opposite effect – they make people do harmful things. The importance placed on dogmas and their claims of truth causes people to put them above their principles; they become emotionally attached, which inevitably leads to conflict and oftentimes to war."

"Good acts result from a good state of mind," says Revata, the disciple the Buddha called 'Foremost in Meditation.' "The Buddha said that a good state of mind comes from meditation, which inevitably leads to a good life. One who practices meditation doesn't have to worry about the next world or depend on external powers of any kind. In this *Kalama Sutta*, particularly, the Buddha stressed the importance of meditating on the Four Sublime States, which are: *metta*, loving-kindness; *karuna*, compassion; *mudita*, appreciative joy; and *upekkha*, equanimity.

"The bottom line is," continues Revata, "the Buddha said that we need to examine our thoughts very carefully, preferably in meditation, to determine their goodness. Then we can decide if the subject is worthy or unworthy, and whether to abandon it – or to act on it. I'm sure we all remember the *Vimansaka Sutta*."⁴

Ananda says, "Allow me to quote the line you are referring to, Venerable Sir:

> "'*Bhikkhus*, a disciple should examine even the Blessed One himself, so that he might be fully convinced of the true value of the teacher before he is followed, and whether or not he is fully enlightened.'"

Revata, sometimes known for his inquiring nature, adds, "You may also recall the 'Four Great References' the Lord gave us when we went to Bhoga, just before he passed away. These guidelines set the standards whenever questions regarding the Dhamma arose."

"Thank you for reminding us, Revata. Please quote that passage from the *Maha Parinibbana Sutta* for us, Venerable Ananda," says the chairman. "It suits the topic of discussion."

Ananda nods and begins reciting:

> "'Now, *Bhikkhus*, I shall make known to you the Four Great References. Listen and pay heed to my words.
>
> "'In this fashion a *bhikkhu* might speak: 'Face to face with the Blessed One, brethren, I have heard and learned thus: This is the Dhamma and the Discipline, the Master's Teaching.' He might also say: 'In an abode of such and such lives a community with elders and a chief' – or – 'In an abode of such and such lives a single *bhikkhu*, or several *bhikkhus*, who are elders, learned, having accomplished their course, and are preservers of the Dhamma, the Discipline and the Summaries. Face to face with those elders, or that single elder, I have heard and learned thus: This is the Dhamma and the Discipline, the Master's Teaching.'
>
> "'In such a case, *bhikkhus*, the declaration of such a *bhikkhu* is neither to be received with approval nor with scorn. Without approval and without scorn, but carefully studying the sentences word by word, one should trace them in the discourses and verify them by the Discipline. If they are

neither traceable in the discourses nor verifiable by the Discipline, one must conclude that these were not the Blessed One's utterances, or the teaching has been misunderstood by that *bhikkhu*, or by that community, or by those elders, or by that single elder. In that way, *bhikkhus*, you should reject it.'

'"On the other hand, if the sentences concerned are traceable in the discourses and verifiable by the Discipline, then one must conclude that this is indeed the Blessed One's utterance, or that the teaching has been well understood by that *bhikkhu*, or by that community, or by those elders, or by that single elder. And in that way, *bhikkhus*, you must accept it on the first, second, third, or fourth references. These, *bhikkhus*, are the Four Great References for you to preserve.'"

Maha Kassapa says, "I thank you, Venerable Ananda. This passage reminds us of the supreme importance the Buddha placed on the process of investigation. Investigation of one's mind, one's emotions, one's beliefs, or the inherent merit or goodness involved, requires an examination of the source of the information, the teacher transmitting the information, and finally an examination using the Dhamma itself as the ultimate comparative reference."

Kumara Kassapa adds, "The Buddha truly understood the damage that could be wrought by a so-called self-professed – or even a certified – teacher; one who was either a charlatan, an egotist, or somehow misguided in his views – innocent or otherwise. The purity of the Dhamma itself could be put in jeopardy causing it to become ineffective, and the course of its transmission derailed."

"Yes indeed, Venerable Sir," says Subhuti, whom the Buddha had declared 'Foremost among Those Who Were of Undefiled Conduct.' "There have been many examples of talented students thrown off the track by their teachers, well-intentioned or not."

"The first one that comes to my mind is Angulimala," says Sunita. "He was certainly derailed by his teacher, but the Lord's compassion enabled him to transform himself into an enlightened being."

"The Angulimala story has many lessons," begins Maha Kassapa. "I realize that we are taking time in the general assembly for these recollections, but I think they are valuable. Perhaps you would like to tell us this tale, Venerable Sunita, since you are the one who mentioned it."

Sunita smiles and the chairman knows he has selected the right person to talk about Angulimala. He also knows that Venerable Sunita had probably been the only close friend the legendary monk had had until his death a few years ago. Their relationship was an odd one, given their diverse backgrounds, but their bond was the fact that they both had been the object of the Buddha's extreme compassion.

"Angulimala," begins Sunita, "was the son of Bhagga, the Brahmin who was Chief Minister of King Pasenadi of Kosala. His mother's name was Mantani. Angulimala wasn't his real name, of course, but one that was given to him later during his violent crime spree. Ironically, his birth name was 'Ahimsaka,' which means 'harmless one.' He was an exceptionally good-looking young man, highly intelligent, and was always at the top of his class in every subject. His parents decided to send him to Taxila, the capital of Gandhara, whose university was and still is the best in the world.

"True to form, Ahimsaka excelled at everything he attempted: mathematics, science, languages, the fine arts, philosophy, competitive sports, and the social arts. At first the gifted young man made many friends, and was immensely popular and highly-admired by his fellow students. However, after the first year his popularity began to wane as his achievements and successes continued to grow. It seemed that no one could surpass him in any area, and that caused a great deal of jealousy among his peers.

"As was the system at Taxila's university, he had one particular teacher who acted as his primary mentor and advisor. This seemingly-wise teacher eventually gained Ahimsaka's total trust, and the young man allowed the older one to mold his mind and shape his thinking. The fact is he had a great deal of influence over his impressionable student from Kosala. A genuine father-son-like bond developed between the student and learned professor, and Ahimsaka was often in the teacher's home. In fact, the teacher encouraged Ahimsaka to think of his home as the young man's home away from home, and he spent most of his free time there.

"Teachers usually married later in life, and Ahimsaka's, who married at forty-five, was no exception. His marriage to a girl of sixteen had only taken place the year before, and the bride was exactly three years older than Ahimsaka," says Sunita.

Upali interjects, "This sounds like a perfect set-up for an unhappy turn of events."

"You are indeed correct, Venerable Sir," says Sunita. "The teacher's wife treated Ahimsaka like a younger brother. The jealous classmates saw the close relationship between the teacher, his wife, and their adversary as an opportunity to destroy him. They started rumors that Ahimsaka was having an affair with the young bride. It didn't take long before these reached the ears of the teacher, who at first didn't believe them, knowing and trusting the young man as he did. But the jealous boys didn't stop with their accusations; they gossiped relentlessly, and even went to the teacher as a group and told him their lies. Still the teacher refused to believe them.

"After about six weeks the teacher began to doubt Ahimsaka; the students' lies began to gradually take effect, poisoning his mind. After all, he was an older man married to a beautiful young woman, and Ahimsaka, in his prime at twenty years old, was very handsome. He could easily imagine the physical attraction that the two could have felt for one another, and his imagination eventually convinced his mind that they were indeed sleeping together. He confronted his young wife, who denied the affair, but by now he was insanely jealous and refused to believe her.

"The teacher decided to take revenge on innocent Ahimsaka. At first he thought he would kill him, or have him killed, but then he didn't think that would reflect very well upon him and his situation as the boy's mentor.

"Finally, he called the young man into his study and said, 'I know you are sleeping with my wife. I can never forgive you for this act of betrayal. You were like part of our family.'

"Ahimsaka, wounded in the heart to be so wrongly accused, said in reply to his teacher's accusations, 'I assure you, Sir, that I have done nothing wrong. I would never do anything to hurt you – or your wife.'

"The teacher didn't believe Ahimsaka; his mind was so poisoned against him that he took the false evidence as true. He told Ahimsaka that the only way to be forgiven was for him to kill one thousand people, saying, 'I will accept those thumbs from their right hand as payment for your sin against me.'"

Kumara Kassapa says, "This teacher obviously didn't investigate the matter very seriously or he would have discovered his student's innocence. This is a perfect example of what I meant earlier when I mentioned the damage a teacher could cause to a student's life."

"Ahimsaka was shocked," continues Sunita. "He knew that he could never do such an evil thing, and he told his teacher as much. Without another word the teacher threw him out of his house, and news of his eviction caused the university authorities to expel him from school. The poor young man was devastated and went home to Kosala to his parents. His father believed the teacher's account, and was furious with his son. Without even listening to the young man, he banished him from the family home. His mother, Mantani, believed Ahimsaka but was helpless to go against her husband's decision; she could do nothing to help her unfortunate son. The situation broke her heart because she loved Ahimsaka dearly.

"The young man then went to the home of his bride-to-be. He had hoped that they would be understanding and take him in. On the contrary, when they heard he was expelled from university they canceled the proposed marriage and forbade Ahimsaka from ever coming to their house again. This was the last straw for the poor boy, and the humiliation, anger, fear, and depression caused his mind to snap.

"The only thing he could think of was his teacher's order to collect one thousand human thumbs so he could buy his forgiveness," says Sunita.

"The poor boy," exclaims Revata. "If only he could have found a good teacher who would have taught him the Dhamma and meditation, he might have been saved at that point."

"Unfortunately he didn't have such a teacher," continues Sunita. "Ahimsaka began his killing spree with a vengeance. He put his whole heart into the act of killing in order to fulfill his teacher's order as quickly as possible. His victims were of every age, caste, and race. After he killed them, he cut off their right thumb with knives and strung them into a garland he wore around his neck. With the passage of time the garland got longer and longer, and eventually he was called 'Angulimala,' which means 'finger garland.' The people feared him greatly, and they barricaded themselves in their homes at night. They were afraid to go into the forest where they knew he lived, and the general situation in Kosala was one of panic and terror.

"The king was under a great deal of pressure to capture this deranged criminal, but all of his attempts thus far had been unsuccessful. The local security forces had not been able to apprehend the killer, so the king organized five hundred royal soldiers to go into the forest to hunt him down and kill him. When Angulimala's mother Mantani heard about the king's plan she decided she had to do whatever she could to save her poor, mentally ill son, so she went into the forest in search of him.

"Right about this time, when the Buddha was surveying the world, he saw Angulimala, who now had nine hundred ninety-nine thumbs on his garland. The Buddha also saw Mantani approaching her son in the forest, and knew that she would very likely be his one-thousandth victim. The Lord knew that killing his mother would bring Angulimala the most severe *kamma* possible, and that he would suffer more for killing her than he would for all of his other innocent victims.

"The Buddha came down from his retreat in the mountain and entered the forest. He saw Mantani approaching from one side and Angulimala from the other, so he stepped in-between them. Angulimala, momentarily distracted, shifted his attention to the monk, immediately deciding that he would kill him. He raised his knife and ran to attack the Buddha. The Buddha, however, using his supernormal powers, leapt forward and Angulimala couldn't reach him. Angulimala ran towards him a second time and the Buddha once again leapt forward. This continued several more times until an angry, frustrated Angulimala shouted at the Buddha, 'O *Bhikkhu*, Stop! Stop!'

"The Buddha turned around and stood face-to-face with Angulimala. He said, 'I have stopped. It is *you* who have not stopped. So now I tell you to stop!'

"Angulimala was confused and didn't understand. He looked up at the Buddha and said, 'O *bhikkhu*! Why do you tell me that you have stopped while I have not?'

"The Buddha replied, 'I say that I have stopped because I do not kill any living creature. I no longer cause harm to anybody. As for you, you have not restrained yourself from harming living beings. Therefore, I say that I have stopped – and you have not stopped.'

"Slowly Angulimala began to calm down, comprehending what the Buddha had said, and he saw that this brave monk was actually the Enlightened One coming to rescue him. Angulimala dropped his knife and flung off his wretched garland of human thumbs. He prostrated himself at the Buddha's feet and sobbing, begged for ordination. The Buddha said, 'Come!' and Angulimala was immediately ordained. When Mantani reached them she was relieved that her son had been restored to his senses, and she thanked the Buddha profusely. The Master and Angulimala returned to the monastery and he gave him instructions in meditation," says Sunita.

Culapantaka exclaims, "This act of compassion was one of the greatest I have ever heard of."

"There are so many acts of compassion in the Buddha's life that we can't possibly mention them all. You all know my story," says Sopaka. "I was almost devoured by ravenous jackals when the Lord rescued me."

"And I was an untouchable who carried away human night soil when the Buddha came to get me," says Sunita. "Angulimala was just about to kill his mother when the Buddha reached out to him. The Lord didn't let anything prevent him from finding those who could be saved from unfortunate circumstances, and turning them around for good."

"What happened when the king went to look for Angulimala?" asks Upali.

Sunita answers, "King Pasenadi stopped at the monastery to see the Buddha before going into the forest with his army. The Buddha asked him, 'Your Majesty, why do you have such an army? Are you going to battle against King Bimbisara, or the Licchavis, or any other king?'

"The king answered, 'No, Lord, we are on our way to capture the murderer Angulimala who has harmed nearly a thousand families in my country.'

"The Buddha looked at the king, smiled, and said, 'If you were to discover that Angulimala was a monk in my Sangha what would you do?'

"The king, surprised, said, 'I would pay all due respect to him as one of your disciples, Lord.'

"The Buddha pointed to Angulimala, who by then was unrecognizable as the former murderer. His head was shaved, he wore the robes of a monk, and he was seated with his eyes half closed in meditation. He looked so calm and peaceful. The Buddha said, 'There is the man you are hunting.'

"The king was frightened, and for a moment he didn't know what to do. The Buddha said, 'There is no more cause for fear. This man Angulimala is a well-subdued monk in my Order.'

"The king, completely relived by this sudden change in events, composed himself and went to where Angulimala was seated. The king very kindly offered to provide Angulimala with robes and other requisites. Finally, King Pasenadi turned to the Buddha and said, 'I thank you, Lord, for subduing a murderer like Angulimala without force or violence.' He bowed before the Master and then departed," says Sunita.

"How did life go for Angulimala as a monk?" asks Upavana.

"Venerable Angulimala did his best to arduously practice meditation. It was hard for him, though, because he kept seeing visions of his violent past deeds, and hearing the screams of pain and torture that he had caused. And when he was collecting his alms food in the streets many relatives of his victims would throw rocks at him and beat him without mercy. They weren't as forgiving as the king, *or* the Buddha,"[5] responds Sunita.

"What finally happened to him?" asks Subhuti.

"He practiced his meditation diligently and eventually attained arahantship, which is a great lesson for all humankind: even a murderer can change and become enlightened," answers Sunita.

"Did his becoming an arahant make his life any easier?" asks Upavana.

"Internally, of course, I'm sure it did – as it has for all of us. Outwardly, however, Venerable Angulimala's former life continued to follow him around; he simply couldn't shake it loose. His reputation was huge as an evil one, and the people could never bring themselves to forget his past deeds," says Sunita.

Ananda says, "If you would, Venerable Sir, please tell us about his particular contribution to the *Sasana*; the one for which he will always be remembered."

"Certainly. One day when Venerable Angulimala was going about Savatthi collecting alms, he heard a woman crying out in pain," begins Sunita. "He followed the sound to its source and discovered that it was a pregnant lady who was having great difficulty delivering her child. Both the mother and the baby appeared to be in grave danger, and thinking they might not survive, Venerable Angulimala went to the Buddha and informed him of what he had found. The Buddha said, 'Go to the woman and recite these words of truth:

"'Sister, since the day I became an arahant, I have not consciously destroyed the life of any living beings. By this truth, may you be well and may your unborn child be well.'"

"Venerable Angulimala bowed before the Buddha and immediately rushed to the poor woman. With a screen separating him from the expectant mother, he chanted the words as the Buddha had instructed him. Instantly the woman delivered her child with ease, and both of them were strong and healthy. To this day the *paritta* known as the *Angulimala Paritta*,[6] is used in similar situations; usually with remarkable efficacy," says Sunita, smiling. "I'm sure that this potent chant will be used for countless generations for the same purpose."

"Venerable Sunita, please tell us what eventually happened to him," says Upali.

"He wanted nothing more than to live in solitude in the forest. Practicing loving-kindness meditation continually for the rest of his life, he learned how to focus it like a great beam to those in trouble. I am convinced he became an unheralded and unseen healer of humans and all other living beings. I was with him when he died a very peaceful death."

Ananda says, "The Buddha once said this of Angulimala:

> "'Whose evil deed is obscured by good,
> He illumines this world like the
> Moon freed from a cloud.'"[7]

"Many *bhikkhus* had often asked the Lord how it was possible that a man who had killed so many people could attain *Nibbana*," continues Ananda. "The Buddha replied, '*Bhikkhus*, Angulimala did many evil things because he did not have good friends and teachers. Their betrayal caused his mind to become cloudy, and he eventually became very ill. Later, however, he found good friends and teachers in the Sangha, and with their help and good advice he became steadfast in his practice of meditation. His evil deeds were ultimately overwhelmed by good *kamma*, and his mind became completely clean – free from all defilements.'"

"So it is possible to overcome the *kammic* effects of just about any condition or past action and become enlightened," says Sopaka. "The lesson is that we can never underestimate the supreme importance of good friends and good teachers."

"The Buddha once said that it was impossible to become enlightened without good friends – spiritual friends," says Revata. "These friends are people who will always tell you the truth; watch your back; keep you from doing wrong; and in all instances help you achieve your highest good. Without friends like that, one has no chance of avoiding misfortune or growing in the light of the Dhamma."

"The teacher issue speaks for itself, I believe," says Subhuti. "The teacher's job is to keep the student on the right track – towards what is good, wholesome, and conducive to enlightenment. A wayward teacher produces wayward students – as was the case with unfortunate Angulimala."

"With the Four Great References we quoted earlier, the Buddha made certain that the Sangha would always produce great teachers who accurately taught the Dhamma," says Kumara Kassapa. "The Buddha wanted to make sure that anyone who taught his Doctrine, in his name, was being totally true to his word, name, intention, and spirit. May the wisdom of the Buddha live in the minds and lives of great teachers – forever."

Maha Kassapa rises from his seat and strikes the gong. It is time for the *dana*, which that day is being provided by a group of King Bimbisara's former courtiers. The arahants quietly file from the assembly hall and make their way to the pavilion in the nearby glade.

Chapter 25
Dr. Jivaka and the Buddha's Daily Routine

"I will next recite the *Kasibharadvaja Sutta*,"[1] says Ananda from the podium.

Punna leans over and whispers to Upali, "This *sutta* has always been one of my favorites because it shows how naturally the Buddha turns a confrontational situation into one that leads ultimately in enlightenment."

Upali nods in agreement, and the two esteemed arahants turns their attention to the speaker. The other arahants in the assembly hall smile in anticipation of hearing one of the Buddha's most brilliant metaphorical discourses.

"Thus I have heard: 'Once the Buddha was dwelling in a Brahmin village called Ekanala in the country of Magadha.

"'At that time, being the sowing season, five hundred plows owned by the Brahmin Kasibharadvaja were set to work. In the morning the Buddha went to that place where Kasibharadvaja's work was in progress. It was lunchtime and the food was being distributed by the Brahmin. When the Buddha arrived at the place where the food was being distributed he stood aside. The Brahmin, seeing the Buddha waiting for alms, said thus: 'O recluse, I plow and sow, and having plowed and sown, I eat. You also, recluse, should plow and sow; and having plowed and sown, you should eat.'

"'I too, Brahmin, plow and sow; and having plowed and sown, I eat.'

"'We see neither yoke, nor plow, nor plowshare, nor goad, nor oxen of the Venerable Gotama, and yet you say: 'I too, Brahmin, plow and sow; and having plowed and sown, I eat.' Thereupon Kasibharadvaja addressed the Buddha in this stanza:

"'You claim to be a farmer, yet we do not see your plowing. Being questioned by us about your plowing, tell us in such a manner that we may know of it.'

""The Buddha replied, 'Confidence is the seed; self-control the rein; wisdom my yoke and plow; modesty is my pole; mind is the rope; mindfulness my plowshare and goad.

"'Bodily action is well-guarded, speech is well-guarded, moderate in food, I make truth the destroyer of weeds and calm my release.

"'Exertion is my yoked-oxen which carries me towards *Nibbana*. It goes onward without stopping; having gone there one has no regrets.

"'In this way the plowing is done; it bears the fruit of immortality. Having accomplished this plowing, one becomes free from all suffering.'"

Ananda continues to the end of the *sutta,* and one of the arahants in the rear of the hall stands up and raises his hand requesting to speak.

The chairman recognizes the monk and he begins to speak, "I am Kasibharadvaja, the former Brahmin farmer in this *sutta*. Before my enlightenment I had such a great sense of remorse and shame for speaking to the Lord in that fashion; I literally questioned his right to eat. My ego, at the time, was so inflated that it actually took pleasure belittling the Buddha, putting him down for not doing hard, honest, farm work like I did. I felt that I deserved to eat, but he didn't. I really believed this at the time, such was my arrogance."

The arahants stir in their seats, deeply moved by this personal testimony of another enlightened one like themselves who through the compassionate and wise teaching of the Master had been utterly transformed.

Maha Kassapa says, "Perhaps you would share more of this experience with us, Venerable Kasibharadvaja, and we can include your statement as part of our record of the life of the Lord."

The former Brahmin farmer then says, "I think it might be important to document our personal impressions of the Buddha's character and his sublime personality, and include them in your recollections. His *parinibbana* was just a few months ago, and we all can still remember him vividly. It won't be too long, however, before we have our own *parinibbanas* and then no one will be around who knew him personally. All we'll have left are the discourses we are classifying at this council – without any recorded evidence of the curative force of his presence."

Maha Kassapa says, "I quite agree with you. We will all be grateful if you would share your impressions with us for our subcommittee's record."

"I look back on that day in my fields and I still can't believe I had the impudence to speak to the Buddha the way I did," begins Kasibharadvaja. "Not a day went by that I didn't think about it. The Buddha was simply standing there silently, majestically, in the place where my staff was distributing the food. The positive energy that radiated from every pore of his body filled the air with perfume and promise. When I walked over and rudely confronted him he remained calm and looked directly into my eyes with a look of almost overwhelming love and understanding. His wide, dark eyes sparkled, and he smiled at me, revealing for just a moment his perfect white teeth, seen through the curve of his blessed mouth.

"When he said, 'I too, Brahmin, plow and sow,' he made a gesture with his exquisitely shaped hand that I will never forget. I felt his movement as if he was stroking the side of my face, even though he stood at least five feet away from me. I could actually feel his hand on my cheek, and the *pranic* energy coursed its way from the top of my head down to the soles of my feet. At that moment I began to clearly understand as I listened to the discourse he created out of thin air just for me; and now thanks to this council, the entire world will benefit from it in the future."

When he finishes speaking Kasibharadvaja bows his head and closes his eyes, silently communicating the vision of that most sacred moment in his life. Each and every one of the arahants is grateful for the remembrance.

"There wasn't a moment's hesitation from the time I uttered my insulting remark to when he began speaking to me in the kindest, most melodic voice imaginable," says Kasibharadvaja. "The metaphors about plowing came out perfectly timed, from some space in infinity, striking dead center at the heart of my being. I begged the Lord for ordination at the end of his discourse, and went with him to his monastery. I practiced meditation diligently, and it wasn't long before I attained arahantship. My gratitude to the Buddha extends to the end of the universe and beyond."

A deep sigh is heard throughout the assembly hall as the arahants echo that same gratitude in their own hearts.

Ananda gestures to the chairman and says, "Venerable Sir, may I share an incident with the Buddha that was similar to the one just described in this last *sutta*? It also demonstrates beautifully how the Lord used common agrarian terms to express truths from the Dhamma."

"Please proceed, Venerable Ananda," answers Maha Kassapa.

"The Lord and I were walking from one destination to another here in Magadha, and we paused for a moment to enjoy the scenery of the endless paddy fields that stretched all the way to the horizon," begins Ananda. "The Master said to me:

> "'Ananda, do you see how the land is laid out in squares, strips, borders, and cross lines?'
>
> "I answered, 'Yes, Lord.'
>
> "Then he said, 'Try to make robes for the monks like that.'[2]
>
> "I didn't quite understand him, so I said, 'I will do as you say, Lord, but I'm not sure what you mean.'
>
> "The Buddha replied, 'Good monks are like farmers, Ananda, so their robes should be designed like paddy fields, which are made up of irrigated segments. Monks cultivate a field of wholesomeness for themselves, as well as for the community in which they live. A good farmer protects the paddy fields, not allowing cows, pigs, elephants, birds, or wild animals to destroy them. He prevents the destruction of the fields in every way he can. Similarly, monks have to prevent the misuse of their five

senses, which helps them to protect themselves from being destroyed by defilements.

"'As a good farmer removes weeds, rocks, and any materials harmful to his field, likewise a monk removes any defilements, such as anger, hate, ill will, and jealousy, from his mind. When a thought comes to his mind that produces defilement, he removes that thought and his mind becomes pure again, just as a field becomes ready for cultivation once weeds and rocks have been removed.

"'In the same way as a farmer cultivates his field with the best rice seed, and plants in the right season at the right time – first fertilizing the soil and making sure the seeds have the best conditions for growth – so monks must cultivate good deeds as well as loving-kindness, compassion, appreciative joy, and equanimity.

"'So you see, Ananda, the robe has an important meaning that we must keep in mind, and by wearing it, we can use it as a tool to teach those around us.'

"The whole time the Lord was telling me the robe metaphor he was gazing out over the paddy fields, but I knew he was not looking at them," says Ananda. "I think he was seeing into the far reaches of time when his Dhamma had taken root in the minds and hearts of humankind; when his example of wholesome, virtuous living had become the standard for all."

Maha Kassapa approaches the podium saying, "Thank you Venerable Ananda and Venerable Kasibharadvaja for sharing your stories with us; the memory monks will add them into our recollected account of the life of the Lord.

"I am happy to announce that our *dana* today is being hosted by our dear friend Jivaka Komarabhacca, who was the Lord's physician. I know you'll all be glad to see him, as will I."

The senior monks lead the way into the *dana* pavilion, which is very simply decorated that day, in sharp contrast to other occasions. There are just a few small baskets of flowers scattered here and there among the banana leaf plates. Jivaka, looking fit and handsome as usual, is waiting at the entrance, and when Maha Kassapa, Ananda, and the other arahants approach him he prostrates himself at their feet.

"It is good to see you again, dear physician," beams Ananda.

"It is always a good day when I see you, Venerable Ananda," replies the doctor, smiling broadly.

"I'm glad you'll be joining us tonight in the sub-committee meeting. I knew you'd be invited – but knowing the way you travel about the country healing the sick, I really wasn't sure if you'd be available," says Ananda.

"Venerable Maha Kassapa invited me some weeks ago, so I dared not venture too far," says Jivaka. "Please, let me escort you to your seat."

Jivaka leads the way to a place of honor for the Buddha's Chief Attendant, and he waits while the revered arahant seats himself. For decades these two had been somewhat of a team taking care of the Buddha's health and well-being, and the bond between them is very strong.

"Today I'm serving the Buddha's favorite healthy foods, Venerable Sir," says Jivaka. "I've added some special herbs I recently discovered that I believe will give added strength and vitality. Nature is truly wonderful to provide us with such gifts!"

Ananda smiles at his friend, expressing gratitude for the healthy *dana* meal that would provide everyone with the added gift of natural energy.

"By the way," says Jivaka, "you don't have to worry about the water today. I pre-filtered it before it was put into the pots."

Maha Kassapa overhears this remark and says, "Thank you for doing so, Jivaka; that will save us one step in the process of preparing for our meal. I'm always amazed at the Buddha's foresight by insisting that one of the eight requisites for monks be a water filter."

"The Lord was always practical in every matter, including the health of his Sangha members," responds the Buddha's physician, "which is just another example of his original, perfectly-rounded character."

When all five hundred arahants are comfortably seated Maha Kassapa begins the chanting. The pavilion fills with the healing energies of sound that radiate out from the slope of Mount Vebhara into the infinitude of space. All living beings are unknowingly benefitting from the loving-kindness generated by the group of enlightened human transmitters:

> "'...By this may you achieve longevity, good health, a rebirth in the heavens, and the attainment of *Nibbana*...'"

Jivaka sits to the side with his eyes closed in meditation while the monks have their meal. He relives in his mind the almost countless opportunities he has had over the years to use his healing art for the Buddha and members of the Sangha. He inwardly expresses his gratitude for the unique *kamma* that had led him to this exact moment in time, serving *dana* to five hundred arahants exactly half a year after the Lord's *parinibbana*.

Later that evening the nine members of the sub-committee convene under the bright full moon on the promontory overlooking the valley vista below. They are joined by the memory monks and Jivaka.

When everyone is focused and ready to begin the chairman says, "Jivaka, before we discuss the Buddha's daily routine, why don't you tell us a bit about your early background so we can preserve your life story along with that of the Lord's."

The humble physician is almost overwhelmed by the chairman's words as he suddenly realizes what they imply: from that moonlit night forward his life story will be forever intertwined with that of the Buddha's.

Jivaka takes a breath and begins, "My mother was the famous courtesan, Salavati. She became the courtesan of Rajagaha after an important man returned from Vesali one day and remarked that the presence of the courtesan Ambapali had greatly enhanced that capital. He suggested to King Bimbisara that he find a courtesan that could enhance his capital city, and so my mother was appointed. She was a great beauty queen, dancer, and musician, and her company was sought by the wealthiest and most powerful men of Rajagaha who paid one hundred gold coins for one night of her company.

"One of the obvious risks involved in being a courtesan, however, is the possibility that she could wind up pregnant. Baby girls are usually raised by their courtesan mothers, but boys are not – for a variety of cultural, social, and sometimes political reasons. It is said that my father was actually Prince Abhaya, a son of King Bimbisara, but this was never proven, of course. Almost immediately after I was born my mother had her trusted servant take me to the rubbish heap outside of town and leave me to my fate, which was, most likely, to die. This maid returned to my mother and told her that no one had seen her perform the deed.

"A few hours later Prince Abhaya, returning to the city from his palace in the countryside, actually saw me – or at least he saw something moving – on the rubbish heap where crows had gathered. He told his men to go and see what it was.

"The captain called to the prince, 'It's a new-born baby boy, Your Highness.'

"The prince asked, 'Is he still alive?'

"'Yes, my lord, he is,' replied the captain.

"So that's how I got my name; 'Jivaka' in the local dialect translates as 'alive.' Do you see the irony in the prince spotting me on the rubbish heap – when he might actually have been my birth father? Another irony is that, my surname, 'Komarabhacca,' translates as 'son of the prince.'" adds the physician.

"The prince raised you as his son, didn't he?" asks Sopaka.

"Yes, Venerable Sir, he did. He had me taken to the palace and from that day forward he brought me up as his own. When I was sixteen years old, realizing that I had no secure position or legal status in the royal household, I decided that I needed to learn a profession so I could earn a living. With the prince's permission I went off to Taxila where I studied medicine under Professor Disapamokkha.

"I studied hard and did my best to learn everything my teacher could teach me. After seven years I asked him when my medical training would be complete.

"In response to my question he handed me a spade and said to travel one mile outside the city, and then circle around it and dig up any plant that didn't have medicinal value. He said to bring these back to him.

"I did as my teacher said, but unfortunately I came back to him empty-handed. I said, 'Master, I found no plants without medicinal value; each and every one of them can cure some malady or disease.'

"My teacher said, 'Congratulations, Jivaka, you have just graduated!'"

Bakkula says, "You learned your lessons well, Jivaka. Everything is useful, and all things are inter-connected in some mysterious way, including a plant's usefulness for healing human bodies."

Jivaka smiles at the elder monk and says, "Yes, even plants are part of conditioned reality – just as the Buddha taught. I sincerely hope that doctors in the future become familiar with nature to the same extent my teacher in Taxila was, so its secrets can be unlocked for the benefit of all humanity. I also hope that nature is respected so that each and every species of plant and animal can be protected, and other, still unknown, inter-connected conditions of reality can be discovered for the purposes of healing."

"Tell us about your early success as a physician," says Bakkula, smiling.

"My teacher gave me some money to get me started in my career," begins Jivaka, "but on the way to Rajagaha my funds ran out. I really wasn't worried, though, because I knew that there were sick people everywhere that could use my services – and that many of them would be able to pay.

"When I got to Saketa, which isn't far from here, I asked around if there was anyone who needed medical treatment. Someone told me about a woman who had suffered from headaches for seven years. She had been treated by the best physicians in the area, but no one had been able to help her. It took me a while to arrange it, but eventually I was able to see this lady for a consultation. I realized that I could heal the woman, and I made my payment conditional on her full recovery. I treated her with some medicinal ghee I made up, and she got well. Her husband, a millionaire, paid me sixteen thousand gold coins, a chariot, and two servants," says Jivaka.

"That's not bad for a young doctor just out of medical school," comments Upali, smiling.

"I was totally overwhelmed," says Jivaka. "I went home and placed these earnings at the feet of my adopted father, Prince Abhaya. I wanted to show my appreciation to him for raising me. He refused to accept the money, though, suggesting that I use it to build myself a house in the city, which I did.

"My next big break came when I was able to cure Avanti's King Canda Pajjota of a life-threatening illness. He paid me five hundred cartloads of rice, sixteen thousand ticals of silver, two priceless pieces of cloth made in Kasi, and a thousand pieces of other fine cloth. Then I performed a surgical procedure on a millionaire from Varanasi who also rewarded me handsomely. Later I successfully treated my grandfather, King Bimbisara, who wished to reward me with five hundred sets of ornaments, but I refused. I accepted instead the office of royal physician; I also became physician for the Buddha and his Sangha," says Jivaka, smiling.

"Wasn't the Buddha staying near these caves at that time?" asks Maha Kaccayana.

"Yes he was," replies Jivaka, "at the old monastery that used to be on the eastern slope of this mountain. King Bimbisara sent me to see the Buddha who was suffering at the time from constipation. I offered him three handfuls of blue lilies, which had been soaked in medicinal water. Something inspired me to ask the Lord to kiss this potion, which he did, and he was cured almost instantly.

"I dearly loved the Buddha, and wanted to do everything I could to accommodate him. I had robes made for him out of the priceless Kasi cloth, and robes for the monks made out of the thousand pieces of other cloth I had received," says Jivaka, smiling.

"I was there when you presented those gifts to him and his Sangha members," begins Anuruddha. "The Buddha preached a sermon to you and instantly you attained *sotapanna*." Jivaka's face radiates happiness as he remembers the sacred occasion vividly.

"The Buddha appreciated your services more than you will ever know, Jivaka," says Ananda. "I don't even have to tell you how grateful I was for your coming to see him almost every day."

"The honor was all mine, Venerable Sir," replies Jivaka. "But, as you know, going to see him on a daily basis at the monastery here on the mountain was time consuming, so I decided to use the money I had earned to build a monastery for him in my mango grove. I wanted the Buddha to be closer to town so I could see him more often."

"That's when you started coming to see him almost three times a day," says Ananda.

"How could I resist going to see the Buddha as often as I could?" asks Jivaka, beaming with joy. "Who in their right mind wouldn't make the best use of their opportunity to be in the presence of a Fully Enlightened Universal Buddha?" Jivaka's voice expressed the devotion he felt for the Buddha, and the tears in his eyes betrayed the fact that he missed him terribly. "Every moment with him was blessed; each time he looked at me with those deep, fathomless eyes was a gift greater than gold."

Maha Kassapa speaks, "Perhaps this would be a good time to recollect the way the Buddha actually spent his time on a daily basis. You and Venerable Ananda were with him every day when he was here in Rajagaha – and, of course, Venerable Ananda was with him every day whether he was here or elsewhere."

"The Buddha was the most disciplined person I have ever known" responds Jivaka, "and his day was very carefully apportioned for the highest and best use possible. Venerable Ananda made sure that the Buddha's schedule was kept according to plan; it would have been impossible without him."

"Since we have just heard how Jivaka came to be the Buddha's physician, maybe Venerable Ananda should tell us how he came to be his personal attendant," suggests Punna.

Maha Kassapa reflects for a moment and then says, "Yes, I think this might be a good place in our recollection for that detail." The chairman looks at Ananda and nods his head for him to proceed.

Ananda begins, "The Buddha had no permanently assigned personal attendant for the first twenty years of his ministry. When he was fifty-five years old the Buddha decided to have one.

"Venerable Sariputta volunteered immediately, but the Buddha declined his offer saying his preaching was far more valuable. Venerable Maha Moggallana also volunteered, and the Buddha refused his services for the same reason. Many of the monks proposed my name, but I waited to be asked by the Buddha himself."

"What did the Buddha do at this point?" asks Sopaka.

"He said, 'It is not necessary for Ananda to be induced by others. He will serve me on his own accord.' I stepped forward agreeing to be the Buddha's attendant, subject to eight conditions," says Ananda.

"For the record," says Maha Kassapa, "what were the eight conditions?"

"The first was that the Buddha should never give me any of the fine robes he received. By the same token, the second was that he should never give me any of the special foods he received. The third was that I not be asked to stay with him in the Fragrant Chamber. The fourth was that he would never ask me to go with him to *dana* ceremonies when he was invited. The fifth condition was that the Buddha should attend *dana* invitations that I accepted on his behalf. The sixth was that the Buddha should see visitors who had traveled a long way to see him. The seventh condition was personal – that I should be allowed to consult the Buddha whenever I had doubts or needed clarification. The last was that he should repeat to me any discourses he gave when I wasn't present."

"And the Buddha accepted these eight conditions?" asks Upali.

"Yes, and from that moment until he passed away just a few months ago I looked after the Lord's personal needs," responds Ananda.

"A more loyal and devoted attendant could never have been found, I assure you," comments Jivaka.

"I understand that Channa, the Buddha's former charioteer, was quite unhappy about your becoming Chief Attendant," says Upali.

"I'm told that he did voice his opinion, claiming that I took his old job," responds Ananda, chuckling.

"As we all know, ever since his ordination when the Buddha first returned to Kapilavatthu, Channa had a problem with overcoming pride and arrogance. He became domineering with the other monks, and he was always demanding preferential treatment because of his former relationship with the Buddha," adds Anuruddha. "Sharing the Buddha's birthday gave him a feeling of being special, which led to a strong sense of entitlement for a place of high rank in the Sangha."

"He often tried to take credit for guiding the Buddha when he experienced the Four Foresigns; and he exaggerated the role he played the night of renunciation when he rode off with Prince Siddhartha on Kanthaka," says Bhaddiya.

"Channa really didn't fit in with the Sangha right from the beginning, or fulfill his duties as a *bhikkhu*," comments Upali, "at least not until a few months ago."

"You're getting a bit ahead of the story, Upali. Let's save word on Channa for later," suggests Maha Kassapa. "Why don't you continue, Jivaka."

"As we said earlier I visited the Buddha three times each day," begins Jivaka, "and I saw with my own eyes how Venerable Ananda scrupulously performed his duties. He brought the Buddha water to wash; he massaged his tired body; and he kept a torch ready in case the Buddha summoned him at night. Before retiring every evening he would circle the Fragrant Chamber nine times – paying obeisance to the Master. He even insisted on sweeping and cleaning the Buddha's private apartment himself; he wouldn't permit anyone else to do this."

"Venerable Ananda was a natural choice to be the Buddha's attendant because they were so close from birth," says Bhaddiya. "Of course, all of us were close in those early days and we knew each other well. It could be said that Ananda served Prince Siddhartha as his personal attendant even when we were children growing up. They had such a close relationship from day one, just as Anuruddha and I have, and it was impossible to imagine seeing one without the other. He was as close as a shadow even then. Many times we were envious of the way the two boys spent so much time together; the love they had for each other was plain for all to see."

Maha Kassapa says, "Now we know how the two main players in the Buddha's daily routine came into the picture. Who will describe his schedule?"

"Having lived that schedule for twenty-five years, I will be happy to begin the description," says Ananda. "Please, Jivaka, don't hesitate to join in and offer details and anything I may overlook." The Buddha's physician smiles warmly at his old friend.

"Basically," begins Ananda, "the Buddha's day was divided into five parts: the forenoon session, the afternoon session, the first watch, the middle watch, and the last watch of the night. Every minute of the day was spent with a purpose, and time was never wasted on fruitless activities.

"His day started at approximately 6:00 a.m. After washing his face and attending to his bodily needs he surveyed the world with his divine eye to see who he could help. If anyone needed him, or if he saw any person ripe for spiritual advancement, the Buddha would immediately go to provide whatever service was necessary. He would reach out to the impure and the wicked, while the virtuous and pure would seek him out. He would visit the sick no matter how far away they were; either going on foot – or by using his supernormal powers," says Ananda.

"Very often he would visit sick monks," says Jivaka.

"That is correct," says Ananda. "I remember on one occasion when I was traveling with him, we visited a secluded monastery. This incident is recorded in the *Mahavagga Vinaya Pitaka*. In the monks' dormitory we came upon a monk who was sick with dysentery, and he was lying in his own excrement. The Lord saw him and asked,

"'Have you anyone to attend to you?'

"The monk said, 'I have not, Lord.'

"The Buddha asked, 'Why don't the other monks take care of you?'

"'I didn't attend to them, so they don't attend to me,' said the monk.

"Then the Buddha said to me, 'Ananda, go and bring water. We will bathe this monk.'

"I brought the water, and the Lord poured it upon the monk. Afterwards we washed his body completely. The Lord took the sick monk by the head and I took his feet, and together we raised him up and laid him on a couch.

"Then the Lord convened the Order of monks and he spoke to them: 'Monks, is there anyone here who is ill?'

"'There is, Lord,' said one of the monks.

"'What, monks, is his disease?' asked the Buddha.

"'Lord, the venerable one has dysentery,' replied the monk.

"'But monks, is there anyone who is tending to the needs of that monk?'

"'There is not, Lord.'

"'Why don't the monks tend him?' questioned the Buddha.

"'Lord, the monk that is ill didn't attend the other monks when they were in need, therefore, the monks do not tend to him.'

"The Buddha then said, 'Monks, you do not have a mother, and you do not have a father who might tend to you. So if you, monks, don't tend to one another, then who is there who will tend to you? Remember this: those monks that take care of the sick are actually taking care of me.'[3]

"When the Buddha said these words the monks who were convened gasped, realizing that the Buddha had known all along about the sick one in their midst. The Buddha had made it very clear that we were all connected by the very fact of our existence, and that doing for one was the same as doing for all – including even an Exalted Buddha," concludes Ananda.

"I may have tended to the physical needs of the Buddha for many years, and healed him when it was necessary," says Jivaka, "but it was nothing compared to the countless times the Buddha himself went forth to heal others. This is why he has been called '*Besajja Guru*,' which means 'Healing Teacher' or the 'Medicine Buddha.'"

"After the Buddha returned from his morning missions, what did he do then?" asks Upali.

"If there was no *dana* ceremony scheduled, then he would get ready to go out for alms collection," replies Ananda. "Sometimes he would go alone, and other times he would go with a group of monks."

"Can you imagine?" exclaims Jivaka. "Great kings throughout all of India prostrated themselves at the Buddha's feet. These same feet walked barefoot from house to house, and he would stand silently without uttering a word, waiting for householders to put food into his bowl. His humility will be a source of inspiration for all of us forever."

"When sufficient food had been placed into his bowl," continues Ananda, "he would return to the monastery. Even in his eightieth year when he was old and his health was failing, he continued to go on alms rounds in Vesali."

"He would finish his meal before mid-day," says Jivaka, "then give a short discourse to anyone who had come to the monastery to see him. He would tailor his talk to suit the people's ability to understand, and each person would feel that he was speaking directly to them – addressing their personal concerns. It was amazing to watch the faces of the individuals who flocked to the Buddha for guidance and refuge."

Ananda says, "He would establish people in the Three Refuges and the Five Precepts, and if any were ready, they were taught the Four Noble Truths. Afterwards he explained the deeper levels of the Dhamma, and then the path to liberation. Sometimes there were men or women who would ask for ordination into the Sangha, and the Buddha would comply if it was appropriate. Later, the Lord would return to the Fragrant Chamber, wash his feet, and take the seat prepared for him."

"Did this conclude the forenoon session?" asks Sopaka.

"Yes," replies Ananda, "but the afternoon session began almost immediately when the *bhikkhus* and *bhikkhunis* assembled to listen to the Buddha's daily Dhamma sermon. Many of the monks and nuns who approached him received suitable objects of meditation, and others just wanted to pay their respects, or simply bask in his powerful energy-field. The Buddha would usually admonish the Sangha members with the following stanza:

> "'Rare it is to be born as a human being.
> Difficult is the life of mortals.
> Rare is the opportunity to hear the Dhamma,
> Rare indeed is the arising of a Buddha.'"[4]

"Afterwards the *bhikkhus* went to suitable places and spent the afternoon on their individual spiritual practices," says Ananda.

"After his discourse to the Sangha," says Jivaka, "the Buddha would return to his Fragrant Chamber to rest. This was usually one of the times I would attend to him. Later he would lay on his right side like a lion and sleep for a while with mindfulness."

"When the Lord concluded his rest period," continues Ananda, "he would rise to the state of *Maha Karuna Samapatti*, or Ecstasy of Great Compassion, and survey the world with his divine eye. He would look for sincere spiritual aspirants. He might pay them a visit using his psychic powers, and offer inspiration and individual spiritual advice."

"Towards evening lay followers would come to the monastery to hear the Buddha's Dhamma sermon, which usually lasted about an hour," says Jivaka. "I would usually try to be there for the sermon so I could attend to him immediately afterwards."

"May I interject a comment here?" asks Maha Kaccayana. "I loved to watch the Buddha win hearts, but he did it by appealing to the intellect and not to the emotions, which was quite different from the approaches of other popular religious leaders. He would often teach in parables using appropriate illustrations, and to the average person he would usually speak about such things as individual discipline, generosity, and loving-kindness. To the more advanced listeners he would teach such subjects as impermanence and the value of renunciation. To the highly advanced he would expound the Four Noble Truths and dependent origination. Everyone from every social stratum benefited from the Buddha's universal message of freedom from suffering, and the possibility of obtaining personal peace."

"The first watch of the night extended from about 6:00 p.m. until 10:00 p.m.," says Ananda. "If the Buddha wished to bathe he would do so at the beginning of this period. Otherwise, these four hours were reserved exclusively for instruction to *bhikkhus*. They would come to him with problems or difficulties, to get their doubts cleared, to ask for suitable objects of meditation, or to obtain answers to questions they had on fine, intricate points of the deeper levels of Dhamma."

"It was fascinating to observe the Buddha give personalized instruction, or offer a specialized technique for the advancement of a particular *bhikkhu*," says Maha Kassapa. "He did this often, as we will continue to see in many of our stories."

"I would usually attend to the Buddha at the end of the first watch," says Jivaka. "Afterwards I would stay nearby to practice meditation for a while before I went home. I knew that during the middle watch the Buddha preached exclusively to *devas* and other celestial beings that approached him with questions about the Dhamma. I enjoyed the radiant, multi-colored lights that would illuminate the monastery when those heavenly beings appeared near the Fragrant Chamber. The Buddha once told me that they came to him daily with a host of questions, and he answered each and every one of them to their satisfaction."

"Many of the well-known discourses such as the *Mangala Sutta* and the *Parabhava Sutta* were expounded during this middle watch," comments Ananda.

"I was never near the Buddha during the last watch of the night," says Jivaka. "If he needed me, the Buddha kindly refrained from calling me until morning."

"The time from 2:00 a.m. to 6:00 a.m. was the last watch, and this was divided into four parts, which were each about an hour long," begins Ananda. "During the first part the Buddha would walk back and forth in the Fragrant Chamber; this was a mild form of exercise to relieve his physical tiredness. The second part would be spent mindfully sleeping on his right side. The third part would be enjoying the bliss of arahantship, which I'm sure re-charged every atom and cell of his body with the energy he needed to maintain his rigorous schedule. During the fourth part he would attain the Ecstasy of Great Compassion again, and radiate loving-kindness toward all living beings in the universe. Also during this hour he would survey the world with his Buddha Eye to see where he could be of service to any that might need his help. Out of compassion for them he would often travel to remote places using his supernormal powers."

"The most amazing thing about the Buddha's schedule," begins Jivaka, "was that he never planned anything in advance – at least not that I could determine. His actions were completely spontaneous and in the present moment; he was able to simply glide through his daily routine with incredible grace and ease. There was never a hint of worry, anxiety, or frustration, of course, as there might have been for ordinary people who wanted to carefully manage their time the way he did."

"And yet," says Ananda, "each and every day everything was accomplished painlessly and successfully, and according to the Lord's moment-to-moment inspirations."

Bakkula says, "I've always been curious about his diet – the eating of meat, especially. As the Lord's physician can you tell me if he ate meat?"

Jivaka answers, "One time the Buddha preached a discourse for me, addressing your question. He said:

"'Jivaka ...there are three instances in which meat should not be eaten: when it is seen, heard, or suspected that the animal has been slaughtered for the *bhikkhu*. When it is not seen, not heard, and not suspected that the living being has been slaughtered for the *bhikkhu*, it may be eaten.'"[5]

"But he wasn't really a meat eater; I know this to be a fact," says Bakkula.

"This is true, he wasn't," says Jivaka. "However, he never wanted to offend either his host at a *dana* ceremony, or anyone who would put food into his alms bowl. He was completely without preferences, but he was also against the taking of life. He usually advised that a vegetarian diet was preferable and healthier."

"That answer is a bit on the ambiguous side, isn't it?" remarks Bakkula, smiling.

"I think it is very typical of the Buddha to not make hard and fast rules about anything, Venerable Sir," answers Jivaka. "Even his precepts are framed more as 'suggestions' than 'mandatory laws.' I think he wanted to make sure that each individual had the freedom to decide what was best for him or her, and to not feel guilty if the precepts were transgressed from time to time. He took into consideration the reality that there would be occasional circumstances or conditions that were beyond our control, or out of the ordinary. He never wanted his followers to obsess about keeping their precepts, or give them undue attention compared to maintaining their more serious practices such as meditation."

"That is perhaps the best explanation I've ever heard on that often misunderstood subject, physician," says Maha Kassapa. "I truly believe that your services greatly enhanced - and perhaps even prolonged – his life, Jivaka. Your loving ministrations did the same, Venerable Ananda. You both made it possible for the Lord not to have to deal with mundane details; he could devote all of his time to spiritual work as it presented itself in each successive moment."

Jivaka instinctively knows that their conversation has reached its end. He bows to the revered chairman and places his palms together in great respect. He turns and does the same to the other arahants who are seated on the moonlit promontory. The sky is clear, and the view is breathtaking; countless stars illuminate the landscape below. After a few moments he turns towards Ananda who notices that there are tears in his eyes again. It is obvious to all of the arahants that for the rest of the kind physician's life nothing will ever fill the void of no longer having the joy of daily contact with the Buddha.

Of course, for the same reason life will never be the same for any of them as well.

Chapter 26
The First Psychologist

"When Jivaka was here we spoke about the Buddha's compassionate power of healing," begins Maha Kassapa. "I think today we should continue in this vein by spending some time talking about the way he healed minds."

"After all," adds Maha Kaccayana, "all human beings are somewhat mentally ill until they are enlightened."[1]

"I suppose you could say that enlightenment is the only cure for mental illness,'" says Bakkula.

"And everyone is afflicted; there are no exceptions. It is only the *extent* to which one is ill that differs," continues Maha Kaccayana with a smile.

The sub-committee members are seated under a canopy in the glade of banyan trees at the base of the mountain. The chairman has called a half-day recess after the *dana* ceremony, and they decide to enjoy the cool breezes of the season while they work on the Buddha's biography.

Anuruddha says, "The Buddha spoke countless times about 'seeing things clearly the way they are.' This is a necessary pre-requisite for attaining enlightenment. 'Not seeing things clearly the way they are' is another way of describing mental illness, which is a major form of human suffering."

"In earlier discussions we talked about several individuals that were cured of mental illness – like Angulimala, Patacara, Kisagotami, and others," says Bhaddiya. "In each of these cases the individual requested ordination into the Buddha's Sangha because they knew that this would greatly benefit their healing process. The safe, spiritual environment of the monastery nurtured their practice of meditation so they could gain the ability to 'see things clearly the way they are,' and eventually attain enlightenment."

"As we all know, however, the Buddha never recommended ordination for everyone," says Punna. "He taught people the truth about the way the mind functions in order to illuminate ways to cure mental diseases, all of which are the result of delusions or distortions of reality."

"The Buddha did teach, of course, that the 'original mind' is luminous, but it is soon spoiled by outside defilements,"[2] says Upali. "Spiritual work is to rid the mind of defilements, which will render it luminous again."

"The Lord once said," begins Ananda:

> "'No other thing I know, O monks, brings so much suffering as an undeveloped and uncultivated mind. An undeveloped and uncultivated mind truly brings suffering. No other thing I know, O monks, brings so much happiness as a developed and cultivated mind. A developed and cultivated mind truly brings happiness.'"[3]

"Ridding the mind of defilements while cultivating and developing the Four Sublime States contributes to the end of suffering," says Maha Kaccayana. "On one side you are purifying the mind by emptying it of negative thoughts and feelings and eliminating unwholesome influences; on the other side you are strengthening the mind by filling it with positive thoughts and feelings, exposing it to wholesome influences."

"The Buddha gave us specific methods for both of these practices," says Punna. "One of them is *vipassana* or insight meditation, which helps us to become aware of exactly what is going on in our minds every instant. It sharpens our focus and keeps our attention on the present moment, which is where reality actually is – rather than getting lost in memories about the past or worries about the future, both of which are tainted, inaccurate mentations and projections that aren't even real."

Ananda speaks, "Another method is *samatha* meditation, which helps develop the power of one-pointedness in concentration with the goal of purifying the mind."

"We can discuss Dhamma references and methodologies for improving the mind and meditation all day, but let's not forget that we are here to discuss the life of the Buddha," says Maha Kassapa. "Perhaps we should focus our attention on stories that illustrate mental healings the Buddha affected during the course of his ministry."

"An excellent suggestion, Venerable Chairman," says Bakkula, "especially since the Buddha taught that health of every kind begins in the mind."

"The variety, complexity, and combination of mental delusions and obsessions are virtually endless," says Upali. "There are as many unique hybrids of afflictions as there are individual humans."

"I have an excellent example of an intense mental obsession that I once witnessed the Buddha cure – in a very unconventional way," says Ananda.

The arahants give the Buddha's Chief Attendant their full attention.

"What reminded me of this particular story was Jivaka's visit here yesterday. This tale is partially about his beautiful sister, Sirima, who was a famous courtesan," says Ananda. "Ironically, she was both the subject and the object of obsession in the same story."

"Please go ahead and share it with us, Venerable Sir," says the chairman.

Ananda begins, "Sirima made the acquaintance of the Buddha through Uttara, one of the Buddha's wealthiest, and most loyal female lay devotees who was a *sotapanna*. Uttara's husband held other beliefs and had forbidden his wife to participate in a traditional observance of the precepts. To circumvent this, Uttara cleverly hired Sirima to amuse her husband for fifteen days in their private chamber while she observed the precepts at the end of the rainy season.

"Unfortunately, after playing the role of wife for those two weeks, Sirima came to believe that she really was the man's wife, and she became deranged. She completely forgot her place in Uttara's house. After the fifteenth day of her retreat Uttara went back home, and Sirima became very angry with her, accusing her that she was trying to take her place as the lady of the house. Sirima went to the kitchen, took a ladle of hot oil from the stove, and poured it on Uttara's head!

"Uttara immediately went into deep meditation on loving-kindness. As a result, the boiling oil passed over her body like water over a lotus flower. Uttara's servants screamed at Sirima and reviled her for her act of violence, which brought Sirima to her senses. She begged Uttara for forgiveness, but Uttara told her to ask the Buddha's forgiveness first," says Ananda.

"This is a truly wild story," says Upali, shaking his head.

Ananda smiles and continues, "Later that day the Buddha came for *dana* at Uttara's house. Sirima was asked to attend, and as soon as she was able, she prostrated herself before him and asked his forgiveness for her transgression against Uttara. The Lord forgave Sirima, of course, and then she went to Uttara and obtained her forgiveness as well.

"The Buddha expounded a discourse, and he uttered the following words:

> "'Conquer the angry one by loving-kindness;
> Conquer the wicked one by goodness;
> Conquer the stingy one by generosity;
> Conquer the liar by speaking the truth.'"[4]

"Sirima attained the state of *sotapanna* when she heard this stanza, and she invited the Buddha and his Sangha members to her house for a *dana* ceremony the next day. The Buddha and his monks attended, and every day from that day forward she started serving eight *bhikkhus* their noonday meal. They would be selected by the abbots of various monasteries in the area, or they would simply show up at her doorstep," says Ananda.

"I was her guest on three or four occasions," says Bhaddiya, "as were many of our Sangha brothers here at this council. We should also mention that from the moment she achieved *sotapanna* she gave up her former life as a courtesan."

"One day a monk who attended the *dana* at Sirima's house went afterwards to visit a monastery about twenty-four miles away," begins Ananda. "That evening the resident monks asked him where he had been for *dana* that day, and he replied that he had been one of the eight highly-fortunate ones to have been to Sirima's. He praised her hospitality, her food, and with perhaps too much enthusiasm he extolled the various aspects of her physical beauty.

"One of the younger resident monks, after hearing about Sirima's extraordinary beauty, fell madly in love with her without even setting his eyes on her. He became completely obsessed thinking about her, and he decided to go to her house the following day for *dana*."

"Tales of young *bhikkhus* falling in love with beautiful former courtesans rarely have happy endings," says Anuruddha thoughtfully.

"He walked all night to Sirima's house in Rajagaha and got there just as the sun was coming up," says Ananda. "He wanted to get there early to make sure he was one of the eight *bhikkhus* invited for *dana* that day, and he got his wish. The day before, however, Sirima had come down with an illness that turned out to be fatal. When the monks came for *dana* she wasn't able to personally serve them, but she had her maids do it on her behalf. Afterwards she had her female attendants carry her to the monks so she could pay her respects before they left her house.

"The monk who had fallen in love with her thought that even though Sirima was ill and was wearing no make-up or golden ornaments, she was still extremely beautiful. He imagined how much more beautiful she would have been if she was in good health and in her full courtesan regalia. At that moment he became totally consumed by a powerful lust for her. He couldn't even eat the food he had been given, so he covered his bowl and walked all the way back to the monastery. He spread out his robe and lay down on the floor. He refused to eat and just lay there dreaming and obsessing about Sirima; he was determined to starve himself to death since he could see no way to end his frustration.

"That night Sirima died. King Bimbisara sent word to the Buddha that Jivaka's sister had passed away, and upon hearing this news he sent a message back to the king asking that he not have her body cremated. He told the king to place her body on its back, and keep it at the charnel grounds. The Buddha also said to make sure it was guarded against predatory animals.

"Her body was kept this way for three days, and on the fourth day it stank and was swollen and putrid; worms crawled in and out of the nine openings. As instructed by the Buddha, King Bimbisara sent drummers all over the city announcing that all citizens, except children, must come to the charnel grounds to see the remains of Sirima – or they would be punished. The Buddha also gave the instruction that all Sangha members must come and observe Sirima's body.

"The Buddha then said, 'Come, monks, let us go to the charnel grounds.'

"One of the monks said to the young passionate monk who had fallen in love with Sirima, 'The Buddha has told us to go and see Sirima. You must come with us.'

"The young monk, who hadn't eaten in four days, reluctantly responded, 'Yes, I will come.' Then he went along with the other monks to the charnel grounds.

"Surrounded by monks and nuns, members of the royalty, common people, male and female lay devotees, the Buddha asked the king, 'Great King, who was this woman?'

"The king answered, 'Her name was Sirima; she was Jivaka's sister, and formerly a great courtesan.'

> "The Buddha said, 'Have the announcement made that anyone who desires her can take her upon the payment of one thousand gold coins.'
>
> "The king did as instructed by the Buddha, but there was no one who stepped forward to take her. The king informed the Buddha, who then said, 'Reduce the price to five hundred.' The announcement was made that the price was now five hundred, but still no one stepped forward. Again the price was dropped – to two-hundred-fifty, then to one-hundred-twenty-five, and it kept being cut in half again and again until it was down to one-sixteenth of one coin. Still there were no takers. It was even announced that anyone could have her for free, but no one approached.
>
> "The king reported this to the Buddha who spoke to the crowd as follows, 'You monks, my dear sons, and other friends! Behold this woman, Sirima, who had been dear to many. Formerly one had to pay one thousand gold coins to be with her for pleasure. Now, there is no one who will take her, even paying nothing at all. The beauty that was so highly valued has now come to destruction. Monks, through your eye of wisdom observe that this body, which was once so desired, is now disgustingly full of loathsomeness. With your penetrating eye, have a look at such a body, studying repeatedly!'[5]

"At the end of the discourse many beings realized various stages of emancipation, including the young monk who attained *sotapanna* and was instantly healed of his obsession," concludes Ananda.

"The Buddha used the tactic of shock to bring this monk to his senses," says Upali, "in combination with revulsion of the human body, of course."

"Meditation on the repulsiveness of the human body was one of the ways the Master taught the doctrine of impermanence," says Bakkula. "His point being that beauty and desirability are nothing but ephemeral illusions; they only mask the underlying reality of dissolution and decay."

"The *Satipatthana Sutta*,[6] *Vijaya Sutta*,[7] and other discourses use the revulsions of the decaying body as objects of meditation," says Punna. "As it was for the monk in the Sirima story, it's a great way to cure lust and carnal obsession. There's nothing more repugnant than seeing or imagining the object of one's desire putrefying into a stinking, festering mess."

"Lust, of course, is one of the major defilements of the mind," begins Upali, "but then so is anger, and the Buddha had many occasions to cure that rather common disease."

"I'll never forget the time the Licchavi 'Prince Wicked,' as he was called, was brought before the Buddha by his parents," says Maha Kaccayana. "He was a fierce, passionate, and cruel young man, always punishing others like an enraged viper."

"Yes, I remember him well," says Bhaddiya. "No one could say more than two or three words to him before his temper went off. His parents were beside themselves trying to find a cure."

"The Buddha basically told this prince that someone as cruelly passionate and fierce as he was would be re-born in hell – and possibly wind up committing suicide to get there," says Maha Kaccayana. "He also said that he would bring his angry deeds from this life into his next one, and suffer even more. The Buddha's powerful message to the young prince totally tamed him in the end, and he did a complete turn-around, becoming subdued and humbled, even kind-hearted."

"The Buddha's antidote for fierce, angry behavior was fear, but he used it in a positive way, and reinforced good behavior by extolling its benefits for this life as well as for future rebirths," says Bhaddiya.

"To some extent he also used fear, along with a great deal of wisdom, to tame Sujata, Anathapindika's daughter-in-law, our hostess at her retreat house by the hot springs," says Maha Kaccayana.

"Indeed. She was a holy terror when she first married and came to Anathapindika's house," says Anuruddha. "She scolded the servants mercilessly, and sorely neglected her husband and his parents; she gave no alms, was faithless and unbelieving, and generally was very difficult to be around."

"That was so until the day the Buddha and a large group of *bhikkhus* went to Anathapindika's house for *dana*," says Ananda. "He could hear Sujata screaming at the servants at the top of her lungs and asked his host about the noise. When Anathapindika, obviously disgusted, said that it was his new daughter-in-law who was making all the racket, the Buddha asked that the woman be brought before him. With your permission, Venerable Chairman, I think it might be good to record the Buddha's wise remarks to Sujata for our recollection."

Maha Kassapa nods his agreement.

"She came before the Buddha with great pride," says Ananda. She saluted him, and stood to one side. Then the Master addressed her thus:

> "'Sujata, there are seven kinds of wife a man may have; of which sort are you?'

> "She replied, 'Sir, I don't understand what you mean; please explain.'

> "The Master said, 'Listen attentively, Sujata,' and then he uttered the following verses:

> "'One is bad-hearted, with no compassion for the good;
> She loves others, but her husband she hates.
> Destroying all that her lord's wealth obtains,
> This wife the title of 'Destroyer' gains.

> "'What'er the husband gets for her by trade,
> Or skilled profession, or the farmer's spade,

She tries to filch a little out of it.
For such a wife the title 'Thief' is fit.

"'Careless of duty, lazy, passionate,
Greedy, foul-mouthed, and full of wrath and hate,
Tyrannical to all her underlings –
All this the title 'High and Mighty' brings.

"'Who evermore has compassion for the good,
Cares for her husband as a mother would,
Guards all the wealth her husband may obtain –
This wife the title 'Motherly' will gain.

"'She who respects her husband in the way
Young sisters reverence to elders pay,
Modest, obedient to her husband's will,
The 'Sisterly' is this wife's title still.

"'She whom her husband's sight will always please
As friend that friend after long absence sees,
High-bred and virtuous, giving up her life
To him – this one is called the 'Friendly' wife.

"'Calm when abused, afraid of violence,
No passion, full of dogged patience,
True-hearted, blending with her husband's will,
'Helpmate' is the title given to her still.

"'These, Sujata, are the seven wives a man may have. The first three are re-born in hell; the remaining four in the Fifth Heaven.'[8]

"While the Master was explaining these seven kinds of wives," continues Ananda, "Sujata attained *sotapanna*. The Master then asked her, 'Once again, Sujata, what kind of wife are you?' This time she answered, 'From this moment, Sir, I am a helpmate!'"

"Sujata was completely transformed," says Anuruddha. "She was tamed, her bad temper was gone, and she became a good wife to her grateful husband, Kala. A bit of fear interjected in the Buddha's discourse won her over, perhaps, but I'm quite sure it was his profound energy of loving-kindness that really cured her of the mental disease of anger."

Punna says, "From my study of the Buddha's Dhamma it appears that there are six distinct *caritas* or character archetypes, each of which is based on temperament. All human beings can be classified as belonging to one of these general categories: the lustful or greedy-natured, the hatred or anger-natured, the stupid or dull-natured, the faithful-natured, the intellectual-natured, and the agitated or pondering-natured. The Buddha addressed and cured mental illnesses according to the characteristics inherent in these broad categories. For example, before hearing the Buddha and becoming a *sotapanna*, Sujata seems to have been an 'anger-natured' individual. The Buddha's antidote for anger, of course, is loving-kindness, and he demonstrated this for her with the discourse on Seven Types of Wives."

The other arahants nod their agreement with Punna's wise assessment of character.

"In the *Sallekha Sutta*[9] the Buddha refers to forty-four illnesses that afflict the human mind," says Ananda. "In the same *sutta* he also gives a cure for each of them. For example, torturing and hurting others is the first disease; non-violence is its cure. Stealing is the second disease; not stealing is its cure. Many other diseases on the list include sexual misconduct, lying, wrong activities, wrong livelihood, egotism, stubbornness, and so forth.

"Another of Sujata's mental illnesses was uttering harsh words. According to this list of remedies, the Buddha's cure for this illness is *not* uttering harsh words. On the surface this remedy seems to be very simplistic, but upon closer examination one will see that for it to be effective, an illumination of the mind is required, along with an intense and vigilant sense of discipline."

Bakkula speaks, "The Buddha talked about another kind of mental disorder called *vancaka dhamma*. This is when thoughts are misidentified or dislocated; when they should be put into one classification of mental attitudes, but they are mistakenly put into another. These can result in 'desires in disguise,' which are sometimes cunning, deceitful, and even trecherous; they can be so subtle and insipid that they completely deceive the one who thinks them. For example, passion is sometimes disguised as *com*passion, and greed is sometimes disguised as generosity. Both of these examples can lead to dire consequences. In her mind, Sujata could have thought of herself as a kind person who was just doing her duty by correcting the people around her. She might never even have seen the effect her anger-natured character had on those around her."

"This is why the Buddha always taught that the mind must be investigated thoroughly in a constant, moment-by-moment practice," says Upali. "It goes right along with the basic teaching of 'seeing things clearly as they are.' There is no escaping this basic tenet of our philosophy, which includes the ensuing training practice of meditation."

"You are correct, Venerable Sir," says Maha Kaccayana. "Since we no longer have the benefit of the Buddha's physical presence for diagnosing mental problems and affecting cures, human beings are now left with the choice of either languishing in their own suffering, or treating themselves by using the methods the Master provided, the foremost of which are *vipassana* and *samatha* meditations."

"Let's not forget what the Buddha truly meant by *bhavana*, or meditation," says Maha Kassapa. "In the fullest sense of the term it means 'mental cultivation.' It aims at cleansing the mind of impurities and disturbances, such as lustful desires, hatred, ill-will, indolence, worries, restlessness, and skeptical doubts. It also aims at cultivating such qualities as concentration, awareness, intelligence, will, energy, the analytical faculty, confidence, joy and tranquility lead finally to the attainment of the highest wisdom, which sees the nature of things as they are, and realizes the ultimate truth, *Nibbana*."[10]

The arahants on the sub-committee nod in complete agreement with the chairman's profound statement.

"The mental illnesses, problems, and delusions we have been discussing today," continues Maha Kassapa, "are nearly all treatable with meditation, and the Master accepted the forty different objects for this practice that were already in existence before his time. The six archetypal characters you mentioned a few moments ago, Punna, are alike in one respect: they will all respond to the positive and uplifting effects of meditation. In fact, different objects of meditation are prescribed for each of these six types of temperaments. The forty-four mental illnesses will eventually disappear when the mind is centered on mindfulness, and is fully-functioning as its own self-investigating mechanism. This keeps it balanced and in harmony with all things."

"After the Buddha renounced the world," begins Bhaddiya, "he was taught *samatha* meditation by his first teachers, Alara Kalama and Uddaka Rama. This form of meditation leads to the development of mental concentration or one-pointedness, and to the highest mystic states: the 'Sphere of Nothingness' or the 'Sphere of Neither-Perception-nor-Non-Perception.' The Buddha found these states were purely mental, mind-created and mind-experienced. They have nothing to do with ultimate reality, truth, or *Nibbana*. The Buddha, not satisfied with these pleasant mystic states went beyond *samatha* meditation and discovered *vipassana*, which develops 'insight' into the nature of things, and leads to the complete liberation of the mind and realization of the Ultimate Truth, *Nibbana*."

"The *Satipatthana Sutta*," begins Ananda, "is the most important discourse the Lord gave on the subject of meditation – particularly on the *Vipassana* technique. It is divided into four parts: the body; the feelings and sensations; the mind; and various moral and intellectual subjects. As you all know, we very oftentimes recite this *sutta* to a dying person to help them purify their thoughts, which helps them achieve a happier rebirth."

"The necessary element in all techniques, subjects, and objects of meditation is mindfulness," says Anuruddha. "Either by developing insight or concentration, the practice is focused on staying in the present moment."

"We all know that the end result of the Buddha's meditation was enlightenment, or *Nibbana*," says Ananda. "The intermediate progressions of meditation training, however, result in a peaceful, happy life and loving-kindness for all. Please allow me to quote the Buddha's words from the *Kakacupama Sutta*:[11]

> "'*Bhikkhus*, even if bandits were to sever you savagely limb by limb with a two-handled saw, he who gave rise to a mind of hate towards them would not be carrying out my teaching. Herein, *bhikkhus*, you should train thus: 'Our minds will remain unaffected, and we shall utter no evil words; we shall abide compassionate for their welfare, with a mind of loving-kindness, without inner hate. We shall abide pervading them with a mind imbued with loving-kindness; and starting with

> them we shall abide pervading the all-encompassing world with a mind imbued with loving-kindness, abundant, exalted, and immeasurable, without hostility and without ill will.' That is how you should train, *bhikkhus*...You should keep this advice on the simile of the saw constantly in mind. That will lead to your welfare and happiness for a long time.'"

"Mental cultivation, in essence, means cultivating *metta*, loving-kindness," says Maha Kassapa. "The Buddha's treatment of every sort of mental illness or delusion was always based on *metta*. Even 'seeing things clearly as they are,' means seeing them through the eyes of loving-kindness, because this is the fundamental fact of the universe, of reality itself.

"Please let me quote one more verse from the Buddha on this subject," continues Maha Kassapa.

The arahants in the clearing of banyan trees smile and then close their eyes to listen carefully.

> "'Sleep and wake in comfort;
> You see no evil dreams;
> You are dear to humans and non-humans;
> Deities protect you;
> Fire, poison and weapons cannot touch you.
>
> "'Your mind quickly concentrates,
> Your countenance is serene,
> And when you die,
> It will be without
> Confusion in your mind.
>
> "'Even if you fail to attain *Nibbana*,
> You will pass to a world of bliss.'[12]

"On that happy note, my brothers, I think we will adjourn for the day," says the chairman, smiling. "We are the lucky ones. We have attained *Nibbana*, and we are experiencing that bliss here, now."

The arahants stand up and stretch their limbs. The sun is setting and the sky is a stunning display of oranges, yellows, and crimson. They walk in silence up the steep path to the cave entrance, and turn occasionally to appreciate the impermanent spectacle of nature. Their inward reflection is on *metta*, the most potent of all energies; the one that powers the entire universe and beyond. They know that *Metta*, in essence, is love.

Chapter 27
Teachers, Reputations, and Tolerance

Ananda stands at the podium facing the five hundred arahants in the assembly hall.

He begins his recitation:

> "Thus have I heard: On one occasion the Blessed One was wandering in the Kosala country with a large number of *bhikkhus*, and eventually arrived at a Kosala village named Nagaravinda.
>
> "Then the Brahmin householders of Nagaravinda went to the Blessed One. When they were seated the Blessed One said to them:
>
> "'Householders, if wanderers of other sects ask you what kind of recluses and Brahmins *should or should not* be honored, respected, revered, and venerated, you should answer them thus: Those recluses and Brahmins who are *not* rid of lust, hate, and delusion regarding forms cognizable by the eye, whose minds are not inwardly peaceful, and who conduct themselves now righteously, now unrighteously, in body, speech, and mind – such recluses and Brahmins *should not* be honored, respected, revered, and venerated.
>
> 'Those recluses and Brahmins, however, who *are* rid of lust, hate, and delusion regarding forms cognizable by the eye, whose minds are inwardly peaceful, and who conduct themselves righteously in body, speech, and mind – such recluses and Brahmins *should* be honored, respected, revered, and venerated.'"[1]

Ananda continues to the end of the *sutta* as Maha Kassapa sounds the gong for the *dana* recess. Sopaka approaches the platform, takes Ananda's elbow, and escorts him from the assembly hall.

"The Lord always behaved with such kindness and generosity to his detractors, as well as to other teachers who 'competed' with him for followers," comments Sopaka as he leads the way down the hill. "He never disparaged anyone, and he always left it up to the listener to decide for himself what made the best sense, what resonated as truth. The *sutta* you just recited is a perfect example."

"We have lived through a very interesting time," responds Ananda. "Rare it is for an Exalted Buddha to make an appearance in the world. It is also rare to have several teachers appear at the same time with varying doctrines – offering the individual so many choices in regards to spiritual paths. This is a great time of change and inner revolution – the likes of which have not been seen for thousands of years. The world will not likely see the appearance of conditions like these again for at least two and a half millennia. Understanding the context of his age, the Buddha was very wise to teach tolerance and forbearance, and to encourage the personal investigation of one's own direct experience using the perfected methods of insight and *samatha* meditations."

Maha Kassapa approaches Ananda and Sopaka on the path and says, "As usual, your morning *sutta* gives us a foretaste of our afternoon's discussions, Venerable Sir. We'll be talking about our competition, of course." The chairman chuckles as he says these last words.

"I know you use that word in jest, dear friend," responds Ananda, chuckling, "although Sopaka just used it a moment ago."

"Of course," says Maha Kassapa. "There never has been – nor will there ever be – any competition for the Lord's incomparable Dhamma. Even using the two words in the same sentence is bordering on the absurd."

"We've encountered our fair share of individuals who felt otherwise, however, as well as jealous teachers from other camps who were under-handed and vicious in their efforts to get back at the Buddha," says Ananda.

"I think this afternoon's sub-committee discussion will be quite interesting," says Maha Kassapa. "We've lived through a remarkable era of transition, and its context should be preserved in our life of the Buddha for future generations."

Ananda and Sopaka look at one another knowingly, and Ananda says, "Your psychic powers are showing again, Venerable Sir; we just said the exact same thing ten minutes ago."

The two old friends smile at one another, and the chairman says, "I know you're looking forward to seeing your devoted friend Visakha again."

Ananda smiles and answers, "As always, and I'm sure the *dana* ceremony she and her husband Dhananjaya are hosting will be lovely. I imagine Visakha has been inspecting the progress on her new monastery."

"I invited Visakha to participate in our sub-committee discussion later – along with Kumara Kassapa," says the chairman. "I figured they would both have input for the stories I know will come up."

"There you go again, my friend, with those psychic powers," says Ananda, "and you are absolutely correct; Visakha's input will be most valuable, as well as humorous, I'm sure. Kumara Kassapa's contribution will also be insightful."

Visakha's and Dhananjaya's *dana* ceremony is elaborate and perfect, which is to be expected. The new pavilion Visakha had built for the previous ceremony is now enhanced with amazing stone and wood carvings of figures from the Buddha's life story. The arahants take a few minutes to tour the splendid new hall before settling down on their mats for the meal.

The host and hostess greet the senior Sangha members with great solemnity and respect, bowing low and touching their feet. They serve the assembled five hundred arahants with the help of many servants, and afterwards offer robes to the monks as they depart.

"May I escort you to the conference pavilion?" Visakha asks Ananda.

"Of course you may, my dear friend. By the way, how is your vast and growing family?" inquires the Buddha's Chief Attendant.

"Everyone is very well, thank you, and they send you their highest regards," says Visakha. "I'm so happy to be able to participate again in your biography of the Buddha. My husband felt left out last time – even though he knew it was for female clan members only. He's glad to be here today, though, not that he'll have that much to say."

"You've always done the talking for both of you, so what else is new?" quips Ananda. Visakha laughs heartily at this remark as they enter the sumptuous new pavilion. They take their places on the colorful display of Kashmiri carpets and silk cushions. Loving, patient husband Dhananjaya seats himself comfortably next to his wife.

The other arahants on the sub-committee, as well as Kumara Kassapa, settle themselves and prepare to begin their discussion. The memory monks close their eyes and go into meditation.

The chairman says, "The Buddha made his appearance in the world just as six other important teachers were making theirs. This occurrence is unprecedented in history."[2]

"These teachers all had substantial followings," begins Upali. "Their doctrines were radically different from one another, and they arrived at their positions as great teachers in a variety of ways – some of them veiled in mystery, and others quite humorously."

Visakha laughs and says, "Like Purana Kassapa. I probably shouldn't be interjecting this story here since it was never proved, but I really can't resist telling it."

The chairman smiles at Visakha indulgently and says, "The origins of these teachers are mostly in the 'gray area' anyway, so you might as well tell your apocryphal story."

Visakha laughs gaily and says, "I heard that one day Purana Kassapa was robbed by some thieves who took all his clothes. He couldn't figure out a way to cover himself, so he simply walked into a nearby village stark naked, unashamed. The people who saw him thought he was a sanctified ascetic who had no attachment to anything, so they started offering him food and looking after him. Even though he was given garments he declined wearing them; he enjoyed the treatment he got as a naked *sadhu*. Believe it or not, this is the rumored beginning of his asceticism, which eventually grew to a following of five hundred naked ones."

The arahants can't help but laugh at this humorous tale, even though its veracity had never been proven.

"Purana Kassapa taught that performing a bad action – even committing murder – wasn't a sin," says Bhaddiya. "He also said that doing a good deed didn't achieve any merit, nor did practicing generosity, self control, or truthfulness. He basically taught that one's actions did not bring any result, either positive or negative."

Understanding very clearly the Buddha's Doctrine about *kamma*, the arahants shake their heads upon hearing this statement relating to Purana Kassapa's unconventional philosophy.

"I also heard that Makkahali Gosala was born in a cattle shed," begins Visakha. "One day he was following his master while carrying a pot of oil on his head. The ground was muddy, and he slipped and fell. He feared his master's wrath for spilling the oil all over the place, so he started to run. The master grabbed Gosala by his loincloth, but Gosala kept running. He wound up leaving his loincloth in his master's hands! Later on he walked into a village naked and received the same reception Purana Kassapa had gotten; and it wasn't long before he was famous!"

The arahants smile and Dhananjaya says, "Please, Visakha, you should show some respect for those teachers. The Buddha would never have said those things."

Visakha looks at her husband with a frown, and says, "You are the father of my children, dear husband, so I have to respect what you say. I do not, however, have to refrain from telling what I've heard about these men. Don't forget – some of them tried to make big problems for the Buddha."

Dhananjaya smiles, shakes his head and keeps silent.

"Gosala taught that everything in life was pre-determined, or foreordained," says Maha Kaccayana. "He also taught that there was no cause and effect, or conditionality behind this pre-determination. I could never figure out how he made that system work – both practically and philosophically. He also taught that the world would eventually come to an end, but he didn't say when."

"Ajita Kesakambali was well-known for wearing a garment made out of human hair. It was supposed to be cool in the cold season and warm in the hot season, which doesn't make much sense to me," says Visakha. "One of my maids encountered him one day in the marketplace and she said he smelled horrible. She also said he was scratching himself like he had slept with fleas."

"Ajita didn't believe in gifts, sacrifice, the fruits of good or bad acts, the existence of heavenly worlds, or in the possibility that people might possess higher powers," says Anuruddha. "He felt that it made no sense to talk of life after death, and said that once the body dies it returns to the four elements and that's that. He was a complete nihilist."

"Pakudha Kaccayana," says Visakha, "always avoided cold water because he believed it contained small life forms that he might inadvertently harm. Whenever he crossed a river or a stream he would build a *stupa* out of sand, which was his way of restoring his vow to not take life."

"According to Pakudha Kaccayana, there are seven immutable elements, and none of them contribute to either pleasure or pain," says Upali. "He said that when the body dies it is ultimately dissolved into these seven eternal elements."

"I'm not sure how he arrived at that theory," says Bhaddiya. "In the Buddha's Dhamma there is no such thing as an 'eternal' element; they're all conditional and relative."

"King Ajatasattu was taken by his ministers to see all of these teachers, and he reported that Sanjaya Belatthiputta was the most foolish and ignorant of them all," says Visakha. "His doctrine seems to purposely divert the mind from the right track, and he never gave solutions to any problems facing the human condition. He was so non-committal and bewildering that it seems to me he didn't really teach anything."

"Jivaka eventually took King Ajatasattu to see the Buddha," says Upali. "The Lord asked him what the six teachers had said to him, and the king shared their theses with the Buddha. The king communicated the fact that he was not impressed by any of the teachers, nor did he accept or reject any of their teachings. The various doctrines simply didn't appeal to him, and he felt the teachers never gave him a straight answer when he asked them direct questions. After he met the Buddha, however, it wasn't long before he became a life-long devotee."

"The one teacher that stands out when compared to the others is Nigantha Nataputta, who is sometimes known as 'Mahavira,'" says Bhaddiya. "He founded the Jain sect right here in Rajagaha – or at least it appears that he did – with the help of another teacher named Parsva, who lived two hundred fifty years ago."

"Either they came up with the same belief system independently," says Maha Kassapa, "or Nataputta embellished and built-upon Parsva's thought. Their beliefs were ultimately united, and their teaching is based on an ethical code that consists of four or five rules – three of them are much like our precepts: refraining from taking life, stealing, and lying."

"The Jainist fourth and fifth rules are about celibacy and not having any possessions," says Bakkula. "Mahavira let those who followed him only have the clothes they wore."

"To be more specific, Venerable Sir, he only allowed clothes if they were *white*," says Upali. "The earlier teacher, Parsva, insisted on complete nudity for his followers."

"Another difference between the Jainist teaching and ours is the concept of prophets. We don't have prophets in the Dhamma," says Visakha. "We have Fully Enlightened Buddhas. Parsva was the twenty-third prophet in their line. Mahavira, or Nataputta, is supposed to be the twenty-fourth; and for some reason that escapes me, he claimed to be the very last prophet that will appear in their lineage."

"These six teachers had been traveling around preaching their doctrines long before the Buddha's enlightenment," says Punna. "They were quite well-known to the people, and they often sought royal patronage, which could bring them an increase in influence and followers – not to mention finances."

"Many of these teachers tried to cause serious harm to the Buddha's reputation," begins Ananda. "They even attempted to set him up in situations that would essentially ruin him, but he never complained or retaliated."

"I'm sure that at least Mahavira, being the non-violent man that he was, would never have attempted to harm the Buddha or his reputation," says Kumara Kassapa with characteristic generosity.

"I agree with you, Venerable Sir. As a matter of fact there is a *sutta* about a man named Upali who was a brilliant, well-respected lay disciple of Mahavira," begins Punna. "Upali was expressly sent by Mahavira himself to meet the Buddha and to defeat him in a debate about *kamma*. At the end of the debate Upali was convinced that the Buddha was correct, and he begged the Lord to be accepted as a lay disciple.

"The Buddha, however, asked him to reconsider his request, and to not be in such a hurry to discard his old teacher. He said, 'Considering carefully is good for well-known men like you.' Upali then made his request a second and third time, and the Buddha advised him to continue to respect and support his old religious teacher. He eventually accepted Upali as a lay disciple, but under the condition that he also respect and support his former teacher,"³ says Punna. "The Buddha would not hurt or offend anyone – including other teachers that differed from him – and even those that attempted to harm him."

Ananda adds, "In the *Brahmajala Sutta* the Buddha even says:

> "'*Bhikkhus*, if others should *malign* the Buddha, the Dhamma and the Sangha, you must not feel resentment, nor displeasure, nor anger on that account. If you do, it will only be harmful to you because then you will not be able to practice the Dhamma. If you feel angry or displeased when others malign the Buddha, the Dhamma and the Sangha, will you be able to discriminate their good speech from bad?'

> "The *bhikkhus* replied, 'No, indeed, Venerable Sir!'

> "'If others malign me, or the Dhamma, or the Sangha, you should explain to them what is false as false, saying 'It is not so. It is not true. It is, indeed, not thus with us. Such fault is not to be found among us.'

> "'*Bhikkhus*! If others should *praise* the Buddha, the Dhamma, and the Sangha, you should not feel pleased, or delighted, or elated on that account. If you do, then it will only be harmful to you. If others praise me, or the Dhamma, or the Sangha, you should admit what is true as true, saying 'It is so. It is true. It is, indeed, thus with us. In fact, it is to be found among us.'"⁴

"So the Buddha counseled us not to react either positively or negatively when someone either praises or criticizes the Buddha, Dhamma, or Sangha," said Sopaka. "I would say that those instructions are quite extraordinary, and probably would never have been made by any of the other teachers."

Kumara Kassapa says, "In that same *sutta* the Buddha talks about sixty-two views – not just the six we mentioned in this discussion. There were and still are many views held by other teachers and their followers. Many adherents of those views still persist in being quite vocal against the Buddha and his teachings."

Visakha speaks up and says, "Even though the Buddha urged the followers of other teachers to continue to respect and patronize them, this was hardly ever the case in reverse. I've had personal involvement in a couple of nasty incidents, and I'd like to tell them now so they can be in the record."

"Please proceed, friend Visakha," says Maha Kassapa. "Your eyewitness accounts will be of great benefit to future historians."

Visakha begins, "One of the teachers we mentioned earlier became exceedingly jealous of the Buddha. Even though you are arahants and can guess who it is, I'm not going to disclose his name. Many of his followers were deserting him to become lay devotees of the Master, and several of his ascetic disciples abandoned him to join the Buddha's Sangha. During one six month period this teacher lost at least ten people a week, which drastically reduced his finances and control over his dwindling community."

"This unnamed teacher you are describing must have become quite upset," says Bhaddiya.

"Upset doesn't even come close to his state of mind," says Visakha, her black eyes gleaming. "He was absolutely livid! He could do nothing but just sit there and watch his previously large spiritual empire vanish before his eyes. The word 'Buddha' became a curse word for him, and he forbade his remaining disciples to use it in his presence. It got to the point where he could barely support himself and his ashram. He finally decided to do something to the Buddha to try to stop his growing influence."

"What was his plan?" asks Punna.

"This teacher had a pupil named Cincamanavika, an extremely beautiful young girl," begins Visakha. "Being very devoted to the teacher she happily became involved in his evil plot to discredit the Master. He called the girl to him and said, 'If you truly believe in me, and in my teaching, then I will give you a chance to prove your loyalty.' The great charlatan teachers always make their followers do things to prove their loyalty. That's how they get them to bed, isn't it? This is what I suspect had already taken place with this girl."

The arahants nod their heads knowing that what she said had happened in the past.

"That very evening she took some flowers and went off towards Jetavana Monastery," says Visakha. "Along the way people asked her where she was going and she replied, 'To spend the night with Gotama Buddha.' This remark raised a number of eyebrows, I'm sure.

"When she got near the monastery she went off to spend the night at the camp of her ascetic group, which was nearby. Early in the morning she got up and made it look as if she had spent the night *inside* the monastery. She walked around outside the gate and announced to the world, 'I slept in the Fragrant Chamber with Gotama Buddha last night.'

"She even said to a few people in the city, 'Gotama Buddha is completely in love with me, but don't tell anyone.' How brazen was that? She must have been completely brainwashed by her teacher, which makes me even more convinced that he had seduced her into being intimate with him. I can't imagine why or how she would have been interested – do you remember what he looked like?"

Visakha starts laughing again and the arahants can't help but laugh along with her. The mental image of the unnamed ascetic teacher – skinny and emaciated and toothless as he was – with the pretty young girl was just too comic and absurd.

"She kept this up for three or four months, and the rumor spread that the Buddha and this girl were a couple. She began to tie cloth around her stomach to make herself look pregnant; and she increased the amount of cloth for eight or nine months – always spreading the word that the Buddha was the father of her child. Cincamanavika even figured out a way to make her hands and feet swollen and red, and she did a great job pretending to be tired and worn out all the time. She played a great pregnant woman in the advanced stage, I'll give her that much."

The arahants shake their heads back and forth recalling the incident.

"One night she came to the monastery while the Buddha was expounding the Dhamma to a group of monks and some lay people; I was there," resumes Visakha. "She walked toward the Buddha, looked him in the eye and said, 'You care nothing for me now that you've made me pregnant! All you ever care about is your own pleasure. You refuse to take responsibility for what you've done – and I'm sure you'll do nothing to take care of your child.'

"The Buddha remained calm and said, 'Sister, only you and I know whether you are speaking the truth or not.'

"The girl answered, 'Yes, you are right. How can others know what only you and I know?'"

Visakha pauses for a moment and then says, "You can't imagine how angry I was by this time. I was fuming. I stood up and faced the girl right on the spot. She tried to look the other way, but I grabbed her chin and made her look at me. I said, 'I'll give you five minutes to apologize to the Lord Buddha. You and I both know you're lying. Ask for his forgiveness now and you might be saved from the wrath of your *kamma*.'

"The girl just stood there trembling. I could tell by the look in her eye that she knew I knew she was lying, and that I wasn't going to let her get away with it. She turned abruptly on her heels and started to walk away, but I grabbed her. I knew she was pretending to be pregnant so I put my hands on her stomach. When she tired to get away I held on tight, and then the rope holding up the cloth around her stomach came loose. Lo and behold, that great big ball of wadded up cloth came loose and rolled out from under her skirt. I went over and picked it up and said, 'Is this your baby?'

"I'm telling you, that girl ran out of there so fast you'd have thought she was on fire. All along the way people started screaming at her, 'Oh, you wicked woman! You shameless liar! How dare you falsely accuse the Buddha!'

"That girl kept running as fast as she could, and you know what? She was never seen or heard from again. It was as if the earth just opened up and swallowed her," says Visakha, almost out of breath.

Ananda speaks, "When the girl ran away the Buddha said, 'The evil person who has given up the virtue of truthfulness has abandoned all hopes of the next world.'"[5]

"It makes me sad to think about Cincamanavika's future rebirths – for having attempted what she did to ruin the Buddha's reputation," says Anuruddha.

"Not to mention the *kamma* of the great ascetic teacher who put her up to it!" exclaims Punna.

"Does anyone here remember the Sundari incident?" asks Maha Kassapa.

"How could we not, Venerable Sir?" exclaims Ananda. "That one really caused a lot of problems for a while."

"Why don't you tell us what happened in just a few words," requests the chairman.

Ananda begins, "Another one of the well-known ascetic groups, finding their numbers shrinking, became exceedingly jealous of the Buddha. They felt they had to do something to damage the Lord's reputation or they would soon be without any followers. They set in motion the same sort of stunt the other teacher pulled with Cincamanavika, using another pretty girl named Sundari."

Visakha arches her eyebrows and with raised voice asks, "Was she sleeping with the great ascetic teacher, too?"

"I'm not sure about that, but I wouldn't have put it past him to use his influence to take advantage of her. I had heard it said that he had done that sort of thing before," answers Ananda. "Anyway, Sundari was a very clever girl and she used her good looks to cause quite a commotion. She walked toward Jetavana Monastery and people asked her where she was going. She said, 'I live with Gotama Buddha in his Fragrant Chamber. I am going to him now.'

"She continued doing this for three days, and the word got around fast that the Buddha had a mistress. She really did a great job carrying on about her intimate relationship with the Lord," says Ananda. "She played the part well."

"The entire city of Savatthi was aflame over this scandal," says Dhananjaya. "Visakha, you went into your mode of damage control and started refuting the rumor, but it continued to spread like wildfire."

"I actually went to see Sundari myself and I confronted her," says Visakha. "She wouldn't even speak to me, the little hussy. She just laughed in my face, turned around and walked off."

Ananda says, "After three days of stirring up the rumor mill to a fever pitch the ascetic leader hired a group of drunkards to kill poor, misguided Sundari. Then they disposed of her body in a rubbish heap near the Jetavana Monastery. The next day they spread the news about Sundari's disappearance, and eventually they found the corpse.'

"The town was literally buzzing with gossip about Sundari's murder, and how it was linked to a cover-up for the affair she was supposedly having with the Buddha," says Ananda.

Visakha speaks up and says, "My maid came running home to tell me what she had heard in the market. I was beside myself with anger."

"The monks went to the Buddha and told him what the ascetics were trying to do to his reputation," says Ananda.

"The Buddha said, 'My sons, you just tell them this:

"'One who tells lies about others goes to hell; one who has done evil and says 'I did not do it,' also goes to hell. Both of them, being evildoers, suffer alike in hell in their next existence.'[6]

"I was so upset by this incident that I suggested that we go to another town," says Ananda.

"The Buddha asked, 'If we get the same treatment in the next town what will we do then, Ananda?'

"I said, 'We can move on to the next town.'

"The Buddha paused for a moment and then said to me, 'Ananda, an elephant trained to fight in a war will never retreat – even though arrows come at him from every direction. We monks should be like such an elephant and go forth, facing criticisms and clearing up misunderstandings.'

"I still wasn't comfortable with the situation," continues Ananda, "so the Buddha said, 'Furthermore, these rumors will last no more than seven days because anyone who falsely accuses a Buddha or an arahant will soon be exposed.'

"So we stayed and waited; it wasn't long before the king ordered his men to further investigate the murder. They soon discovered that Sundari had died at the hands of hired brigands. They had gotten drunk in a tavern and were bragging out loud about ruining the Buddha's reputation," says Ananda.

"When they brought this news to the king he had them hauled before him. They confessed their crime – admitting that the ascetics were the ones who had paid them to kill the girl. The king then ordered them to go about the city and proclaim the truth to everyone.

"So they went around and yelled, 'We are the ones who killed Sundari. We have falsely accused the disciples of Gotama just to bring disgrace to him. They are innocent, and the Buddha is innocent. We are the guilty ones.'"

Visakha says, "The whole scheme backfired on the ascetics and they were punished severely by the king. They were completely ruined and the Buddha's reputation grew even bigger."

Maha Kassapa speaks up, "Venerable Kumara Kassapa, you have remained unusually silent throughout this meeting. Have you been saving your energy to tell *your* tale?"

Kumara Kassapa says, "I was actually reflecting on the sad fact that those under the influence of negative defilements will stop at nothing to succeed."

"Well said, Venerable Sir," says Visakha. "In the case of the Buddha, however, those with defilements were always defeated. Your own life is a perfect example."

"You were there at the beginning, dear friend, and that was thirty years ago," replies Kumara Kassapa, "and I'll always be grateful for the friendship you offered my mother when she needed it most."

"It was just a case of being in the right place at the right time, Venerable Sir," replies the kind Visakha, "and besides, your mother became one of the greatest friends of my life. I miss her more than I can tell you."

Visakha's eyes fill with tears as she thinks about the passing of her friend, Kumara Kassapa's mother. She had died only the year before.

"Why don't you tell the tale of your origin," suggests Maha Kassapa, smiling. "I'm sure Visakha will help you."

"My mother was the daughter of a wealthy merchant," begins Kumara Kassapa, "and from an early age she wanted nothing more than to become a spiritual aspirant. She would have been perfectly happy becoming a *bhikkhuni* and living happily ever after, but her father had other plans for her. He insisted that she marry the son of one of his wealthy merchant friends and she couldn't refuse.

"The marriage was consummated, and in the beginning my parents got along reasonably well. After a while, however, my mother realized that she could never be happy as a married woman. She convinced my father that she had no choice but to leave him to become a nun. She was one of those women who wanted the spiritual life so desperately that she would have willingly died to get it. My father was a kind man, and he eventually gave her the permission she sought," says Kumara Kassapa.

"If Visakha had asked me for permission to do the same thing," begins Dhananjaya, "I don't think I could have given it to her. Your father seems to have been a very noble person indeed, Venerable Kumara Kassapa."

Visakha gives her husband a look filled with great love and affection. It is obvious to the arahants that Visakha and Dhananjaya have a true and lasting partnership – even after the birth of twenty children and many years of her habit of speaking for both of them.

Kumara Kassapa nods in appreciation for Dhananjaya's kind words and says, "Unfortunately, when she left my father she sought refuge in Venerable Devadatta's nunnery, of all places. After a few weeks my mother discovered she was pregnant, and when Devadatta was told about it she was immediately and mercilessly expelled."

"The Buddha's former brother-in-law was nothing, if not cruel, as we shall soon see when we get to his chapter in the Buddha's life story," says Maha Kassapa.

"My mother, a young pregnant *bhikkhuni*, left Devadatta's nunnery in disgrace. She found her way, however, to a nunnery of *bhikkhunis* who were disciples of the Buddha," continues Kumara Kassapa. "The nuns reported her pregnancy to the Buddha, who authorized Venerable Upali to investigate and render a decision on the matter."

Upali says, "I immediately called Visakha and asked her to get a group of her respectable lady friends together to help us find out if your mother's pregnancy took place before or after her ordination."

"That was the first time I met your dear mother," says Visakha. "She was so frightened that day, and very shy – painfully shy. She said she had been with your father shortly before she left him, but had never been with him or with any other man since then. I could tell by the look on her face and the sincerity of her voice that she was telling us the truth."

"You and your lady friends examined her and found that she had, indeed, been telling the truth. Her pregnancy definitely had occurred *before* she was ordained," says Upali.

"When you reported our findings to the Buddha," begins Visakha, "I remember that he praised you for your good judgment and the way you handled the case."

"I, of course," begins Kumara Kassapa, "am grateful to both of you for the compassion you showed my mother. I don't know what would have happened to us if the Buddha's nunnery hadn't been available – and if you hadn't been on the scene, dear friend."

"As you well know," says Visakha, "your mother and I were like sisters, remaining so until the day she died. She was on hand to help me through many of my children's births, and I was always so happy that she and Dhananjaya got along so well."

"I was actually getting to know your father a little," says Dhananjaya, "but then he died; you were only a year-old infant."

"I was so fortunate that King Pasenadi raised me like a prince until I was seven years old," says Kumara Kassapa.

"That's how you were called 'Kumara,' Venerable Sir," says Ananda. "It can mean 'prince,' or 'boy,' and I was never sure which one the Buddha actually meant when he gave you that name."

Visakha smiles saying, "You were such a beautiful child, Venerable Sir. You looked like a little golden statuette when you were born. Your mother loved you dearly, and was so happy when the Buddha arranged to have you brought up by the king. We all participated in raising you in one way or another – you had a whole community of monks and nuns looking after your welfare – including the Buddha himself."

"Not to mention Venerable Ananda – and me, of course," says Upali. "I always took a special interest in you, you know."

"I know that very well Venerable Upali," says Kumara Kassapa, "and I always thought of you as one of my four fathers: my merchant birth father, King Pasenadi, the Buddha, and you."

Upali beams, remembering the time when the infant Kumara Kassapa was born.

"I was ordained as a *samanera* at the age of seven, so the entire Sangha became my family," says Kumara Kassapa with a big smile. "And I got to go on the road and travel with my Sangha fathers from time to time, and I was schooled by some of the greatest scholars in the Order. My gratitude for all of you has no limits."

The arahants in the elegant pavilion breathe deeply and reflect on the many years they have been brothers in the Sangha, and the scores of other youthful *samaneras* they have helped raise. Kumara Kassapa was one of the best examples of Sangha culture and education that had yet been produced. They are all fond of him, and admire his great accomplishments preaching the Dhamma. Kumara Kassapa had been an arahant himself for many years by this time; they had all rejoiced when that blessed event had taken place.

"This whole discussion about how the Buddha was often maligned can be concluded with a simple statement he once made," begins Maha Kassapa. "I think you know the one I'm thinking about, Venerable Ananda. Will you quote it for us?"

"I believe I do know the statement you are referring to. It goes like this:

> "'At Savatthi the Buddha once said, '*Bhikkhus*, I do not dispute with the world; rather it is the world that disputes with me. A proponent of the Dhamma does not dispute with anyone in the world.'⁷"

"No matter how often the Buddha or his reputation was attacked by some jealous or vengeful opponent," begins Maha Kassapa, "he never reacted in any negative way. Instead, he would use the occasion to teach the Dhamma to the individual or group, and he usually gained followers during the process. He never argued, he never lost his temper, he never sought revenge, and he never, ever punished."

"If he had done any of those things," says Visakha, "he wouldn't have been the Fully Enlightened Buddha, and none of you would be arahants. We owe him so much."

As Maha Kassapa rises from his seat, he says, "I think this is a good place to break for the day, dear friends. I am forever grateful to you, our special guests, for your participation and for your on-going contributions to the Buddha *Sasana*."

"Don't hesitate to invite me back if I can be of use, Venerable Sir," says Visakha.

The chairman smiles at the Buddha's chief female lay disciple and blesses her with his eyes. Visakha and Dhananjaya bow low in front of the arahants, and reach out to touch their feet with great respect.

The sun has long since gone down, the moon has risen in the east, and the peace of the Buddha descends on the land. The First Sangha Council has finished its work for the day, and all is well.

Chapter 28
Sigala and Friends

"On one occasion the Blessed One was dwelling at Kapilavatthu in the Banyan Tree Monastery," begins Ananda as he addresses the assembly. "It was there that Mahanama, the Sakyan, approached the Blessed One and, after paying homage to him, sat down at one side. So seated, he addressed the Blessed One and asked:

"'How, Lord, is one a lay follower?'

"'If, Mahanama, one has gone for refuge to the Buddha, the Dhamma and the Sangha, one is a lay follower.'

"'But how, Lord, is a lay follower virtuous?'

"'If, Mahanama, a lay follower abstains from the destruction of life, from taking what is not given, from sexual misconduct, from false speech and from wines, liquor and intoxicants which are a basis for negligence, the lay follower is virtuous.'

"'And how, Lord, does a lay follower live for the welfare of both himself and others?'

"'If, Mahanama, a lay follower himself has faith, virtue and generosity, and also encourages others in gaining them; if he himself likes to visit monks and to listen to the good Dhamma, and he also encourages others to do so; if he himself retains in mind the teachings heard and carefully examines their meaning, and he also encourages others to do so; if, having understood both the letter and the meaning, he himself practices in accordance with the Dhamma and also encourages others to do so – in such a case, Mahanama, a lay follower lives for the welfare of both himself and others.'"[1]

Maha Kassapa announces, "Today's *dana* is being offered by Sigala, a local Rajagaha lay disciple to whom the Buddha gave his definitive treatise on lay life. He will be serving the Sangha members in the *dana* pavilion with four of his lifelong friends: Sanjaya, Anup, Dilip, and Pradeep. This will conclude our morning council proceedings." He sounds the gong and the five hundred arahants rise from their seats.

On his way out of the assembly hall Ananda is joined by his cousin, Anuruddha, who says, "My brother, Mahanama, was forever changed by that discourse you just recited."

"I know, Venerable Sir," replies Ananda. "After he heard that discourse he was prepared to become king in your stead. It rooted him firmly in the precepts, and it gave him the proper perspective for sharing the Dhamma with his subjects."

"It also made him aware of his responsibility to lead his people along the path of virtue and purification by his own example," replies Anuruddha.

"And I know it taught him a greater appreciation for the practice of encouragement," says Ananda. "He learned to rule by encouraging the positive qualities in an individual – rather than proscribing the negative."

The three arahants join the other members of the Sangha council and proceed to the *dana* pavilion where Sigala and his four childhood friends are waiting to greet them.

"Friend Sigala," begins Ananda, "it is good to see you again, as always."

Sigala immediately goes down on his knees before Ananda and touches his feet in respect. His friends do the same.

When they stand up there are broad smiles on their faces. The senior monks can't help but notice the clean, healthy demeanor of the five handsome householders in the prime of their lives. Each of them exudes a quality of freshness and purity that demonstrates their adherence to the Five Precepts and their practice of meditation.

"You do us great honor by allowing us to serve you today, Venerable Sirs," says Sigala to the senior monks.

"And you do the *Sasana* a great honor by living the advice the Buddha gave you," responds Maha Kassapa. "None of you seem to have changed a bit since I saw you five years ago. You are as youthful and prosperous-looking as ever."

"We owe our happiness to the teaching of the Buddha, Venerable Sir, and we support each other to our highest good – just as the Lord taught us when we were still wayward young rascals," replies Sigala, smiling.

The men, now in their mid-forties, escort the revered elders to their seats, making sure they are comfortable. When all of the arahants are seated Maha Kassapa begins the chanting, which fills the *dana* pavilion with a vibrant sweetness that matches the cheerful, positive attitudes of the hosts.

The five friends are joined by their wives and children to help serve their esteemed guests, and the arahants happily return the smiles of the many family members who graciously portion food onto their banana leaf plates.

When the *dana* ceremony is over Maha Kassapa rises from his seat and announces to the Assembly, "Sigala and his friends will be joining the sub-committee recollecting the life of the Buddha later this afternoon. We wish to add the context of the well-known *Sigalovada Sutta*[2] to our record. This *Sutta* has become the standard for Buddhist families to insure that they and their associates lead happy, productive lives."

The arahants stand to their feet and return to the assembly hall for another afternoon of recitations.

At about three o'clock the chairman sounds the gong and the council is adjourned for the day. The majority of the arahants go alone or in small groups to the forest for a period of meditation and relaxation, while several return to their cave chambers where they will remain in deep *samadhi* until the following morning. The members of the sub-committee begin their stroll down the hillside to the hot springs, where Sigala and his friends have set up a large canopy with a view of the valley below.

"Visakha's new monastery is really taking shape," says Anuruddha to Punna, pointing to the large construction site next to the mountain. "At the rate they're going, it looks like it might be completed within a few weeks."

"I believe that large building to the left will have chambers for the resident monks," responds Punna. "I hear that it will accommodate nearly one thousand *bhikkhus*."

"I'm told that the building to the right of the new assembly hall will be used specifically for instruction in meditation," comments Anuruddha.

Ananda walks over to the two arahants. "Visakha sent me word that she will make another appearance here before the council closes. She has made a special request, which was granted, to be present when we review the *Parinibbana Sutta*. She is still having a hard time adjusting to the loss of the Master."

The two arahants nod in agreement, and Punna says, "Perhaps her new monastery will be completed by that time, and we can all participate in the dedication ceremony. That might cheer her up."

Ananda smiles and says, "Maybe she will sing and dance again." The three senior monks smile, remembering her happiness during the dedication of the first monastery she built years before.

Maha Kassapa steps into the canopied enclosure and says, "Venerable Sirs, please make yourselves comfortable. I believe we can begin our meeting now."

The monks are seated on the large blue and crimson carpet, which had been placed on a raised wooden dais overlooking one of the hot springs; Sigala and his four friends sit facing them.

"Well, Friend Sigala, tell us how you came to know the Buddha," requests the chairman.

Sigala, who is sitting cross-legged directly opposite Maha Kassapa, straightens his posture and smiles warmly while remembering that sacred moment nearly twenty years before, "I was the product of two wealthy merchant families and my parents did all within their power to raise me correctly. They gave me every possible advantage, which unfortunately I didn't really appreciate. I had a mind of my own, and I was what you might call a 'free spirit,' which means that I was incorrigible and listened to no one. My good parents were both lay disciples of the Buddha, but no matter how hard they tried I wouldn't go to see him."

Sigala pauses for a moment while he lowers his head and discreetly wipes a tear from his eye. "I wish now that I had listened to them and gone to the monastery to hear his discourses much earlier. It would have saved all of us a great deal of unnecessary heartache if I had learned the lesson on friends much earlier."

"What do you mean by that, Sigala?" asks Upali as he shifts from one elbow to the other, listening intently to Sigala's story.

"Do you see my four friends here with me? They are all the sons of wealthy merchants from Rajagaha, as am I. We were all spoiled by the good life our parents so generously offered us, and I am sorry to say that we used their wealth and social position merely to indulge all of our sensual urges. We had no sense of family responsibility whatsoever."

Sanjaya speaks up and says, "That's putting it mildly, Sigala. We first tasted alcohol when we were about thirteen, and our first courtesan a year later. We were committed gamblers the year after that. We made a career out of wasting our time. We never took anything or anyone seriously, and our only thoughts were for momentary, reckless amusement."

"You were our leader, Sigala, the one that led us down that road. Fortunately, you also led us back after you met the Buddha," says Dilip, smiling.

"To be fair to Sigala, all three of you must admit that we were willing participants in all of his crazed misadventures," adds Anup. "We're lucky the Buddha found him that morning. If he hadn't, we might not even be alive today."

Pradeep speaks, "We were all on the verge of being expelled from our houses by our parents. In my case, they were completely fed up with my not coming home at night, wasting their money gambling, and refusing to comply with the family rules. The day before Sigala met the Buddha I had just been given my last warning."

No one speaks for a few moments, and the only audible sound is the gentle gurgle of one of the hot springs, just ten feet away. All five of the men hang their heads and look down at the plush, colorful carpet upon which they sit.

"So, Venerable Sirs," begins Sigala, "this is the way our lives were going when I met the Buddha. My father's death sobered me up to some extent for a while, but soon I was back to my old habits – full steam ahead. I have to admit that I influenced my friends in very negative ways, and for this I am truly sorry."

"Did your father's death greatly affect you?" asks Maha Kaccayana.

"It really shook me up, Venerable Sir," replies Sigala, seriously. "His death was very sudden – none of us expected it. One day he came home from his warehouse and complained of a headache. He took to his bed and my mother called the physician. By the following morning he was dead."

"I understand that before he died he gave you an instruction," says Bhaddiya.

"He told me that from that day forward I must pay homage every morning at dawn to the six directions. He knew I didn't know anything about the Buddha, the Dhamma or anything religious, so he told me to honor the gods of the directions. The truth is I didn't know anything about the gods he spoke of either – and didn't care. I think he just said that to try to make me wake up and worship something – at least until I might have the chance to meet the Master. I have a strong feeling that he had faith I would one day become the Buddha's disciple. I know that was his dying wish; my mother told me so later."

"So how did you worship the gods of the six directions?" asks Bakkula.

"After the initial shock of my father's sudden death I soon slipped back into my old habits," begins Sigala. "I just told you about my worthless lifestyle, which meant that I stayed out late every night drinking, gambling, womanizing, loitering in the streets, and carousing with my friends here.

"In our society, as you know, one cannot ignore the last instructions of one's dying father, so I gave orders to my servant to literally drag me out of bed every morning and pour a bucket of cold water on me. Then I would go outside the city walls, which weren't that far from our house, and bow to the six directions. I had seen the Brahmins do this since I was a child, so I tried to imitate them – not having a clue what I was doing. I only knew that I was obeying my dying father's last command."

"Maybe your father was thinking that practicing the yoga sun salutation would at least give you some physical exercise," adds Bakkula, always looking at the health angle.

"That may have been part of it – since he used to begin every day of his life with meditation and yoga *asanas*," agrees Sigala.

"So how did you come to meet the Buddha?" asks Maha Kaccayana.

"One morning I was standing in my spot outside the city walls, dripping wet from my servant's dousing, and the Buddha walked up to me on his way to collect alms. At first I wasn't aware of his presence, but then I heard a voice saying, 'Young householder, rising early in the morning, having come out from Rajagaha, in wet clothes and with wet hair, wherefore do you worship with palms together the various directions such as the East, the South, the West, the North, the Nadir, and the Zenith?'

"Through my morning haze I looked up at him, and for a moment I couldn't make any words come out of my mouth. I was completely awestruck by his aura; his divine body emanated a glow that equaled the rising sun. I simply stared at his radiant form for a few moments while trying to gather my wits. I felt a loving energy enveloping me that calmed me and made me feel safe. I had never seen a man whose body was so elegant and perfectly formed; grace flowed from his very fingertips. His eyes were shining with compassion, and his faint smile told me that he knew everything about me," says Sigala.

"What was your answer?" asks Anuruddha.

"I told him that I was worshipping the six directions, and that it was the last command of my dying father," answers Sigala.

"He said, 'Young householder, in the noble teaching, the six directions are not to be worshipped in this manner.'

"'How then, Venerable Sir, are the six directions to be worshipped in the noble teaching? May it please the *Bhagava* to teach me the proper way.'"

"The Buddha said, 'In that case, young householder, listen and bear it well in mind. I shall teach you.' Little did I know at that moment that what he told me would turn my wretched life completely upside down," says Sigala. "By this time there was quite a crowd around us. His holy presence had attracted a number of early-rising townspeople, and my servant had run back to my house to tell my mother the Buddha was talking to me. I spread out my cloak on a large rock, and offered it to the Buddha while I sat on the ground in front of him."

"Your mother came immediately, didn't she?" asks Sopaka.

"Even at her age, she practically ran all the way to where I sat with the Buddha," answers Sigala. "She came close to me, but the Buddha gave her a signal with his eyes not to come nearer. Then she stepped back and listened with all the others. I didn't know what to make of the whole scene."

"How did he begin his explanation?" asks Punna.

"He began by saying,

> "'Young householder, the noble disciple refrains from four acts of defilement, which are killing, stealing, telling lies, and committing sexual misconduct. The wise never praise them.
>
> "'He does no evil which is instigated by four factors, which are partiality, anger, ignorance of what is right or wrong, and fear. As the noble disciple is not led astray by these four factors...he does not commit evil.
>
> "'He does not indulge in six practices causing dissipation of wealth, which are indulgence in intoxicants that cause inebriety and negligence, sauntering in the streets at unseemly hours, frequenting shows and entertainments that promote inferior morality, addiction to gambling, associating with bad companions, and habitual idleness.
>
> "'Thus avoiding these fourteen evil things he covers the six directions and follows the path for success in both worlds. He has accomplished his tasks for this world as well as for the next. After death and dissolution of the body he is reborn in a happy *deva* world.'

"The Buddha's words stopped my mind dead in its tracks. I looked at my life and realized that I had indulged in all fourteen of those evil things. Quite frankly, I was so ashamed I didn't know what to say to him," says Sigala.

"According to the now-famous *sutta*, the Buddha went on to amplify the six practices causing the dissipation of wealth," comments Bakkula.

"Yes, he did," says Sigala. "He first explained the six evil consequences of indulgence in intoxicants, which cause inebriety and negligence, and inevitably the actual loss of wealth in this very life. These are: the liability to become involved in quarrels, susceptibility to illness and disease, loss of good name and reputation, indecent exposure of the body, and impairment of intelligence.

"He next explained the six evil consequences of sauntering in the streets at unseemly hours. This practice causes one to be unprotected and unguarded, one's children and wife to be unprotected and unguarded, one's property to be unprotected and unguarded, to be open to suspicion in regard to crimes and evil deeds, subject to false accusations, and having to face many troubles.

"Then he explained the six evil consequences of frequenting shows and entertainments that promote inferior morality. These are caused by one habitually enquiring: Where is the dancing? Where is the music? Where is the recitation? Where is the playing of cymbals? Where is the beating of drums?'"

Bhaddiya chuckles and speaks, "In other words, 'where is the action'?"

Sigala and his friends nod their heads in the affirmative.

"I think we should make it clear that the Buddha wasn't condemning dancing, music, and dramatic performances in general," interjects Punna. "He was referring to being addicted to entertainments that were unwholesome and led to suffering."

"Thank you for that clarification," says Maha Kassapa. "Please proceed, Sigala."

"When the Buddha explained the six evil consequences of gambling I felt great remorse for having wasted so much of my family's money. These six are: 'As a winner he begets enmity; as a loser he grieves over his loss; there is actual loss in this very life; his word is not relied upon in a court of law; he is despised by his friends and companions; he is not sought after as a partner in marriage or business.'"

Sigala hangs his head in remorse as he reflects on the impact gambling and its six evil consequences had had on his own life.

In a few moments Sigala begins again, "The Buddha then explained the six evil consequences of associating with bad companions." Sigala looks at his four friends and gives them a warm smile. They look back at him with compassion and understanding. "He said that one suffers greatly in this life and the next when he associates only with gamblers, libertines, drunkards, swindlers, cheats, and those who are aggressive and violent.

"He explained the six evil consequences of habitual idleness next, and it made me realize that in my twenty-something years I had accomplished nothing. My privileges and advantages had only made me lazy. These six are: 'He does no work, saying it is too cold; he does no work, saying it is too hot; he does no work, saying it is too late in the evening; he does no work, saying it is too early in the morning; he does no work, saying he is too hungry; he does no work, saying he is too full.' He also said, 'Thus making such lame excuses he leaves many duties undone, not acquiring new wealth, but wasting away such wealth as he has already accumulated.'

"Then the Buddha began to tell me all about bad friends and practices. He uttered these verses for my benefit – and I'm sure for the benefit of all miscreants in the future:

> "'There are drinking companions, and there are those who are friends only in one's presence. These are not true friends. There is one who proves to be a comrade in times of crisis. This is indeed a true friend.
>
> "'Sleeping 'till the sun is high, committing adultery, begetting enmity, engaging in unbeneficial activities, keeping evil companions and being extremely stingy: these are the six causes that bring ruin to a man.
>
> "'He who has bad friends and evil companions, who is given to bad ways and is moving in bad circles is heading for ruin both in this world and the next.
>
> "'Playing dice, womanizing, drinking, dancing and singing, sleeping during the daytime, sauntering at unseemly hours, having evil companions, and stinginess: these six causes bring a man to ruin.'

"He told me:

> "'Playing dice, indulging in drinking, misbehaving with women who are dear as life to other men, and with women who are sought after by the base and are shunned by the wise: the fame and following of such people fade away just like the moon in the waning half of the month.
>
> "'The destitute drunkard, feeling thirsty, frequents liquor shops. As a stone sinks in water, he becomes immersed in debt to be soon disowned and rejected by his relatives.

"'He who habitually sleeps in the day, indulges in immoral entertainments at night, is always drunk, and is debauched cannot manage a household.

"'Chances and opportunities pass by the young man who says it is too hot, too cold, too late, and leaves things undone.

"'But for him who does not consider cold or heat any more than a blade of grass, and who dutifully attends to the affairs of men: happiness and prosperity do not decline.'"

Sigala pauses and lowers his head, deep in thought.

Maha Kassapa says, "I guess the Buddha really gave you a lot to think about that morning, didn't he?"

"Indeed he did, Venerable Sir. I was practically reeling from the force of his powerful words. I tried my best to absorb it all. I covered my head in shame in front of this perfect human being. I felt that I had wasted everything, and that I could never make a new start," says Sigala with great sadness. "I also realized that I had dragged my four best friends down the road of depravity with me."

Sanjaya raises his voice, "You really didn't have to drag us too hard, Sigala. We were willing participants in your lifestyle, and we happily accepted your ways."

"We've been over this many times, Sigala," adds Dilip. "You don't need to feel guilty about anything. At the time we were not only grown men, but false friends as well. We didn't know any better until you taught us what the Buddha explained to you that morning."

"Speaking of 'false friends,' the Buddha's next message that fateful day was on this very subject," begins Sigala. "He said:

"'Young householder, these four types should be regarded as false friends pretending to be true friends:

"'The friend who only takes, the friend who only renders lip service, the friend who flatters, and the friend who brings about loss of wealth – the wise should know these four as false friends and avoid them from a distance as from a path of danger.'

"The next thing the Buddha said was, 'Young householder, these four should be regarded as true-hearted friends:

"'The friend who is helpful, the friend who is the same in prosperity and adversity, the friend who gives good counsel, and the friend who understands and sympathizes – the wise should know these four as true-hearted friends and cherish them with devotion as a mother cherishes the child of her own bosom.

"'The wise man of virtue shines bright like a blazing fire.

"'The riches of a person who acquires his wealth in harmless ways is like a bee which gathers honey without damaging the flowers, and grows, little by little, as an anthill grows.

"'Having acquired wealth in this manner, the young man able to set up a household should divide his wealth into four portions:

"'He should spend and enjoy one portion; he should use two portions to run his business; and the fourth should be reserved for use in emergencies.'

"The Buddha explained false friends and true-hearted friends in detail, using many useful examples. Later this same day I gathered my four friends that are here with me today and told them what the Buddha taught me," says Sigala.

Anup speaks, "This was a true day of reckoning for all of us, and we made a pact that we would change."

"We decided that we only wanted to be true-hearted friends for one another, and we have been ever since that day," adds Pradeep.

"We chose to give up our unwholesome lifestyle and stop gambling, lazing around, womanizing, and drinking. The four of us sought the Buddha that very night and asked him if we could become lay disciples," says Sanjaya.

Ananda looks at the other members of the sub-committee and says, "The Master never failed to reach the heart of the person he sought – as he did in Sigala's case. He knew that Sigala was ripe for change. He also knew the ripple effect his words would have, and he foresaw that Sigala's false friends would become these true-hearted friends who are here with him today."

"Look at what they have become, too," says Bakkula with a big smile. "They look as healthy as teenagers, having reversed the negative effects of their unwholesome habits by adopting wholesome ones."

"Not just their wholesome physical habits, mind you," says Bhaddiya, "but their mental habits as well. I can tell by looking at them that they have practiced the Dhamma thoroughly to the best of their abilities, and have shared it with their beautiful families. We saw the results today at the *dana* ceremony when they served us so graciously. The purity of their hearts was visible on their faces, and the virtue of their lives shone in their clear, clean auras."

"Tell us now about the Buddha's instructions on the six directions," says Maha Kassapa.

Sigala begins by saying, "When the Buddha finished telling me about true-hearted friends he said:

> "'Young householder, how does the noble disciple cover the six directions? Young householder, these six directions should be known thus: the parents should be looked upon as the East, the teachers as the South, wife and children as the West, friends and associates as the North, servants and employees as the Nadir, and *samanas* and *brahmanas* as the Zenith.'"

"Didn't the Buddha's explanation include reciprocal instructions for the six groups he mentioned?" asks Punna.

"Yes it did, Venerable Sir, and I will share the way the instructions work both ways. First of all, the Lord said in regards to the parents:

> "'…In five ways should a son minister to the parents as the Eastern quarter thus: My parents have supported me, therefore, I shall support them in return; I shall manage affairs on their behalf; I shall maintain the honor and tradition of the family; I shall make myself worthy of their inheritance; and furthermore, I shall offer alms on behalf of the departed parents.

> "'Young householder, the parents look after the children in five ways: they restrain them from evil, they encourage them to do good, they give them education and professional training, they introduce suitable partnerships for the children, and they hand over property as inheritance to them at the proper time.'"

Ananda says, "It seems that the Buddha chose the Eastern direction for the parents because the sun rises in the east. The symbol of the rising sun represents life coming from the parents, a new beginning, the passing on of old tools, lifestyles, and traditions to the newborn son or daughter."

The arahants on the sub-committee smile with appreciation for Ananda's metaphor, as do Sigala and his four true-hearted friends.

"The Buddha then said," begins Sigala:

> "'Young householder, in five ways should a pupil minister to a teacher as the Southern quarter: by rising from the seat to greet and salute the teacher; by attending and waiting upon the teacher; by paying close attention to the words of the teacher; by offering personal service to the teacher; and by learning and receiving the teacher's instructions with respectful attention.
>
> "'Young householder, the teacher looks after the pupil in five ways: he instructs the pupil well in what should be instructed; he teaches well what should be taught; he trains the pupil in all the arts and sciences; he entrusts the pupil to his friends and associates, and provides for protection in every quarter.'"

Anuruddha turns to Ananda and asks, "Do you have a metaphor for what the teacher represented by the South?"

"I always thought the Buddha referred to the teachers as the right hand, which in our society is the hand one always puts forward – in greeting, in accepting things, and even when eating. The teacher becomes the right hand of the pupil's training, which in turn becomes the right hand of his entire life. Another way of looking at it is, if one stands in the center of the circle and faces the parents in the East; the South is directly on the right hand."

"Very good analogy, Venerable Sir," says Maha Kassapa. "Please continue, Sigala."

"Then the Buddha said:

> "'Young householder, in five ways should a husband minister to a wife as the Western quarter: by being courteous to her and addressing her in endearing terms; by showing respect to her and not disparaging her; by being faithful to her; by giving her control and authority over domestic matters; by providing her with clothing and ornaments.
>
> "'Young householder, the wife attends upon the husband in five ways: she discharges well her various duties; she is hospitable and generous to kith and kin from both sides of the family; she is faithful to her husband; she manages well what he earns and brings to her; she is skilled and industrious in performing all her tasks.'"

Without being asked, Ananda volunteers, "The Buddha used the symbol of the West because the sun sets in the west at the close of every day. Ideally, the husband and the wife will be together until death separates them at the end of their lives."

"All of us learned this lesson well," says Anup, "and we have never been unfaithful to our wives from that day to now."

"Speaking of wives," interjects Dilip, "up until that time I had never so much as given my wife a single flower for her birthday. You can imagine how cranky she was about my poor treatment of her. Since the Buddha's discourse to Sigala, I remember her every year with jewels and silks. You saw earlier today how happy she is." The arahants smile and nod their approval of Dilip's generosity towards his wife.

"The Buddha next explained the five ways a man of good family should minister to his friends and associates in the Northern quarter," begins Sigala. "He said that he should give generously; be pleasant and courteous in speech; be helpful; treat them as he treats himself; be true to his words and promises.

> "'Young householder, the friends and associates should look after him in return in these five ways: they protect the inebriated or the temporarily mentally impaired friend; they guard over his property when he is

inebriated or impaired; they become a refuge when he is in trouble; they do not forsake him in troubles; they even help his descendants whenever they can.'"

"The Buddha compared friends and associates to the North because the needle of the compass always points to the northern direction," says Ananda. "I believe that he felt that true friends would never waver – they would always be there to support one another in times of need, and point them down the right path in all instances."

"When we made our pact that day to help keep each other on the right path, Venerable Ananda, I myself thought about your example of the compass, and I mentioned it to my friends," says Dilip. "I am very happy that you and I share the same idea."

Ananda smiles at the prosperous householder and says, "The North, therefore, represents the quality of loyalty, which you and your friends have consistently proven by your actions. You have demonstrated your loyalty to one another, and your loyalty to living the precepts and following the Dhamma." Dilip smiles at his four friends, and it is clear to the arahants that their pact of loyalty is secure and will not be broken.

"The Buddha next explained how one should minister to his servants and employees as the Nadir, or the direction below:

> "'In these five ways: by assigning the work in accordance with their ability and physical strength; by giving them food and remuneration; by looking after them in sickness; by treating them the same way they would their own family; by granting them leave from time to time.
>
> "'Young householder, the servants and employees should attend upon the employer in five ways: they rise before him; they go to sleep after him; they take only what is given; they perform their duties well; they uphold his good name and reputation.'"

Ananda adds, "I believe that the Buddha used the direction below, the earth or ground, as the symbol for servants and employees because it represents the foundation of our earthly activities and pursuits. Without the earth we can do nothing. The earth brings forth food, shelter, clothing, and all forms of material wealth."

"Most of us have farms," adds Pradeep, "and we depend on our employees to care for what nature gives us. Everything in the physical realm comes from the earth, and we depend on those in our employ to help us manage the blessings that it brings forth. We five friends understand this principle, and this is why we never have a problem finding employees. Everyone knows that we look after our people better than anyone else does. Our employees are like our own families in this respect, and we cherish them."

Sigala smiles at his friends and says, "Before meeting the Buddha that fateful day I barely even noticed my family's servants and employees. I took what they offered as if I was entitled to it, and I lived off the fruits of their labor because I felt it was my birthright. It was only after the Buddha's discourse that I learned that employer and employee are actually a team; there cannot be one without the other; we each depend upon one another for our mutual survival and benefit."

"Now, Sigala, please tell us about the last direction – the Zenith," requests Maha Kassapa.

"The Buddha said:

"'Young householder, in five ways should a man of good family minister to the *samanas* and *brahmanas* as the Zenith, the direction above: by deeds of loving-kindness; by words of loving kindness; by thoughts of loving-kindness; by keeping the house open to them; by supplying them with material needs such as alms food.

"'Young householder, the *samanas* and *brahmanas* bring benefit to you in six ways: they restrain you from evil; they exhort you to do good; they protect you with loving kindness; they teach you the profound matters that you *have not* heard before; they explain and make clear to you the profound matters which you *have* heard before; they show you the path to the realm of the *devas*.'"

"The Zenith or direction above is the sky, or the heavens above," begins Ananda. "It is also the direction of the sun, the source of all life on earth. The Buddha always exhorted us to 'look up' and strive for the heights of spiritual wisdom and understanding. Religious teachers are represented by the sky because we are taught to look to them for guidance. They are the keepers of the knowledge of the universe, and without them we have no way to rise above mundane earthly matters and strive for *Nibbana*, or universal perfection, as exemplified by the Buddha himself."

"Well said, Venerable Sir," says Maha Kassapa. "The Buddha's emphasis on *metta*, or loving-kindness, is also a very important element to mention. This is the energy that powers the universe, and the one we can all tap into when we deal with associates from all six directions."

Everyone in the tented enclosure nods in agreement with the wise chairman. It is obvious from the demeanor of the five true-hearted friends that they practice loving-kindness toward themselves, as well as toward all beings in all directions.

"From that day onward I held the Buddha and members of his Sangha in a completely new light," says Anup. "All five of us have since offered *dana* to the Sangha members on a daily basis, and we have reserved time out of our busy schedules for Dhamma study with the *bhikkhus*, and for meditation."

"If I may," says Sigala, "I would like to quote the verses that the Buddha gave me after passing on all of this information. I might add that after he recited these words I prostrated myself before him and asked to become a lay disciple for life."

"Sigala immediately ran to us to share the good news that changed all our lives after the Buddha accepted him," says Anup, beaming.

"Please proceed, Sigala," says the chairman who is smiling broadly.

Sigala closes his eyes, and prepares himself for the recitation. Ananda looks at the wise householder with great admiration for the fact that he has memorized these important sacred verses – as well as the many he had already quoted.

> "'The mother and the father are the East; the teachers are the South; wife and children are the West; friends and associates are the North.
>
> "'Servants and employees are the Nadir; *samanas* and *brahmanas* are the Zenith; the man of good family who is the head of a household should worship these six directions.
>
> "'Whoever is skilled and wise in worshiping these six directions, and is full of moral virtues, is gentle and keen-witted, meek and humble, gains fame and followers.

"'Whoever is energetic and not indolent, unshaken in adversity, constantly employed in making a livelihood, endowed with resourceful intelligence, gains fame and followers.

"'Whosoever is benevolent, seeks and makes good friends, understands what is spoken by a benefactor, is not stingy or jealous, leads and guides by giving helpful counsel and reasoned advice, gains fame and followers.

"'There are these benevolent practices, namely, generosity and charitableness, pleasant speech, helpfulness to others, impartial treatment to all as to oneself as the case demands; in this world these four benevolent practices are like the lynchpin of a moving carriage.

"'Were these benevolent practices non-existent in the world, the mother would not receive honor and respect from her children; the father would not receive honor and respect from his children.

"'Because the wise observe these four benevolent practices in every way, they reach eminence, and gain praise and admiration.'"

The arahants in the enclosure smile in appreciation for Sigala's obvious compliance with the wise advice of the Buddha. They can see that he has taken the Master's message to heart and has inculcated it into his life.

Upali, who has been silent during this discussion, speaks, "This *sutta* could be called the 'guidelines of discipline for lay people.' In a single discourse the Buddha set down suggestions for creating a happy life so lay people can gain the fruits of virtuous living."

"Very true, Venerable Upali," says Maha Kassapa. "Sigala, your transformation led to the transformation of your four friends here, and theirs to their families and countless others within their spheres of influence."

"Don't forget to tell us about your dear mother," says Punna knowingly.

"Yes, my wonderful mother," responds Sigala. "When she heard this discourse she immediately attained *sotapanna* and asked the Buddha for ordination as a *bhikkhuni*."

Ananda says, "She became known as Sigalamatu Theri, 'The *Bhikkhuni* Mother of Sigala.' I knew her very well, as did many here in this council. She had great faith, meditated on insight, and eventually attained arahantship. The Lord declared that she was the 'Foremost in Conviction Among the *Bhikkhunis.*'"[3]

"She made many priceless contributions to the Buddha *Sasana* during the course of her life," adds Maha Kaccayana. "We know that she passed into *parinibbana* just a year ago, Sigala. You must still feel her loss."

"She and my father remain forever in my heart, Venerable Sir. I know that I am now living the life they always wished for me. I will always be grateful for their patience and forbearance when I wasn't," replies Sigala with great emotion.

The chairman says, "The sun is now setting; it is time for the five of you to get back to your wives and families. Your contribution today to this recollection of the life of the Buddha has been invaluable, and we offer you our sincere gratitude. The example of your lives will demonstrate to lay people of future generations the benefits of living by the words of the Buddha. The happy, prosperous, healthy lives you have created are a testament to his great wisdom."

Sigala and his friends rise from the carpet and approach the dais where the eight esteemed arahants are seated. One by one they prostrate themselves and receive their silent blessings.

The faces of the five friends are radiant as they stand. There are tears of gratitude in all of their eyes, which reflect the timelessness of the words of the Buddha that have forever changed their lives. When they walk from the canopied enclosure the only sound is the gurgling of the hot springs just beyond.

After the footsteps of Sigala, Sanjaya, Anup, Dilip, and Pradeep are heard below on the path Ven. Maha Kassapa says, "Those five fine householders in the prime of their lives were given a second chance, thanks to the intervention of the Buddha. How many more can achieve the same by hearing the Master's sacred words?"

The other arahants nod their agreement, and then stand to leave the pleasant enclosure. They pause for a moment to observe the setting of the sun, and in unison they themselves turn around silently to pay homage to the symbols of unity represented by the six directions.

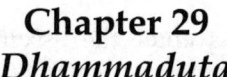

Chapter 29
Dhammaduta

Ananda and Maha Kassapa sit side by side on a large boulder on the edge of a promontory overlooking the lush green valley below Mount Vebhara. The sun is just about to rise and a dark blue glow fills the eastern sky. The two arahants are wrapped tightly in their outer robes to protect themselves against the morning chill, and they look up just in time to see a shooting star arc across the sky. Ananda points to it and Maha Kassapa smiles.

"The council has been a big success so far, my friend. The Buddha *Sasana* of the past, present, and future owes you a monumental debt for organizing it," says Ananda. "The Dhamma could have quickly-faded like that meteor – had it not been for your diligence in protecting it by bringing us together to preserve it forever in a codified system."

"I just couldn't sit by and watch the Dhamma deteriorate after so many *bhikkhus* and *bhikkhunis* spent their lives walking barefoot throughout India teaching it to whoever wanted to listen," replies the chairman. "Many of our Sangha brothers from the early days have already passed away, as has the Lord. The younger ones and the ones who haven't yet ordained – or who haven't yet been born – need to have a solid foundation in Dhamma when they travel the world and propagate the Buddha's message."

"And travel they will, I'm sure; just as we have. The Buddha called us swans: plain birds that have the capacity to venture far," says Ananda.

"And he called lay people peacocks: beautiful birds encumbered by their luxuriant tails – unable to fly great distances," adds Maha Kassapa.

The two arahants chuckle over the avian metaphors, and stand up to begin their walk toward the assembly hall.

"I'm amazed whenever I think about the wanderers we have become. We were once so ensconced in our luxurious, comfortable lives as lay people that such a life never even occurred to us," says Ananda, smiling. "For over four decades we have essentially been without permanent homes. I could never have imagined that it would have turned out this way, or that I would be this happy."

The two senior monks enter the assembly hall. They take their places and the chairman begins the devotional chants. Afterwards, Ananda stands and says, "Today I will begin by reciting a short discourse the Buddha delivered to me about teaching the Dhamma to others:

> "'On one occasion while the Blessed One was dwelling at Kosambi...he said:
>
> "'It is not easy to teach the Dhamma to others. To teach the Dhamma to others one should set up in oneself five standards for doing so. What five?
>
> "'I shall give a gradual discourse.'
>
> "'I shall give a well-reasoned discourse.'
>
> "'Moved by sympathy I shall speak.'
>
> "'Not for the sake of worldly advantage I shall speak.'
>
> "'Without alluding to myself or to others I shall speak.'
>
> "'In these five ways should the Dhamma be taught to others.'" [1]

Ananda continues reciting until it is time for the morning break. When he steps down from the podium Maha Kassapa approaches him and says, "When we meet this evening, I think it might be a good idea to continue your theme of teaching the Dhamma."

"Once again we share the same thought, Venerable Sir," replies Ananda. "The Buddha taught many Dhamma teachers in his forty-five-year ministry, and they have traveled like swans spreading his message to many lands. I think our recollection of the life of the Lord should include some of his special instructions, and some examples of those who taught."

The two arahants proceed from the enclosure to where cool drinks are being served by a group of lay devotees from the city.

Late that evening in the chairman's cave chamber the nine arahants re-convene to continue their discussions. The memory monks are ready to receive their sacred transmissions.

"How did the Buddha determine who should teach the Dhamma and who should not?" asks Maha Kassapa.

Ananda replies, "Please allow me to quote a very short discourse the Buddha delivered on the subject of 'Messages.' I think this will help answer that question."

"'Monks, a monk endowed with eight qualities is worthy to be a Dhamma messenger. With what eight?

"'Herein, a monk is both a listener and one who makes others listen; both a learner and an instructor; both a knower and an expounder; one skilled in recognizing nonconformity from conformity, and not given to quarrelling.

"'Monks, Sariputta is so endowed and he is worthy to be a Dhamma messenger.

"'Who, to some high assembled council come,
Wavers not, nor in discourse fails, nor hides
The Master's word, nor speaks in doubtfulness,
Whoso by question ne'er is moved to wrath –
Worthy to be a Dhamma messenger is that monk.'" [2]

Bhaddiya says, "The Buddha was certainly right about Sariputta being such a well endowed and worthy Dhamma messenger. If the *Sasana* had a hundred monks who could teach at his level the world would already be completely Buddhist."

"As you know, Venerable Sir, making the world completely Buddhist was never the Lord's ambition," says Upali. "He knew well the fact that the world is ensnared by a vast diversity of opinions that could never be united as one. He never advised any of us to try to convert anyone."

"What you say is very true, Upali," responds Bhaddiya. "What I meant was, if there were a hundred monks with the enthusiasm, Dhamma knowledge, and talent for teaching that Sariputta had, the world could become free from suffering by following the Buddha's teaching." Upali seems satisfied with this clarification.

"We have come to call Buddhist propagation activities '*Dhammaduta*,'" says Punna. "Most of us here at this council, with the exception of a few meditation arahants, have spent our lives engaged in *Dhammaduta*. We have traveled throughout the land with only our alms bowls in our hands, doing our best to spread the truth contained in the Buddha's teachings."

"From our perpetual journeying we've all come to realize that the Dhamma spreads naturally through the living example of the Buddha's Sangha members," adds Anuruddha. "Even though doubts have been raised regarding the value of the Sangha, I think we have proven our worth just in terms of the countless lives we have helped."

Ananda speaks, "The Buddha once addressed this issue when he responded to a question made by a Brahmin named Sangarava. If you'll allow me, I'll quote briefly from the discourse." The arahants voice no objection, so Ananda begins:

> "The Brahmin stated, 'We are Brahmins, Master Gotama. We sacrifice and enjoin others to make sacrifices, so both engage in a meritorious practice; the offering of sacrifice extends to many persons. But a monk, one who goes forth from home into the ascetic life, he tames himself alone, calms himself alone, attains *Nibbana* for himself alone. If this is so, he then engages in a meritorious practice involving only one person.'
>
> "The Buddha answered: 'Well, Brahmin, I shall ask you a question and you may answer as you think fit. Now, Brahmin, what do you think of this: A *Tathagata* arises in the world, an arahant, fully enlightened...the Blessed One. He speaks thus: 'Come! This is the way; this is the path treading which I have directly known and realized that highest consummation of the holy life which I now proclaim. Come! You too should practice thus, so that you too, by your own effort, may directly know and realize this highest consummation of the holy life and dwell in its attainment!'
>
> "'Thus this teacher shows the Dhamma, and others too practice in that way. And of such who do so, there are many hundreds, many thousands, many hundreds of thousands. What do you think, Brahmin: since this is so, is that act of going forth into the ascetic life a meritorious practice involving only one person or many people?'
>
> "The Brahmin answered: 'Since it is so, Master Gotama, the going forth is a meritorious practice extending to many people.'"[3]

"This discourse demonstrates that the Buddha's teaching helps the world one heart and mind at a time," began Maha Kaccayana. "No lasting changes are ever made by using force; only by using the power of compassion and by illuminating the minds of willing listeners."

"The Buddha once gave a discourse to me regarding advice for new monks," says Ananda. "The Master knew that before they went out to perform *Dhammaduta* they should be thoroughly trained. He foresaw that they would experience many challenges, and he wanted them to be prepared for whatever they encountered."

"Why don't you quote a bit of this discourse for the record," requests Maha Kassapa.

Ananda begins, "The Buddha told me:

"'Ananda, those monks who are newcomers, who have recently gone forth and have just come to this Dhamma and Discipline, should be exhorted, settled and established...in five things. What five?

"'Come, friends, be virtuous, dwell restrained from unwholesome conduct, perfect in conduct and comportment, seeing danger in the slightest faults. Having undertaken the training rules, train yourselves in them;

"'Come, friends, dwell guarding the doors of the sense faculties, with mindfulness as guard, with discerning mindfulness, with a well-protected mind, with a mind maintaining mindfulness;

"'Come, friends, do not talk much, place limits on your talking;

"'Come, friends, be forest dwellers. Resort to remote lodgings in the forests and woodlands;

"'Come, friends, be of right view, of right perspective;

"'Those monks, Ananda, who are newcomers, who have recently gone forth and have just come to this Dhamma and Discipline, should be exhorted, settled, and established...in these five things.'"[4]

Upali says, "It has been proven that those five points of advice will establish new *bhikkhus* on the right path and keep them there through thick and thin."

"Some have better luck than others – like Sivali," begins Anuruddha. "He was a special case, though, and was blessed with abundance in this life because of a surfeit of meritorious deeds in the past. He never wanted for anything whenever he went abroad."

"Remember how other monks always wanted him to travel with them?" asks Bakkula. "If Sivali was part of the group there was never any shortage of alms food – no matter where they were."

"The words 'shortage' and 'Sivali' do not even belong in the same sentence," laughs Bhaddiya. "The Buddha called him the disciple who was 'Foremost in Abundance' for very good reasons."[5]

"Very few of the traveling *bhikkhus* consistently had the pleasant experiences Sivali did," adds Sopaka. "There are countless stories of hardship – some of them even involving death threats – that tell of what was endured by Sangha members on the *Dhammaduta* road."

"If I may," says Punna, "I'll share with you one of my favorites of those stories." The arahants smile at the venerable monk, encouraging him to speak.

"Do any of you remember Manikara Kulupaga Tissa?" asks Punna. Three of the arahants nod their heads in the affirmative.

"While on *Dhammaduta*, Venerable Tissa made friends with a goldsmith. While the other monks went out to collect alms food Tissa was invited to lunch by a friend of his, who also happened to be a royal jeweler. When Tissa arrived for the mid-day meal the goldsmith was cutting meat, and the man offered the monk a seat in the kitchen so they could chat while he cooked. The goldsmith's pet falcon was seated on a perch nearby – overseeing the kitchen operations with a keen eye.

"A messenger arrived from the palace with a large precious jewel that the king wanted to have mounted. The goldsmith accepted it from the messenger with a bloody hand, and set it down on the kitchen table. When he finished cutting the meat the man covered the jewel with a cloth and he left the room to wash his hands.

"When the goldsmith came back to the kitchen he picked up the cloth and discovered that the precious stone was missing. He asked his wife about it, but she knew nothing. The man and his wife searched the entire building, but it was nowhere to be found. He came back into the kitchen and said angrily to Tissa, 'Did you take the jewel that was sitting here?'

"The monk said, 'No, friend, I did not.'

"The goldsmith yelled at Tissa and said, 'Then what happened to it? It was here a few minutes ago, and no one has been in here but you!'

"Tissa kept quiet and said nothing. The goldsmith became very fearful for his life; the precious stone had been left in his care and he knew he would surely be put to death if it went missing. For a moment he completely lost his mind with fear and he struck the monk with his fist and tied him up. He threatened to kill him if he didn't admit where he had hidden the stone.

"The poor *bhikkhu* was bleeding copiously, and blood dripped onto his shoulder. Seeing the blood, the hungry falcon came to drink it. This made the goldsmith even more enraged so he struck the bird with his fist and it fell to the ground.

"The goldsmith picked up the bird and realized it was dead. Tissa then told his friend to examine the contents of the bird's stomach. When the goldsmith did this he discovered the precious gemstone; the bird had obviously swallowed it.

"The monk said, 'I saw your pet bird swallow the stone, but I kept silent, fearing for its life. As a monk, we have to keep quiet if we witness any event that may cause the taking of life.'

"The poor goldsmith was overcome by grief for what he had done not only to the bird, but to the monk. He begged Tissa for forgiveness, which was instantly granted."[6]

The arahants reflect quietly upon hearing this reminiscence. "Thank you for that wonderful story, Punna. I'm sure it will become a favorite of lay disciples down through the ages," comments Maha Kassapa.

"Let's not forget that the Buddha himself spent forty-five years doing *Dhammaduta*. He traveled continuously when it wasn't the rainy season," says Sopaka.

"He, too, had to put up with hardships of all sorts – even abuse from time to time," adds Bakkula.

"I remember a story that is recorded in one of the discourses," says Ananda. "It goes like this:

"'Thus I have heard: On one occasion when the Blessed One was dwelling in the Alavi country, he rested on a heap of leaves spread on a cattle track in a *simsapa* forest. At that time Hatthaka of Alavi passed that way while taking a walk, and there he saw the Blessed one. He said:

"'Venerable Sir, has the Blessed One slept well?'

"'Yes, prince, I have slept well. Among those in the world who always sleep well, I am one.'

"'But, Lord, the winter nights are cold and this is a week of frost. Hard is the ground trampled by the hoofs of the cattle, thin is the spread of leaves, sparse are the leaves on the trees, thin are the tawny monk's robes and cold blows the wind. Yet the Blessed One says that he has slept well and that he is one of those in the world who always sleeps well.'

"'Now, prince, I shall put a question to you about this and you may reply as you think fit. What do you think of this, prince? Suppose there is a householder living in a house with a gabled roof, plastered inside and out, protected against the wind, with fastened door bolts and windows closed. And there is a couch in the house, covered with a long-fleeced, black woolen rug, with a bedspread of white wool...Also a lamp is burning there and his four wives attend on him pleasantly. What do you think, prince: would that person sleep well or not, or what is your opinion about this?'

"'He will surely sleep well, Lord. He will be one of those in the world who sleeps well.'

"'What do you think, prince? Might there not arise in that householder vexations of body or mind caused by lust, hatred and delusion, which torment him so that he would sleep badly?'

"'That may well be so, Lord.'

"'Now, prince, the lust, hatred and delusion by which that householder is tormented, and which would cause him to sleep badly, have been abandoned by the *Tathagata*, cut off at the root, made barren like palm-tree stumps, obliterated so that they are no more subject to arise in the future. Therefore, prince, I have slept well.'

> "'The Brahmin who is quenched within
> Always sleeps happily;
> He does not cling to sensual desire,

> Free from props, one cool in mind.
> Having cut all straps of attachment,
> Removed care deep within the heart,
> The peaceful One sleeps happily,
> Attained to perfect peace of mind.'" [7]

When Ananda finishes reciting the discourse all of the arahants in the cave chamber smile with pleasure. They, too, always sleep well.

"Even though the Buddha was out in the cold, sleeping on a heap of leaves, he never complained," begins Bhaddiya, "he turned that hardship into an opportunity to teach the Dhamma. This is the true spirit of *Dhammaduta!*"

"Sleeping on a heap of leaves reminds me of another short discourse the Buddha once delivered from the *Dighacarika Sutta*. If I may?" asks Ananda.

"Of course, dear friend, and who would want to stop you?" jokes Maha Kassapa.

Ananda kindly ignores the remark and begins, "The Lord said:

> "'Monks, there are these five advantages to one who spends his days wandering afield. What five?
> "'One hears what one has not heard before;
> "'One gets rid of unnecessary things that one has already heard;
> "'One becomes an expert on things that you hear again;
> "'One will never be stricken with some chronic disease;
> "'And one will always have friends.' [8]"

Bakkula speaks, "Perfect health in body, mind, and spirit are the possessions of one who keeps on the move. Each one of us is a perfect example of this teaching of the Master."

"Perhaps you more than the rest of us," says Bhaddiya. "You've never had a single sick day in your entire life of one hundred-five years!"

"I attribute that to good *kamma*, and happy travels," replies the revered elder monk with a twinkle in his eye.

"The short discourse I just recited goes along well with this one," says Ananda:

"'Monks, there are these five advantages from not staying too long in one place. What five?'

'One doesn't collect a massive amount of belongings;
'One doesn't collect an over-abundance of medicine;
'One doesn't have many duties, things to do, or any concern about them;
'One doesn't have to live with householders and wanderers, mix with them frequently, or become averse to the company of laymen;
'When one leaves that place, one leaves it happily and with no regret.'9"

"Each phrase of that discourse is absolutely true from my perspective," says Bhaddiya. "The eight requisites for a monk is all I've owned for over four decades, and I'll never own more; my only duty is to share the Dhamma, which is a joy; I never wear out my welcome, so people are always happy to see me when I return; and since I'm always in the present moment, I'm happy wherever I am. This is a grand life!" He smiles blissfully, expressing great joy for his *Dhammaduta* lifestyle, which is in a constant state of motion.

"Not everyone is happy to be a wandering *bhikkhu* like you," says Maha Kaccayana.

"That is very true," says Bhaddiya. "It takes a certain type of man or woman to dedicate him or herself to wandering the earth and putting up with all sorts of difficulties just to share the Dhamma. Not everyone is cut out for it."

"Do you remember Sunakkhatta?" asks Ananda. "He was never able to achieve the full fruit of enlightenment, so he left the Order and wound up suffering, deluded, and gravely disappointed." The majority of the nine arahants in the cave chamber shake their heads in the affirmative, recalling their memory of the unhappy monk from Vesali.

Upali speaks, "I remember him very well. He didn't like living by the disciplinary rules of the *Vinaya*, and he was obsessed with miracles."

"Why don't you share his story with us, Ananda, since you brought up his name," suggests Maha Kassapa.

"I will recite from the *Patika Sutta*," responds Ananda. "I always find the words in the *suttas* are better than mine, so I prefer to use them whenever I can."

"Go right ahead," says Maha Kassapa. "You're the one who has all of them memorized." The arahants laugh softly at the chairman's remark.

Ananda begins his recitation:

"'...the wanderer Bhaggavagotta said: 'Come, Blessed Lord, welcome. At last the Blessed Lord has gone out of his way to come here. Be seated, Lord.' The Lord sat down on the prepared seat, and Bhaggavagotta took a low stool and sat down to one side. Then he said: 'Lord, a few days ago Sunakkhatta the Licchavi came to me and said: 'Bhaggavagotta I have left the Blessed Lord. I am no longer under his rule.' Is that really so, Lord?'

"'It is true, Bhaggavagotta. A few days ago Sunakkhatta came to me and said: 'Lord, I am leaving the Blessed Lord; I am no longer under the Lord's rule.'

"'So I said to him: 'Well, Sunakkhatta, did I ever say to you: 'Come, Sunakkhatta, and be under my rule'?'

"'No, Lord,' responded Sunakkhatta.

"'So, Sunakkhatta, if I did not say that to you and you did not say that to me – you foolish man, who are you and what are you giving up? Consider, unwise man, how far the fault is yours.'

"'Well, Lord, you have not performed any miracles.'

"'And did I ever say to you: 'Come under my rule, Sunakkhatta, and I will perform miracles for you'?'

"'No, Lord,' replied Sunakkhatta.

"'Or did you ever say to me: 'Lord, I will be under your rule if you will perform miracles for me'?'

"'No, Lord.'

"'Then it appears, Sunakkhatta, that I made no such promises, and you made no such conditions. Such being the case, you unwise man, who are you and what are you giving up? ...

"'...And I say to you, I declare to you, Sunakkhatta, there will be those who will say: 'Sunakkhatta the Licchavi was unable to maintain the holy life under the ascetic Gotama, and being thus unable he abandoned the training and reverted to a base life.' That, Sunakkhatta, is what they will say.' And, Bhaggavagotta, at my words Sunakkhatta left this Dhamma and discipline like one condemned to hell.'" [10]

"Thank you for quoting that discourse, Ananda," says Anuruddha. "Even though the Buddha knew how to perform miracles, he had no intention of displaying them just to gain fame or followers. As we all know, he forbade us to perform them as well – for the same reason. Monks who are obsessed by miracles have no place in the Sangha."

Ananda says, "The Lord often stated that he was only interested in having monks in the Order that truly wanted to be there; those that chose to live by the Dhamma. Sunakkhatta made it very clear that the Dhamma wasn't enough for him, so he decided to leave. The Buddha's policy, as we all know, was never to try to keep someone in the Order forcefully, or against their will."

"Not to change the subject, but it's interesting to see how the varying temperaments of the monks gradually evolved into two basic groups: meditators, and Dhamma scholars who did *Dhammaduta* activities," says Punna. "I wonder if this will persist in the future, or if this is only a passing phase of Sangha evolution."

"Only time will tell, dear friend," responds Bhaddiya.

"This subject reminds me of a discourse delivered by Maha Cunda," begins Ananda.

> "'Thus I have heard. On one occasion the Venerable Maha Cunda was dwelling at Sahajati among the Ceti people. There he addressed the monks thus:
>
> "'There are Dhamma-experts who praise only monks who are also Dhamma-experts, but not those who are meditators. And there are meditators who praise only those monks who are also meditators but not those who are Dhamma-experts. Thereby neither of them will be pleased, and they will not be practicing for the welfare and happiness of the multitude, for the good of the multitude, for the welfare and happiness of *devas* and humans.

"'Therefore, friends, you should train yourselves thus: 'Though we ourselves are Dhamma-experts, we will also praise those monks who are meditators.' And why? Such outstanding men are rare in the world who have personal experience of the deathless *Nibbana*.

"'And the other monks, too, should train themselves thus: 'Though we ourselves are meditators, we will also praise those monks who are Dhamma experts.' And why? Such outstanding persons are rare in the world who can, by their wisdom, clearly understand a difficult subject.'" [11]

Maha Kassapa says, "I know recitation is your specialty, Venerable Sir, and you are quoting a lot this evening, which is unusual. Please allow me to quote one short verse that encourages the monks to be well-rounded in both the Dhamma – and in the solitary practice of meditation."

Ananda smiles and says kindly, "Of course, Venerable Chairman, I didn't mean to dominate the meeting with so many recitations. Please quote to your heart's content."

Maha Kassapa raises his eyebrows, then smiles at his friend's comment and begins,

"'...Take the case of the monk who masters the Dhamma: the discourses, the sayings, the verses, and so forth. He does not spend the whole day only engaged in the mastery of the Dhamma, he does not neglect seclusion, he applies himself to internal tranquility of mind, and he further understands its meaning with wisdom. Verily, such a monk is one who lives by the Dhamma.'"[12]

"I think the true spirit of the monk living by the Dhamma, living on the road in *Dhammaduta* activities, and still keeping up his practice of meditation, is well-expressed by the determined example of Venerable Punna. Not you, Venerable Punna Mantaniputta, but another by the same first name," says Bakkula, nodding to his brother monk.

"Why don't you tell us about him," says Maha Kassapa.

"I don't pretend to have the greatest of memories for recitation, as do my esteemed colleagues, but I will do my best – paraphrasing the *Salayatanavagga* if I need to. I knew this determined, dedicated monk very well, and it pleases me that his account will be recorded in our recollections," answers Bakkula in his robust voice. The other arahants turn their attention to Bakkula, and he begins:

"Venerable Punna approached the Blessed One and asked him to teach the Dhamma in brief so that he could go forth to share it with others.

"'Now ...Punna, in which country will you dwell?'

"'There is, Venerable Sir, a country named Sunaparanta. I will dwell there.'

"'Punna, the people of Sunaparanta are wild and rough. If they abuse and revile you, what will you think about them?'

"'Venerable Sir, if the people of Sunaparanta abuse and revile me, then I will think: 'These people of Sunaparanta are excellent, truly excellent, because they do not give me a blow with the fist.'

"'But Punna, if they do give you a blow with the fist, what will you think about them then?'

"'Venerable Sir, I will still think they are excellent because they do not give me a blow with a clod.'

"'But, Punna, if they give you a blow with a clod, what will you think about them then?'

"'Venerable Sir, I will still think they are excellent because they do not give me a blow with a rod.'

"'But, Punna, if they give you a blow with a rod, what will you think about them then?'

"'Venerable Sir, I will still think they are excellent because they do not stab me with a knife.'

"'But, Punna, if they stab you with a knife, what will you think about them then?'

"'Venerable Sir, I will still think they are excellent because they do not take my life with a sharp knife.'

"'But, Punna, if the people of Sunaparanta do take your life with a sharp knife, what will you think about them then?'

"'Venerable Sir, if they take my life with a sharp knife, then I will think: There have been disciples of the Blessed One who, being repelled, humiliated, and disgusted by the body and by life, sought for an assailant. But I have come upon this assailant even without a search.'

"'Good, Punna! Endowed with such self-control and peacefulness, you will be able to dwell in the Sunaparanta country. Now, Punna, you may go at your own convenience.'

"'Wandering by stages, he eventually arrived in the Sunaparanta country, where he dwelt establishing five hundred male lay followers and five hundred female lay followers in the practice, and he himself, during that same rains, realized the three true knowledges and he attained final *Nibbana*.' [13]"

When the arahants hear Bakkula relate this story they smile in appreciation for a hero of the *Sasana* who risked his life to spread the Dhamma.

"During these past four decades there must have been countless Sangha members who were just as fearless, just as dedicated, and just as full of loving-kindness, who gave up their comfortable lives at home – and then at their monasteries – to lead the *Dhammaduta* life," says Bhaddiya.

"And not one of them ever coerced anyone to change their beliefs, or ever spilled one drop of blood in their efforts to teach a single person the Dhamma," says Maha Kassapa. "Our record is blameless and spotless. May it be so for all time to come."

The arahants instinctively know that their discussion has come to a close. The story of *Dhammaduta* has been told, and it is now time for rest and meditation.

They rise from their seats, bow to their seniors and then silently file from the torch-lit cave. They know that as soon as their work at the First Sangha Council comes to an end, most of them will be happily back on the road.

Chapter 30
Ajatasattu

King Ajatasattu and his retinue of royal guards and attendants wait respectfully at the entrance to the *dana* pavilion adjacent to the assembly hall. He has come to serve the Sangha members with his own hand on this particular day. The queen isn't with him on this occasion, and he looks like he hasn't slept well. His mood is pensive and he seems somewhat distracted.

Ananda and Maha Kassapa, leading the procession, are deep in discussion. "I hope I made the right decision inviting the king to our sub-committee meeting this afternoon," says Maha Kassapa.

"Even though King Ajatasattu has done his best to make amends for his father's death eight years ago, I know he must be nervous about having his story recorded in our recollections," responds Ananda.

"It is impossible to talk about the rebellion and eventual demise of Devadatta without exposing the king's role in those sordid events; and I think it will be good for him to tell the truth about it," says the chairman. "Even though he alone has to live out the consequences of his past *kammic* actions, I believe his confession to the sub-committee will be cathartic, and will help to relieve him of some of the guilt he carries."

"He has been a completely devoted disciple of the Buddha, the Dhamma, and the Sangha ever since those dark days, and he has acquired considerable merit by performing countless good deeds – including sponsoring this council," says Ananda. "However, if he wants to experience a healing from that tragic period, I agree that his participation at our proceedings this afternoon will be of great benefit for him."

"I know he is feeling very vulnerable today, which is an unusual feeling for a king," says Maha Kassapa. "I have nothing but compassion for the man, as you know, but in life we all have to be accountable for our actions – no matter who we are."

The two senior Sangha members nod at one another and then approach King Ajatasattu who bows low to them and touches their feet with great respect. His chief ministers do the same.

"I am honored to have the opportunity to personally serve you again, Venerable Sirs," says the king.

"Thank you for the *dana*, and for agreeing to attend our sub-committee proceedings this afternoon, Your Majesty. I have no doubt that your contribution will be most valuable," says Ananda. "Your willingness, especially as a king, to subject yourself to scrutiny regarding that painful time in your life shows the courage and humility you have developed in the interim."

The king becomes flustered and is suddenly at a loss for words. He hangs his head, and with nervous hands he motions for the two arahants to enter the *dana* hall.

King Ajatasattu manages to conduct himself well during the ceremony, albeit with a certain reserve, and the arahants notice that the luncheon he provides is even more elaborate than usual. Hundreds of attendants have busied themselves cooking and serving the food, and making sure the king's revered guests are taken care of in the best possible way.

When *dana* is over the king leads the way up the steep solitary path to the top of the mountain where he has had a canopied enclosure erected for the sub-committee's discussion. It is comfortably carpeted, and contains a raised dais on one side where the monks will sit. Flowing white curtains are tied back so the tent is open on all four sides, and thanks to the clear day, it provides its occupants with a vista of nearly the entire kingdom of Magadha. The king has instructed his guards to come up no further than a certain point, wishing to insure the greatest possible privacy for the discussions. Before ascending to the summit he gives his ministers orders that they are to return to the capital.

Sopaka gently holds the elbow of Ananda as they scale the rocky path. When they reach the top the Buddha's Chief Attendant pauses to appreciate the view. "It is interesting that the king chose this mountaintop as the place to tell his story," says Ananda in a whisper. "All that we see is land over which he rules. It was given to him freely by his father, King Bimbisara, who only felt great love for his son – in spite of his exposed treachery."

"Perhaps his choice of locations is to remind us all that in spite of his past actions, he is still the king," responds Sopaka in a serious tone.

"That's exactly what I am thinking," says Ananda. "It indicates that he still doesn't seem to understand that kings come and go with the passage of time, leaving no more than footnotes in history. The Buddha's legacy, however, is forever and will far out-live us all."

King Ajatasattu escorts the nine members of the sub-committee to their places, and then sees that the ten memory monks are comfortably seated. Afterwards he takes his place below the raised, carpeted dais. He faces the members of the sub-committee alone, and with no outside witnesses to hear his personal account of the sordid tale of the Devadatta insurgency.

Maha Kassapa begins the discussion by saying, "Venerable Devadatta, as Venerables Ananda and Bhaddiya have earlier told us, was prone to being a bully from his youth. He felt acutely that he was doomed to live his life in the shadow of Prince Siddhartha's greatness. Jealousy arose in him as a child, and even after he was ordained in the Sangha with you, Venerable Upali, and his Sakyan relations, he craved attention." Upali, Ananda, Anuruddha, and Bhaddiya nod their heads in agreement.

"Even though he did attain considerable psychic powers after being admitted to the Order, he never progressed much further on the path to spiritual fruition," says Anuruddha.

"He was raised in a very political household," says Bhaddiya. "Don't forget that his father was a king. His primary orientation was the politics of a royal court, and the fickle popularity that came with it – along with the occasional act of treachery, of course. As a monk he did his best to make himself popular with the common people by always showing up at funerals, weddings, and other public gatherings. He didn't realize, however, that the public clamored for particular Sangha members because of their spiritual realization, or because of the wisdom they could impart that would benefit their lives. It had nothing to do with personality or popularity; it was guidance in the Dhamma that sincere devotees wanted. But Devadatta took everything as a slight, as he would have in the royal courts, and his ego began demanding an ever-increasing amount of flattery. He couldn't bear it if the five men he had entered the Sangha with were sometimes getting more notice than he was."

"This was when he turned his attention to you, Your Majesty," says Maha Kassapa. "His wounded ego and his twisted, self-centered views led him to believe that he needed to find a political champion if he were to get recognition. He knew he couldn't undermine your father's loyalty to the Buddha, so unfortunately, you became Devadatta's target."

King Ajatasattu puts his face in his hands and weeps. He starts to sob violently, and his body is wracked by convulsive shaking. After a few minutes he manages to somewhat regain his composure, and through his tears says, "Not an hour passes that I don't think about Devadatta's early advances that eventually led to my crimes. He used his psychic powers to demonstrate his greatness, and then he manipulated my ego to make me feel entitled to my father's throne."

"You started visiting Venerable Devadatta twice a day, and you sent him hundreds of pots of food on a daily basis as well," says Upali. "That certainly demonstrated your attachment to him."

"It didn't take long before I was completely under his control, I'm sorry to admit," says the king. "I stoked his ego by lavishing attention on him, and he stoked mine by telling me wonderful things about myself that weren't quite true."

"You knew the Buddha most of your life," says Bakkula. "Your father was one of the Buddha's closest friends from even before the time of his enlightenment. You had to know the story of the astrologers' prediction at your birth that you would be a patricide. Your own mother wanted to have you put to death to prevent you from killing your father. King Bimbisara, out of his love for you, forbade your being killed, and he raised you with all honor and respect as Crown Prince. How did it come to pass that you turned against not only your father, but the Buddha as well? You aligned yourself with Venerable Devadatta and his nefarious schemes. Why?"

The king shakes his head in shame, visibly upset, unable for a while to answer the arahant's pointed questions.

Eventually he says, "I made the mistake of having a bad friend and a misguided teacher. The Buddha often talked on both of these subjects, and I am a good example of someone falling prey to bad advice. Devadatta puffed up my ego; I sent him hundreds of pots of food every day which inflated *his* ego. I provided him with great material gains, and his ambition became insatiable. He set his sights on the leadership of the Sangha. What more can I say?"

Ananda speaks, "The Buddha explained how the love of fame leads to suffering, and Devadatta is a prime example."

"That statement certainly turned out to be true," says Upali. "The Buddha saw Devadatta racing head-long down the path of self-destruction, and he knew the sordid outcome could not be averted; it could only run its course, and unfortunately it did."

"Several of us were there on the day the Buddha was preaching to a large assembly," begins Ananda. "Kings and princes were present, as were many monks of the Order. Devadatta stood up, approached the Lord, and paid his respects. Then he said, 'Glorious Buddha, you are now old, far advanced in years, and on the threshold of the last stage of your life. Venerable Sir! Let the Exalted Buddha now live in peace without having to bother with so many responsibilities. Let him hand over the Sangha to me. I will look after it and lead it.'"

"I've always thought it so strange that Devadatta would try to get the Buddha to retire based on his age when, in actuality, Devadatta was *older* than the Buddha," says Bhaddiya, incredulous.

The arahants concur with this inconsistency in Devadatta's argument, and Anuruddha asks, "What was the Buddha's response to his former brother-in-law's arrogant request?"

Ananda speaks, "The Buddha answered, 'Devadatta! That is not proper. Do not think of taking charge of the Sangha.' You could almost see the steam building up in Devadatta's head. He asked him a second time and the Buddha again rejected his request. His anger was growing, and Devadatta's composure took on a look of defiance. He had the nerve to ask a third time, and the Master said, 'Devadatta! I will not hand over the charge of the Sangha even to Sariputta or Moggallana. Why should I hand it over to you, one whose conduct is unwholesome and improper?'"

Punna says, "I was present that day and I can attest to the fact that Devadatta's anger was beyond intense, and his jealousy was obvious to everyone. His rage at being embarrassed before such an illustrious crowd caused his mind to fill with hate, which quickly turned into desire for revenge. It was palpable. He stormed out of the assembly after perfunctorily paying his respects to the Buddha."

King Ajatasattu begins, "He immediately came to the palace to see me, and he started venting about the Buddha, calling him all sorts of horrible names," says the king. "Finally he said, 'In ancient times people lived longer, but today they are short-lived. You might not even live long enough to be king. Why don't you kill your father and become king now, and I will kill the Buddha and take his place.'"

"He actually came right out and suggested those murderous acts?" asks Bhaddiya, his eyes wide in disbelief.

King Ajatasattu's expression is full of pain and remorse. "Yes…he did. The Buddha and my father were such close friends that I couldn't help but associate one with the other. I could never have imagined having my father around without the Buddha – and vice versa. I reasoned that if one were to go, they both had to go. Devadatta convinced me that the two of them were redundant old men whose power had lost its potency, and they had to be replaced. He said their time had already passed like the ancient animals of old. Besides, I felt neglected whenever my father and the Buddha got together; I had no place in their conversations. Devadatta, on the other hand, always praised me and made me feel like a great man."

"Didn't you have any feelings for your father and the Buddha? What harm had either of them ever done you?" asks Punna directly.

"At that moment, given the fact that Devadatta and the Buddha were now at the point of splitting, I thought my own days were somehow numbered," answers the king. "I had so closely associated myself with Devadatta, much to my father's displeasure, that I thought he would surely disinherit me. Now that the Buddha had openly been challenged by Devadatta, I thought that there was very little chance that I would ever be king. Did I have any feelings for them? I have to admit that at that time I was only thinking about myself."

"In actual fact, Your Majesty, your father and the Buddha hadn't given you any cause to think this way. It was all based on your own distorted perceptions, which had nothing to do with reality," says Maha Kaccayana.

"I see that now," says the king, "but at the time I was completely under Devadatta's control, and all I could see was his point of view. Unfortunately, his egotistical demand for revenge became my own."

"So what did you do at that point?" asks Sopaka.

"It was as if Devadatta had cast a magic spell over me. I grabbed a dagger, tied it to my thigh, and ran at once to my father's palace. It was broad daylight! I had stupidly forgotten that the king's guards searched everyone who approached him – even me, every time I visited. They did their duty when I arrived at my father's door and they soon found the weapon. They asked me what I intended to do with it, and I insanely answered that I wanted to use it to kill my father. The ministers were brought to the scene and started to interrogate me. One of them said, 'Who put you up to this, Prince?' After some prodding I eventually told them that it had been Devadatta."

"I remember this incident very well," says Anuruddha. "Some of King Bimbisara's ministers thought that the Prince, Devadatta, and all his monks should be put to death. Some of them thought that only Devadatta and the Prince should be executed, and the monks should be spared. Some of the more level-headed ministers suggested that no one should be killed, and the matter should be brought before the king for resolution. It didn't take long for word of this incident to leak out of the palace, and before too long the entire city of Rajagaha was in an uproar."

"I was taken by the guards and the ministers before my father, the king, and they showed him the dagger and told him what I had intended to do with it," began King Ajatasattu. "My father very calmly stated that since Devadatta had publicly shown his true feelings for the Buddha, the monks couldn't possibly be held responsible. Right on the spot he fired the group of ministers who wanted to have the monks killed. Then he demoted the ministers that wanted to have me and Devadatta executed, and he turned around and promoted those that said that no one should be killed."

"How did you feel at that moment?" asks Bakkula. "Didn't you have any fear or remorse for trying to murder your own father in cold blood?"

"I felt no remorse," answers the king, sadly. "I just glared at my father and said nothing. I didn't fear for my life, because in my heart I knew he would never harm me. In my distorted state of mind, however, I actually felt that *I* was the one who had been wronged – and Devadatta, too."

"What did your father say to you after that?" asks Bhaddiya.

"He said, 'Son, why do you want to kill me?'

"I answered very plainly, 'Because I want to be king.'

"Then he said, 'Son, if this is what you want – to be king – then the kingdom is yours from this moment.'

"Can you believe it? Right then and there he abdicated the throne and handed his kingship over to me. It was only hours before that I had tried to murder him and violently take his throne, but he simply gave it to me for the asking," says King Ajatasattu. At this point the king breaks down in a fit of tears. He collapses on the plush crimson carpet and sobs uncontrollably.

When the king eventually finishes weeping he catches his breath and sits upright. Maha Kassapa says, "I see how you feel about your act of treachery now, but how did you feel when you were suddenly king?"

"To be honest, I was absolutely delighted – almost giddy," says King Ajatasattu, his voice shaking. "I don't think I even bothered to thank my father for stepping aside – in fact I'm sure I didn't. I couldn't wait to run to Devadatta and tell him the good news. Don't forget that I followed him as my teacher – not only as my friend. My father's ministers were completely aghast by my horrible actions, of course. They forced themselves to bow to me with deference, but I knew they were in a state of shock. I decided at that moment that I would have to replace all of them because they were loyal to my father, and not to me. My ego was inflated, that's for sure, and I know I behaved arrogantly. I dismissed the ministers, turned and frowned at my father, and abruptly left the palace."

"What did Venerable Devadatta have to say to you when you told him?" asks Anuruddha.

"Devadatta was very shrewd. He knew exactly how to play me," answers the king with self-loathing. "With just a few words he turned my moment of triumph into a stab of fear. He made me feel like a fool for not having thought the whole thing through. He said fiercely, exposing his teeth, 'Like a man who has covered his drum with a fox inside it you think you have achieved the object of your goal. After two or three days your father will have second thoughts about your impudence – not to mention your attempt on his life – and he'll take away your crown and make himself king again. He still has the power, you fool. Nothing's changed.'"

"What did you do then?" asks Upali, obviously disgusted by the king's foul tale.

"I went back to the palace and gave the order for my father to be put in an iron cage," replies the king, nearly breaking down again with grief.

"I exiled the ministers that I knew were loyal to him, and I had his private cadre of guards put in prison because I was sure they would try to assassinate me. I gave the instruction that no one was allowed to see my father except my mother. I also forbade anyone from taking him food since my intention was to starve him to death."

"I must say, Your Majesty, that your candor in retelling these painful memories is admirable," says Maha Kassapa, looking with kindness at the distraught king.

"I feel that this is the only way that I could even begin to make amends for my evil deeds. Knowing that this recollection of the life of the Buddha is for all posterity, I'm hoping that future generations will learn from my mistakes," replies the king. "I'm not making any excuses for my actions, mind you. I'm telling you the truth so at least *that* fact will be recorded. I hope they will say that thanks to the Buddha's grace, he learned to tell the truth about himself, and to see things clearly as they really were."

"I have a feeling that will be the world's ultimate opinion of you, Your Majesty. When people down through the ages learn about the circumstances surrounding your crimes, and know that the information came from your own lips, I think they will be kinder to your memory" says Punna. "Opinions about you won't necessarily be favorable, but I think that they may perhaps be merciful and understanding." King Ajatasattu heaves a sigh of relief when he hears these kind words from the wise arahant.

As the sun is setting, the members of the sub-committee turn and face the west. The sky has turned a brilliant deep orange, and the view from the mountaintop is clear and unobstructed. The king pauses to watch the sun disappear on the horizon, and a tear trickles down his cheek.

"My father would probably be here today if it hadn't been for my treachery," says King Ajatasattu. "Undoubtedly, he would have been proud and honored to host this council. I wish there was some way he could know…"

"Who says he doesn't know?" asks Ananda. "The Buddha said that what he had told us about the universe could be compared to a handful of leaves. The rest, he felt, was incomprehensible to us mortal humans, so why bother telling? In fact, he refused to answer questions about other dimensions whenever he was asked. Perhaps in that remaining forest of leaves is a mystery that somehow allows your father to witness all of this. Perhaps one day you'll find out."

These words seem to comfort the saddened king. The arahants intuit that Ananda has told him this beautiful simile to fortify him for the remainder of his confession.

The reality of the chairman's next words brings everyone back to the subject at hand. "Tell us what happened to your father once you had him imprisoned in the iron cage with no food."

King Ajatasattu catches his breath and begins, "As you all know, my mother, Queen Videhi, was an advanced student of the Dhamma and a loyal follower of the Buddha. She couldn't believe that I would listen to someone like Devadatta and lock up my dear father in a cage. She begged me to reconsider my cruel and reckless actions, and to show him mercy and compassion. I wouldn't hear her words, but she was so persistent I finally forbade her to come near me. Since she was the only person I allowed to visit my father, she hid food in a golden bowl and snuck it in to him. I didn't know about this at the time, but when my father was still living after several weeks I couldn't understand why. When I asked, the guards told me my mother brought food to keep him alive. That was when I gave the order that no food whatsoever should enter his cage."

"Didn't you have any sympathy at all for the man who sired you?" asks Upali with wide eyes.

"I'm sorry to admit that at the time I had none," responds the king, hanging his head. "I only wanted the king to be dead so I could feel that I was really king of Magadha. Besides, as long as he was alive there was a chance that his loyal ministers would stage a revolt against me. My ego told me that I would never have the satisfaction of being king until he was gone."

"What happened next?" asks Sopaka.

"When the king stayed alive for another three weeks I discovered that my mother was getting food into him by hiding it in a container in the knot of her hair. I put a stop to this immediately, and ordered the guards to take further precautions before her visits."

King Ajatasattu is obviously in great mental pain. The arahants, living beings of realized compassion and loving-kindness, can feel his agony as if it is their own. They want to release him from this painful process of confession, but they know that it is the best way for him to come to terms with his *kamma;* the confession must be endured.

"After another three or four weeks, I became increasingly more frustrated and impatient that my father should be dead. I became angrier by the day. I gave orders that my mother be searched even more thoroughly before she came near the cage. I have to commend my clever mother; the guards found food inside her golden shoes. I forbade this, of course, and ordered greater inspection of everything she wore," said the king.

"Your dear mother, the queen of Magadha, was indeed a great lady," recalls Punna.

The king breaks down in tears again. He experiences almost unendurable remorse as he reflects on the extreme grief he inflicted on his own mother.

When he recovers enough to speak he says, "My father still refused to die in his solitary iron cage, and no matter how thoroughly they searched my mother they could find nothing. They finally figured out that she was bathing herself in fragrant water and then covering her body in oil, honey, molasses, and butter, which was enough to sustain my father when he licked it from her. When I heard this news I went into a complete rage and forbade my mother to ever see my father again."

The arahants look at one another in dismay, shaking their heads.

The king continues, "I later learned from the guards that when the queen heard this order she stood outside my father's iron cage and said to him, 'O Great King! You yourself did not allow this wicked son Ajatasattu to be killed when he was young. You yourself raised your own potential enemy. Now, this is the last time that I will see you. Forgive me for anything that I have done wrong.' My mother was wailing as she was physically dragged away from the prison, and my father wept uncontrollably."

"I heard that even though King Bimbisara had no food," adds Bakkula, "he kept alive by walking back and forth in his cage in the bliss of *sotapanna*. He stayed absorbed in that spiritual state of fruition and his body seemed to thrive in spite of being starved to death. You know, your father never even thought badly of you during his entire ordeal,

King Ajatasattu. He even considered his incarceration in that cage like time spent in a monastery, and he used each and every hour to meditate on loving-kindness, sending it out to you and to all beings everywhere."

The king is sobbing again as he says, "I don't think I can continue, Venerable Sirs. The memory of what I did to my family is just too painful."

"I will continue for you, Your Majesty, if my fellow sub-committee members have no objection," says Punna. The other arahants look at their revered colleague and nod for him to proceed. The king remains silent, unable to look the monks in the eye.

Punna, using a slow, somber voice says, "When your guards reported to you that your father's physical appearance seemed even healthier than it was before he was imprisoned – that he was keeping himself alive by walking back and forth in his cage – you ordered an end to his exercise. You sent your barbers to the king, and when he saw them coming he thought you had returned to your senses, and decided to end his torture. He assumed that you were sending them to trim his beard and hair so he could return to court.

"His optimism was short-lived, however, because you had instructed the barbers to gash the soles of his feet and smear them with oil and salt. Then you told them to broil them over red-hot coals," says Punna, who pauses for a moment while the king relives his act of horror.

"I was a very close friend of King Bimbisara, so I will continue from here," says Ananda in a soft voice. "Your father endured this excruciating pain without harboring any ill-will towards you, Your Majesty. He concentrated on sending you loving-kindness while contemplating the sublime attributes of the Buddha, the Dhamma, and the Sangha.

"On the very same day your father finally passed away, your wife gave birth to a son. Two separate messages reporting these events reached the palace at the same time. Your ministers thought that it would be kinder to report your child's birth before reporting your father's death. When you heard the good news about the birth of your heir, you were filled with an excitement and joy that penetrated to the very marrow of your bones. You suddenly became aware of the gratitude you felt for your own father, which had been hidden in the depths of your mind, buried under the rubbish heap of your ego. At that moment you ordered your father's release from his iron cage," concludes Ananda who can go no further.

Maha Kassapa speaks up, "Your dear mother, Queen Videhi, who had been told of her husband's death, approached you at the height of her grief and said, 'You foolish son! You have no idea what you are doing. When you were a young child you had an infected boil on your finger, which caused you great pain and suffering. The royal nurses didn't know what to do, and they couldn't stop your crying. They took you to your father who sat in the courts of law. He held you on his lap and put your inflamed finger in his mouth. Because of the warmth your pain was eased and you fell asleep. After a while the boil erupted in his mouth and since he didn't want you to wake up he swallowed the poison rather than spitting it out. This is how your father loved you, foolish man! And now he is dead by your own hand!"

"After a few days your mother collapsed and died of grief," says Anuruddha very slowly.

King Ajatasattu, by this time, is writhing on the floor in emotional and mental torment. His sobs come from the depths of his being, and it seems like they will never stop. The king is allowed to have his catharsis, and to slowly come face-to-face with his crimes. The arahants respect him for the way he turned around his life to become a good man; one who is devoted with all his heart to the Triple Gem. Bakkula rises from his seat and goes to the pot of water in the center of the enclosure. He dips the corner of his robe into the cool liquid and walks over to the suffering king. He wipes the poor man's forehead and strokes his hair.

"Even the birth of your son didn't cure you of your attachment to the evil ways of your teacher and friend, Venerable Devadatta," says Maha Kassapa. "You continued to go along with his schemes until the public outcry against you became almost overwhelming. At that moment you were forced to abandon Devadatta or face the destruction of your prized kingship. We won't put you through that part of the telling, Your Majesty, since I can see that you have reached the limit of your emotional endurance. We will finish the story of your involvement with Devadatta without you."

Ananda speaks, "To end this discussion I will quote from the sayings of the Buddha for inclusion in our recollection:

"'Ill-done is that action, doing which one repents later and the fruits whereof one reaps with tears weeping.'[1]"

After a minute's pause Maha Kassapa says, "Thank you, Your Majesty, for going through this painful ordeal with us today. The memory of your part in the life of the Buddha will be greatly enhanced by your courage in facing your past actions. In closing this discussion I will add another verse to the one you just quoted, Venerable Ananda, even though it has been quoted before. Perhaps this will help our king regain some of his peace of mind:

"'He by his good deeds covers the evil he has done,
illuminates this world like the moon freed from clouds.'"[2]

King Ajatasattu finally sits up and wipes the tears from his face with the backs of his hands. His suffering is obvious, but the arahants all know that there is nothing further they can do for the reformed monarch of Magadha. His *kamma* is defiled to the point where he will suffer for eons in future rebirths. For the rest of this life he will have to live with the memory of having murdered his own father. The only thing he can do is to stay on the path following the Buddha's teaching, and rule his people with the compassion and loving-kindness that he had denied the very man who gave him life.

The members of the sub-committee stand and walk as a group to the edge of the canopied enclosure. Night has fallen, torches have been lit in Visakha's unfinished new monastery, and the brightest stars they have ever seen illuminate the cloudless sky.

The king sends a signal to his guards who quickly ascend to the peak with torches to escort the arahants down the steep path. One by one he bows before the revered enlightened masters and touches his forehead to their feet.

King Ajatasattu spends the rest of the night in the canopied enclosure, alone with his troubled memories. He orders his guards to stay below, and tells them that he is not to be disturbed. This makes him laugh silently to himself knowing that his mind and its thoughts of remorse would disturb him until the day he died.

His night is sleepless, but he knows that he has done the right thing by being honest with the arahants. He has held nothing back in his telling, which is to his credit. He knows, however, that he will have to pay for the ill-conceived, ego-driven acts of his past in this life, and perhaps the next; for how many lives, he does not know. He does know, however, that if he ever finds peace it will be due to the healing grace of the Buddha, the Dhamma, and the Sangha.

Chapter 31
Gain, Honor, and Praise:
The Devadatta Insurgency

Ananda stands at the podium reciting from the *Labha Sakkara Sutta*. The memory of the discussion two days before with King Ajatasattu is still fresh in his mind.

"At Savatthi... '*Bhikkhus*, dreadful are gain, honor, and praise; bitter, vile, obstructive to achieving the unsurpassed security from bondage. Suppose a fisherman would cast a baited hook deep into a lake, and a fish on the lookout for food would swallow it. That fish, having swallowed the fisherman's hook, would meet with calamity and disaster, and the fisherman could do with it as he wishes.

"'*Bhikkhus*, '*fisherman*' is a designation for Mara the Evil One. '*Baited hook*" is a designation for gain, honor, and praise. Any *bhikkhu* who relishes and enjoys the arisen gain, honor, and praise is called a *bhikkhu* who has swallowed the hook, who has met with calamity and disaster, and the Evil One can do with him as he wishes.[1]

"'*Bhikkhus*, once in the past there was a large family of turtles that had been living for a long time in a certain lake. Then one turtle said to another: 'Dear turtle – do not go to such and such a region.'

"'But that turtle went to that region anyway, and a hunter struck him with a corded harpoon.

"'Then that turtle approached the first one, and when he saw him coming in the distance he said to him: 'I hope, dear turtle, that you didn't go to that region.'

"'I did go to that region, dear.'

"'I hope you haven't been hit or struck, dear.'

"'I haven't been hit or struck, but there is this cord constantly following behind me.'

"'Indeed you've been struck! Your father and grandfather also met with calamity and disaster on account of such a cord. Go now, dear turtle, you are no longer one of us.'

"'*Bhikkhus*, '*hunter*' is a designation for Mara the Evil One. '*Corded harpoon*' is a designation for gain, honor, and praise. '*Cord*' is a designation for delight and lust. Any *bhikkhu* who relishes and enjoys the arisen gain, honor, and praise is called a *bhikkhu* who has been struck with a corded harpoon, or who has met with calamity and disaster, and the Evil One can do with him as he wishes.

"'So dreadful, *bhikkhus*, are gain, honor, and praise; so bitter, vile, obstructive to achieving the unsurpassed security from bondage. Therefore, *bhikkhus*, you should train yourselves thus: 'We will abandon the arisen gain, honor, and praise, and we will not let the arisen gain, honor, and praise persist obsessing our minds.'"[2]

Ananda recites several more discourses until *dana*, which is being hosted by King Ajatasattu's wife, Queen Vajira. She is the mother of his son, Prince Udayibhadda, and the daughter of King Pasenadi of Kosala.

When the senior arahants approach the *dana* pavilion they notice the profusion of floral arrangements that abound throughout the enclosure. It is as if the queen has brought the entire contents of her palace garden to grace her offering to the monks. The flowers are of every hue and variety, and there are even individual bouquets in front of each of the five hundred seats for the arahants. Special arrangements of pure white lotus flowers are also placed on the banana leaf plates of the nine members of the sub-committee.

Maha Kassapa, Ananda, and other elders approach the hall where the queen stands with her group of female attendants to greet them.

"Is there a single flower left blooming in your garden?" asks Maha Kassapa as he approaches the regal personage of the queen, who is dressed in a flowing white sari trimmed in gold.

"Not one, Venerable Sir," answers the Queen as she bows low to pay her respects. "My husband the king requested that I offer every blossom to his esteemed guests to express his gratitude for showing him such great compassion two days ago. For the first time in years he was able to sleep well last evening, after having spent the previous night alone on top of this mountain. He said that his spirit has been refreshed by the experience of participating in your candid discussion, and he wanted me to tell you that he is re-inspired to dedicate the rest of his life to making his kingdom bloom for the greater glory of the *Sasana*."

Maha Kassapa and the other arahants smile at the queen, pleased that King Ajatasattu has benefitted from his excruciating emotional ordeal before the sub-committee.

"King Ajatasattu has become a good man," begins Ananda, "and I am sure that he will become an even better king, given his new understanding." The queen bows in thanks for the kind compliment to her troubled husband. The arahants are escorted to their seats and Maha Kassapa begins the chants of blessing.

That evening in the chairman's torch-lit cave chamber the nine members of the sub-committee and ten memory monks gather to continue their work.

"I'm glad you chose to spare King Ajatasattu from this part of the Devadatta discussion," says Ananda to Maha Kassapa.

"I felt that he could be spared the ending of this tale, given what he went through two days ago," responds the chairman. "Besides, apart from assisting Devadatta in two misguided attempts to murder the Buddha, the king had little to do with the way it ended."

"Perhaps I should preface this discussion with a quote from the *Devadatta Sutta*, which foreshadows his demise," says Ananda.

"Please proceed, Venerable Sir," says Maha Kassapa.

Ananda pauses for a moment and then begins:

> "'As its own fruit brings destruction
> To the plantain, bamboo, and reed,
> As its embryo destroys the mule,
> So do honors destroy the scoundrel.'"[3]

"That verse so completely describes the fate of Devadatta after he succumbed to gain, honor, and praise, just as the fish by the fishhook and the turtle by the corded harpoon," says Punna.

After a moment Maha Kassapa says, "Going back to our recollections, Devadatta was frustrated and enraged by the Buddha's public refusal to allow him to take charge of the Sangha. Before he carried out his murderous attempts on the Buddha's life he tried one last time to gain honor, praise, and power, which resulted in a schism in the Sangha."

"I heard that Devadatta consulted with a number of religious leaders from other sects that are still popular in this area. Many of them have harsh rules for members of their orders; one of them even forbids walking on the grass because it might kill harmless insects. I think that's how he came up with the idea that imposing new and constricting rules on the monks might gain him a greater following," said Punna. "His ego was the sort that demanded there always be followers behind him."

"Even though he was no longer really welcome in the Sangha, Devadatta actually had the nerve to approach the Buddha again – and to make five new demands," says Upali. "They were proposed additions to the *Vinaya* code of discipline that he used as a ruse in his attempt to divide the Order."

"Since this area is your specialty, Upali, why don't you tell us about those five demands, as well as the Buddha's responses," requests Maha Kassapa.

Upali sits up straight and begins, "Devadatta's first request was that monks should live in a forest hermitage all their lives. He said that any monk who lives in a monastery near a village would be guilty of an offense.[4]

"His second request was that all monks should only eat food they collected on alms rounds; any monk who accepted an invitation from lay people would be guilty of an offense.

"The third new rule was that all monks should only wear robes made from old rags sewn together. He proposed that a monk who accepts new robes offered by laypeople would be committing an offense.

"Devadatta's fourth new rule was that all monks should always dwell at the base of trees, and that any monk who goes and lives in a monastery would be guilty of breaking the code of discipline.

"His fifth request was that all monks should never eat meat or fish, and that any monk who did so would be committing an offense.

"Upon hearing these demands the Buddha knew instantly that Devadatta's intention was to create a schism in the Sangha. He also knew that agreeing to these five demands would possibly create hindrances to spiritual progress.

"The Buddha responded to the five demands by saying, 'Devadatta, your demands are not proper or reasonable.' He continued to explain:

> "'I say, let the monk live in a forest hermitage or in a monastery near a village as he pleases.
>
> "'Let the monk either eat food he collects from alms, or at the invitation of laypeople in their homes or other places, as he chooses.
>
> "'Let the monk either wear robes made of rags, or new robes sewn and offered by laypeople, according to his choice and the circumstances.
>
> "'Devadatta, I have permitted the monks to dwell at the base of trees for eight months out of each year. The other four months are in the monsoon season, and it is more convenient for monks to live indoors where they are protected from the elements.
>
> "'I have permitted the monks to eat meat or fish provided they don't see or hear or have any suspicion about any creature being killed for their food. As you know, however, I have always advocated a vegetarian diet.'"

When the expert on the *Vinaya* concludes his explanation he sits back and rests on one elbow.

"Thank you, Upali. I might add that the Buddha, in his wisdom, knew that monks were of varying strengths, temperaments, and inclinations," adds the chairman. "To impose restrictions on where they could live would undoubtedly harm a great many of them."

"He also knew that when a monk accepted a *dana* invitation from a layperson he would have the opportunity to teach the Dhamma to them afterwards, be it in their homes or in other places. This would be of great benefit for the laypeople," adds Bakkula.

"The Buddha felt that offering new robes to the monks gave laypeople the chance to practice generosity, and to him a new robe or one made of old rags represented the same thing, which is membership in the Sangha," says Bhaddiya.

"The Buddha knew that to put strict restrictions on the eating of meat and fish might place an unnecessary burden on laypeople. They may have these items in their own diets and might include them in their food offerings, but might not know that Sangha members generally avoid them," says Anuruddha. "As long as the monk doesn't know or suspect that life had been taken on his behalf, the existing rule is satisfied. The Buddha was always thinking of the convenience, inclinations, and welfare of others – both the monks' and the laypeople."

"The five demands made by Devadatta were purposefully designed to cause a schism in the Sangha, and it came to pass that he did, in fact, attract a following of several hundred monks," says Sopaka.

"I was there the day Devadatta made these five demands to the Buddha," says Punna. "It was obvious that he was very pleased by the Buddha's flat refusal to accept them. He had achieved his intended purpose, and immediately afterwards he and his two closest disciples, Kokalika and Katamodaka Tissaka, paid their off-hand respects to the Lord and left the monastery."

"Devadatta and his followers went directly to Rajagaha and expounded their new doctrine. They hoped it would appeal to those that were disciples of the popular ascetic teachers that advocated strict rules for members of their clergies," says Bhaddiya. "They announced to the populace that the Buddha had rejected rules that would contribute to non-attachment, and that they themselves would live by these 'purer' rules they advocated."

"He got a mixed reaction, though," begins Anuruddha. "Those that lacked faith and intellectual discernment extolled Devadatta's new doctrine and called the Buddha lax and attached to comforts. Those that were more intelligent and had faith, criticized Devadatta for trying to create a division in the Sangha, and for undermining the existing *Vinaya* code of conduct and discipline."

"The monks who heard Devadatta's pronouncements in the city streets came back to the Buddha and reported to him," says Sopaka.

"Then the Buddha called an assembly of the monks and summoned Devadatta to his presence. He asked him directly, 'Devadatta, are you trying to create a schism in the Sangha and destroy its authority?'

"Devadatta's eyes gleamed, and with great flourish and arrogance he said, 'Yes I am, Sir.'

"The Buddha responded calmly, 'Devadatta, what you are doing is not proper. One who causes a schism in a united Sangha bears a grave responsibility, and commits an evil that will cause him to suffer in hell for an entire eon. Do not do this.' Devadatta looked directly at the Buddha with undisguised enmity, and then turned around and walked out of the assembly, followed by his two disciples."

"It was then that the Buddha requested that a resolution based on the rules of the *Vinaya* be declared," says Sopaka. "It stated that 'the bodily or verbal actions of Venerable Devadatta should not be identified with the Buddha or the Dhamma or the Sangha.' This was also publicly announced."

"Afterwards Devadatta went even further in his attempt to divide the Sangha," says Ananda. "The next day while I was in Rajagaha collecting alms food I met him in the streets and he informed me that he would be performing religious services on his own – separately from the Buddha Sangha. I reported this matter to the Buddha and he said this verse:

> "'It is easy for a good man to do a good deed
> It is hard for an evil man to do a good deed
> It is easy for an evil man to do an evil deed
> It is hard for a good man to do an evil deed.'"[5]

"A couple of days later it was the full moon, and we were conducting our services for the laypeople to observe Eight Precepts," begins Upali. "Devadatta had the nerve to enter the service and participate as if he hadn't been expelled from the Order. At the end of the ceremony he stood up and announced that the Buddha had rejected his demand for five new *Vinaya* rules that would lead to non-attachment and greater and speedier spiritual development. He said that he and his followers would abide by these five rules, and he invited any monks who would also like to observe them to follow him. Around five hundred young, inexperienced monks from Vesali, who were ignorant of the *Vinaya* teaching, chose to go with Devadatta. Devadatta, pleased with himself for his victory, marched out of the assembly hall with the five hundred monks following him. They departed for Gaya Head."

Maha Kaccayana speaks up, "I remember that Sariputta and Maha Moggallana went to the Buddha and told him of this incident because the Lord had not been present in the Eight Precepts assembly. The Buddha reproached them for their lack of compassion for the young monks, and he urged them to go to Gaya Head and save them from spiritual ruin. The two Chief Disciples immediately left on their mission."

Bakkula chuckles, saying, "One uninformed monk went directly to the Buddha and told him that Sariputta and Maha Moggallana had defected. He reported that they had gone over to the side of Devadatta because they preferred his teaching. The Buddha smiled and quickly straightened him out, telling him the real reason they were going to Gaya Head."

"Maha Moggallana later told me how it went when he arrived in Devadatta's camp," says Bakkula.

"Please tell us, friend, so we can record this important part of the story in our recollection," requests the chairman.

Bakkula smiles at Maha Kassapa and begins, "When the two Chief Disciples approached the camp, Devadatta was preaching to a large group of his followers. When he saw the elders coming he yelled out, 'Monks! Look over there! Even Gotama Buddha's two most senior disciples have seen the light. They prefer my teaching over the Buddha's and are joining me!'"

The arahants on the sub-committee begin to laugh at Devadatta's ridiculous assumption that two self-realized, fully-enlightened monks like Sariputta and Maha Moggallana would even *consider* joining Devadatta's break-away sect.

"How could Devadatta have even thought this?" asks Sopaka, incredulous.

"He so craved gain, honor, and praise that he had been blinded to reality, that's how," answers Anuruddha. "He knew, of course, that if the Buddha's two Chief Disciples did defect to his camp, his new movement would gain both credibility and great esteem. His presumption just shows how deluded he had become."

Bakkula begins again, "The monk Kokalika, Devadatta's primary confidante, walked up to Devadatta and said, 'Do not associate with Sariputta and Moggallana. They have evil desires, which they will implement here.' Devadatta calmly replied, 'My friend, what you say is not true or proper. They came here because they appreciate the true value of my teaching, and recognize its superiority over the Buddha's Dhamma.'

"When the two esteemed monks came close to Devadatta he said, 'Come, Sariputta, sit here,' and he moved over to share his seat with him. Sariputta kindly refused to accept his offer and took a seat to the side – so did Maha Moggallana. Devadatta behaved as if he hadn't noticed the slight.

"Devadatta continued preaching in earnest to his group of monks the whole night. Finally, because he was tired, he said to Sariputta, 'Friend Sariputta, these monks have become free from sloth and torpor. You carry on with a talk on the Dhamma. My neck is stiff and cramped, and I need to stretch my back,'" says Bakkula. "Sariputta agreed, smiling."

"Sorry to interrupt you, Bakkula," says Ananda, "but Maha Moggallana told me this part of the story, which is priceless." Bakkula smiles at his dear, old friend, and nods for him to go ahead.

"Devadatta actually tried to imitate the Buddha in front of his flock," begins Ananda. "He spread out his big four-fold robe on the ground and lay down on his right side – exactly as the Buddha would have done. Before too long, however, he fell fast asleep – something the Buddha would *never* have done." The arahants laugh again at this part of the account. The thought of Devadatta trying to act like the Fully Enlightened Buddha was indeed comical.

Ananda begins again, "Sariputta began to preach the true Buddha Doctrine to the five hundred monks. He began his discourse by helping the monks to become aware of their current mental states. Then he taught them the difference between Dhammas they should practice, and ones they should discard. Maha Moggallana then got up and piqued their interest by performing a small miracle or two, and then he expounded on which teaching they should follow, and which to shun. Right there on the spot these five hundred young, inexperienced *bhikkhus* attained the state of *sotapanna*.

"After their spiritual attainment Sariputta announced that he and Maha Moggallana were leaving to return to the Buddha. He invited them to go with them if they liked his teaching. Every single one of those young monks picked up their alms bowls and followed the distinguished Chief Disciples back to the Buddha's monastery," concludes Ananda with satisfaction.

Bakkula speaks, "After the departure of the five hundred members of Devadatta's new sect, Kokalika, in a fit of rage, went over to where Devadatta was sound asleep and struck him in the breast. He said, 'Get up, Venerable Devadatta! Sariputta and Moggallana have taken away the five hundred young disciples. I told you not to associate with Sariputta and Moggallana, and that they had evil desires to destroy you; but did you listen to me?' Devadatta suddenly became so inflamed with anger and revenge that he vomited hot blood."

"I can only imagine how Devadatta felt when he woke up from his peaceful slumber to the news that he had been deserted – and that his careless falling asleep had been the cause of it," comments Bhaddiya.

"Indeed," says Anuruddha. "The monks living at Veluvana Monastery rejoiced when they saw our two esteemed brothers returning with their inexperienced, misguided brethren." The arahants in the torch-lit cave chamber smile when they recall this event, and reflect on the fact that the talents of Sariputta and Maha Moggallana seemed almost limitless.

Maha Kassapa, who has been silent through most of this telling speaks, "This catastrophe didn't deter Devadatta from continuing his clamor for gain, honor, and praise. In fact, it turned him into an attempted murderer."

"That is quite accurate, Venerable Sir," says Maha Kaccayana. "And he realized that he only had one real ally left – besides his two chief disciples, Kokalika and Kadamodaka Tissaka."

"The events we just recollected all happened before the death of King Bimbisara while he was still in prison," says Ananda. "Devadatta, enraged and jealous to the point of insanity, persuaded that last ally, the unfortunate King Ajatasattu, to send assassins to kill the Buddha. He convinced him by saying that they had earlier made a pact, and the king had to do his part to help him."

"I'm still amazed that the king would agree to assist in such a despicable scheme," comments Bhaddiya, shaking his head. "But I guess I shouldn't be surprised at anything after the way he treated his father."

"He thought he could distance himself from the actual act if he sent the assassins to Devadatta for instructions. He ordered them to do whatever his traitorous teacher wanted – rather than to dispatch them to do the evil deed himself," says Anuruddha. "It's almost like he felt he wouldn't be guilty of the crime by keeping himself one step removed. It just demonstrates how thoroughly Devadatta had the deluded king under his control."

Ananda says, "When the king's assassins met with Devadatta he arranged to see them separately and give each of them different instructions. He told the first man to arm himself with a sword and bow; then told him where to go to kill the Buddha. He also told him which path to use going, and to use a different path after he had done the deed. He next told two other assassins to use the path upon which the first assassin would be returning, and to kill him. Then he told four of the other assassins to go and wait on that same path and kill the two returning assassins, and another eight to kill the previous four. Then he instructed sixteen more to go the same way and kill the eight who would be returning. In this way he hoped to keep his murder of the Buddha a secret from everyone. Only he and King Ajatasattu would actually know the truth – everyone else would be dead."

"A very clever plan indeed, albeit soaked in blood," comments Sopaka. "It just shows how vicious and full of revenge Devadatta's warped mind had become."

"The first man reached the spot where the Buddha was peacefully enjoying the bliss of solitude. The poor man stood there trembling with fear, experiencing great apprehension for what he was about to to do," continues Ananda. "The Buddha saw him and said, 'Have no fear, man. Come here.' The man put down his weapons and tentatively approached the Lord. He was frightened and bewildered and didn't know how to behave.

"Overcome by the Buddha's powerful presence, the would-be assassin went on his knees and bowed before him in reverence. He also confessed that he had been sent to murder him, and he asked for forgiveness. The Buddha preached to him about generosity, morality, and other good deeds that lead to the Path and Fruition; then he gave him a short discourse on the Four Noble Truths. The assassin attained *sotapanna* and took refuge in the Triple Gem.

"The Buddha blessed the man and told him to return to Rajagaha by another path," says Ananda.

"The Master had obviously seen the whole plot from the beginning," says Maha Kaccayana, "and, as usual, he turned the deathly situation into one of benefit for the individual and the *Sasana*."

"The pair of assassins who had been sent to kill the first one waited for him to come back on the designated path," begins Ananda. "They waited for several hours and finally decided they couldn't wait any longer. They proceeded up the path in search of the man and eventually came face to face with the Buddha, who was seated at the foot of a large banyan tree. They approached the Lord and sat down near him. The Buddha preached the Dhamma to them and they, too, achieved *sotapanna* and became lay disciples."

"The second two men, of course, had no idea that the man they were dispatched to kill had been sent to murder the Buddha," adds Anuruddha.

"Correct. They didn't know why they were sent to kill the first man – it could have been for any reason," says Ananda. "The same scene was repeated by the next group of four, then the following group of eight, and finally the last group of sixteen men. Each new batch of assassins, completely ignorant of their part in the real mission, was won over by the Buddha and attained *sotapanna*. They all became lay disciples."

"All together that fateful day gained thirty-one new members for the *Sasana*," says Bakkula. "The Buddha, motivated by the purest form of compassion, prevented those men from creating bad *kamma*."

Ananda pauses for a moment while the arahants reflects on this observation, and then begins again. "The first assassin returned to Devadatta and told him that he couldn't possibly kill the Buddha. The other thirty assassins never went back to Devadatta. It was at this point, in a state of total rage, and frustrated beyond endurance by this failure, that he decided to kill the Buddha himself."

The arahants look back and forth at one another in dismay, trying to imagine Devadatta's twisted mental state at this time.

"A few days after this incident," begins Ananda, "the Buddha was taking some exercise on Vultures Peak, which is not far from here. Devadatta climbed to a spot directly above the Buddha's path and rolled a huge boulder down the mountain towards the Lord. The large rock hit another stone as it descended the hill and it was deflected from hitting the Buddha; however, a small piece chipped off and struck the Master in the foot, which caused him to bleed. The Buddha looked up and saw Devadatta above him and said, 'Foolish man! You, who can make no spiritual progress, have gathered much evil *kamma* as you have caused bleeding on the body of the Buddha with a corrupt and murderous intention.' Devadatta, terrified, turned and fled from the scene.

"A group of monks gathered by the Buddha's side and he said to them, 'Devadatta has committed the first evil act of *anantarika-kamma* by spilling my blood," says Punna. "I was one of those monks. We carried him to Jivaka's mango grove so he could get medical attention and rest. Jivaka came at once and applied a highly potent medicine to the wound and wrapped it in a bandage.

"Word of Devadatta's assassination attempt on the Buddha's life quickly spread to the other monks and they immediately went to the Lord's chamber. They formed three protective rings around his dwelling, and prepared to defend him with their lives. He summoned them and said, 'Have no fear, monks. It is impossible for anyone to kill the Buddha. Go back to your residences. The lives of Buddhas do not depend on other people's protection.' Reluctantly, the monks left the Buddha alone."

"I was with the Buddha that night, of course, and I removed the bandage from his injured foot," says Ananda. "I assure you that the Lord was not the least bit worried or concerned about his safety."

"How long was it before Devadatta made his next attempt?" asks Upali.

"Not more than a few days," answers Ananda. "In the meantime, word about Devadatta and his attempt to kill the Buddha had spread throughout Magadha. The people already knew, of course, that he had tried his best to create a schism in the Sangha, but failed. Public opinion against Devadatta was growing, and with it their dislike of the king's association with him."

"King Ajatasattu, unfortunately, didn't pay any attention to popular opinion, and he foolishly agreed to Devadatta's next, and final, demand for his help," says Sopaka.

"Still under the evil spell of his teacher and friend the king allowed him to use the royal elephant, Nalagiri, who was known to be vicious, wild, and homicidal," adds Anuruddha.

"With King Ajatasattu's permission Devadatta summoned the elephant's custodians," says Bakkula. "He told the men to feed Nalagiri sixteen pots of potent, intoxicating liquor. He assured them that they would be promoted if they could incite the drunken elephant's temper with spears. Then he wanted them to encourage Nalagiri to break open his shed, charge in the direction of Gotama Buddha, and kill him."

"Word got out about this plan, of course, given the natural tendency of humans to gossip," begins Upali. "The Buddha's lay devotees in Rajagaha came and told the Lord of Devadatta's plan. They urged him to not come into the city for alms, and said they would bring *dana* to him and the monks at the monastery. They were very worried about his safety."

"The Buddha accepted their offer of bringing food, so the townspeople went back home. The Buddha, however, had other thoughts on his mind," says Sopaka.

"As usual, the Buddha taught the monks during the first watch of the night," begins Ananda. "The remainder of the night was spent in his usual fashion. Later, when he surveyed the world, he saw Nalagiri. He realized that his message to the elephant that day would be important for multitudes of people for all time to come. He asked me to assemble all of the monks from the eighteen monasteries that surrounded Rajagaha. He wanted them to go with him into the city."

"Meanwhile, the elephant's custodians carried out Devadatta's instructions and got Nalagiri intoxicated and in a rage," says Bhaddiya.

"Throngs of people began to gather to witness the confrontation between the Buddha and the massive bull elephant," adds Anuruddha. "They climbed on the turreted mansions, on the city walls, the roofs of houses - anywhere they could find good viewing places. A carnival atmosphere filled the air."

"Followers of the Buddha believed that he would win the battle," says Punna. "The others who had no faith in the Buddha thought they would witness the Lord's destruction."

"I entered the city with the Buddha and the thousands of monks who had been summoned," says Ananda. "Before too long Nalagiri tore down the door to his shed and stormed out into the street. He charged toward the Buddha at full speed knocking down anything in its way, crushing and casting aside vendor carts as if they were toys.

"When the monks saw the elephant rushing toward them like an unstoppable tsunami, they begged the Buddha to get out of the way and take cover. With total calmness and composure the Buddha said, 'Monks! Put aside your fear. I will tame the elephant Nalagiri.'

"Sariputta stepped forward at this point and said, 'Glorious Buddha, as your eldest son it is my duty to tame the elephant in your stead.' The Buddha replied, 'Sariputta, the power of the Buddha and the power of the disciple are different matters. Please do not trouble yourself on my behalf. I can handle the elephant myself.' Most of the other senior monks made the same request, but the Lord turned them all down. He simply stood there and exuded the brilliant confidence of one who knows the universe first-hand.

"Finally, I couldn't take it any longer," exclaims Ananda. "I went and stood in front of the Buddha with the intention of sacrificing my life for him. The Buddha merely said, 'Get back, Ananda. Do not stand there in front of me.' I said to him, 'Glorious Buddha, this elephant Nalagiri is bent on destroying you. Please let him kill me instead.' I begged him three times, but in each instance he rebuffed me. He finally took me by the arm and moved me to the side."

"That must have been quite a moment!" says Bakkula with great excitement. "Your courage is commendable, my dear friend, not in regards to the elephant, but in your disobedience to the Lord!"

The arahants laugh at Bakkula's humorous comment. In truth, however, none of them had ever dared to disobey the Lord – danger or no danger.

Ananda laughs along with his colleagues and then continues. "Just at that moment a young child ran away from his mother and headed directly for the elephant. The terrified mother ran after her child, and

Nalagiri charged at her in a rage. The young mother ran faster than the drunken elephant, so he turned around and started walking toward the tot, menacingly waving his huge white tusks back and forth in the air.

"Without getting the least bit flustered the Buddha focused his loving-kindness on the elephant and said in a very sweet voice, 'O Nalagiri, they served you sixteen pots of liquor and made you drunk to kill me and not anyone else. Please don't harass the people on the street. Come to me now.'

"Hearing the Buddha's melifluous voice the wild, ferocious beast turned his head and opened his eyes wide. He focused on the form of the Buddha and immediately sobered up. He dropped his trunk to the ground, lowered his head in reverence, and walked directly to where the Buddha stood. People in the crowd held their collective breaths as they watched the mammoth Nalagiri humble himself and bow before the Buddha.

"Our dear Lord stretched out his right hand and stroked the elephant's forehead lovingly. He said, 'Nalagiri, I am a Buddha and you are now an animal. From this point on, do not behave like a violent killer. Do your best to cultivate loving-kindness towards all living beings.' Then the Buddha quoted the following verses:

> "'Do not approach the Buddha, O elephant, with the idea of harming him, for that will cause you suffering. A killer of the Buddha will find no good state either here or after death.
>
> "'Be free from intoxication and indolence. The indolent cannot go to a good state. You must act in such a way that you will go to a good happy state.'"[6]

The arahants in the cool, dim cave chamber smile inwardly as they hear these sweet verses. They all have memories of being in the presence of their Lord when he focused his loving-kindness on a single individual. The transformation that unfailingly took place was always rapid, visible, and permanent.

"By the time the Buddha finished these verses Nalagiri was in a state of spiritual ecstasy," concludes Ananda. "He bent down and took dust off the Buddha's feet with his trunk and then sprayed it on himself. This gesture did not go unnoticed by anyone."

"It is my humble opinion that if that elephant had been human he would have attained the state of *sotapanna*," says Punna, smiling.

"Undoubtedly," agrees Upali as the other arahants nod their heads in full agreement.

Ananda continues, "The people in the city of Rajagaha that had witnessed this miracle with Nalagiri were filled with joy. They stood and applauded the Buddha and the elephant with great enthusiasm. Many of the people came forward and adorned the elephant with golden ornaments."

"On the other hand," begins Bhaddiya, "the people also booed and shouted obscenities at Devadatta and the king. This public demonstration caused a sense of general unrest, and before too long it escalated to an all-out uproar."

"A well-deserved uproar at that!" exclaims Upali.

"To complete the story, Nalagiri bowed to the Buddha one last time and then backed away from him. He waved his trunk in the air in a grand salute and trumpeted. The sound was almost deafening. Then the powerful elephant turned and walked quietly back to his stable," concludes Ananda.

"I remember that after this memorable event the Buddha led us all back to the monastery where the townspeople served a great *dana*," adds Sopaka.

"Devadatta must have been devastated by the taming of Nalagiri," says Anuruddha. "Did anyone see him there that day? Did he witness the event himself?"

"I'm told that he watched it from the balcony of King Ajatasattu's palace," replies Bakkula.

"As we said earlier, public opinion against the king and Devadatta was growing very strong by this time," says Punna. "When Devadatta used the king's own elephant to try to kill the Buddha, this became the last straw. The spontaneous public demonstration against this ill-fated pair, the teacher and his student, nearly ignited a revolt in the kingdom. King Ajatasattu saw the danger he was in, and the possible end of his short rule. He knew that he needed to immediately and publicly sever his ties with his teacher. This was a huge realization for the king. He had

Devadatta thrown out of his palace and announced that he would never again be allowed to enter. From that day forward they never spoke. By the way, the king also cut off Devadatta's daily supply of sumptuous food."

"Things in Rajagaha gradually returned to normal, and the king did his best to demonstrate to the public that he had reformed," says Bhaddiya. "As we know, he eventually won back the hearts and loyalty of his subjects, but in the beginning it wasn't easy for the king to prove that he had become a faithful supporter of the Triple Gem. The events we've recollected this evening took place eight years ago. The king is now secure on his throne and walking the Buddha's noble path. He came very close, however, to losing it all."

"Devadatta's health began to decline over the next nine months, and he was never able to recover any of his lost gains, honors, or praises," says Ananda. "When he became desperately ill he knew that his end was near, and for some reason he developed a desire to see the Buddha again. He told his remaining disciples to take him to the Buddha. The surprised disciples said, 'You were the Buddha's enemy. We dare not take you to him now!'

"Devadatta answered, 'It was only I who bore the grudge against the Buddha. He did not have the slightest ill-will for me. Take me now to my brother, the Exalted Buddha.'

"They put his body on a couch and started carrying him all the way to Savatthi, where the Buddha was residing at the time," continues Ananda.

"How ironic and presumptuous for Devadatta to call the Buddha 'brother' after all he had done," says Upali.

"Devadatta knew that the Buddha was compassion personified, and I believe that at the end of his days he regretted his unfortunate past actions," says Anuruddha.

"What do you think he hoped to gain by seeing the Buddha again?" asks Punna.

"The usual: absolution, forgiveness, deathbed blessings. Probably all of the above," answers Maha Kassapa. "As fate would have it, however, he got none of these."

"When Devadatta was just a few hundred yards away from Jetavana monastery his disciples set his couch down on the bank of a small pond. The disciples entered the pond to bathe while Devadatta sat up and put his two feet on the ground. In a matter of seconds his feet began to sink into the sand. The earth sucked him right off the couch and devoured him whole. First went his ankles, then his knees, his waist, his chest, his neck, and finally up to his chin. His arms flailed above his head in a state of abject fear.

"As he was about to be completely consumed he screamed out, 'I, Devadatta, on my deathbed seek refuge in the Exalted One with all my remaining strength.'

"Almost immediately after uttering these words the earth took the rest of him," concludes Ananda.

The arahants in the cave chamber sit still for a moment, thinking about Devadatta's horrible death. Each of them had known him; three of them had been related to him. What distinguished these elders from other men, though, was the fact that they had no negative feelings toward him; the programmed mental reaction of judgment had ceased long ago. They were fully-enlightened beings, never to return, and never to revert to using any base human thinking mechanism that might produce anything other than loving-kindness.

Maha Kassapa breaks the silence saying, "The Buddha summed it all up in the following verse:

> "'Do not associate with evil companions,
> Nor seek the fellowship of the vile.
> Associate with good friends, and
> Seek the fellowship of noble men.'[7]

"I think this should conclude our discussion this evening, my friends. We've had two long conversations about King Ajatasattu and his companion, Devadatta. Their two names will be forever linked in the history of the *Sasana*."

The arahants rise from their seats and pay their respects to their seniors. One by one they leave Maha Kassapa's chamber and return to their own for rest and meditation.

Ananda, however, asks Sopaka to join him outside for a breath of fresh air and a look at the stars. Sitting on a large boulder across from the cave entrance they turn their gaze toward the sky and after a few moments Ananda says, "No matter how vile Devadatta became, I can never forget the Buddha saying that one day – eons from now – he would eventually become a Pacceka Buddha named Satthissara. Universal compassion has no limits."

The two arahants continue to sit on the huge stone and meditate until the rising sun stirs them into waking consciousness.

Chapter 32
The Passing of Sariputta and Moggallana

"'Cultivate the friendship of Sariputta and Moggallana, *bhikkhus*; associate with Sariputta and Moggallana. They are wise and helpful to their companions in the holy life. Sariputta is like a mother; Moggallana is like a nurse. Sariputta trains others for the fruit of stream-entry [*sotapanna*], Moggallana for the supreme goal. Sariputta, *bhikkhus*, is able to announce, teach, describe, establish, reveal, expound, and exhibit the Four Noble Truths.'"

Ananda continues reciting to the end of the *Saccavibhanga Sutta*,[1] and is escorted from the podium by Sopaka.

During the morning tea break Maha Kassapa says to his old friend, "We are getting close to the end of the council meeting and our recollection of the life of the Buddha. Hearing your recitation this morning reminded me that before we record our account of the passing away of the Lord, we should pay our final respects to the Buddha's Chief Disciples."

Ananda smiles and says, "As usual, dear friend, your thoughts are mine."

The chairman ends the council proceedings in the middle of the afternoon and the members of the sub-committee meet for discussions in the shady glade of banyan trees at the edge of the forest below the mountain. This site is chosen because Ananda is curious to see the progress of Visakha's new monastery, and it gives them an opportunity for an impromptu inspection.

"It's just the finishing touches now," says Bhaddiya to the other sub-committee members as they tour the grounds.

"I think Visakha has outdone herself with this project," comments Anuruddha as he closely examines the intricate stone carvings on the gatehouse. "The only word that comes to mind is 'magnificent.'"

Ananda and the other arahants gaze with appreciation at the carvings and murals depicting scenes from the life of the Buddha; they cover nearly every square inch of the many structures. Hundreds of craftsmen and builders are still busy at work completing the roofs, footpaths, landscaping, and other details of the new complex.

"I think I will invite Visakha to be present for at least part of our discussion on the *parinibbana* of the Buddha," says the chairman. "I have a feeling she would like that."

"An excellent idea," responds Ananda with a smile. "We should be able to have our final committee meeting coincide with the dedication of her new monastery. I think we should make this our goal." The arahants smile at one another and everyone's agreement is evident.

After their tour of the new monastery the nine members of the subcommittee meet in the shade of the wide, verdant trees. Simple mats have been spread for them on the ground, and they take their seats along with the ten memory monks.

"The contributions made to the Buddha *Sasana* over the years by Sariputta and Maha Moggallana were enormous," begins Maha Kassapa. "They entered the Order one year after the Lord's enlightenment, and worked tirelessly in *dhammaduta* activities until just moments before they passed away. The Buddha repeatedly held them up as the ideal examples for all Sangha members to emulate. We have already recorded their early lives, their entrance into the Order, and many references to their great service; therefore, a record of their passing is essential in this recollection, and that will be the topic of our discussion this afternoon. Ananda, if you would be so kind as to begin..."

"After the Buddha observed his forty-fifth rains retreat in Vesali we moved with him to Jetavana monastery in Savatthi," begins Ananda. "Sariputta was with us, of course, and his routine then was the same as always: teaching his students, serving the Buddha, preaching the Dhamma to both monks and lay people, making sure the monastery was swept and kept clean, and solitary contemplation.

"One day after enjoying the bliss of meditation Sariputta arose with a question in his mind: who would attain *parinibbana* first, the Buddha or himself? When he examined the question he came to know that he would be first, and that it would take place in just seven days. He fully accepted this eventuality and further examined where his *parinibbana* would occur. He saw that it would be in his hometown of Upatissagrama in the outskirts of Rajagaha. Sariputta understood that this culmination of his life – and all his past rebirths – would happen in the very bed in which he was born, in the home of his mother, Rupasari. We have already recollected how this devout, but bitter, Brahmin woman still held a grudge against her revered son because he not only became a monk himself, but all his siblings followed him into the Order as well." Ananda pauses for a moment before continuing.

Punna speaks, "Sariputta saw with his inner vision that by having compassion for his mother on his deathbed, she would join the Buddha's path to enlightenment and become a *sotapanna*."

"He also knew that her embrace of the Buddha Dhamma would only take place if he himself preached it to her," adds Bhaddiya. "She was still very resistant and angry, feeling that she had been robbed of all her children by the *Sasana*."

Ananda begins, "Sariputta felt that he had to ask the Buddha's permission to attain *parinibbana*, and he had to carefully frame his request in such a way that the Lord's response would not be perceived by the lay people as either praising death or praising suffering."

"Sariputta always thought of all the angles when it came to the image and perception of the *Sasana* – right to the end," says Maha Kaccayana, shaking his head in amazement.

"An idea occurred to him," continues Ananda. "He called his younger brother, Cunda, and told him to gather all of his monks and tell them to prepare for a journey. They stood around him while he swept out his dwelling, packed his bedding, and gathered his eight requisites. When he was finished he looked around his small room and said, 'This is the last time I will see you; I won't be coming back.'"

"I was there the day Sariputta approached the Lord," says Bakkula. "He said to him, 'Exalted Buddha, I ask your permission to leave. The time has come for my *parinibbana*; my lifespan on this earth is coming to an end.'"

"Then the Buddha asked, 'Where will you attain *parinibbana*?'"

"Sariputta answered him, 'My birthplace, Upatissagrama, in the country of Magadha.'

"Then the Buddha said, 'Since you are aware that your time for *parinibbana* is near, your brother monks may not be able to meet again a man of your stature. I suggest that you preach to them.'"[2]

"Sariputta then preached one of the most inspiring sermons I have ever heard – with the exception of the Buddha's own, of course," says Bakkula. "He preached to the monks for several hours using a stunning variety of styles, many of them demonstrating his extraordinary supernatural powers."

"Afterwards the Buddha praised Sariputta's preaching, and then the loyal Chief Disciple went down on his knees and grasped the Buddha's sacred feet," continues Ananda. "He asked the Lord's for forgiveness if he had ever done anything wrong. The Buddha maintained that Sariputta had been blameless, but was forgiven nonetheless. Then he told the captain of the Dhamma that he could go wherever he wished.

"Sariputta then stood and circled the Buddha while bowing to him on all sides. He said, 'It was my sincere wish in a former rebirth eons ago to be able to see you in the future, and this wish has been fulfilled. There will not be a chance for me to see you again.' Then he raised his graceful hands and joined them as he bowed to the Buddha for the last time. He backed away slowly, never taking his eyes off the Lord's form." Ananda concludes this part of his recollection and pauses for a moment. Even though the parting of his dear friend Sariputta had taken place a year and a half before, it was still fresh in his mind.

Maha Kaccayana continues by saying, "The Buddha then said to the many monks surrounding them, 'Dear sons, go and see your elder brother on his way.' Every monk in the surrounding monasteries went out with Sariputta to give him a send-off, leaving the Buddha alone. The townspeople learned that the Buddha's Chief Disciple was leaving, and they gathered in the streets in great multitudes with flowers and perfumes, wailing, and they followed him to the city gates.

"Sariputta turned to them and said, 'No one is able to overcome the final destination on the human path, which is death and dissolution of the body. Be mindful, and understand that all conditioned things, whether they are mental, emotional, or physical, pass away after they arise.' After these words he persuaded both the monks and the laypeople that had followed him to go back to their homes and monasteries," concludes Maha Kaccayana.

Anuruddha speaks, "I walked with Sariputta on this last journey, and witnessed everything that happened. It took us seven days to reach Upatissagrama from Savatthi; we stopped only to sleep each night. When he arrived at his hometown he paused to rest under a banyan tree near the village gate.

"While he was sitting there his nephew, Uparevata, happened to be walking by, and when he saw the venerable he immediately paid his respects. Sariputta asked him, 'Is your grandmother at home?' When the young man said that she was, Sariputta told him to go and inform her of his arrival and that he had his student monks with him. He said to ask her to prepare the room where he was born. He also asked that she arrange for the accommodation of the monks who accompanied him. Uparevata immediately went to his grandmother and relayed his uncle's messages. She asked her grandson why he wanted his old room, but he only shrugged his shoulders, not knowing the reason,"[3] concludes Anuruddha.

"I was later told by one of Sariputta's student monks that the mother actually hoped that after all those years he was giving up his robes and returning home," says Bhaddiya. "She went off and happily had his room prepared."

"Afterwards she made arrangements for the housing of his student monks, lit the standing lamps in her home, and sent for her son," says Anuruddha. "Uparevata accompanied his uncle back to the house and escorted him to his chamber. Sariputta dismissed his student monks and told them to go to their places for rest. Within a few minutes after issuing this instruction he fell ill and suffered great pain. Rupasari stood leaning against the door of the chamber, worried for her son.

"Before long the *devas* and the great *deva* kings came in succession to Sariputta's side, to watch over him," continues Anuruddha. "To each one of these brilliant celestial beings he said that he had a nurse monk to look after him, and not needing them he sent them away. I recognized these deities immediately, and was in awe that they had come to bid their farewells."

"Rupasari approached her son and said, 'Who are those persons who just visited you?'

"Sariputta answered, 'They are the Four Great *Deva* Kings.'

"Surprised, the Brahmin lady asked, 'Are you superior to those *Deva* Kings, son?'

"He replied, 'Mother, those four *Deva* Kings are like the guards who watch our house. Since the Buddha was born they have always been around, armed with their swords to protect him.'

"Rupasari could hardly believe what her son had just said to her. She asked, 'Who was that who came immediately after the Four *Deva* Kings?'

"Sariputta said, 'That was Sakka.'

"She said, 'Are you superior to Sakka as well?'

"'Sakka is like a novice *samanera* who carries my bowl and other requisites,' answered the dying monk.

"'Who was it who followed him to your bedside?' asked Rupasari, incredulous.

"'That was Maha Brahma, your god and master,' said Sariputta to his mother who was a Brahmin worshiper of the gods.

"She stood there with her mouth agape and said, 'Dear Son, are you superior to our god, Maha Brahma, too?'

"'Yes, mother, I am. When the Exalted Buddha became enlightened Maha Brahma came to worship him, and he invited the Buddha to teach his Dhamma to the world,' replied Sariputta.

"Rupasari had to pause and reflect for a moment on what her son had just told her. She realized that she had only now seen her own son's magnificence and it made her wonder what the Buddha himself must be like. Thinking these thoughts she became filled with an immense joy, which Sariputta immediately perceived. He used this emotional opening as an opportunity to extol the Buddha's attributes and virtues, and he gave his mother a Dhamma talk, which included the Four Noble Truths," concludes Anuruddha.

"Cunda told me that at the end of this talk Rupasari attained the state of *sotapanna* and said, 'My dear son, Sariputta, why didn't you give me this happiness before? Why did you wait so late to do this?'" adds Ananda. "Then her eyes filled with tears of regret. When he saw this Sariputta looked at his mother with great compassion and said, 'Go now, mother.' She looked at her son with longing, and then reluctantly walked out of the room."

"Sariputta realized that he had accomplished his last mission, which was to establish his mother on the path to spiritual fruition," begins Anuruddha. "Then he asked his brother, Cunda, what time it was. He replied, 'Almost daybreak, Venerable Sir.' Then the Buddha's captain of the Dhamma asked Cunda to assemble all of the monks, and quickly they gathered around him.

"He requested that he be helped to sit up in the bed, and Cunda raised him. He said to the assembly, 'If I have ever said or done anything unpleasant during our long years of association, please forgive me.' The monks assured him that he had never said or done anything to warrant forgiveness, and they told him that they should be the ones to be asking him instead." Anuruddha pauses for a moment to reflect on the purity and compassion of his close friend of decades.

Ananda says, "I am told that after this last exchange Sariputta rearranged his robe, covered his face, and turned to lay on his right side. He immediately entered the four *jhanas* and then the four advanced achievements of fruition, one by one, and then *Nirodha-Samapatti*; afterwards he did the same thing in reverse. He next went progressively from the first up to the fourth *jhana* and shortly afterward attained *parinibbana*. His physical and mental aggregates were extinguished with no remnants, and he was free forever."

"The earth quaked when he passed from this life," says Anuruddha. "All of us felt the ground tremble and the house shake. When his mother Rupasari realized that her son was gone she wailed and lamented the fact that she had never taken an opportunity to offer *dana* to him or to his fellow Sangha members. She sobbed until dawn, regretting that she had wasted all those years in darkness, never accepting the Buddha's teaching or offering robes to the monks."

"Regret is a very painful emotion," comments Sopaka. "Only by living in gratitude for the present, appreciating fully 'what is,' and understanding the impermanent nature of all things, is one able to avoid regret and self-recrimination when a loved one is gone."

"The funeral rites for Sariputta lasted for seven days," begins Anuruddha. "On the site where the cremation took place various monks gave Dhamma talks throughout the night. At daybreak I myself extinguished the fire with scented water. Then Cunda sifted through the ashes and put the relics in his water filter. He collected Sariputta's few possessions, which consisted of nothing more than his robe and bowl, and started out for Savatthi to present them to the Buddha."

"Your statement about regret is very true," agrees Ananda, nodding at Sopaka. "When the party of monks arrived at the monastery in Rajagaha, Cunda came immediately to inform me of my dear friend's *parinibbana*. He bowed and reverently presented his brother's relics and requisites to me. Then we went to inform the Buddha. When we approached the Lord I introduced him to Cunda and handed him Sariputta's bowl and robe. I put the water filter containing his relics into the Buddha's long, slender hands.

"Then the Buddha said, 'Dear monks! Behold the relics of Sariputta who was of great wisdom! Behold the relics of Sariputta who was of vast wisdom, of active wisdom, of quick wisdom, of sharp wisdom...of few wants, easily contented...and highly energetic. He admonished others by pointing out their faults, and condemned evil deeds and evil doers regardless of their social position!

"'O my dear sons, monks! To him who has attained *parinibbana* and ceased the cycle of rebirth and suffering, bow your heads in homage, with faith, and with conceit destroyed.'

"From this point on, my dear colleagues, the Buddha praised the virtues of Sariputta in five hundred more verses," adds Ananda. "The more he praised him the more helpless I felt. The Buddha immediately understood my grief and helplessness so he said to me:

"'My dear Ananda, while a big substantial tree is standing, its largest branch might come to destruction; similarly, while the community of worthy monks exists, Sariputta has attained *parinibbana* and ceases to live as a human being. Herein how would it be possible to wish that something, having the nature of newly coming to life, clearly coming into existence and being subject to conditioning and destruction, should not pass away? Indeed there is no such possibility.

"'My dear Ananda, if monks at present or after my demise, who live not depending on others but by depending on themselves, who dwell with the Dhamma as their only refuge, all of them will become arahants.'"[4]

When Ananda finishes these verses he closes his eyes and lowers his head. Even though he himself is now an arahant, it is clear to everyone sitting with him in the shade of the banyan tree that he was missing his old friend.

"The Buddha then instructed that the relics of Sariputta be interred in a *stupa* in Savatthi," says Punna.

Ananda says, "It's only a little over a year and a half since his *parinibbana*, but there was such great admiration and respect for him that this *stupa* is now one of the most sacred places in the country, and a popular destination for pilgrims."

"Tell us now about Maha Moggallana so an account of his *parinibbana* can also be recorded in our recollections of the life of Buddha," requests Maha Kassapa, bowing his head, knowing what was to come.

"After the enshrinement of Sariputta's relics, the Buddha indicated that he wished to move to Rajagaha and take up residence at the Veluvana monastery," begins Ananda. "I informed the monks of his intention, and a great number of us accompanied the Lord to that favored location.

"Only two weeks had passed since Sariputta's *parinibbana*. At that time, Maha Moggallana was living in solitude here in Magadha at the Kalasila stone slab on Mount Isigili. He had gained a great reputation among the people for being able to tell them where their deceased loved ones had been reborn. Maha Moggallana's supernormal powers were fully developed, and the people were in awe of him. Because of Maha Moggallana many people had left their former teachers and now followed the Buddha; the *Sasana* had consistently grown in strength and numbers," adds Ananda.

"The naked ascetics got tired of losing their devotees to the Buddha," says Bakkula. "They realized it wouldn't be long before they had no followers at all; that there wouldn't be donors to support them with money and food. Jealousy finally raised its ugly head and conquered the minds of these ascetic teachers. They got together as a group and decided to murder the saintly Maha Moggallana."

"They paid a thousand coins to a criminal named Samamaguttaka and told him who his target was and where he was staying," says Punna. "This man was a professional murderer, and would have killed his own mother if given enough gold."

"Samanaguttaka took his band of killers and climbed up to the Kalasila stone slab on Mount Isigili. Maha Moggallana saw them coming and using his psychic powers he disappeared into thin air," says Ananda. "They came back the next day and tried it again, but the venerable monk evaded them the same way. For the next four days they tried again and again but without success; each time Maha Moggallana saw them approaching and vanished."

"The seventh time, however, turned out differently," says Anuruddha in a somber tone.

"Indeed it did," exclaims Ananda. "The seventh time Maha Moggallana's psychic powers failed to work. An unresolved *kammic* action from a distant past life finally caught up with him, and he had no choice but to face the killers with no supernormal protection. He knew immediately that he had been caught by his past, and the tremendous power that he had once used to tame the Naga King Nandopananda failed to ignite.

"Samanaguttaka and his men grabbed the monk, bound him, and pounded him with clubs until his bones were crushed. Thinking that he was dead they picked up his crumbled, bloody body and threw it into a thicket of brambles."

"What was that past-life act that came back to haunt him in the end?" asks Bakkula, almost wincing as he felt his old friend's pain.

"I'll answer that question, if I may," says Maha Kassapa. "This is the way the Buddha explained it after Maha Moggallana's death. In one of his past lives he was the good, devoted son of two elderly parents who were blind. He cheerfully did everything he could to care for them, and he made their lives as comfortable as possible. His mother and father kept telling him he needed a wife; that he was working too hard in the house and at his trade. He repeatedly told them that he was happy doing the work alone, and that taking care of them was no hardship. Finally, he could no longer stand their constant pleading on this subject, so he gave in to their request. He agreed to accept a wife, so his parents found a young woman and brought her home to him.

"She tended to the house and his parents for a while, but soon grew tired of all the work and complained bitterly about his blind parents. She began to hate the elderly couple, and made no attempt to hide her ill feelings, even in front of them. She said to her husband, 'Your old parents are messy and make trouble for me. I can no longer live in the same house with them.'

"The poor man tried to pacify her, but she was relentless and bitter. She would even litter the house herself and blame the mess on the poor old man and woman. All along she kept repeating, 'I can no longer live in the same house with them.'

"After a while the wife's incessant complaining got to be too much for the man so he agreed to do something. He put his father and mother in his cart and told them he would take them to see their relatives in a village on the other side of the nearby forest. When they got into the forest he told them that he was stopping the cart to scout the area for robbers; at the time they were known to frequent the dense jungle. He got down from the cart and started making noise as if robbers were attacking him. Thereafter he began to beat his mother and father mercilessly. They called out, 'Kill us, if you will, but please spare our good son!'

"Even while hearing his parents' pleas for his own life he continued to beat them until they were dead. Then he threw their bodies into a ditch in the underbrush. After he did this he returned home to his wife,"[5] concludes Maha Kassapa. "This is what happened to cause Maha Moggallana's gruesome demise."

"Like King Ajatasattu, the man didn't understand the dire *kammic* consequences of murdering his parents," comments Punna. "He suffered in hell for many, many lifetimes before he was finally reborn as Maha Moggallana."

"Our revered Sangha brother didn't die right away, did he?" asks Punna.

"That is correct," answers Ananda. "He eventually regained consciousness and knew that he was about to pass away. He thought about seeing the Buddha one last time, so he used his now-restored psychic powers to go to the Lord at Veluvana monastery. He paid homage to the Master and said, 'Exalted Buddha, this body is about to die, and I am going to attain *parinibbana*.'

"The Buddha replied, 'Where will you go and do that?'

"'At the Kalasila stone slab, Exalted Buddha,' answered the Chief Disciple.

"Then the Buddha said, 'In that case, dear son Moggallana, give the Sangha members a Dhamma talk before you go. I will not have another opportunity to have a disciple like you.'"

"So Maha Moggallana, in his astral body, gave an inspiring Dhamma talk that was accompanied by several demonstrations of his vast psychic powers," says Ananda. "After he finished preaching he paid homage to the Lord one last time and then went back into his physical body at the Kalasila stone slab and attained *parinibbana*."

"An earthquake occurred at that moment, and a great cry was heard throughout the *deva* worlds that Maha Moggallana had passed into *parinibbana*," says Bhaddiya solemnly.

"Maha Moggallana's remains were brought down from Mt. Isigili, and a great pyre of sandalwood was prepared. The Buddha himself came with his large retinue of monks," adds Bakkula, "and he personally arranged and conducted the funeral rites, which lasted for seven days."

"Afterwards the Buddha had the relics of Maha Moggallana enshrined in a large *stupa* here in Rajagaha, and it, too, has become a well-visited place of worship and veneration," says Ananda.

"What about the murderers?" asks Sopaka?

"King Ajatasattu, enraged by this assault on the Buddha's Chief Disciple, immediately sent his security forces to investigate," answers Ananda. "They discovered the murderers in a tavern when the men were overheard boasting among themselves about their evil deed. They were even vying for who could take the credit."

"What happened to them?" asks Sopaka.

Ananda quickly responds, "They were brought before the king and he asked them, 'Did you kill Venerable Maha Moggallana?'

"The men hung their heads and said, 'Yes, we killed him, Great King.'

"'Who put you up to it?' asked King Ajatasattu.

"'Great King, those naked ascetics paid us to do it,' they finally answered after a bit of torture.

"Then the king rounded up the scores of naked ascetics who were responsible, and along with the band of murderers, he had them executed," says Ananda.

The arahants in the shade of the banyan trees sigh and take a deep breath. There are a few moments of silence while they reflect on the fates of their two most eminent Sangha brothers.

Anuruddha is the first to speak. "Both of these esteemed arahants attained *parinibbana*, but in very different circumstances, which were based on past rebirths. Any reverberations from past negative actions had been extinguished prior to Sariputta's *parinibbana*. Maha Moggallana, on the other hand, had to face just one more that had been left unresolved, which he paid for with his painful death."

Maha Kassapa says, "The Buddha summed it all up when he made this statement about *kamma*, that applies to everyone alike – layman, monk, criminal, king, or arahant:

> "'According to the seed that is sown,
> So is the fruit you reap.
> The doer of good will gather good result,
> The doer of evil reaps evil result.
> If you plant a good seed well,
> Then you will enjoy the good fruits.'"[6]

"We have now almost completed our council proceedings, and our recollections as well," continues the chairman. "Our final committee meetings will focus on the *parinibbana* of the Buddha himself."

The arahants close their eyes, and go into the bliss of deep meditation.

The sun is just about to set, and a soft breeze rustles the leaves in the banyan trees. By their own efforts they had scaled to the zenith of spiritual attainment, and are ready for their own *parinibbanas* whenever the moment is right. Each of them wonder if they, too, might have just one last bit of negative *kamma* to account for before the deaths of their physical forms, as did the great Chief Disciple of the Buddha, Maha Moggallana.

They knew that if they did have to pay for some as yet unknown past action, they would welcome it with courage, and willingly face the challenge knowing that it would be their last on earth, or on any other world. They had righteously earned their final release.

Chapter 33
The Final Year

"After staying at Natika village for as long as he wished, the Buddha said to me, 'Come, Ananda, let us go to Vesali.' I agreed, of course, so we departed with a large company of *bhikkhus*, young and newly-ordained in the Sangha. We set up our residence at Ambapali's mango grove.

"The Buddha wanted to make sure that the fresh, youthful *bhikkhus* wouldn't be tempted to lose their mindfulness and become captivated by the courtesan Ambapali's seductive beauty," says Ananda. "He preached to them thus:

> "'*Bhikkhus*, a *bhikkhu* should dwell in mindfulness and clear comprehension. This is my exhortation to you. A *bhikkhu* keeps his mind on the body with diligence, comprehension and mindfulness, steadfast by contemplating it as body, so as to keep away sense-desires and distress that would otherwise arise in him. A *bhikkhu* also keeps his mind on sensation, the mind, and mind objects in the same way and for the same reasons. *Bhikkhus*, this is how a *bhikkhu* remains mindful.'"[1]

Maha Kassapa picks up the large mallet and sounds the gong. The day's council proceedings are officially ended. He and Ananda step down from the platform and Sopaka escorts them from the hall.

A few minutes later they are in the chairman's chamber deep inside the mountain and the members of the sub-committee, along with the memory monks, are ready for their discussion.

Maha Kassapa says, "We are in the final phase of our recollections. As you gathered from Ananda's closing recitation just now, we will recount the story of Ambapali this evening, and continue with the events leading up to the Buddha's *parinibbana*. Ananda, would you care to begin?"

Ananda bows his consent, "Ambapali was the foremost courtesan of Vesali. This high rank was given to her by the king, who appointed her when she was of age. Legend says that she suddenly materialized out of thin air in the king's gardens, but she was probably an unwanted orphan who was left there by parents who could no longer afford to take care of her. One of the king's gardeners found her at the foot of a mango tree, and she was given to a childless couple to raise as their daughter.

"She grew up to become the reigning beauty of her time; no other young woman could even begin to compete with her physical perfection. Even when she was very, very young her grace captivated the attention of many of the Licchavi princes who wanted to marry her. Not being able to make up her mind, and shunned by many of the royal families who said she had no pedigree, the king made her the city's chief courtesan, wanting to make sure she could provide for herself."

"And provide for herself she did!" exclaims Anuruddha. "She became very wealthy, and I'm told that those princes and rich merchants of Vesali paid hundreds of gold coins for one night with her."

"You may recall from one of our earlier discussions that a rich traveling merchant from Vesali suggested to King Bimbisara that his kingdom of Magadha would be greatly enhanced if he had a courtesan equal to the high-ranking Ambapali," says Bhaddiya.

"That is correct, Venerable Sir. That's when King Bimbisara appointed Salavati, Jivaka's and Sirima's mother," agrees Punna. "She, too, became one of the most famous courtesans of her era, commanding vast sums of money for her services here in Rajagaha."

"Ambapali also entertained King Bimbisara whenever he was in Vesali, and several years before he died she gave birth to his son," adds Anuruddha. "He must be in his late teens by now."

"He's actually in his early thirties, Venerable Sir; Ambapali had him when she was at the maximum age for a woman to conceive," says Upali. "He ordained in the Order and now his name is Venerable Vimala-Kondanna. He's living a solitary life in the jungle engaged in meditation, and I hear he's doing very well in his practice."

"Ambapali must be much, much older than I thought she was," says Bakkula, raising his eyebrows. The other arahants in the cave chamber express the same surprise.

"As physically beautiful as she once was, I don't think her looks matter to her any more," says Upali. "Just a few months before the Buddha passed away Ambapali finally retired from her profession and ordained as a *bhikkhuni*."

"You're getting slightly ahead of our story, Upali," says Maha Kassapa. "Why don't you proceed on your timeline, Ananda."

Ananda nods his head and begins, "Ambapali was very smart with her money and invested it well. Many years ago she bought a beautiful parcel of land on the outskirts of the city that was planted in mango trees. I believe that all of my Sangha brothers know that place very well." The arahants in the cave chamber smile, reflecting on their memories of the lovely, shady grove that had the sweetest golden mangoes in the kingdom.

"Through King Bimbisara and other patrons she became acquainted with the Buddha," says Ananda. "She gave him permission to stay in her mango grove with his Order of *bhikkhus* whenever he liked. Ambapali had built a country retreat house there that the trees covered like an umbrella. This became a favorite place for the Lord to stay when he was in Vesali.[2]

"A little more than a year ago we had just taken up residence in the mango grove and Ambapali was soon given the news. This is when the Buddha gave the discourse I recited earlier to the young monks who had accompanied us. She had several of her elegant, ornate carriages made ready, and came at once to see the Lord in the company of her male and female attendants. When she entered the grove she stopped the carriages and then went the rest of the way on foot, as was proper when approaching the Buddha. She bowed low to him, as did her retainers, and then she sat to one side.

"The Buddha greeted her with a gentle smile and then preached to her from the Doctrine. He told her to set herself up in the practice of the Dhamma, and he made her heart glad when he said that she could one day attain the fruits of a spiritual life.

"Afterwards she graciously invited him for the mid-day meal on the following day. The Buddha accepted her invitation with his customary silence, and she bowed respectfully and departed," says Ananda.

"I understand she was in quite a hurry to get home," says Upali, smiling.

"She was so excited to be the first in Vesali to offer *dana* to the Lord that she literally took off at a run," answers Bhaddiya, laughing. "She hopped up into her carriage and told the driver to hurry. On the way home she came upon a group of Licchavi princes; some were dressed in blue, some in yellow, and others in red. She tried to overtake them."[3]

"I heard that her wheels, yokes, and axles bumped into the carriages of the Licchavis, nearly causing an accident," adds Anuruddha. "One of the princes dressed in blue yelled out to her driver and ordered him to stop the carriage. When everyone came to a halt he said, 'Ambapali, why is your man driving so recklessly? You almost got us all killed.'

"Nearly out of breath she answered, 'O my princes! I have invited the Buddha and his *bhikkhus* for *dana* tomorrow and I have much to do.'

"Another prince, attired in a red costume, considered this bit of news, frowned, and then said, 'Ambapali, we'll give you a hundred thousand gold coins if you let us have the privilege of serving *dana* to the Buddha tomorrow.'

"Ambapali proudly said, 'O my princes! Even if you were to give me the entire kingdom of Vesali – along with its five territories – I would not give up my chance to offer this meal.'

"Another of the princes, this one dressed from head to toe in yellow, exclaimed, 'Men! We have been outdone by this woman!' Then the other princes joined in shouting, 'We have been outdone by this woman!' It was always considered an honor – you might even say a status symbol – to be the first to offer *dana* to the Buddha whenever he took up residence in a new city. These princes had been outdone by their chief courtesan; you can imagine how this wounded their proud egos, and how they feared their reputations would suffer," says Anuruddha.

"In order to try to salvage their image they went at once to visit the Buddha in Ambapali's mango grove," says Ananda. "When the Lord saw them approaching he said to us *bhikkhus*, 'Let those *bhikkhus* who have never seen the *Tavatimsa devas* look at that array of the Licchavis; let them look carefully; let them feast their eyes on the Licchavis.' I must say that they looked magnificent. The princes dressed in blue uniforms were in blue carriages studded with precious blue stones. Their helmets, armor and everything they wore was vivid blue. They had even applied blue pigment to their skin. The red ones and the yellow ones were the same – completely monochromatic down to the last detail. All of them were tall and grand, having the regal demeanor of the princes they were."

"It's the first time I had ever heard the Buddha make such a statement like that about someone's appearance – even going so far as comparing them to the *devas*," says Bakkula.

"I'm quite sure he was giving the monks a lesson in impermanence," says Maha Kassapa. "No matter how great and glorious the princes were at that time, their appearance could change in an instant on the battlefield, or slowly in the process of aging."

"The magnificent Licchavi princes approached the Buddha, paid their obeisance to him, and sat down to one side," begins Ananda. "The Buddha preached to them from the Doctrine, and then the tallest one in red said to him, 'Venerable Sir, please accept our offering of food tomorrow together with your company of *bhikkhus*.'

"The Buddha answered, 'O Licchavi princes, I have already accepted an invitation tomorrow from Ambapali.'

"In unison the frustrated Licchavi princes excitedly waved their arms in the air and exclaimed, 'Men! We have been outdone by this woman! We have been outdone by this woman!'"

"The Licchavi princes must not have believed Ambapali when she told them she was offering *dana* the following day," comments Maha Kaccayana.

"Either that, or they hoped to pull rank on her," says Bhaddiya.

"The Buddha would never cancel on one person for *dana* in favor of another," says Anuruddha emphatically. "I'm convinced that he wanted to prove to the princes that he was no respecter of a person's status. Whether one is a prince or a courtesan, the sincerity of a lay person's devotion to the Triple Gem is all that matters."

"The following morning Ambapali sent a messenger saying that *dana* was ready, so the Buddha and the rest of us *bhikkhus* accompanied him to the retreat house where it was to be served," says Ananda. "Ambapali had outdone herself that day in terms of the quality and varieties of food that were offered. She served us with her own hand, and afterwards she said, 'Venerable Sir, please accept this mango grove as a gift for you and your Sangha members.' The Buddha accepted the grove and expounded a discourse to a happy Ambapali and her attendants. Shortly afterwards we all departed for our lodging places."

"A lot happened during the intervening year," says Maha Kassapa. "Why don't you tell us Ananda."

"Looking back, I can see why the Buddha wanted the majority of the *bhikkhus* to be in the Vesali area during the rains retreat. He knew that he would attain *parinibbana* in ten months, and he wanted them to have as many opportunities as possible to hear his discourses and be in his sacred presence. He also knew that when he passed away they would all want to come and pay their respects, but if they were in far away places that would be impossible."

"So once again the Lord showed his infinite compassion by confining the *bhikkhus'* travel for a while so they could be near him at the end," says Maha Kaccayana.

"Almost as soon as the retreat season began the Buddha came down with a very serious illness," begins Ananda. "He was in great pain most of the time, and it grieved me to see him suffer so much. He was able to bear the pain by practicing insight meditation and *phala-samapatti*, which is contemplation of the fruition of knowledge. He wanted to postpone his *parinibbana* for ten months so he could properly take leave of his Sangha."

"He eventually recovered enough to resume his schedule, and we were able to see him again," says Bhaddiya.

"I told him I was so worried about him that my mind had become befuddled," says Ananda. "I knew, however, that he would not leave us without any instruction concerning his Order. He knew my thoughts so he explained:

> "'Ananda, what more does the Sangha expect from me? In the matter of the Dhamma, I have held back nothing. I have no desire to have sole control over the monks, so why should I leave instructions? I have grown old, and am in the last stage of life. I will turn eighty years old this year, and my body is kept going like putting straps on an old worn-out cart through my effort of practicing *phala-samapatti*. It is only when in this state that the *Tathagata's*

body is comfortable. Ananda, let yourselves be your own refuge – yourselves and no one else. Let the Dhamma, and only the Dhamma be your foundation. This goes for all of the *bhikkhus* as well.'"[4]

"Not too long after the passing away of Sariputta and Maha Moggallana the Buddha made his announcement about his imminent *parinibbana*," says Anuruddha. "It has been rumored that he gave you clear hints that you didn't catch because you were blinded by Mara."

Ananda looks up and says, "I know that many people – some *bhikkhus* included – have blamed me for not asking the Buddha to live for an eon. They say that he would have done so if I had asked him to. Venerable Maha Kassapa, you and I had a conversation about this before my enlightenment a few months ago. In the *Mahapadana Sutta* the *devas* say, 'In this fortunate eon now the Lord Buddha has arisen in the world. He was born of the Khattiya caste; he is of the Gotama clan. In his time the life-span is short, limited and quick to pass. It is seldom that anyone lives to be a hundred.'[5] The Buddha actually lived to complete four-fifths of this maximum range for his time."

"In addition," begins Maha Kaccayana, "even if it was the Buddha's *kamma* to be able to prolong his life, then that ability would be limited to the maximum lifespan of the time; in this case probably no more than one hundred years."

"If I was somehow blinded by Mara and didn't seize an opportunity to ask the Buddha to live, please forgive me," says Ananda with great humility. "Now that I have become an arahant, however, I truly believe that this was not the case. I felt guilty about it until I achieved spiritual fruition, but now I understand that everything worked out perfectly – exactly as the Buddha intended."

"We are in agreement with you, Venerable Sir," says Punna, "and this recollection of the Lord's life will set this issue straight."

Maha Kassapa says, "Speaking of Mara, I believe it is recorded that the Evil One approached the Buddha during this time."

Ananda says:

"He came to him and said, 'Venerable Sir! Let the *Bhagava* realize *parinibbana* now, let the well-spoken one pass away! Venerable Sir! It is time.' On this occasion the Buddha answered Mara by saying, 'I shall not pass away as long as my *bhikkhus, bhikkhunis,* and lay disciples are not yet well-disciplined, sure of themselves in their conduct, possessed of wide knowledge, able to memorize the Teaching, able to practice according to the Teaching, able to expound and elucidate the Teaching, and not yet able to thoroughly refute on righteous grounds other doctrines that may arise.' Mara argued with the Lord saying that these groups were, in fact, so established. The Buddha finally dismissed Mara by saying, 'Don't worry, Evil One. The *parinibbana* of the *Tathagata* will not be long in coming. Three months from now the *Tathagata* will pass away.'" [6]

"I'm told that the earth quaked violently at the very moment the Master made that announcement," says Upali.

"That is true, Venerable Sir, it did," says Ananda. "The Buddha explained to me why the earth quaked, actually there were eight reasons for this; almost all of them having to do with Buddhas or great *Bodhisattas* being born, dying, expounding the Dhamma, or attaining enlightenment. When I heard his explanation I knew without him telling me that he had just relinquished the life-maintaining mental process that sustained him. I knew that he would soon pass away. I looked at the Buddha and realized immediately that he knew I understood."

"I remember that he spoke to us on a variety of subjects," says Anuruddha. "He spoke about the eight categories of assemblies, the eight ways of mastering the mind through concentration, the eight stages of release, and about relinquishing the life-maintaining mental process. He related the discussion he had just had with Mara, and told Ananda that he had made the decision to pass away in three months time."

"I said to the Lord," begins Ananda, "'Venerable Sir, for the welfare of mankind, and for the benefit and happiness of *devas* and humans, please live the maximum life span. Out of compassion for the world, live as long as you can.'

"The Buddha said, 'Enough, Ananda. Do not implore the *Tathagata* now.' I asked a second and then a third time. At the end he said, 'Ananda, have I not said in the past that it is the very nature of things that we must someday part with them, even if they are near and dear to us? Ananda, the *Tathagata* has discarded the life-maintaining mental process and has said under no uncertain terms that the *parinibbana* will be realized in three months time. There is no possibility for the *Tathagata* to go back on his word. Let us now go to the pinnacled hall in the Mahavana forest.'

"I went with him to the pinnacled hall and he asked me to assemble all of the Sangha members living in the Vesali area. When they were all gathered in the hall I went to him, paid my obeisance and said, 'Venerable Sir, the Sangha members are ready to be addressed whenever you wish,'" concludes Ananda.

"The Buddha came into the hall and we all bowed before him," says Punna. "I knew instinctively that he had something important to say to us, and I was prepared for what we all heard, knowing the poor state of his health during the past several months."

"He exhorted the monks in many aspects of the Doctrine," begins Ananda, "and then finally said at the end:

> "'O *Bhikkhus*, I now say this to you: all conditioned and compounded things, *sankhara*, have the nature of decay and disintegration. With mindfulness, endeavor diligently to complete the task. The *parinibbana* of the *Tathagata* will take place before long. Three months from this day the *Tathagata* will realize *parinibbana* and finally pass away.'

"The ensuing silence that prevailed in the hall was profound," continues Ananda. "When the reality of what the Lord had just said finally penetrated their minds, there was a collective gasp from the *bhikkhus*, and then a great many tears and pleas for him not to leave them. The Buddha held up his hand to quiet them and said in verse:

> "'I am now quite ripe in age.
> Only a little of my life remains.
> I shall soon have to depart, leaving you behind.
> I have made a refuge of myself.
> '*Bhikkhus*, vigilantly and with mindfulness be of pure virtue.
> Being composed and collected of mind,
> Thinking right, watch over your own mind.

> "'*Bhikkhus*, in this Teaching, this Doctrine and Discipline,
> He who is heedfully vigilant will be able to escape
> From the round of repeated rebirths
> And make an end to all suffering.'[7]

"The following morning the Buddha rearranged his robe and with us behind him, he entered the city of Vesali for alms collection. After he took his meal he turned around and looked at the fair city where we had spent so much time over the years. At that moment he stood like a noble elephant; I'll never forget his royal appearance. He said to me, 'Ananda, this will be the last time the *Tathagata* looks on Vesali. Come, let us go to Bhandu village.'"

"The Buddha had never made a comment like that whenever he left any of the other places we would visit," says Anuruddha. "I think that turning back to look at Vesali had some special significance as yet unknown to us. At the time I had a strong feeling that the Buddha saw some dark future ahead for Vesali. I realize now that he also foresaw that the Licchavi princes would commemorate his turning back to view their city by building a place of reverence, which they have since done on that very spot where he stood."

"When we got to Bhandu village," begins Ananda, "the Buddha gave a discourse similar to the one he had given the monks in Vesali. He would continue to preach on these same themes throughout this last tour. We passed through Hatthi, Amba, Jambu, and finally reached the village of Bhoga. He delivered a discourse there that we have already covered in one of our earlier recollections, which was about determining whose words should be accepted or rejected in regards to the Dhamma. After we stayed in Bhoga for a while the Buddha said, 'Come, Ananda, let us go to Pava.' I said, 'Very well, Venerable Sir,' and soon we were on our way."

"Throughout this journey hundreds, if not thousands, of Sangha members came from nearby forests and monasteries to pay their last respects to the Buddha," says Upali.

"Except for one named Venerable Dhammarama!" exclaims Bakkula. "He steadfastly maintained that he would not travel to visit the Lord."

Maha Kaccayana smiles and says, "Yes, this is true; I know that monk very well. Some of the *bhikkhus* reported Venerable Dhammarama's refusal to the Buddha. The Lord then asked that this *bhikkhu* be brought to him. Many of the finger-pointing monks expected Dhammarama to get a scolding, so they stood on the sidelines waiting to see him get his due. When the monk went before the Buddha he bowed low and touched the Lord's feet. When he stood up the Buddha said, 'Why didn't you want to come and pay your last respects to me?'

"Humble Venerable Dhammarama said, 'Venerable Sir, I have heard the news that you would pass away in a short time. I thought the best way to honor you would be to attain arahantship before you enter *parinibbana*. I have been striving day and night.'

"The Buddha exclaimed, 'Excellent! Excellent! Anyone who wishes to honor me should emulate this *bhikkhu*. He who practices my teaching best, honors me best.' The monks who were watching on the side felt ashamed for criticizing this devoted disciple. They began following his example and increased their own efforts toward realizing the ultimate goal," concludes Maha Kaccayana.

"In Pava, as you all know, we stayed in the mango grove donated by Cunda, the goldsmith's son," begins Ananda. "He was a very rich man, and from an earlier exchange with the Buddha had become a *sotapanna*. When Cunda heard the news that the Buddha was residing at the mango grove he came immediately and paid his respects by touching the ground with his forehead. The Buddha preached a discourse to him, and afterwards this devoted lay disciple invited the Lord to his home for *dana* the following day. The *Tathagata* accepted the invitation with his usual silence." The arahants in the cave chamber go silent for a moment as they reflect on that ill-fated *dana*.

"Cunda went home and instructed his staff to begin preparing choice foods for the Buddha's lunch, which included a special dish prepared with *kukurumuttu*, a particular variety of wild mushroom that had been gathered from the edge of a pond in the jungle," says Bakkula. "Cunda had heard that this particular ingredient might be helpful for the Buddha since his health was failing."

"We suspect that wild pigs might have been rutting in that pond, in which case they would have fouled the water near the mushrooms," says Punna.

"If pigs had been in that pond, then the *kukurumuttu* could easily have become contaminated. Otherwise, these rare mushrooms are usually very good for the health," adds Bakkula.

"The following day a large company of *bhikkhus* went with the

Buddha to Cunda's home for the mid-day meal," says Ananda. "When Cunda was serving the Buddha, he offered the wild mushroom dish to him first. The Buddha said, 'Cunda, serve this dish only to me;

serve the other dishes to my *bhikkhus.*' Cunda looked surprised, but he did as he was instructed; the Buddha proceeded to eat what he was offered.

"After finishing his meal the Buddha said to his host, 'Cunda, bury the remaining *kukurumuttu* dish in a pit. I see no one else but me in all the celestial worlds of *devas, maras,* and *Brahmas,* or in this human world of *samanas* and *brahmanas,* rulers and men, who if they were to eat it would be able to digest it well.'[8]

"Cunda said, 'Very well, Venerable Sir.' Even though I'm sure he had no idea why he was doing it, he did as he was told and went out and buried the remainder of the dish he had so thoughtfully ordered for the Buddha. Afterwards the Buddha taught Cunda a discourse on the Doctrine, and then he rose from his seat and we all departed.

"It didn't take long before the Buddha suddenly came down with a violent case of dysentery. There was a discharge of blood, and it caused the Lord great pain. I thought he would surely die that day, but he endured the pain using concentration and mindfulness. He never complained," says Ananda with tears in his eyes. "Then he said to me, 'Ananda, let us go to Kusinara.' Somehow the Lord found the strength to walk all the way to Kusinara in the company of the many *bhikkhus* who were traveling with us."

"Is it possible that the Buddha became ill not because of the meal, but because he was coming down with something anyway?" asks Bakkula. "If that had been the case, then the meal prepared with the special mushrooms actually might have fortified him; it actually could have given him the strength to make that journey on foot to Kusinara."

"It is possible, Venerable Sir," answers Ananda, "but we will never know the answer to that question."

"Tell us the story of the water," requests Punna.

Ananda smiles and says, "With pleasure, Venerable Sir. It is one of my fondest memories of the Lord. On the road to Kusinara we stopped to rest for a while at the foot of a big tree. The Buddha was still weak from the dysentery, and I'm sure he was dehydrated. He said, 'Ananda, I am weary. I shall sit down for a while.' He placed his fourfold robe on the ground and seated himself. Then he said, 'Ananda, go and get some drinking water; I am thirsty.'

"I was very concerned about the available water supply so I said, 'Venerable Sir, five hundred carts have just crossed over the stream and it is muddy. The Kukudha River is not far away, and the water is clean and clear of mud. Perhaps the *Tathagata* would like to go there and drink, and maybe cool his limbs for a while.'

"Right away the Buddha said emphatically, 'Ananda, go and get me some water; I am very thirsty.'

"I repeated the same thing about the muddy water, and once again urged him to visit the narby Kukudha River. A third time he said to me, 'Ananda, go and get me some water; I am thirsty and want water.' After being commanded by the Lord three times I took his alms bowl and went to the muddy stream. I couldn't believe my eyes when I watched the water suddenly start flowing clear and pure – there was no mud in it at all! I marveled at the way nature cooperated with the Lord's every request.

"I filled the alms bowl with clean, cool water and brought it to the Buddha. When I handed him the bowl I said, 'Wonderful indeed is the great power of the Buddha!' The Buddha smiled at me fondly and drank from the bowl," concludes Ananda.

"What about the Malla prince? Didn't he show up right about that time?" asks Bhaddiya.

"Yes, he did," answers Ananda. "Right after I gave the Buddha his water, Pukkusa, the Malla prince who was a devoted disciple of Alara Kalama, passed by on his journey from Kusinara to Pava. He saw the Buddha sitting peacefully under the tree and he approached him and paid obeisance to him. Then he said to the Buddha, 'Wonderful it is, Venerable Sir, how recluses remain in such a tranquil state. It reminds me of the time my teacher, Alara Kalama, sat down by a tree next to the road and five hundred carts passed by very close to him; he heard nothing – even though he was still conscious.

"Then the Buddha said,

> "'Pukkusa, at one time I was living in a straw hut in the town of Aluma. During that time there was a violent thunderstorm and four oxen and two farmers were struck by lightning right next to my hut. A large number of people came from the town to survey the destruction, and by that time I was walking back and forth outside my small

dwelling. A man from the crowd came over to me and paid his respects. I asked the man, 'Friend, why are so many people gathered here?'

"The man said, 'Just hours ago four oxen and two farmers were struck dead from lightning bolts right by your hut. Where were you during the violent storm?'

"'Friend, I have been here the whole time.'

"'Venerable Sir, did you see it happen?'

"'Friend, I didn't see anything.'

"'Venerable Sir, you must have heard the crashing sounds!'

"'Friend, I didn't hear anything either.'

"Incredulous, the man looked at the Lord and said, 'Were you able to sleep through the whole thing?'

"'Friend, I wasn't sleeping.'

"'Venerable Sir, were you conscious at all?'

"'Yes, friend, I was completely conscious.'[9]

"'Venerable Sir, even though you were conscious and awake you didn't see or hear anything. How wonderful and marvelous it is that recluses can remain in their tranquil state!' Then the man paid his respects to the Buddha and walked away.

"After the Buddha told this story, the Malla Prince Pukkusa turned to a servant and said, 'Bring me the two pieces of golden-hued cloth that I just purchased for my ritual.' The servant brought the beautiful cloth to Pukkusa who then held them out to the Buddha and said, 'Venerable Sir, out of compassion for me please accept these.'

"Without even glancing at the cloth the Buddha said to him, 'Present one piece to me and the other one to Ananda.'

"So with great respect Pukkusa presented one to the Lord, and then turned and presented the other to me. I was very surprised that the Buddha made the request that one of them should be given to me, but I had no choice but to accept it," concludes Ananda. "You all know that one of the agreements I had made with the Buddha when I took on the post of Chief Attendant was that I would refuse any and all gifts that were offered to the Lord. It seemed that he wished to make an exception in this particular instance."

"You had never accepted any gifts in your twenty-five years of faultless, loyal service, Venerable Sir, and the Buddha knew that you would immediately present it right back to him any way," says Upali.

"Perhaps it was also a symbolic offering to the Sangha, and you accepted it on the Order's behalf," suggests Punna.

Ananda looks at the two sub-committee members who have voiced opinions about him accepting the gift and says, "After the Buddha preached the Doctrine to Pukkusa, and he had gone on his way, it is true that I placed both brilliant, golden robes over the Lord's shoulder. Then an amazing thing happened. The two robes immediately lost their luster and looked dull, like any other ordinary cloth. The Buddha's countenance, however, was radiant, and it was as if some brilliant light was shining from within his body. I was so awestruck that I just stepped back and stared at him.

"Then the Lord said to me, 'Ananda, there are two occasions when the body of the Buddha shines with such brilliance. The first is when the *Tathagata* attains supreme enlightenment, and the other is on the night when he attains *parinibbana*. Today, in the last watch of the night, in the *sala* grove of the Malla princes where the road turns to Kusinara, the *Tathagata's* realization of *parinibbana* will take place. Come, Ananda, let us go to the Kukudha River.' With great sadness I said, 'Very well, Venerable Sir.'

"Then the Buddha and I with the large retinue of *bhikkhus* went to the Kukudha River. The Buddha entered the river, bathed in it, and drank from it. Then he went up to the mango grove by the river while I wrung out his loin cloth and spread it out to dry. He said to Venerable Cunda, not the goldsmith's son who had served him his last meal, 'Cunda, fold my robe in four and place it on the ground. I need to lie down.'

"Venerable Cunda did as he was instructed and the Buddha lay down on his right side in a noble posture. The Lord then said to me, 'Ananda, it may happen that people may cause Cunda, the goldsmith's son, to be unhappy because he served me my last meal. Please tell them that in the life of the *Tathagata* there are two most important meals, which bestow great merit upon the donors. They are the meal just before the *Tathagata's* supreme enlightenment; and the last meal before the *Tathagata* attains *parinibbana*. These two meritorious deeds were performed by Sujata, who offered me milk-rice just before my enlightenment, and Cunda, who served me my final meal earlier today. Please make this clear to all.'

"The Buddha rested for a while and then he said, 'Come, Ananda, let us go to the *sala* grove of the Malla princes on the far bank of the Hiraññavati River.'

"I said, 'Very well, Venerable Sir,' and we departed for the place the Buddha wished to go," says Ananda with a voice full of great emotion.

Maha Kassapa says, "I thank you, Ananda, for so carefully and respectfully recollecting your memories of the Buddha up to this point. All of posterity will be grateful for your faithful telling. I suggest that we break here for the night, as it is now quite late, and we all need time to reflect on what we have heard.

"Visakha and her husband will be arriving tomorrow to hear the account of the Buddha's *parinibbana*, and then afterwards she will host a great *dana* celebration to dedicate her new monastery in the valley below. We still have a great deal of work to do organizing the Dhamma and the *Vinaya* before our final presentation to the general assembly. Ananda and Upali, you will co-chair that sub-committee, if you will." The two arahants nod their heads in acceptance of the great responsibility the chairman has just given them.

Without another word, eight of the nine arahants and ten memory monks rise from their seats and depart from Maha Kassapa's cave chamber. Each of them is pondering their own remembrance of the event that would be talked about on the following day.

They know that one day that same event will occur to them, and then they will be no more.

Chapter 34
Parinibbana

The next morning Maha Kassapa sends word to the arahants that the general assembly has been canceled for the day. At nine o'clock the sub-committee will hold its meeting in the glade of shady trees at the base of Mount Vebhara where they have met many times. The five hundred arahants will meet afterwards for a grand procession into the new monastery constructed and donated by the Buddha's Foremost Female Lay Disciple, Visakha. Then she and her family will host a *dana* ceremony in the seven-storied main pavilion, which will be formally dedicated and offered to the Sangha members at that time.

Wanting to make sure they have plenty of time, Ananda and Sopaka start their descent down the steep mountain path at eight o'clock. About half way down the two arahants stop to view the crowd that is gathering near the new monastery's entrance. Hundreds of servants are bringing in supplies for the ceremony, and hundreds more are busy putting up flags, banners, and other decorations on the structure's exterior and interior walls.

Ananda points to the caravan of carriages and carts, which is being led by twenty-one caparisoned elephants. Visakha and her husband Punnavardhana are riding atop the lead beast in a golden lacquered seat canopied in gold and red embroidered silk. The elephant's caparison is fashioned in rich gold and red brocades, and it is studded with countless rubies, diamonds, and pearls. On the elephant's forehead, and hanging from both of its sides are red silk panels emblazed with her "V" monogram outlined with precious gems. Plumes dyed red crown the elephant's regal head as well as the elegant miniature palace on its back in which ride the hosts. Dozens of maidens dressed in white silk saris walk before, beside, and behind the massive elephant, scattering flower blossoms and singing. The mahout, in a red and gold turban, sits astride the elephant with his legs behind its ears, encouraging it forward with his knees and a gilded metal prod paved in diamonds.

"She always did know how to make a spectacular entrance," comments Ananda, laughing and pointing at the display below. Sopaka simply smiles and shakes his head. The other arahants on the subcommittee catch up with the two monks and join them in watching the awesome pageant unfolding in the valley.

Bhaddiya says, smiling, "I see that we have quite a day in store for us."

"I never saw such a procession in my life – not even in the days of our uncle, King Suddhodana, in Kapilavatthu," says Anuruddha, shaking his head.

Dozens of drummers in white silk pants, bare above the waist, and wearing massive golden collars studded with precious gems, wildly beat their ancient instruments as they lead the way. They are accompanied by conchs and trumpets being sounded by scores of other musicians who trail close behind.

The other twenty elephants carry members of Visakha's family, as do the horse-drawn carriages that follow the elephant carrying Visakha and Punavardhana. One hundred carts laden with treasure are next: gifts of gold and silver bullion that will be presented to the Sangha as an endowment for the monastery's long life and well-being. Carriages transporting guests are arriving from several directions. A huge white canopy has been erected just outside the entrance of the monastery where guests will be entertained until the monks have entered the new sanctuary.

The eight arahants and the ten memory monks join Maha Kassapa at their designated spot in the shady glade just as the elephant carrying Visakha and Punnavardhana arrives. A golden staircase is immediately placed by the elephant's side and a male servant walks up to safely escort his masters to the ground. When they alight Visakha and her husband approach the arahants and bow low in respect.

"You look radiant today, Visakha," says Ananda when his friend rises to her feet. He turns to her husband and says, "I'm so happy you could accompany your wife today, Punnavardhana."

Visakha beams and says, "Even though it won't be easy, I promise that I will restrain myself from singing and dancing until all hours, Venerable Sir. This is one of the most joyful days of my life."

"Thank you for including us in your recollections today, Venerable Maha Kassapa," says Punnavardhana. "We wouldn't have missed this opportunity for anything."

Maha Kassapa smiles warmly and says, "Let's take our seats and begin our discussion, shall we?"

The arahants, memory monks, and Visakha and her husband seat themselves on carpets that have been spread out on the grass.

At just that moment Jivaka walks up to the group and says, "Sorry I'm a bit late. I had a sick patient at the last minute." He bows to the arahants and then greets Visakha and Punnavardhana cordially.

"Glad you could make it, Doctor," says the chairman, smiling. "You aren't late at all."

Maha Kassapa's mood becomes serious when he turns to the group and says, "In our discussion last night we came to the point where the Lord had reached his final destination of Kusinara. Today we will cover the Buddha's *parinibbana*, his funeral rites, and the distribution of his relics. Venerable Ananda, will you please begin?"

Ananda pauses for a moment to collect his thoughts, and then says, "The Buddha instructed us to accompany him to the *sala* grove of the Malla princes. He was weak from dysentery, and the journey on foot to Kusinara had consumed the last of his physical energy. On the way we had to pause twenty-five times so he could rest, and we finally arrived just as the sun was setting. When we got to his chosen spot he said to me, 'Ananda, prepare a place for me to lie down with my head to the north between the twin *sala* trees. I am weary and wish to lie down.'

"'Very well, Venerable Sir,' I answered. "I placed the robe according to his wishes and he lay down on his right side in a noble posture, with his left foot on the right foot, placed slightly beyond it, with mindfulness and clear comprehension. The *sala* trees were called 'twin' because their roots were intertwined. By this time countless numbers of Sangha members had gathered near this spot, and they prepared to stay until the end."

Tears are already streaming from Visakha's eyes as she listens intently to this story of the last hours of her Master. Her husband Punnavardhana takes her hand in his and squeezes it gently.

Jivaka's eyes are watering as well, and he lowers his head in reverence, deeply moved.

"Almost as soon as the Buddha lay down," begins Anuruddha, "the twin *sala* trees suddenly burst into bloom even though it wasn't the season for them to do so."

"From that moment onward large, celestial *mandarava* flowers began to fall from the sky," says Maha Kaccayana. "They continued to fall until the *parinibbana* took place."

"Many of us went into meditation," says Bakkula, "and our inner ears were filled with choruses of celestial melodies."

"The fragrance of sandalwood was everywhere," says Punna. "The perfume drifted in the soft breezes."

Ananda begins:

> "The Buddha said to me, 'these offerings of *sala* blossoms, *mandarava* flowers, sandalwood, and celestial music are hardly sufficient acts of reverence for the *Tathagata*. Ananda, the *Tathagata* is best honored and revered when the *bhikkhus*, *bhikkhunis*, male and female lay disciples practice and conduct themselves according to the Doctrine, which leads to enlightenment. Ananda, train yourself diligently and practice with a firm resolve.'"[1]

"He had spoken almost these same words to Venerable Dhammarama: he who practices the Doctrine honors the teacher best," says Sopaka.

"Venerable Upavana was standing in front of the Buddha fanning him," begins Ananda. "The Buddha said, 'Move away, *bhikkhu*.' Venerable Upavana immediately dropped the palm frond fan and moved off to the side. This loyal *bhikkhu* had served the Lord for over twenty years and I couldn't understand why the Buddha had spoken to him in such a brusque manner. I voiced my thoughts and said, 'Venerable Upavana has been serving you for two decades, and yet at this time of your passing you tell him to move away. Why did you ask him to do that?'

"The Buddha smiled faintly and answered, 'Ananda, most of the *devas* and *Brahmas* of ten world-systems are here in Kusinara to pay their last respects to the *Tathagata*. Within ninety-six miles of this *sala* grove there isn't a single space bigger than the width of a hair that isn't occupied by one of these divine beings. These *devas* are complaining that the arahant Upavana, who is an unusually large man, is obstructing their last view of the *Tathagata*, so I asked the loyal *bhikkhu* to move aside. He has done nothing wrong.'"

"The Lord had once said that eons ago Venerable Upavana was the guardian spirit assigned to watch over the relics of former Buddha Vipassi," says Punna. "Therefore, in this lifetime he spent over twenty years serving the Master."

Ananda continues by saying, "At this time I asked the Lord where Sangha members and lay devotees should go after his *parinibbana* if they wished to pay homage to him, and be inspired in their practice with the aim of spiritual awakening. He said, 'Ananda, there are four places where they might go that will inspire them: the *sala* grove in Lumbini where the *Tathagata* was born, the *bodhi* tree in Bodh Gaya were the *Tathagata* attained supreme enlightenment, the Migadavana forest in Sarnath where the *Tathagata* preached his first sermon that set the Wheel of Dhamma into motion, and here in Kusinara where the *Tathagata* will soon realize *parinibbana*. These four places are worthy of pilgrimage by sincere devotees who wish to deepen their spiritual understanding and further their quest for perfect enlightenment. Persons who visit these four sacred shrines will be bound for a fortunate destination after the death and dissolution of their bodies.'

"I understand that at this point you asked the Lord some additional questions," says Upali.

"That is correct," responds Ananda. "The first question I asked was, 'Venerable Sir, how should we conduct ourselves with regard to women?'

"'By not seeing them, Ananda,' was his response. I understood that by not seeing women there would be no cause to desire them.

"'Venerable Sir, if we unavoidably see a woman what should we do?' I asked.

"'Do not speak to them, Ananda,' was the Lord's reply. The Buddha knew that *bhikkhus* encountered women every day during their alms collections, so it was impossible to avoid seeing them. I took his reply to mean that speaking with women would breed familiarity, and familiarity would lead to attachment, which might lead to desire.

"'Venerable Sir, if we cannot avoid an occasion when we must speak to them, what should we do?'

The Lord replied, 'Ananda, consider every woman to be your mother, your aunt, your daughter, or your sister; and remember to be mindful.'"

Visakha smiles at this answer and says, "I am a woman and I have been in the presence of *bhikkhus* nearly all my life. I have always thought of myself as a mother or a sister to each and every one of the monks. I'm happy to hear that the Lord gave this helpful advice that applies to both *bhikkhus* and the women who wish to serve them. After all, the Buddha taught that men and women are the same; it's just our temporary physical costumes that are different."

Ananda breathes deeply again and says, "My next question was regarding how we should honor the remains of the Buddha after he passed away. He answered me by saying, 'Ananda, do not trouble yourself about honoring the remains of the *Tathagata*. Instead, strive in earnest and without negligence in your pursuit of attaining *Nibbana*. When the Buddha passes away there will be Brahmins and wise householders who will see to the task of honoring the *Tathagata's* remains.'

"My next question followed along the lines of the last one since I wanted to know how the Brahmins and householders should conduct his funeral rites. He answered, 'Ananda, the rites should be performed as in the case of honoring a Universal Monarch.'

"I then asked very respectfully, 'Venerable Sir, what is the procedure in the case of treating the remains of a Universal Monarch?'

"The Buddha said, 'Ananda, the body of a Universal Monarch is wrapped up in new cloth from the province of Kasi. Then it should be wrapped in cotton wool. Over that there should be another layer of Kasi cloth, and then one more of cotton wool. A total of five hundred alternating layers of Kasi cloth and cotton wool should be wrapped around the body of a Universal Monarch. Then it should be put in a vat of oil; both the vat and the lid should be made of gold. Afterwards it should be placed on a funeral pyre built from various kinds of scented woods and then cremated. Then a *stupa* should be built in memory of the Universal Monarch at the intersection of four highways and the relics be interred. People will come to make offerings at this shrine with flowers, incense, or scented powder, and they will show their reverence and reflect on the Buddha's greatness. For such acts of devotion people will enjoy benefit and happiness for a long time.'[2]

"The Buddha continued to explain the four types of persons who are worthy of having their remains honored in a *stupa*," continues Ananda. "He said that these four classes are: a *Tathagata*, a Pacceka Buddha, an arahant disciple of a Buddha, and a Universal Monarch."

"How did you feel when the Buddha answered your questions?" asks Bakkula.

"I was absolutely miserable," is the Buddha's Chief Attendant's honest answer. "I knew I was just about to break down into sobs, and I also knew I shouldn't be seen doing this in the Buddha's presence. I rushed as quickly as I could to a quiet place behind a nearby pavilion and stood by a wooden post. It was there that I cried and wailed and lamented the fact that I was still training, still striving hard in my practice, and my teacher, who had always been so compassionate toward me, was about to pass away."

"Then the Buddha asked where you were," says Anuruddha. "He knew that you were grieving and feeling helpless."

"Yes, and one of the *bhikkhus* went and found me and said, 'Venerable Ananda, the Buddha calls you.'

"I gathered my wits about me and went before the Lord, trying to stifle my sobs. He said, 'Ananda, do not grieve or weep. Haven't I told you before that there must be separation while living, severance through death, and sundering through being in different states of existence from all that are dear and beloved? Ananda, everything that has the nature of arising, of appearing, and of being compounded, is subject to decay and dissolution. How then can even the body of the *Tathagata* not disintegrate and disappear? There can be no such possibility.'

"He said, 'For a long time now you have served the *Tathagata* faithfully both in his presence and in his absence and with unbounded lovingkindness…You, Ananda, have gained much merit. Exert yourself in *vipassana* meditation. You will soon become an arahant, free from defilements.'

"I brightened up a bit upon hearing these words, but I still felt depressed and overwhelmed. I looked at the Buddha and he smiled at me with his radiant eyes. I could feel his energy and compassion flowing toward me.

"Then the Lord spoke to the monks: 'O *Bhikkhus*, Ananda is wise and intelligent. He knows that this is the proper time for *bhikkhus*, *bhikkhunis*, male and female lay disciples, kings, their ministers, teachers of other sects or their followers to approach and see the *Tathagata*.'

"After the Lord praised my qualities and described the four qualities of a Universal Monarch I asked him, 'Why do you wish to enter *parinibbana* in a small, insignificant town like Kusinara when there are so many other larger cities?'

"The Buddha said, 'Ananda, do not say that this is a small, insignificant town. In the far distant past there was a king named Maha Sudassana, a Universal Monarch, and this Kusinara was his capital city. It was once a flourishing and prosperous economic center; and it resounded with the pleasant sounds of life.' He described the glories of ancient Kusinara and then said, 'Ananda, go to Kusinara and announce to the Malla princes that in the third watch of this night the *parinibbana* of the *Tathagata* will take place. Tell them to come and pay their respects to the *Tathagata* in his last hour, lest one day they regret not having taken the opportunity to do so when I was in their midst.'³

"Even though the hour was very late I did as the Lord requested. When I entered Kusinara I learned that the Malla princes were having a meeting in their council chamber. I entered the chamber and stood before them, making my announcement just as the Buddha had instructed me. Upon hearing the message the princes, their wives, and their sons and daughters were grief-stricken. They started sobbing and lamenting because the *Tathagata* was going to pass away. Then they headed off at once to the *sala* grove to pay homage to him.

"When they arrived I realized that it would take too much time to let them approach the Buddha one by one, so I organized them into families and groups. This special event for the Mallas was finished before the end of the first watch of the night."

"Tell us about Subhadda, the wandering ascetic," requests Maha Kaccayana.

"We should clarify for the record that this is not the same Venerable Subhadda who commented to me upon hearing of the Buddha's demise, and said that the *bhikkhus* would now be free to conduct themselves any way they wanted," interjects Maha Kassapa. "We covered his small role in the life of the Lord very early on by mentioning that his ill-advised remarks were the motivation for holding this very council in the first place. Venerable Ananda, will you please continue?"

Ananda nods to Maha Kassapa and begins, "Subhadda was an ascetic who had originally come from a well-known, wealthy Brahmin family. He had been a wandering hermit for years, and followed the doctrines of various teachers, some of whom we have discussed in our recollections. On the day the Buddha was about to enter *parinibbana* the thought occurred to Subhadda that he should visit the Lord."

"Interesting the way Subhadda's *kamma* unfolded for him," comments Anuruddha.

Ananda continues, "Subhadda approached me in the *sala* grove of the Malla princes and said, 'I have heard it said by old and venerable wandering ascetics, teachers of teachers, that Perfectly Self-Enlightened

Tathagatas arise in the world only rarely. Today, in the last watch of the night, the *parinibbana* of the *Samana* Gotama will take place. An uncertainty, a problem, has arisen in my mind, and I have faith that the *Samana* Gotama will be able to teach his Doctrine to me so this uncertainty can be removed and my mind can be made clear. Venerable Ananda, please let me see the *Samana* Gotama.'

"I perceived Subhadda as one of those ascetics who clung to their own views no matter who preached to them, so I answered, 'Friend Subhadda, this cannot be allowed. The *Bhagava* is very weary, so don't bother him.' He wouldn't take 'no' for an answer, so he asked me two more times to see the Buddha, and both times I refused to allow it. We weren't standing very far away from the Buddha and he overheard our conversation. The Lord called out to me and said, 'Ananda, it is not fitting to hinder the ascetic from seeing me. He's not trying to harass me; he just wants to clear his doubts. I will answer his questions and he will understand.'

"I told Subhadda that the Buddha had given him permission to speak, and then led him forward to the Lord's presence. Subhadda offered courteous greetings to the Master and then sat to one side. He said, 'O Venerable Gotama, there are a variety of religious leaders who have sects, followers, good reputations, schools, and fame. Do all of them, some of them, or none of them have the knowledge and understanding of the truth they claim?'

"The Buddha answered, 'Subhadda, do not ask this question about other teachers; it is not fitting and proper. Besides, I don't have the time to discuss the other teachers. Listen to my Doctrine and bear in mind what I tell you.' At this point the Buddha explained the Noble Eightfold Path to Subhadda.

"The Buddha continued by saying, 'In whatever Doctrine you find that does not include the Noble Eightfold Path, then it is useless in terms of reaching the four stages of spiritual fruition, namely: *sotapanna, sakadagami, anagami,* and arahant. In my Doctrine alone you will find Sangha members who have attained these stages, and if they pass on my Teachings correctly, then the world will always have arahants.'

"When this was said Subhadda addressed the Buddha, 'Venerable Sir! The Blessed One has expounded the Dhamma clearly, excellently. I now go to the Buddha, the Dhamma, and the Sangha for refuge, and I humbly ask for ordination in your Order.'

"The Buddha answered Subhadda by saying, 'If a person who previously had been a believer in other doctrines wishes to be initiated and ordained into this Order as a *bhikkhu*, he has to live under probation for four months. After these four months have passed and the *bhikkhus* are satisfied with him, then that person will be admitted into the Order.'[4]

"Subhadda, ecstatic with happiness, said, 'I am prepared to live under probation for four years if necessary.'

"Then the Lord said, 'Since that is so, Ananda let Subhadda be ordained as a member of the Sangha.' I answered, 'Very well, Venerable Sir.'

"Subhadda bowed low before the Buddha and his eyes were filled with tears. When he raised himself up I took him outside, poured water on his head, made him repeat the formula of the impermanence of the body, shaved off his hair and beard, and dressed him in yellow robes. I had him repeat the Three Refuges, and then led him back to the Buddha. The Buddha himself admitted Subhadda to the higher ordination and gave him a subject for meditation. Venerable Subhadda then took himself to a solitary part of the grove and directed his mind towards the attainment of *Nibbana* without any remission of awareness and with vigorous resolution."

"It wasn't very long before Venerable Subhadda achieved arahantship," says Bakkula, smiling.

"He was the very last *bhikkhu* that was ordained in the presence of the Buddha," adds Maha Kaccayana.

"Didn't the Buddha give you some instructions at this point?" asks Upali.

"Yes, he did, Venerable Sir," answers Ananda. "He said that after he passed away, if the Sangha wished to abolish any of the lesser and minor rules of discipline then it may do so."

"The Buddha didn't give this as a direct instruction, and you didn't ask him which rules he was referring to," says Upali to Ananda, who nods his head.

"This is why earlier in this council we agreed to keep the *Vinaya* rules of discipline and conduct in tact," says Maha Kassapa.

"A very wise decision," says Upali, satisfied.

"The Buddha also told me that he wished to change the way Sangha members addressed one another," begins Ananda. "At the time senior monks and junior monks were casually calling one another '*avuso*,' or friend. The Buddha instructed that from that time forward senior monks could call junior monks by their name, their clan name, or simply as 'friend.' Junior monks should call their seniors *'bhante,' ayasma,'* or 'Venerable Sir.' Senior nuns could call junior nuns by their name, their clan name or *'bhagini.'* Junior nuns should call their seniors *'ayya.'*[5]

"Didn't you have a conversation about Channa at this point?" asks Sopaka.

"Yes. Many of us had been troubled by the fact that Channa, the Buddha's former charioteer, had never gotten over his pride and arrogance and his false perception that his status should have been higher than it was. Even though he had been ordained for nearly forty-five years he still behaved in a domineering fashion with the other *bhikkhus*.

"So I said to the Lord, 'What should be done about Channa?'

"After my passing, the monk Channa is to receive the *Brahmadanda* penalty,' he answered.

"'But, Lord, what is the *Brahmadanda* penalty?' I asked, since the Buddha had not used this term before.

"Whatever the monk Channa wants or says, he is not to be spoken to, admonished, or instructed by the monks,' was his reply. This penalty has since become known as the 'silent treatment.' Even though it is rarely imposed, it essentially creates a pariah in the Sangha, which either forces the errant monk to change his ways – or leave the Order for good.'"

"This was the last disciplinary act of the Buddha, and you Ananda, were entrusted with carrying it out," says Bhaddiya.

"After the Lord's *parinibbana* I did, in fact, carry out this last request, and Channa was devastated. He lived for a while in seclusion at Varanasi and pondered over his sentence," answers Ananda.

"He did come to his senses, however, and then go to you for help, didn't he?" asks Maha Kaccayana.

"Channa had the intuition that I might be the one who could preach the Dhamma to him in such a way that he could understand it, and then perhaps he could change his life. He approached me at the monastery in Ghosita's Park in Kosambi and said, 'Let the Venerable Ananda exort me, let him instruct me, let him give me a Dhama talk in such a way that I might see the Dhamma.' I was pleased that Channa had opened his mind enough to have this breakthrough. His biggest affliction was pride and thinking that he was special, which gave him a sense of entitlement.

I said to him, 'Lend your ear, friend Channa; you are capable of understanding the Dhamma.'"

"Apparently Channa had a clear realization at that moment that he was, in fact, capable of understanding the Dhamma," says Bakkula.

"I saw the rapturous feelings that had welled up in him, so the idea came to me to relate the discourse the Lord had given to the monk Kaccanagotta. This *sutta* explains the illusion of duality and the cessation of the mass of suffering," answers Ananda.

"After hearing your recitation, Venerable Sir, Channa became an arahant. Hearing the Dhamma from you was just the boost he needed to allow his ego to die," says Sopaka, smiling.

"Even though I wasn't yet an arahant myself, the powerful words of the Lord made such an impact on Channa that he did attain enlightenment. I witnessed his transformation with own eyes," adds Ananda with humility.

The arahants and guests bow their heads for a moment. All of them remember Channa, and reflect how his memory would be forever associated with the Four Foresigns and Prince Siddhartha's flight from the palace on the night of his renunciation.

Maha Kassapa speaks up and says, "Thank you for that recollection, Ananda. The Lord knew that you would be able to help his old friend, so he gave you this one last mission. Please continue with your story from where you left off."

"Then the Buddha addressed the monks and said, 'O *Bhikkhus*, if any of you should have any uncertainties or doubts regarding the Buddha, the Dhamma, the Sangha, the Path, or the Practice, ask me questions now. I don't want you to regret later that you had me in your presence and you didn't ask.'

"I remember the utter silence that filled the space," says Anuruddha. "No one said a word."

"I thought it must have been out of courtesy," says Bakkula, "that the monks didn't want to tire the Lord on his deathbed."

"Then the Buddha asked the *bhikkhus* the same question again," begins Ananda, "and still no one spoke up. He asked it a third time and the monks remained silent.

"Then the Buddha said, 'Perhaps it may be out of respect for the Teacher that you do not question me. Then let a friend, O disciples, tell it to another.' Still there was silence.

"Finally I said to him, 'How wonderful it is, Venerable Sir, that not a single monk in this community has any uncertainty or doubts regarding the Buddha, the Dhamma, the Sangha, the Path, or the Practice.'

"The Lord looked at me with the kindest expression in his eyes and said, 'Ananda, you say this out of your faith. Indeed, the *Tathagata* knows for certain that not a single *bhikkhu* here has any uncertainties or doubts regarding the Buddha, the Dhamma, the Sangha, the Path, or the Practice. Ananda, amongst this multitude of *bhikkhus* the least is a *sotapanna*, and will never be reborn in any realm of misery. He is assured of reaching desirable realms of existence, or of reaching the end of suffering, bound for the three higher levels of insight, culminating in enlightenment.'[6]

"Then the *Bhagava* said to the *bhikkhus*:

> "'O *Bhikkhus*, I say this to you now: All conditioned and compounded things have the nature of decay and disintegration. With mindfulness, endeavor diligently to complete the task.'"[7]

When Ananda finishes this phrase he closes his eyes and bows his head. "These were the Buddha's last words," he says in a whisper.

After a few moments he begins again, "The Buddha, still reclining like a noble lion on his right side, went into deep meditation. He entered the first *jhana*, then the second, third, and finally the fourth. Rising from the fourth *jhana* he became absorbed in the sphere of infinity of space. From his sustained absorption of infinite space he entered into the sphere of infinity of consciousness. Soon he became absorbed in the sphere of nothingness, and then the sphere of neither consciousness nor non-consciousness. From this absorption he finally entered the state of *Nirodha-Samapatti*, in which consciousness ceases.

"I can tell you about these states now because I have been there. At the time, however, I wasn't an arahant. I didn't know if the Lord was alive because his body was so still, and he didn't seem to be breathing. So I asked you, Venerable Anuruddha, 'Has the *Bhagava* passed away?'"

"And I answered, '*Avuso* Ananda, the *Bhagava* has not passed away. He is absorbed in *Nirodha-Samapatti*, the Attainment of Extinction. I was also in meditation, and I was with the Buddha up until he reached this state, so I knew what was happening. At this point I withdrew, and the Buddha moved onwards alone," responds Anuruddha.

Ananda begins speaking very slowly, "Then the Lord reversed the order of his absorption and entered the Sphere of Neither Conscious Nor Non-Consciousness, then the Sphere of Nothingness, then the Sphere of Infinite Consciousness, then the Sphere of Infinite Space, and then into the fourth *jhana*. From there he descended to the third, second, and finally the first *jhana*, and then back up again to the fourth. Immediately after rising from the fourth *jhana* the Buddha passed away, realizing *parinibbana*."

There is complete silence as the arahants and their guests contemplate the sacred event that has just been recollected.

Finally, Anuruddha breaks the spell, "When the Buddha passed away I said to the assembled monks, 'The exhaling and inhaling of the passionless Buddha of steadfast mind has ceased, and he has passed away into the final state of bliss. With an open mind he bore no pain, and the release of his mind was like the extinction of a flame.'"

Visakha, Punnavardhana, and Jivaka are in tears. The arahants on the sub-committee are deep in thought. The cool breeze that has been blowing through the trees above them has subsided, as if it, too, is stilled in remembrance of the Buddha's last breath.

Ananda waits a few moments before speaking, "At the instant of the Buddha's passing away there was an earthquake, great enough to make one's hair stand on end, and the god Brahmasahampati uttered this stanza:

> "'In this transient world
> Even such an incomparable person
> As the Self-Enlightened *Tathagata*,
> The teacher of *devas*, humans, and Brahmas,
> Endowed with Ten Powers,
> Has to pass away.
> All beings in this world,
> When the time of death is due,
> Must lay down this body,
> A composite of mental and physical phenomenon.'

"And then Sakka, King of the *devas*, uttered this stanza:

> "'Impermanent indeed are all conditioned things.
> They are in the nature of arising and dissolution.
> Having arisen, they cease to be.
> The realization of *Nibbana* on their utter cessation
> Is perfect bliss.'"[8]

"The monks who had gathered that had not yet attained the final fruition of arahantship began wailing and lamenting," says Anuruddha. "The emotional display reached such fervor that I had to exhort them to get hold of themselves. I said to them, 'Friends, *devas* are reproachful saying that if even the venerable ones cannot bear with it, how could they give comfort to others?' The *bhikkhus* finally calmed down and then Venerable Ananda and I spent the rest of that night discussing spiritual matters – particularly the omnipresence of death. I said to him, 'Friend, death has no shame to snatch away even the Buddha. How could any common being escape such a fate?' At one point I suggested that the news of the Buddha's passing should be conveyed to the Malla princes of Kusinara."

"I took it upon myself to convey this news," begins Ananda, "and so I set out at once to tell them. They were in their council chamber discussing how to proceed with the Lord's funeral services after his imminent passing away. When I made my announcement about the Buddha's *parinibbana* the princes and the others were overcome with grief. They immediately began to sob and lament.

"When the Malla princes asked me how the Buddha's body should be handled, I told them that it should be treated as if for a Universal Monarch. They made the proper arrangements just as the Buddha had instructed before his passing away.

"The Mallas collected all of the flowers and perfumes in their kingdom, as well as five hundred pieces of cloth. With a large contingent of musicians they went to pay homage to the body of the Lord and prepare it for cremation. After completing their preparations, in accordance to the Buddha's wishes, they placed a canopy over his bier and *bhikkhus* sat at each of its four corners in meditation. For seven days the Mallas and countless numbers of people paid their highest respects to the sacred body. On the seventh day eight Malla leaders put on clean white garments and intended to take the body through the southern gate for cremation."

"For some reason, no matter how hard they tried they were unable to lift the body. They came to me to find out why," says Anuruddha. "I told them that their intention to bring the funeral procession through the southern gate was contrary to the wishes of the *devas*. They wanted to know what those wishes were, so I explained that the *devas* wanted the body to first be carried northward and to enter Kusinara through the northern gate. Then they wanted it to be carried through the middle of the city and out the eastern gate to the Makutabandhana Shrine. They also wanted it to be accompanied by musical instruments, and have homage paid to it the entire length of the way. With this new intention in mind they were easily able to lift the Buddha's body and proceed along the alternate route according to the wishes of the *devas*.

"Thousands upon thousands of people gathered in Kusinara to pay their last respects to the Buddha," continues Anuruddha. "Lines of sobbing mourners dressed in white garments waited for hours just to pass and bow before him one last time. The funeral rites continued and eventually it was time to light the funeral pyre."

"It wouldn't light, though, would it?" asks Punna.

"Let me explain this part, Venerable Sirs," says Maha Kassapa. "At the time I was traveling from Pava to Kusinara accompanied by several hundred *bhikkhus*, many of them newly ordained. Along the way I stopped to rest under a shade tree and cool my limbs with water from my pot. Before too long a wandering ascetic approached us from the opposite direction, heading for Pava. He was holding over his head a large celestial *mandarava* flower, which was supported by a stick like an umbrella. I knew very well the rare occasions when such a flower would appear, and I realized that it could only mean that the Buddha had passed away. I was suddenly reminded of the earth tremors we had felt the week before, and the two signs together convinced me that he was gone.

"I stood and addressed the ascetic and said, 'Friend, do you know our Teacher?'

"He answered, 'Yes, Friend, I know of him. It has been seven days since *Samana* Gotama passed away.' He pointed to the *mandarava* flower and said, 'I brought this blossom from the place where his funeral is being held.'

"Many of the monks that were traveling with me had never seen the Buddha before," says Maha Kassapa. "I knew that if they weren't told of his death before we arrived in Kusinara their grief would cause them to act in an unseemly way before the people. I would be responsible for their behavior, so I figured I had better tell them the sad news then and there. This way, they could sob and wail to their hearts content and not be seen by others."

"So you told them?" asks Sopaka.

"Yes, and I'm glad I did because those that were still new and had not yet abandoned attachment were overwhelmed by grief and could not control their emotions," answers Maha Kassapa. "The others bore the news with fortitude, understanding that there was no such thing as permanence in conditioned things – including the human life of a Fully Enlightened Buddha."

"This is when Venerable Subhadda said he was relieved and happy the Buddha had passed away, wasn't it?" asks Punna.

"Yes, and his vulgar remarks are the reason we are here now at this council," responds the chairman. "After I admonished all the monks on their behavior and their need for discipline we continued on our way to Kusinara."

"What happened when the Malla princes couldn't ignite the Buddha's funeral pyre?" asks Bakkula.

"The funeral bier, as you all know, was one of the most magnificent ever constructed – fit for a Universal Monarch," relates Ananda. "Four men were assigned to the task of lighting it – one at each corner of the pyre – but it wouldn't ignite no matter what they tried. Then eight men approached the pyre – each one carrying a flaming torch. They put their torches into the pyre simultaneously, but it still refused to catch fire. More and more men tried, but no matter what they did it wouldn't burn."

"A group of the Malla princes approached me and asked what was happening," says Anuruddha. "I told them that it was the wish of the *devas* that the funeral pyre could not be lit at that time. They asked me when it could be fired and I explained that Venerable Maha Kassapa and his *bhikkhus* were on their way, and it could be lit after they arrived."

"When we got to Kusinara I led my group of *bhikkhus* into the Makutabandhana Shrine and immediately approached the Lord's bier," begins Maha Kassapa. "I put my palms together and walked around the structure three times, keeping it on my right side. Then I stood at the feet of the Buddha and slowly became absorbed in the meditative fourth *jhana*. I expressed the intention that the Buddha's feet should cut through the five hundred layers of wrapped cloth so I could place them on my head. Almost immediately the wrapped cloth burst open and the Buddha's sacred feet were exposed. Then I grabbed his ankles and placed his feet on my forehead." Maha Kassapa pauses to remember that solemn moment.

"A thunderous roar went up in the crowd of thousands," resumes the chairman. "Almost in unison everyone bowed low to the ground and paid their humblest respects to the Lord for the final time. The *bhikkhus* who had accompanied me from Pava adjusted their robes and walked around the Master's bier three times, just as I had done. During this time I kept my firm hold on the Buddha's feet, which were still placed on my forehead. There are no words to describe what transpired within the void of my mind during that time. When the *bhikkhus* finally finished paying their respects I released the Lord's holy feet, and in that same instant the funeral pyre ignited on its own. The flames soon shot up to the canopy above the bier and quickly consumed the carefully-wrapped body."

"When the Buddha's feet disappeared from view," says Anuruddha, "the people wailed and lamented even louder than they had when he passed away. It was pitiful, really, to see how they grieved for the great teacher that had lived in their midst for forty-five years. Many of them perhaps thought that they hadn't taken full advantage of his presence while he was alive. This is often the case when loved ones pass away; the grief is even greater than it would have been if they had shown their devotion when their dear ones were still living."

"The lay people and monks who had gathered to witness the funeral rites stayed for many hours, until the last ember had lost its light," says Ananda. "Streams of water from above and below shot upwards and downwards – to and from the earth – and extinguished the dying fire. Then the Malla princes brought scented water and poured it over the ashes before sifting through them to gather up the Lord's sacred relics. They placed the remains in a golden casket and then put it on top of an elephant. Then the princes and their families and guards guided the elephant through streets that had been canopied and strewn with flowers. When they reached the town square the princes lifted the casket from the elephant's back and carried it into their council chamber. They placed it on a raised platform covered in golden silk, and throngs of people came for seven days to pay their respects."

"They set up guards to protect the relics, didn't they?" asks Upali.

"Yes, Venerable Sir, they did," answers Anuruddha. "Three rings of elephants were stationed around the council chamber – each with guards astride who watched the crowd below. The princes were fearful of thieves who might attempt to steal the relics and take them away to their own kingdoms for enshrinement."

Jivaka says, "King Ajatasattu heard the news of the Buddha's passing from one of his ministers and he immediately fainted. The ministers called for me so I could be on hand in case the king fell ill. Once he regained consciousness he looked around him with a questioning expression, and he was told the same news again. He immediately went into another swoon. When he awakened the next time he remembered what he had been told, and he lamented the Buddha's death, sobbing and wailing, overcome with grief. Later, when his head had cleared, he said that he must depart at once for Kusinara to claim a portion of the Buddha's relics. He felt that he was entitled to them, and he declared that he would even use force against the Malla princes if it became necessary. He was determined to get what he felt was his due."

"The same thoughts were also on the minds of the kings and princes of other kingdoms in the region," adds Bhaddiya. "Fully-armed envoys were dispatched from Vesali, Kapilavatthu, Allakappa, and Koliya as well. All of them were prepared to fight the Mallas to get their share of the relics."

"The Brahmin of Vetthadipa also sent an envoy. He claimed that since the Buddha was from the ruling class, the Brahmin caste was entitled to a share of the relics for enshrinement," adds Punna.

"The Malla princes of Pava also sent a whole regiment of soldiers to Kusinara – in full battle array – to claim their share," says Sopaka. "There were a total of seven armed forces that soon marched on Kusinara to fight for the relics of the Lord."

"A representative of the Malla princes, seeing that Kusinara was surrounded by hostile armies, brazenly shouted out that the Buddha's relics were the most precious thing on earth; there was no way they would share them with anyone," says Anuruddha.

"Tensions rose to an extremely high level, and we all expected a fierce battle to break out at any moment," says Ananda.

"Then the shrewd, diplomatic Brahmin Drona showed up on the scene," says Maha Kassapa. "In his heart he felt that fighting over the relics would be doing the Buddha's memory a great disservice. He knew that the Lord, after all, was the consummate proponent of peace, and had been a light of harmony in the world for forty-five years."

"The Brahmin Drona came with the intention of pacifying all parties and getting them to calm down and be reasonable," begins Ananda. "He stood on a small mound and started reciting extemporaneous verses on the glory and virtues of the Buddha. The angry, squabbling princes didn't even hear the first half of his speech; they were too busy hurling vitriolic words at one another. It wasn't until the second half of Drona's recitation that they paused to pay attention. Many of the princes had been Drona's students; finally recognizing his voice, the tumult ceased almost at once.

"When he knew he had their complete attention Drona said in a loud voice, 'O Sirs, listen to these words of mine. Our Beloved *Bhagava* was an upholder of forbearance. It would not be proper to make war over the matter of sharing his relics, and it would dishonor his noble nature. Let us all be united and in harmonious agreement to divide the relics into eight parts. There are multitudes devoted to the Buddha, and there will be more in times to come. Let there be *stupas* built in his honor everywhere across the land!'"

"'The princes who had been shouting at one another said, 'Brahmin Master! We will agree if you yourself divide the relics fairly into eight parts,'" adds Anuruddha. "The Brahmin Drona, relieved, had the golden casket containing the Lord's relics opened. While the princes were overcome with grief, however, he thought that no one would notice if he quickly grabbed the Buddha's right canine tooth from the casket and hid it under his hat. I saw him, though, and so did others. None of us said a word, of course, for fear that blood might be shed."

"Sakka, the king of *devas*, had also been watching and he saw the thieving act," says Maha Kassapa. "He snatched the tooth out from under Drona's hat and brought it to the *Tavatimsa* heavens where he enshrined it in the Culamani Shrine. Drona didn't even know it had happened."

"That canine tooth will undoubtedly wind up somewhere else over time," says Punna, with a knowing grin. The other arahants smile at Punna, sharing his knowledge, but they say nothing.

"The Brahmin Drona divided up the eight portions and handed them over to the representative princes," says Ananda. "When he was finished Drona surreptitiously reached up and felt his hat to make sure the canine tooth was still there. You should have seen the shock on his face when he realized it was gone! He kept his composure, though, and didn't say anything – knowing that it was in his best interest to keep quiet about his theft. He did, however, claim for himself the casket the relics had been kept in, and no one opposed him."

"This is when the Mauriyan princes of Pippalivana showed up in full battle gear," says Anuruddha. "They had heard about the Lord's *parinibbana* and came at once to claim their share of the relics. The Malla princes explained that they were too late; every last portion had already been distributed. They made it clear that no one should dare to desecrate them by reapportioning them. One of the Malla princes said, 'Here, take the charred pieces of firewood from the cremation.' This token seemed to satisfy the Mauriyans, and they reverently packed up the charcoal."

"All eight claimants of the Buddha's relics took them to their capitals and erected *stupas* in which to enshrine them," says Anuruddha. "Drona also built a *stupa* to enshrine the golden casket that had contained the relics, and the Mauriyans did the same with the charred firewood. This made a total of ten *stupas* for honoring the Lord's remains."

"Great care and ample security measures were taken to safeguard the relics in the various places where they were enshrined," says Upali. "You, Venerable Maha Kassapa, foresaw the need for this given the evil nature of unbelievers that might want to steal them and desecrate them."

"Later on, as a precaution, I took back the majority of the relics – leaving only a small portion in each *stupa*," begins the chairman. "I took the remainder and buried it in a secret depository here in Rajagaha with the help of King Ajatasattu. They now rest under eighty *stupas* – one for each of the Buddha's senior disciples."

The arahants, Visakha, Punavardhana, and Jivaka pause for a few moments to collect their thoughts. They now have the complete story of the Buddha's *parinibbana*, having heard it from unreproachable eyewitnesses.

Maha Kassapa speaks up and says, "Our recollection of the life of the Buddha is now complete; therefore, this sub-committee is officially adjourned. I humbly thank all of you for your valuable contributions."

After a moment the chairman continues, "It is time now to turn our attention to the dedication of Visakha's new monastery. She has prepared a commemorative *dana* celebration for us, and there are countless guests waiting for us to proceed."

Visakha, her husband, and doctor Jivaka go before the chairman and the other arahants and prostrate themselves at their feet. When Visakha rises from the floor there are tears streaming down her face, and at the same time she is wearing a broad smile.

"You have given us a great honor today by allowing us to hear you recount the story of the Buddha's *parinibbana*. Any words of thanks I might offer would be inadequate, but you already know the fullness of my heart," says Visakha with great humility. Punnavardhana and Jivaka are so filled with emotion that they can only put their hands together as they bow again low to the ground, their tears falling to make darkened spots on the crimson carpet.

Maha Kassapa and the other arahants rise from their seats and proceed from the now-sacred glade of shady trees where the *parinibbana* has been told for the benefit of all posterity. A cool breeze blows through the leaves as if offering a farewell blessing to the enlightened *bhikkhus* and their devoted friends.

The chairman leads the way to the entrance of the new monastery. When they reach the gate they are joined by the other arahants from the council, and the special guests who will participate in the grand dedication and *dana* ceremonies.

Bhikkhuni Kalyani steps forward and is first to bow to the Sanga members. A smile is on her serene, unlined face as the senior monks warmly return her greeting.

King Ajatasattu and his Queen Vajira are at the head of the receiving line, and Anathapindika's son Kala and his wife Sujata are next. Visakha's and Punnavardhana's twenty children follow with their children – all dressed in white. Each one bows and pays their respects to the Noble Ones.

Maha Kassapa gathers all five hundred arahants around him and together they chant the *paritta* of protection and blessings for the new monastery. The many guests and friends stand silently, joining their hands together in front of them as the sonorous tones fill the morning air.

> "'May there be timely rain,
> May the harvest be abundant;
> May the world prosper,
> And the rulers be righteous.'"[9]

Finally, the chairman nods at Visakha, which is the signal for her to lead the way through the towering nine-tiered gates. She smiles at the senior monk and the grand procession follows her to the magnificent new *dana* hall. She is accompanied by the multitude of musicians and drummers who elevate the energy of the moment to match the joy in her heart.

A soft misty rain begins to fall even though the sun is shining brilliantly. All heads look up to see the fleeting glimpse of a multi-hued rainbow. A promise is felt, and the Buddha's blessings are bestowed on all.

Chapter 35
Epilogue

During the six month course of the First Sangha Council, the *Vinaya* Code of Discipline and Conduct as well as the Dhamma teachings have all been recited, thoroughly discussed, and carefully examined.

The work of the sub-committee recollecting the life of the Buddha has also been presented and critiqued. These efforts resulted in a complete biography of the Buddha that would be transmitted to faithful followers for generations to come. Seekers of truth will be able to know the source of the Dhamma, and to have a glimpse of the divine personality that realized it in his moment of supreme enlightenment.

During the past three weeks each saying and discourse of the Buddha has been vetted and approved for inclusion in the body of work that will ultimately become the Buddhist Canon. The final task of the arahants participating in the council has been to organize the eighty-four thousand individual elements of the Dhamma teachings into categories. This will insure its preservation, and make it more convenient for memorization and oral transmission. A system has also been devised that organizes the various monasteries in regards to being responsible for memorizing specific sections of the Canon. These sections will be passed down through successive generations of monks. The division of labor throughout the Sangha's monastery system will prevent overlaps, and ensure that there will be no gaps in content as well.

Upali and Ananda have been in charge of the monumental task of organization, under the guidance of the chairman, Maha Kassapa. They have ceaselessly used their combined right efforts to accomplish this task, and they have had the full cooperation and participation of each of the five hundred eminent arahants in the council. Their meetings were held in open assembly, and the input of every member of the Sangha was both welcomed and appreciated.

The last day of the council has finally arrived and the arahants are gathered to hear the summary reports. Maha Kassapa sounds the gong and its deep, rich tone reverberates throughout the hall and to the valley below. The morning devotional chants start almost at once, and fill the atmosphere with protection, blessings, and peace.

The chairman stands at the podium and begins, "My Sangha brothers, I thank all of you for contributing your knowledge, wisdom, and insight during these past seven months. The *Vinaya* rules of discipline and the teachings of the Buddha are now sorted and codified for transmission down through the ages. Venerable Upali and Venerable Ananda will now present their summaries, and we will vote on whether or not to accept them."

Upali approaches the podium and says, "The *Vinaya Pitaka*, now called the 'Basket of Discipline,' has been organized into the following sub-headings:

"The first is the *Parajika Pali*, or the Major Offences.
"The second is the *Pacittiya Pali*, or the Minor Offences.
"The third is the *Mahavagga Pali*, or the Greater Section.
"The fourth is the *Cullavagga Pali*, or the Lesser Section.
"The fifth is the *Parivara Pali*, or the Epitome of the *Vinaya*."

Maha Kassapa says in a loud voice, "Please indicate your approval of this system as stated by Venerable Upali by remaining silent; if any of you disapprove, please speak."

There is silence in the assembly hall. This request is repeated three times and no one voices disapproval.

"The systematized *Vinaya Pitaka* is thereby approved unanimously by the First Sangha Council," announces Maha Kassapa.

Upali bows to his fellow arahants and walks away from the podium.

Ananda steps forward and says, "The Buddha's Dhamma or Teachings has been called the *Sutta Pitaka*, or 'Basket of Discourses,' and has been codified into five collections based on length and subject matter.

"The first is the *Digha Nikaya*, the Collection of Long Discourses. These may also be called the 'Dialogues of the Buddha.' There are thirty-four discourses in this grouping.

"The second is the *Majjhima Nikaya*, the Collection of Middle-Length Discourses. These may also be called the 'Middle Length Sayings.' There are one-hundred fifty-two of these.

"The third category is the *Samyutta Nikaya*, the Collection of Connected Discourses. These may also be called the 'Kindred Sayings.' In this there are seven-thousand seven-hundred sixty-two discourses, which are divided into fifty-six related groups of subjects.

"The fourth is the *Anguttara Nikaya*, the Collection of Numerical Discourses. These may also be called the 'Gradual Sayings.' There are nine-thousand five-hundred fifty-seven discourses in this category, which is divided into eleven *Nipatas*, or books.

"The fifth is the *Khuddaka Nikaya*, the Minor Collection, which has been sub-divided into the following fifteen groupings: *Khuddaka Patha*, or Shorter Texts; *Dhammapada*, or The Way of Truth; *Udana*, or Paeans of Joy; *Itivuttaka*, or 'Thus Said' Discourses; *Sutta Nipata*, or Collected Discourses; *Vimana Vatthu*, or Stories of Celestial Mansions; *Peta Vatthu*, or Stories of Ghosts; *Theragatha*, or Verses of the Elder Monks; *Therigatha*, or Verses of the Elder Nuns; *Jataka*, or Former Birth Stories; *Niddesa*, or Expositions; *Patisambhida Magga*, or The Book of Analytical Knowledge; *Apadana*, or Lives of Arahants; *Buddhavamsa*, or Lineage of the Buddhas; and *Cariya Pitaka*, or The Basket of Good Conduct."[1]

Maha Kassapa's voice rings out in the assembly hall, "All of those who approve of this new system of organization for the Dhamma as stated by Venerable Ananda, please remain silent; anyone who disapproves, please speak up."

Venerable Kumara Kassapa stands up and says, "May I be recognized, Venerable Sir?"

Maha Kassapa looks out into the assembly and says to the standing *bhikkhu*, "Yes, Venerable Sir. Do you have a question?"

Kumara Kassapa says, "Yes, Venerable Chairman. I do not see what we have learned to call the '*Abhidhamma*' included in any of these categories. Have you left it out for a reason?"

There is a stir of whispering back in forth in the hall as the arahants wait in anticipation to see how Ananda will answer this question. There has been a great deal of discussion about what to do with these valuable teachings.

Ananda pauses for a moment before responding, and then says, "What you call the *Abhidhamma* was reputedly taught by the Buddha to his mother, Queen Maha Maya, in the *Tavatimsa* Heaven. It is said that Venerable Maha Moggallana related these sermons to us on earth so they could be remembered and recorded.

"These are profound teachings of Buddhist philosophy that focus primarily on the subject of psychology. There is a great deal of wealth to be found in them, and I'm quite sure that they will be discussed, debated, amplified, and commented upon for many generations.

"Many of the discourses in the five collections of the *Sutta Pitaka* already contain parts, seeds, or roots, of what is in the *Abhidhamma*. In our organizational discussions these past three weeks it was decided that we would not create a separate category for it at this time, and to leave it to later councils and Buddhist scholars to perhaps do that one day," concludes Ananda.

"Does that answer your question, Venerable Kumara Kassapa, and do you agree with this decision?" asks Maha Kassapa.

"Yes, Venerable Chairman, it both answers my question and meets with my approval." He bows to the assembly and respectfully takes his seat.

"Once again," begins Maha Kassapa, "all who approve of this organization of the *Sutta Pitaka*, please remain silent; those of you who disapprove may voice your objections."

The arahants in the assembly hall remain silent, and the chairman repeats his request two more times.

"Since there are no objections, the organization of the *Sutta Pitaka* thus stands as approved by the First Sangha Council," announces Maha Kassapa.

"A later arising *de facto* project of this council was the development of an eye-witness recollection of the life of the Buddha. The biography has been presented and discussed here in the assembly, and we will now vote on its acceptance. Venerable Ananda, you told me you wished to speak a few words before we vote on this great work, which was truly an act of devotion by the nine sub-committee members who took part in its creation," concludes the chairman.

Ananda steps over to the podium and says, "Thank you, Venerable Chairman, for agreeing to undertake this project at the last minute. I know that we have had more than enough to do at this council without adding an additional task, but your vista on the future, as usual, prompted you to allow us to formally organize our recollections while eye-witness accounts are still available. We are grateful to you for taking a leadership role in this endeavor." Ananda bows to Maha Kassapa, and their eyes meet for a moment in an embrace of joy.

"Recollections of the life of Buddha wouldn't have been possible without your memory, Venerable Sir," responds Maha Kassapa. "And it wouldn't have been complete without your and your cousins' accounts of those twenty-nine years before renunciation."

Ananda says, "When the idea of creating a biography first presented itself I thought it would be a relatively simple task. But as we got deeper into it – especially after the time of enlightenment – I realized that it wouldn't be so easy, given the fact that we weren't discussing an ordinary human being. If I may, I would like to quote one of the *suttas* we recited earlier that sums this up as well as it can be said:

> "One day the Buddha walked along the road from the city of Ukkattha to the city of Setavya. A Brahmin named Drona, traveling along the same road behind the Buddha was amazed when he saw his footprints. He thought, 'These could never be the footprints of a human being.' He continued following the footprints and finally saw the Buddha seated under a tree. The Buddha looked very calm and serene.
>
> "'The Brahmin asked the Buddha, 'Are you a *deva*, a god?'
>
> "'No, Brahmin, I am not a *deva*,' answered the Buddha.
>
> "'Are you a *gandhava*, a celestial musician?'
>
> "'No, Brahmin, I am not a *gandhava*.'
>
> "'Are you a *yakkha*, a devil?'

"'No, Brahmin, I am not a *yakkha*?'

"'Are you a human being?'

"'Brahmin, I am not a human being either.'

"'Then the Brahmin said, 'When I ask you whether you are a *deva*, *gandhava*, *yakkha*, or human being, you say, 'No.' If that were so, who are you?'

"The Buddha replied, 'O Brahmin, if I am a *deva*, then I must have the sense-desires of a *deva*. But I have eradicated sense-desires fully; therefore, I am not a *deva*. If I am a *gandhava*, I must have the sense-desires of a *gandhava*. But I have eradicated those fully; therefore, I am not a *gandhava*. If I am a *yakkha* then I must have the sense-desires that a *yakkha* should have. But I have eradicated all of that fully; therefore, I am not a *yakkha* either. If I am an ordinary human being, then I must have the sense-desires of ordinary men. But I have totally eradicated those; therefore, I am not a human being like other human beings.'

"The Buddha continued, 'O Brahmin, a blue lotus, red lotus, or white lotus is born in the water. It grows in the water; but it remains uncontaminated and untouched by water. I, too, am like that. I was born among men of this world. I grew up among men in this world. But I have risen above the world and ordinary men and women. I am not attached to the world. Therefore, O Brahmin, I am a superior human being who has destroyed all the weaknesses of ordinary human beings. In short, I am a Buddha. The best way to describe me is 'Buddha.' O Brahmin, please call me 'Buddha.'"[2]

The arahants in the assembly hall are stilled and silent when Ananda finishes reciting these words. Each of them reflects on who, and what, the Master has been to them; and each one comes to the same conclusion: he was the Buddha. They realize that he was the solitary occupant of a very rare category of beings, and even though each and every arahant was fully enlightened, there was only one Buddha. He had reached a highly-advanced level of spiritual attainment and universal understanding which essentially had no peers.

Ananda says, "While we attempted to tell the story of the Buddha's life it became increasingly more apparent that we weren't merely recording the tale of Prince Siddhartha, a human being from Kapilavatthu who was my cousin.

"That 'person' transcended and challenged every future human description during his realization of truth that full-moon night under the Bodhi tree. Everything human about him disappeared at that moment – even his brilliant, unique personality that I had known and loved all my life. From that time forward he was no longer a 'person,' he was the Buddha. He behaved like the Buddha. He spoke like the Buddha. He taught like the Buddha. He had the power of the Buddha. In short, he was *Tathagata*: one who had 'gone beyond.' As such, he defies description of any kind.

"Our sub-committee has tried its best to convey the essence of the indescribable Buddha in all of his unparalleled aspects. Since the mere convention of language cannot possibly convey the experience of enlightenment, how could it even attempt to convey an accurate description of one who had attained it? After saying this I sincerely hope that our efforts came somewhat close in this attempt, and I hope that future listeners or readers of our biography will forgive us if we have fallen short of describing the impossible."

The chairman walks over and stands next to Ananda at the podium. "Venerable Sir, the sub-committee's recollections of the life of the Buddha require no forgiveness. I feel confident that future generations will be grateful for the knowledge and blessings this biography brings them, and that they will enjoy the experience of hearing or reading it as well."

Ananda smiles at his dear old friend, and the arahants in the audience begin loudly exclaiming, "*Sadhu! Sadhu! Sadhu!*" This is their way of showing their great appreciation for the extraordinary and heroic work of the sub-committee, and in particular for the accurate and devoted remembrances of their brother, Ananda.

"I will take your enthusiasm as unanimous approval for our recollections of the life of Buddha," announces Maha Kassapa, beaming with joy. "I thank you all for your assistance and participation."

For a while all of the arahants enjoy the tremendous energy they have spontaneously generated in appreciation for the great work of the council.

After a few minutes the chairman sounds the gong for the last time. In a deep resounding voice he proclaims to the assembly, "This First Sangha Council is hereby adjourned."

The arahants, who are all still standing, continue to chant, "*Sadhu! Sadhu! Sadhu!*"

When the chanting finally subsides, each one of the monks approaches Maha Kassapa, Ananda, and Upali to pay their respects, and to convey their gratitude for their hard work and service to the *Sasana*.

Blessings and farewells are offered and exchanged, and after a while the *bhikkhus* retire to their cave chambers for a final meditation and to pack their meager belongings.

The members of the sub-committee gather one last time to take their leave before they go their separate ways. They exchange smiles and good wishes for a happy and successful life of *Dhammaduta*.

The three cousins of the Buddha, Ananda, Anuruddha, and Bhaddiya embrace one another and silently say their good-byes. A few minutes later Upali, Bakkula, and Maha Kaccayana pay their deepest respects to one another and start off on different paths.

Sopaka bows low to Ananda, and the Buddha's Chief Attendant thanks him for his faithful service. "You were there to help whenever I needed assistance, my dear friend; you never missed a single time. I'm so grateful for you."

Sopaka says, "Are you sure you can get along without me?"

Ananda smiles and answers, "Where I'm going there are no podiums or steep trails, so I'll be fine. You know, you've always been like a son to me – ever since that first night. You were a frightened, naked little boy of seven when you came to me hand-in-hand with the Buddha."

Sopaka looks deeply into Ananda's eyes and smiles. Then he puts his hands together in front of him, bows, and walks away. When he has gotten about twenty paces he turns and waves goodbye.

It doesn't take long for the five hundred arahants to disperse from their cave dwellings on the slopes of Mount Vebhara. King Ajatasattu's crews rapidly dismantle the assembly hall, and when everyone is gone there is barely a trace that anyone had even been there.

Maha Kassapa and Ananda are the very last to depart.

"Where will you go from here?" asks Ananda.

"I yearn for a long period of quiet and solitude in the forest, my dear brother," responds Maha Kassapa. "I think I'll visit the Kusinara area so I can be close to the spot where the Buddha attained *parinibbana*. After that I think I'll visit the other three places the Lord suggested for pilgrimage: Sarnath, Bodh Gaya, and finally Lumbini. What about you?"

"I was thinking along those same lines, friend," answers Ananda. "These physical forms won't be here forever, as we both know, and while this one still functions I think I'll make the same pilgrimage, but in the reverse order. I want to see my birthplace of Kapilavatthu once more before my *parinibbana*, and then walk quietly and alone to Lumbini, where I'll meditate under the *sala* tree where the Buddha was born. If I still have the strength I will visit the other three places in the course of time. No rush."

"No rush, indeed," chuckles Maha Kassapa. "Don't forget that you're going to live another forty years."

"I'll do my best to make sure they're good ones," replies Ananda. "'Till my last breath I'll continue working for the *Sasana* in one way or another. I'm sure it will all be good."

The two esteemed arahants salute each other with great admiration and respect. Then they turn and begin to walk their separate ways, both knowing that it might be the last time they ever meet. Neither one, however, even gives this a second thought. They have scaled the heights, achieved their goal, and are prepared to never return when the moment of their passing comes.

The story of Prince Siddhartha, the 'person' who became the Buddha, will live and inspire forever.

Dukkhappatta ca nidukkha
Bhayappatta ca nibbhaya
Sokappatta ca nissoka
Hontu sabbepi panino

May all beings be free from Suffering.
May all beings be free from Fear.
May all beings be free from Grief.
May all beings be Well and Happy[3]

Glossary of Terms

Abhidhamma —— "Higher Teachings," one of the three main categories of the *Tripitaka*, the "Three Baskets" of the Buddhist Canon

Adhitthana——Determination; resolution

Avihimsa——Non-violence

Ajjava——Honesty and integrity

Akkodha——Freedom from hatred, ill-will, and enmity

Anagami——Non-returner; the third phase of spiritual development on the path to enlightenment

Anantarika-kamma——An action that finds consequences without delay

Anapanasati——Mindfulness on breathing

Anguttara Nikaya——"Collection of Numerical Discourses"; also called the "Gradual Sayings"; one of the five divisions of the *Sutta Pitaka*

Anicca——Impermanence

Apadana— — "Lives of the Arahants"; one of the groupings of teachings from the *Khuddaka Nikaya*, the Minor Discourses of the *Sutta Pitaka*

Avirodha——Non-opposition and non-obstruction

Anatta——Not self; the concept of "I" and "my" is an illusion

Arahant——One who is liberated; a fully-enlightened person; the fourth and final stage of the path to enlightenment

Asana——A seat; a yoga posture or position

Ashram——Hermitage of a community of spiritual aspirants or ascetics

Avuso——Friend; brother; a form of respectful address for elder monks to use with younger monks

Ayasma—— "Venerable Sir"; a form of respectful address for monks

Ayya——Lady; nuns; an appellation for junior nuns to use for their seniors

Besajja Guru—— "Medicine Buddha"; teacher

Bhagava—— "Blessed One"; an appellation for the Buddha

Bhagini——Younger sister; an appellation for a junior *bhikkhuni*, as called by her senior

Bhanaka——Monks who are trained to memorize the Buddhist teachings for oral transmission
Bhante—— "Venerable Sir"; a form of respectful address for monks
Bhavana——Mental development; meditation
Bhikkhu——A male member of the Sangha; a Buddhist monk
Bhikkhuni——A female member of the Sangha; a Buddhist nun
Bodhi——Enlightenment; Bo Tree
Bodhisatta——A being destined to attain Buddha-hood
Brahmadanda——The highest penalty for monks; "Silence Treatment"; from the *Vinaya*
Brahmana——One of the Brahmin, or highest caste in India
Brahma——Celestial "gods" of the ten-thousand world systems; supreme God (for Brahmins); a class of deities (for Buddhists)
Brahmi——An ancient alphabet/script
Brahmin——A member of the highest caste in India
Buddha——A "Fully Enlightened One"; "Awakened One"
Buddhavamsa—— "Lineage of the Buddhas"; one of the groupings of the the *Khuddaka Nikaya*, the Minor Discourses of the *Sutta Pitaka*
Buktanumodana——A sermon usually given after a *dana* ceremony
Candala—— "Untouchable"; outcaste
Caritas——Character archetypes
Cariya Pitaka—— "The Basket of Good Conduct"; one of the groupings of the the *Khuddaka Nikaya*, the Minor Discourses of the *Sutta Pitaka*
Caste——A system of social stratification in India; the four castes are Brahmins (ritualists, members of the priesthood), *Kshatriyas* (kings and warriors), *Vaishyas* (agriculturalists and traders), and *Shudras* (service providers and laborers), and those without caste
Crore——In the Indian measuring system, a unit of 10 million
Cullavagga Pali—— "The Lesser Section"; one of the five sections of the *Vinaya Pitaka*
Dana——Generosity
Deva——A "god"
Dhamma——The teachings of the Buddha
Dhammaduta——The act of spreading the Buddha's teachings
Dhammapada—— "The Way of Truth"; one of the groupings of teachings from the *Khuddaka Nikaya*, the Minor Discourses of the *Sutta Pitaka*

Digha Nikaya—— "Collections of Long Discourses"; also called "Dialogues of the Buddha"; one of the five groupings of the *Sutta Pitaka*

Dukkha——Suffering; stress

Gandhava——Celestial musician

Iddhi——Supernormal power; spiritual power; success

Itivuttaka—— "Thus Said' Discourses"; one of the groupings of teachings from the *Khuddaka Nikaya*, the Minor Discourses of the *Sutta Pitaka*

Jambudipa——Ancient word for "India"

Jataka—— "Former Birth Stories" of the Buddha; one of the groupings of teachings from the *Khuddaka Nikaya*, the Minor Collection of the *Sutta Pitaka*

Jatilas——A sect of wandering ascetics, distinguished by the turbans they wore

Jhana——Meditative absorption

Kalyana mitta——Spiritual or "noble" friends

Kamma——Action

Kammic——Adj. pertaining to *kamma*

Kappa——An eon

Karuna——Compassion

Khanti——Patience or forbearance

Khuddaka Nikaya—— "Minor Discourses"; the fifth collection in the *Sutta Pitaka*; it is subdivided into fifteen categories

Khuddaka Patha—— "Shorter Texts"; one of the groupings of teachings from the *Khuddaka Nikaya*, the Minor Collection of the *Sutta Pitaka*

Kukurumuttu——A type of wild mushroom

Lakh——In the Indian measuring system, a unit of 100 thousand

Maddava——Kindness or gentleness

Maha——Great

Maha Karuna Samapatti——Ecstasy of Great Compassion

Mahavagga Pali—— "The Greater Section"; one of the five sections of the *Vinaya Pitaka*

Majjhima Nikaya—— "Collections of Middle-Length Discourses"; also called "Middle Length Sayings"; there are one hundred fifty-two discourses in this collection; one of the five groupings of the *Sutta Pitaka*

Mandarava——Celestial flowers that only bloom on rare occasions, such as when a Buddha passes away

Mara—— "The Evil One"

Metta——Loving-kindness; universal benevolence for all

Mudita——Appreciative joy

Nandana Vana——A celestial garden or resort; where the *Bodhisatta Deva Setaketu* rested prior to taking human form as Prince Siddhartha

Neem——*Azadirachta Indica*, a tree in the mahogany family; twigs from the tree are used for cleaning the teeth, and are one of the "eight requisites" for a Buddhist monk.

Nekkhamma——Renunciation

Nibbana——Final deliverance from suffering; emancipation; enlightenment

Niddesa—— "Expositions"; one of the groupings of teachings from the *Khuddaka Nikaya*, the Minor Collection of the *Sutta Pitaka*

Nirodha-Samapatti——The meditative absorption of "cessation of consciousness" or "Attainment of Extinction"

Pacittiya Pali—— "The Minor Offences"; one of the five sections of the *Vinaya Pitaka*

Panna——Wisdom

Parajika Pali—— "The Major Offences"; one of the five sections of the *Vinaya Pitaka*

Pariccaga——Personal sacrifice for the good of the people

Parinibbana——Final attainment of *Nibbana*

Parivara Pali—— "Epitome of the *Vinaya*"; one of the five sections of the *Vinaya Pitaka*

Paritta——Protective chants

Patisambhida Magga—— "The Book of Analytical Knowledge"; one of the groupings of teachings from the *Khuddaka Nikaya*, the Minor Collection of the *Sutta Pitaka*

Pacceka Buddha——A fully-enlightened Buddha that does not teach; a solitary enlightened one

Peta Vatthu—— "Stories of Ghosts"; one of the groupings of teachings from the *Khuddaka Nikaya*, the Minor Collection of the *Sutta Pitaka*

Phala-samapatti——Contemplation of the fruition of knowledge

Pice——A coin of very small monetary value

Prana (pranic) ——Life force energy

Pubbacariya——One's first teachers

Puja——Worship; offerings

Sacca——Truths; truthfulness

Sadhana——Spiritual practice

Sadhu——Holy one; reverend; sometimes used as an adulatory exclamation of praise and rejoicing

Sakadagami—— "Once-Returner"; the second phase of spiritual development on the path to enlightenment

Sakya——The royal clan of Kapilavatthu into which Prince Siddhartha was born

Sala——A semi-deciduous tree in India with small yellow flowers; bloomed out of season when the Buddha was born and passed away

Samadhi——Concentration

Samana——Recluse; hermit

Samanera——Novice Buddhist monk

Samatha——Serenity; stilling of formations; concentrated, one-pointed meditation

Samsara——The cycle of life (birth, old age, sickness, death, rebirth, etc.)

Samyutta Nikaya—— "Collection of Connected Discourses"; also called "Kindred Sayings"; there are seven-thousand seven-hundred sixty-two discourses in this collection, which are divided into fifty-six related groups of subjects; one of the five groupings of the *Sutta Pitaka*

Sangha——The Order of Buddhist monks and nuns

Sasana——Buddhism

Sila——Virtue

Sotapanna—— "Stream-Enterer"; the first stage on the path to enlightenment

Stupa——Pagoda; a dome-like structure built to house the relics of the Buddha or one of his senior Sangha members

Sutta——Discourse

Sutta Pitaka—— "Basket of Discourses"; codified into five collections based on length and subject matter.

Sutta Nipata—— "Collected Discourses"; one of the groupings of teachings from the *Khuddaka Nikaya*, the Minor Collection of the *Sutta Pitaka*

Tapa——Austerity

Tathagata—— "The One Who Has Gone Beyond" or "Thus Gone One"; the Buddha referred to himself as the *Tathagata*

Tavatimsa——A celestial abode

Theragatha—— "Verses of the Elder Monks"; one of the groupings of teachings from the *Khuddaka Nikaya*, the Minor Collection of the *Sutta Pitaka*

Therigatha—— "Verses of the Elder Nuns"; one of the groupings of teachings from the *Khuddaka Nikaya*, the Minor Collection of the *Sutta Pitaka*

Tusita——A celestial abode

Udana—— "Paeans of Joy"; one of the groupings of teachings from the *Khuddaka Nikaya*, the Minor Collection of the *Sutta Pitaka*

Upekkha——Equanimity

Vancaka dhamma——Misidentified or mis-categorized thoughts and attitudes

Vandana——To pay homage; devotional chants

Vedas——Ancient Indian scriptures

Vesakha——Fifth month of the year

Vimana Vatthu—— "Stories of Celestial Mansions"; one of the groupings of teachings from the *Khuddaka Nikaya*, the Minor Collection of the *Sutta Pitaka*

Vinaya——The *Vinaya Pitaka*, the "Basket of Discipline"; the rules of conduct and discipline for Sangha members; divided into five groupings

Vipassana——Insight; a form of meditation practiced by the Buddha

Viriya——Committed Energy

Yakkha——A devil

Yuva raj——Crown Prince

Endnotes

CHAPTER 1
[1] *Mahapadana Sutta,* in *Digha Nikaya,* (Rangoon: Burma Pitaka Assoc., 1984).
[2] Pali Text Society, trans., *Itivuttaka,* (London: Pali Text Society) sec. 92.
[3] Pali Text Society, trans., *The Gradual Sayings,* (London: Pali Text Society), I:19-20.
[4] Vinaya ii, 284 f.
[5] Pali Text Society, trans., *The Gradual Sayings,* (London: Pali Text Society), I: 20.

CHAPTER 2
[1] Pali Text Society, trans., *The Gradual Sayings,* (London: Pali Text Society), I: 16.
[2] Pali Text Society, trans., *The Gradual Sayings,* (London: Pali Text Society), II: 20.
[3] Samantapasadika I, p. 161 and Papancasudani (Majjhima Nikaya Commentary) Vol. I, p. 103.
[4] Narada Thera, The Buddha and His Teachings, Ch. 41.
[5] Majjhima Nikaya Commentary, Vol. I, p. 103
[6] Professor E. B. Cowell, editor, *Mahahamsajataka,* in *The Jataka,* (Delhi: Motilal Banarsidass Publisher, 1994), V:186.
[7] Pali Text Society, trans., *The Book of the Discipline,* (London: Pali Text Society), IV: 9.
[8] Pali Text Society, trans., *Rathavinita Sutta,* in *The Middle Length Sayings,* (London: Pali Text Society), I:187-194.

CHAPTER 3
[1] Digha Nikaya Mahapadana Commentary and *Canki Sutta* of the Majjhima Nikaya Commentary.
[2] Sutta Nipata Commentary Vol. II, p. 483. Asitadevala also called Kaladevala (Jataka I, #54).
[3] Sarattha Dipani Vinaya sub-commentary.
[4] Digha Nikaya Commentary Vol. II in the exposition of the Bodhisatta dhammata.
[5] *Sukhumala Sutta,* Devaduta Vagga Tikanipata, Anguttara Commentary, Vol. II.

CHAPTER 4
[1] Bhikkhu Nanamoli and Bhikkhu Bodhi, trans., *Alagaddupama Sutta,* in *The Middle Length Discourses of the Buddha,* (Boston: Wisdom Publications, 1995) 224.
[2] Ibid.
[3] Burma Pitaka Association, trans. *Brahmajala Sutta,* in *Digha Nikaya,* (Rangoon: Burma Pitaka Assoc., 1984), 3-69.
[4] Ibid.
[5] B. Ananda Maitriya, *Buddhajanma (Khemendra)* in *Buddhacaritaya,* (Sinhala), 262.
[6] Pali Text Society, trans., *Devdutavagga Sutta,* in *The Gradual Sayings,* (London: Pali Text Society).

CHAPTER 5

[1] *Ariyapariyesana Sutta*, Majjhima Nikaya.

[2] Buddhavansa Commentary account is incomplete. It mentions old man and monk. Jataka Nidana is more complete. The four fore signs story based on *Mahapadana Sutta* of the Digha Nikaya.

CHAPTER 6

[1] Pali Text Society, trans., *Maha Saccaka Sutta*, in *The Middle Length Sayings*, (London: Pali Text Society), I:291-305.

[2] Story based on *Ariyaparisana Sutta* in Majjhima Nikaya.

CHAPTER 7

[1] Suttanipata Commentary, II: 386; Suttanipata, Mahavagga pabbja sutta.

[2] B. Ananda Maitriya, *Buddhacaritaya*, (Sinhala), 35.

[3] Ibid.

[4] Ibid.

[5] *Lalita Vistara*, Ch. 16; Pali Text Society, trans., *Maha Saccaka Sutta*, in *The Middle Length Sayings*, (London: Pali Text Society), I:207-214.

[6] Ibid.

[7] Pali Text Society, trans., *Mahasīhanuda Sutta*, in *The Middle Length Sayings*, (London: Pali Text Society), I:97-110.

[8] Pali Text Society, trans., *Maha Saccaka Sutta* and *Sangarava Sutta*, in *The Middle Length Sayings*, (London: Pali Text Society), I:291-305.

CHAPTER 8

[1] Pali Text Society, trans., *Dvedhavitakka Sutta*, in *The Middle Length Sayings*, (London: Pali Text Society), I:148-152.

[2] *Lalita Vistara*, Ch. 18 and Buddhawansa Commentary.

[3] H. Saddhatissa, trans., *Padhana Sutta*, in *Sutta Nipata*, (London: Curzon Press Ltd., 1985), 48.

[4] Verse 153-154, *Dhammapada*.

[5] Anguttara Nikaya 4:23; II 23.

CHAPTER 9

[1] *Mahaparinibbana Sutta*, Digha Nikaya.

[2] Pali Text Society, trans., *Bahudhatuka Sutta*, in *The Middle Length Sayings*, (London: Pali Text Society), I:104-110.

[3] Pali Text Society, trans., *Dependent Origination*, in *The Book of the Discipline*, (London: Pali Text Society), IV:11-12.

[4] Suttanipata, *Vasettha Sutta*.

[5] Samyutta Nikaya, Marasamyutta, *Sattavassani Sutta*. Vol. I, p 122.

[6] Ibid.

[7] Fa-Hien, Ch. 31, Hiun-Tsisang, Vol. 2.

[8] Buddha Caritaya (Sinhala Ananda Maitriya, p. 64, 276).

Endnotes   535

⁹ Pali Text Society, trans., *Mahavagga Pali,* in *The Book of Vinaya*, (London: Pali Text Society), IV:10.

CHAPTER 10
1. Bhikkhu Bodhi, trans., *Anattalakkhana Sutta,* in *The Connected Discourses of the Buddha,* (Boston, Mass: Wisdom Publications, 2000), I:901.
2. Pali Text Society, trans., *Mahavagga Pali,* in *The Book of the Discipline*, (London: Pali Text Society), IV:11-12.
3. Mahavagga, 1 Mahakhandaka
4. Vinaya Mahavagga I, 10. No. 17.
5. Pali Text Society, trans., *Anattalakkhana Sutta,* in *The Book of Kindred Sayings*, (London: Pali Text Society), III:59-60.
6. H. Saddhatissa, trans., *Nalaka Sutta,* in *Sutta Nipata,* (London: Curzon Press Ltd., 1985), 79-83.

CHAPTER 11
1. Pali Text Society, trans., *Sabbasava Sutta,* in *The Middle Length Sayings*, (London: Pali Text Society), I:8-16.
2. Pali Text Society, trans., *The Book of Vinaya,* (London: Pali Text Society), IV:28.
3. Pali Text Society, trans., *Dasadhamma Sutta,* in *The Gradual Sayings,* (London: Pali Text Society), V:62-63.
4. Verse 183-185, *Dhammapada.*
5. Mahavagga Mahakhandaka
6. Samyutta Nikaya, Marasamyutta.
7. Verse 50, *Dhammapada.*

CHAPTER 12
1. *Ariyapariyesana Sutta,* Majjhima Nikaya.
2. Pali Text Society, trans., *The Book of Vinaya,* (London: Pali Text Society), IV:32-38.
3. Dr. Henepola Gunaratana, complier, *Loving Kindness Meditation,* in *Bhavana Vandana,* (West Virginia: The Bhavana Society), 45.
4. Pali Text Society, trans., *The Book of Vinaya,* (London: Pali Text Society), I.

CHAPTER 13
1. Pali Text Society, trans., *Attahamahapurisa Sutta,* in *The Gradual Sayings,* (London: Pali Text Society), IV:332.
2. Pali Text Society, trans., *The Gradual Sayings,* (London: Pali Text Society), I:16.
3. Pali Text Society, trans., *The Book of Vinaya,* (London: Pali Text Society), IV:53.
4. Maurice Walshe, trans., *Payasi Sutta,* in *The Long Discourses of the Buddha,* (Boston, Mass.: Wisdom Publications, 1995), 351.
5. Theragatha 995
6. H. Saddhatissa, trans., *Nava Sutta,* in *Sutta Nipata,* (London: Curzon Press Ltd., 1985), 35.
7. Dhammapattha Katha, 26 Brahmana Vagga 7.
8. Tittira Jataka, #37.
9. *Rathavinita Sutta,* Majjhima Nikaya.

[10] Bhikkhu Nanamoli and Bhikkhu Bodhi, trans., *Mahagosinga Sutta,* in *The Middle Length Discourses of the Buddha,* (Boston: Wisdom Publications, 1995), 307.
[11] Bhikkhu Bodhi, trans., *The Barrel,* in *The Connected Discourses of the Buddha,* (Boston, Mass: Wisdom Publications, 2000), II:715.

CHAPTER 14
[1] Pali Text Society, trans., *Paharada Sutta,* in *The Gradual Sayings,* (London: Pali Text Society), IV:197.
[2] Samyutta Nikaya Vol. II, p. 219.
[3] Manoratha Purani, Ekanipata Vannana.
[4] Dhammapada Atthakata Vol. III, 3.
[5] Pali Text Society, trans., *The Gradual Sayings,* (London: Pali Text Society), I:19.
[6] Samyutta Atthkata, Vol. II, 130.
[7] Pali Text Society, trans., *The Book of Kindred Sayings,* (London: Pali Text Society), II:137.
[8] Visuddhimagga

CHAPTER 15
[1] Pali Text Society, trans., *The Gradual Sayings,* (London: Pali Text Society), I:56.
[2] Dhammapadattha Katha, #9 and #137.
[3] Verse 168, *Dhammapada.*
[4] Yasodhara's Utterings, Pujavaliya (Sinhala), 297-298.
[5] Verse 16, *Dhammapada.*
[6] Professor E. B. Cowell, editor, *The Jataka,* Vol. II-IV, #485.

CHAPTER 16
[1] Thanissaro Bhikkhu, trans., *The Buddhist Monastic Code,* 530-557.
[2] Pali Text Society, trans., *Sattadana Sutta,* in *The Gradual Sayings,* (London: Pali Text Society), IV:45
[3] Pali Text Society, trans., *The Vinaya,* (London: Pali Text Society), IV:104.
[4] Professor E. B. Cowell, editor, *Maha Dhammapala Jataka,* in *The Jataka,* (Delhi: Motilal Banarsidass Publisher, 1994), No. 447.
[5] Bhikkhu Nanamoli and Bhikkhu Bodhi, trans., *Ambalatthikarahulovada Sutta,* in *The Middle Length Discourses of the Buddha,* (Boston: Wisdom Publications, 1995), 523.
[6] Ibid, *Maharahulovada Sutta,* 527.

CHAPTER 17
[1] Pali Text Society, trans., *Vasettha Sutta,* in *The Middle Length Sayings,* (London: Pali Text Society), II:379-385.
[3] Dhammapadattha Katha, Vol. IV, #124.
[3] Pali Text Society, trans., *Vinaya Pitaka,* Vol. II, p. 180.
[4] Pali Text Society, trans., *Mahasunnata Sutta,* in *The Middle Length Sayings,* (London: Pali Text Society), III:152-162.
[5] H. Saddhatissa, trans., *Karaniya Metta Sutta,* in *Sutta Nipata,* (London: Curzon Press Ltd., 1985), 15-16.

CHAPTER 18
[1] Bhikkhu Bodhi, trans., *Anattalakkhana Sutta*, in *The Connected Discourses of the Buddha*, (Boston, Mass: Wisdom Publications, 2000), I:164-194.
[2] Bhikkhu Bodhi, trans., *The Connected Discourses of the Buddha*, Vol. II, p. 1816.
[3] Ibid., *Sudatta* in *Yakkhasamyutta*, I:311.
[4] *Majjhimanikaya Atthakatha*, Vol. I, p. 50.
[5] Pali Text Society, *Vinaya Pitaka*, Vol. II, p. 158.
[6] Nyanaponika Thera and Bhikkhu Bodhi, trans. and edited, *Numerical Discourses of the Buddha, An Anthology of Suttas from the Anguttara Nikaya*, p. 99.

CHAPTER 19
[1] Verses 209-216, *Dhammapada*.
[2] Verses 13-14, *Dhammapada*.
[3] *Theragatha*, verses 33; *Theragatha Atthakatha*, Vol. I, p. 94.
[4] Pali Text Society, trans., *The Gradual Sayings*, (London: Pali Text Society), V:35-37.
[5] Pali Text Society, trans., *Therigatha*, (London: Pali Text Society), 620-631.

CHAPTER 20
[1] H. Saddhatissa, trans., *Kalahavivada Sutta*, in *Sutta Nipata*, (London: Curzon Press Ltd., 1985), 101-103.
[2] Ven. Ananda Maitreya, *Buddhacarita*, Sinhalese, p. 123-4.
[3] Professor E. B. Cowell, editor, *Vattak Jataka*, in *The Jataka*, (Delhi: Motilal Banarsidass Publisher, 1994), Vol. V, p. 261, No. 118.
[4] H. Saddhatissa, trans., *Attadanda Sutta*, in *Sutta Nipata*, (London: Curzon Press Ltd., 1985), 109-110.
[5] Verse 201, *Dhammapada*.
[6] Bhikkhu Bodhi, trans., *Brahmasamyutta*, in *The Connected Discourses of the Buddha*, (Boston, Mass: Wisdom Publications, 2000), I:231-253.
[7] Pali Text Society, trans., *Akkosaka Bhardvaja*, in *The Kindred Sayings*, (London: Pali Text Society), I:256-257.
[8] H. Saddhatissa, trans., *Salla Sutta*, in *Sutta Nipata*, (London: Curzon Press Ltd., 1985), 68-69.

CHAPTER 21
[1] Bhikkhu Nanamoli and Bhikkhu Bodhi, trans., *Vatthupama Sutta*, in *The Middle Length Discourses of the Buddha*, (Boston: Wisdom Publications, 1995), 118-119.
[2] Bhikkhu Bodhi, trans., *Kosalasamyutta Sutta*, in *The Connected Discourses of the Buddha*, (Boston, Mass: Wisdom Publications, 2000), I:179.
[3] Pali Text Society, trans., *The Book of the Vinaya*, (London: Pali Text Society), V:354-355.
[4] Verse 236, *Dhammapada*.
[5] Pali Text Society, trans., *Dhammapada-attha Katha*, (London: Pali Text Society), IV:168.
[6] Pali Text Society, trans., *Bhikkhu Uppalavanna*, in *Therigatha*, (London: Pali Text Society), 55:224-235.
[7] Pali Text Society, trans., *Therigatha*, (London: Pali Text Society), 157-162.
[8] *Dhammapadattha Katha*, II:260 and *Anguttara Atthakatha*, 2:108.

CHAPTER 22
[1] Nyanaponika Thera and Bhikkhu Bodhi, trans., *A Woman's Success,* in *Numerical Discourses of the Buddha,* Walnut Creek: Altamira, 1999), 218-220.
[2] Dhammapada Atthakatha, *Visakhavattu.*
[3] Pali Text Society, trans., *Dhammapada-attha Katha,* (London: Pali Text Society), I:403.

CHAPTER 23
[1] Maurice Walshe, trans., *Cakkavatti Sihanada Sutta,* in *The Long Discourses of the Buddha,* (Boston, Mass: Wisdom Publications, 1995), 395.
[2] Bhikkhu Nanamoli and Bhikkhu Bodhi, trans., *Dhatuvibhanga Sutta,* in *The Middle Length Discourses of the Buddha,* (Boston: Wisdom Publications, 1995), 1087 and *Papanccha Sudani,* II:979.
[3] W. Sarada, trans., *Treasury of Truth,* (Taipei: Corporate Body of the Buddha Educational Foundation, 1993), 44-45.
[4] Professor E. B. Cowell, editor, *Dalitadhamma Jataka,* in *The Jataka,* (Delhi: Motilal Banarsidass Publisher, 1994), No. 409, III:233.
[5] Bhikkhu Bodhi, trans., *A Bucket Measure of Food,* in *Kosalasamyutta,* in *The Connected Discourses of the Buddha,* (Boston, Mass: Wisdom Publications, 2000), I:176.
[6] Ibid., *Battle (1),* I:177 and Verse 201, *Dhammapada.*
[7] Ibid., *Battle (2),* I:178
[8] Ibid., *Sacrifice,* I:171-2.
[9] Ibid., *Mallika,* I:171.
[10] H. Saddhatissa, trans., *Ratana Sutta,* in *Sutta Nipata,* (London: Curzon Press Ltd., 1985), 24
[11] Burma Pitaka Assn., trans., *Mahaparinibbana Sutta,* in *Digha Nikaya,* (Rangoon: Burma Pitaka Assoc., 1984), 188-191.

CHAPTER 24
[1] Nyanaponika Thera and Bhikkhu Bodhi, trans., *To the Kalamas,* in *Numerical Discourses of the Buddha,* Walnut Creek: Altamira, 1999), 64-66.
[2] Udanapali, p. 68-9.
[3] Pali Text Society, trans., *The Gradual Sayings,* (London: Pali Text Society), I:227.
[4] Bhikkhu Nanamoli and Bhikkhu Bodhi, trans., *Vimansaka Sutta,* in *The Middle Length Discourses of the Buddha,* (Boston: Wisdom Publications, 1995), 415.
[5] W. Sarada, trans., *Treasury of Truth,* (Taipei: Corporate Body of the Buddha Educational Foundation, 1993), 371.
[6] Piyadassi Thera, trans., *Angulimala Paritta,* in *The Book of Protection,* 115.
[7] Verse 173, *Dhammapada.*

CHAPTER 25
[1] Bhikkhu Bodhi, trans., *Kasi Bharadvaja Sutta,* in *Brahmanasamyutta,* in *The Connected Discourses of the Buddha,* (Boston, Mass: Wisdom Publications, 2000), I:266-268
[2] T. W. Rhys Davis, trans., *Maha Vagga Kandhaka,* in *The Sacred Books of the East,* 208.
[3] Pali Text Society, trans., *Maha Vagga,* (London: Pali Text Society), VIII: 431.

⁴ Verse 182, *Dhammapada*.
⁵ *Jivaka Sutta*, in Majjhima Nikaya.

CHAPTER 26

¹ Sabbe puthujjana ummattaka.
² Nyanaponika Thera and Bhikkhu Bodhi, trans., *The Mind II*, in *Numerical Discourses of the Buddha*, Walnut Creek: Altamira, 1999), 36.
³ Ibid., *The Mind I*, 35.
⁴ Verse 223, *Dhammapada*.
⁵ *Sirima*, in *Dhammapada Commentary*, (Cambridge, Mass.: Harvard University Press, 1999), Part 3, 189-191.
⁶ Pali Text Society, trans., *Satipatthana Sutta*, in *The Middle Length Sayings*, (London: Pali Text Society), I:70-82.
⁷ H. Saddhatissa, trans., *Vijaya Sutta*, in *Sutta Nipata*, (London: Curzon Press Ltd., 1985), 20-21.
⁸ Nyanaponika Thera and Bhikkhu Bodhi, trans., *Numerical Discourses of the Buddha*, Walnut Creek: Altamira, 1999), 190-1.
⁹ Pali Text Society, trans., *Sallekha Sutta*, in *The Middle Length Sayings*, (London: Pali Text Society), I:51-57.
¹⁰ Dr. Walpola Rahula, *What the Buddha Taught*, (London: Gordon Frazer, 1978), Chap. VII.
¹² Bhikkhu Nanamoli and Bhikkhu Bodhi, trans., *Kakacupama Sutta*, in *The Middle Length Discourses of the Buddha*, (Boston: Wisdom Publications, 1995), 223.
¹³ Pali Text Society, trans., *Mettanisanse Sutta*, in *Anguttara Nikaya*, (London: Pali Text Society), V:382

CHAPTER 27

¹ Bhikkhu Nanamoli and Bhikkhu Bodhi, trans., *Nagaravindeyya Sutta*, in *The Middle Length Discourses of the Buddha*, (Boston: Wisdom Publications, 1995), 1140.
² *Samannaphala Sutta* in Digha Nikaya.
³ Ibid., *Upali Sutta*, 484.
⁴ Burma Pitaka Assn., trans., *Brahmajala Sutta*, in *Digha Nikaya*, (Rangoon: Burma Pitaka Assoc., 1984), 5.
⁵ Verse 176, *Dhammapada*.
⁶ Eugene W. Burlingame, trans., *Dhammapada Commentary, Buddhist Legens*, (Cambridge, Mass.: Harvard University Press, 1990), 189-190.
⁷ Bhikkhu Bodhi, trans., *Flowers*, in *The Connected Discourses of the Buddha*, (Boston, Mass: Wisdom Publications, 2000), I:949.

CHAPTER 28

¹ Pali Text Society, trans., *Mahanama Sutta*, in *Anguttara Nikaya*, (London: Pali Text Society, 1973), III:204-205.
² Maurice Walshe, trans., *Sigalaka Sutta*, in *The Long Discourses of the Buddha*, (Boston, Mass: Wisdom Publications, 1995), 461-469.
³ Pali Text Society, trans., *Bhikkhuni Sigalamata*, in *Anguttara Nikaya*, (London: Pali Text Society, 1973), I: 29.

CHAPTER 29
[1] Nyanaponika Thera and Bhikkhu Bodhi, trans., *The Right Way of Teaching the Dhamma*, in *Numerical Discourses of the Buddha*, Walnut Creek: Altamira, 1999), 140.
[2] Pali Text Society, trans., *Eight Qualities of a Dhamma Messenger*, in *Anguttara Nikaya*, (London: Pali Text Society, 1973), IV:134.
[3] Nyanaponika Thera and Bhikkhu Bodhi, trans., *Do Monks Benefit Others?*, in *Numerical Discourses of the Buddha*, Walnut Creek: Altamira, 1999), 58.
[4] Ibid., *Advice to New Monks*, 138.
[5] Pali Text Society, trans., *Sivali*, in *The Gradual Sayings*, (London: Pali Text Society, 1973), I-18.
[6] Eugene W. Burlingame, trans., *Dhammapada Commentary, Buddhist Legends*, (Cambridge, Mass.: Harvard University Press, 1990), 284-286.
[7] Nyanaponika Thera and Bhikkhu Bodhi, trans., *Good Sleep*, in *Numerical Discourses of the Buddha*, Walnut Creek: Altamira, 1999), 50.
[8] Pali Text Society, trans., *Dighacarika Sutta*, in *The Gradual Sayings*, (London: Pali Text Society, 1973), III:188.
[9] Ibid., III:189.
[10] Maurice Walshe, trans., *Pitaka Sutta*, in *The Long Discourses of the Buddha*, (Boston, Mass: Wisdom Publications, 1995), 371-383.
[11] Nyanaponika Thera and Bhikkhu Bodhi, trans., *Scholars and Meditators*, in *Numerical Discourses of the Buddha*, Walnut Creek: Altamira, 1999), 163.
[12] Ibid., *Living by the Dhamma*, 137-138.
[13] Bhikkhu Bodhi, trans., *Punna*, in *The Connected Discourses of the Buddha*, (Boston, Mass: Wisdom Publications, 2000), II:1167-8.

CHAPTER 30
[1] Verse 67, *Dhammapada*.
[2] Verse 173, *Dhammapada*.

CHAPTER 31
[1] Bhikkhu Bodhi, trans., *The Hook*, in *The Connected Discourses of the Buddha*, (Boston, Mass: Wisdom Publications, 2000), I:682-683.
[2] Ibid., *The Turtle*, I:683.
[3] Ibid., *Devadatta*, I:247.
[4] *Cullavagga* 7:3, Vinaya Pitaka, Sutta Vibhanga Sangha 10.
[5] *Sanghabhada Sutta*, in the Sona Vagga of the *Udana Pali*.
[5] Pali Text Society, trans., *The Book of Discipline*, (London: Pali Text Society, 1975), V:274.
[7] H. Saddhatissa, trans., *Mangala Sutta*, in *Sutta Nipata*, (London: Curzon Press Ltd., 1985), 29.

CHAPTER 32
[1] Pali Text Society, trans., *Saccavibhanga Sutta*, in *The Middle Length Sayings*, (London: Pali Text Society), III:295.299.
[2] *Sangiti Sutta*, Digha Nikaya.

³ Samyutta Atthakata (Sarathappa Kasani.)
⁴ Ibid.
⁵ W. Sarada, trans., *Treasury of Truth,* (Taipei: Corporate Body of the Buddha Educational Foundation, 1993), 295.
⁶ Pali Text Society, trans., *Samyutta Nikaya,* (London: Pali Text Society, 1973), I:293.

CHAPTER 33
¹ Burma Pitaka Assn., trans., *Mahaparinibbana Sutta,* in *Digha Nikaya,* (Rangoon: Burma Pitaka Assoc., 1984), 250-251.
² Ibid., 161-5.
³ Ibid., 219.
⁴ Ibid., 267.
⁵ Burma Pitaka Assn., trans., *Mahapadana Sutta,* in *Digha Nikaya,* (Rangoon: Burma Pitaka Assoc., 1984).
⁶ Burma Pitaka Assn., trans., *Mahaparinibbana Sutta,* in *Digha Nikaya,* (Rangoon: Burma Pitaka Assoc., 1984), 228.
⁷ Pali Text Society, trans., *The Sacred Books of the Buddhists,* (London: Pali Text Society, 1977), III:128.
⁸ Burma Pitaka Assn., trans., *Mahaparinibbana Sutta,* in *Digha Nikaya,* (Rangoon: Burma Pitaka Assoc., 1984), 258.
⁹ Ibid., 261-263.

CHAPTER 34
¹ Burma Pitaka Assn., trans., *Mahaparinibbana Sutta,* in *Digha Nikaya,* (Rangoon: Burma Pitaka Assoc., 1984), 292.
² Ibid., 295.
³ Ibid., 279-280.
⁴ Ibid., 285-286.
⁵ Ibid., 287.
⁶ Ibid., 287-288.
⁷ Ibid., 289.
⁸ Ibid., 290-291.
⁹ *Buddha Vandana,* (Los Angeles: Dharma Vijaya Publication, 1990) 19.

CHAPTER 35
¹ Dipak Kumar Barua, *The Four Nikayas,* (Calcutta, 1971).
² Pali Text Society, trans., *The Book of Gradual Sayings,* (London: Pali Text Society, 1982) II:43-45.
³ *Buddha Vandana,* (Los Angeles: Dharma Vijaya Publication, 1990) 19.

About the Authors

Bhante Walpola Piyananda is the author of **Saffron Days in LA** and **The Bodhi Tree Grows in LA** – both of them subtitled "**Tales of a Buddhist Monk in America**." "Saffron Days in LA" has become a classic in American Buddhist literature, often used as a textbook in Buddhist Studies courses in universities; it has been translated into Mandarin, Korean, and Sinhalese.

Bhante Piyananda was ordained in 1955 as a novice monk in Sri Lanka at the age of twelve. He graduated with Honors with a BA from Kelaniya University in 1967. He received post-graduate degrees from the University of Calcutta in India and from Northwestern University in Chicago; completing his doctoral coursework at the University of California, Los Angeles. Bhante also received an honorary Ph.D. from the University of Oriental Studies in Los Angeles. He received the title of "Tripitaka Dharma Visarada" from the University of Ruhuna in Sri Lanka.

He first came to America on July 4, 1976 and founded Dharma Vijaya Buddhist Vihara in Los Angeles in 1980. He is the President of the Sri Lankan Buddhist Sangha Council of America and Canada, Chief Sangha Nayake of America, and Abbot of Dharma Vijaya Buddhist Vihara.

Dr. Stephen Long *(Bodhicari Dharmapala)* is the author of **Karmic Ties: A Novel of Modern Asia**, first published in the U.S. in 1999, and again in Asia in 2005. He is also a business consultant, screenwriter, journalist, editor, and meditation practitioner. In 1998 he was ordained a Buddhist lay minister *(Bodhicari)* at Dharma Vijaya Buddhist Vihara in Los Angeles; and in 2009 he received a Doctorate of Dharma from Buddhist Studies International, Los Angeles. He is Chairman of the Board of Captive Daughters, an all-volunteer California non-profit, which is dedicated to ending sex trafficking in the world. (www.captivedaughters.org)